Examkrackers MCAT®

101 PASSAGES:
BIOLOGY 2
SYSTEMS

OSOTE
PUBLISHING

Major Contributors:

Austin Mattox
Jay Li
Leena Asfour
Kaitlyn Barkley
Jennifer Birk Goldschmidt, M.S.
Andrew Elson
Kaitlin Shinn

Contributors:

Christina Snider
Christopher Stewart
Darren Sultan

Art Director:

Erin Daniel

Designer:

Dana Kelley

ISBN 13: 978-1-893858-93-0

To purchase additional copies of this book or other books of the 101 Passage series, call 1-888-572-2536.

Examkrackers.com
Osote.com

FAIR USE NOTICE. This book is an independent educational guide for students who are preparing to take the Medical College Admission Test® exam, also known as the MCAT® exam. This book has been prepared and published by Examkrackers, Inc. and is not endorsed or sponsored by, or otherwise affiliated with, the Association of American Medical Colleges (AAMC), which publishes the MCAT® exam and owns the foregoing trademarks. The trademarks owned by AAMC are used for information and identification only, and are not intended to claim or suggest any affiliation with AAMC.

Printed and bound in the United States of America.

PHOTOCOPYING & DISTRIBUTION POLICY

Read this First

Practice is essential to success on the MCAT®. MCAT® practice is the best way to develop the key skills you will need to get a high score.

The 101 passages and associated questions in this book were carefully designed to simulate exactly the content, length, style, tone, difficulty and format of real AAMC MCAT® passages, questions, and answer choices. Each chapter in this book has two tests. The first one is of exact MCAT® section length and the second is a mini-MCAT® section for additional practice. Both passage-based questions and stand-alone questions are just like the questions you'll see on MCAT® day, and are included in a 3:1 ratio, just like the real MCAT®.

The Examkrackers 101 series covers every single topic and subtopic tested by the MCAT®. Topics that require more drilling and topics that are especially difficult are covered by multiple questions. Each chapter in *101 Passages: Biology 2 Systems* tests the content covered by the corresponding chapter in Examkrackers *Biology 2 Systems* manual. To maximize your MCAT® preparation, take the tests in each chapter following your review of that chapter in the manual. To stay in touch with how the science you review is tested on the MCAT®, coordinate your content review with simulated MCAT® practice, chapter by chapter.

The MCAT® is all about how flexible and adaptable you are with the basics. Real MCAT® passages and questions will always present you with new and unfamiliar situations. It is only through simulated MCAT® practice that you will learn to see what simple science is relevant and then recall and apply the basics with confidence. Through practice and focus on the questions you get wrong, you will develop essential skills that bring a high score on MCAT® day.

In this section you will find information on:

- Using the warm-up passage to assess your skills
- MCAT® Timing
- MCAT® Simulation
- How to use this book to increase your MCAT® score
- Scoring your practice tests
- Complete MCAT® preparation with Examkrackers

How to Begin: Assessing Your Skills

This book begins with one "warm-up" passage. Use it to familiarize yourself with the look, feel, and format of MCAT® biological passages and questions. Give yourself about eight minutes to take the warm-up test. While working through the passage and the associated questions, observe yourself and notice your own approach. Immediately after taking the warm-up test, look at the following checklist of strategies and skills. Based on the passage and questions in the warm-up, evaluate which skills come naturally to you and which skills you will work to build as you continue through this book.

- Energy
- Focus
- Confidence
- Timing
- Narrating the passage
- Identifying and answering research questions
- Applying simple science in new situations
- Clear, simple, and connected organization of the content in your mind
- Simplifying the questions and answers
- Eliminating weak answer choices

Choose two or three skills to focus on throughout Test 1 and continue to build new skills as you proceed through the book. Return to this page and check off strategies and skills as you master them.

MCAT® Timing

Examkrackers 101 books are great tools with which to master MCAT® timing before MCAT® day. The tests can be taken untimed or timed. As you initially practice brand-new skills, go slowly in order to master them. Take timed tests to prepare for timing on MCAT® day. The practice tests in this book are exactly like the real MCAT®: 10 passages and 59 questions in 95 minutes. The mini-tests are precisely scaled to AAMC MCAT® timing: 41 questions in 65 minutes. Timing on MCAT® day is a skill that you will build through timed practice.

Take a 5 second break before reading each passage. Look at the clock only once, at the halfway point (the 29th question). If you are before the 47-minute mark, slow down. If you are after the 47-minute mark, speed up. Developing an intuitive sense for good MCAT® timing and pace is an essential skill. Eventually, you will come to know whether you are on pace as you go without looking at a clock. You will know when you are getting sandbagged in order to speed up and when you are rushing so that you can slow down.

After you take a test, assess your timing skills. If you did not finish the test before the allotted time, determine where you are spending time that you could save. If you finished with time to spare, determine how you could spend more time toward a higher score on your next practice test.

Plan a schedule in advance. Choose a distribution for these tests throughout your study period. For example, if you are studying over a ten-week period, take one test from this book every week on the same day. Do not save all the tests for the weeks immediately prior to the MCAT®, as MCAT® skills require time and practice to develop. It is important to stay in touch with the MCAT® and MCAT® practice throughout your study period. Between tests, give yourself adequate time to review the test you take each week. Consciously plan what you will do differently on the next test in order to increase your MCAT® score.

MCAT® SIMULATION

When you are ready to take your first simulated, full-length test, choose an environment that is not familiar or comfortable, e.g. a public library, not your couch at home. Ensure that you will maximize focus and minimize distraction for one sitting of at least 95 minutes. If needed, you may use disposable earplugs, just as on MCAT® day. During the test, do not look at or answer the telephone, do not sit and stare out the window, and do not get up for any reason, such as to get a drink or to go to the bathroom. Treat each practice test like the real thing.

It is always a good idea to mark up the multiple choice questions *on the test itself* as you go through them. If 'A' can't be correct, then mark it off and go to 'B'. If 'B' is *possible*, circle it, and go to 'C', and so on. That way you are eliminating and narrowing choices that are *not possible* or are *less likely*. Using the process of elimination is a very helpful technique on the MCAT®. The computer-based test allows the use of strikethrough and highlight functions right on the screen to help with narrowing down choices. It is not very practical or helpful to write your answers or considerations on a piece of notebook paper as this does not simulate MCAT® day.

How to Use This Book to Increase Your MCAT® Score:

REVIEW

Test and question review is the single most important thing you will do to change your MCAT® score.

Always leave time for review of each test. Your score will change through careful review of each practice test you take, not through repetitive practice.

Every question you get wrong is a gift, an opportunity to increase your score. Always think about how questions you get wrong are valuable – they are the pearls that will lead you directly to a high MCAT® score.

You will need ninety-five minutes to take the test and at least ninety minutes to review it.

Immediately after completing each test, take notes on what happened during the test.

Then, take a short break for an hour or less. Next sit down and check your answers. At the end of each test, you will be directed to the page in the back of the book where you can find the answers, and answer explanations, for that test. Every page of the tests has a tab and footer telling you what test you're working on. Every page of the answers and explanations has a tab and footer telling you which test is being covered. Always be sure these match when checking your answers. No need to flip through pages and pages of explanations looking for the right test.

Make a list of question numbers you marked and/or got wrong. Do not yet read the answer explanations.

Compare your score to the last practice test you took. Your raw score is the number you answered correctly out of 59. Did your raw score increase since the last test? If yes, what did you do differently? Make a note to keep doing what worked. If no, what was different today? Make a commitment to change strategies that did not work.

Make time to retake the questions you answered incorrectly before looking at the answer explanations. This allows you to build the most important MCAT® muscles of all: problem solving and independent thinking. Once you see the answer explanation, you lose the opportunity to learn how to solve the MCAT® question yourself. This may sometimes require multiple attempts or reinforcement of science, but the purpose of practice is for you to learn how to *solve* the questions. Reading the explanation of how to get to the right answer should come only after you have tried your hardest to find your own way there.

Once you have made a second attempt, read the answer explanation for each question you got wrong in order to learn to think in ways that will get you a high score. Examkrackers answer explanations are uniquely process-oriented, meaning that they reveal the way to think like the MCAT®. The answer explanations show you the reasoning process that leads to the elimination of each weak answer and the selection of the best answer. Our answer explanations will help you identify new strategies that work and will help you learn to think in ways that bring a high score.

It can also help to review those questions you got right in order to reinforce the skills, confidence and concepts that allowed you to solve those problems.

SMART PRACTICE

There are two kinds of practice: practice that is repetitive and practice that is smart. Practice that is repetitive, in which you do the same thing over and over again, will reinforce skills that you already have and will also reinforce any habits you may have that are not working.

1. Before each test, plan on what skills you want to add, build, reinforce or replace with this practice test. Use the list provided above as well as any skills you have added. Make specific "When... Then..." commitments (see below).

2. Be conscious or self-aware during each test, in order to evaluate what you are doing while you are doing it. Take notes during the test on what you are thinking or feeling, what skills you are struggling with, what is happening that you notice, etc.

3. Smart practice finally means evaluating immediately *after* each test how the commitments helped. If your score increased, what did you do differently that accounts for the increase—commit to continuing with this new skill. If your score decreased, what in your approach or environment was different— commit to replacing what is not working.

4. Repeat this process throughout the study period.

MAKING COMMITMENTS

Immediately after each test, make specific commitments for what you plan next – what will you keep doing more of and what still needs to change?

Commitments work best if new, good habits are linked to old, bad habits. I can make a commitment not to speed on the highway tomorrow, but inevitably I will find myself speeding yet again. Change comes when I decide that

> **When** I speed, **then** I will immediately slow down to 54 mph.
> Similarly:
> **When** I fall into negative thinking while taking the test,
> **Then** I will take a five-second break and refocus on the question in front of me.
> Or
> **When** I have trouble understanding what I am reading,
> **Then** I will take a five-second break and resume reading, narrating with the basics that I know

When you commit to avoiding the mistakes that led you to incorrect answers in one test, you will see improvement in your raw score on the next test.

Look toward the next date you will take a practice test. Document your commitments and keep them ready at hand to review before you begin your next practice test.

Scoring Your Practice Tests

The goal is to see your scores on Examkrackers practice materials improve over time.

The best way to utilize your raw score is to be sure it increases with each practice test you take, whether as skill-building or simulation. The best way to do this is to make specific commitments to replace what isn't working with effective MCAT® skills.

Note: Even if Examkrackers derived a scaled score from thousands of our students, it would not accurately predict your AAMC MCAT® score. Unlike the AAMC MCAT® which includes easy questions, Examkrackers practice questions simulating the MCAT® are largely of the medium and difficult level, in order to improve your MCAT® skills and to help you learn how to think like the MCAT®. Our students are at different stages of preparation for the MCAT® and do not represent the MCAT® day student population. Any scaled score other than that directly from the AAMC does not correlate to AAMC MCAT® scores. Only a scaled score from the AAMC can accurately predict your AAMC MCAT® score.

Your goal should be to get more items right and fewer wrong with each Examkrackers practice test you take. A higher score with each practice test reflects that you are using the questions you get wrong and those you get right to learn and practice new skills that will increase your score.

Complete Your MCAT® Preparation

Note: *101 Passages: Biology 2 Systems* contains only systems biology passages and questions to maximize your biology practice. The AAMC MCAT® integrates biological systems with biochemistry. For integrated MCAT® simulation, use our full-length, online *EK-Tests®*. Visit www.examkrackers.com for details.

To complete your preparation for the Biological and Biochemical Foundations MCAT® section, use this book along with the Examkrackers *Biology 1: Molecules*, *Biology 2: Systems*, and *Reasoning Skills* manuals, and *MCAT® 101 Passages Biology 1: Molecules*. Together these tools provide in-depth instruction in the skills needed to get a high score on the "Biological and Biochemical Foundations" MCAT® section.

To prepare fully for the four sections of the MCAT®, Examkrackers *Complete Study Package* includes six manuals packed with content review, MCAT® strategy, and guided practice. The corresponding *MCAT® 101 Passages* series allows you to practice the methods and build the skills taught in Examkrackers study manuals. Take an online or in person Examkrackers Comprehensive MCAT® Course (information available at our website, below).

Examkrackers Live MCAT® Hotline is a service available ten hours per week so your questions can be addressed directly and interactively by expert, high scoring MCAT® instructors.

EK-Tests® are the best full length simulated MCAT® product available on the market. Each electronic test matches the MCAT® in sources, style, format, question types, length, skills and content tested. Tools to maximize review and score improvement are built-in.

Regularly visit the Examkrackers Forums where students' questions are answered and any errata are posted.

Go to www.examkrackers.com or call 1.888.KRACKEM to learn more about Examkrackers materials, support and live MCAT® preparation, both online and in-person.

Toward your success!

TABLE OF CONTENTS

BIOLOGICAL SCIENCES

DIRECTIONS. Most questions in the Biological Sciences test are organized into groups, each preceded by a descriptive passage. After studying the passage, select the one best answer to each question in the group. Some questions are not based on a descriptive passage and are also independent of each other. You must also select the one best answer to these questions. If you are not certain of an answer, eliminate the alternatives that you know to be incorrect and then select an answer from the remaining alternatives. A periodic table is provided for your use. You may consult it whenever you wish.

PERIODIC TABLE OF THE ELEMENTS

1 H 1.0																		2 He 4.0
3 Li 6.9	4 Be 9.0											5 B 10.8	6 C 12.0	7 N 14.0	8 O 16.0	9 F 19.0	10 Ne 20.2
11 Na 23.0	12 Mg 24.3											13 Al 27.0	14 Si 28.1	15 P 31.0	16 S 32.1	17 Cl 35.5	18 Ar 39.9
19 K 39.1	20 Ca 40.1	21 Sc 45.0	22 Ti 47.9	23 V 50.9	24 Cr 52.0	25 Mn 54.9	26 Fe 55.8	27 Co 58.9	28 Ni 58.7	29 Cu 63.5	30 Zn 65.4	31 Ga 69.7	32 Ge 72.6	33 As 74.9	34 Se 79.0	35 Br 79.9	36 Kr 83.8
37 Rb 85.5	38 Sr 87.6	39 Y 88.9	40 Zr 91.2	41 Nb 92.9	42 Mo 95.9	43 Tc (98)	44 Ru 101.1	45 Rh 102.9	46 Pd 106.4	47 Ag 107.9	48 Cd 112.4	49 In 114.8	50 Sn 118.7	51 Sb 121.8	52 Te 127.6	53 I 126.9	54 Xe 131.3
55 Cs 132.9	56 Ba 137.3	57 La* 138.9	72 Hf 178.5	73 Ta 180.9	74 W 183.9	75 Re 186.2	76 Os 190.2	77 Ir 192.2	78 Pt 195.1	79 Au 197.0	80 Hg 200.6	81 Tl 204.4	82 Pb 207.2	83 Bi 209.0	84 Po (209)	85 At (210)	86 Rn (222)
87 Fr (223)	88 Ra 226.0	89 Ac= 227.0	104 Unq (261)	105 Unp (262)	106 Unh (263)	107 Uns (262)	108 Uno (265)	109 Une (267)									

	58 Ce 140.1	59 Pr 140.9	60 Nd 144.2	61 Pm (145)	62 Sm 150.4	63 Eu 152.0	64 Gd 157.3	65 Tb 158.9	66 Dy 162.5	67 Ho 164.9	68 Er 167.3	69 Tm 168.9	70 Yb 173.0	71 Lu 175.0
*														
=	90 Th 232.0	91 Pa (231)	92 U 238.0	93 Np (237)	94 Pu (244)	95 Am (243)	96 Cm (247)	97 Bk (247)	98 Cf (251)	99 Es (252)	100 Fm (257)	101 Md (258)	102 No (259)	103 Lr (260)

WARM-UP

Passage: 1

Time: 8 minutes

DIRECTIONS: Use this warm-up passage and questions to become familiar with MCAT® biological science questions and to assess your skills before beginning Practice Test 1A.

Read the passage, then select the best answer to each associated question. If you are unsure of an answer, rule out incorrect choices and select from the remaining options. Indicate your selection beside the option you choose. A periodic table can be found on the last page of this book for you to use at any point during this test section.

Passage 1 (Questions 1-5)

Human immunodeficiency virus (HIV) infection can lead to reactivation and spread of herpesviruses, including HSV-1and HSV-2, in oral and genital mucosa, causing ulcers that are difficult to treat. HIV infection causes attenuation of the immune system by substantially depleting immune cells that target these viruses. In addition, HIV infection can impair the barrier function of various mucosal epithelia, including oral and intestinal mucosa. This in turn may facilitate the spread of opportunistic infections, such as HSV-1 or HSV-2, throughout the epithelium. HIV tat and gp120 proteins lead to disruption of tight junctions (TJ) through aberrant internalization of TJ proteins and their down-regulation.

Researchers were interested in exploring the role of HIV-associated disruption of oral mucosal epithelium in HSV-1 infection by using polarized oral keratinocytes, which resemble the oral epithelia, as a model system. The polarity of epithelial cells was confirmed by immunodetection of the TJ protein zonula occludens-1 and measurement of paracellular permeability, or the permeability of the junctions between adjacent cells. Polarity refers to the difference between the apical and basolateral surfaces of the cells, where the tight junctions form the dividing barrier.

Polarized tonsil cells were treated with active or inactive mutant tat/gp120 or HIV virions for 5 days and were subsequently infected with HSV-1. HSV-1 infection was quantitatively determined by measuring levels of an HSV glycoprotein inside the cells. The results are shown in Figure 1.

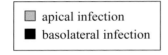

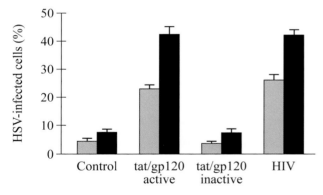

Figure 1 HSV-1 infection following treatment with tat/gp120 proteins or HIV virions

In an additional experiment, the researchers studied how the mechanism for the increased spread of HSV may be mediated by exposure of Nectin-1, an epithelial protein that is sequestered in the adherens junctions. Nectin-1 binds to HSV glycoprotein D (gD), facilitating both the entry of the viruses into epithelial cells and the cell-to-cell spread of the progeny. Quantitative analysis of HSV-infected cells showed that antibodies to Nectin-1 reduced HSV-1 infection in cells treated with active tat/gp120 and HIV virions by approximately 70%.

This passage was adapted from "HIV-Associated Disruption of Tight and Adherens Junctions of Oral Epithelial Cells Facilitates HSV-1 Infection and Spread." Sufiawati I, Tugizov SM. *PLoS ONE.* 2014. 9(2) doi:10.1371/journal.pone.0088803 for use under the terms of the Creative Commons CC BY 4.0 license (http://creativecommons.org/licenses/by/4.0/legalcode).

Question 1

Researchers add anti-donkey IgG antibodies conjugated with horseradish peroxidase to the apical surfaces of the oral keratinocytes and measure for the enzymatic activity of the peroxidase surrounding the basolateral surfaces likely in order to:

○ **A.** assess the efficacy of the anti-Nectin-1 antibodies.

○ **B.** visualize the tight junction protein zonula occludens-1.

○ **C.** establish a baseline of tight junction permeability to water.

○ **D.** determine the similarity of the experimental model to oral epithelia.

Question 2

The information in the passage suggests that the disruption of the barrier function of oral epithelial cells is a consequence of:

○ **A.** lysosome degradation of tight junction proteins.

○ **B.** HIV tat and gp120 downregulation.

○ **C.** increased Nectin-1 exposure facilitating viral entry.

○ **D.** increased fluid transport through leaky tight junctions.

Question 3

Evidence shows that HIV increases the severity of hepatitis C through signaling interactions of gp120 with membrane receptors. Which of the following stages of the HIV life cycle is likely mediated through gp120?

○ **A.** Self-assembly of the outer viral envelope

○ **B.** Integration of the retroviral genes into the host genome

○ **C.** Invasion of the HIV virus into the host cell

○ **D.** Reactivation of the provirus following a dormant phase

Question 4

The data in the passage would best support the finding that the control group used in the experimental design:

○ **A.** was subjected to mutant forms of the HIV proteins.

○ **B.** was infected with HIV but not HSV.

○ **C.** had preserved function of zonula occudens-1.

○ **D.** downregulated the expression of Nectin-1.

Question 5

Which of the following reflects the sequence of changes to the HIV genome during an HIV infection?

○ **A.** Single-stranded RNA to double-stranded RNA to DNA

○ **B.** Single-stranded RNA to mixed DNA and RNA to DNA

○ **C.** Double-stranded RNA to DNA

○ **D.** Double-stranded RNA to mixed DNA and RNA to DNA

STOP. If you finish before time is called, check your work. You may go back to any question in this test.

ANSWERS & EXPLANATIONS for the Warm-Up Passages can be found on p. 187.

LECTURE 1

The Cell

TEST 1A

Time: 95 minutes
Questions 1–59

DIRECTIONS: Most of the questions in this test section are grouped with a passage. Read the passage, then select the best answer to each question. Some questions are independent of any passage and of one another. Select the best answer to each of these questions. If you are unsure of an answer, rule out incorrect choices and select from the remaining options. Indicate your selection beside the option you choose. A periodic table can be found on the last page of this book for you to use at any point during this test section.

Passage 1 (Questions 1-4)

Epstein-Barr virus (EBV) is a double-stranded DNA, enveloped virus that infects over 90% of the adult population worldwide. Its acute infection sometimes causes infectious mononucleosis, or "mono," though most of the time its infection is asymptomatic. Symptoms of mononucleosis include swollen neck lymph nodes, fever, and fatigue. EBV adopts a biphasic life cycle and persists in a latent form in infected cells after initial infection, expressing only a limited number of viral proteins and transcripts. Reactivation of the latent virus into a lytic cycle induces the expression of approximately 80 lytic proteins.

EBV may underlie the development of various lymphoid and epithelial cancers. Lytic induction therapy, where a combination of a lytic inducer and antiviral drug is employed for the specific killing of EBV-positive tumor cells, is a novel strategy to fight EBV-positive cancers. Induction of the lytic cycle allows virus-specific antigens to be expressed on the epithelial cell surface, triggering an immune response. Additionally, antiviral drugs act to decrease the concentration of infectious viruses, limiting spread of EBV within the body.

High-throughput screening utilizing epithelial cells latently infected with EBV identified compound E11 (Figure 1) as a potent lytic inducer.

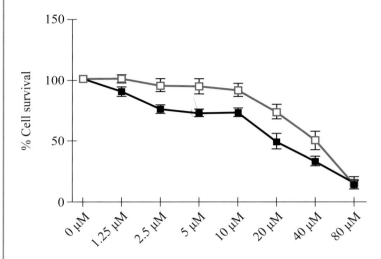

Figure 1 Structure of compound E11

Uninfected epithelial cells and epithelial cells latently infected with EBV were treated with compound 11 at various concentrations and co-incubated with B and T cells. The amount of cell death was determined by an MTT assay. An MTT assay is a colorimetric assay that relies on NADPH. Healthy cells that maintain adequate NADPH levels can reduce the colored compound, causing it to appear colorless. The results are presented in Figure 2.

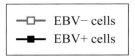

Figure 2 Cytotoxicity of compound E11 in EBV negative and positive cells

This passage was adapted from "Identification of Novel Small Organic Compounds with Diverse Structures for the Induction of Epstein-Barr Virus (EBV) Lytic Cycle in EBV-Positive Epithelial Malignancies." Choi C, Ho D, Hui K, Kao R, and Chiang A. *PLoS ONE*. 2015. 10(12) doi:10.1371/journal.pone.0145994 for use under the terms of the Creative Commons CC BY 4.0 license (http://creativecommons.org/licenses/by/4.0/legalcode).

Question 1

Insertion of the EBV genome into the human genome often disrupts the transcription of tumor suppressor genes and increases the risk of developing cancer. EBV is most likely to insert its genomic sequences into the:

○ **A.** 5′ promoter region.

○ **B.** 3′ untranslated region.

○ **C.** 3′ enhancer region.

○ **D.** splice site of exon 1.

Question 2

EBV is LEAST likely to employ which of the following mechanisms during the lysogenic phase of its life cycle?

   I. Methylation of C bases

  II. Acetylation of histone H3

 III. Methylation of histone H2A

○ **A.** I only

○ **B.** II only

○ **C.** III only

○ **D.** I and III only

Question 3

Compound 11 is likely to induce the lytic phase of EBV via:

○ **A.** inhibiting host DNA-methyltransferase by associating with phenylalanine in the active site.

○ **B.** inhibiting the viral reverse transcriptase by associating with tryptophan in the active site.

○ **C.** activating the viral ribosome by associating with glutamate in the active site.

○ **D.** inhibiting the host RNA polymerase by associating with serine in the active site.

Question 4

Which of the following statements best interprets the findings of Figure 2?

○ **A.** Decreasing the concentration of compound 11 increases lysis of non-infected cells over EBV-infected cells.

○ **B.** Decreasing the concentration of compound 11 has no effect on the cell death of EBV-infected cells.

○ **C.** Increasing the concentration of compound 11 results in targeted killing of EBV-infected cells.

○ **D.** Increasing the concentration of compound 11 increases lysis of non-infected cells over EBV-infected cells.

Passage 2 (Questions 5-8)

Several viral pathogens cause malignant disease in humans (pandemic influenza virus) and animals (Newcastle disease virus, a negative-sense, ssRNA virus), resulting in significant mortality and economic losses. Although various therapeutic drugs and vaccines have been developed to prevent and treat these diseases, the emergence of novel mutants and resistant strains reduces their efficacy. For centuries, herbal medicines have been traditionally utilized for the treatment of various ailments, including viral diseases. The discoveries of effective Western medicines, such as aspirin, which can be obtained from white Willow bark, or quinine, an antimalarial drug derived from the bark of *Cinchona officinalis*, have increased the interest for more elaborate research on herbal medicines and paved the way toward the acceptance of the efficacy of using standardized herbal preparations.

KIOM-C is a compound mixture of herbal medicine. Previous studies have shown that pigs supplemented with KIOM-C restored their viability from porcine circovirus-associated disease (PCVAD). Other studies have shown increased production of antiviral cytokines leading to clearance of the Influenza virus in the respiratory tracts of mice due to the oral administration of KIOM-C. Although these traditional herbal medicines from various herbal plants have been tested and proven to have potential uses against diseases, the breadth of their protection against a wide range of viruses and mechanisms of action has remained largely unknown.

To further study the efficacy of KIOM-C as a possible treatment for viral infection, researchers measured cell viability and viral count following viral infection with PR8 or VSV viruses and subsequent KIOM-C treatment (Figure 1).

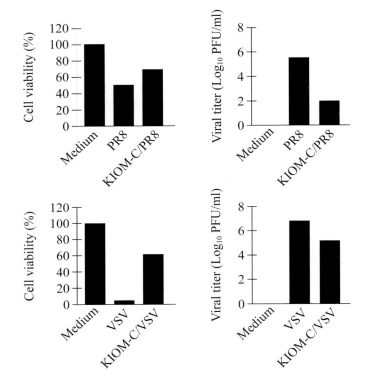

Figure 1 Cell viability and viral titer following viral infection and KIOM-C treatment

Question 5

Which of the following best explains the relationship shown in Figure 1?

○ **A.** KIOM-C increases cell viability in VSV-infected cells by reducing the number of viruses in the lytic cycle.

○ **B.** KIOM-C increases cell viability in VSV-infected cells by reducing the number of viruses in the lysogenic cycle.

○ **C.** KIOM-C does not affect cell viability in VSV-infected cells because VSV is in the lytic cycle.

○ **D.** KIOM-C does not affect cell viability in VSV-infected cells because VSV is in the lysogenic cycle.

Question 6

Which of the following correctly shows the path of Newcastle disease virus reproduction?

○ **A.** Viral RNA is used as a template to generate complementary RNA that can be used to generate more genomic RNA

○ **B.** Viral RNA is used directly by host machinery to generate viral proteins and RNA-dependent RNA polymerase replicates the genomic RNA.

○ **C.** Viral DNA is used as a template to generate RNA, and then this RNA is used by host machinery to generate protein.

○ **D.** Viral DNA is used by host machinery to generate protein, and then this protein is used to generate RNA by reverse transcriptase.

Question 7

A researcher wants to transduce cells growing in a culture containing KIOM. Which viruses could serve as an effective vector in this experiment?

○ **A.** PR8 and VSV

○ **B.** PR8 only

○ **C.** VSV only

○ **D.** Neither PR8 nor VSV

Question 8

Which of the following could be a possible way by which KIOM-C changes viral titer?

○ **A.** By increasing apoptosis signaling in infected cells

○ **B.** By increasing apoptosis signaling in healthy cells

○ **C.** By decreasing apoptosis signaling in infected cells

○ **D.** By decreasing apoptosis signaling in healthy cells

Passage 3 (Questions 9-13)

Dengue virus (DENV) is one of the most prevalent mosquito-borne viruses that causes roughly 390 million infections in humans annually. Neither effective therapeutics nor approved vaccines exist, and clinical manifestation ranges from unapparent infection to a mild febrile syndrome or even a more serious presentation with a mortality rate of 5% to 30%.

In rare cases, a more sudden onset and extensive syndrome might progress to shock or even death, which is referred to as dengue shock syndrome (DSS). Endothelial cells are regarded as the primary cellular barrier and the major defense system of the vasculature to resist viral infection and prevent DSS. However, the potential mechanisms of DENV receptor binding and infection of endothelial cells, especially at early stages of disease, remain obscure.

Type I interferon plays a crucial role in the ability of the endothelium to withstand DENV infection. Scientists were interested in further understanding how Type I interferon signaling mediated protection against DENV and observed that IFN-α inducible gene 6 (IFI6) was increased in DENV infected human vascular endothelial cells. Scientists used plasmids to overexpress IFI6 in non-infected cells and noted that the activation of caspase-3, an effector protein for apoptosis, was decreased in IFI6$^{+/+}$ but increased in IFI6$^{-/-}$ cells at 24–48 hrs. The scientists also found that after incubation with DENV for 48 hours, the mitochondrial membrane potential ($\Delta\psi$) was stable in IFI6$^{+/+}$ cells but reduced in IFI6$^{-/-}$ cells.

In a separate experiment, scientists measured the level of X-linked Inhibitor of Apoptosis (XIAP)-Associated Factor 1(XAF1), a pro-apoptotic protein, in the presence and absence of IFI6 overexpression. The results are shown in Figure 1. In endothelial cells with enhanced expression of XAF1, as much as 28% of the cells had entered irreversible apoptosis by 72 hours post-infection.

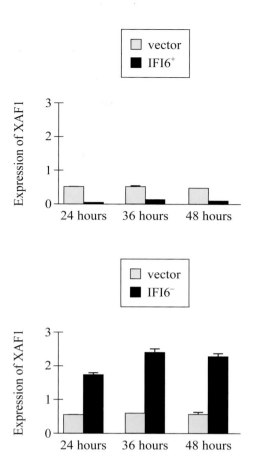

Figure 1 Effect of IFI6 on the expression of XAF1

This passage was adapted from "IFI6 Inhibits Apoptosis Via Mitochondrial Dependent Pathway in Dengue Virus 2 Infected Vascular Endothelial Cells." Qi Y, Li Y, Zhang Y, Zhang L, Wang Z, et al. *PLoS ONE.* 2015. 10(8) doi:10.1371/journal.pone.0132743 for use under the terms of the Creative Commons CC BY 4.0 license (http://creativecommons.org/licenses/by/4.0/legalcode).

Question 9

According to information contained in the passage, viral binding of which of the following molecules on the endothelial cell is likely important for DENV infection?

○ **A.** PC, a lipid in the outer phospholipid leaflet

○ **B.** NF1, a glycoprotein on the outer phospholipid leaflet

○ **C.** GADT2, a protein on the inner phospholipid leaflet

○ **D.** HAT14, a carbohydrate on the inner phospholipid leaflet

Question 10

Epidemiologic studies have demonstrated that some people display immunity to Dengue virus infection. Mutation of which of the following is likely responsible for this finding?

○ **A.** Clathrin

○ **B.** Cholesterol

○ **C.** Tubulin

○ **D.** Myosin

Question 11

Type I interferon has been shown to induce the expression of over 50 genes that mediate antiviral protection. Which of the following is LEAST likely responsible for mediating increased transcription?

○ **A.** cAMP

○ **B.** INFR, the type I interferon receptor

○ **C.** Ca^{2+}

○ **D.** 22-hydroxycholesterol

Question 12

According to information contained in the passage, IFI6 prevents which of the following mitochondrial functions?

○ **A.** Programmed cell death

○ **B.** Defending endothelial cells against viral infection

○ **C.** Upregulating the expression of IFI6

○ **D.** Generating heat

Question 13

In a follow-up experiment, scientists treated normal endothelial cells with a non-competitive inhibitor of IFI6. Based on Figure 1, the scientist most likely observed:

○ **A.** the formation of the mitotic spindle complex.

○ **B.** multiple protrusions of the plasma membrane.

○ **C.** an increased number of ribosomes.

○ **D.** uncoiling of mitochondrial DNA.

Questions 14 - 17 do not refer to a passage and are independent of each other.

Question 14

How can the mechanism of infection in prion diseases be studied using a plausible experimental method?

○ **A.** DNA from affected cells can be sequenced to look for mutations.

○ **B.** Markers for increased transcription can be measured in affected cells.

○ **C.** The conformation of the proteins in affected cells can be analyzed.

○ **D.** The ability to self-replicate can be measured using plates with different nucleic acid combinations.

Question 15

A doctor conducts several tests to identify the causative agent of his patient's illness. Which of the following could be used to distinguish whether the pathogen is a bacteria or a virus?

○ **A.** A test that determines the presence of deoxyribose nucleic acid

○ **B.** A test that determines the presence of proteins

○ **C.** A test that determines the presence of a nucleus

○ **D.** A test that determines the presence of ribosomes

Question 16

Consanguinity results from the mating of closely-related individuals and has been tied to a number of rare genetic disorders. This is likely the result of the:

○ **A.** increased polymorphisms within the inbred population.

○ **B.** decreased gene flow within the inbred population.

○ **C.** increased homozygosity within the inbred population.

○ **D.** decreased diversity within the inbred population.

Question 17

Allopatric speciation is the process by which adaptation occurs through geographic distribution. How does this concept relate to the definition of evolution?

○ **A.** Evolution is defined by changes in the gene pool over time, and this causes speciation through selection.

○ **B.** Evolution reflects the sum of gradual random changes over time, and this occurs through natural selection.

○ **C.** Evolution refers to adaptations arising within populations, and these adaptations can lead to speciation.

○ **D.** Evolution occurs through selection by differential reproduction, and this is determined by distinct pressures.

Passage 4 (Questions 18-21)

HIV-1 is a virus that selectively infects certain cells of the immune system. Current antiretroviral therapy (ART) effectively suppresses HIV-1 plasma viremia by inhibiting viral replication. In most patients, plasma viremia is suppressed below the limit of detection. However, even in the settings of optimal therapy, residual low-level viremia persists in a large subset of patients.

Cell-associated (CA) HIV-1 RNA is a possible predictive marker of ART outcome. Expression of CA HIV-1 RNA is believed to directly reflect the reactivation of latent HIV. The role of CA HIV-1 RNA and its potential use as a virological biomarker for monitoring the response to ART and to novel therapeutic strategies has recently been reviewed in depth elsewhere. In this framework, CA HIV-1 RNA is a promising candidate biomarker for future diagnostic purposes.

In recent years, quantification of CA HIV-1 RNA has been performed using assays based on quantitative reverse transcription real-time PCR (RT-qPCR). However, this technique suffers from increased technical variation at the lower ranges of detection. To overcome these shortcomings, a new qPCR procedure that enables CA HIV-1 RNA measurement in patient samples has been developed with a lower limit of quantification and with increased accuracy at the lower quantitative. By performing two successive PCR reactions, the specificity is maintained and the limit of quantification is considerably reduced.

This passage was adapted from "Comparison of Droplet Digital PCR and Seminested Real-Time PCR for Quantification of Cell-Associated HIV-1 RNA." Kiselinova M, Pasternak AO, Spiegelaere WD, Vogelaers D, Berkhout B, et al. *PLoS ONE*. 2014. 9(1) doi:10.1371/journal.pone.0085999 for use under the terms of the Creative Commons CC BY 4.0 license (http://creativecommons.org/licenses/by/4.0/legalcode).

Question 18

The amount of CA HIV-1 RNA detected in a subject is most likely:

○ **A.** directly correlated to the rate of apoptosis.

○ **B.** inversely correlated to the rate of apoptosis.

○ **C.** unrelated to the rate of apoptosis.

○ **D.** unrelated to the number of infected cells.

Question 19

Which of the following is true about CA HIV-1 RNA?

○ **A.** It is found in higher levels in the lysogenic phase, as the virus prepares to exit the host cell.

○ **B.** It is found in higher levels in the lysogenic phase, as the virus lies dormant.

○ **C.** It is found in higher levels in the lytic phase, as the virus prepares to exit the host cell.

○ **D.** It is found in higher levels in the lytic phase, as the virus lies dormant.

Question 20

Which of the following organelles is most important to the reproductive process of HIV-1?

○ **A.** Nucleus and ribosomes

○ **B.** Nucleus and rough ER

○ **C.** Ribosomes and rough ER

○ **D.** Golgi apparatus and rough ER

Question 21

Which of the following is most likely true regarding HIV-1 infection?

○ **A.** The virus uses a receptor that is constitutively expressed throughout the body.

○ **B.** The specific cells that are infected most likely have the same type of membrane-bound receptor.

○ **C.** The switch from the lysogenic phase to the lytic phase is mediated by the viral enzyme, reverse transcriptase.

○ **D.** HIV-1 can infect all cells of the body.

Passage 5 (Questions 22-25)

The obligate human pathogen *Neisseria gonorrhoeae* is a Gram-negative obligate aerobe that colonizes mucosal tissues in the urogenital tracts to cause the sexually transmitted disease gonorrhea. Although gonorrhea can still be treated with antibiotics, it has progressively accumulated resistance against many antibiotics. Horizontal gene transfer in *N. gonorrhoeae* is driven by its high rates of natural transformation and recombination. Three types of gonococcal conjugative plasmids have been described in *N. gonorrhoeae*; a 24.5 MDa plasmid with no detectable marker, and two 25.2 MDa plasmids which contain the *tetM* determinant.

TetM determinants are transposon-borne determinants found in many organisms and are responsible for high levels of tetracycline resistance. Gonococcal isolates resistant to high doses of tetracycline and carrying 25.2 MDa plasmids have been isolated. Restriction endonuclease mapping and Southern blotting of conjugative plasmids from different isolates revealed two different 25.2 MDa conjugative plasmids, which were named the "American" and "Dutch" type plasmids. The restriction map of the Dutch type plasmid strongly resembled the restriction map of the 24.5 MDa conjugative plasmid, and it is possible that the Dutch type 25.2 MDa plasmid is a derivative of the 24.5 MDa plasmid via an insertion of the *tetM* determinant. Sequencing of the *tetM* regions of American and Dutch type plasmids also revealed differences within the two *tetM* determinants.

This passage was adapted from "Conjugative Plasmids of *Neisseria gonorrhoeae.*" Pachulec E and van der Does C. *PLoS ONE*. 2010. 5(4) doi:10.1371/journal.pone.0009962 for use under the terms of the Creative Commons CC BY 3.0 license (http://creativecommons.org/licenses/by/3.0/legalcode).

Question 22

A common research technique for gene manipulation of human cells is to make the cell membrane slightly porous and allow the DNA fragments from the environment to enter the cell. What type of prokaryotic gene transfer is this most similar to?

○ **A.** Conjugation

○ **B.** Transformation

○ **C.** Transduction

○ **D.** Binary Fission

Question 23

If medical professionals stopped using tetracycline entirely, which of the following would most likely occur?

○ **A.** Level of *tetM*-containing plasmids in *N. gonorrhoeae* would decrease because they no longer give a selective advantage.

○ **B.** The population of *N. gonorrhoeae* would remain roughly the same.

○ **C.** Level of *tetM*-containing plasmids in *N. gonorrhoeae* would increase because they no longer give a selective advantage.

○ **D.** *TetM* bacteria would mutate and no longer resist tetracycline.

Question 24

Which of the following statements best explains the high level of 25.2 plasmids in *N. gonorrhoeae*?

○ **A.** The bacteria wanted to gain tetracycline resistance, leading to the creation of more 25.2 plasmids.

○ **B.** 25.2 plasmids were artificially inserted into the bacteria by researchers.

○ **C.** There is not a high level of 25.2 plasmids in the bacteria.

○ **D.** Bacteria with the 25.2 plasmids survived high levels of tetracycline and successfully reproduced.

Question 25

A bacterium moves down the concentration gradient of tetracycline. Which of the following correctly describes this phenomenon?

○ **A.** Flagellar propulsion

○ **B.** Ciliary beating

○ **C.** Chemotaxis

○ **D.** Tumbling

Questions 26 - 29 do not refer to a passage and are independent of each other.

Question 26

The growth of an particular bacterial strain is illustrated by the graph below. If a student initially plated 6,400 colonies and returned to find 102,400 colonies, how much time elapsed?

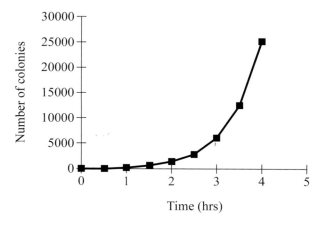

Time (hrs)

- **A.** 0.5 hrs
- **B.** 1.0 hrs
- **C.** 2.0 hrs
- **D.** 2.5 hrs

Question 27

Sodium thioglycolate is a reducing agent that converts atmospheric oxygen into water. Bacteria from which of the following tubes containing sodium thioglycolate does NOT require an anoxic environment to survive? (Each black dot represents a bacterial colony)

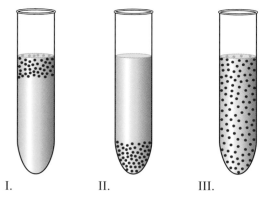

I.   II.   III.

- **A.** I only
- **B.** II only
- **C.** I and III only
- **D.** II and III only

Question 28

Which of the following would provide evidence against endosymbiotic theory? Observing that:

- **A.** mitochondria do not contain histone bound DNA.
- **B.** mitochondria are capable of surviving and reproducing outside of a cell.
- **C.** lysosomes contain compounds that are toxic to most prokaryotes.
- **D.** the endoplasmic reticulum is bound by a monolayer.

Question 29

Researchers identify a strain of bacteria which causes painful gastric ulcers. A sample is cultured, and the bacteria are found to have a very high surface area to volume ratio, and do not aggregate into clusters or chains. Which of the following is likely to be true of these bacteria?

- **A.** The bacteria are unable to tolerate environments with low pH.
- **B.** The bacteria are helical in shape.
- **C.** The bacteria are similar to *Streptococcus aureus*.
- **D.** The bacteria would be indistinguishable from *Lactobacillus* under a microscope.

Passage 6 (Questions 30-33)

N. gonorrhoeae (GC) is a Gram-negative bacterium, human-specific pathogen and the etiological agent of gonorrhea. The sexually transmitted infection (STI) is a global health burden. If left untreated, GC infection can lead to long-term health consequences including pelvic inflammatory disease and infertility. Effective antibiotic treatment of GC is becoming limited by the development of antibiotic resistance, which is made more precipitous by the misuse of antimicrobial drugs. Antibiotic resistant infections, such as those caused by GC and methicillin-resistant *Staphylococcus aureus* (MRSA), result in prolonged illness with potentially greater mortality and morbidity as well as added healthcare expenditure.

Scientists have recently proposed that the Obg protein is a potential molecular target for the development of new therapeutic interventions against drug-resistant bacteria. Obg and Obg-like proteins are highly conserved GTPases, present in bacteria, archaea, and eukaryotes. G proteins typically display high affinities for nucleotides, low dissociation rates in the absence of exogenous exchange factors, and low intrinsic hydrolysis activity.

Obg homologs are essential for the survival of both Gram-positive and Gram-negative bacteria, with depletion of the protein resulting in species-specific pleiotropy. Bacterial Obg proteins have been associated with a variety of cellular functions, including ribosome biogenesis and maturation, DNA synthesis and replication, and chromosomal segregation. Both the association between Obg and ribosome assembly and its proposed role in inducing bacterial multidrug tolerance make Obg a promising drug target.

This passage was adapted from "Targeting an Essential GTPase Obg for the Development of Broad-Spectrum Antibiotics." Bonventre J, Zielke R, Korotkov K, and Sikora A. *PLoS ONE*. 2016. 11(2) doi:10.1371/journal.pone.0148222 for use under the terms of the Creative Commons CC BY 4.0 license (http://creativecommons.org/licenses/by/4.0/legalcode).

Question 30

Researchers often stain clinical samples provided by patients in order to determine the most likely cause of infection. By Gram stain, GC would most likely appear:

○ **A.** purple due to a thick peptidoglycan cell wall.

○ **B.** purple due to a thin peptidoglycan cell wall.

○ **C.** pink due to a thick peptidoglycan cell wall.

○ **D.** pink due to a thin peptidoglycan cell wall.

Question 31

Development of methicillin resistance in *Staphylococcus aureus* strains most likely arose due to:

○ **A.** a mutation that altered the confirmation of the active site of transpeptidase.

○ **B.** a mutation that increased the methylation of the transpeptidase gene on the bacterial genome.

○ **C.** a mutation that deleted the TATA box of the transpeptidase promoter.

○ **D.** a mutation that created a new repressor of the transpeptidase gene.

Question 32

Obg inhibitors are LEAST likely to:

○ **A.** prevent docking of ribosomes at the rough endoplasmic membrane, limiting translation.

○ **B.** inhibit formation of the septal ring.

○ **C.** interfere with topoisomerase enzymes.

○ **D.** prevent the association between the large and small ribosomal subunits.

Question 33

Obg inhibitors are most likely to resemble which of the following molecules?

○ **A.** ATP

○ **B.** Ca^{2+}

○ **C.** Ubiquitin

○ **D.** Glucose-6-phosphate

Passage 7 (Questions 34-39)

Pseudomonas aeruginosa is a gram-negative pathogen capable of causing chronic respiratory infections in patients with cystic fibrosis. These bacteria are associated with the rapid development of resistance to antibiotics including the carbapenems, making eradication of this microorganism from the airways of cystic fibrosis patients exceedingly difficult. Carbapenems, such as imipenem, meropenem, and doripenem are frequently used as drugs of last resort for the treatment of multidrug-resistant infections. These drugs work by inhibiting multiple penicillin-binding proteins responsible for constructing the bacterial cell wall.

In non-carbapenemase-producing strains of bacteria, meropenem and doripenem resistance is associated with the overexpression of the *mexAB-oprM* efflux pump and concomitant loss of the carbapenem-specific porin OprD. Porins are transmembrane proteins that form wide channels for the diffusion of large molecules. Imipenem resistance has only been associated with the down-regulation of OprD. Mutations such as nucleotide substitutions, deletions, and insertion sequence (IS) elements within the *oprD* gene or its promoter region can decrease or cause a loss of OprD production, resulting in significant reductions in susceptibility of the bacteria to carbapenem antibiotics.

Experiment 1

A clinical isolate of the bacteria PA42 was challenged with subinhibitory levels of meropenem in agar plates. To determine whether nucleotide changes within *oprD* had occurred, the gene and its flanking regions were amplified by PCR and sequenced for the clinical strain as well as for selected mutant strains isolated from the meropenem agar plates (Figure 1).

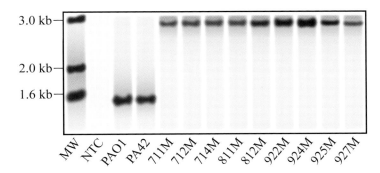

Figure 1 PCR amplification and sequencing of *oprD* in strains of *P. aeruginosa* (Note: MW: molecular weight; NTC: no template control)

Experiment 2

PCR primers ISPa8F1 and OprDRTR3 were used to map the approximate location of the insertion sequence, IS*Pa*8, within the *oprD* gene. The smaller PCR products indicate an insertion by the 3′ end of *oprD* (Figure 2).

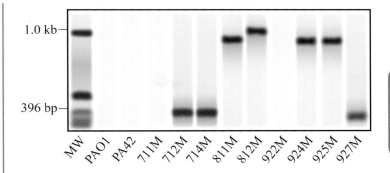

Figure 2 PCR amplification and sequencing of IS*Pa*8 within the *oprD* gene (Note: MW: molecular weight)

Experiment 3

Outer membrane proteins were isolated and stained with Coomassie Blue R-250 dye (Figure 3).

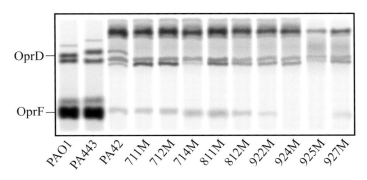

Figure 3 Outer membrane analysis of *P. aeruginosa* PA42 and nine isogenic mutants

This passage was adapted from "Emergence of Carbapenem Resistance Due to the Novel Insertion Sequence IS*Pa*8 in *Pseudomonas aeruginosa*." Fowler RC and Hanson ND. *PLoS Medicine*. 2014. 9(3) doi:10.1371/journal.pone.0091299 for use under the terms of the Creative Commons CC BY 4.0 license (http://creativecommons.org/licenses/by/4.0/legalcode).

Question 34

The acquisition of antibiotic resistance in *P. aeruginosa* specifically through nucleotide substitutions is best characterized as:

○ **A.** genetic polymorphism.

○ **B.** speciation through gradual random changes.

○ **C.** genetic drift.

○ **D.** evolutionary adaptation.

Question 35

Based on the information in the passage, the drug meropenem used in the experimental setup is LEAST likely to be:

○ **A.** effective against bacteria with thin peptidoglycan layers in their cell walls.

○ **B.** effective in treating respiratory infections in patients with cystic fibrosis.

○ **C.** ineffective against *Streptococcus*, which are gram-positive cocci.

○ **D.** ineffective against carbapenemase-producing strains of *P. aeruginosa*.

Question 36

P. aeruginosa is typically classified as an aerobic organism. Which of the following observations would serve to indicate that the current classification is misleading?

○ **A.** The bacteria are found to be lacking mitochondria for cellular respiration.

○ **B.** The bacteria are able to survive in thick mucus in the airways of patients with cystic fibrosis.

○ **C.** The bacteria generate ATP from ATP synthase along the cellular membrane.

○ **D.** The bacteria are found to be rod-shaped bacilli.

Question 37

Which of the following findings, when combined with the data in the passage, would support the conclusion that the development of antibiotic resistance in the mutant strains is caused by the insertion of a large segment of DNA?

○ **A.** The expression of the porin OprD on the outer membrane is found to be significantly decreased compared to non-mutant strains.

○ **B.** A sequence of DNA within the *oprD* gene of one of the mutants is found to have similarity to a transposase gene.

○ **C.** An increase in *mexA* mRNA transcript levels is found in mutant strains.

○ **D.** No PCR product was observed for mutant 711M in the second experiment.

Question 38

The amino acids facing the inner channel of the porin OprD are best described as having which of the following types of R groups?

○ **A.** Aromatic

○ **B.** Aliphatic

○ **C.** Polar

○ **D.** Hydrophobic

Question 39

Which of the following accurately describes the sample labeled PAO1 and its purpose in the experiments described in the passage?

○ **A.** It is a control sample with no DNA and is meant to validate the experiment.

○ **B.** It is a control sample containing DNA taken from a different species and is meant to validate the experiment.

○ **C.** It is a sample for comparison and contains DNA from an isolate of bacteria that was exposed to high doses of meropenem.

○ **D.** It is a sample for comparison and contains DNA from an isolate of bacteria that is susceptible to meropenem.

Passage 8 (Questions 40-43)

Chlamydia trachomatis is a Gram negative, obligate intracellular pathogen responsible for millions of cases annually of sexually transmitted diseases. Throughout evolution, these bacteria have undergone extensive genome reduction, leading to the loss of several biosynthetic pathways. Regarding lipid synthesis, they possess the enzymes to synthesize some phospholipids, but lack genes to make others. Early studies demonstrate the transfer of typical eukaryotic host lipids to the bacteria, including phosphatidylcholine, sphingophospholipid and cholesterol. Interestingly, host lipids are not merely incorporated into the bacteria's plasma membrane, but some serve as precursors for bacteria-specific ether lipids called plasmalogens.

The developmental cycle of these intracellular bacteria takes place within a membrane-bound compartment, sometimes called the inclusion. Some of the host lipids reach the lumen of the inclusion in the form of lipid droplets (LD). These are made up of a core of triacylglycerol and sterol esters surrounded by a phospholipid monolayer and a coat of proteins. LD are often situated adjacent to peroxisomes and are thought to furnish substrates to some peroxisomal enzymes. Peroxisomes harbor enzymes engaged in an array of metabolic functions, including the oxidation of fatty acids, the biosynthesis of ether lipids, the metabolism of reactive oxygen species, and the synthesis of bile acids. Since LD are imported into inclusions, and peroxisomes are often associated with LD, researchers investigated whether peroxisomes might also be imported into inclusions and exploited by the bacteria.

Figure 1 shows the results of a quantitative image analysis where bacteria and peroxisomes are fluorescently tagged and visualized by fluorescent microscopy within a region of interest (ROI).

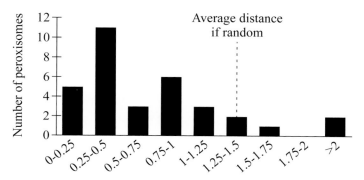

Figure 1 Quantification of the distances between intra-inclusion peroxisomes and bacteria

Human fibroblasts lacking peroxisomes due to a defective *PEX19* gene, which is essential for assembling the peroxisome membrane, and control human fibroblasts were infected with *C. trachomatis*. Cells were fixed, and the number of inclusion-forming units was determined (Figure 2).

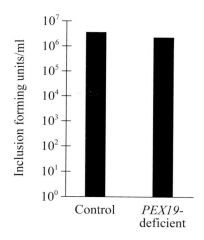

Figure 2 The effect of peroxisomes on *C. trachomatis* infection and development

This passage was adapted from "The Intracellular Bacteria *Chlamydia* Hijack Peroxisomes and Utilize Their Enzymatic Capacity to Produce Bacteria-Specific Phospholipids." Boncompain G, Muller C, Meas-Yedid V, Schmitt-Kopplin P, Lazarow PB, et al. *PLoS Medicine*. 2014. 9(1) doi:10.1371/journal.pone.0086196 for use under the terms of the Creative Commons CC BY 4.0 license (http://creativecommons.org/licenses/by/4.0/legalcode).

Question 40

Of the three types of eukaryotic host lipids discussed in the passage, two of them share which of the following characteristics?

○ **A.** They lack a polar phosphate group.

○ **B.** They are classified as hydrophobic.

○ **C.** They form micelles with a core of water.

○ **D.** They are considered amphipathic.

Question 41

The information and data in the passage best support the conclusion that the lack of host cell peroxisomes due to a defective *PEX19* gene:

○ **A.** results in no change to the bacteria *C. trachomatis*.

○ **B.** affects the ability of the bacteria to replicate.

○ **C.** leads to a loss in the exploitation regarding ether lipids.

○ **D.** is the result of extensive genome reduction.

Question 42

The information in the passage helps to support the hypothesis that *C. trachomatis* have evolved to be highly adapted to human cells through:

○ **A.** random mutations resulting in altered replication.

○ **B.** viral transduction of DNA through bacteriophages.

○ **C.** loss of genetic material carried on plasmids.

○ **D.** a symbiotic relationship between the bacteria and human cells.

Question 43

The information in the passage suggests that peroxisomes in eukaryotic host cells have which of the following functions in the synthesis of plasmalogens by the bacteria?

○ **A.** They store lipids and proteins within a single bilayer membrane.

○ **B.** They break down hydrogen peroxide to avoid cell damage.

○ **C.** They contain enzymes involved in the formation of specific lipids.

○ **D.** They self-replicate and grow by taking up lipids in the cytosol.

Questions 44 - 47 do not refer to a passage and are independent of each other.

Question 44

A researcher is trying to grow *E.coli*, but the bacteria continually fail to grow on agar. He suspects that there may be a bacteriophage contaminating his samples. Which of the following might confirm this hypothesis?

○ **A.** Stain the bacteria with a gram stain and examine under a light microscope.

○ **B.** Introduce a molecule that causes proteins with signal sequences to aggregate into toxic clusters.

○ **C.** Re-incubate the cell plates at a higher temperature.

○ **D.** Use a fluorescent binding molecule to tag the 3′ end of DNA and view microscopically.

Question 45

Which of the following is NOT expected to be affected by an experimental drug that binds cholesterol and increases its level of elimination via the digestive tract?

○ **A.** The signaling between cells through lipophilic hormones

○ **B.** The synthesis of steroids in the rough endoplasmic reticulum

○ **C.** The structure of the inner leaflet of the plasma membrane

○ **D.** The transcription of genes regulated by intracellular receptors

Question 46

A cell's surface proteins are tagged with blue fluorescent dye and fused with a separate cell whose surface proteins are tagged with a red dye. Immediately after fusion, one half of this cell appears red while the other half appears blue. Which of the following is most likely to be observed under a fluorescence microscope over time?

○ **A.** The color labels remain segregated due to stable intermolecular interactions between membrane components.

○ **B.** The color labels intermix due to stable intermolecular interactions between membrane components.

○ **C.** The color labels remain segregated due to transient intermolecular interactions between membrane components.

○ **D.** The color labels intermix due to transient intermolecular interactions between membrane components.

Question 47

The cristae of steroid producing cells are tubular and more developed. Which of the following would be viable explanations for this phenomenon?

    I. Exporting cells require more ATP, and more membrane surface area allows greater rates of oxidative phosphorylation

    II. Cholesterol synthesis occurs on the inner mitochondrial membrane

    III. Ketone body synthesis occurs on the inner mitochondrial membrane

  ○ **A.** I only

  ○ **B.** I and II only

  ○ **C.** II and III only

  ○ **D.** I and III only

Passage 9 (Questions 48-52)

A change in the intracellular calcium concentration is an important signal that controls versatile cellular processes, including muscle contraction and neurotransmitter release into neural synapses. At the plasma membrane, activation of Na^+ gradient-dependent Ca^{2+} transporters is one main mechanism for exporting calcium out of cells when its concentration is elevated. Mutations in these transporters have been shown to increase the risk of heart attacks and seizures.

One transporter responsible for Na^+ gradient-dependent Ca^{2+} transport is NCX1.1, which exchanges one calcium ion for three sodium ions. Deletion of a calmodulin binding site (CaMS) or mutations in the ion pore may significantly reduce exchange activity. However, the membrane orientation of the exchanger and its regulation by calmodulin (CaM) have not been experimentally determined. A predicted schematic of NCX1.1 is shown in Figure 1.

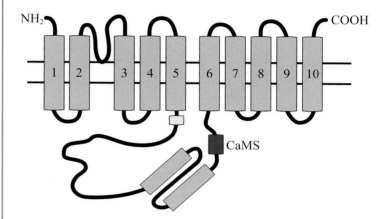

Figure 1 Predicted schematic illustration of NCX1.1

In order to understand whether the CaMS affects the localization of NCX1.1 to the plasma membrane, scientists expressed NCX1.1 with or without CaMS in human embryonic kidney (HEK293T) cells and stained the cells with an antibody against NCX1.1. After fixation and permeabilization, images showed that wild-type NCX1.1 was largely present on the exoplasmic side of the plasma membrane. NCX1.1 mutants that lack the CaMS (NCX1.1ΔCaMS) were mostly distributed in a cytosolic region near the membrane.

To further characterize the importance of the CaMS in CaM-mediated regulation, scientists mutated the three conserved amino acid residues in the CaMS from F, V, and L to A, A, and D respectively (named F1A, V5A, L8D) and monitored the calcium efflux activity of NCX1.1. The results are shown in Figure 2.

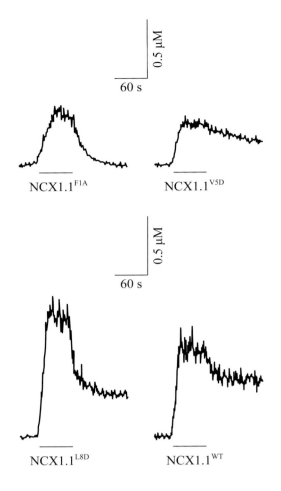

Figure 2 Calcium efflux for F1A, V5D, and L8D mutant NCX1.1 compared to wild-type NCX1.1

Question 48

NCX1.1 domains 4 and 5 are LEAST likely to contain with of the following amino acids in their alpha helices?

- **A.** R
- **B.** V
- **C.** I
- **D.** S

Question 49

Which additional experimental evidence would best support the role of CaMS in NCX1.1 membrane localization?

- **A.** Deletion of CaMS allows NCX1.1 localization to the exoplasmic side of the plasma membrane.
- **B.** CaMS is found to associate with a protein responsible for flipping charged proteins across the plasma membrane.
- **C.** N-terminal mutation of NCX1.1 prevents its localization to the cytosolic side of the plasma membrane.
- **D.** CaMS is found to associate with Golgi transport vesicles.

Question 50

NCX1.1 is likely to assist the:

- **A.** simple diffusion of Ca^{2+} across the membrane.
- **B.** the passive diffusion of Ca^{2+} across the membrane.
- **C.** the primary active transport of Ca^{2+} across the membrane.
- **D.** the secondary active transport of Ca^{2+} across the membrane.

Question 51

In a follow-up *in vivo* experiment, scientist expressed V5A CaMS instead of wild-type CaMS in mouse cardiac myocytes. Which of the following physiologic findings was likely observed?

- **A.** Bradycardia, a heart rate lower than normal
- **B.** Tachycardia, a heart rate higher than normal
- **C.** Tachypnea, a breathing rate higher than normal
- **D.** Bradypnea, a breathing rate lower than normal

Question 52

Cellular fluorescence staining on cardiac myocytes showed that F-actin co-localized with mutant NCX1.1 on the cytosolic side of the plasma membrane. The cellular activities of actin include:

- I. the intracellular transport of vesicles.
- II. mediating muscle contraction.
- III. providing structural support to the plasma membrane.

- **A.** I only
- **B.** I and II only
- **C.** II and III only
- **D.** I, II, and III

Passage 10 (Questions 53-56)

Autophagy is a well-conserved cellular catabolic process of self-degradation through the lysosomal machinery and plays an important role in both normal physiology and diseases. During autophagy, an autophagosome filled with organelles marked for destruction is fused with a lysosome, forming an autophagic vacuole (AV).

Flow cytometry has been used to monitor autophagy by using the LC3B fluorescence molecule, which allows researchers to bypass counting individual AVs in a sample. Additionally, FAOS (fluorescence-activated organelle sorting) allows researchers to sort labeled and gradient-purified organelles such as endosomes or lysosomes, and is sometimes referred to as SOFA (single organelle flow analysis). Flow analyses of purified organelles, such as endosomes, mitochondria, phagosomes, and more recently autophagosomes and lysosomes, have been reported using various fluorescent probes. These reports relied on the established preparative methods for isolation and characterization of pure organelle fractions, including autophagosomes, which usually involve elaborate procedures that take several days and are designed to isolate pure fractions from a single sample, which often requires a large amount of starting material.

Researchers developed a method to detect AVs in cell homogenates as a population of particles that were labeled fluorescently. Inhibition of autophagy induction with 3-methyladenine or knockdown of ATG proteins prevented the accumulation of these AVs. This assay can be easily performed in a high-throughput format and opens up previously unexplored avenues for autophagy analysis. Researchers used this assay to measure the degree of autophagy following treatment with a lysosomal protease inhibitor (Figure 1).

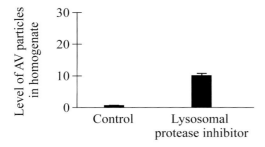

Figure 1 AV particles in homogenate following treatment with an autophagy inhibitor

This passage was adapted from "Novel Quantitative Autophagy Analysis by Organelle Flow Cytometry after Cell Sonication." Degtyarev M, Reichelt M, and Lin K. *PLoS ONE.* 2014. 9(1) doi:10.1371/journal.pone.0087707 for use under the terms of the Creative Commons CC BY 4.0 license (http://creativecommons.org/licenses/by/4.0/legalcode).

Question 53

Which of the following statements correctly describes the relationship between ATG proteins and AVs?

- ○ **A.** ATG proteins are unimportant to AVs because AV detection was increased following knockdown of ATG proteins.
- ○ **B.** ATG proteins are unimportant to AVs because AV detection was reduced following knockdown of ATG proteins.
- ○ **C.** ATG proteins are important to AVs because AV detection was unaffected following knockdown of ATG proteins.
- ○ **D.** ATG proteins are important to AVs because AV detection was reduced following knockdown of ATG proteins.

Question 54

Which of the following is correct based on the results of Figure 1?

- ○ **A.** When autophagy is inhibited, the cells compensate by increasing production of AVs.
- ○ **B.** When autophagy is increased, the cells compensate by increasing production of AVs.
- ○ **C.** Following treatment with the inhibitor, the cells end up with a net increase in autophagy levels.
- ○ **D.** AVs are found in higher levels in the control.

Question 55

The researchers use a molecule called LC3B in some of their experiments. LC3B could be:

- ○ **A.** an antibody against a protein only found on AVs.
- ○ **B.** a fluorescent molecule that binds to all DNA.
- ○ **C.** a fluorescent molecule that binds to all mRNA.
- ○ **D.** an antibody against a protein found on all vacuoles.

Question 56

Based on the passage, which of the following could be a role of autophagy in the cell?

   I. Destruction of intracellular infected organelles

   II. Recycling of components from worn out organelles

   III. Apoptosis

- ○ **A.** I only
- ○ **B.** II only
- ○ **C.** I and III only
- ○ **D.** I, II, and III

Questions 57 - 59 do not refer to a passage and are independent of each other.

Question 57

The production of which of the following will be most impacted by a deficiency in the smooth ER?

○ **A.** Alcohol

○ **B.** Lactate

○ **C.** Glucose

○ **D.** Triglycerides

Question 58

A researcher exposes a sample of human cells to an antibody against tubulin that is conjugated to a green fluorescent probe. Which of the following statements is true regarding this experimental plan?

○ **A.** Human cells infected with bacteria will fluoresce strongly green due to the bacterial flagella.

○ **B.** Ciliated cells obtained from the respiratory tract will not fluoresce.

○ **C.** The experiment will be unsuccessful because tubulin is found in prokaryotic cilia.

○ **D.** Cells that have motile functions are more likely to fluoresce green.

Question 59

Which of the following has the same structure as a micelle?

○ **A.** Nuclear membrane

○ **B.** Cell membrane

○ **C.** Mitochondrial outer membrane

○ **D.** Digested fats in the lumen of the small intestine

STOP. If you finish before time is called, check your work. You may go back to any question in this test.

ANSWERS & EXPLANATIONS for Test 1A can be found on p. 190.

The Cell

MINI-TEST 1B

Time: 65 minutes
Questions 1–41

DIRECTIONS: Most of the questions in this test section are grouped with a passage. Read the passage, then select the best answer to each question. Some questions are independent of any passage and of one another. Select the best answer to each of these questions. If you are unsure of an answer, rule out incorrect choices and select from the remaining options. Indicate your selection beside the option you choose. A periodic table can be found on the last page of this book for you to use at any point during this test section.

Passage 1 (Questions 1-5)

Mitochondria are multifunctional organelles that play a key role in the metabolism of reactive oxygen species (ROS). Manifestations of the aging process include, among other things, a progressive loss of cells due to apoptosis induced by oxidative damages. Initial ROS are generated mainly by complexes I and III of the mitochondrial respiratory chain in the form of superoxide, which is then converted to hydrogen peroxide by superoxide dismutase (SOD2). The mitochondrial genome is extremely susceptible to the damaging effects of ROS produced in mitochondria as it has a limited DNA repair capacity. Impaired mitochondria with mutated mtDNA tend to accumulate in aging tissues, further contributing to the aging process.

Hydrogen peroxide (H_2O_2) serves as a signaling molecule and participates in numerous physiological responses. NADPH-dependent oxidases (NOXs) coupled to many membrane-bound receptors are believed to be a major source of physiologically produced ROS.

The use of ROS in physiological signaling may be associated with a trade off in protection against oxidative damage, which contributes to an acceleration of aging and a shorter lifespan. A possible mediator of the mechanism is p66Shc, a product of an alternatively spliced transcript from the *SHC1* gene. A fraction of p66Shc isoform is targeted to the mitochondrial matrix where it is implicated in the regulated increase in intracellular ROS levels. Researchers studied the effect of p66Shc knockout on cell viability following exposure to hydrogen peroxide (Figure 1).

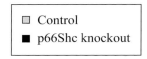

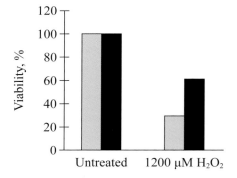

Figure 1 Effect of oxidative stress on p66Shc knockout

This passage was adapted from "Prooxidant Properties of p66shc Are Mediated by Mitochondria in Human Cells." Galimov ER, Chernyak BV, Sidorenko AS, Tereshkova AV, and Chumakov PM. *PLoS ONE*. 2014. 9(3) doi:10.1371/journal.pone.00866521 for use under the terms of the Creative Commons CC BY 4.0 license (http://creativecommons.org/licenses/by/4.0/legalcode).

Question 1

Which of the following is true of mitochondrial proteins based on the passage?

- **A.** All mitochondrial proteins are generated from mtDNA.
- **B.** All mitochondrial proteins are generated from nuclear DNA.
- **C.** Some mitochondrial proteins are generated from mtDNA, while others are generated from nuclear DNA.
- **D.** There are no proteins in the mitochondria.

Question 2

Which of the following best summarizes the results of Figure 1?

- **A.** p66Shc makes cells more resistant to ROS and oxidative stress since the knockout has lower viability.
- **B.** p66Shc makes cells more resistant to ROS and oxidative stress since the knockout has higher viability.
- **C.** p66Shc makes cells more vulnerable to ROS and oxidative stress since the knockout has lower viability.
- **D.** p66Shc makes cells more vulnerable to ROS and oxidative stress since the knockout has higher viability.

Question 3

Which of the following mutations to mtDNA could be inherited by the next generation?

    I. Mutation in the mtDNA of a somatic cell
    II. Mutation in the mtDNA of an egg
   III. Mutation in the mtDNA of a sperm

- **A.** I only
- **B.** II only
- **C.** II and III only
- **D.** I, II, and III

Question 4

Hydrogen peroxide generated by the mitochondria would do the most damage to the cell in the:

- ○ **A.** nucleolus.
- ○ **B.** rough ER.
- ○ **C.** lysosome.
- ○ **D.** nucleus.

Question 5

A cell with high levels of ROS would most likely have an increased count of:

- ○ **A.** lysosomes.
- ○ **B.** ER.
- ○ **C.** Golgi bodies.
- ○ **D.** vacuoles.

Passage 2 (Questions 6-9)

Mitochondria are important organelles for the cell as they produce energy, regulate redox balance and maintain Ca^{2+} homeostasis. Mitochondrial dysfunction is associated with numerous diseases such as neurodegenerative diseases, diabetes and cancer. Among the factors leading to mitochondrial dysfunction are depolarization of the mitochondrial transmembrane potential, mutations in mtDNA, oxidative stress, and alterations in mitochondrial number.

Many viral proteins target the mitochondria and interfere with their functions, contributing to the pathology of some viral diseases. For example, association of hepatitis C virus (HCV) proteins with the mitochondria plays an important role in the pathogenesis of HCV induced chronic liver diseases and liver cancer. HCV proteins enter the mitochondria causing an increase in mitochondrial Ca^{2+} uptake, reactive oxygen species production and mitochondrial permeability transition.

Viruses can modulate mitochondrial functions for their benefit. ERK1/2 signal cascade activates cytoplasmic and nuclear substrates that promote cell survival, cell division, differentiation and cell motility. As a result of its functions, activation of ERK1/2 signaling has been reported to be an important mediator in the pathogenesis of a number of viruses (Figure 1).

Parvoviruses are small non-enveloped viruses with linear ssDNA genome. Pathology of parvoviral infection is often directly connected to the cytotoxic nature of infection. Enteritis, myocarditis, hepatitis and reticulocytopenia are consequences of parvovirus induced cell death. The mechanisms of cell death have been reported to be apoptosis, necrosis and death by cytoskeletal rearrangements. Canine parvovirus (CPV) was used by researchers as a model to study the effect of viruses on mitochondria.

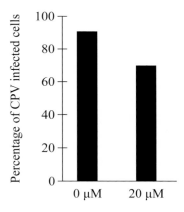

Figure 1 Effect of U0126, an inhibitor of ERK1/2 activation, on CPV infection

This passage was adapted from "Role of Mitochondria in Parvovirus Pathology." Nykky J, Vuento M, and Gilbert L. *PLoS ONE*. 2014. 9(1) doi:10.1371/journal. pone.0086124 for use under the terms of the Creative Commons CC BY 4.0 license (http://creativecommons.org/licenses/by/4.0/legalcode).

TEST 1B

Question 6

What is the most likely reason that it would be favorable for viruses to activate ERK1/2 signaling? During infection:

○ **A.** ERK1/2 activation prevents apoptosis and ensures destruction of viral progeny.

○ **B.** ERK1/2 activation prevents apoptosis and ensures production and release of viral progeny.

○ **C.** ERK1/2 activation causes apoptosis and ensures destruction of viral progeny.

○ **D.** ERK1/2 activation causes apoptosis and ensures production and release of viral progeny.

Question 7

Which of the following statements correctly describes the relationship between U0126 and apoptosis?

○ **A.** U0126 reduces apoptosis through an increase in ERK1/2 signaling.

○ **B.** U0126 reduces apoptosis through a decrease in ERK1/2 signaling.

○ **C.** U0126 induces apoptosis through an increase in ERK1/2 signaling.

○ **D.** U0126 induces apoptosis through a decrease in ERK1/2 signaling.

Question 8

Which of the following is true regarding the mitochondria?

I. The mitochondria has a double membrane.

II. mtDNA is inherited from the father.

III. The mitochondria contains folds called cristae.

○ **A.** I only

○ **B.** II only

○ **C.** I and III only

○ **D.** II and III only

Question 9

CPV can alter the lipid content of the mitochondria drastically. If this is not due to the presence of CPV in the mitochondria, then what organelle is likely to also be impacted directly by CPV infection?

○ **A.** Golgi apparatus

○ **B.** Nucleolus

○ **C.** Ribosome

○ **D.** Smooth ER

Questions 10 - 13 do not refer to a passage and are independent of each other.

Question 10

Flattening of cristae in the mitochondria would have which of the following effects?

○ **A.** Increased import of glucose into the mitochondria from the cytoplasm

○ **B.** Decreased level of glycolysis in the mitochondria

○ **C.** Decreased generation of ATP by oxidative phosphorylation

○ **D.** Decreased import of fatty acids into the cell

Question 11

During dehydration, cells in the brain may attempt to compensate for the lack of water in the body in order and maintain their size by:

○ **A.** increasing osmotic pressure in the cells by briefly becoming hypertonic to the extracellular fluid.

○ **B.** decreasing osmotic pressure in the cells by briefly becoming hypertonic to the extracellular fluid.

○ **C.** increasing osmotic pressure in the cells by briefly becoming hypotonic to the extracellular fluid.

○ **D.** decreasing osmotic pressure in the cells by briefly becoming hypotonic to the extracellular fluid.

Question 12

Digitalis inhibits the NKA (Na^+/K^+ ATPase) pump by binding to the open K^+ binding face and irreversibly inhibiting it. This in turn reverses the polarity of a Na^+/Ca^{2+} exchanger (a secondary active transporter). In small doses, this would mostly likely be used therapeutically to achieve:

○ **A.** decreased neurotransmitter release at synapses.

○ **B.** increased muscle contractility.

○ **C.** stronger action potentials.

○ **D.** localized pain relief.

Question 13

Disruption of the rough endoplasmic reticulum is LEAST likely to impact:

○ **A.** the concentration of albumin the blood.

○ **B.** the acid hydrolase composition of lysosomes.

○ **C.** the rate of nuclear protein synthesis.

○ **D.** the concentration of glycosylation enzymes in the Golgi apparatus.

Passage 3 (Questions 14-17)

The biogenesis of a ribosome in the eukaryotic cell can be detected at the start cell cycle checkpoint, and it involves many aspects of the cellular machinery. There is much known about membrane-bound ribosomes, but practically nothing is known about the cytoplasmic distribution of free ribosomes. Ribosomes are thought to redistribute such that they accumulate at the site of protein synthesis, implying that the ribosome population undergoes dynamic movement as required. An understanding of how a cell can command ribosome movement in the cytoplasm to allow translation is of significant interest due to the potential effect of ribosomal distribution on health and disease. Proper distribution has a great impact on the survival of daughter cells formed in mitosis, which need an adequate number of ribosomes to ensure the synthesis of important proteins for future physiological events.

To study the localization of ribosomes throughout the cell cycle, researchers examined HeLa cancer cells through various stages of the cell cycle. Ribosomes were stained and counted near the nuclear membrane (NM) and cell membrane (CM), as seen in Table 1. During the M phase, a fairly consistent cytoplasmic dispersion pattern was found. When the ribosomal staining of each daughter cell during late telophase was measured, the ratio between the two new cells was close to one.

Table 1 Ribosome Count Near NM and CM during G_1 and G_2

Phase of cell cycle	Ribosomes	
	Near NM	Near CM
G_1	17.9	18.9
G_2	23.0	12.6

This passage was adapted from "Ribosome Distribution in HeLa Cells during the Cell Cycle." Tsai YJ, Lee HI, and Lin A. *PLoS ONE*. 2012. 7(3) doi:10.1371/journal. pone.0032820 for use under the terms of the Creative Commons CC BY 3.0 license (http://creativecommons.org/licenses/by/3.0/legalcode).

Question 14

Which of the following is true of the ribosomes studied in this experiment?

I. These ribosomes are composed of rRNA.

II. These ribosomes consist of 2 subunits of different size.

III. These ribosomes independently produce secreted proteins.

- **A.** I only
- **B.** III only
- **C.** I and II only
- **D.** II and II only

Question 15

Damage to which of the following would most likely cause impairment of a cell's ability to localize and redistribute ribosomes?

- **A.** Microtubules
- **B.** Flagella
- **C.** Cilia
- **D.** Nucleolus

Question 16

The ratio of ribosome staining in daughter cells following mitosis reveals that ribosomes:

- **A.** are degraded prior to mitosis and resynthesized after the cell completes mitosis.
- **B.** move to opposite poles during anaphase.
- **C.** line up in the center of the dividing cell during metaphase.
- **D.** are evenly divided between the two daughter cells.

Question 17

Which of the following is a conclusion that can be drawn from Figure 1?

- **A.** Ribosomes aggregate near the NM during both phases.
- **B.** Ribosomes aggregate near the CM during both phases.
- **C.** Ribosomes migrate towards the CM between G_1 and G_2.
- **D.** Ribosomes migrate towards the NM between G_1 and G_2.

Passage 4 (Questions 18-22)

Human African trypanosomiasis, also known as sleeping sickness, is a vector-borne parasitic disease in sub-Saharan Africa with very limited medical resources. *Trypanosoma brucei gambiense* and *Trypanosoma brucei rhodesiense* are the etiological unicellular eukaryotic parasites of sleeping sickness in humans. These parasites live and grow extracellularly in the blood and tissue fluids of humans or cattle and are transmitted between hosts by tsetse flies. At the beginning of the infection, trypanosomes proliferate in the bloodstream and lymphatic system. Eventually, these parasites cross the blood-brain barrier and enter the central nervous system. At this stage, patients show a variety of neurological symptoms and often exhibit an alteration of the circadian sleep/wake pattern, which is why the disease is called "sleeping sickness."

If the patient does not receive treatment before the parasites invade the central nervous system, neurological damage caused by parasites is irreversible. Current drugs are not successful in the treatment of the disease, but some scientists have suggested using tubulin inhibitors to treat trypanosomiasis. The fast population doubling rate of trypanosomes makes them highly dependent on tubulin polymerization and depolymerization. More importantly, tubulin is critical for trypanosome locomotion, which is critical for trypanosome survival.

In order to determine whether tubulin inhibitors are an effective treatment for trypanosomiasis, scientists screened a library of compounds similar to the one presented in Figure 1, using various functional groups at the R_1, R_2, R_3, and R_4 positions.

Figure 1 General structure of screened anti-trypanosome agents

After identifying three potential compounds, the scientists treated cultured trypanosomes with DMSO (Control) or compounds 11, 12, or 79. After isolating cellular protein, they measured the level of tubulin in the cell to determine whether the compounds blocked tubulin polymerization, induced the degradation of tubulin, or had no effect on tubulin levels. The results are shown in Figure 2.

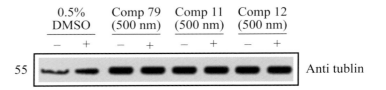

Figure 2 Western blot for tubulin in cultured trypanosomes

This passage was adapted from "Orally Active and Selective Tubulin Inhibitors as Anti-Trypanosome Agents." Nanavaty V, Lama R, Sandhu R, Zhong B, Kulman D, et al. *PLoS ONE*. 2016. 11(1) doi:10.1371/journal.pone.0146289 for use under the terms of the Creative Commons CC BY 4.0 license (http://creativecommons.org/licenses/by/4.0/legalcode).

Question 18

Which of the following statements best describes the mechanism of action of the various anti-tubulin compounds in Figure 2?

- **A.** Compound 79 decreases the transcription of *TUBB*, resulting in a reduction in the protein levels of TUBB
- **B.** Compound 11 decreases the translation of the *TUBB* mRNA, resulting in a reduction in the protein levels of TUBB
- **C.** Compound 12 destabilizes tubulin polymers but does not result in a decrease in overall TUBB levels
- **D.** Compound 12 increases ubiquitination of TUBB to prevent cellular proliferation

Question 19

Some trypanosomes become resistant to tubulin inhibitors, even when they are used at high concentrations. Multidrug Resistance Protein 1 (MDR1) is a plasma membrane protein that most likely exports tubulin inhibitors by:

- **A.** hydrolyzing ATP to drive the anti-tubulin compound up its chemical gradient.
- **B.** hydrolyzing ATP to drive the anti-tubulin compound down its chemical gradient.
- **C.** stabilizing the hydration shell of the anti-tubulin compound, allowing it to flow down its concentration gradient.
- **D.** stabilizing the hydration shell of the anti-tubulin compound, allowing it to flow up its concentration gradient.

Question 20

Selective pressure caused by the presence of the tubulin inhibitor often selects for:

- **A.** silent mutations that create a new gene.
- **B.** silent mutations that create a new allele.
- **C.** missense mutations that create a new gene.
- **D.** missense mutations that create a new allele.

Question 21

Trypanosomes are LEAST likely to contain which of the following features compared to central nervous system neurons?

- O **A.** Non-membrane bound nucleus
- O **B.** Histones that bind DNA
- O **C.** mRNA with a 5′ cap and poly-A tail
- O **D.** Golgi apparatus and mitochondria

Question 22

Which of the following is the most likely conclusion that could be drawn from the results of the following additional experiment?

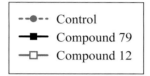

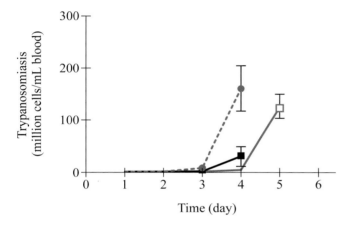

- O **A.** Compound 12 is the most effective at preventing the separation of sister chromatids
- O **B.** Compound 79 is the most effective at preventing flagellar motion in trypanosomes
- O **C.** Neither compound 12 nor 79 are effective at reducing the proliferation of trypanosomes in the blood
- O **D.** Resistance to compound 12 likely takes 30 days or longer to develop

Passage 5 (Questions 23-26)

The maintenance of a resting plasma membrane potential is critical to many processes in the human body such as the transmission of nerve action potentials and the contraction of the heart. The membrane potential is tightly regulated by the passage of ions across the membrane as well as by the transport of much larger charged molecules such as hyaluronan.

Hyaluronan is a glycosaminoglycan synthesized on the inner side of cell membranes and exported by the cystic fibrosis transmembrane conductance regulator (CFTR) of epithelial cells and other cell types. It can be retained by the CD44 receptor on the external portion of the cell membrane, where it alters the membrane potential. To make transport of polyanions possible, the law of electroneutrality must be obeyed, so cations must follow with hyaluronan or even drive hyaluronan export from the cytosol into the extracellular matrix. The most likely cation to generate this effect is K^+ because it is the only cation that the cell passively extrudes in significant quantities.

Three major classes of K^+ channels exist and can be expressed simultaneously. The first category is the voltage-gated channels, which open once the membrane is depolarized. They govern the repolarization of neurons after an action potential.

The second type is the K_{ir} channels (inwardly rectifying potassium channels), which are activated during hyperpolarization. The K_{ir} channels are separated into different subgroups consisting of the ATP-dependent K^+ channel and the G-protein-activated K_{ir} channel.

The third category includes the calcium-activated K^+ channels, which are activated by high intracellular Ca^{2+} concentrations. For all three categories of channels, there are specific inhibitors that can be used. These inhibitors were used to analyze the influence of these channels on the resting membrane potential and hyaluronan export (Table 1).

Table 1 The Effects of K_{ir}, Na^+ and Ca^{2+} Channel Blockers on Inhibiting Hyaluronan Export and on Membrane Potential (Note: Potential difference reflects the change in the potential difference following administration of the inhibitor.)

Channel inhibitor	K_{ir}		Na^+	Ca^{2+}	HA-inhibition (%)	Potential difference (mV)
	K_{ATP}	K_G				
BaCl$_2$	+	+			50	-2
Glibenclamide	+				50	5
Verapamil				+	20	0
Ropivacain	+	+			80	18
Amiloride			+		20	6

This passage was adapted from "Hyaluronan Export through Plasma Membranes Depends on Concurrent K^+ Efflux by K_{ir} Channels." Hagenfeld D, Borkenhagen B, Schulz T, Schillers H, Schumacher U, et al. *PLoS Medicine*. 2012. 7(6) doi:10.1371/journal.pone.0039096 for use under the terms of the Creative Commons CC BY 3.0 license (http://creativecommons.org/licenses/by/3.0/legalcode).

Question 23

The voltage-gated potassium channels of the first group that are activated after membrane depolarization are LEAST likely to be characterized as:

○ **A.** membrane channels carrying out diffusion akin to glucose transport.

○ **B.** channels that open in response to binding of an external molecules

○ **C.** membrane channels carrying out transport of ions down an electrochemical gradient.

○ **D.** channels made of protein subunits that are integral membrane proteins.

Question 24

Which of the following represents a possible step that may occur to a CFTR protein complex following the translation of the gene in airway epithelial cells?

   I. Degradation by hydrolytic enzymes in a lysosome

   II. Glycosylation within mature secretory vesicles

   III. Attachment to the inner leaflet of the plasma membrane

   IV. Glycan processing in the Golgi apparatus

○ **A.** I and IV only

○ **B.** II and III only

○ **C.** II, III, and IV only

○ **D.** I and II only

Question 25

The purpose of using the drug amiloride, which is used to treat high blood pressure, in the experimental setup was likely to:

○ **A.** provide a control group in order to validate the experiment.

○ **B.** analyze the effects of sodium channel inhibition on hyaluronan export.

○ **C.** study the mechanism of sodium ion transport in cultured cells.

○ **D.** assess how common therapeutics influence membrane channels and resting potential.

Question 26

Glibenclamide is a popular drug that is used to treat diabetes. Based on the data in the passage, which of the following likely reflects the mechanism of action of the drug?

○ **A.** It inhibits the activation of the G protein complex to inactivate the associated channel.

○ **B.** It blocks ATP synthase in the cell to prevent the K_{ATP} channel from being activated.

○ **C.** It inhibits the flow of calcium ions into the cell to stimulate the release of insulin.

○ **D.** It alters the membrane potential by inhibiting the passage of ions.

Questions 27 - 29 do not refer to a passage and are independent of each other.

Question 27

Marfan syndrome is an autosomal dominant disorder characterized by the misfolding of a glycoprotein that makes up elastic fibers throughout the body, including in the aorta. This disorder can best be studied using:

○ **A.** skeletal muscle cells.

○ **B.** cardiac muscle cells.

○ **C.** epithelium.

○ **D.** fibroblasts.

Question 28

Connexins are proteins that make up the subunits of gap junctions. How might mutations in the genes for these proteins lead to skin diseases?

○ **A.** The lack of proper gap junctions results in poor epithelial cell attachments.

○ **B.** The lack of proper gap junctions results in altered basal lamina formation.

○ **C.** The lack of proper gap junctions results in impaired intercellular signaling.

○ **D.** The lack of proper gap junctions results in leakage of fluid between cells.

Question 29

A single bacterial colony is removed from a cell plate, resuspended in a liquid solution and plated on an agar medium. After three days of incubation, two colonies growing on opposite ends of the plate are removed and re-plated on agar that contains antibiotic. Colony 1 does not grow on the new plate while Colony 2 shows prolific growth. Which of the following would explain this observation?

○ **A.** Because of outbreeding, Colony 2 is a different species from Colony 1.

○ **B.** Conjugation occurred between Colony 1 and Colony 2.

○ **C.** Colony 2 passed on random mutations through binary fission.

○ **D.** Colony 1 was affected by the bottleneck effect, but Colony 2 was not.

Passage 6 (Questions 30-34)

Lung cancer is one of the most common diseases in the world and the leading cause of cancer related death. *Daphne genkwa* is a well-known traditional medicinal plant distributed mainly in Korea, and its flower has been reported to exhibit anti-cancer activities. Yuanhuacine (YC) is a major component isolated from the flower buds of *Daphne genkwa* (Figure 1).

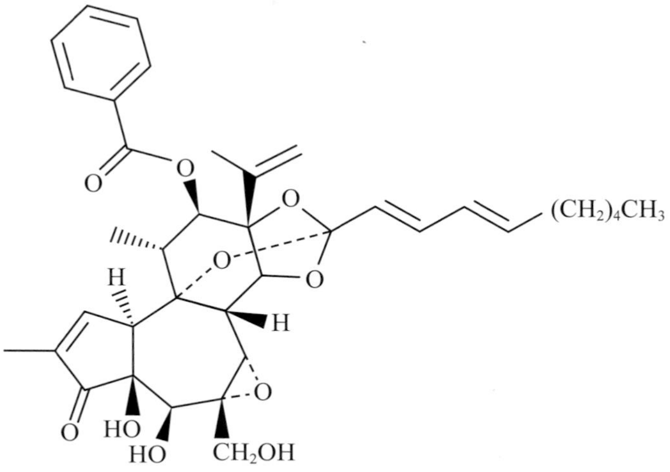

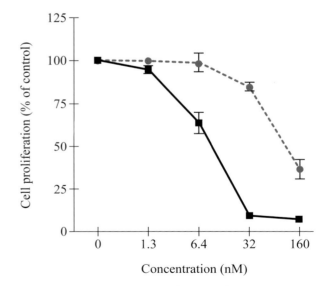

Figure 1 Structure of YC

Experiment 1

In order to test the effect of YC on the proliferation of a non-small cell lung cancer cell line, H1993, scientists treated cultured H1993 cells with increasing concentrations of YC and a chemotherapeutic nucleoside analogue, gefitinib and stained the cells with trypan blue, a dye that stains apoptotic cells. The results are shown in Figure 2.

Figure 2 Effect of YC on cell proliferation in H1993 NSCLC cells

Experiment 2

YC is predicted to interact with AMP-activated protein kinase (AMPK), a ubiquitous serine/threonine protein kinase consisting of a catalytic α subunit and two regulator subunits (β and γ). AMPK controls mTORC2, a key regulator of the actin cytoskeleton that is correlated with cancer metastasis.

It is well known that the asymmetric accumulation of F-actin is associated with cell invasion and migration. To investigate the effect of YC on cancer cell invasion and migration, H1993 cells were treated with YC for 24 hours and the amount of migration was measured (Figure 3). Scientists predicted that AMPK regulation of mTORC2 affected the organization of the actin cytoskeleton, leading to rearrangements of extracellular adhesion proteins and the initiation of events leading to de-differentiation and metastasis.

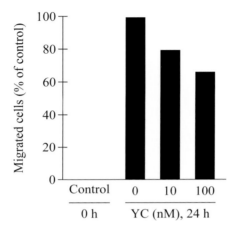

Figure 3 Effect of YC on cell migration and invasion in H1993 cells

Question 30

Based on the structure in Figure 1, YC is most likely to bind which of the following amino acids in AMPK?

- **A.**
- **B.**
- **C.**
- **D.**

Question 31

Trypan blue-stained H1993 cells are likely to show:

 I. condensed chromatin.

 II. fragmented DNA.

 III. membrane blebbing.

- **A.** I only
- **B.** I and II only
- **C.** II and III only
- **D.** I, II, and III

Question 32

The intracellular cytoskeleton is LEAST likely to be composed of:

- **A.** microtubules.
- **B.** intermediate filaments.
- **C.** actin.
- **D.** glycoproteins.

Question 33

Cellular movement that results in metastasis of lung cancer cells requires that the cells dissociate from the basement membrane of the alveolus. Disassembly of which of the following structures would be most important in this process?

- **A.** Gap junctions
- **B.** Desmosomes
- **C.** Hemidesmosomes
- **D.** Tight junctions

Question 34

Increased inhibition of AMPK by higher doses of YC is most likely to:

- **A.** decrease mTORC2-mediated actin polymerization.
- **B.** increase mTORC2-mediated microtubule polymerization.
- **C.** decrease mTORC2-mediated ubiquitination of cell cycle protein cdk2.
- **D.** increase mTORC2-mediated ubiquitination of intermediate filaments.

Passage 7 (Questions 35-38)

Extracellular matrix (ECM) glycoproteins participate in many physiological and pathological processes, including ischemic vascular diseases, inflammation, tumor growth and metastasis. Endothelial cell (EC)-ECM interactions play a key role in cellular functions by binding multiple cell surface receptors and are critical for the activation of cell signal transduction pathways. One of the components of the ECM, vitronectin (VN), is incorporated into the ECM with exposed binding sites that interact with integrins and cell surface receptors that regulate cell adhesion and cellular motility. Levels of VN are increased in patients with various cardiovascular diseases, tumor growth and metastasis.

Angiogenesis, the growth of new blood vessels, encompasses cell proliferation, migration, and differentiation. Loosening of cell-to-cell contacts is the key initial event that causes normally quiescent ECs to initiate angiogenesis. Cell-to-cell adhesion is mainly achieved by vascular endothelial (VE)-cadherin, which is a critical adhesion molecule. Activation of avb3 by integrin antagonists disrupts VE-cadherin and enhances vascular permeability.

Vitronectin has been shown to be involved in promoting transendothelial migration by interacting with leukocyte Mac-1 during adhesion and extravasation (Figure 1). Although ECM-derived VN multimerizes in response to various types of tissue injury, and this transition involves functional changes in the vessel such as angiogenesis, the role of VN in VE-cadherin-mediated cell-to-cell contacts and vascular permeability remain unknown. In the present study, whether VN is implicated in the regulation of cell-to-cell contacts and vascular permeability was evaluated (Figure 2). It was found that VN redistributes VE-cadherin by promoting internalization of VE-cadherin and increases vascular permeability.

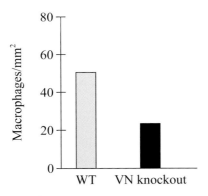

Figure 1 Macrophages exiting blood vessels following injury in Wild-type or VN knockout

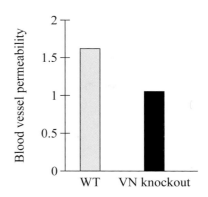

Figure 2 Blood vessel permeability in Wild-type or VN knockout

This passage was adapted from "Vitronectin Increases Vascular Permeability by Promoting VE-Cadherin Internalization at Cell Junctions." Li R, Ren M, Chen N, Luo M, Zhang Z, et al. *PLoS ONE*. 2012. 7(5) doi:10.1371/journal.pone.0037195 for use under the terms of the Creative Commons CC BY 3.0 license (http://creativecommons.org/licenses/by/3.0/legalcode).

Question 35

Which of the following organelles is most likely to have an inverse relationship with the quantity with VE-cadherin?

○ **A.** Rough ER

○ **B.** Smooth ER

○ **C.** Flagella

○ **D.** Nucleus

Question 36

Which of the following is a conclusion that could be drawn from the results of Figure 1 and Figure 2?

○ **A.** VN knockout could reduce immune response to a pathogen by decreasing vessel permeability.

○ **B.** VN knockout could reduce immune response to a pathogen by increasing vessel permeability.

○ **C.** VN knockout could enhance immune response to a pathogen by decreasing vessel permeability.

○ **D.** VN knockout could enhance immune response to a pathogen by increasing vessel permeability.

Question 37

Which of the following is true about intercellular junctions?

   I. Tight junctions form a seal that prevents transcellular movement of most molecules.

   II. Gap junctions can be found in cardiac muscle.

   III. Tight junctions are found in many epithelial tissues.

○ **A.** I only

○ **B.** II only

○ **C.** I and III only

○ **D.** I, II, and III

Question 38

Which of the following statements is true about vitronectin binding to its receptor?

- ○ **A.** Vitronectin binds to a membrane receptor and enters the cell by pinocytosis.
- ○ **B.** Vitronectin binds to a cytoplasmic receptor and subsequently exits the cell by exocytosis.
- ○ **C.** Vitronectin binds to a membrane receptor and enters the cell by endocytosis.
- ○ **D.** Vitronectin binds to a nuclear receptor and subsequently exits the cell by exocytosis.

Questions 39 - 41 do not refer to a passage and are independent of each other.

Question 39

Which molecule is LEAST likely to passively diffuse through a cell membrane?

○ **A.** ○ **B.**

○ **C.** ○ **D.**

Question 40

The HPV vaccine contains hollow, virus-like particles made of recombinant coat proteins. Why might this type of vaccine be ineffective against HIV?

- ○ **A.** HIV contains reverse transcriptase, allowing it to rapidly mutate.
- ○ **B.** HIV targets cells of the immune response that are important to vaccine-induced immunity.
- ○ **C.** The HIV particle has a capsid and an envelope.
- ○ **D.** HIV has a long latent period and can remain undetected in host cells.

Question 41

The cells primarily associated with the production of extracellular matrix components such as glycosaminoglycans are:

- ○ **A.** epithelial cells.
- ○ **B.** lymphocytes.
- ○ **C.** fibroblasts.
- ○ **D.** neurons.

STOP. If you finish before time is called, check your work. You may go back to any question in this test.

ANSWERS & EXPLANATIONS for Test 1B can be found on p. 190.

The Nervous System

TEST 2A

Time: 95 minutes
Questions 1–59

DIRECTIONS: Most of the questions in this test section are grouped with a passage. Read the passage, then select the best answer to each question. Some questions are independent of any passage and of one another. Select the best answer to each of these questions. If you are unsure of an answer, rule out incorrect choices and select from the remaining options. Indicate your selection beside the option you choose. A periodic table can be found on the last page of this book for you to use at any point during this test section.

Passage 1 (Questions 1-4)

Every year, millions of patients around the world are given general anesthesia during major surgeries. Diverse ion channels in the nervous system are major targets of general anesthetics. Among them, neurotransmitter-gated ion channels and voltage-gated K^+ channels are the important players in general anesthesia. Kv1.2 channels encoded by *KCNA2* gene are widely expressed in the brain and mainly localize in the axon initial segment and axon terminals. In these locations, Kv1.2 channels help regulate action potential threshold, repolarization, propagation, and firing patterns.

Sevoflurane is commonly used in human general anesthesia. At relevant concentrations, it increases the maximum conductance. Kv1.2 channels undergo complex and strongly voltage-dependent activation gating involving sequential transitions between multiple closed states and a final cooperative opening step. This mechanism has two major steps. The first corresponds to a major conformational change of the voltage sensors, which unlocks the gating machinery. The second corresponds to a final cooperative rearrangement of the voltage sensors, which ultimately opens the intracellular activation gate.

The S4-S5 transmembrane linker connects the voltage-sensing domain to the pore domain of the Kv1.2 channel and is responsible for the electromechanical coupling that controls voltage-dependent gating. Normalized dose-inhibition of sevoflurane on Kv1.2 follows the Hill equation:

$$\frac{I}{I_0} = \frac{x}{K + x}$$

Equation 1 The Hill Equation

where I/I_0 is the normalized current, x is the drug concentration, and K is the apparent dissociation equilibrium constant between the drug and the protein. To investigate the role of the S4-S5 linker in the modulation of Kv1.2 by sevoflurane, five amino acid residues were mutated in Kv1.2 (Figure 1).

- ■ Wild type
- □ Substituted amino acids

Mutant Kv	314GLKILIQTFRASAKELTLL332
Kv Wild Type	313GLQILGQTLKASMRELGLL331

Figure 1 Amino acid sequence of the mutant and wild type Kv1.2 channels

Reconstituted liposomes with membrane imbedded Kv1.2 channels were used to detect current flowing through the channel after exposure to sevoflurane. The results are shown in Figure 2.

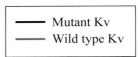
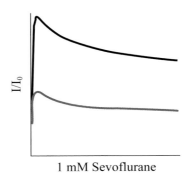

Figure 2 Modulation of Kv mutant and Kv wild type conductance by sevoflurane

Question 1

The resting membrane potential of a neuron is around −70 mV. A mutation in Kv1.2 that increases the resting permeability of the channel to K^+ is likely to give a resting potential of:

- ○ **A.** −120 mV.
- ○ **B.** −80 mV.
- ○ **C.** −40 mV.
- ○ **D.** −20 mV.

Question 2

Kv1.2 channels are likely to be found at the:

  I. axon hillock.
  II. synaptic button.
  III. cell body.

- ○ **A.** I only
- ○ **B.** I and II only
- ○ **C.** I and III only
- ○ **D.** II and III only

Question 3

Kv1.2 is most likely to contain which of the following amino acids in the pore domain of the channel?

○ **A.** R

○ **B.** K

○ **C.** A

○ **D.** E

Question 4

Mutation of the voltage-sensing domain of Kv1.2:

○ **A.** increases the repolarization time of the neuron.

○ **B.** decreases the repolarization time of the neuron.

○ **C.** increases the repolarization time of the neuron.

○ **D.** decreases the repolarization time of the neuron.

Passage 2 (Questions 5-9)

A 44 year-old male patient presents with paralysis that began in the legs and is progressing upwards. The patient recently had a stomach bug and all imaging of the head and spine is normal. With this information, a diagnosis of Guillain-Barré syndrome (GBS) is expected.

Although not completely supported by current evidence, GBS is thought to be the result of antibodies causing demyelination in the peripheral nervous system. To assess the frequency of glycolipid complex antibodies in a cohort of patients, GBS researchers used a newly developed combinatorial glycoarray methodology to screen against a large range of antigens. Serum samples of 181 patients with GBS were analyzed, along with 161 control sera.

The detection of antibodies against specific complexes was associated with particular clinical features including disease severity, requirement for mechanical ventilation, and axonal electrophysiology. This work confirms the activation of the humoral immune system in the dysimmune disease process in GBS, and correlates patterns of antigen recognition with different clinical features.

This passage was adapted from "Antibodies to Heteromeric Glycolipid Complexes in Guillain-Barré Syndrome." Rinaldi S, Brennan KM, Kalna G, Walgaard C, van Doorn P, et al. *PLoS ONE*. 2013. 8(12) doi:10.1371/journal.pone.0082337 for use under the terms of the Creative Commons CC BY 3.0 license (http://creativecommons.org/licenses/by/3.0/legalcode).

Question 5

Damage to which of the following cells is expected in GBS?

○ **A.** Neurons

○ **B.** Astrocytes

○ **C.** Oligodendrogytes

○ **D.** Schwann cells

Question 6

By which mechanism may a person with GBS need to be placed on a ventilator?

○ **A.** GBS Ig attack the autonomic nervous system.

○ **B.** GBS Ig attack the sympathetic nervous system.

○ **C.** GBS Ig attack the parasympathetic nervous system.

○ **D.** GBS Ig attack the somatic nervous system.

Question 7

If examined under the microscope, damage to the spinal cord in a person with GBS should be seen:

○ **A.** in the inner layer of white matter.

○ **B.** in the outer layer of white matter.

○ **C.** in the inner layer of gray matter.

○ **D.** in the outer layer of gray matter.

Question 8

Which of the following neurotransmitters would have a diminished concentration in the intersynaptic cleft in a person with GBS?

  I. Acetylcholine
  II. Epinephrine
  III. Norepinephrine
  IV. Dopamine

○ **A.** I only

○ **B.** I and II only

○ **C.** I, II, and III only

○ **D.** I, II, III, and IV

Question 9

Which of the following would have the same end result as GBS?

○ **A.** A drug that increases the frequency of excitatory signals

○ **B.** A drug that blocks Ca^{2+} influx in the presynaptic neuron

○ **C.** A drug that decreases metabolism of ACh in the synaptic cleft

○ **D.** A drug that prolongs the relative refractory period

Passage 3 (Questions 10-13)

Diabetes mellitus (DM) is a disease that is commonly associated with peripheral neuropathy and subsequent impaired sensation. The meibomian and lacrimal glands are responsible for the secretion of the lipid and aqueous portions of the preocular tear film, respectively. Meibomian glands are innervated primarily by parasympathetic fibers.

To investigate the association between peripheral neuropathy and ocular surface characteristics in patients with type 1 DM versus healthy controls, tear film interferometry and noncontact corneal anesthesiometry, which measure characteristics of the tear film and corneal thickness, respectively, were performed in patients with type 1 DM versus control.

The reduced tear production identified in patients with diabetes in the current study lends support to the concept that lacrimal gland function might be adversely affected by a neuropathic mechanism, resulting in dysfunction of the ocular surface secretory glands via their innervation. Such dysfunction could arise from a peripheral neuropathy involving the afferent sensory nerves from the ocular surface affecting corneal sensitivity and the autonomic (efferent) nerves responsible for innervating the tear component secreting glands and the lacrimal and meibomian glands.

Table 1 Comparison of Symptoms and Tear Characteristics for Control and Patient Groups. (NIBUT = Noninvasive Tear Breakup Time; * indicates statistically significant difference)

	Diabetes	Healthy controls	ANOVA/ Friedmann (P values)
Lipid layer thickness grade (median)	2*	3	0.02
NIBUT (s) (mean ± SD)	6.0 ± 1.9*	8.2 ± 2.5	<0.0001
Corneal sensitivity threshold (mBAR)	1.3 ± 1.3*	0.2 ± 1.3	<0.001

Table 2 Correlation Analysis between Diabetes Duration, Tear Film Stability (NIBUT), and Total Neuropathy Score (TNS) in Patients with DM (* indicates statistically significant correlation)

	Correlation (r values)
Lipid layer thickness versus NIBUT	0.56*
NIBUT versus diabetes duration	−0.29*
NIBUT versus TNS	−0.29*

Question 10

In general, which of the following is NOT a property of reflexes?

○ **A.** Reflexes may operate in a negative feedback loop.

○ **B.** Reflexes may involve excitation of one muscle group plus inhibition of its antagonistic muscle group.

○ **C.** Reflexes may operate without the central nervous system.

○ **D.** Reflexes may be modulated by the central nervous system.

Question 11

The corneal reflex involves the cranial nerves of the peripheral nervous system without involving the spinal cord, and stimulates blinking if the nerve endings on the cornea experience sensation. The passage shows that, compared to healthy controls, patients with diabetes were more likely to:

○ **A.** have more sensitive corneas than control.

○ **B.** have equally sensitive corneas as control.

○ **C.** take longer to become desensitized to corneal stimuli than control.

○ **D.** have weaker corneal reflexes.

Question 12

This passage shows that decreasing tear film stability in diabetic patients is LEAST likely to be associated with changes in the properties of:

○ **A.** photoreceptors.

○ **B.** mechanoreceptors.

○ **C.** nociceptors.

○ **D.** thermoreceptors.

Question 13

The nervous system may adapt to external influences by:

   I. changing levels of neurotransmitters released at synapses.

   II. changing the activity of other organ systems.

   III. changing the processing of sensory input.

○ **A.** I only

○ **B.** III only

○ **C.** I and II only

○ **D.** I and III only

Questions 14 - 17 do not refer to a passage and are independent of each other.

Question 14

Nervous system dysfunction, as in neurofibromatosis, can often lead to lower quality of life. The primary function of the nervous system is:

○ **A.** sensing stimuli.

○ **B.** information processing.

○ **C.** mediating internal communication and external interactions.

○ **D.** facilitating movement.

Question 15

Which of the following is NOT an example of the nervous system serving as a high level regulatory center for the body's organ systems?

○ **A.** The hypothalamus sets body temperature, thus determining the temperature at which enzymatic reactions such as glycolysis take place.

○ **B.** The parasympathetic nervous system stimulates the urinary and gastrointestinal systems.

○ **C.** The auditory system receives external stimuli and sends them to the brain for further processing.

○ **D.** Through voluntary control, the brain can suppress some physiological processes like holding one's breath.

Question 16

Which of the following channels is responsible for maintaining the voltage in section A of the neuron action potential?

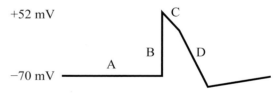

○ **A.** Voltage-gated K^+ channel

○ **B.** Ligand-gated Na^+ channel

○ **C.** Na^+/K^+ pump

○ **D.** Voltage-gated Ca^{2+} channel

Question 17

Chemical synapses that utilize neurotransmitters differ from electrical synapses in that they:

○ **A.** only function within the central nervous system.

○ **B.** only function within the peripheral nervous system.

○ **C.** are bidirectional.

○ **D.** are unidirectional.

Passage 4 (Questions 18-22)

Age-related hearing loss (presbyacusis) affects about half the population over 75 years of age. Studies of older human donors have shown that one of the most common pathological changes is the degeneration of spiral ganglion neurons (SGNs). Two populations of SGNs are present in the mammalian ear. Bipolar type I neurons comprise about 95% of the neurons in the cochlea. Their peripheral processes synapse both directly and indirectly with a single inner hair cell, which in turn constitute the primary sensory receptors in the cochlea.

Researchers hypothesized that age-related degeneration of myelin sheaths may occur in the human auditory nerves and that these changes may contribute to presbyacusis. Defining the cellular and molecular mechanisms underlying human SGN degeneration is an important step toward improved methods of diagnosis and treatment.

The mean auditory brainstem responses (ABR) thresholds for young and old subjects were compared. ABR is an indicator of auditory nerve activation and ABR threshold is the minimum intensity level required to elicit an ABR. Researchers also employed ABR wave I amplitude input/output (I/O) functions to assess the gross activity of the auditory nerve at various frequencies. The maximum wave I amplitudes and slopes of the I/O functions is an indicator of auditory nerve activity at various decibel levels.

Additionally, researchers studied changes in myelin basic proteins (MBPs). MBPs are the major constituents of the myelin sheath produced by the nervous system. It was found that changes in the MBP immunostaining pattern and loss of MBP nerve fibers are associated with structural changes in the myelin sheath and a significant decline of auditory nerve function in aged subjects.

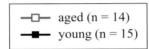

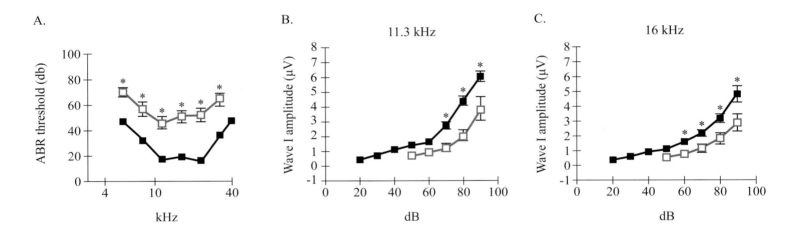

Figure 1 ABR threshold and wave I amplitude at 11.3 kHz and 16 kHz (Note: Star indicates p < 0.05)

This passage was adapted from "Age-Related Changes of Myelin Basic Protein in Mouse and Human Auditory Nerve." Xing Y, Samuvel D, Stevens SM, Dubno J, Schulte B, et al.. *PLoS ONE*. 2012. 3(5) doi: 10.1371/journal.pone.0034500 for use under the terms of the Creative Commons CC BY 3.0 license (http://creativecommons.org/licenses/by/3.0/legalcode).

Question 18

Reduction of MBPs in bipolar type I neurons results in hearing deficits because:

○ **A.** post-synaptic neurons are not sufficiently depolarized.

○ **B.** loss of myelin increases the threshold necessary for action potentials.

○ **C.** MBPs are essential components of ion channels that cause action potentials.

○ **D.** loss of myelin results in destruction of the resting membrane potential.

Question 19

Which of the following would most strongly challenge the researchers' hypothesis that myelin sheath damage of the auditory nerve contributes to presbyacusis?

○ **A.** Patients with presbyacusis show decreased auditory cortex activation.

○ **B.** Patients with presbyacusis have damage to the semicircular canals.

○ **C.** Patients with presbyacusis have a reduced number of hair cells.

○ **D.** Patients with presbyacusis have increased action potential frequency.

Question 20

According to Figure 1A, over which frequency range will dendrites of bipolar type I neurons become most depolarized in young subjects?

○ **A.** 10 kHz to 30 kHz

○ **B.** 5 kHz to 10 kHz

○ **C.** 5 kHz to 10 kHz and 30 kHz to 40 kHz

○ **D.** Equal depolarization over entire range

Question 21

Recent studies have shown that ANS neurons synapse on bipolar type I neurons. Respectively, how should ANS neurons and bipolar type I neurons be classified?

○ **A.** Afferent; efferent

○ **B.** Sensory; effector

○ **C.** Efferent; afferent

○ **D.** Neuroglia; sensory

Question 22

Bipolar type I neurons can be described in terms of a concentration cell. During a high intensity auditory stimulus, which of the following best describes the flow of negative charge in the axon?

○ **A.** Only positively charged ions are exchanged during an action potential.

○ **B.** Current first flows into the neuron and then flows out.

○ **C.** Negatively charged proteins cannot pass through the membrane.

○ **D.** Electrons first flow from the cytosol to the extracellular space.

Passage 5 (Questions 23-26)

The oxidative stress or free radical theory of aging suggests that free radicals cause oxidative damage to proteins, DNA, and lipids. Oxidative stress is the result of an imbalance between pro-oxidants and antioxidants. To date, both invertebrate and vertebrate models have been generated in which one or more antioxidants are either ablated or overexpressed. However, the role of oxidative stress in aging remains unclear, likely due to the complexity of the aging process. In neurons, this process can lead to a decline in nerve conduction velocities, increasing the time it takes to send signals within the nervous system.

All cells contain multiple enzymes that target and neutralize free radicals. Superoxide dismutase (SOD) partners with another antioxidant enzyme, catalase, to defend against oxidative damage by converting the free radical pro-oxidant superoxide anion into molecular oxygen and hydrogen peroxide. There are three mammalian forms of SOD: cytoplasmic copper/zinc or SOD1, mitochondrial manganese or SOD2, and extracellular or SOD3. SOD1-deficient ($Sod1^{-/-}$) mice appear normal at birth, but over time exhibit increased levels of oxidative stress in muscle and plasma, display a chronic peripheral neuropathy, accelerated age-associated hind limb muscle mass loss, neuromuscular junction degeneration, muscle weakness, and a 30% reduction in lifespan.

Researchers studied the effects of SOD1 on neurons by measuring oxidative damage and levels of cleaved caspase 3 (casp3), a marker of apoptosis, relative to levels of actin.

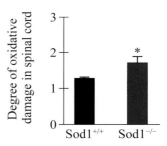

Figure 1 Effect of SOD1 on oxidative stress levels

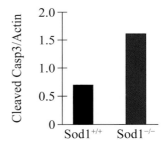

Figure 2 Levels of cleaved casp3 are affected by SOD1

This passage was adapted from "The Role of Oxidative Stress in Nervous System Aging." Sims-Robinson C, Hur J, Hayes JM, Dauch JR, Keller PJ et al. *PLoS ONE.* 2013. 8(7) doi:10.1371/journal.pone.0068011 for use under the terms of the Creative Commons CC BY 3.0 license (http://creativecommons.org/licenses/by/3.0/legalcode).

Question 23

SOD1 deficient mice have been observed to have deficits in cholinergic neurons throughout the nervous system. Based on this information, which of the following components of the nervous system could be affected?

    I. Somatic motor

    II. Sympathetic

    III. Parasympathetic

○ **A.** I only

○ **B.** II only

○ **C.** II and III only

○ **D.** I, II, and III

Question 24

A dysfunction in which of the following cells would most greatly exacerbate the changes shown in Figure 2 in SOD1 deficient mice?

○ **A.** Microglia

○ **B.** Schwann cells

○ **C.** B lymphocytes

○ **D.** Neutrophils

Question 25

Researchers wanted to test conduction velocity of simple two-neuron reflexes in SOD1 deficient mice. In what location could the recording device be placed to yield useful information?

    I. On the axon of the sensory neuron

    II. On the axon of the interneuron

    III. On the axon of the motor neuron

○ **A.** I only

○ **B.** II only

○ **C.** I and III only

○ **D.** I, II, and III

Question 26

SOD1 deficient cells are often unable to maintain the integrity of their membranes due to lipid damage. Which of the following statements is most likely to be true in SOD1 deficient neurons?

○ **A.** Increased neurotransmitter concentration at the synaptic cleft

○ **B.** Reduced neuron death as a result of decreased damage to DNA

○ **C.** Inability to maintain resting potential and an increase in membrane potential

○ **D.** Inability to maintain resting potential and a decrease in membrane potential

Questions 27 - 30 do not refer to a passage and are independent of each other.

Question 27

Cancer of ependymal cells can result in an overgrowth of these cells, but also a loss of their function. This would most likely lead to:

○ **A.** an inability to fight off infection in the nervous system.

○ **B.** a reduction in conduction velocity along neuron processes.

○ **C.** a loss of integrity of the blood brain barrier.

○ **D.** an inability to produce cerebrospinal fluid.

Question 28

Which of the following cell types is most important to the maintenance of nerve conduction velocity within the peripheral nervous system?

○ **A.** Oligodendrocytes

○ **B.** Schwann cells

○ **C.** Microglia

○ **D.** Ependymal cells

Question 29

Which of the following correctly identifies the role of astrocytes in the CNS?

○ **A.** Phagocytic cleanup

○ **B.** Formation of myelin sheaths

○ **C.** Maintenance of brain barrier formation

○ **D.** Circulation of cerebrospinal fluid

Question 30

The presence of the myelin sheath in bipolar type I neurons increases action potential velocity through:

○ **A.** nodes of Ranvier.

○ **B.** saltatory conduction.

○ **C.** glial cells.

○ **D.** electrical synapses.

Passage 6 (Questions 31-35)

Parkinson's disease (PD) is the second most common neurodegenerative disorder after Alzheimer's disease and afflicts millions of people worldwide. The primary clinical symptoms are resting tremor, rigidity, and postural instability. These symptoms are caused by the loss of dopaminergic innervation of the striatum and increase in severity over time due to progressive failure of dopaminergic neurons. Loss-of-function mutations in the Parkin and DJ-1 genes were the first mutations to be causally linked to recessive PD. Both genes are widely expressed throughout the brain and other tissues. The mechanism by which loss of Parkin or DJ-1 function causes Parkinsonism remains unclear. Parkin knockout and DJ-1 knockout mice are susceptible to PD-related neurodegeneration induced by various stresses including exposure to neurotoxins or to lipopolysaccharide (LPS), a bacterial endotoxin.

Overexpression of Parkin or DJ-1 is neuroprotective both *in vitro* and *in vivo*. Parkin has been found to function as an E3 ubiquitin ligase and is known to promote destruction of dysfunctional mitochondria, which are major cellular sources of free radicals and oxidative stress. Mutations in Parkin result in impaired mitochondrial respiration and increased markers of oxidative stress. It is quite possible that oxidative damage is an important factor in the development of PD. Researchers developed a transgenic knockout (KO) mouse deficient in Parkin, DJ-1, and SOD1, an antioxidant protein that protects neurons from oxidative stress, and analyzed dopamine levels in the striatum (Figure 1).

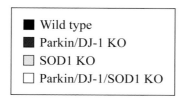

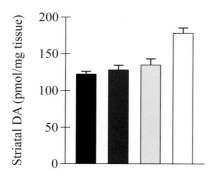

Figure 1 Dopamine (DA) levels in the striatum

This passage was adapted from "Behavioral and Neurotransmitter Abnormalities in Mice Deficient for Parkin, DJ-1 and Superoxide Dismutase." Hennis MR, Seamans KW, Marvin MA, Casey BH and Golberg MS. *PLoS ONE*. 2013. 7(8) doi:10.1371/journal.pone.0084894 for use under the terms of the Creative Commons CC BY 3.0 license (http://creativecommons.org/licenses/by/3.0/legalcode).

Question 31

Based on information in the passage and Figure 1, which of the following best explains the dopamine levels observed in the triple mutant?

○ **A.** Decreased dopamine results from compensation for increased dopaminergic signaling.

○ **B.** Increased dopamine occurs as a result of an inability to reuptake dopamine following release into the synapse.

○ **C.** Increased dopamine results from compensation for decreased dopaminergic signaling.

○ **D.** Increased dopamine results from an inability to combat pathogens.

Question 32

Following the conditions in the striatum observed in the Parkin/DJ-1/SOD1 KO mouse, which of the following would happen to striatal dopaminergic neurons?

○ **A.** Increase in receptor count and decreased resistance to oxidative stress

○ **B.** Increase in receptor count and increased resistance to oxidative stress

○ **C.** Decrease in receptor count and decreased resistance to oxidative stress

○ **D.** Decrease in receptor count and increased resistance to oxidative stress

Question 33

Which of the following would have the same impact as triple KO on activity?

○ **A.** Overactive potassium channels

○ **B.** Oversensitive voltage-gated sodium channels

○ **C.** Blockage of calcium channels

○ **D.** Decreased mobility of vesicles containing DA

Question 34

PD is also marked by migroglial activation in the CNS. Which of the following serves to recreate this in the model?

- ○ **A.** Knockout of DJ-1
- ○ **B.** Knockout of Parkin
- ○ **C.** Injection of LPS
- ○ **D.** Knockout of SOD1

Question 35

A mutation in a key amino acid prevents SOD1 from performing its regular function and directly interacting with the major pathways that generate oxidative stress in neurons. Which of the following is wild type SOD1 most likely to bind to?

- ○ **A.** Membrane lipids
- ○ **B.** Nuclear proteins
- ○ **C.** Mitochondrial proteins
- ○ **D.** Membrane proteins

Passage 7 (Questions 36-39)

Depression is one of the most prevalent psychiatric disorders and is a leading cause of mortality. The lifetime prevalence of depression in the general population is 4.4–20% and suicide occurs in up to 15% of individuals with severe major depression. Therefore, major depression is a serious public health problem and causes a considerable psychological and economic burden for families. To solve this severe public health problem, it is urgent to keep studying the pathophysiology of major depression and to develop new therapeutic targets and strategies. Many animal models of depression have been developed including environmental stress models, social stress models, pharmacological models and genetic models. Among all these models, genetic models have more stable phenotypes and are becoming a more common way to study the mechanisms of major depression.

The mutation of Abelson helper integrationsite-1 (Ahi1) gene is one of the causes of Joubert syndrome, a neurodevelopmental disorder characterized by congenital malformation of the brainstem and agenesis or hypoplasia of the cerebellar vermis. The increasing lines of evidence indicate that Ahi1 is associated with psychiatric diseases. Conditional Ahi1 knockout (KO) in mice causes depressive behaviors that are common symptoms in human psychiatric diseases. Since depression can be caused by multiple pathogenic pathways, it is important to investigate whether different mechanisms underlie the depressive phenotypes of Ahi1 KO mice. Along this line, researchers examined the impact of Ahi1 deletion on neurotransmitter release throughout the brain. The results are shown in Figures 1 and 2.

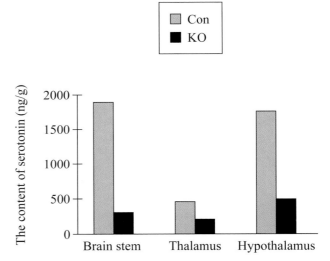

Figure 1 Serotonin levels throughout the brain in Ahi1 KO

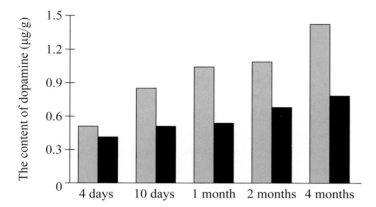

Figure 2 Dopamine levels in the brainstem following birth in Ahi1 KO

Question 36

Which of the following could explain the effect of Ahi1 KO on serotonin release?

- ○ **A.** Ahi1 KO reduces calcium channel expression on postsynaptic neurons.
- ○ **B.** Ahi1 KO reduces calcium channel expression on presynaptic neurons.
- ○ **C.** Ahi1 plays a vital role in serotonin release.
- ○ **D.** Ahi1 increases reuptake of serotonin by the presynaptic neuron.

Question 37

Researchers found that imipramine, an antidepressant, works by increasing levels of serotonin in the brain. How does this finding affect the results of this study?

- ○ **A.** Supports the results because the results indicate depression could be caused by increased serotonin levels.
- ○ **B.** Contradicts the results because the results indicate depression could be caused by decreased serotonin levels.
- ○ **C.** Contradicts the results because the results indicate depression could be caused by increased serotonin levels.
- ○ **D.** Supports the results because the results indicate depression could be caused by decreased serotonin levels.

Question 38

Researchers investigated the brainstem due to its high expression of Ahi1. Damage to the brainstem would most strongly impair which of the following activities?

- ○ **A.** Remembering a childhood experience
- ○ **B.** Combating hypothermia
- ○ **C.** Storing water while dehydrated
- ○ **D.** Regulation of heart rate

Question 39

What is the function of the brain region where dopamine release is least affected by Ahi1 KO?

- ○ **A.** Processing sensory information
- ○ **B.** Memory
- ○ **C.** Maintenance of homeostasis
- ○ **D.** Cannot be determined

Passage 8 (Questions 40-44)

The importance of the neurovascular unit in the preservation of the normal functions of the central nervous system (CNS) is well documented. Cross talk between different cell types within this unit is critical, and its dysfunction has been linked to several human pathologies of the brain including Alzheimer's and Parkinson's disease. Astrocyte dysfunctions may promote neurodegenerative pathologies.

To better elucidate the role of astrocytes in promoting both normal and pathological processes, efficient gene transfer and gene manipulation of these cells is highly beneficial. Gene delivery into astrocytes and other cells of the CNS remains challenging. The presence of the blood-brain barrier and the lack of tools to target gene expression hamper progress in astrocyte research.

Viral vectors that carry a transgene of interest and deliver them into defined areas and cells in the CNS are a well-established practice. Lentiviral vectors are highly attractive because they are easy to manipulate and transduce both dividing and nondividing cells. In the past, glycoproteins from the vesicular stomatitis virus (VSV-G) have been incorporated onto lentiviruses, and these displayed non-selective and broad tropism towards a wide variety of cells. VSV-G pseudotyped lentiviruses only facilitate non-specific marking of cells.

Reporter viral particles that expressed the ZsGreen fluorescent gene were pseudotyped with a modified lentiviral envelope, resulting in sindMu-ZsGreen. Attachment of viral particles to astrocytes was complemented by a soluble antibody that bound the glutamate transporter GLAST, a unique surface astrocyte marker. This resulted in sindMu-Zsgreen/IgG GLAST, a viral vector targeted towards astrocytes (Figure 1).

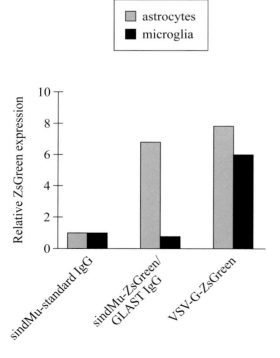

Figure 1 Relative ZsGreen expression in different glia types

This passage was adapted from "Preferential Lentiviral Targeting of Astrocytes in the Central Nervous System." Fassler M, Weissberg I, Levy N, Diaz-Griffero F, Monsonego A et al. PLoS ONE. 2013. 8(10) doi:10.1371/journal.pone.0076092 for use under the terms of the Creative Commons CC BY 3.0 license (http://creativecommons.org/licenses/by/3.0/legalcode).

Question 40

Which of the following statements best summarizes the results of Figure 1?

○ **A.** sindMu-ZsGreen/GLAST IgG decreases the population of astrocytes.

○ **B.** sindMu-ZsGreen/GLAST IgG increases the population of astrocytes.

○ **C.** sindMu-ZsGreen/GLAST IgG is successful in specific targeting of astrocytes.

○ **D.** sindMu-ZsGreen/GLAST IgG is not successful in specific targeting of astrocytes.

Question 41

Which of the following is true regarding the ability of lentiviruses to transduce human CNS cells?

○ **A.** Lentiviruses can transduce neurons only.

○ **B.** Lentiviruses can transduce glia only.

○ **C.** Lentiviruses can transduce neither neurons nor glia.

○ **D.** Lentiviruses can transduce both neurons and glia.

Question 42

Suppose a group of lentiviruses escapes the CNS and circulates in the bloodstream. Which of the following cells would be activated in the body's response to the escaped viruses?

○ **A.** Neurons

○ **B.** Microglia

○ **C.** Beta cells

○ **D.** NK Cells

Question 43

Which of the following results would be expected if VSV-G-ZsGreen was used to transduce a population of astrocytes and neurons?

○ **A.** Equal transduction of neurons and astrocytes

○ **B.** Preferential transduction of astrocytes

○ **C.** Preferential transduction of neurons

○ **D.** Sole transduction of astrocytes

Question 44

A deficiency in astrocytes can result in a disruption of ion homeostasis. Which of the following ionic changes would slow down the action potential firing of a neuron?

○ **A.** Increase of the sodium gradient between the inside and the outside of the cell

○ **B.** Reduction of the sodium gradient between the inside and the outside of the cell

○ **C.** Increase of the potassium gradient between the inside and the outside of the cell

○ **D.** Reduction of the potassium gradient between the inside and the outside of the cell

Questions 45 - 48 do not refer to a passage and are independent of each other.

Question 45

Which of the following types of neurons is not involved in a reflex arc?

○ **A.** Sensory neurons

○ **B.** Interneurons

○ **C.** Motor neurons

○ **D.** None of the above

Question 46

Gymnasts often need to contort their bodies in positions that would typically cause a reflex. How is it that gymnasts are able to achieve these positions?

○ **A.** Interneurons between sensory and motor neurons can facilitate movement.

○ **B.** Supraspinal input inhibits motor neurons from sending action potentials.

○ **C.** The gymnasts are lacking typical reflex arcs that prevent injury.

○ **D.** Sympathetic nervous system innervation allows for extra mobility.

Question 47

In which of the following situations would autonomic innervation to the body primarily be sympathetic?

○ **A.** Directly following a meal

○ **B.** While running a marathon

○ **C.** During sleep

○ **D.** While reading a book

Question 48

What major central nervous system structure is NOT likely to be involved in the sensory pathways related to the consumption of sweet fruits?

○ **A.** The thalamus

○ **B.** The cerebellum

○ **C.** The olfactory cortex

○ **D.** The temporal lobe

Passage 9 (Questions 49-52)

Graves' ophthalmopathy (GO), an eye disease caused by aberrant thyroid hormone activity, occurs in up to 45% of patients with Grave's disease, a common thyroid autoimmune condition. GO may compromise the quality of life of affected individuals by causing vision impairment. The impairment is a result of cornea, lens, and vitreous humor clouding due to altered metabolism and high levels of fibroblast proliferation.

Over the past few years, several fibrin-forming factors including fibronectin, apolipoprotein J, and connective tissue growth factor (CTGF) have been identified. Among them, CTGF has been shown to be most critical. Recently, CTGF has also been shown to play a role in ocular fibrosis process of human lens epithelial cells. Reactive oxygen species (ROS) levels are an important inducer of CTGF expression and may be increased by exposure to high levels of UV radiation.

Experiment 1

To determine whether CTGF and other fibrin-forming factors were aberrantly expressed in GO patients, the total cellular RNA from orbital fibroblasts lysates was extracted with a chloroform solution and was then precipitated with isopropanol solution. An aliquot of 5 μg RNA was reverse-transcribed to cDNA at 42°C for at least 16 hr. The cDNA was used in PCR with primers designed to amplify fibronectin, apolipoprotein J, and CTGF. The results are shown in Figure 1. Additionally, the protein expression levels of fibronectin, apolipoprotein J and CTGF were also measured by western blot and the results are shown in Figure 2.

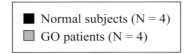

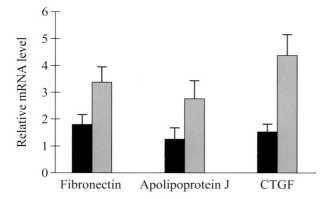

Figure 1 mRNA expression of fibronectin, apolipoprotein J, and CTGF in normal subjects and GO patients

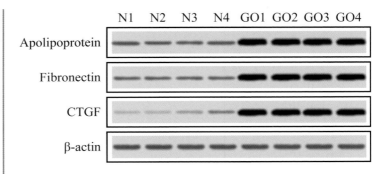

Figure 2 Protein expression levels of fibronectin, apolipoprotein J, and CTGF in normal subjects and GO patients

Experiment 2

To determine whether or not ROS contributed to CTGF expression, orbital fibroblasts were cultured with 200 μM hydrogen peroxide (H_2O_2) for 1 hour and the secretion of CTGF was measured in normal subjects and GO patients. The results are shown in Figure 3.

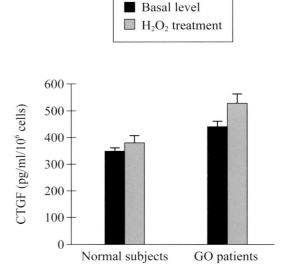

Figure 3 Effect of ROS on CTGF protein levels in the primary culture of normal subject orbital fibroblasts and GO orbital fibroblasts

Question 49

Increased expression of fibronectin would cause light to:

○ **A.** refract more when it enters the cornea.

○ **B.** refract less when it enters the cornea.

○ **C.** reflect more when it enters the cornea.

○ **D.** reflect less when it enters the cornea.

Question 50

Thyroid autoimmune diseases often affect multiple organs, compounding the visual deficits produced by GO. Autoimmune disease of which of the following organs would be likely to further reduce vision in GO patients?

    I. Heart

    II. Liver

    III. Small intestine

○ **A.** II only

○ **B.** III only

○ **C.** I and II only

○ **D.** II and III only

Question 51

Excitation of a rod cell is most likely to produce which of the following curves in a voltage recording?

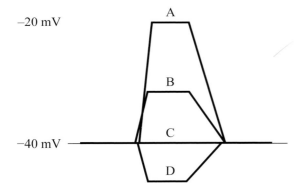

○ **A.** Curve A

○ **B.** Curve B

○ **C.** Curve C

○ **D.** Curve D

Question 52

H_2O_2 treatment of fibroblasts derived from GO patients is more likely to cause:

○ **A.** acetylcholine-mediated inhibition of on bipolar cells.

○ **B.** glutamate-mediated inhibition of on bipolar cells.

○ **C.** acetylcholine-mediate stimulation of on bipolar cells.

○ **D.** glutamate-mediated stimulation of on bipolar cells.

Passage 10 (Questions 53-56)

The vast majority of degenerative retinal diseases lead either directly or indirectly to the loss of photoreceptor cells. As degeneration progresses, the microenvironment of the retina undergoes a number of significant changes. In addition, Müller glial cells undergo reactive gliosis, leading to the formation of a glial scar that can envelope the entire retina at late stages of degeneration. This scar can act as a reservoir for the accumulation of extracellular matrix (ECM) proteins including chondroitin sulfate proteoglycans (CSPGs), which are known to be inhibitory to axonal regeneration. Formation of a glial barrier around a lesion can be an advantage because it isolates the still intact CNS tissue from secondary lesions. Reactive astrocytes in the glial barrier can also provide a platform for neurite extension.

Gliosis is characterized by a dramatic increase in intermediate filament expression and a pronounced hypertrophy of Müller cells. These processes lead to proliferation of fibrous structures and deposition of CSPGs at the retina. This process of gliosis is characteristic of many retinal disease models, although the temporal relationship between the onset of gliosis and degeneration may vary between disease models. Researchers compared retinal characteristics of various disease models at early, middle, and late stages in order to examine the role of gliosis in these diseases. These diseases were retinitis pigmentosa, a progressive rod degeneration disease, and Leber congenital amaurosis, a rare inherited eye disease that appears very early in life. The results are shown in Figure 1.

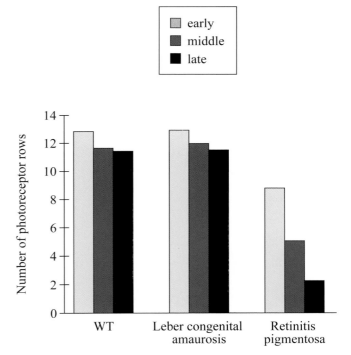

Figure 1 Photoreceptor row count in various diseases and stages

This passage was adapted from "Muller Glia Activation in Response to Inherited Retinal Degeneration Is Highly Varied and Disease-Specific." Hippert C, Graca AB, Barber AC, West EL, Smith AJ. *PLoS ONE*. 2015. 10(3) doi:10.1371/journal.pone.0120415 for use under the terms of the Creative Commons CC BY 4.0 license (http://creativecommons.org/licenses/by/4.0/legalcode).

Question 53

Which of the following lines of mice would be most useful in studying the mechanism by which glial scars lead to blindness?

○ **A.** Mice whose rods degenerate with age.

○ **B.** Mice whose cones degenerate with age.

○ **C.** Mice who develop obstructive lesions on the retina.

○ **D.** Mice whose retinal glia degenerate with age.

Question 54

Gliosis leads to which of the following changes to the cell?

○ **A.** Increased cytoskeleton rigidity

○ **B.** Decreased motility

○ **C.** Increased motility

○ **D.** Inability to form an intact cell membrane

Question 55

Which of the following statements is true regarding photoreceptor loss?

○ **A.** Photoreceptor loss does not occur in the WT mice.

○ **B.** Photoreceptor loss is most pronounced in the model of Leber congenital amaurosis.

○ **C.** The mutations do not lead to a decrease in photoreceptors.

○ **D.** Photoreceptor loss is most pronounced in the model of retinitis pigmentosa.

Question 56

A disease of the ciliary muscles would most likely have what impact on vision:

   I. Inability to adjust to darkness

   II. Inability to adjust between viewing distances

   III. Color blindness

○ **A.** I only

○ **B.** II only

○ **C.** III only

○ **D.** I and II only

Questions 57 - 59 do not refer to a passage and are independent of each other.

Question 57

In damage to the structure of the brainstem that lies closest to the diencephalon, which of the following senses are most likely to be affected?

   I. Hearing

   II. Smell

   III. Vision

○ **A.** I only

○ **B.** II only

○ **C.** III only

○ **D.** I and III only

Question 58

Which of the following functions is correctly paired with the side of the brain in which it primarily takes place?

○ **A.** Negative emotion, right hemisphere

○ **B.** Negative emotion, left hemisphere

○ **C.** Positive emotion, right hemisphere

○ **D.** Language, right hemisphere

Question 59

A marker of Parkinson's disease in the asymptomatic stage is the appearance of protein accumulations called Lewy bodies in the medulla. As more accumulation occurs, which of the following functions is most impaired due to these changes in the medulla?

○ **A.** Temperature control

○ **B.** Control of blood pressure

○ **C.** Coordination and movement

○ **D.** Water balance

STOP. If you finish before time is called, check your work. You may go back to any question in this test.

ANSWERS & EXPLANATIONS for Test 2A can be found on p. 214.

LECTURE

The Nervous System

MINI-TEST 2B

Time: 65 minutes
Questions 1–41

DIRECTIONS: Most of the questions in this test section are grouped with a passage. Read the passage, then select the best answer to each question. Some questions are independent of any passage and of one another. Select the best answer to each of these questions. If you are unsure of an answer, rule out incorrect choices and select from the remaining options. Indicate your selection beside the option you choose. A periodic table can be found on the last page of this book for you to use at any point during this test section.

Passage 1 (Questions 1-4)

Activation of NMDA-type glutamate receptors (NMDARs) plays a pivotal role in synaptic transmission by allowing calcium entry into the neuronal cells. However, over-activation of NMDARs leads to a rise in intracellular calcium levels and promotes the degeneration of neuronal cells in the central nervous system (CNS), as well as in the retina. In support of this, a number of previous studies have documented that the activation of NMDARs increases calcium influx and promote apoptotic death of retinal ganglion cells (RGCs), as well as of other neuronal cells in the retina. However, the intrinsic mechanisms that promote the degeneration of RGCs following the activation of NMDARs are still unclear.

Neuronal calcium sensing (NCS) proteins may play an important role in this process. Four NCS proteins that belong to a group of K-channel interacting proteins 1 to 4 (KChIP-1 to -4) have been identified to date in the CNS. A member of this family, DREAM also known as calsenilin or KChIP-3, is highly expressed in sensory neurons including RGCs. Researchers carried out a study designed to investigate whether DREAM is expressed in the retina, and whether the expression of DREAM plays a role in NMDA-mediated degeneration of retinal neurons. NMDA was injected into the vitreous humor of mice, with phosphate-buffered saline (PBS) being used as a control. DREAM expression was then detected by immunohistochemistry (Figure 1), and apoptotic cell death was determined by TUNEL assay (Figure 2), a method that labels DNA nicks found in apoptotic cells.

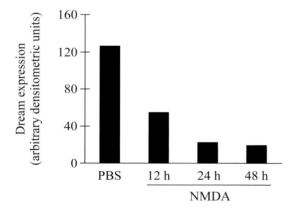

Figure 1 DREAM expression following NMDA treatment

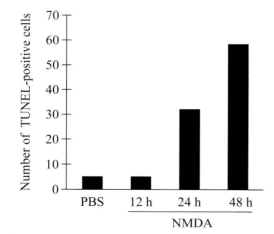

Figure 2 TUNEL assay following NMDA treatment

This passage was adapted from "Decreased Expression of DREAM Promotes the Degeneration of Retinal Neurons." Chintala S, Cheng M and Zhang X. *PLoS ONE*. 2015. 10(5) doi:10.1371/journal.pone.0127776 for use under the terms of the Creative Commons CC BY 4.0 license (http://creativecommons.org/licenses/by/4.0/legalcode).

Question 1

Which of the following would occur in a transgenic mouse lacking a retina?

- **A.** Inability of light to enter the eye
- **B.** Improper refraction of light onto the back of the eye
- **C.** Inability to transmit light signals from the eye to the brain
- **D.** Inability to adjust to different viewing distances

Question 2

Which of the following changes would most strongly reduce cell death related to over-activation of NMDARs?

- **A.** Increase in excitatory signaling
- **B.** Increase in inhibitory signaling
- **C.** Reduction in extracellular sodium
- **D.** Increase in extracellular sodium

Question 3

When NMDARs are activated, they open channels that allow positively charged ions to flow down their gradients. Which of the following occurs following NMDAR activation?

   I. NMDA reuptake by the postsynaptic neuron
   II. Potassium ion influx into the postsynaptic neuron
   III. Sodium ion influx into the postsynaptic neuron

- **A.** II only
- **B.** III only
- **C.** I and II only
- **D.** II and III only

Question 4

Which of the following would occur if retinal degeneration was selective to cones?

- **A.** Reduction of color in the eye
- **B.** Reduced peripheral vision
- **C.** Major effects in the fovea, leading to color blindness
- **D.** Major effects in the optic nerve, leading to color blindness

Passage 2 (Questions 5-9)

In everyday life, individuals are typically exposed to multiple stimuli within their visual field simultaneously. For example, a person's face is usually surrounded by objects and other faces, such as when a person is in a crowd. Previous studies have shown that multiple stimuli presented within the visual field compete for neural representations in the visual cortex. Theories of sensory competition suggest that the processing capacity of multiple simultaneously presented stimuli within the receptive field of a given neuron is limited, presumably due to the mutual suppressive interactions among them.

Signs of such interactions have been found in several areas of both the ventral and dorsal visual pathways, including the fusiform face area (FFA) and parahippocampal place area (PPA). Studies of object, scene and face processing suggest that contralateral, meaning opposite visual fields, and ipsilateral stimuli, meaning same visual field, are processed differentially and object and face processing are, to a large extent, position-dependent. Therefore, scientists designed an experiment to test the sensory competition among stimuli falling into the same category (faces) within the ipsilateral visual field.

Previous studies showed that the degree of competitive interactions changes as a function of the spatial separation of the competing stimuli in the array: the larger the spatial separation among the stimuli, the lower the magnitude of competitive interactions. The researchers maintained the light intensity of the images but varied the number of intervening noise images (consequently the distance) among the face stimuli and measured the reduction in brain activity using PET imaging. Positron emission tomography (PET) imaging highlights metabolic activity in the brain based on the use of a radioactive analogue of glucose, fludeoxygluose (FDG). Highly active areas show a strong signal, due to rapid use of glucose. The images shown to participants, as well as the relative signal recorded from the FFA are shown in Figure 1.

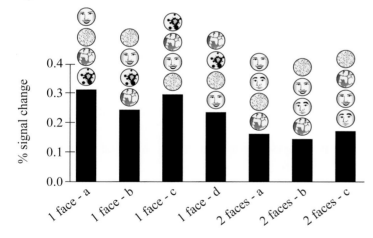

Figure 1 The average signal change from the right FFA in the four possible conditions shown above the figure

Question 5

Which of the following regions of the brain would show the greatest change in signal in the one face experiment between conditions A and B?

- ○ **A.** Ventral pathway
- ○ **B.** Dorsal pathway
- ○ **C.** Optic nerve
- ○ **D.** Lateral geniculate nucleus

Question 6

Additional research has shown that the location of noise made by an object's movement may play a role directing the eyes towards a particular visual field. In order to confirm these findings, scientists should measure FDG use in:

- ○ **A.** the parietal lobe only.
- ○ **B.** the cerebellar lobe only.
- ○ **C.** the parietal lobe and the temporal lobe.
- ○ **D.** the frontal lobe and the parietal lobe.

Question 7

The results of the experiment presented in the passage are most likely to:

- ○ **A.** support the assertions of the signal detection theory.
- ○ **B.** refute the assertions of the signal detection theory.
- ○ **C.** support the assertions of Weber's Law.
- ○ **D.** refute the assertions of Weber's Law.

Question 8

The two face experimental condition is likely to involve activity of:

- ○ **A.** ganglion cells, but not bipolar cells and horizontal cells.
- ○ **B.** bipolar cells and ganglion cells, but not horizontal cells.
- ○ **C.** bipolar cells and horizontal cells, but not ganglion cells.
- ○ **D.** bipolar cells, horizontal cells, and ganglion cells.

Question 9

Research participants' awareness of the spatial relationship between themselves and the faces displayed on the screen involves:

    I. transmission of neuronal action potentials from the retina.
    II. vestibular nerve tract fibers to the abducens nucleus.
    III. afferent neurons from the quadriceps muscles.

- ○ **A.** I only
- ○ **B.** II only
- ○ **C.** II and III only
- ○ **D.** I, II, and III

Questions 10 - 12 do not refer to a passage and are independent of each other.

Question 10

Magnetic resonance imaging is a technique used to visualize blood flow in the brain during normal functioning or while one is asked to perform a task. A patient with a lesion in an area of the brain used for language, when compared to a healthy control, may show:

○ **A.** increased blood flow while reading.

○ **B.** decreased blood flow while speaking.

○ **C.** increased blood flow while listening.

○ **D.** decreased blood flow while awake.

Question 11

Which of the following is NOT a function of the forebrain?

○ **A.** Controlling movement via the motor cortex

○ **B.** Regulating the cardiovascular system via chemoreceptors

○ **C.** Processing visual input via the occipital lobe

○ **D.** Cognition

Question 12

Photoreceptors behave quite differently depending on the conditions of light. In conditions of darkness:

○ **A.** photoreceptors will divide more.

○ **B.** photoreceptors will divide less.

○ **C.** photoreceptors action potentials will initiate more often.

○ **D.** photoreceptors action potentials will initiate less often.

Passage 3 (Questions 13-16)

A four-day-old baby failed to respond to verbal cues or turn his head in response loud noises. The attending physician suspected the baby had a congenital form of hearing loss because, in addition to these symptoms, he had a maternal grandfather that was born deaf, though the parents were unaffected.

Deafness is a condition in which a defect in the anatomy of the ear or in the neural pathway transmitting information from the ear to the brain results in hearing loss. Almost all babies with hearing loss have a congenital form of the disease. Prestin is the molecular motor essential for sound amplification in the cochlea and is expressed in hair cells and possibly neurons. Normally, prestin maintains stiffness of the hair cells, allowing small changes in the fluid waves of the cochlea to move hair cells embedded in the tectorial membrane. It also helps regulate the density of the cochlear fluid.

In deafness due to a mutation in *SLC26A5,* which is the gene that produces prestin, the ability of prestin to maintain hair cell stiffness is compromised, leading to failed transmission of sound waves in the cochlea. Many hair cells at the apical end of the cochlea are also only 60% of the length of normal hair cells, which further complicates discrimination of tone in individuals with congenital hearing loss. Some mutations in the prestin gene, such as a V to G amino acid substitution at position 499, are less severe than the protein-shortening mutation that characterizes the majority of cases. Patients with the V499G mutation often have relatively normal hearing early in life but are unable to discriminate between sounds with similar frequencies and develop progressive hearing loss later in life. Recent studies have implicated oxidative stress in hair cell death and auditory nerve degeneration in patients with V499G mutations. The increase in oxidative stress is thought to be due to an increased number of radical oxygen species (ROS) in the hair and nerve cells.

This passage was adapted from "Prestin-Dependence of Outer Hair Cell Survival and Partial Rescue of Outer Hair Cell Loss in Prestin[V499G/T501H] Knockin Mice." Cheatham M, Edge R, Homma K, Leserman E, Dallos P, et al. *PLoS ONE.* 2015. 10(12) doi:10.1371/journal.pone.0145428 for use under the terms of the Creative Commons CC BY 4.0 license (http://creativecommons.org/licenses/by/4.0/legalcode).

Question 13

Prestin-deficient hair cells are likely to display:

○ **A.** decreased potassium current compared to normal hair cells.

○ **B.** increased potassium current compared to normal hair cells.

○ **C.** decreased calcium current compared to normal hair cells.

○ **D.** increased calcium current compared to normal hair cells.

Question 14

Familial hearing loss caused by mutations in prestin are most likely segregate in what manner?

   I. Autosomal dominant

   II. Autosomal recessive

   III. X-linked recessive

○ **A.** II only

○ **B.** I and II only

○ **C.** II and III only

○ **D.** I, II, and III

Question 15

Which of the following findings from an additional experimental test would further confirm the role of prestin in hearing loss?

○ **A.** Patients with mutated prestin are able to distinguish between low frequency but not high frequency sounds.

○ **B.** Patients with normal prestin are able to distinguish between both high and low frequency sounds.

○ **C.** Patients with mutated prestin are able to distinguish between high frequency but not low frequency sounds.

○ **D.** Patients with normal prestin are able to distinguish changes in body position.

Question 16

Transcranial stimulation produces small vibrations on the skull that are able to vibrate the incus and malleus of the middle ear. What effect is transcranial stimulation likely to have on patients with prestin-dependent congenital hearing loss?

○ **A.** Transcranial stimulation would restore the ability to hear high but not low frequency sounds

○ **B.** Transcranial stimulation would restore the ability to hear both high and low frequency sounds

○ **C.** Transcranial stimulation would fail to restore the ability to hear high but not low frequency sounds

○ **D.** Transcranial stimulation would fail to restore the ability to hear both high and low frequency sounds

Passage 4 (Questions 17-21)

Neurofibromatosis type 2 (NF2) is an autosomal dominant heritable neoplasia syndrome. It results from a germline mutation of the NF2 tumor suppressor gene located on the long arm of chromosome 22. NF2 has a penetrance of nearly 100% by age 60 years. While the clinical manifestations of NF2 include central and peripheral nervous system tumors, including cancer of ependymal cells, the hallmark of NF2 is the development of tumors on the nerves between the inner ear and the brain called bilateral cochleovestibular schwannomas (CVSs). Although CVSs are benign tumors, they cause significant audiovestibular morbidity, including deafness. While complete hearing loss occurs in nearly all NF2 patients, its progression remains unpredictable and therefore management paradigms have remained inconsistent.

Variable patterns of hearing loss suggest that complex mechanisms of hearing loss such as disruption of cochlear vascular supply, and alteration in the biochemical milieu of inner ear fluids result in cochlear hair cell degeneration and dysfunction may play a critical role in the pathophysiology of hearing loss in patients with NF2. Because of the incomplete understanding of the pathophysiologic mechanisms underlying onset and variable progression of hearing loss in NF2 (even between ears in the same patient), the optimal management of CVSs in NF2 has not been determined. To identify markers for hearing loss and underlying pathophysiological mechanisms, researchers analyzed the clinical, imaging, and audiologic findings in a large cohort of NF2 patients. They found that hearing loss was most associated with a buildup of intralabrynthine protein in the inner ear fluid, resulting in damage to surrounding cells.

This passage was adapted from "Mechanisms of Hearing Loss in Neurofibromatosis Type 2." Asthagiri AR, Vasquez RA, Butman JA, Wu T, Morgan K et al. *PLoS ONE*. 2012. 7(9) doi:10.1371/journal.pone.0046132 for use under the terms of the Creative Commons CC BY 3.0 license (http://creativecommons.org/licenses/by/3.0/legalcode).

Question 17

A father heterozygous for NF2 and a mother homozygous for NF2 have a child. What is the probability that the child is healthy?

○ **A.** 100%

○ **B.** 50%

○ **C.** 25%

○ **D.** 0%

Question 18

Which of the following comparisons would be the most ideal model when studying the differences between deaf and hearing NF2 cases?

○ **A.** Two cousins with NF2, with one hearing and one deaf

○ **B.** Unrelated hearing and deaf cases of NF2

○ **C.** Twins with NF2, with one hearing and one deaf

○ **D.** An NF2 patient with one hearing ear and one deaf ear

Question 19

Hair cell degeneration may play a large role in NF2-linked deafness. In what part of the ear are hair cells located?

○ **A.** Organ of Corti

○ **B.** Semicircular canals

○ **C.** Malleus

○ **D.** Pinna

Question 20

All of the following are impaired in NF2 patients except:

○ **A.** balance.

○ **B.** speech.

○ **C.** sensory transmission to the brain.

○ **D.** taste.

Question 21

Which of the following models is most appropriate to study NF2?

○ **A.** A transgenic rat with no hair cells

○ **B.** A transgenic mouse with no hair cells

○ **C.** A transgenic mouse constitutively overexpressing intralabrynthine protein

○ **D.** A transgenic mouse overexpressing intralabrynthine protein specifically in the inner ear

Passage 5 (Questions 22-25)

Radiation is a treatment modality used for tumors of the head, neck and central nervous system. One of the clinical challenges of radiation to these sites is that the inner ear (cochlea and vestibular organs), temporal bone, and brain are within the radiation field, which may result in hearing loss and balance disorders. Generally, radiation induced hearing loss is a result of degeneration of the outer and inner hair cells within the organ of Corti, which respond primarily to changes in potassium levels in the cochlear fluid, and spiral ganglion neurons.

Radioprotective drugs may help prevent hearing loss during cancer therapy. A newly synthesized radioprotective drug PrC-210 was administered prior to radiation either directly into the ear (intra-tympanic) or into the abdomen (intra-peritoneal) of guinea pigs to determine whether it could prevent radiation-induced hearing loss. Guinea pigs treated with an IP or IT injection but not control animals were noted to have normal cochleae and did not demonstrate quantitative hair cell loss in any of the cochlear turns.

In addition to inspecting for physical damage, the hearing thresholds were assessed at three different frequencies, 8 kHz, 16 kHz, and 32 kHz, to determine if the range of hearing was protected by PrC-210. The results are shown in Figure 1.

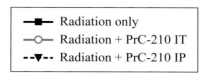

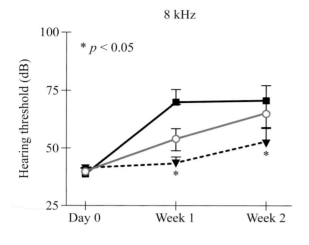

8 kHz

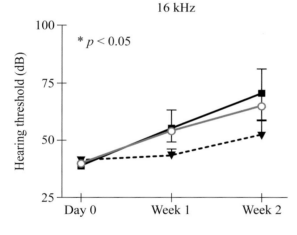

16 kHz

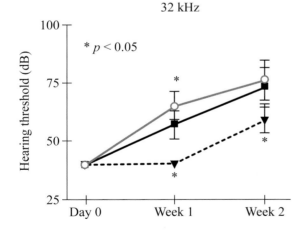

32 kHz

Figure 1 Hearing thresholds of irradiated adult guinea pigs treated by intra-peritoneal or intra-tympanic injection of PrC-210

This passage was adapted from "Radioprotective effect of aminothiol PrC-210 on irradiated inner ear of guinea pig." Giese A, Guarnaschelli J, Ward J, Choo D, Rizauddin S, et al. *PLoS ONE*. 2015. 10(11) doi:10.1371/journal.pone.0143606 for use under the terms of the Creative Commons CC BY 4.0 license (http://creativecommons.org/licenses/by/4.0/legalcode).

Question 22

In addition to the inner ear, ionizing radiation may damage which of the following structures to cause difficulties with balance?

○ **A.** Cerebellum

○ **B.** Occipital lobe

○ **C.** Frontal lobe

○ **D.** Parietal love

Question 23

Compared to guinea pigs treated only with radiation, guinea pigs treated with radiation + PrC-210 intra-peritoneally:

○ **A.** have vibration of the organ of Corti at lower sound intensity.

○ **B.** have vibration of the organ of Corti at higher sound intensity.

○ **C.** have movement of otoliths at lower sound intensity.

○ **D.** have movement of otoliths at higher sound intensity.

Question 24

In a second experiment, scientists sought to understand whether radiation induced damage in auditory processing and pattern recognition. They are most likely to stain for neuron apoptosis in the:

○ **A.** cochlear nuclei.

○ **B.** inferior colliculus.

○ **C.** medial geniculate nucleus.

○ **D.** temporal lobe.

Question 25

A person that experiences dizziness and difficulty walking but is able to distinguish between high and low pitched sounds is most likely to have damage in which of the following structures?

○ **A.** Organ of Corti

○ **B.** Otolith organs

○ **C.** Semicircular canals

○ **D.** Stapes

Questions 26 - 29 do not refer to a passage and are independent of each other.

Question 26

Vitreous humor clouding often results in lens flattening. What effect is this likely to have on the image formed at the retina?

- ○ **A.** The upright, imaginary image is formed closer to the lens.
- ○ **B.** The inverted, imaginary image is formed further from the lens.
- ○ **C.** The upright, real image is formed closer to the lens.
- ○ **D.** The inverted, real image is formed further from the lens.

Question 27

Electrolyte abnormalities in the blood have been shown to cause decreased hearing sensitivity. Which of the following conditions would be expected to result in decreased audition?

- ○ **A.** Hypokalemia, a condition of abnormally low potassium levels
- ○ **B.** Hypophosphatemia, a condition of abnormally low phosphate levels
- ○ **C.** Hypercalcemia, a condition of abnormally high calcium levels
- ○ **D.** Hypermagnesemia, a condition of abnormally high magnesium levels

Question 28

Damage to which of the following structures would be most likely to impair detection of object orientation in the visual field?

- ○ **A.** Lateral geniculate nucleus
- ○ **B.** Primary visual cortex
- ○ **C.** Medial geniculate nucleus
- ○ **D.** Semicircular canal

Question 29

Pheromones:

- ○ **A.** are only involved in conscious behavior.
- ○ **B.** may be involved in menstrual cycle timing.
- ○ **C.** are processed by the amygdala and thalamus.
- ○ **D.** are detected by olfactory chemoreceptors.

Passage 6 (Questions 30-34)

Neurofibromatosis type 1 (NF-1) is an autosomal dominant genetic disorder that affects 1 in 3500 individuals worldwide. Patients with high levels of the NF-1 protein develop malignancies and complex cognitive symptoms that include learning disabilities, attention deficit hyperactivity disorder and motor coordination problems.

To determine regulation of NF-1 expression throughout the nervous system, a recent study profiled the levels of mature miR-103, miR-137, miR-128 and *NF1* mRNA in cells of the cortex and hippocampus at different ages. Since neural tissues are a mixed population of neurons and glial cells, including astrocytes and Schwann cells, the levels of mature miR-103, miR-137, miR-128 and *NF1* mRNA were also quantified in these different cell types. The results are shown in Figure 1.

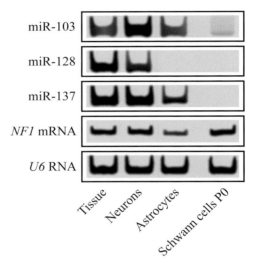

Figure 1 Levels of miR-103, miR-137, miR-128 and *NF1* mRNA in various cell types

Researchers theorized that the three miRNAs, miR-128, miR-103 and miR-137 bind directly to the terminal uridine residues of *NF1* mRNA and significantly reduce its protein levels. To test this, hippocampal neurons were transfected with miR-128 alone or in combination with miR-103 and miR-137 vectors, and Nf1 protein levels were assessed 48 hours later (Figure 2).

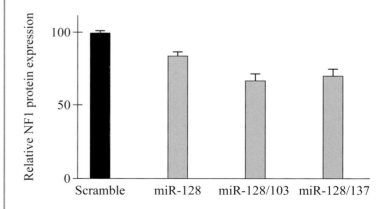

Figure 2 Levels of NF-1 expression in transfected hippocampal neurons

MiR-103, miR-128, and miR-137 all have ascribed functions apart from regulating *NF1* expression. MiR-103 is down regulated in neuropathic animals, while intrathecal applications relieve pain. MiR-128 regulates the formation of fear-extinction and memory. MiR-137 is enriched in synaptic fractions and has been shown to regulate neuronal maturation and dendritic morphogenesis.

This passage was adapted from "Neurofibromin 1 Is a miRNA Target in Neurons." Paschou M, Doxakis E. *PLoS ONE*. 2012. 7(10): doi:10.1371/journal.pone.0046773 for use under the terms of the Creative Commons CC BY 3.0 license (http://creativecommons.org/licenses/by/3.0/legalcode).

Question 30

According to Figure 1, which nervous tissue cells are most likely to become cancerous in a person with neurofibromatosis type 1?

- ○ **A.** Glial cells of the peripheral nervous system
- ○ **B.** Neuronal cells of the optic nerve
- ○ **C.** Glial cells of the central nervous system
- ○ **D.** Neuronal cells of the forebrain

Question 31

Neurofibromatosis type 2 patients have a high incidence of tumors involving the peripheral vestibular system. The associated symptoms would most likely include which of the following?

- I. Loss of sense of smell
- II. Hearing loss
- III. Gait instability

- ○ **A.** II only
- ○ **B.** I and III only
- ○ **C.** II and III only
- ○ **D.** I and II only

Question 32

Nociceptors most likely interact with the products of which of the following mRNAs?

- ○ **A.** miR-103
- ○ **B.** miR-137
- ○ **C.** miR-128
- ○ **D.** *U6* RNA

Question 33

Based on the information in the passage, absence of miR-137 would most directly cause which of the following?

- ○ **A.** Tumors precipitated by NF-1
- ○ **B.** Dysfunction of neuronal input integration
- ○ **C.** Slower action potential propagation in the peripheral nervous system
- ○ **D.** Speech disabilities

Question 34

One of the earliest signs of NF-1 is hypotonia, or decreased muscle tone, which can sometimes lead to diminished deep tendon reflexes. Upon stretching a muscle, hypotonia might result in a less robust:

- ○ **A.** positive feedback loop to contract the muscle.
- ○ **B.** inhibitory input from supraspinal circuits.
- ○ **C.** response, increasing the risk for tissue damage.
- ○ **D.** activation of the parasympathetic nervous system.

Passage 7 (Questions 35-38)

In the peripheral gustatory system, ATP plays a crucial role in the transmission of information from taste buds to the gustatory nerve fibers. ATP is released from taste receptor cells and activates P2X2/P2X3 receptors, which contain ion channels, on taste nerves. The importance of such transmission is evidenced by the loss of essentially all gustatory neural responses in P2X2/P2X3 double knockout (KO) mice.

Mature taste cells can be classified into three distinct types based on morphologic, molecular, and functional features. Type I cells express the glial glutamate/aspartate transporter (GLAST), which serves as a molecular marker for this cell type. Type II cells express the G protein-coupled receptors for umami (T1R1/T1R3), sweet (T1R2/T1R3) or bitter (T2Rs) transduction. These taste receptors are expressed in largely non-overlapping subsets of Type II taste cells, but all couple to the same downstream signaling effectors including phospholipase C-β2 (PLCβ2), inositol 1,4,5-trisphosphate receptor type 3 (IP3R3) and transient receptor potential channel M5 (TrpM5). Type III cells are responsible for sour taste transduction and express carbonic anhydrase isoenzyme 4 (Car4). Type III cells accumulate and release several transmitters, including 5-HT, GABA, and noradrenaline. Whereas Type III cells form classical synapses onto nerve fibers, Type II cells instead release ATP to activate purinergic P2X2 and P2X3 receptors on afferent nerve fibers.

The action of extracellular ATP is terminated by enzymes that convert ATP to adenosine, which itself can activate one or more G-protein coupled adenosine receptors including the A2B receptor. A2BR is expressed in the subset of taste cells that contain the sweet taste receptors. Researchers sought to test the function of these receptors by analyzing the nerve responses to sweet and other taste stimulants in A2BR KO mice exposed to different compounds (Figure 1).

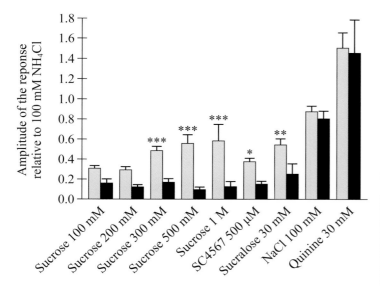

Figure 1 Glossopharyngeal nerve recordings from WT and A2BR KO mice

This passage was adapted from "A2BR Adenosine Receptor Modulates Sweet Taste in Circumvallate Taste Buds." Kataoka S, Baquero A, Yang D, Shultz N, Vandenbeuch A, et al. *PLoS Medicine*. 2012. 3(5) doi:10.1371/journal.pone.0030032 for use under the terms of the Creative Commons CC BY 3.0 license (http://creativecommons.org/licenses/by/3.0/legalcode).

Question 35

How might the quinine test serve as an effective control to demonstrate that differential nerve responses in the presence of sucrose are mediated by the A2B receptor?

○ **A.** Nerve signaling in the presence of quinine is identical in the two mouse types, proving that synaptic transmission is intact in KO mice.

○ **B.** Quinine is a potent antimalarial with a bitter taste, so its use indicates that there is intact action potential formation in KO mice.

○ **C.** The mice treated with NaCl already serve as an effective control, making the quinine test redundant.

○ **D.** Quinine leads to gustatory signaling by a unique pathway unrelated to the sweet taste response.

Question 36

The mechanism underlying the salty taste is somewhat unknown to researchers. One proposed mechanism involves the entry of sodium ions into taste receptor cells. This would be expected to:

○ **A.** hyperpolarize the taste cell, thereby leading to an action potential in the gustatory neurons.

○ **B.** depolarize the taste cell, thereby leading to potassium influx into the taste cell.

○ **C.** depolarize the taste cell, thereby leading to vesicle exocytosis in the synapse.

○ **D.** hyperpolarize the taste cell, thereby disinhibiting the activity of tonically active neurons.

Question 37

The response to sucrose appears to be muted but still present in A2BR KO mice. Based on the passage, how might the addition of a potent T1R2/T1R3 blocker affect the ability to differentiate between the two study populations?

○ **A.** The blocker would eliminate the response in the KO group, thereby widening the gap between the responses in the two populations.

○ **B.** The blocker would affect the wild-type and KO groups equally, slightly diminishing the response in either case.

○ **C.** The blocker would primarily diminish the strong response in the wild-type group, making the responses for the two populations similarly low.

○ **D.** The blocker would eliminate the response in both populations, making it impossible to distinguish between the groups.

Question 38

Sucralose is a commonly used non-nutritive sweetener that is not metabolized well by the body. Based on Figure 1, it is reasonable to conclude that sucralose:

○ **A.** is equally effective in generating a sweet response as is sucrose.

○ **B.** is more effective than sucrose in terms of generating a sweet response.

○ **C.** acts through a unique gustatory pathway that does not involve an adenosine receptor.

○ **D.** acts similarly to quinine, though quinine is more effective at generating a sweet response.

Questions 39 - 41 do not refer to a passage and are independent of each other.

Question 39

After exposure of olfactory chemoreceptors to a specific competitive inhibitor, olfaction would be:

○ **A.** diminished greatly, because the inhibitor would block all chemicals with a specific olfactory stimulus.

○ **B.** diminished somewhat, because the inhibitor would block a certain chemical but perception of smell integrates many types of olfactory chemoreceptors.

○ **C.** enhanced; the inhibitor would block chemicals with a specific olfactory stimulus so chemicals that are not blocked have a greater effect.

○ **D.** None of the above

Question 40

Which of the following depicts the correct olfactory pathway in the brain?

○ **A.** Olfactory chemoreceptors → olfactory nerve → olfactory bulb → piriform cortex

○ **B.** Olfactory chemoreceptors → olfactory nerve → olfactory bulb → thalamus → piriform cortex

○ **C.** Olfactory bulb → olfactory nerve → piriform cortex

○ **D.** None of the above

Question 41

Which of the following is FALSE according to classic psychophysics?

○ **A.** The experimental measurement of perception is not prone to subjectivity.

○ **B.** Signals need a minimal threshold to be detected by the human body.

○ **C.** Signals can escape detection in the presence of conflicting stimuli.

○ **D.** Depending on neighboring cues, signals can register inaccurately.

STOP. If you finish before time is called, check your work. You may go back to any question in this test.

ANSWERS & EXPLANATIONS for Test 2B can be found on p. 214.

The Endocrine System

TEST 3A

Time: 95 minutes
Questions 1–59

DIRECTIONS: Most of the questions in this test section are grouped with a passage. Read the passage, then select the best answer to each question. Some questions are independent of any passage and of one another. Select the best answer to each of these questions. If you are unsure of an answer, rule out incorrect choices and select from the remaining options. Indicate your selection beside the option you choose. A periodic table can be found on the last page of this book for you to use at any point during this test section.

Passage 1 (Questions 1-4)

Cushing syndrome (CS) is a metabolic disorder caused by overproduction of the hormone cortisol. CS increases cardiovascular risk factors (CVRF), including impaired glucose tolerance and obesity.

Telomere length (TL) shortening is a novel CVRF marker, associated with inflammatory biomarkers. Premature cell senescence and oxidative stress are both the cause and consequence of several CVRFs and their complications. In humans it is widely accepted that TL is affected by oxidative stress and is considered a novel marker of cardiovascular risk.

As telomere shortening is approximately the same in different tissues, circulating white blood cells are used as easily accessible surrogate tissue for TL assessment when analyzing systemic effects of chronic diseases, like cardiovascular disease. Telomeres are shortened by oxidative stress, which preferentially damages guanine-rich sequences to a greater extent than non-telomeric DNA.

Experiment 1

In a cross-sectional study, 77 patients with Cushing Syndrome and 77 age-, gender-, smoking-matched controls were included. Total white blood cell TL was measured by first using a telomere restriction fragment assay, separating the fragments using agarose gel electrophoresis, and measuring using Southern Blot. In addition, blood samples were collected to asses for dyslipidemia (DLP), metabolic syndrome (MetS), and type 2 diabetes mellitus (T2DM) Any correlations between TL and clinical features were examined. The results are shown in Figure 1.

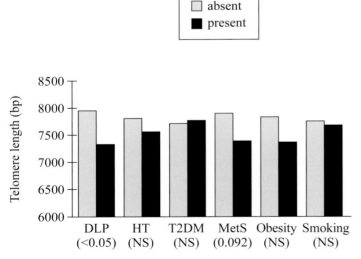

Figure 1 Mean telomere length according to different cardiovascular risk factors in Cushing's syndrome patients

Experiment 2

Cured and active CS participants were evaluated in the presence and absence of dyslipidemia for telomere length (Figure 2).

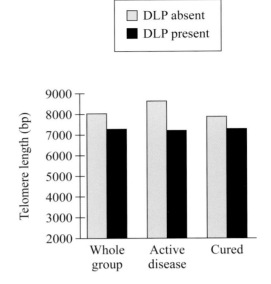

Figure 2 Mean telomere length in patients with Cushing's syndrome according to the presence or absence of dyslipidemia

This passage was adapted from "Dyslipidemia and Chronic Inflammation Markers Are Correlated with Telomere Length Shortening in Cushing's Syndrome." Aulinas A, Ramírez M-J, Barahona M-J, Valassi E, Resmini E, et al. *PLoS ONE*. 2015. 10(3): doi:10.1371/journal.pone.0120185 for use under the terms of Creative Commons License Attribution 4.0 License (www.biomedcentral.com/pdf/Creative_Commons_Attribtion_4.0_International_CC_BY_4.0.pdf).

Question 1

Based on the information in Figure 2, which of the following is likely to be found in participants with telomere lengths of over 8000 bp?

   I. Rapid and fleeting elevation in heart rate

   II. Increased gluconeogenesis

   III. Enhanced immune function

   IV. Increased blood volume

○ **A.** II only

○ **B.** I, II, and III only

○ **C.** I and III only

○ **D.** II, III and IV only

Question 2

Which of the following would be most likely to cause an overproduction of cortisol as seen in Cushing's syndrome?

○ **A.** Dysfunction in cell migration of neural tissue

○ **B.** A tumor on the posterior pituitary gland

○ **C.** Abnormally high GnRH secretion

○ **D.** A tumor on the anterior pituitary gland

Next ▶

Question 3

The control of which hormone is MOST similar to that of cortisol?

- ○ **A.** ADH
- ○ **B.** Prolactin
- ○ **C.** Estrogen
- ○ **D.** FSH

Question 4

Which of the following additional experiments would be LEAST likely to strengthen the conclusions of this study?

- ○ **A.** A study displaying a reduction in healing time in patients with hypertension
- ○ **B.** A study correlating reduced cell division and dyslipidemia
- ○ **C.** A study displaying an increase in heart disease in elderly patients
- ○ **D.** A study correlating increased cellular senescence and repeated stressful environmental stimuli

Passage 2 (Questions 5-8)

Congenital adrenal hyperplasia (CAH) is an autosomal recessive disorder of adrenal steroidogenesis. In 95% of cases, it is caused by 21-hydroxylase deficiency. Deficiency of 21-hydroxylase results in impaired adrenal synthesis of cortisol and often also of aldosterone leading to increased secretion of ACTH by the pituitary gland, adrenal hyperplasia, and excessive production of adrenal androgens. Current treatment of CAH consists of administration of glucocorticoids and, if necessary, of mineralocorticoids to prevent adrenal crises and to suppress the abnormal secretion of adrenal androgens. Long-term treatment, in particular the chronic over-treatment with glucocorticoids, may have an adverse effect on the cardiovascular risk profile in adult CAH patients.

Experiment 1

On the first day, participants visited the hospital in the morning after abstinence of caffeine containing substances and an overnight (10-hour) fast. All participants (those with CAH and controls) received a physical examination, and blood was drawn to assess several circulating cardiovascular risk markers.

Experiment 2

Blood pressure was measured twice supine and once in upright position. Mean supine office blood pressure was calculated (Table 1).

Table 1 Office Blood Pressure Measurements and (Standard Deviation) of Patients with CAH and Controls in Supine and Upright Positions

	CAH	Controls
Office systolic blood pressure (mmHg)		
Supine	133 ± 12	133 ± 12
Upright	138 ± 13	131 ± 12
Office diastolic blood pressure (mmHg)		
Supine	83 ± 10	80 ± 10
Upright	91 ± 10	90 ± 10

Experiment 3

Ambulatory blood pressure was monitored for 24 hours. On the second day, participants returned to the hospital for disconnection of the ambulatory blood pressure monitoring device (Figure 1).

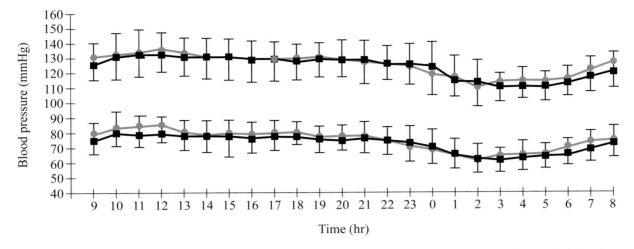

Figure 1 Mean ambulatory blood pressure measurements in CAH patients (open squares) and controls (closed squares)

This passage was adapted from "Adult Patients with Congenital Adrenal Hyperplasia Have Elevated Blood Pressure but Otherwise a Normal Cardiovascular Risk Profile." Mooij C.F., Kroese J.M., Sweep F.C.G.J., Hermus A.R.M.M. 2011 *PLoS ONE* 6(9): e24204. doi:10.1371/journal.pone.0024204 for use under the terms of the Creative Commons CC BY 3.0 license (http://creativecommons.org/licenses/by/3.0/legalcode).

Question 5

Based on the findings in Experiment 2, investigators could conclude which of the following?

○ **A.** The patients with CAH had significant aldosterone deficiencies compared to controls.

○ **B.** The patients with CAH may not have significant aldosterone deficiencies compared to controls.

○ **C.** CAH does not significantly change cardiovascular risk factors compared to controls.

○ **D.** The patients with CAH experienced negative side effects as a result of glucocorticoid treatment.

Question 6

In a patient with low cortisol due to CAH, what would be the expected effect on adrenocorticotropic hormone (ACTH)?

○ **A.** ACTH would be decreased via a negative feedback mechanism.

○ **B.** ACTH would be decreased due to the lack of a positive feedback mechanism.

○ **C.** ACTH would be increased due to the lack of a negative feedback mechanism.

○ **D.** ACTH would be increased via a positive feedback mechanism.

Question 7

Two healthy participants, Individual A and Individual B have their blood pressure measured. Which of the following would best describe the aldosterone levels present in an individual with a blood pressure of 95/60 (Individual A) relative to the average individual in the control group (Individual B)?

○ **A.** Individual B would have higher aldosterone levels due to having a higher blood pressure.

○ **B.** Individual A would have higher aldosterone levels due to having a higher blood pressure.

○ **C.** Individual A would have higher aldosterone levels due to having a lower blood pressure.

○ **D.** Their aldosterone would measure about equal assuming they have comparable renal function.

Question 8

Based on the information provided in paragraph 1, which of the following findings might support the diagnosis of CAH specifically in a female patient?

○ **A.** A lack of measurable cortisol in the blood

○ **B.** Closed epiphyseal plates

○ **C.** Hair growth on the chin and lip

○ **D.** Low systolic and diastolic blood pressure

Passage 3 (Questions 9-12)

Huntington's disease (HD) is an inherited neurodegenerative disease, caused by a CAG triplet repeat expansion in the gene encoding huntingtin. Classical features of HD include motor manifestations, cognitive and psychiatric symptoms. However, these are not the sole manifestations in HD, and disruption of circadian rhythms, alterations in sleep patterns, altered glucose homeostasis, muscle atrophy and weight loss may also impact on the quality of life of the patients and can precede motor symptoms by many years.

The hypothalamus exerts control over many bodily functions via three major outputs: autonomic, endocrine and behavioral systems. Hypothalamic endocrine efferent output is mediated through the hypothalamic pituitary axes, regulating the function of the thyroid gland, the adrenal gland, and the gonads, and, thereby, the circulating levels of growth hormone, thyroid hormones, cortisol, testosterone and estrogens. Alterations of the hypothalamic-pituitary-adrenal (HPA) axis have been shown in HD patients and in HD mouse models. Interestingly, increased cortisol levels can cause symptoms that are common in HD patients such as depression, skeletal muscle atrophy, altered glucose tolerance and memory impairment.

Scientists interested in the HPA axis in HD patients conducted a study to analyze the corticotropic axes in detail over a 24-hour period in a controlled environment, using cohorts of pre-manifest and moderate HD subjects and healthy controls. Pre-manifest subjects contained the unstable CAG triplet repeat but did not yet display symptoms. Stage II/III HD patients presented with marked tremors, along with decreased cognitive functioning. Blood was drawn every hour for 24 hours and the mean plasma ACTH and cortisol levels are presented in Figure 1.

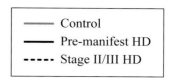

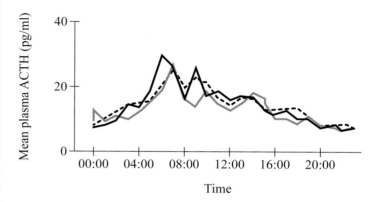

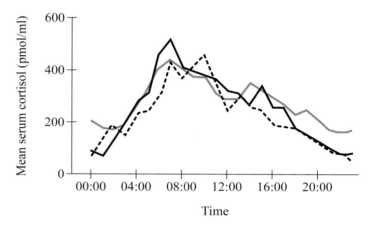

Figure 1 Analysis of ACTH and cortisol in control, pre-manifest, and stage II/III HD cohorts

This passage was adapted from "A 24-hour study of the hypothalamo-pituitary axes in Huntington's disease." Kalliolia E, Silajdzic E, Nambron R, Costelloe S, Martin N, et al. *PLoS ONE*. 2015. 10(10) doi:10.1371/journal.pone.0138848 for use under the terms of the Creative Commons CC BY 4.0 license (http://creativecommons.org/licenses/by/4.0/legalcode).

Question 9

How do corticotropin-releasing hormone (CRH) levels compare between the three trial groups?

○ **A.** Healthy controls > pre-manifest > stage II/III

○ **B.** Healthy controls < pre-manifest < stage II/III

○ **C.** Healthy controls = pre-manifest > stage II/III

○ **D.** Healthy controls = pre-manifest = stage II/III

Question 10

Negative feedback on the HPA axis is likely strongest at which time of day?

○ **A.** 12:00 AM

○ **B.** 8:00 AM

○ **C.** 2:00 PM

○ **D.** 9:00 PM

Question 11

Cushing's disease, which is caused by excess ACTH secretion due to a pituitary tumor, is also likely to result in:

○ **A.** low levels of blood glucose.

○ **B.** increased levels of circulating insulin.

○ **C.** increased levels of circulating glucagon.

○ **D.** increased levels of portal CRH.

Question 12

Overproduction of cortisol in end-stage Huntington's disease likely requires:

○ **A.** increased transcription and translation of carrier proteins in the liver.

○ **B.** decreased synthesis of CRH in the hypothalamus.

○ **C.** increased FSH synthesis in the anterior pituitary.

○ **D.** increased TSH synthesis in the thyroid gland.

Questions 13 - 16 do not refer to a passage and are independent of each other.

Question 13

Which of the following describes all endocrine glands?

○ **A.** Their products are fast-acting and quickly degraded.

○ **B.** They are inhibited by positive feedback loops using hormones released by other glands.

○ **C.** They control transcription and translation of DNA using their products.

○ **D.** They are collections of secretory cells controlled by nervous tissue.

Question 14

Which statement best describes the adrenal cortex?

○ **A.** It is an exocrine gland that is rich with ducts.

○ **B.** It is an endocrine gland that is rich with ducts.

○ **C.** It is an exocrine gland that has rich blood supply.

○ **D.** It is an endocrine gland that has rich blood supply.

Question 15

Epinephrine is best described as a:

   I. Neurotransmitter

   II. Hormone

   III. Second messenger

   IV. Peptide

○ **A.** I and IV only

○ **B.** I and II only

○ **C.** I, II, and III only

○ **D.** I, II, III, and IV

Question 16

Which statement best describes the mechanism of action of ACTH?

○ **A.** ACTH binds an extracellular receptor, triggering G-protein coupled signaling.

○ **B.** ACTH binds a cytosolic receptor, triggering G-protein coupled signaling.

○ **C.** ACTH binds a nuclear receptor, triggering translocation to the nucleus and gene transcription.

○ **D.** ACTH binds a cytoplasmic-facing endoplasmic reticulum receptor, triggering G-protein coupled signaling.

Passage 4 (Questions 17-21)

Thyroid hormone receptors (TRs) are ligand-dependent transcription factors that mediate the actions of the thyroid hormone (T_3) in cellular development, growth and differentiation. The role of TRs in human cancer is not well understood. The reduced expression of TRs because of differential methylation or deletion of TR genes in human cancers suggests that TRs could function as tumor suppressors. A close association of somatic mutations of TRs with thyroid cancers further supports the notion that the loss of normal functions of TR could lead to uncontrolled growth and loss of cell differentiation.

To understand the functional consequences of ligand-bound TR effects on downstream signaling pathways in thyroid cancer cells, scientists investigated RhoB, a member of the Ras superfamily of isoprenylated small GTPases, which regulate actin stress fibers and vesicle transport. In contrast to other Rho family members, RhoB has anti-proliferative and pro-apoptotic effects in cancer cells. Membrane association is required for proper RhoB protein functioning and occurs through modification with a fatty acid, farnesyl.

Experiment 1

Scientists first sought to characterize the presence of two TR isoforms, TRα and TRβ in the thyroid and a liver cancer cell line, HEPG2. They plated 1×10^6 cells isolated from patient biopsy specimens and the HepG2 cell line and allowed the cells to grow for 48 hours. After lysis of the cells, anti-TRα and anti-TRβ antibodies were used to characterize receptor expression levels (Figure 1).

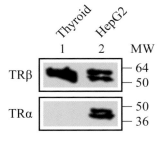

Figure 1 Expression of TRα and TRβ in the human thyroid and liver cancer cell line HepG2

Experiment 2

Following a similar procedure to Experiment 1, scientists then analyzed the effect of T_3 treatment with and without farnesyl-transferase inhibitor (FTI) co-treatment on RhoB activity (Figure 2). In the active GTP-bound form, RhoB specifically binds to the Rho-binding domain (RBD) of a membrane protein to regulate downstream signaling cascades.

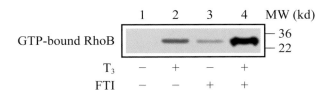

Figure 2 Expression and activation of GTP-bound RhoB

This passage is adapted from "Activation of the RhoB Signaling Pathway by Thyroid Hormone Receptor β in Thyroid Cancer Cells." Ichijo S, Furuya F, Shimura H, Hayashi Y, Takahashi K, et al. *PLoS ONE*. 2014. 9(12) doi:10.1371/journal.pone.0116252 for use under the terms of the Creative Commons CC BY 4.0 license (http://creativecommons.org/licenses/by/4.0/legalcode).

Question 17

Which of the following co-factors is most critical for the functioning of T_3?

- ○ **A.** I^-
- ○ **B.** Co^{2+}
- ○ **C.** Mg^{2+}
- ○ **D.** Cl^-

Question 18

Decreased expression of TR by thyroid cancer cells correlates with abnormally low levels of circulating T_4. Which of the following statements best describes predicted alterations of an additional hormone marker?

- ○ **A.** The level of TSH is lower than normal
- ○ **B.** The level of TRH is higher than normal
- ○ **C.** The level of CRH is higher than normal
- ○ **D.** The level of prolactin is lower than normal

Question 19

T_4 has been shown to nearly exclusively bind TRα receptors compared to TRβ receptors. Increased release of TSH is most likely to lead to:

- ○ **A.** increased cell death in liver cancer cells compared to thyroid cancer cells.
- ○ **B.** increased cell death in thyroid cancer cells compared to liver cancer cells.
- ○ **C.** increased cell death in both liver cancer and thyroid cancer cell lines.
- ○ **D.** decreased cell death in both liver cancer and thyroid cancer cell lines.

Question 20

Patients diagnosed with hyperthyroidism are NOT likely to experience which of the following symptoms?

- ○ **A.** Rapid heartbeat
- ○ **B.** Decreased blood glucose levels
- ○ **C.** Decreased body weight
- ○ **D.** Elevated body temperature

Question 21

According to information contained in the passage, FTI acts:

- ○ **A.** as a direct inhibitor of T_3.
- ○ **B.** as a synergistic agonist along with T_3.
- ○ **C.** to increase TSH expression.
- ○ **D.** to decrease TRH degradation.

Passage 5 (Questions 22-26)

Obesity is a major problem in the Western world and an increasing challenge in the developing countries. In particular, abdominal obesity is linked to chronic diseases such as type 2 diabetes, hypertension and cardiovascular disease, which are both currently recognized as major public health concerns. Adipose tissue is one of the most dynamic tissues of the body, expanding and shrinking in response to various hormonal, neurogenic and nutritional stimuli. The number of adipocytes is set before adolescence, and stays relatively constant throughout the adulthood, while adipose stem cells are mainly committed in utero. Prenatal stress is known to increases the risk of obesity and diabetes in the progeny. However, how stress affects adipogenic commitment in embryos, and contributes to the adult obesity, remains unclear.

Adipogenesis is a developmental process by which mesenchymal stem cells (MSCs) differentiate into mature adipocytes. Very little is known about the molecular mechanisms and the cellular intermediates responsible for the transitions from undifferentiated embryonic stem cells (ESCs) to MSCs, and from MSCs to preadipocytes. Adipocytes arise from MSCs, a common precursor for myocytes, chondrocytes and osteocytes.

To further investigate the effects of stress on adipocyte formation, researchers measured levels of FABP4, a marker of adipocytes, mRNA in ESCs following treatment with hormones (Figure 1). These hormones included epinephrine, a major stress hormone, and insulin.

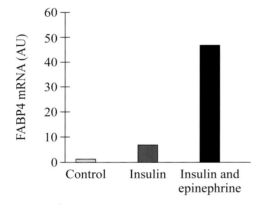

Figure 1 FABP4 mRNA levels following hormone treatment

Question 22

In an adult, the majority of adipocytes are in the:

- A. S phase.
- B. M phase.
- C. G_1 phase.
- D. G_0 phase.

Question 23

Which of the following conclusions is supported by Figure 1?

- A. Stress increases adipocyte formation in the womb.
- B. Stress decreases adipocyte formation in the womb.
- C. Stress increases adipocyte formation in adults.
- D. Stress decreases adipocyte formation in adults.

Question 24

FABP4 mRNA levels were used by researchers to detect adipocytes. The detected level of FABP4 mRNA is:

- A. directly correlated with growth rate.
- B. inversely correlated with growth rate.
- C. directly correlated with ability to differentiate.
- D. inversely correlated with ability to differentiate.

Question 25

Receptors for hormone are found in various locations depending on the characteristics of the hormone. The receptor for insulin is most likely located:

- A. in the cytoplasm.
- B. on the nuclear membrane.
- C. on the cell membrane.
- D. in the nucleus.

Question 26

Epinephrine is a major hormone and neurotransmitter in the body. The effects of epinephrine include:

  I. vasoconstriction of internal organs.
  II. vasodilation of skeletal muscles.
  III. increasing water retention.

- A. I only
- B. III only
- C. I and II only
- D. I, II, and III

Questions 27 - 30 do not refer to a passage and are independent of each other.

Question 27

End-stage liver disease often presents with multiple endocrine abnormalities. Which of the following best explains this finding?

○ **A.** The liver is responsible for solvating steroid hormones.

○ **B.** The liver is the major producer of insulin and glucagon.

○ **C.** The liver is responsible for excreting water-soluble hormone metabolites.

○ **D.** The liver is the site of negative feedback for the majority of endocrine pathways.

Question 28

Which of the following is NOT true about the hormone cortisol?

○ **A.** Cortisol is a steroid hormone secreted by the adrenal medulla.

○ **B.** Cortisol regulates glucose mobilization.

○ **C.** Cortisol's hydrophobicity allows it to traverse membranes and act in cell nuclei.

○ **D.** Cortisol is likely to be elevated in response to chronic stressors.

Question 29

The researchers most closely studied P, E_2, FSH, and LH. What characteristic is shared by all four of these molecules?

○ **A.** Binding to a cytosolic receptor

○ **B.** Use of a binding protein

○ **C.** Transport through the blood

○ **D.** Membrane-bound receptor

Question 30

cAMP is upregulated in a localized tissue by an intracellular receptor protein, but nonadjacent tissues do not experience any stimulus. Which of the following is most likely responsible for this phenomenon?

○ **A.** FSH

○ **B.** Prostaglandins

○ **C.** Cortisol

○ **D.** Calcitonin

Passage 6 (Questions 31-34)

Type 1 diabetes (T1D) results from autoimmune destruction of certain pancreatic cells and current treatments for T1D include administration of exogenous insulin or islet transplantation. Therapeutic benefit has been obtained with islet transplantation, but complications associated with long-term immunosuppression have hampered its broad clinical application.

The conversion of non-insulin-producing cells into insulin-producing cells *in vivo* is an innovative approach to treat diabetes. *In vivo* reprogramming has been achieved by adenoviral (Ad)-mediated gene transfer of the transcription factors (TFs) *Pdx1*, *Ngn3* and *MafA* (PNM) into two cell lines, AR42J and B13. AR42J is a rat cell line that can synthesize, store, and secrete digestive enzymes and has an electrically excitable membrane and B13 cells are derived from pancreatic progenitor cells.

Scientists wanted to gain further insight into the mechanisms underlying the reprogramming of exocrine cells towards an insulin-secreting phenotype. To compare their efficiencies of reprogramming into insulin-producing cells, B13 cells were transduced with adenoviral vectors bearing a polycistronic expression cassette that encoded *Pdx1*, *Ngn3*, and *MafA*, as well as a GFP marker gene, all of which were under the control of a CAG promoter (Ad-PNM). mRNA levels of *Glut2*, a glucose transporter, and *Gck*, glucokinase, were measured in B13 cells to determine whether overexpression of *Pdx1*, *Ngn3*, and *MafA* resulted in changes in glucose processing. The results are shown in Figure 1.

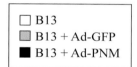

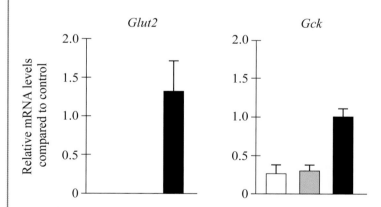

Figure 1 Expression levels of *Glut2* and *Gck* in reprogrammed B13 cells

The development of insulin-producing cells in the pancreas is not only controlled by TFs but also by microRNAs (miRNAs). Mature miRNAs are short (~22 bp), non-coding RNAs that can negatively or positively regulate gene expression at the post-transcriptional level. Scientists measured the expression levels of two miRNAs in various regions of the pancreas, as well as in B13 and AR42J cells. The results are shown in Figure 2.

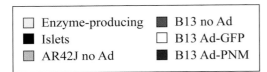

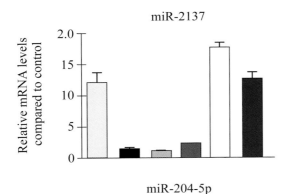

miR-2137

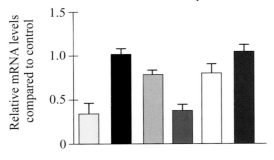

miR-204-5p

Figure 2 Relative mRNA levels of two miRNAs

Question 31

After conducting the experiment presented in Figure 1, scientists would most likely:

○ **A.** stain for insulin protein levels by western blot in B13 cells.

○ **B.** stain for glucagon mRNA levels by northern blot in B13 cells.

○ **C.** replicate the experiment in AR42J cells.

○ **D.** use fluorescent hybridization to assay for an increased number of *Glut2* gene copies.

Question 32

Type 1 diabetes is most likely caused by:

○ **A.** a person's killer T cells recognizing antigens on the surface of pancreatic β cells.

○ **B.** a person's B cells generating antibodies against antigens on the surface of pancreatic α cells.

○ **C.** viruses or bacteria invading the exocrine tissue of the pancreas, eliciting an innate immune system reaction.

○ **D.** macrophages attacking lipid antigens on the surface of pancreatic α and β cells.

Question 33

Which of the following statements best summarizes the findings of Figure 2?

   I. miR-2137 is more likely to affect chymotrypsin than miR-204-5p.

   II. miR-204-5p is more likely to affect insulin secretion than miR-2137.

   III. miR-2137 is more likely to affect somatostatin secretion than miR-204-5p.

○ **A.** I only

○ **B.** I and II only

○ **C.** I and III only

○ **D.** II and III only

Question 34

Increased secretion of insulin from the pancreas is most likely to coincide with:

○ **A.** increased sympathetic stimulation of cardiac muscle.

○ **B.** decreased parasympathetic stimulation of smooth muscle.

○ **C.** increased parasympathetic stimulation of the ciliary muscle.

○ **D.** increased sympathetic stimulation of the gut muscles.

Passage 7 (Questions 35-38)

Telomeres consist of repetitive DNA sequences, thousands of "TTAGGG" tandem repeats, which are located at the ends of linear chromosomes in most somatic cells. Although the potential relationship between telomere length and growth hormone (GH) and insulin-like growth factor-1 (IGF-1) axis has been investigated, telomere length in patients with abnormally long bone growth (acromegaly) has not been reported. Acromegaly is characterized by the over-secretion of GH, mostly caused by GH-producing pituitary adenomas.

Scientists examined the telomere length in peripheral leukocytes in patients with acromegaly and control patients with non-functioning pituitary adenoma (NFPA). To explore the underlying mechanisms of telomere shortening in acromegaly, they analyzed the effect of GH or IGF-1 treatment on telomere length in cultured human skin fibroblasts (Figure 1).

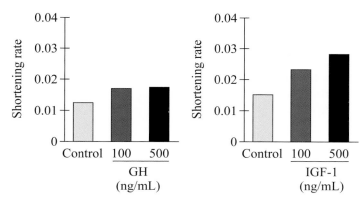

Figure 1 Telomere shortening rate in human fibroblasts with GH and IGF-1 treatment

Patients with Laron syndrome are GH receptor (GHR) deficient, have low serum IGF-1 levels, and have a low prevalence of cancer and diabetes. Interestingly, serum from subjects with GHR deficiency showed differences in the incidence of DNA breaks (as measured by p53 protein levels) but increased apoptosis (Figure 2). Scientists constructed a theoretical explanation of the effect of telomere shortening in acromegaly patients (Figure 3).

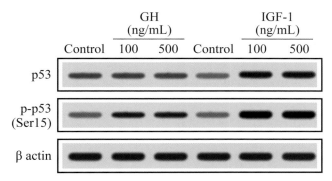

Figure 2 Incidence of DNA breaks in Laron syndrome patients and patients with normal (100 ng/ml) and elevated (500 ng/ml) levels of GH and IGF-1

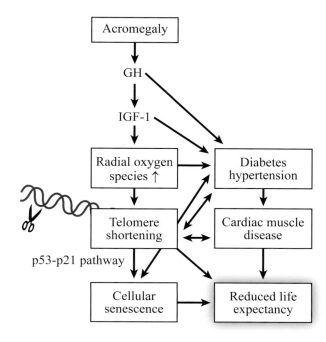

Figure 3 Hypothesized pathway leading to decreased life expectancy in acromegaly patients

This passage is adapted from "Accelerated Telomere Shortening in Acromegaly; IGF-I Induces Telomere Shortening and Cellular Senescence." Matsumoto R, Fukuoka H, Iguchi G, Odake Y, Yoshida K, et al. *PLoS ONE.* 2015. 10(10) doi:10.1371/journal. pone.0140189 for use under the terms of the Creative Commons CC BY 4.0 license (http://creativecommons.org/licenses/by/4.0/legalcode).

Question 35

Increased secretion of which of the following hormones would also lead to acromegaly?

- **A.** GHRH
- **B.** GnRH
- **C.** Calcitonin
- **D.** Prolactin

Question 36

Telomere length is most likely:

- **A.** decreased by GH, which interacts with a cell-surface receptor.
- **B.** decreased in IGF-1, which interacts with a cytoplasmic receptor.
- **C.** increased by GH, which interacts with a cytoplasmic receptor.
- **D.** increased by IGF-1, which interacts with a cell-surface receptor.

Question 37

In a separate experiment, scientists measured the mRNA levels of p53, a transcription factor, and p21, the target gene of p53, under conditions of various levels of GH and IGF-1. These data are most likely to:

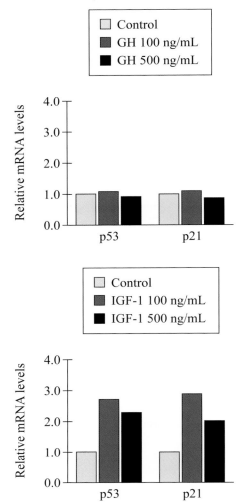

O **A.** support the conclusion of the scientists that increased GH but not increased IGF-1 leads to acromegaly.

O **B.** refute the conclusion of the scientists that both increased GH and increased IGF-1 lead to acromegaly.

O **C.** support the conclusion of the scientists that increased IGF-1 but not increased GH leads to acromegaly.

O **D.** neither support nor deny the conclusion of the scientists that increased IGF-1 but not increased GH leads to acromegaly.

Question 38

A pituitary adenoma compressing the posterior pituitary is LEAST likely to result in:

O **A.** increased blood pressure.

O **B.** constriction of the peripheral vasculature.

O **C.** increased transport of sodium in the ascending loop of Henle.

O **D.** decreased filtration in the glomerulus.

Passage 8 (Questions 39-42)

Primary hyperparathyroidism (PHPT) is a common endocrine disorder characterized by increased levels of parathyroid hormone (PTH) and, occasionally, abnormalities in prolactin levels. In addition to its normal physiologic roles, prolactin has calciotropic effects in the intestine, kidney and skeleton and has also been associated with cancer development in the breast and ovary. Increased levels of prolactin and/or increased expression of the prolactin receptor is thought to predispose patients to developing gynecologic and other malignancies.

Previous observations have also suggested a role for the prolactin receptor (PRLr) in parathyroid cells. Given the frequent occurrence of PHPT in women and the role of PRLr in other tumors, scientists aimed to assess PRLr expression and functionality in human parathyroid tumors.

Experiment 1

Using biopsy samples of breast, normal parathyroid tissue, parathyroid tumor, and cells from the T47D breast cancer cell line, scientists determined PRLr isoform expression by western blot. Five tumor specimens were used, corresponding to parathyroid tumors from five different patients. The nuclear extract of normal parathyroid tissue was found to be negative for PRLr expression (Figure 1).

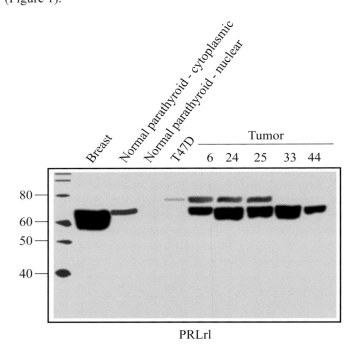

Figure 1 Western blot analysis of protein expression for isoforms (approximate molecular weight indicated by arrows) of the prolactin receptor

Experiment 2

In a second experiment, cells obtained from a parathyroid tumor were co-cultured with two concentrations of prolactin. Over the course of an hour, the PTH secretion and intracellular concentration of calcium were determined. The results are presented in Figure 2.

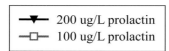

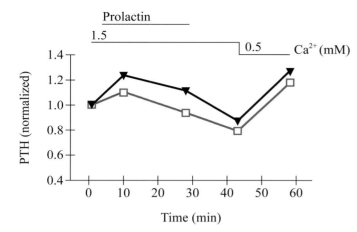

Figure 2 Analysis of PTH secretion and intracellular calcium after prolactin treatment

Question 39

In individuals without PHTP, prolactin functions to:

○ **A.** increase the breakdown of bone.

○ **B.** increase the basal metabolic rate.

○ **C.** increase the production of milk from breast mammary glands.

○ **D.** increase the release of milk from breast mammary glands.

Question 40

Parathyroid cancer growth may also be stimulated by thyroid hormone. Which of the following findings would most likely be seen if Experiment 1 was repeated with antibodies directed against T_3 and thyroid hormone receptor?

○ **A.** Parathyroid hormone staining would be the strongest in the cytoplasm of parathyroid cancer cells.

○ **B.** Thyroid hormone staining would be the strongest in the nucleus of parathyroid cancer cells.

○ **C.** Prolactin staining would be the strongest in the nucleus of parathyroid cancer cells.

○ **D.** Thyroid hormone receptor staining would be strongest at the cellular membrane of parathyroid cancer cells.

Question 41

Which of the following symptoms is LEAST likely to be seen in PHPT patients?

○ **A.** Increased stimulation of osteoclasts to release phosphate

○ **B.** Decreased levels of phosphate in the kidney collecting duct

○ **C.** Increased absorption of calcium in the small intestine

○ **D.** Decreased bone density in the femur, a long bone of the leg

Question 42

Which of the following statements best explains the results of tumor six in Experiment 1?

○ **A.** The antibody binds to two unique epitopes on a single protein that binds a hormone released by the posterior pituitary.

○ **B.** The antibody binds one shared epitope on two isoforms of a protein that binds a hormone released from the anterior pituitary.

○ **C.** The antibody binds three unique epitopes on two proteins, one that is released from the anterior pituitary and its receptor.

○ **D.** The antibody binds a shared epitope on one isoform of a protein that binds the receptor released from the anterior pituitary.

Questions 43 - 46 do not refer to a passage and are independent of each other.

Question 43

Transcription of the *DOI2* gene, which is responsible for the conversion of T_4 to T_3, would be increased by:

○ **A.** increasing TSH release and decreasing methylation of the *DOI2* promoter.

○ **B.** decreasing TRH release and increasing methylation of the *DOI2* promoter.

○ **C.** decreasing T_3 ubiquitination and increased methylation of the *DOI2* promoter.

○ **D.** increasing T_3 mRNA transcription and increasing methylation of the *DOI2* promoter.

Question 44

Constantly increased GH levels are most likely to increase:

    I. longitudinal growth at epiphysis.

    II. H^+ production in the stomach.

    III. lipogenesis in yellow bone marrow.

○ **A.** I only

○ **B.** II only

○ **C.** I and II only

○ **D.** II and III only

Question 45

Which of the following blood ion values would most likely be seen in a patient with elevated parathyroid hormone?

○ **A.** Increased calcium and increased phosphate

○ **B.** Increased calcium and decreased phosphate

○ **C.** Decreased calcium and increased phosphate

○ **D.** Decreased calcium and decreased phosphate

Question 46

A scientist is examining the effects of testosterone use on body builders by sampling the body fluids of 100 men who admit to currently using testosterone supplements. Analysis of these samples is expected to show:

○ **A.** elevated testosterone levels in the blood due to an increase in the level of production by the testes.

○ **B.** an high level of luteinizing hormone being released from the anterior pituitary gland.

○ **C.** a decreased amount of hormones secreted by the hypothalamus.

○ **D.** an increased level of the hormone that stimulates the hypothalamus to release more luteinizing hormone into the systemic blood.

Passage 9 (Questions 47-50)

Estrogens comprise a group of steroid hormones with a pivotal role in physiological processes. In the anterior pituitary, in addition to well-characterized estrogenic actions on gonadotropins and prolactin secretion, estrogens are involved in control of cell fate acting as either pro-survival, anti-proliferative or pro-apoptotic factors. Estrogens thereby remodel and reshape the cells of the anterior pituitary by regulating anterior pituitary structural and functional plasticity so that the gland is able to adapt dynamically to changing physiological status and environmental stimuli in several physiological conditions such as pregnancy, lactation and the estrous cycle.

17β-estradiol (E2) is the prevailing endogenous estrogen in adult females before menopause. It elicits its multiple actions via binding to and activating intracellular estrogen receptors (ER), ERα and ERβ. ERα protein is found primarily in lactotropes, cells that secrete prolactin, followed by somatotropes, cells that secrete GH, and, to a lower extent, gonadotropes, cells that secrete LH and FSH, and thyrotropes, cells that secrete TSH. The expression of ERα varies along the estrous cycle, reaching minimum levels at diestrus and maximum at proestrus, which can be positively correlated with estrogen circulating levels.

Other mechanisms of estrogen action involving rapid activation of membrane-associated ERs (mERα and mERβ) and triggering of second-messenger pathways have also been described. E2 exerts a rapid pro-apoptotic action in anterior pituitary cells, especially in lactotrope and somatotrope populations, through activation of membrane-associated ERs. The involvement of mERα in the rapid pro-apoptotic action of estradiol was measured by TUNEL in primary cultures of anterior pituitary cells from rats that lacked ovaries using a cell-impermeable E2 conjugate (E2-BSA) and an ERα selective antagonist (MPP dihydrochloride).

This passage was adapted from "Estrogens Induce Expression of Membrane-Associated Estrogen Receptor a Isoforms in Lactotropes." Zarate S, Jaita G, Ferraris J, Eijo G, Magri M, et al. *PLoS*. 2012. 7(7) doi: 10.1371/journal.pone.0041299 for use under the terms of the Creative Commons CC BY 3.0 license (http://creativecommons.org/licenses/by/3.0/legalcode).

Question 47

Which statement best describes the mechanism of apoptosis in the anterior pituitary described in the passage?

○ **A.** External signaling induces internal digestive elements to break down a healthy cell body.

○ **B.** External signaling induces internal digestive elements to break down a damaged cell body.

○ **C.** Internal preprogrammed signaling induces a complete lysis in response to normal cell components.

○ **D.** Internal preprogrammed signaling induces a complete lysis in response to damaged cell components.

Question 48

Which mechanism of cellular signaling best describes how the hormone secreted by experimental lactotropes travels to and affects its target tissue?

- A. Hypophyseal portal system and intracellular receptors respectively
- B. Carrier proteins and membrane-bound receptors respectively
- C. Carrier proteins and intracellular receptors respectively
- D. Free floating in the bloodstream and membrane-bound receptors respectively

Question 49

Which experiment would best support the proposed role of mERα in cellular apoptosis?

- A. Keep E2 and E2-BSA concentration constant and measure the rate of apoptosis in the presence and absence of mERα.
- B. Keep E2-BSA concentration constant and measure the rate of apoptosis in increasing concentrations of E2 in the presence and absence of mERα.
- C. Keep mERα and E2 concentration constant and measure the rate of apoptosis in increasing concentrations of E2-BSA.
- D. Keep mERα and E2-BSA concentration constant and measure the rate of apoptosis in increasing concentrations of E2.

Question 50

Researchers measure the rate of estrogen-induced apoptosis and evaluate lactotrope activity in mice immediately following parturition. Which of the following is likely true of the results of this experiment?

- A. Lactotrope secretion is elevated due to elevated levels of serum estrogen.
- B. Lactotrope secretion is elevated due to inhibition of the hypothalamus.
- C. Lactotrope apoptosis is elevated due to elevated levels of estrogen.
- D. Lactotrope apoptosis is elevated due to stimulation of the hypothalamus.

Passage 10 (Questions 51-56)

Polycystic Ovary Syndrome (PCOS) is a widespread reproductive disorder characterized by a disruption of follicular growth and anovulatory infertility. In women with PCOS, follicular growth and ovulation can be induced by subcutaneous injections of low doses of follicle stimulating hormone (FSH).

The aim of this study was to determine the effect of oral administration of recombinant human FSH (rhFSH) on follicle development in a PCOS murine model. Female peripubertal mice were injected with dehydroepiandrosterone (DHEA) to induce the symptoms of PCOS. To study the effect of oral administration of recombinant human FSH on PCOS-induced animals, three groups of eight mice each were orally treated with a solution of rhFSH.

Experiment 1

After 20 consecutive days of treatments, blood samples were collected from each mouse before sacrifice. Analysis of testosterone (T) was performed employing a competitive inhibition enzyme immunoassay technique. Levels of progesterone (P4), estradiol (E2) and LH were measured using a magnetic bead immunoassay based on Luminex Multiplex System (Figure 1).

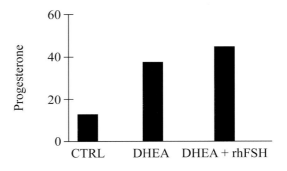

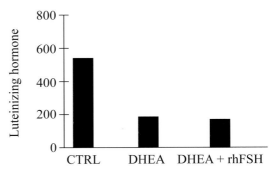

Figure 1 Blood serum levels of progesterone and luteinizing hormone following 20 days of treatment

Experiment 2

The ovaries were collected immediately after sacrifice and fixed in 10% neutral buffered formalin overnight. The ovaries were dehydrated and serially sectioned at 4 μm. Slices were placed on glass microscope slides and analyzed under light microscopy to assess follicles diameter and morphological features. Two investigators performed morphological analysis independently (Figure 2).

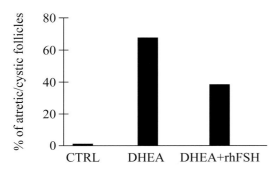

Figure 2 Effect of different hormonal treatments on the percentage of follicles presenting atretic/cystic signs

This passage was adapted from "Effect of Oral administration of Low-Dose Follicle Stimulating Hormone on hyperandrogenized mice as a model of PCOS." Tessaro I, Modina S, Franciosi F, Sivelli G, Terzaghi L, et al. *Journal of Ovarian Research*. 8(64) doi: 10.1186/s13048-015-0192-9 for use under the terms of the Creative Commons CC BY 4.0 license (https://creativecommons.org/licenses/by/4.0/legalcode).

Question 51

Which mechanism best explains how an injection of FSH mitigates the infertility caused by PCOS?

○ **A.** FSH stimulates the corpus luteum, thickening the endometrium

○ **B.** FSH causes a dramatic decrease in the level of LH, inhibiting the luteal surge

○ **C.** FSH facilitates the conversion of androgen into estradiol, increasing estrogen production

○ **D.** FSH causes the growth of the cells around the primary oocyte which create the zona pellucida

Question 52

The stimulation of which of the following structures of the female reproductive system is increased in the DHEA-treated mice?

○ **A.** Follicle

○ **B.** Endomysium

○ **C.** Fimbraie

○ **D.** Endometrium

Question 53

PCOS is also associated with metabolic dysfunction, often leading to obesity and chronic high serum glucose levels. The activity of which hormone is MOST likely to be increased in the DHEA-treated mice?

○ **A.** Cortisol

○ **B.** Glucagon

○ **C.** Epinephrine

○ **D.** Insulin

Question 54

Which aspect of the experiment would most WEAKEN the conclusion that administration of rFSH was unsuccessful in alleviating the symptoms of PCOS?

○ **A)** Increased presence of atretic cysts in mice treated with the recombinant protein

○ **B)** No change in serum LH between DHEA-treated mice and DHEA + rFSH treated mice

○ **C)** Diminished presence of atretic cysts in mice treated with the recombinant protein

○ **D)** Increased serum progesterone in DHEA-treated mice vs DHEA + rFSH treated mice

Question 55

The hormone whose production is decreased with the administration of DHEA + rFSH communicates with its target cells by binding with which type of receptor?

○ **A.** Intracellular receptor proteins

○ **B.** Membrane-bound receptor

○ **C.** Extracellular matrix proteins

○ **D.** Nuclear receptor sequences

Question 56

Researchers develop a new experiment in which male mice are treated with DHEA instead of females. Which of the following is the most likely consequence of administration of this compound in the mice?

○ **A.** Development of secondary sex characteristics such as growth of the seminal vesicles and penis would be slowed

○ **B.** Inhibin production is slowed, decreasing negative feedback on GnRH production

○ **C.** Differentiation of germ cells into sperm would be stimulated

○ **D.** Luteal phase of sperm development is lengthened due to increased progesterone

Questions 57 - 59 do not refer to a passage and are independent of each other.

Question 57

Hypopituitarism is an endocrine disorder resulting in the release of little to no hormones from the pituitary gland. Which hormone would most likely be elevated in such a case?

○ **A.** GnRH

○ **B.** FSH

○ **C.** Oxytocin

○ **D.** Estrogen

Question 58

Which of the following represents the correct pathway of seminal fluid through the male reproductive tract?

○ **A.** Epididymis, vas deferens, urethra

○ **B.** Vas deferens, epididymis, ejaculatory duct

○ **C.** Seminal vesicles, urethra, bulbourethral gland

○ **D.** Seminal vesicles, ejaculatory duct, urethra

Question 59

Prior to ovulation:

○ **A.** the corpus luteum is producing large quantities of progesterone and estrogen to prevent the endometrial lining from shedding.

○ **B.** a large increase in the amount of estrogen initiates the production of luteinizing hormone.

○ **C.** the egg completes meiosis II in preparation for fertilization.

○ **D.** a large increase in secretion of luteinizing hormone, called the luteal surge, triggers the proliferation of the uterine endometrium.

STOP. If you finish before time is called, check your work. You may go back to any question in this test.

ANSWERS & EXPLANATIONS for Test 3A can be found on p. 238.

The Endocrine System

MINI-TEST 3B

Time: 65 minutes
Questions 1–41

DIRECTIONS: Most of the questions in this test section are grouped with a passage. Read the passage, then select the best answer to each question. Some questions are independent of any passage and of one another. Select the best answer to each of these questions. If you are unsure of an answer, rule out incorrect choices and select from the remaining options. Indicate your selection beside the option you choose. A periodic table can be found on the last page of this book for you to use at any point during this test section.

Passage 1 (Questions 1-4)

Triclosan (TCS) is a broad-spectrum antimicrobial agent that is used in clinical settings and in various personal care and consumer products, including soaps, hair products, toothpaste, medical devices, plastics, textiles, children toys, and others. Currently, TCS is one of the more frequently detected and highly concentrated contaminants in aquatic and terrestrial environments.

Analysis of the chemical structure of TCS implies that it may have chemical properties related to many toxic compounds. The placenta is an important endocrine organ that connects the developing fetus to the maternal uterus. The placenta can synthesize a number of hormones, such as hCG, progesterone (P), and estrogen (E_2), which play important roles in implantation, pregnancy maintenance and embryo development. Toxic and foreign chemicals may interfere with placental hormone secretion and further result in abortion, stunted fetal growth and intrauterine fetal death.

Researchers aimed to study the potential effects of TCS on the endocrine environment in pregnant rats. Serum levels of hormones are shown below in Figure 1. Additionally, transcriptional levels of estrogen receptor (ER) and progesterone receptor (PR) were quantified through quantitative reverse transcriptase polymerase chain reaction (Q-RT-PCR). Increases in expression of these receptors in placental tissue were observed. In contrast, levels of HSD11B1 mRNA, the enzyme that produces cortisol, were unchanged.

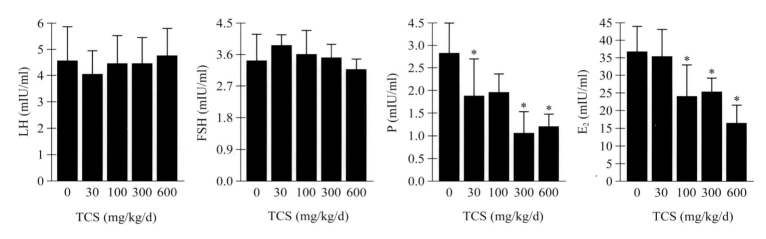

Figure 1 Levels of various hormones following TCS administration

Question 1

The information in the passage most strongly suggests that TCS could have what effect on reproductive processes during pregnancy?

○ **A.** Degeneration of the corpus luteum

○ **B.** Increased input from the hypothalamus onto the anterior pituitary

○ **C.** Decreased frequency of LH surges

○ **D.** Increased thickness of the uterine wall

Question 2

Which of the following results would most strongly support the study's findings related to ER and PR levels following TCS treatment?

○ **A.** E_2 exhibits negative feedback on levels of ER, while P exhibits positive feedback on levels of PR.

○ **B.** E_2 exhibits negative feedback on levels of ER, while P exhibits negative feedback on levels of PR.

○ **C.** E_2 exhibits positive feedback on levels of ER, while P exhibits positive feedback on levels of PR.

○ **D.** E_2 exhibits positive feedback on levels of ER, while P exhibits negative feedback on levels of PR.

Question 3

What abnormality would be expected in an individual with mutations in HSD11B1 rendering it nonfunctional?

○ **A.** Increase in plasma proteins

○ **B.** Decreased blood glucose

○ **C.** Decreased inflammation

○ **D.** Increased blood lipid content

Question 4

TCS can disrupt signaling related to endoderm differentiation and development. Based on this information, which of the following could be observed in a child exposed to TCS?

   I. Recurrent infections

  II. Inability to control glucose levels

 III. Deafness

○ **A.** I only

○ **B.** III only

○ **C.** I and II only

○ **D.** I, II, and III

Passage 2 (Questions 5-8)

Hypothalamic and pituitary hormones are key regulators of the entire endocrine system. The hypothalamic-pituitary-gonadal axis refers to the pulsatile hypothalamic gonadotropin-releasing hormone (GnRH), which stimulates the secretion of the pituitary gonadotropins, luteinizing hormone (LH) and follicle-stimulating hormone (FSH). These hormones in turn, stimulate the production of gonadal hormones, such as estrogen and testosterone.

Rheumatoid arthritis (RA) symptoms may develop or flare during stimulation of the hypothalamic-pituitary-gonadal axis or when GnRH and gonadotropin secretion increases. This may occur during the menopausal transition, postpartum, or in patients with polycystic ovarian syndrome (PCOS). In contrast, improvement in RA disease activity is associated with suppression of the hypothalamic-pituitary-gonadal axis. In this study, researchers investigated the safety and efficacy of a GnRH-antagonist, cetrorelix in RA.

Experiment 1

Patients were randomly assigned in a 1:1 ratio to receive 5 consecutive days of daily subcutaneous injections of cetrorelix acetate or corresponding volumes of saline placebo. LH levels were measured throughout the treatment period and following up until day 15 (Figure 1).

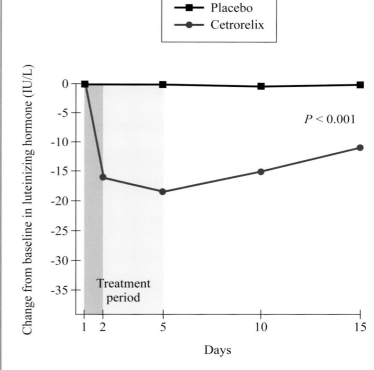

Figure 1 Change in hormonal levels of LH measured from baseline

Experiment 2

Multiplex technology measured serum cytokines, C-reactive protein, Tumor Necrosis Factor (TNF), and IL-1β using high sensitivity assays in order to determine the effect of cetrorelix treatment on markers of inflammation associated with RA (Table 1).

Table 1 Change in Interleukin Factor 1β (IL-1β) and Tumor Necrosis Factor (TNF) from Baseline During Treatment Period

Cytokine (log pg/mL)	Baseline day 1	Final day 15	Change from baseline by day 15
TNF Cetrorelix	0.46 ± 2.3	0.01 ± 2.1	−0.45
TNF Placebo	0.97 ± 3.0	0.99 ± 3.1	+0.02
IL-1β Cetrorelix	−1.48 ± 1.5	−1.68 ± 1.4	−0.20
IL-1β Placebo	−1.21 ± 2.4	−1.11 ± 2.4	+0.10

This passage was adapted from "Rapid Anti-Inflammatory Effects of Gonadotropin-Releasing Hormone Antagonism in Rheumatoid Arthritis Patients with High Gonadotropin Levels in the AGRA Trial." Kåss A, Hollan I, Fagerland MW, Gulseth, HC, Torjesen PA,et al. *PLoS ONE.* 2015. 10(10) doi:10.1371/journal.pone.0139439 for use under the terms of Creative Commons License Attribution 4.0 License (www.biomedcentral.com/pdf/Creative_Commons_Attribtion_4.0_International_CC_BY_4.0.pdf).

Question 5

Based on the results in Figure 1, which of the following would be the most likely side effect of cetrorelix for male participants?

- **A.** Inhibition in production of spermatocytes and spermatids
- **B.** Inhibition in production of testosterone
- **C.** Upregulation of production of semen and seminal fluid
- **D.** Upregulation of secondary male sex characteristics

Question 6

Worsening symptoms of rheumatoid arthritis are most likely correlated with:

- **A.** elevated serum estrogen.
- **B.** low serum estrogen.
- **C.** low serum GnRH.
- **D.** low serum FSH.

Question 7

What is the most likely reason serum LH was measured during days 1-5 in Experiment 1?

- **A.** To determine the extent of the effect of cetrorelix on participant's symptoms of RA
- **B.** To determine if cetrorelix successfully suppressed the production of estrogen
- **C.** To determine if cetrorelix successfully mimicked the effect of ovulation
- **D.** To determine if cetrorelix successfully mimicked the effect of the follicular phase

Question 8

Which of the following would decrease the serum concentration of the dependent variable in Experiment 2?

- **A.** A reduction in protein receptors for cortisol
- **B.** An increase in protein receptors for cortisol
- **C.** A reduction in protein receptors for antidiuretic hormone
- **D.** An increase in protein receptors for antidiuretic hormone

Questions 9 - 11 do not refer to a passage and are independent of each other.

Question 9

A rare genetic disorder causes production of sperm lacking the enzymes of the acrosome. What aspect of fertilization would be most affected by this deficit?

○ **A.** Motility of sperm through the vaginal canal

○ **B.** Production of sperm in the seminiferous tubules

○ **C.** Penetration of sperm through the zona pellucida

○ **D.** Fusion of male and female genetic information

Question 10

A compound that inhibits the cortical reaction is most likely to have which of the following direct effects?

○ **A.** A fertilized zygote with too many chromosomes

○ **B.** Failure to implant the blastocyst into the uterine wall

○ **C.** The inability of the blastocyst to hatch from the zona pellucida

○ **D.** Infertility due to the sperm cells being unable to break through the zona pellucida

Question 11

Placodal cells are thought to play an important role in the physiological development of the special sensory systems. The greatest proliferation of placodal cells most likely occurs during the:

○ **A.** first and second trimesters.

○ **B.** first and third trimesters.

○ **C.** second trimester only.

○ **D.** third trimester only.

Passage 3 (Questions 12-16)

Fluorides are inorganic and organic fluorine compounds that are widely used in numerous dental products for the prevention and remineralization of dental caries. Numerous epidemiological and clinical studies have demonstrated that high-dose fluorides could lead to changes in teeth and bone structure and adversely affect neurodevelopment by lowering the intelligence quotient (IQ) in children. Additional findings suggested that high-dose fluoride could influence the development of the human embryo.

The successful *in vitro* culture of pluripotent human embryonic stem cells (hESCs) isolated from human blastocyst created a new avenue to analyze the cytotoxicity and embryotoxicity of chemical compounds and substances in humans, as the *in vitro* differentiation of hESCs can partially recapitulate cellular developmental processes and gene expression patterns of early human embryogenesis.

The effects of sodium fluoride (NaF) were investigated on the proliferation, differentiation and viability of H9 hESCs. A 1 mM NaF did not significantly affect the proliferation of hESCs but did disturb the gene expression patterns of hESCs during embryoid body (EB) differentiation, a process mimicking *in vivo* gastrulation. At high magnification, the untreated hESCs exhibited typical hESC morphology (small and tightly packed with prominent nuclei), but the NaF-treated hESCs became larger and flattened. Moreover, 1 mM NaF significantly up-regulated the expressions of the ectoderm marker NeuroD1 in 14D EB and the mesoderm marker Brachyury in 7D and 14D EB but markedly decreased the expression of the endoderm marker AFP in 14D EB.

Higher doses of NaF (2 mM and above) markedly decreased the viability and proliferation of hESCs. The experimental findings suggest that NaF might interfere with early human embryogenesis by disturbing the specification of the three germ layers as well as osteogenic lineage commitment, and that high-dose NaF could cause apoptosis through a JNK-dependent pathway in hESCs.

This article was adapted from "High-Dose Fluoride Impairs the Properties of Human Embryonic Stem Cells via JNK Signaling." Fu X, Xie F-N, Dong P, Li Q-C, Yu G-Y, Xiao R. *PLoS ONE*. 2015. 11(2): doi:10.1371/journal.pone.0148819 for use under the Creative Commons Attribution 4.0 License (www.biomedcentral.com/pdf/Creative_Commons_Attribtion_4.0_International_CC_BY_4.0.pdf.)

Question 12

An increase in which of the following is LEAST likely to be the mechanism by which NaF alters differentiation of hESCs into EBs?

○ **A.** Methylation of CpG islands

○ **B.** Acetylation of histone tails

○ **C.** Cell to cell communication in adjacent cells

○ **D.** Replication mutations and deletions

Question 13

Which of the following would be found in the same structure as that from which the experimental hESCs were derived?

   I. Totipotent stem cells

  II. Inner cell mass

 III. HCG

- **A.** I only
- **B.** I, II, and III
- **C.** II only
- **D.** II and III only

Question 14

Which characteristic best displays alterations in the cellular specialization of the experimental developing embryonic cells?

- **A.** A larger and flattened shape
- **B.** Decreased proliferation
- **C.** Increased induction into the JNK pathway
- **D.** Differing protein translation patterns

Question 15

Normal differentiation of the hESCs into EBs would include which of the following changes?

- **A.** First cell movements
- **B.** Formation of inner cell mass
- **C.** Overproduction of NeuroD1
- **D.** Organogenesis

Question 16

Which study would best support the claim that fluoride exposure directly affects the IQ of developing children?

- **A.** A study displaying altered acidity in the amniotic fluid
- **B.** A study measuring a downregulation of cell to cell communication around the neural plate
- **C.** A study measuring upregulation of the transcription factor Brachyury
- **D.** A study displaying inhibition of neural crest cell migration throughout the body

Passage 4 (Questions 17-20)

Concerns about the increasing incidence of abnormalities in human and animal male reproductive function have been steadily increasing. Some of these issues have been hypothesized to be the expression of one common underlying disorder, testicular dysgenesis syndrome (TDS) that arises during fetal life. One theory proposes that TDS can result from alterations of the function of fetal Leydig cells. Leydig cells produce testosterone that is responsible for the masculinization of the male urogenital system and external genitalia. This process usually begins sometime between the 6th and 8th week of development. Several findings have suggested a link between deterioration of reproductive health and environmental factors, particularly endocrine disruptors (EDs).

Among such EDs, the estrogenic activity of bisphenol A (BPA, 4,4′-duhydroxy-2,2-diphenylpropane, Figure 1) has been the focus of considerable discussion about its toxicity at low doses.

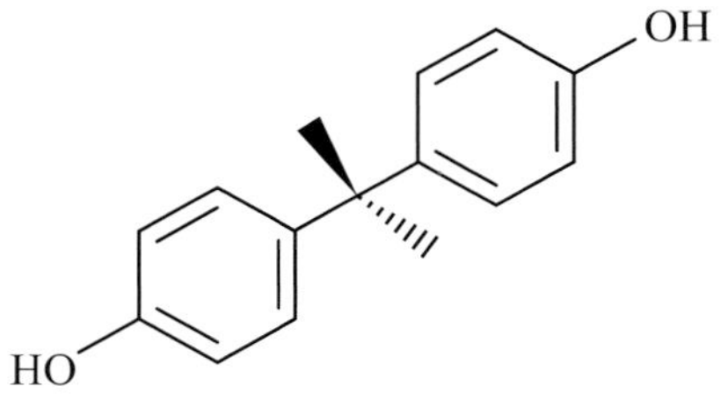

Bisphenol A

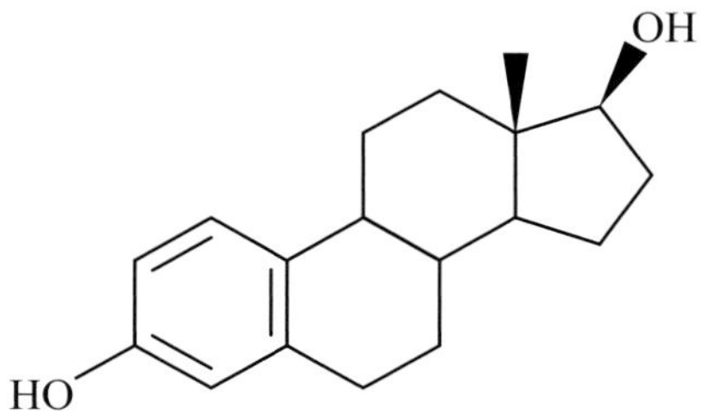

Estradiol

Figure 1 The structure of bisphenol A and estradiol

To test the effect of BPA on Leydig cell endocrine function, cultures of human fetal testes were exposed to various BPA concentrations for three days. The amount of testosterone secreted into the culture medium was measured every 24 hours by radioimmunoassay.

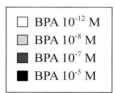

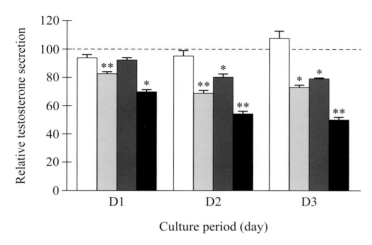

Figure 2 Effect of BPA on testosterone secretion by human fetal testes

Samples taken from fetuses at different gestation weeks were exposed to BPA for two days and the production of testosterone was quantified. The results of the testosterone assay were recorded as a function of the gestation week of the fetus from which each sample was acquired (Figure 3).

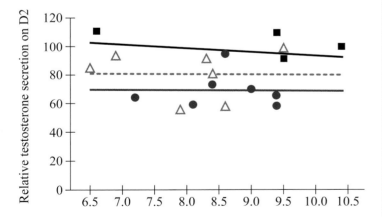

Figure 3 Effect of BPA on testosterone secretion by human fetal testes as a function of their developmental stage

Question 17

Which of the following conditions could serve as the best positive control for the experiment described in the passage?

○ **A.** BPA at a concentration of 1 M

○ **B.** Testosterone at a concentration of 10^{-5} M

○ **C.** Diethylstilbestrol, a synthetic estrogen analog, at 10^{-6} M

○ **D.** Dibutly Pthalate, a potential ED also found in plastics, at a concentration of 10^{-5} M

Question 18

The *SRY* gene becomes activated in males during the 6th week of gestation and initiates the differentiation of the gonads into testes. How does the *SRY* gene elicit this response?

○ **A.** Transcription of the *SRY* gene produces testosterone which binds to a nuclear receptor in the gonads and increases transcription of male-specific proteins.

○ **B.** Translation of the *SRY* mRNA produces a transcription factor necessary for the activation of a family of genes required for the development of the male reproductive organs.

○ **C.** The *SRY* gene codes for an estrogen receptor that is inserted into the plasma membrane.

○ **D.** *SRY* mRNA produces a protein that degrades DNA in the developing fetus that could be transcribed and translated to produce proteins unique to females.

Question 19

If the Leydig cells are permanently affected by the BPA exposure described in the passage, which of the following might occur?

○ **A.** Late onset of puberty with above average levels of testosterone produced by the Leydig cells

○ **B.** Indeterminate sex of the newborn because of a mutation on the *SRY* gene

○ **C.** Inability to produce high levels of testosterone due to a decreased amount of ribosomes in the Leydig cells available for the synthesis of the hormone

○ **D.** Infertility in post-puberty life due to a decreased ability of the testes to produce sperm

TEST 3B

Question 20

Which of the following when combined with the data in the passage would best support the conclusion that fetal exposure to BPA contributes to the development of TDS?

○ **A.** Researchers demonstrated that BPA was unable to cross the umbilical cord.

○ **B.** Monozygotic twins exposed to high levels of BPA always resulted in similar levels of testosterone production in both offspring.

○ **C.** Infertility due to low sperm production is diagnosed after puberty in 90% of dizygotic twins with a high level of BPA measured in the amniotic fluid.

○ **D.** A national survey of amniotic fluid of pregnant woman found no change in the concentration of BPA when compared to samples from twenty years prior.

Passage 5 (Questions 21-25)

Duchenne muscular dystrophy (DMD) is a devastating X-linked recessive genetic myopathy that is caused by mutations in the *DMD* gene and results in dysfunction or absence of the protein dystrophin. Since its first description in the mid-1800's, DMD physiopathology has not been fully understood. Interestingly, analyses of X-linked muscular dystrophy (mdx) mice showed that the onset of pathology can be observed in utero with abnormal myogenesis.

Experiment One

In order to further explore the effects of DMD in utero, researchers used human induced pluripotent stem cells (hiPSCs) from healthy and DMD muscular cells to compare the two genetic contexts during the early steps of myogenesis, A member of the transforming growth factor beta (TGF-β) superfamily, bone morphogenetic protein 4 (BMP4), was used to induce differentiation of the hiPSCs toward mesodermic lineage.

The analysis showed, on BMP4-treated hiPSCs 1, the downregulation of pluripotency markers (e.g., SOX2, POU5F1) and upregulation of markers specific to mesoderm (e.g., T, EOMES, CDX2, GATA binding protein 4 (GATA4), and actin alpha cardiac muscle 1 (ACTC1)). In addition, it showed upregulation of markers specific to the endoderm (such as SOX17) but none to ectoderm (such as paired box 6 (PAX6)) (Figure 1).

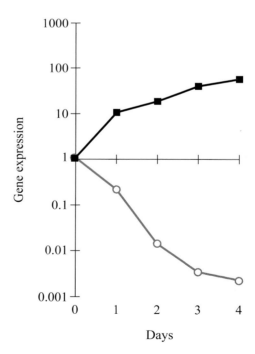

Figure 1 Changes in protein folding over a 4 day period of BMP4 treatment in SOX2, ACTC1

Experiment Two

72 hours following BMP4 treatment a new long DMD transcript was detected in all tested hiPSCs and hESCs, at levels similar to that found in adult skeletal muscle. The novel dystrophin protein Dp412e was characterized by an N-terminal-truncated actin binding domain. In addition, Dp412e has the same apparent molecular weight as a recently identified highly functional dystrophin. Quantitative RT-PCR was used to determine the expression level of Dp412e transcripts in hiPSCs 1 and hESCs 1 EBs from day 0 to day 10 of differentiation with or without BMP4 treatment (Figure 2).

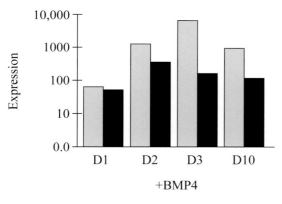

Figure 2 Expression of Dp412e in hiPSCs and hESCs in the presence and absence of BMP4

Question 21

Cells treated with BMP4 would most likely first migrate into a specific region of the developing embryo during which stage of embryogenesis?

○ **A.** Morulation

○ **B.** Blastulation

○ **C.** Gastrulation

○ **D.** Neurulation

Question 22

Researchers hypothesize that dysfunction in embryogenesis in DMD patients could also affect other germ layers besides the mesoderm. Which of the following additional studies would most strengthen this hypothesis?

○ **A.** A study showing elevated creatine kinase in cardiac tissue in DMD newborns

○ **B.** A study showing disorganized brain structure in dystrophin-deficient infants

○ **C.** A study of altered gene expression in skeletal muscle in presymptomatic DMD patients lacking dystrophin

○ **D.** A study in zebrafish showing dysfunction in ureter attachment due to the absence of dystrophin

Question 23

In additional experiment, researchers treat only one stem cell in a group of cells with BMP4, but later find that the entire sample is induced into the mesodermal cell lineage. What is the most likely reason for this outcome?

○ **A.** Cell specialization

○ **B.** Migration of cells

○ **C.** Cell-cell communication

○ **D.** Downregulation of pluripotency markers

Question 24

hiPSCs are used in Experiment 1 because:

○ **A.** they can differentiate into any cell type, including placental tissue.

○ **B.** they can differentiate into any cell type except that of the placenta.

○ **C.** they will differentiate into only cell types found in the mesoderm.

○ **D.** they will differentiate into only muscle cells.

Question 25

A student hypothesizes that BMP4 induces the differentiation of hiPSCs towards mesodermic cell lineage through the deletion of unnecessary genetic information. Is the student's hypothesis reasonable?

○ **A.** No; cellular determination is caused by silencing of regions of the genome.

○ **B.** No; cellular determination is predetermined and is unaffected by external factors.

○ **C.** No; cellular determination arises primarily through apoptosis.

○ **D.** Yes; cellular determination is caused by deletion of promoter regions not needed in the differentiated cell.

Questions 26 - 29 do not refer to a passage and are independent of each other.

Question 26

Which of the following statements about zygotic cleavage is true?

 I. It occurs when cells multiply, but the size of the embryo remains relatively constant

 II. Cleavage occurs in the fallopian tube

 III. During the second trimester, mitosis is occurring rapidly with no change in the size of the developing fetus

 ○ **A.** I only

 ○ **B.** III only

 ○ **C.** I and II only

 ○ **D.** II and III only

Question 27

Which of the following characteristic is most likely to change about the zygote as a result of the initial stages of cleavage?

 ○ **A.** Cellular potency

 ○ **B.** Structural shape

 ○ **C.** Location in the fallopian tube

 ○ **D.** Cellular surface area

Question 28

After injury, which of the following is NOT possible?

 ○ **A.** Complete regeneration in a human liver

 ○ **B.** Regrowth of body parts in salamanders

 ○ **C.** Formation of new organisms in flatworms

 ○ **D.** Leukocyte re-differentiation in humans

Question 29

Which process does NOT play an important role in gastrulation?

 ○ **A.** Differentiation

 ○ **B.** Determination

 ○ **C.** Cell migration

 ○ **D.** Cell-cell communication

Passage 6 (Questions 30-33)

The use of *in-vitro* fertilization (IVF) to treat infertility has become increasingly common since its introduction. IVF is sometimes performed without a definitive diagnosis of the underlying cause of the infertility. Issues arising in the preimplantation phase of development can prevent the developing blastocyst from attaching to the uterus. The ultimate goal of the mammalian preimplantation development is the formation of a hollow shaped embryo called a blastocyst. The blastocyst contains three distinct cell lineages—the epiblast, which will give rise to the embryo proper, the primitive endoderm, which forms some of the extraembryonic structures and the trophectoderm (TE), which contributes to the placenta. The formation of a proper blastocyst strongly depends on tightly controlled cell adhesion mainly mediated by E-cadherin (E-cad). In contrast, N-cadherin (N-cad), another type of cadherin is first detected after implantation. Insulin-like growth factor 1 (Igf1) signaling provides growth promoting, anti-apoptotic functions in almost all tissues and treatment of mouse preimplantation embryos with Igf1 enhanced blastocyst formation *in vitro*. A role of E-cad in promoting cell survival of the TE by facilitating Igf1r activity has been proposed in addition to its function in cell adhesion. If better understood, this research could assist in improving the implantation rate for IVF.

To elucidate the function of E-cad during TE formation, E-cad was divided into two parts, its extracellular adhesive region (Eo) and its transmembrane and intracellular portion (Ei). These regions were fused with the opposite portion of the N-cad molecule, either extracellular region (No) or intracellular portion (Ni), to generate artificial chimeric cadherins. Expression, synthesis, and insertion into the plasma membrane were not altered in these chimeric cadherins. Table 1 shows the resulting phenotypes when these proteins were integrated into the genome (ki) of preimplantation embryos.

Table 1   Effect of Cadherin Genotype on the Formation of Blastocysts

Genotype of embryo	% of embryos forming blastocysts under normal conditions	% of embryos forming blastocysts after addition of extra Igf1
E-cad$^{+/+}$ (WT)	99	98
E-cad$^{-/-}$	0	0
EoNi$^{+/ki}$	95	96
NoEi$^{+/ki}$	93	92
EoNi$^{ki/ki}$	80	84
NoEi$^{ki/ki}$	0	83

This passage was adapted from "Igf1r Signaling Is Indispensable for Preimplantation Development and Is Activated via a Novel Function of E-cadherin." Bedzhov I, Liszewska E, Kanzler B, Stemmler MP. *PLoS Genet.* 2012. 8(3) doi: 10.1371/journal. pgen.1002609 for use under the terms of the Creative Commons CC BY 3.0 license (http://creativecommons.org/licenses/by/3.0/legalcode)

Question 30

A fertilized egg with complete loss of N-cadherin function would most likely develop all of the following except:

- ○ **A.** a neural tube.
- ○ **B.** trophoblasts.
- ○ **C.** the zona pellucida.
- ○ **D.** an inner cell mass.

Question 31

Caspase-3, a protein activated during apoptosis, was measured in each of the developing embryos. Which of the following findings is most likely?

- ○ **A.** A higher level of caspase-3 production due to more efficient Igf1 signaling is measured in EoNi embryos when compared to wild-type.
- ○ **B.** Caspase-3 production in NoEi is similar to that observed in cells that have been severely damaged.
- ○ **C.** Caspase-3 activity is the highest when the NoEi ki/ki genotype is developing into a morula.
- ○ **D.** An increase in Caspase-3 production after treatment of NoEi embryos with Igf1 will be noted.

Question 32

Aside from their proposed role with Igf1 signaling, cadherins have a critical function in embryologic development by:

- ○ **A.** binding to molecules found on other cells and in the ECM and transmitting information about the environment to the cell.
- ○ **B.** receiving lipophilic hormone signals and altering gene expression.
- ○ **C.** attaching the embryo to the endometrium and establishing a connection through which nutrients and waste can be exchanged.
- ○ **D.** acting as transcription factors to alter gene expression and initiation cell differentiation.

Question 33

The receptor for Igf1 is inhibited using Tryphostin AG1024. Administration of this drug on developing embryos would produce a phenotype similar to which of the following ?

- ○ **A.** E-cad$^{+/+}$
- ○ **B.** E-cad$^{-/-}$
- ○ **C.** EoNi$^{ki/ki}$
- ○ **D.** NoEi$^{ki/ki}$

Passage 7 (Questions 34-38)

The peripheral nervous system arises from neural crest and placodal cells derived from neural plate border cells. Placodal cells are collections of cells that give rise to the structures of the sensory systems. Neural crest cells are generated along the entire rostro-caudal neuraxis, except at rostral forebrain levels, where neural plate border cells generate placodal but no neural crest cells. The specification of both neural crest and placodal cells is ongoing at the late gastrula stage, and BMP2 and BMP4 are expressed in the ectoderm surrounding the entire neural plate. Studies conducted later in development suggest that both BMP and Wnt signals induce neural crest character in caudal neural cells. Thus, it remains unclear whether BMP and Wnt signals act in parallel or have separated roles during the initial induction of neural crest cells.

To address how Wnt and BMP signaling interact during the initial specification of olfactory/lens placodal and neural crest cells, scientists established explant assays of neural crest and placodal cell differentiation using late gastrula stage chick embryos (Figure 1). In chick embryos, the specification of neural crest cells has been initiated at the late gastrula stage, stage 4.

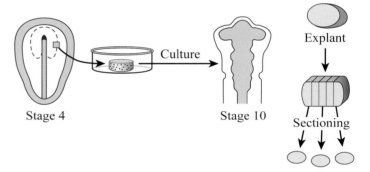

Figure 1 Experimental overview of explant assays from chick embryos

To examine whether Wnt signals are required for the initial induction of neural crest cells at the late gastrula stage, scientists cultured stage 4 caudal border (CB) explants in the presence of soluble mFrz8CRD, which blocks Wnt, but not BMP signaling. They stained the explants for various protein markers, including: Snail2, which is expressed in pre-migratory and early migratory neural crest cells, HNK-1, which is expressed in all migratory neural crest cells, and Ker, which is expressed in epidermal cells. The results are shown in Figure 2.

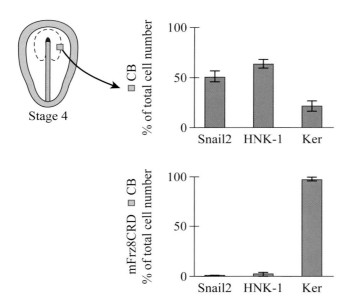

Figure 2 Relative cell number of Snail2, HNK-1, and Ker positive cells in the caudal border with and without exposure to mFrz8CRD

Researchers also tested whether Wnt activity was sufficient to induce caudal border character in rostral border cells fated to generate lens and olfactory placodal cells by exposing stage 4 prospective rostral border (RB) explants to Wnt3A, an active isoform of the Wnt protein. The results are shown in Figure 3.

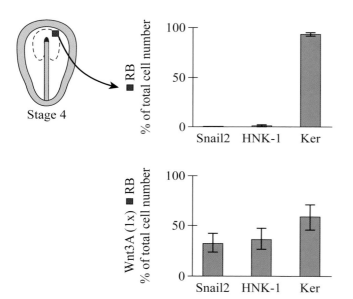

Figure 3 Relative cell number of Snail2, HNK-1, and Ker positive cells in the rostral border with and without exposure to Wnt3A

Question 34

mFrz8CRD treatment of CD cells is LEAST likely to prevent formation of:

○ **A.** cells of the adrenal medulla.

○ **B.** the C cells of the thyroid.

○ **C.** cells that myelinate the peripheral nervous system.

○ **D.** the lining of the ileum.

Question 35

A chick embryo observed at stage 5 would be most likely to show:

○ **A.** thickened and rounded ectoderm.

○ **B.** formation of the primitive streak.

○ **C.** migration of endodermal cells from the primitive streak.

○ **D.** formation of the mesodermal layer.

Question 36

Snail2[+] cells are likely to support the controlled contraction of which of the following muscles first in a developing child?

○ **A.** The pectoralis major muscle of the chest

○ **B.** The biceps muscle of the arm

○ **C.** The sternocleidomastoid muscle of the neck

○ **D.** The gastrocnemius muscle of the lower leg

Question 37

Exposure of the RB to Wnt3A in the stage 4 embryo would be most likely to cause:

○ **A.** an increased number of neural crest cells to develop following fertilization.

○ **B.** a decreased number of epidermal cells to develop following implantation.

○ **C.** an increased number of neural crest cells to develop after neurulation.

○ **D.** a decreased number of epidermal cells to develop following birth.

Question 38

During adolescence, HNK-1 positive cells are LEAST likely to play a role in:

○ **A.** increasing the production of dopamine, a hormone associated with increased risk-taking and novelty seeking.

○ **B.** providing increased control of sexual maturation.

○ **C.** stimulating increases in circulating calcitonin.

○ **D.** increasing serotonin expression in the hippocampus.

Questions 39 - 41 do not refer to a passage and are independent of each other.

Question 39

The proper development of which of the following structures relies most on cell migration during embryogenesis?

O **A.** Neurula

O **B.** Notochord

O **C.** Neural crest

O **D.** Adrenal medulla

Question 40

The cells that differentiate into adipocytes are most similar to what germ layer?

O **A.** Ectoderm

O **B.** Mesoderm

O **C.** Endoderm

O **D.** Both ectoderm and endoderm

Question 41

Which of the following statements accurately represents *in utero* development?

O **A.** The first trimester is characterized by growth of the brain.

O **B.** Organs begin to develop in the second trimester.

O **C.** Migration of cells is a major component of the third trimester.

O **D.** At parturition, the brain is incompletely developed.

STOP. If you finish before time is called, check your work. You may go back to any question in this test.

ANSWERS & EXPLANATIONS for Test 3B can be found on p. 238.

LECTURE

4

The Circulatory, Respiratory, and Immune Systems

TEST 4A

Time: 95 minutes
Questions 1–59

DIRECTIONS: Most of the questions in this test section are grouped with a passage. Read the passage, then select the best answer to each question. Some questions are independent of any passage and of one another. Select the best answer to each of these questions. If you are unsure of an answer, rule out incorrect choices and select from the remaining options. Indicate your selection beside the option you choose. A periodic table can be found on the last page of this book for you to use at any point during this test section.

Passage 1 (Questions 1-4)

Cigarette smoke (CS) is considered to be the main causative factor of chronic obstructive pulmonary disease (COPD) in humans. Reactive oxygen species (ROS) and cytotoxic by-products of oxidation reactions are the most recognized mediators of lung cell damage under smoking conditions. Accumulating evidence suggests that the adaptor protein p66Shc, recently involved in lung development, regulates intracellular oxidant levels in mammalian cells through the regulation of a forkhead related transcription factor (FOXO3a), which regulates the transcription of a gene *p66Shc*, which may also modulate response to oxidative stress.

Scientists investigated whether p66Shc knockout mice showed a modified cellular and molecular response to CS to explore whether p66Shc knockout confers protection against the pulmonary changes induced by CS exposure. After 7 months of CS exposure, the lungs of p66Shc knockout mice showed trivial patchy areas of air space enlargement, while WT mice showed significant areas of alveolar wall breakdown, similar to emphysema, a condition found in human cigarette smokers. To quantify the breakdown of the alveolar walls, the scientists measured cross-linked desmosine levels, which are an important component of elastin in the alveolar wall. The results are shown in Figure 1.

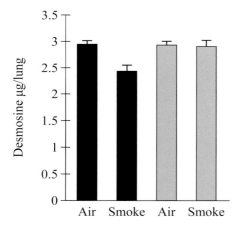

Figure 1 Relative desmosine levels in the lungs of WT and p66Shc knockout mice after exposure to room air and cigarette smoke

While p66Shc knockout mice exposed to CS for 7 months did not result in emphysema, the mice developed bronchiolar fibrosis, characterized by progressive deposition of collagen that expanded to contiguous alveolar septa. Alveolar lumens were frequently lined by hyperplastic epithelial cells, and were filled with macrophages.

Question 1

Compared to WT mice exposed to CS, p66Shc KO mice exposed to CS are likely to show:

- ○ **A.** increased elastic recoil of the lungs during expiration.
- ○ **B.** decreased elastic recoil of the lungs during inspiration
- ○ **C.** increased elastic recoil of the lungs during expiration and increased elastic recoil of the lungs during inspiration.
- ○ **D.** decreased elastic recoil of the lungs during expiration and increased elastic recoil of the lungs during inspiration.

Question 2

Which of the following statements best describes the differences in hematocrit and blood oxygen levels in WT and p66Shc KO mice after 7 months of exposure to CS?

- ○ **A.** WT mice would have increased hematocrit and increased blood oxygen levels compared to p66Shc KO mice.
- ○ **B.** WT mice would have decreased hematocrit and decreased blood oxygen levels compared to p66Shc KO mice.
- ○ **C.** WT mice would have increased hematocrit and decreased blood oxygen levels compared to p66Shc KO mice.
- ○ **D.** WT mice would have decreased hematocrit and increased blood oxygen levels compared to p66Shc KO mice.

Question 3

After 9 months of exposure to CS, the blood acid/base balance of WT and p66Shc KO mice is best characterized respectively as:

- ○ **A.** acidosis and normal.
- ○ **B.** alkalosis and normal.
- ○ **C.** normal and acidosis.
- ○ **D.** alkalosis and acidosis.

Question 4

Increased mucus production is one of the contributors to the chronic cough often seen in COPD patients. CS is most likely to increase the:

- ○ **A.** apoptosis of tracheal Goblet cells.
- ○ **B.** proliferation of bronchiolar epithelium.
- ○ **C.** proliferation of bronchiolar Goblet cells.
- ○ **D.** apoptosis of tracheal epithelium.

Passage 2 (Questions 5-9)

High altitude pulmonary edema (HAPE) is a potentially life-threatening condition that occurs after rapid ascent to high altitude. Mountaineers with a previous history of HAPE are at particular risk. In individuals with HAPE, fluid accumulates in the alveoli. The diagnosis at high altitude is based on the presence of tachypnea (rapid breathing), pulmonary crackles, and cyanosis (blue discoloration of the skin). A chest radiograph demonstrates pulmonary infiltrates but this is rarely available in the mountains. Currently, it is unknown why some individuals are more susceptible to HAPE than others.

In 18 mountaineers, forced vital capacity (FVC) (Figure 1), residual volume (RV) (Figure 2), diffusion capacity (Figure 3), nitrogen washout, and pulse oximetry (Table 1) were recorded at 490 m and then again at 4559 m after a rapid ascent over the course of 3 days. Oxygen saturation was measured by pulse oximetry in the sitting position after 15 min of quiet rest. Spirometry and single breath diffusing capacity were performed according to standard techniques. Findings were compared among subjects developing HAPE and those remaining well (controls).

Spirometers measure lung volumes, including tidal volume, inspiratory capacity, expiratory reserve volume, and vital capacity. FVC is the maximum volume of air that can be exhaled after a full inhalation. RV defines the volume of the lungs after a full exhalation. Spirometers cannot measure residual volume, so RV can be calculated by subtracting expiratory reserve volume from the functional residual capacity (FRC). FRC can be measured by helium dilution or body plethysmography.

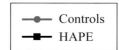

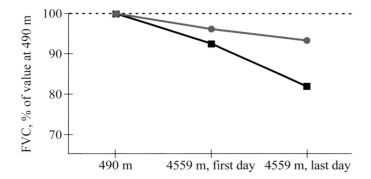

Figure 1 Changes in forced vital capacity (FVC) in subjects developing HAPE and in healthy controls

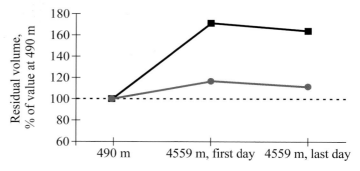

Figure 2 Changes in residual volume (RV) in subjects developing HAPE and in healthy controls

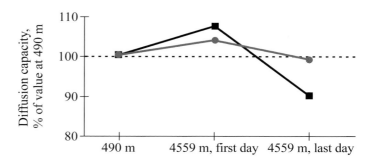

Figure 3 Changes in diffusion capacity in subjects developing HAPE and in healthy controls

Table 1 Pulmonary Function and Arterial Blood Gas Analysis

	Controls (n = 10)		HAPE-group (n = 8)	
	490 m, baseline	4559 m, day 3	490 m, baseline	4559 m, day 3
FVC, L	5.64 ± 0.56	$5.26 \pm 0.53^*$	5.07 ± 1.32	$4.07 \pm 0.93^*$
FEV1, L	4.35 ± 0.43	4.12 ± 0.46	3.85 ± 1.30	$3.23 \pm 0.89^*$
RV, L	1.52 ± 0.31	1.60 ± 0.37	1.63 ± 0.45	1.59 ± 0.37
Pulse oximetry, $SpO_2\%$	96 ± 2	$77 \pm 8^*$	96 ± 1	$68 \pm 11^*$
$PaCO_2$, mmHg	40.2 ± 2.6	$30.3 \pm 1.7^*$	40.1 ± 2.3	$28.8 \pm 2.0^*$
PaO_2, mmHg	100 ± 7.3	$46.1 \pm 2.9^*$	100 ± 3.6	$30.1 \pm 3.6^*$

$^*p<0.05$ vs. 490 m within the group
$^\P p<0.05$ vs. controls.

Question 5

The law of Laplace is given by: $P = 2 \times$ tension/radius. If HAPE causes small amounts of water to replace the surfactant in alveoli, individuals with HAPE would be expected to:

○ **A.** have difficulty breathing because of increased pressure and increased surface tension.

○ **B.** have difficulty breathing because of decreased pressure and decreased surface tension.

○ **C.** have difficulty breathing because of decreased pressure and increased surface tension.

○ **D.** have difficulty breathing because of increased pressure and decreased surface tension.

Question 6

Which of the following would likely lead to a change in diffusion capacity similar to the change seen in the diffusion capacity of HAPE patients?

  I. Administration of oxygen through nasal cannula

  II. Increased alveolar wall thickness

  III. Reduction of PO_2 in the pulmonary artery

  IV. Reduction of PO_2 in the pulmonary vein

○ **A.** I only

○ **B.** II only

○ **C.** I and III only

○ **D.** II and IV only

Question 7

If the concentration of dissolved O_2 for the HAPE group at 490 m is 3 mL O_2/L, what is the concentration at 4559 m, assuming constant solubility at 490 m and 4559 m?

○ **A.** 1.50 mL O_2/L

○ **B.** 1.38 mL O_2/L

○ **C.** 1.20 mL O_2/L

○ **D.** 0.90 mL O_2/L

Question 8

Which of the following would most likely cause the most rapid change in respiration rate?

○ **A.** Decreased blood pressure near the central baroreceptors

○ **B.** Decreased blood pressure near the peripheral baroreceptors

○ **C.** Decreased pH near the medulla

○ **D.** Decreased PO_2 near the hippocampus

Question 9

According to Figure 1, HAPE most likely interferes with:

○ **A.** diaphragm contraction.

○ **B.** diaphragm relaxation.

○ **C.** external intercostal contraction.

○ **D.** development of negative intrapleural pressure.

Passage 3 (Questions 10-13)

Asthma is a common disease affecting 5–10% of people and an important cause of morbidity and mortality at all ages. Asthma is defined by the severe inflammation-induced narrowing of the airway, leading to difficulty breathing that can be rapidly fatal if untreated. The airway epithelium is at the interface between the airway and the external environment and is the first structure to interact with noxious stimuli such as allergens, viruses and pollutants. Not only does the columnar epithelium tend to shed from the basal layer, but the airway epithelium is also functionally abnormal in asthma.

Ion channels are emerging as interesting therapeutic targets in asthma and the Ca^{2+}-activated K^+ channel $K_{Ca}3.1$ is of particular interest as a novel target for asthma therapy. The proposed role for $K_{Ca}3.1$ in the epithelium is to reduce bicarbonate secretion and increase Cl^- secretion to promote airway surface liquid hydration. Increased hydration is thought to worsen asthma symptoms. It has therefore been suggested that inhibitors of $K_{Ca}3.1$ might be useful in the treatment of asthma.

Experiment 1

In a process similar to a western blot, scientists stained tissues from normal and asthmatic patients to determine the relative expression of $K_{Ca}3.1$ in the bronchial epithelium (Figure 1). Given that $K_{Ca}3.1$ channels are predicted to increase Cl^- secretion, which would result in greater release of mucus into the bronchioles, scientists stained for MUC5AC, a glycoprotein found in mucus secretions (Figure 2).

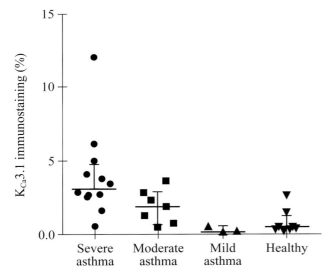

Figure 1 Relative KCa3.1 expression in healthy and asthmatic tissues

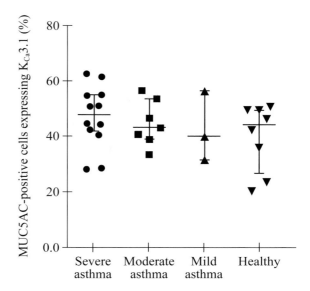

Figure 2 Relative MUC5AC-positive cells that express $K_{Ca}3.1$

Experiment 2

To measure the relative current through a single $K_{Ca}3.1$ channel in normal and asthmatic patients, a synthetic compound 1-ethyl-2-benzimidazolinone (1-EBIO) was introduced in the culture medium of human bronchial epithelial cells. A patch clamp, a tube that surrounds and insulates one single ion channel, was used to measure the current flowing through the $K_{Ca}3.1$ channel immediately upon introduction of 1-EBIO into the culture mix. The results are presented in Figure 3.

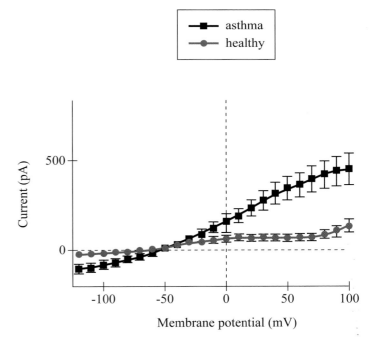

Figure 3 Current flow through $K_{Ca}3.1$ in healthy versus asthmatic patients

This passage is adapted from "$K_{Ca}3.1$ K^+ Channel Expression and Function in Human Bronchial Epithelial Cells." Arthur G, Duffy S, Roach K, Hirst R, Shikotra A, et al. *PLoS ONE*. 2015. 10(12) doi:10.1371/journal.pone.0145259 for use under the terms of the Creative Commons CC BY 4.0 license (http://creativecommons.org/licenses/by/4.0/legalcode).

Question 10

$K_{Ca}3.1$ channels are also thought to help regulate surfactant levels. Which of the following statements would best describe an unintended side-effect of $K_{Ca}3.1$ channel inhibitors?

○ **A.** Increased difficulty breathing during inspiration

○ **B.** Increased difficulty breathing during expiration

○ **C.** Decreased difficulty breathing during inspiration

○ **D.** Decreased difficulty breathing during expiration

Question 11

Blocking which of the following receptors would prevent asthmatics from forcibly exhaling trapped air in their lungs?

○ **A.** Dopamine receptor

○ **B.** Epinephrine receptor

○ **C.** Norepinephrine receptor

○ **D.** Acetylcholine receptor

Question 12

Patients with severe asthma are:

○ **A.** more likely to clear allergens due to thinner mucus.

○ **B.** less likely to clear allergens due to thicker mucus.

○ **C.** more likely to clear allergens due to an increased number of cilia.

○ **D.** less likely to clear allergens due to a decreased number of cilia.

Question 13

Due to increased stress on the lung by recurrent asthma attacks, alveolar walls of severe and moderate asthmatics are often slightly thicker than the alveolar walls of non-asthmatics. This is likely to affect:

   I. the amount of CO_2 exhaled from the lungs.

   II. the amount of O_2 dissolved in the blood.

   III. the efficacy of the circulatory system.

○ **A.** I only

○ **B.** I and II only

○ **C.** II and III only

○ **D.** I, II, and III

Questions 14 - 16 do not refer to a passage and are independent of each other.

Question 14

A bioengineer attempting to build a synthetic lung asks for advice for the initial design. All of the following would be recommended EXCEPT:

○ **A.** a large surface area for gas exchange.

○ **B.** a way to create negative pressure.

○ **C.** a button to initiate inspiration.

○ **D.** a means for ample vascularization.

Question 15

The most ATP is burned during which phase of the respiratory cycle?

○ **A.** The beginning of inhalation

○ **B.** The end of inhalation

○ **C.** The beginning of exhalation

○ **D.** The end of exhalation

Question 16

Acute bronchospasm, a condition that occurs when the trachea narrows in an asthma or allergy attack, is likely to:

○ **A.** increase the pH of the blood.

○ **B.** increase the clearance of foreign particles from inhaled air.

○ **C.** decrease the breathing rate.

○ **D.** decrease the heart rate.

Passage 4 (Questions 17-20)

Pulmonary diseases such as asthma, acute lung inflammation and chronic obstructive pulmonary disease (COPD) represent major threats to human health. They often involve complex immune responses in which inflammatory and epithelial cells release elevated levels of pro-inflammatory cytokines such as IL-6, TNF-α, IL-4 and also the anti-inflammatory cytokine IL-10. Constant inflammation induces pulmonary structural changes, including fibroblast activation and extracellular matrix (ECM) fiber deposition, which impair lung function.

The cholinergic anti-inflammatory pathway is a modulator of innate immune responses. During the inflammatory process, acetylcholine (ACh) released by the vagus nerve acts via α7 nicotinic receptors (α7nAChR) on macrophages and other immune cells to inhibit cytokine production and counteract an ongoing state of inflammation.

ACh storage in secretory vesicles in neurons depends on the activity of the vesicular acetylcholine transporter (VAChT). ACh is also synthesized and released by non-neuronal cells, including immune and epithelial cells, but the exact mechanism involved in non-neuronal ACh release is not known. In the lung, ACh is released from parasympathetic nerve fibers to induce bronchoconstriction. Acute lung inflammation is also associated with reduced lung cholinergic markers. Researchers used genetic VAChT knockout (KO) mice to investigate the role of ACh and VAChT in lung inflammation and immunity. They measured levels of cytokines in these mice and compared these levels to those found in wild-type mice. The results are shown below in Figure 1.

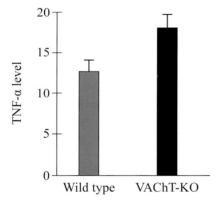

Figure 1 TNF-α levels in VAChT-KO

Question 17

The results of Figure 1 suggest that ACh might do which of the following during inflammation?

    I. Inhibit macrophage activation

    II. Increase capillary permeability

    III. Reduce neutrophil recruitment

○ **A.** I only

○ **B.** II only

○ **C.** I and III only

○ **D.** I, II, and III

Question 18

A sudden increase in ACh to the lungs would most likely result in:

○ **A.** reduced ventilation.

○ **B.** increased blood pH.

○ **C.** increased total lung capacity.

○ **D.** decreased residual volume.

Question 19

Which of the following adaptive immune cells would be most instrumental in maintaining a state of constant inflammation?

○ **A.** Macrophage

○ **B.** B cell

○ **C.** CD8$^+$ T cell

○ **D.** CD4$^+$ T cell

Question 20

Due to COPD, the entire right lung is blocked off at the right bronchus. Which of the following is likely to occur?

○ **A.** Reduced ability to oxygenate the blood due to more blood flow than air flow in the right lung

○ **B.** Reduced ability to oxygenate the blood due to more air flow than blood flow in the right lung

○ **C.** Reduced ability to oxygenate the blood due to reduced hematocrit

○ **D.** Reduced ability to oxygenate the blood due to reduced cardiac output

Passage 5 (Questions 21-25)

A 40-year-old female presented to the emergency department 36 hours after arriving in a high-altitude city with delayed breathing, headache, and dizziness. She reported taking ibuprofen over the past 24 hours to treat the headache. The physician suspected that the ibuprofen interfered with her acclimatization to the high altitude.

The body's first line of defense to decreased oxygen levels is the hypoxic ventilatory response (HVR), which is a reflex change in breathing in response to low arterial partial pressure of oxygen (PO_2) and high CO_2, stimulating carotid body (arterial) chemoreceptors. If hypoxia is sustained, both ventilation and ventilatory sensitivity to acute changes in O_2 (i.e. the HVR) increase. Collectively these changes are termed ventilatory acclimatization to hypoxia (VAH). VAH is observed 24 to 48 hours after ascent to high altitude and persists for at least 8 weeks at an altitude of 3,800 m. VAH is thought to be advantageous because it can increase arterial O_2 levels over time at a given altitude.

Ibuprofen is an anti-inflammatory drug commonly used by people in sustained hypoxia to alleviate headache from acute mountain sickness. Recent evidence suggests that ibuprofen may blunt the HVR. The physiological mechanisms of VAH are not completely understood but considerable progress has been made in animal studies. Cytokines expressed in chronically hypoxic carotid bodies, which can be blocked by ibuprofen, cause increased gene expression for chemical and voltage-sensitive ion channels that increase O_2-sensitivity. Plasticity in central nervous system (CNS) respiratory centers with chronic sustained hypoxia involves changes in glutamatergic neurotransmission, ion channels that increase synaptic transmission and intrinsic neuronal excitability, and neuron-glia interactions. Glial cells are an important source of cytokines in neuropathic pain. Neuropathic pain is hypothesized to share common mechanisms with carotid body acclimatization to hypoxia and is also sensitive to ibuprofen.

This passage is adapted from "Ibuprofen Blunts Ventilatory Acclimatization to Sustained Hypoxia in Humans." Basaran K, Villongco M, Ho B, Ellis E, Zarndt R. *PLoS ONE*. 2016. 11(1) doi:10.1371/journal.pone.0146087 for use under the terms of the Creative Commons CC BY 4.0 license (http://creativecommons.org/licenses/by/4.0/legalcode).

Question 21

Sustained exposure to cytokines released from hypoxic carotid bodies is known to induce vasodilation of peripheral arterioles. Which of the following statements best explains this finding?

- **A.** Eosinophils release histamine in response to cytokines, leading to increased blood pressure.

- **B.** B cells traffic to the lungs in response to high cytokine levels.

- **C.** Macrophage-released IL-2 stimulates proliferation of T cells.

- **D.** Mast cells release prostaglandins in response to cytokines, leading to decreased blood pressure.

Question 22

Which of the following curves most likely represents the oxyhemoglobin dissociation curve of the patient in this passage?

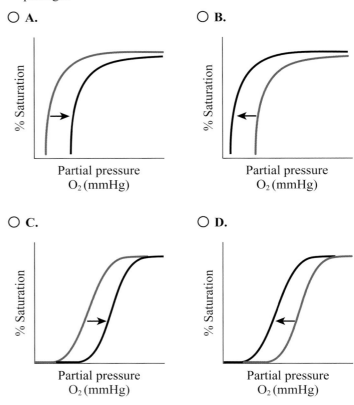

Question 23

The initial response to decreased concentrations of atmospheric oxygen is likely to include:

- **A.** increased breathing rate and increased heart rate.

- **B.** increased breathing rate and decreased heart rate.

- **C.** decreased breathing rate and increased heart rate.

- **D.** decreased breathing rate and decreased heart rate.

Question 24

Acetazolamide, an oral medication used to prevent altitude sickness, helps impair breakdown of HCO_3^- in the kidney proximal convoluted tubule. What is the most likely effect of acetazolamide on breathing rate?

- ○ **A.** Increased rate of breathing compared to the rate at high altitude
- ○ **B.** Decreased rate of breathing compared to the rate at high altitude
- ○ **C.** Maintenance of breathing rate compared to the rate at high altitude
- ○ **D.** Acetazolamide is unlikely to affect the rate of breathing.

Question 25

Administration of which of the following hormones could serve to prevent altitude sickness?

- ○ **A.** Erythropoietin
- ○ **B.** Epinephrine
- ○ **C.** Glucagon
- ○ **D.** Acetylcholine

Questions 26 - 29 do not refer to a passage and are independent of each other.

Question 26

During exercise, active skeletal muscle releases CO_2 and H^+. Which of the following would be the most likely effect on hemoglobin?

- ○ **A.** K_a would decrease
- ○ **B.** K_D would decrease
- ○ **C.** K_a would increase
- ○ **D.** K_a and K_D would remain unchanged since K is an equilibrium constant

Question 27

A patient with rheumatic fever may eventually develops mitral valve stenosis. Which of the following structures will blood pass through after the diseased valve?

- ○ **A.** Tricuspid valve
- ○ **B.** Bicuspid valve
- ○ **C.** Pulmonary vein
- ○ **D.** Right ventricle

Question 28

In the capillary bed, a hydrophilic drug LEAST likely reaches its target tissue by:

- ○ **A.** moving through the spaces between endothelial cells.
- ○ **B.** pinocytosis.
- ○ **C.** diffusing through endothelial cell membranes.
- ○ **D.** moving through fenestrations in the endothelial cells.

Question 29

Which of the following is most likely to occur in a person on a cold day?

- ○ **A.** Increase in respiratory rate
- ○ **B.** Vasodilation of nasal capillary beds
- ○ **C.** Vasoconstriction of tracheal capillary beds
- ○ **D.** Vasodilatation of arterioles leading to the skin capillaries

Passage 6 (Questions 30-33)

Ethanol effects on human physiology is an important research topic, given the pervasiveness of alcohol abuse and the myriad of health and social problems associated with heavy drinking. Ethanol and similar anesthetic drugs cause significant alterations of cells, tissues, and organs. In particular, ethanol exposure induces cell membrane remodeling in various cell types and lipid vesicles, including membrane fluidization.

While red blood cells (RBCs) experience the greatest exposure to ethanol, little is known about the morphological properties of individual human RBCs exposed to increasing doses of ethanol. The deformability of RBCs is crucial to their ability to pass through capillaries in microvasculature, and thus essential for oxygen transport to various organs. Oxygen delivery is particularly important around lethal doses (0.5% volume per volume (v/v)) of ethanol.

Using spectroscopy, dynamic membrane fluctuations of individual RBCs exposed to various ethanol concentrations were measured. The amplitude of the membrane fluctuation in nm is shown in Figure 1 and is proportional to the fluidity of the plasma membrane and the ability of the RBC to adopt a spherical shape, and inversely proportional to the surface area of the RBC.

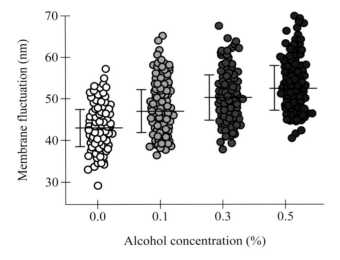

Figure 1 Membrane fluctuation of individual red blood cells exposed to various ethanol concentrations

The highest ethanol concentration (0.5%) represents a dose associated with severe intoxication and marked by muscular incoordination, blurred vision, stupor, and death. To determine whether the oxygen carrying capacity of RBCs was altered at various concentrations of alcohol, spectroscopy was used to determine the hemoglobin (Hb) concentration and content. The results are shown in Figure 2.

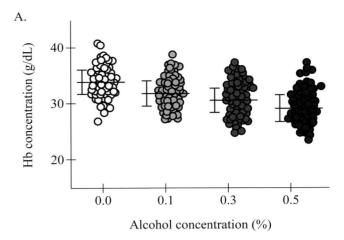

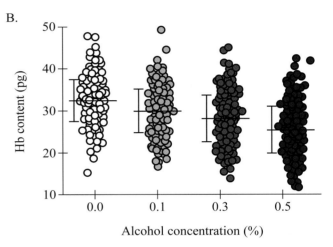

Figure 2 Hemoglobin concentration (A) and content (B) in RBCs at various ethanol concentrations

Question 30

Longitudinal studies on patients with chronic alcoholism exhibit stiffer RBC membranes than those of control RBCs, despite the membrane fluidizing properties of ethanol molecule. What statement best explains this finding?

○ **A.** Chronic alcoholics have impaired cholesterol synthesis due to extensive liver damage.

○ **B.** The RBC membranes of chronic alcoholics are unlikely to have ever experienced increased membrane fluidity.

○ **C.** RBCs of chronic alcoholics are more likely to be spherical than those of control cells.

○ **D.** RBCs of chronic alcoholics are more likely to have a decreased surface area than those of control cells.

Question 31

Over secretion of erythropoietin is most likely to:

○ **A.** increase the hematocrit of a patient.

○ **B.** decrease the hematocrit of a patient.

○ **C.** increase the plasma volume of a patient.

○ **D.** decrease the blood volume of a patient.

Question 32

The association of oxygen with hemoglobin is necessary for oxygen to be transported from the lungs to other organs in the body. What force mediates the binding of oxygen to hemoglobin?

○ **A.** Hydrogen bonding

○ **B.** Metallic bonding

○ **C.** Covalent bonding

○ **D.** Ion-induced dipole bonding

Question 33

Which statement is best supported by the data in the passage?

○ **A.** High blood alcohol levels are likely to increase RBC membrane fluidity and decrease delivery of oxygen to tissues.

○ **B.** Low blood alcohol levels are likely to have no effect on RBC shape or oxygen transport.

○ **C.** Intermediate blood alcohol levels are likely to decrease RBC membrane fluidity and increase delivery of oxygen to tissues.

○ **D.** Blood alcohol levels are unlikely to affect carbon dioxide transport by RBCs.

Passage 7 (Questions 34-37)

Platelets are small, anucleate cells in the blood that can sense environmental changes. Platelets are versatile cells and play important roles in thrombosis, inflammation, and atherosclerosis. Platelet adhesion and subsequent aggregation at the site of vascular injury are key events for healing. Excessive platelet accumulation and thrombus formation may result in thrombotic diseases such as myocardial infarction or stroke, the two leading causes of morbidity and mortality worldwide. Many cardiovascular diseases (CVDs), including atherosclerosis, are linked to platelet hyperactivity, the abnormal, excessive activation of platelets, which is considered an independent risk factor for CVDs.

Mounting epidemiological information suggests that dietary intake of plant foods rich in phytochemicals is negatively associated with CVDs. The polyphenols are a well-studied group of phytochemicals. It has been demonstrated that intake of anthocyanin-rich beverages or pure anthocyanins inhibits atherosclerosis through anti-oxidative and anti-inflammatory properties, and through improving lipid profiles and endothelium-dependent vasodilatation. Delphinidin-3-glucoside (Dp-3-g) is a natural colorant found in bilberries and other fruits and flowers. It has been shown to have beneficial effects on human low-density lipoprotein cholesterol oxidation. However, its roles in platelet function and thrombosis are completely unknown. Along this line, researchers investigated the effects of Dp-3-g on platelet aggregation and clot formation. The results are shown below in Figure 1 and Figure 2.

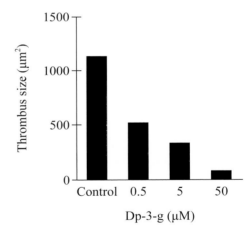

Figure 1 Size of thrombus formed during *in vitro* blood flow following Dp-3-g administration at varying doses

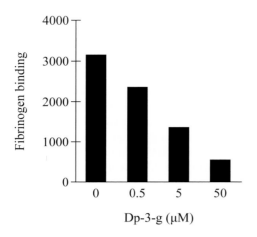

Figure 2 Fibrinogen binding to clot following Dp-3-g treatment

This passage was adapted from "Plant Food Delphinidin-3-Glucoside Significantly Inhibits Platelet Activation and Thrombosis: Novel Protective Roles against Cardiovascular Diseases." Yang Y, Shi Z, Rehema A, Jin JW, Li C et al. *PLoS ONE.* 2012. 7(5) doi:10.1371/journal.pone.0037323 for use under the terms of the Creative Commons CC BY 3.0 license (http://creativecommons.org/licenses/by/3.0/legalcode).

Question 34

How does Dp-3-g affect fibrinogen and what impact does this have on clotting?

- **A.** Dp-3-g increases fibrinogen binding to the clotting site and inhibits formation of a tight plug.
- **B.** Dp-3-g increases fibrinogen binding to the clotting site and facilitates formation of a tight plug.
- **C.** Dp-3-g decreases fibrinogen binding to the clotting site and inhibits formation of a tight plug.
- **D.** Dp-3-g decreases fibrinogen binding to the clotting site and facilitates formation of a tight plug.

Question 35

A clot forms, sticks to the side of an arteriole and partially blocks blood flow through it. Which of the following occurs in the arteriole?

I. Increased resistance

II. Decrease in cross-sectional area

III. Decrease in blood pressure

- **A.** I only
- **B.** I and II only
- **C.** II and III only
- **D.** I, II, and III

Question 36

If clotting were studied in stationary blood samples, which of the following is a factor that makes this model less relevant to biological systems?

- **A.** Lack of resistance in the vessels
- **B.** Lack of megakaryocytes
- **C.** Lack of plasma proteins
- **D.** Lack of shear stress

Question 37

Which of the following actions could be used by researchers to induce thrombus formation?

I. Administration of peptide X, a signal that activates the receptor that Dp-3-g blocks

II. Increase the pressure within the damaged vessel

III. Injection of albumin into the bloodstream

- **A.** I only
- **B.** II only
- **C.** I and III only
- **D.** I, II, and III

Passage 8 (Questions 38-42)

The erythrocyte membrane consists of a phospholipid bilayer with integral proteins associated to cytoskeleton through a proteins network underlying the cytoplasmic side of the membrane. Frequently exposed to oxidative events, the erythrocyte membrane represents a model to study the effect of oxidative stress. H_2O_2, Cu^{2+} ascorbic acid, Fe^{2+} ascorbic acid, azocompounds, and their effects, such as methemoglobin production, lipid peroxidation and spectrin-hemoglobin (Hb) complexes, have been previously investigated. Membrane rigidity induced by oxidative stress has been also observed, mainly due to a reduction in mobility of the proteins embedded in the phospholipid bilayer.

Experiment 1

The aim of this investigation was to verify the effect of H_2O_2–induced oxidative stress on SO_4^{2-} uptake through Band 3 protein. The protein is responsible for Cl^-/HCO_3^- as well as for cell membrane deformability, due to its cross link with cytoskeletal proteins. Oxidative conditions were induced through 30 min of exposure of human erythrocytes to different H_2O_2 concentrations (10 to 300 μM), with or without GSH (glutathione, 2 mM) or curcumin (10 μM), compounds with proved antioxidant properties. Since SO_4^{2-} influx through Band 3 protein is slower and better controllable than Cl^- or HCO_3^- exchange, the rate constant for SO_4^{2-} uptake was measured to prove anion transport efficiency. The results are shown in Figure 1.

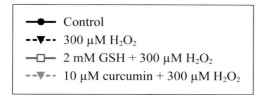

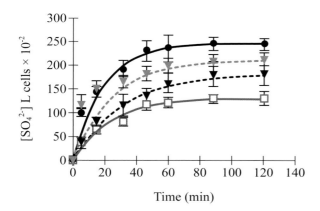

Figure 1 Uptake of SO_4^{2-} under H_2O_2 plus GSH or curcumin treatment

Experiment 2

Next, MDA (malondialdehyde) levels and –SH groups were estimated to quantify the effect of oxidative stress. The results are shown in Figure 2.

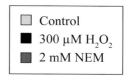

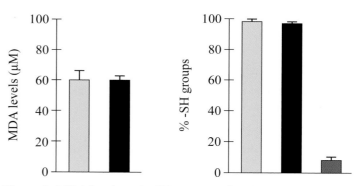

Figure 2 MDA levels and –SH groups estimation under H_2O_2 treatment

Question 38

In Figure 1, the sulfate anion is:

○ **A.** crossing the plasma membrane of an anucleated cell.

○ **B.** a strong acid and nucleophile.

○ **C.** utilizing a sulfate specific ion channel.

○ **D.** bound to albumin.

Question 39

Physiologically, GSH may be responsible for:

○ **A.** converting deoxyhemoglobin to oxyhemoglobin.

○ **B.** converting oxyhemoglobin to deoxyhemoglobin.

○ **C.** converting methemoglobin to oxyhemoglobin.

○ **D.** converting oxyhemoglobin to methemoglobin.

Question 40

If researchers used sulfuric acid as the source of sulfate anion, which of the following would be expected?

○ **A.** A leftward shift in hemoglobin saturation curve corresponding to oxygen onloading.

○ **B.** A leftward shift in hemoglobin saturation curve corresponding to oxygen offloading.

○ **C.** A rightward shift in hemoglobin saturation curve corresponding to oxygen onloading.

○ **D.** A rightward shift in hemoglobin saturation curve corresponding to oxygen offloading.

Question 41

Which of the following could be a physiological source of H_2O_2?

- A. Neutrophils
- B. Mast cells
- C. B cells
- D. Platelets

Question 42

If scientists find that the ion channel is releasing Cl⁻ which of the following must be true?

- A. The red blood cell must be in the tissue.
- B. The blood is becoming more basic.
- C. The blood is experiencing an increase in osmolarity.
- D. Carbonic anhydrase is producing water.

Questions 43 - 46 do not refer to a passage and are independent of each other.

Question 43

What statement best describes the role of the autonomic nervous system in maintaining body temperature?

- A. Acetylcholine release from sympathetic neurons dilates skin epithelial blood vessels to decrease body temperature.
- B. Acetylcholine release from parasympathetic neurons dilates skin epithelial blood vessels to increase body temperature.
- C. Norepinephrine release from sympathetic neurons dilates skin epithelial blood vessels to decrease body temperature.
- D. Norepinephrine release from parasympathetic neurons constricts skin epithelial blood vessels to decrease body temperature.

Question 44

A genetic disorder leads to extra functional copies of the gene that codes for albumin and a subsequently higher level of albumin in the blood. Which of the following is true regarding the blood in this disorder?

   I. Increased blood volume
  II. Decreased blood pressure
 III. Decreased hematocrit

- A. I only
- B. II only
- C. I and III only
- D. I, II, and III

Question 45

A researcher synthesizes a type of blood vessel lined only with a layer of endothelial cells. Which of the following is NOT a function of these vessels in the human body?

- A. Nutrient and gas exchange
- B. Thermoregulation
- C. Fluid exchange
- D. Diffusion of albumin

Question 46

Peripheral resistance experienced by erythrocytes would be highest in:

- A. arterioles.
- B. venuoles.
- C. capillaries.
- D. lymphatics.

Passage 9 (Questions 47-50)

Doxorubicin (Dox) is one of the most effective and commonly used chemotherapeutic drugs to treat cancer patients. Unfortunately, a notorious side-effect of Dox is its cardiotoxicity, which often results in reduced blood flow to the heart muscle ultimately causing heart attacks. Despite advances in medical and catheter-based therapies for these side effects, doxorubicin treatment decreases survival after cancer treatment by up to 10 years.

New cell therapies are needed to protect the heart from chemotherapy. c-kit$^+$ cardiac stem cells (CSCs) seem to be one of the most promising cell types used in clinical trials to repair ischemic heart failure, likely because of their cardiac origin and their capability of being transplanted without immunorejection. In animal studies, human c-kit$^+$ CSCs demonstrated the ability to differentiate into cardiac myocytes, smooth muscle, and endothelial cells, restoring cardiac structure and function.

A small molecule, Y-27632, has been demonstrated to protect single cells from apoptosis and maintain the self-renewal of other stem cells. To determine whether Y-27632 could be used as a preconditioning reagent to protect human CSCs from apoptosis induced by doxorubicin, scientists first sought to establish how doxorubicin affected CSC populations.

Experiment 1

Scientists plated 4×10^4 CSCs on a petri dish and allowed them to rest for 24 hours before exposing them to increasing concentrations of doxorubicin. After 48 hours of treatment, cells were stained with a fluorescent dye that is retained in cells that are alive. The results of the experiment are shown in Figure 1.

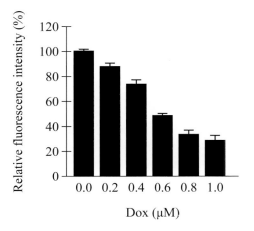

Figure 1 Effect of doxorubicin (Dox) on the survival of CSCs

Experiment 2

Next, scientists sought to examine whether Y-27632 could protect CSCs from apoptosis. 5×10^4 CSCs were pretreated with Y-27632 at various concentrations followed by 0.6 μM Dox. Cellular extracts from cells were collected and the number of apoptotic cells determined. The results of their study are shown in Figure 2.

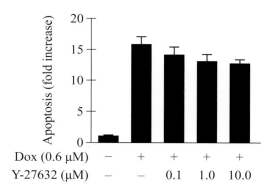

Figure 2 Effect of pretreatment with Y-26732 on apoptosis induced by Dox

This passage is adapted from "Rho-Associated Kinase Inhibitor (Y-27632) Attenuates Doxorubicin-Induced Apoptosis of Human Cardiac Stem Cells." Kan L, Smith A, Ledford B, Fan H, Liu Z, et al. *PLoS ONE*. 2015. 10(12) doi:10.1371/journal. pone.0144513 for use under the terms of the Creative Commons CC BY 4.0 license (http://creativecommons.org/licenses/by/4.0/legalcode).

Question 47

Based on information contained in the passage, Dox is most likely to affect endothelial cells of the:

○ **A.** pulmonary artery.

○ **B.** coronary artery.

○ **C.** pulmonary vein.

○ **D.** vena cava.

Question 48

Which of the following cardiac structures is responsible for determining the resting heart rate?

○ **A.** Sinoatrial node

○ **B.** Atrioventricular node

○ **C.** Purkinje fibers

○ **D.** Bundle of His

Question 49

Verapamil, a calcium channel blocker, is most likely to block which part of the cardiac action potential after CSCs differentiate into cardiac myocytes?

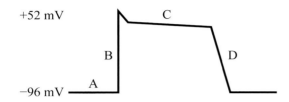

- ○ **A.** A
- ○ **B.** B
- ○ **C.** C
- ○ **D.** D

Question 50

Which of the following vessels is likely to have the LEAST number of hemoglobin molecules bound to oxygen?

- ○ **A.** Pulmonary artery
- ○ **B.** Pulmonary vein
- ○ **C.** Vena cava
- ○ **D.** Aorta

Passage 10 (Questions 51-55)

A 26-year-old male motorcyclist was taken to the nearest trauma center after being involved in a head-on collision at 40 mph. The patient is confused, has a heart rate of 140 bpm, cool and clammy skin, and multiple open lacerations. There are significant internal injuries causing hemorrhagic shock, which is defined by a large amount of blood loss.

Uncontrolled hemorrhage, resulting from traumatic injuries, continues to be the leading cause of death in civilian (40% of total deaths) and military (50% of total deaths) environments. According to US military reports, 15-30% of all deaths are potentially preventable, and of those 80-87% are deaths occurring from hemorrhage. Hemorrhagic deaths usually occur very early, within the first 6 hours of admission to a hospital. Hence, early identification of patients who are at risk for developing shock and death is imperative in order to maximize effective treatments to preserve vital cardiovascular and metabolic function. Several parameters were proposed as indicators of the patient's condition after traumatic hemorrhage: mean arterial pressure (MAP), heart rate, urine output, cardiac index, oxygen consumption, oxygen delivery, base excess (BE) or base deficit, lactate, and mucosal gastric pH.

This topic is of special interest since the traditionally used parameters, such as blood pressure and heart rate, may mask activation of compensatory mechanisms and do not necessary reflect the severity of the traumatic injury. Moreover, late identification of massive internal bleeding may lead to transportation of these patients to inadequately equipped medical centers and consequently delay treatment.

This passage was adapted from "Potential Early Predictors for Outcomes of Experimental Hemorrhagic Shock Induced by Uncontrolled Internal Bleeding in Rats." Abassi ZA, Okun-Gurevich M, Abu Salah N, Awad H, Mandel Y, et al. *PLoS ONE*. 2013. 8(11) doi: 10.1371/journal.pone.0080862 for use under the terms of the Creative Commons CC BY 4.0 license (https://creativecommons.org/licenses/by/4.0/legalcode).

Question 51

If normal blood pressure is 120/80, what blood pressure would corroborate the diagnosis of hemorrhagic shock?

- ○ **A.** Systolic of 140, diastolic of 100
- ○ **B.** Systolic of 100, diastolic of 140
- ○ **C.** Systolic of 100, diastolic of 60
- ○ **D.** Systolic of 60, diastolic of 100

Question 52

After being delivered to the emergency department, the patient is given intravenous Lactated Ringer's solution (an isotonic electrolyte solution) to help compensate for the blood loss. The hematocrit will:

- ○ **A.** increase.
- ○ **B.** decrease.
- ○ **C.** remain unchanged.
- ○ **D.** increase or decrease depending on the osmolality of the solution.

Question 53

The kidneys play a key role in regulating blood pressure. The urine of a hemorrhaging patient would most like have:

○ **A.** decreased $[Na^+]$.

○ **B.** increased K^+.

○ **C.** increased volume.

○ **D.** increased ADH.

Question 54

The figures below display the arterial blood gas levels of a patient during hypovolemic shock.

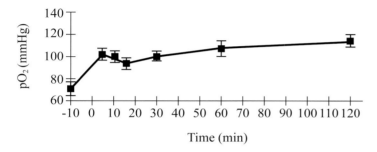

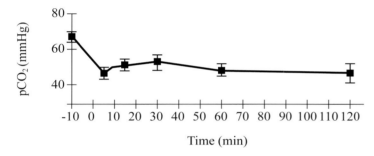

Additional signs that would likely be seen are:

○ **A.** increased blood pH and increased respiration rate.

○ **B.** decreased blood pH and decreased respiration rate.

○ **C.** increased blood pH and decreased respiration rate.

○ **D.** decreased blood pH and increased respiration rate.

Question 55

The hormone ADH was found to be elevated in the patient. ADH is released from the:

○ **A.** anterior pituitary and increases aquaporins in the collecting duct.

○ **B.** hypothalamus and decreases aquaporins in the collecting duct.

○ **C.** juxtaglomerular apparatus and decreases aquaporins in the collecting duct.

○ **D.** posterior pituitary and increases aquaporins in the collecting duct.

Questions 56 - 59 do not refer to a passage and are independent of each other.

Question 56

When inspecting a histological specimen, which of the following would NOT help to differentiate a venule from an arteriole?

○ **A.** Presence of a smooth muscle layer

○ **B.** Presence of a fibrous endothelial layer

○ **C.** Presence of endothelial valves

○ **D.** Presence of accompanying lymphatics

Question 57

A synthetic capillary has endothelial cells with plasma membranes that are twice as thick as those of human capillaries. The transport of which substance would be most affected by this change?

○ **A.** Albumin

○ **B.** Sodium chloride

○ **C.** Carbon dioxide

○ **D.** Potassium ion

Question 58

Elephantiasis is a condition caused by parasitic obstruction of the lymphatic system. If obstruction occurred at the right lymphatic duct, which of the following would occur?

○ **A.** The right arm and head would have a shriveled appearance.

○ **B.** The rest of the body, excluding the right arm and head, would have a shriveled appearance.

○ **C.** The right arm and head would have a swollen appearance.

○ **D.** The rest of the body, excluding the right arm and head, would have a swollen appearance.

Question 59

Which of the following mechanisms opposes hydrostatic pressure in arterioles and capillaries?

○ **A.** Increased albumin content in the surrounding tissue

○ **B.** Constriction of the arteriole

○ **C.** Constriction of the venule

○ **D.** Fluid flow through the thoracic duct

STOP. If you finish before time is called, check your work. You may go back to any question in this test.

ANSWERS & EXPLANATIONS for Test 4A can be found on p. 262.

LECTURE

4

The Circulatory, Respiratory, and Immune Systems

MINI-TEST 4B

Time: 65 minutes
Questions 1–41

DIRECTIONS: Most of the questions in this test section are grouped with a passage. Read the passage, then select the best answer to each question. Some questions are independent of any passage and of one another. Select the best answer to each of these questions. If you are unsure of an answer, rule out incorrect choices and select from the remaining options. Indicate your selection beside the option you choose. A periodic table can be found on the last page of this book for you to use at any point during this test section.

Passage 1 (Questions 1-4)

Melanoma is one of the most common cancers and it is increasing at a faster rate than any other malignancy. Patients who are at highest risk for recurrence require not only routine skin examinations, but also costly and potentially harmful radiologic imaging. These methods are effective in finding recurrences and new melanomas once they are visible on imaging or on dermatologic exam, but other types of monitoring in these patients may provide important prognostic and diagnostic information at an earlier time than traditional methods.

The ability to measure circulating tumor cells (CTCs) represents a potentially powerful method for monitoring patients with known malignancies with minimal morbidity. Many studies have demonstrated the diagnostic and prognostic value of CTCs in cancer patients, with much of the work focused on CTCs as biomarkers in breast and prostate cancers. CTCs are individual or small groups of 4-10 cells that break away from a vascularized tumor and travel through the blood. They are often responsible for forming distant metastases, but they may also be useful for recurrence screening. Larger CTC clusters are thought to be more likely to establish metastatic tumors.

Researchers performed CTC measurements on a series of melanoma patients. They used a simple porous membrane gradient centrifugation device to isolate a fraction from whole blood which is enriched 400–500 times for CTCs (Figure 1). CTCs are thought to have a lighter buoyant density than peripheral blood mononuclear cells (PBMCs). They then isolated RNA and measured melanoma marker RNAs MLANA and MIF using quantitative PCR for several genes implicated in melanoma progression. The results of their study are found in Figure 2.

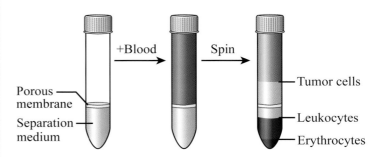

Figure 1 Enrichment and Recovery of Melanoma CTCs

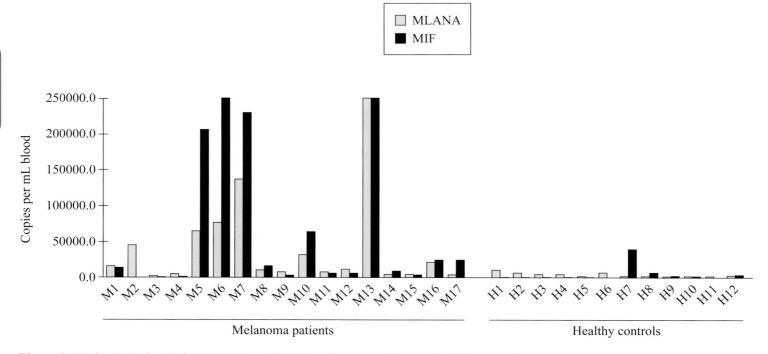

Figure 2 Marker RNA levels for MLANA and MIF in melanoma patients vs. healthy controls

Next ▶

TEST 4B

Question 1

Recent studies have shown that platelets may also contain transformed RNA from melanoma cells. Scientists interested in measuring gene levels in platelets would most likely:

○ **A.** isolate platelets from the buffy coat portion of blood and use reverse transcriptase to create cDNA of the mRNA.

○ **B.** isolate platelets from the plasma portion of blood and use RNA polymerase to create more copies of the mRNA.

○ **C.** isolate platelets from the erythrocyte portion of blood and use reverse transcriptase to create cDNA of the mRNA.

○ **D.** isolate platelets from the erythrocyte portion of blood and use reverse transcriptase to create cDNA of the mRNA.

Question 2

Metastatic tumors that arise from CTCs from melanoma are most likely to be found in tissue that is adjacent to:

○ **A.** the aorta.

○ **B.** the renal artery.

○ **C.** lung capillaries.

○ **D.** the vena cava.

Question 3

Clonal expansion of which of the following cell types in the leukocyte later could be used to treat melanoma patients?

○ **A.** Killer T cells

○ **B.** Macrophages

○ **C.** Helper T cells

○ **D.** Natural killer cells

Question 4

Tumor metastasis is also known to occur through the lymphatic system. Which of the following explanations is LEAST likely to support this finding?

○ **A.** The low pressure of the lymphatic system allows slow transport of CTCs to distant organs.

○ **B.** The low velocity of the lymphatic system allows CTCs to remain clustered.

○ **C.** The lymphatic system contains low levels of immune system cells that can detect cancer cells.

○ **D.** High levels of triglycerides and cholesterol support the metabolism of CTCs.

Passage 2 (Questions 5-8)

Mammalian survival is dependent on a rapid system to neutralize the potent immunostimulatory effects of Gram-negative bacterial endotoxin, which is a lipopolysaccharide found on the bacterial membrane. This multifaceted system includes several cell types expressing toll-4 receptors, degradation enzymes and binding proteins. Early after exposure, "natural antibodies" form an important component of the innate response. Natural antibodies are IgM molecules with broad specificity against pathogen-associated molecular patterns (PAMPs).

An acute exposure to endotoxin can result in life-threatening sepsis while chronic exposure has been implicated in several disease states including inflammatory bowel disease (IBD). IBD is characterized by chronic inflammation of the gastrointestinal tract that can result in abdominal pain, diarrhea and malnutrition. Crohn's Disease (CD) and ulcerative colitis (UC) are the two major types of IBD. CD results in deep, patchy regions of inflammation separated by healthy tissue while UC causes superficial inflammation over large, continuous regions.

Inflammation associated with IBD causes a disruption in the natural intestinal barrier leading to increased permeability. This leakiness leads to issues such as diarrhea as well as significant increases in bacterial antigen exposure in the bloodstream.

Circulating endotoxin is elevated in IBD patients and correlates with disease severity. To measure the immune reaction against Gram-negative bacteria, specifically, researchers examine total endotoxin neutralization (TEN) by adding endotoxin to a sample of a patient's blood and determining what percentage of the endotoxin was neutralized by natural antibodies. Researchers interested in determining which IBD patients had a more robust immune reaction to endotoxin measured TEN in various groups of IBD patients. The results are shown in Figures 1 and 2.

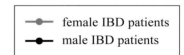

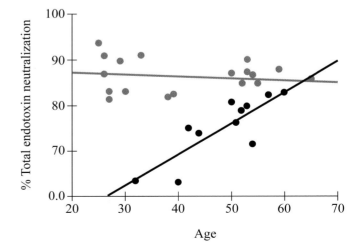

Figure 1 TEN percentage in male (A) and female (B) IBD patients

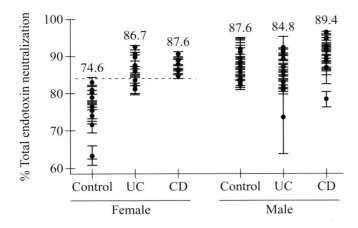

Figure 2 TEN percentage in male (A) and female (B) control, UC and CD patients

Question 5

Which of the following might you expect to see if the Gram-negative endotoxin were suddenly introduced to a person's bloodstream for the first time?

○ **A.** The person's blood pressure may drop.

○ **B.** Natural antibodies are synthesized as part of the primary response.

○ **C.** Antibodies specific to the endotoxin neutralize it.

○ **D.** The endotoxin will be redirected to the stomach for degradation.

Question 6

IBD is considered an autoimmune disease. It is most likely precipitated by a failure in which of the following processes?

○ **A.** Antigen presentation

○ **B.** Positive selection

○ **C.** Negative selection

○ **D.** Clonal selection

Question 7

A woman with a high TEN % mostly likely has which of the following conditions?

○ **A.** UC

○ **B.** CD

○ **C.** Impaired macrophage function

○ **D.** Not enough information is given to determine the answer

Question 8

Which of the following claims is best supported by the data from Figure 1 and Figure 2?

○ **A.** Men have a more robust innate immune response to endotoxin.

○ **B.** Women have a more robust innate immune response to endotoxin.

○ **C.** Women experience a more severe form of IBD than men.

○ **D.** Men experience a more severe form of IBD than women.

Questions 9 - 12 do not refer to a passage and are independent of each other.

Question 9

Langerhans cells of the skin often migrate to regional lymph nodes. Which of the following statements best describes the likely function of these cells?

○ **A.** Langerhans cells are responsible for inducing B cell differentiation in the germinal center of lymph nodes.

○ **B.** Langerhans cells process antigens and present them to CD4$^+$ helper T cells.

○ **C.** Langerhans cells directly activate plasma cells to secrete antibodies against a new antigen.

○ **D.** Langerhans cells secrete granzyme and perforin to lyse invading bacteria in the regional lymph nodes.

Question 10

Damage to the left thoracic duct is LEAST likely to impact which of the following values?

○ **A.** Blood cholesterol levels

○ **B.** Blood triglyceride levels

○ **C.** Blood glucose levels

○ **D.** Blood lymphocyte count

Question 11

Which of the following is most likely to increase lymphatic fluid flow?

○ **A.** A decrease in capillary permeability

○ **B.** An increase in blood pressure

○ **C.** A drop in interstitial pressure

○ **D.** An increase in capillary osmotic pressure

Question 12

The lymphatic system is most likely to remove which of the following from the blood?

○ **A.**

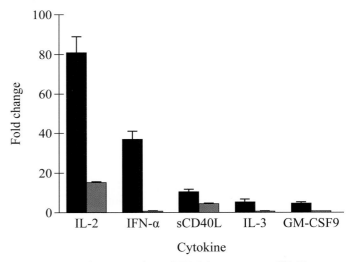

○ **B.** O = O

○ **C.** O = C = O

○ **D.**

$$^+H_3N - \overset{\displaystyle COO^-}{\underset{\displaystyle H}{\overset{|}{\underset{|}{C}}} } - H$$

Passage 3 (Questions 13-17)

Immune checkpoint receptors expressed on T cells have emerged as important targets for the development of cancer immunotherapies. Under physiological conditions, immune checkpoint proteins serve to attenuate sustained immune cell activation, thus regulating normal immune homeostasis. However, during cancer, a sustained state of T cell dysfunction emerges in which the normal effector functions of individual T cell subsets are lost. Referred to as T cell exhaustion, this phenotypic change is characterized by a gradual loss in cytokine secretion, mainly IFNγ, TNFα, IL-2, and an increase in inhibitory receptors, CTLA-4, PD-1, LAG-3, and TIM-3, which eventually results in a loss of function.

Little is known about the role of TIM-3 in this process. In order to gain a better understanding of TIM-3 function, scientists overexpressed TIM-3 in T cells and measured the secretion of five cytokines after stimulation of T cells with anti-CD3/CD28 beads (Figure 1). In a follow-up experiment, scientists mutated two conserved cytoplasmic tyrosine residues at positions 265 & 272 to better understand if they are required for TIM-3 function. Missense mutation of either residue restored cytokine secretion to parental levels.

Figure 1 Ectopic expression of TIM-3 suppresses CD69 expression and IL-2 secretion

Scientists concluded that TIM-3 serves to attenuate signals emanating from the TCR by sequestering the available pools of Lck kinase and phospholipase C (PLC), preventing the activation of the calcium-dependent NFAT pathway. They predicted that phosphorylation of the Y residues on TIM-3 sequestered key proteins, making them unavailable to carry out the necessary activation steps required for full TCR signaling.

This passage is adapted from "TIM-3 suppresses anti-CD3/CD28-induced TCR activation and IL-2 expression through the NFAT signaling pathway." Tomkowicz B, Walsh E, Cotty A, Verona R, Sabins N, et al. *PLoS ONE*. 2015. 10(10) doi:10.1371/journal.pone.0140694 for use under the terms of the Creative Commons CC BY 4.0 license (http://creativecommons.org/licenses/by/4.0/legalcode).

Question 13

Increased activity of which of the following molecules would likely hinder TIM-3 activity?

O **A.** Cdk 4, a cell cycle kinase

O **B.** CD45, a phosphatase

O **C.** PLC, an enzyme involved in cleavage of membrane lipids

O **D.** LCK, a kinase involved in T cell activation

Question 14

Which of the following innate immune system cells would best serve to activate antigen-specific CD4$^+$ T helper cells?

O **A.** Eosinophils

O **B.** Basophils

O **C.** Macrophages

O **D.** Mast Cells

Question 15

Which additional experimental finding would best support the role of NFAT in activating T cell responses to novel cancer antigens?

O **A.** TIM-3 activity decreases activation of the NF-κB reporter.

O **B.** High EDTA, a calcium binder, prevents CD8$^+$ T cell killing of tumor cells.

O **C.** Exogenous application of IL-2 stimulates robust CD4$^+$ T cell proliferation.

O **D.** CTLA-4 expression hinders B cell antibody production.

Question 16

Overexpression of TIM-3 by tumor-associated macrophages would likely result in:

O **A.** rapid proliferation of cancer cells.

O **B.** small to moderate increases in tumor cell volume.

O **C.** regression of tumor volume due to increased immune system recognition.

O **D.** stable disease as noted by neither increased nor decreased tumor volume.

Question 17

Increased transcription of the *TIM-3* gene likely leads to:

O **A.** decreased recruitment of plasma cells to the tumor microenvironment.

O **B.** decreased apoptosis of basophils.

O **C.** decreased transcription of MHC Class II in CD103$^+$ Langerhan's dendritic cells.

O **D.** increased chemotaxis of B cells from the bone marrow.

Passage 4 (Questions 18-21)

Common variable immunodeficiency (CVID) is a relatively common primary immune deficiency characterized by low levels of serum immunoglobulin G, A, and/or M, coupled with a lack of production of specific IgG antibodies. While mutations in autosomal genes leading to loss of B cell function have been identified in a few rare cases, for the great majority of patients, the genetic basis remains unknown. The current best treatment for B cell defects is immunoglobulin (Ig) replacement. While this therapy effectively reduces the incidence of bacterial infections, it does not prevent non-infectious complications. These complications include organ-specific autoimmunity, interstitial lung disease, lymphoid hyperplasia, gastrointestinal inflammatory disease, and lymphoma. As bacterial infections have become less common, these inflammatory conditions have been shown to lead to significantly increased morbidity and earlier mortality.

To explore the dysregulated networks in these subjects, researchers compared characteristics of CVID subjects with and without inflammatory conditions. Chronic up-regulation of innate immune pathways is known to occur in autoimmune disease. It was found that subjects with inflammatory complications were also more likely to have reduced B cell and T cell numbers. It is possible that the more impaired adaptive immunity in these subjects may lead to chronic activation of innate pathways in response to environmental antigens.

This passage was adapted from "Interferon Signature in the Blood in Inflammatory Common Variable Immune Deficiency." Park J, Munagala I, Xu H, Blankenship D, Maffucci P et al. *PLoS ONE*. 2013. 8(9) doi:10.1371/journal.pone.0074893 for use under the terms of the Creative Commons CC BY 3.0 license (http://creativecommons.org/licenses/by/3.0/legalcode).

Question 18

A person with inflammatory CVID is shown to have a complete lack of B and T cells. Which of the following is true regarding this patient?

  I. A vaccine would not work on this patient.

  II. This patient will develop immunity to a flu virus after initial exposure.

  III. There will be reduced housekeeping function by macrophages.

O **A.** I only

O **B.** II only

O **C.** I and III only

O **D.** II and III only

Question 19

Which of the following would be most effective in treating a transgenic mouse with a B cell deficiency?

O **A.** Injection of antibodies

O **B.** Injection of pro-inflammatory cytokines

O **C.** Injection of plasma cells

O **D.** Injection of memory cells

Question 20

A scientist analyzes a sample of immune cells in a CVID patient with inflammation. Which of the following would be expected?

    I. Lowered levels of MHC I
    II. Lower levels of B cell receptors
    III. Increased numbers of granules

○ **A.** I only

○ **B.** II only

○ **C.** III only

○ **D.** II and III only

Question 21

Aplastic anemia is a disease that damages the bone marrow stem cell population and potentially causes immune insufficiency. Which of the following would be expected in a person with aplastic anemia?

    I. Increased oxygen carrying capacity due to higher hematocrit
    II. Thrombocytopenia, or low platelet count
    III. Increased risk of infection

○ **A.** I only

○ **B.** III only

○ **C.** I and II only

○ **D.** II and III only

Passage 5 (Questions 22-26)

Evading immune destruction is an emerging hallmark of cancer. The absence of strong cancer antigens, loss of MHC class I, or inhibitory molecules can result in the failure of T cell recognition, antigen presentation, and tumor elimination. Numerous nutritional interventions have demonstrated potential in modulating the dysregulated immune response. Mushroom derivatives, which contain protein-bound polysaccharides (PSPs), have been well studied and are known to possess immune-stimulatory effects. PSPs may be potent immunomodulatory agents that strengthen the immune response against cancers.

In T cell dependent B cell antibody responses, an antigen taken up by a dendritic cell (DC) or macrophage is presented to naïve T helper cells where cognate interaction between B cells can occur. The B cell with the same specificity as a particular T cell engulfs and digests the antigen and displays the antigenic fragments on its surface for further presentation. A mature matching T cell interacts with the B cell and secretes cytokines leading to cell division of B cells and antibody production. The grouping of interacting T cells, DCs, and B cells is commonly called the "immunological synapse" (Figure 1).

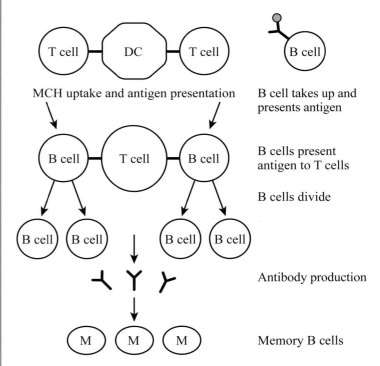

Figure 1 Schematic diagram of the events that give rise to cognate interactions between T cell and B cells

Additional data suggest an augmentation of cytokine levels and immunological subsets conferred by PSP's non-specific but broad ranging activities. After exposure to PSP, T cells experience an initial 3-4 day phase of non-proliferation, called T cell priming. After exposure to artificial antigen that mimics a cancer antigen and expansion of the T cell pool, antigen-specific B cells are activated. These B cell clones then either develop into short-lived antibody-secreting cells or migrate into follicles, where they form germinal center long-lived plasma cells. These plasma cells may produce high-affinity antibodies against cancer cell antigens, strengthening the immune response to cancer cells.

This passage is adapted from "Evaluation of Selected Immunomodulatory Glycoproteins as an Adjunct to Cancer Immunotherapy." Sekhon B, Roubin R, Li Y, Devi P, Nammi S, et al. *PLoS ONE.* 2016. 11(1) doi:10.1371/journal.pone.0146881 for use under the terms of the Creative Commons CC BY 4.0 license (http://creativecommons.org/licenses/by/4.0/legalcode).

Question 22

The T cell receptor (TCR) on T helper cells most likely recognizes:

- ○ **A.** short peptides inside a non-enzymatic protein.
- ○ **B.** long peptides inside an enzymatic protein.
- ○ **C.** short polysaccharides inside an enzymatic protein.
- ○ **D.** long-chain fatty acids inside a non-enzymatic protein.

Question 23

IgM, the antibody initially produced by B cells before germinal center maturation, has high avidity but low affinity for cancer antigens. IgG, shown in Figure 1, is the final antibody that has lower avidity but higher affinity. Which of the following sets of characteristics best matches IgM and IgG?

○ **A.**

Characteristic	IgM	IgG
K_m per binding site	1×10^{-4}	1×10^{-8}
Number of binding sites	10	2

○ **B.**

Characteristic	IgM	IgG
K_m per binding site	1×10^{-7}	1×10^{-3}
Number of binding sites	1	1

○ **C.**

Characteristic	IgM	IgG
K_m per binding site	1×10^{-3}	1×10^{-3}
Number of binding sites	5	2

○ **D.**

Characteristic	IgM	IgG
K_m per binding site	1×10^{-7}	1×10^{-5}
Number of binding sites	2	10

Question 24

Some pro-inflammatory cytokines, such as TNFα, bind cell surface receptors, causing translocation of cytosolic proteins into the nucleus. Which of the following statements best describes TNF?

- ○ **A.** TNFα is a steroid-derived cytokine that decreases translation of target genes.
- ○ **B.** TNFα is a peptide-derived cytokine that increases transcription of target genes.
- ○ **C.** TNFα is a lipid-derived cytokine that increases transcription of target genes.
- ○ **D.** TNFα is a polysaccharide-derived cytokine that increases translation of target genes.

Question 25

Based on information in the passage, which of the following best explains T cell priming?

- ○ **A.** Maturation of DCs into macrophages that are able to present antigen more effectively
- ○ **B.** Migration of naïve B cells to germinal centers
- ○ **C.** Accelerated selection of T cell clones with the lowest dissociation constant for the cancer antigen
- ○ **D.** Direct activation of naïve B cells by DCs

Question 26

Immunotherapy agents used in cancer treatment prevent the inactivation of cytotoxic T cells by blocking inhibitor interactions between the tumor and T cell. What experimental finding would best support this mechanism?

 I. Patients receiving immunotherapy have increased rates of autoimmune disease.

 II. Patients not receiving immunotherapy have increased rates of infection.

 III. Patients receiving immunotherapy have increased diversity of T cell receptor sequences.

- ○ **A.** II only
- ○ **B.** I and II only
- ○ **C.** I and III only
- ○ **D.** II and III only

Questions 27 - 29 do not refer to a passage and are independent of each other.

Question 27

Intravenous immunoglobulins are given to patients who experience sepsis due to acute exposure to endotoxin. If the patient were also given a blood transfusion, which of the following blood type samples would be safe to give to a person with a B, Rh (−) blood type?

   I. O, Rh (−)

  II. AB, Rh (−)

 III. B, Rh (+)

○ **A.** I only

○ **B.** II only

○ **C.** I and III only

○ **D.** I, II and III

Question 28

Which cell type can make a soluble antigen receptor?

○ **A.** T Cell

○ **B.** B Cell

○ **C.** Neutrophil

○ **D.** NK Cell

Question 29

Molecular mimicry occurs when pathogen antigens closely resemble peptides normally present in the human body. Which of the following is LEAST likely to result from molecular mimicry?

○ **A.** Elimination of host peptides from the body

○ **B.** The development of a sustained autoimmune disease

○ **C.** Clonal expansion of plasma cells

○ **D.** Increased proliferation of host T cells

Passage 6 (Questions 30-33)

Regulatory T cells (Tregs) are key players in maintaining immune homeostasis and provide protection from auto-immunity and chronic inflammatory diseases. The major regulator of Treg suppressive function is the forkhead box P3 (FoxP3) transcription factor. FoxP3 initiates the differentiation of CD4$^+$ T cells into Treg cells. FoxP3 is activated by MEK, a protein that transfers phosphate groups.

Persistent immune activation is a hallmark of chronic infectious diseases such as tuberculosis (TB) and human immunodeficiency virus (HIV). Tregs protect tissue from damage caused by infection induced inflammation, but at the same time suppress effector T cell immune responses and facilitate pathogen persistence. Tregs are responsible for whole body dissemination of TB and, depending on the phase of infection, Tregs may play different roles in HIV pathogenesis. While they control viral replication in early infection, they potentially have a negative impact on immune responses in later stages.

Experiment 1

MEK inhibitors are commonly used in cancer treatment but their role in Treg regulation is unknown. Scientists tested the hypothesis that inhibition of MEK would affect Treg differentiation by inhibiting FoxP3 activity. They cultured naïve human CD4$^+$ T cells in the presence of a TB antigen and two different concentrations of MEK inhibitor (MEKI). The results are shown in Figure 1.

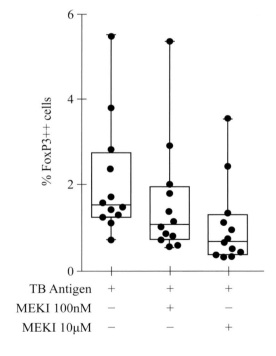

Figure 1 Effect of TB antigen and MEK inhibition on FoxP3 expression in naïve CD4$^+$ T cells

Experiment 2

Scientists were also interested in the effect of MEK inhibition on Treg differentiation in the setting of HIV infection. Scientists cultured naïve human CD4$^+$ T cells in the presence or absence of Gag or Pol, an HIV glycoprotein and polymerase, respectively, and two different concentrations of MEKI. The results are shown in Figure 2.

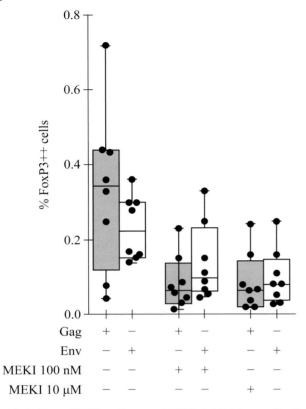

Gag	+	−	+	−	+	−
Env	−	+	−	+	−	+
MEKI 100 nM	−	−	+	+	−	−
MEKI 10 μM	−	−	−	−	+	−

Figure 2 Effect of HIV antigen and MEK inhibition on FoxP3 expression in naïve CD4$^+$ T cells

This passage was adapted from "Targeting Tuberculosis and HIV Infection-Specific Regulatory T Cells with MEK/ERK Signaling Pathway Inhibitors." Lieske N, Tonby K, Kvale D, Dyrhol-Rilse A, and Tasken K, et al. *PLoS ONE*. 2015. 10(11) doi:10.1371/journal.pone.0141903 for use under the terms of the Creative Commons CC BY 4.0 license (http://creativecommons.org/licenses/by/4.0/legalcode).

Question 30

Treatment of patients with MEK inhibitors is likely to increase susceptibility to:

    I. lupus, an autoimmune disease.

    II. influenza, a viral illness.

    III. otitis media, a bacterial middle ear infection.

○ **A.** I only

○ **B.** I and II only

○ **C.** II and III only

○ **D.** I, II, and III

Question 31

CD4$^+$ T helper cells are LEAST likely to:

○ **A.** stimulate macrophages to endocytose TB bacteria.

○ **B.** stimulate B cells to exocytose TB antigen-specific antibodies.

○ **C.** directly cause cytolysis of TB bacteria.

○ **D.** indirectly stimulate CD8$^+$ T cells to lyse cells infected with the flu virus.

Question 32

Phagocytosis is an important mechanism of presenting extracellular antigens on MHC Class II molecules. Which of the following cells is LEAST likely to phagocytize the HIV virus?

○ **A.** Macrophages

○ **B.** Dendritic cells

○ **C.** B cells

○ **D.** T cells

Question 33

Which of the following statements best describes the evolution of the CD4$^+$ T helper cell population throughout the course of TB infection?

○ **A.** The number of antigen-specific T helper cells remains relatively constant and the affinity of the T cell receptor population decreases over time.

○ **B.** The number of antigen-specific T helper cells increases and the affinity of the T cell receptor population remains relatively constant.

○ **C.** The number of antigen-specific T cells increases and the affinity of the T cell receptor population increases over time.

○ **D.** The number of antigen-specific T cells decreases and the affinity of the T cell receptor population decreases over time.

Passage 7 (Questions 34-38)

Cervical cancer is the fourth most common type of epithelial cancer among women worldwide. Persistent infection with high-risk human papillomavirus (HPV) is the primary risk factor for the development of the disease. Although two vaccines have proven to be highly effective in preventing HPV infection, neither one shows therapeutic effects to established HPV infections. Unlike anti-virus prophylactic vaccines based on the induction of neutralizing antibodies, therapeutic anti-tumor vaccines require induction of cell-mediated immune responses capable of identifying and eliminating abnormal cells. To achieve an effective treatment, the therapeutic vaccines depend on a close cooperation between the innate and adaptive immune system, in particular, antigen-presenting cells (APC), CD4+ helper T cells, and CD8+ cytotoxic T lymphocytes (CTLs).

E6 and E7 oncoproteins are the targets for immunotherapy against tumors induced by papillomavirus. To increase the magnitude and quality of E6 and E7-specific immune response, scientists developed a therapeutic vaccine candidate employing a recombinant protein consisting of a string of multi-immunogenic T cell epitopes of E6 and E7 (E6E7 vaccine). The results indicate that this approach may contribute to the development of vaccines targeting tumors induced by papillomavirus.

Approximately 7.5×10^4 TC-1 cancer cells were injected into groups of five C57BL/6 mice. After three days, animals were injected with three doses of E6E7 (18 µg/dose) at 7 days intervals. Tumor growth was monitored daily and the results are presented in Figure 1. Additionally, the antigen-specific responses to E6, E7, and E6E7 were measured in T cells isolated from vaccinated mice. IFNγ levels are proportional to levels of T cell activation (Figure 2).

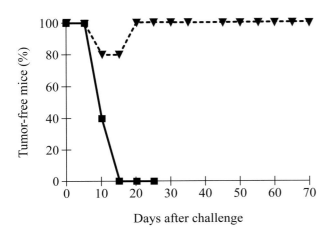

Figure 1 Therapeutic anti-tumor responses elicited in mice immunized with E6E7

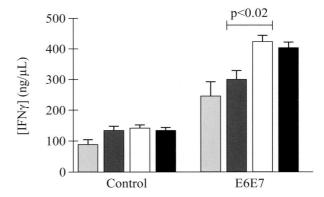

Figure 2 Induction of IFNγ secretion after antigen-specific challenge with E6, E7, or E6E7 in control mice and E6E7 vaccinated mice

This passage was adapted from "Design, Immune Responses and Anti-Tumor Potential of an HPV16 E6E7 Multi-Epitope Vaccine." de Oliveira L, Morale M, Chaves A, Cavalher A, Lopes A, Diniz M, et al. *PLoS ONE*. 2015. 10(9) doi:10.1371/journal.pone.0138686 for use under the terms of the Creative Commons CC BY 4.0 license (http://creativecommons.org/licenses/by/4.0/legalcode).

Question 34

Cervical cancer cells are most likely to present mutant peptides at the highest concentrations on:

○ **A.** MHC Class I

○ **B.** MHC Class II

○ **C.** TCR

○ **D.** BCR

Question 35

Which of the following curves best represents the number of antigen-specific CD8+ T cells against HPV, the viral cause of cervical cancer?

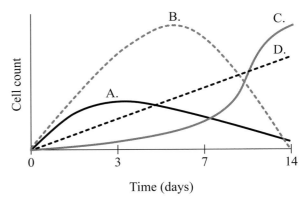

○ **A.** Curve A

○ **B.** Curve B

○ **C.** Curve C

○ **D.** Curve D

Question 36

The decrease in number of tumor-free mice around days 10 in Figure 1 is best explained by what additional experimental evidence?

○ **A.** The antigen-specific CD8⁺ T cell response is strongest around day 15 after TC-1 cell injection.

○ **B.** Natural killer cell populations decline around day 30 after TC-1 cell injection.

○ **C.** Macrophages are most efficient at presenting cancer cell antigens around day 1 after TC-1 cell injection.

○ **D.** TC-1 cells are incapable of establishing a tumor in C57BL/6.

Question 37

According to information contained in the passage, the K_m of the TCR for which of the following molecules is the lowest?

○ **A.** E6

○ **B.** E7

○ **C.** E6E7 Fusion

○ **D.** Cannot be determined

Question 38

Antibodies produced by tumor-specific plasma cells aid macrophages in removing cancer cells in the primary tumor. Which of the following sites is most important for recognition of cancer-specific antigens?

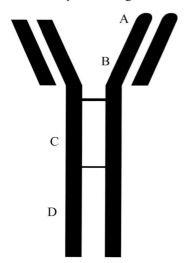

○ **A.** Site A

○ **B.** Site B

○ **C.** Site C

○ **D.** Site D

Questions 39 - 41 do not refer to a passage and are independent of each other.

Question 39

Antibodies would likely be able to bind and recognize:

   I. carbohydrates.

   II. lipids.

   III. proteins.

○ **A.** I only

○ **B.** III only

○ **C.** I and III only

○ **D.** I, II, and III

Question 40

Primary and secondary antibodies are commonly used in immunohistochemical staining. If a scientist wished to generate secondary antibodies (antibodies that bind antibodies) in a mouse against a range of human primary antibodies, she would create:

○ **A.** Mouse α Human Fc.

○ **B.** Mouse α Human Fab.

○ **C.** Mouse α Human light chain.

○ **D.** Mouse α Human heavy chain.

Question 41

Antibodies are able to decrease the concentration of infectious bacteria in the bloodstream of a septic patient by:

   I. increasing receptor-mediated endocytosis by macrophages.

   II. increasing lysis of bacteria by activating the complement system.

   III. preventing adherence of bacteria at mucosal membranes.

○ **A.** I only

○ **B.** II only

○ **C.** I and II only

○ **D.** I, II, and III

STOP. If you finish before time is called, check your work. You may go back to any question in this test.

ANSWERS & EXPLANATIONS for Test 4B can be found on p. 262.

LECTURE

5

The Digestive and Excretory Systems

TEST 5A

Time: 95 minutes
Questions 1–59

DIRECTIONS: Most of the questions in this test section are grouped with a passage. Read the passage, then select the best answer to each question. Some questions are independent of any passage and of one another. Select the best answer to each of these questions. If you are unsure of an answer, rule out incorrect choices and select from the remaining options. Indicate your selection beside the option you choose. A periodic table can be found on the last page of this book for you to use at any point during this test section.

Passage 1 (Questions 1-4)

Crohn's Disease (CD) and ulcerative colitis (UC) are two inflammatory bowel diseases (IBD), characterized by chronic inflammation of the small bowel and/or colon. Ileocecal resection (ICR) is a commonly required surgical intervention in unmanageable Crohn's disease and necrotizing enterocolitis (NEC). However, the impact of ICR and concomitant antibiotics on intestinal commensal microbiota has not been determined.

ICR can be required to remove regions of seriously inflamed, fibrotic or necrotic bowel. Complications that may be associated with ICR include the loss of ileum tissue, which can reduce or prevent efficient reabsorption of bile acids, and the possibility that ICR may alter the microbiota in the jejunum and colon.

The present study analyzed the effect of antibiotic dose on the microbiota in mouse jejunum and proximal colon following ICR. Intestinal lumen contents were collected from jejunum and colon at 7, 14, and 28 days after resection and compared to non-ICR controls. The intestinal microbiota was altered by 7 days after ICR and antibiotic treatment, with decreased diversity in the colon. Moreover, colon and jejunum bacterial populations were remarkably similar 28 days after resection, whereas the initial communities differed markedly. The changes in jejunal and colonic microbiota induced by ICR and concomitant antibiotics may therefore be considered as potential regulators of post-surgical adaptive growth or function. In a setting of active IBD, these changes could act as potential contributors to post-surgical pathophysiology of disease recurrence.

This passage was adapted from "Impact of Ileocecal Resection and Concomitant Antibiotics on the Microbiome of the Murine Jejunum and Colon." Devine AA, Gonzalez A, Speck KE, Knight R, Helmrath M, et al. *PLoS ONE*. 2013. 8(8) doi:10.1371/journal. pone.0073140 for use under the terms of the Creative Commons CC BY 3.0 license (http://creativecommons.org/licenses/by/3.0/legalcode).

Question 1

A follow-up study of patients with ICR was performed. Investigators likely did NOT conclude that:

○ **A.** patients are often found to be vitamin K deficient.

○ **B.** ICRs lead to an increased percentage of certain microbiotic species.

○ **C.** patients have a surplus of vitamin B12 that cannot be broken down.

○ **D.** over time patients have diminished levels of bile.

Question 2

Both the small intestine and colon are divided into a series of subdivisions, with the terminal small intestine connected to the most proximal section of the colon. Ileocecal resection, the surgical intervention for unmanageable Crohn's disease, describes removal involving which of the following areas?

○ **A.** Terminal colon

○ **B.** Mid-colon

○ **C.** Terminal small intestine

○ **D.** Proximal small intestine

Question 3

Studies have shown that individuals with ulcerative colitis often have rectal involvement in addition to inflammation in other parts of the GI tract. Damage to the rectum would lead to:

○ **A.** difficulty absorbing water.

○ **B.** an extremely acidic GI tract.

○ **C.** inability to store feces.

○ **D.** problems absorbing electrolytes.

Question 4

Which of the following is NOT true about the movement of contents through the large intestine?

○ **A.** It is controlled by enteric innervation.

○ **B.** It would not be possible without smooth muscle.

○ **C.** The movement is involuntary.

○ **D.** It is controlled by the somatic nervous system.

Passage 2 (Questions 5–8)

Like other bacterial pathogens, multidrug resistance in toxigenic *Vibrio cholerae*, the causative agent of cholera epidemics, is a growing concern. In addition to using cholera toxin (CT), *V. cholerae* causes diarrheal diseases by using another virulence factor toxin-coregulated pilus (TCP). Diarrhea is characterized by significant water and electrolyte loss due to watery stools. ToxT is the direct transcriptional activator of the genes *ctxA* and *tcpA*, encoding CT and TCP, respectively.

Due to declining performance of traditional antibiotics, use of antivirulence drugs could be a novel therapeutic approach to combat diseases caused by toxigenic *V. cholerae*. Previous studies demonstrated that bile repressed *ctxA* and *tcpA* transcription in a ToxT-independent manner, but a natural compound, anethole, isolated from sweet fennel and star anise seeds, mildly inhibited CT production in a ToxT-dependent manner in *V. cholerae*.

To better understand the role of anethole in CT and TCP production, the dose-dependent effect of anethole on CT production was analyzed in a representative high CT-producing O1 El Tor variant strain CRC41. The results of CT quantitation and the number of bacterial colonies (CFU) are shown in Figure 1. The relative amount of TCP was measured by western blot for the same strain, and the results are shown in Figure 2.

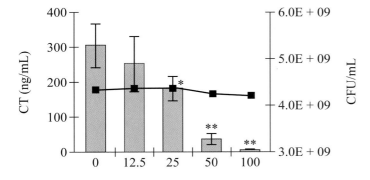

Figure 1 Dose-dependent effects of anethole on CT and TCP production in *V. cholerae* O1 El Tor variant strain CRC41

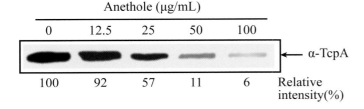

Figure 2 Dose-dependent effect of anethole on *tcpA* expression

Based on their experimental results, scientists concluded that anethole may serve as an adjunct therapy to antibiotics in treating cholera-induced diarrhea.

This passage was adapted from "Suppression of virulence of toxigenic *Vibrio cholerae* by anethole through cyclic AMP (cAMP)-cAMP receptor protein signaling system." Zahid M, Awasthi S, Asakura M, Chatterjee S, Hinenoya A, et al. *PLoS ONE*. 2015. 10(9) doi:10.1371/journal.pone.0137529 for use under the terms of the Creative Commons CC BY 4.0 license (http://creativecommons.org/licenses/by/4.0/legalcode).

Question 5

V. cholerae is transmitted through contaminated water that has come into contact with sewage. The path of *V. cholerae* is best described as:

- **A.** mouth → esophagus → stomach → jejunum → cecum → colon.
- **B.** mouth → esophagus → jejunum → duodenum → cecum → colon.
- **C.** esophagus → stomach → ileum → descending colon → transverse colon.
- **D.** esophagus → ileum → jejunum → ascending colon → descending colon.

Question 6

CT and TCP are likely to mediate their effects via G-protein coupled receptors in the:

- **A.** jejunum.
- **B.** descending colon.
- **C.** fundus of the stomach.
- **D.** ileum.

Question 7

Exposure of the intestinal tract to 300 ng/μL of CT is LEAST likely to affect the absorption of:

    I. Ca^{2+}.

    II. K^+.

    III. Na^+.

- **A.** I only
- **B.** I and II only
- **C.** I and III only
- **D.** II and III only

Question 8

CT and TCP mediate diarrhea by binding the cyclic AMP (cAMP)-receptor protein (CRP) complex, leading to phosphorylation and ubiquitination of aquaporin channels. How does this finding impact the authors' conclusions?

- **A.** It supports the authors' conclusion that anethole decreases CT production.
- **B.** It supports the authors' conclusion that anethole decreases TCP production.
- **C.** It weakens the authors' conclusion that anethole strengthens ToxT binding.
- **D.** It neither supports nor weakens the authors' conclusion that anethole decreases CT production.

Passage 3 (Questions 9-13)

Ulcerative colitis (UC) is a chronic condition of the human colon which affects the superficial mucosal layer from the rectum and extending proximally for variable distances, typically terminating before reaching the ileum. The possibility of infection as a trigger event for, or indeed as the cause of, inflammatory bowel disease (IBD) has long been debated with various organisms suggested as pathogens.

Studies examining the diversity of bacteria in IBD have shown increased cell counts of bacteria and reduced species diversity. Changes in bacterial populations to the detriment of the host have been termed "dysbiosis" and this type of change is thought to be central to IBD pathogenesis. IBD onset following infectious episodes is well described and one possibility is that gastrointestinal infection may facilitate dysbiosis and ultimately IBD.

The discovery that *Helicobacter pylori* is the causative agent underpinning gastric and duodenal ulceration and ultimately gastric cancer revolutionized scientific understanding of these conditions. The possibility that a similar agent is responsible for IBD warrants consideration and exploration. Isolation of these organisms from colonic tissue is needed to enable interrogation of pathogenicity against established criteria. The difficulties in isolating and culturing non-*pylori Helicobacter* from human colonic tissue highlight the importance of molecular approaches as viable alternatives to facilitate the study of the role of several species of *Helicobacter* in extra-gastric diseases.

This passage was adapted from "Enterohepatic Helicobacter in Ulcerative Colitis: Potential Pathogenic Entities?" Thomson JM, Hansen R, Berry SH, Hope ME, Murray GI, et al. 2011. *PLoS ONE*. 6(2): e17184. doi:10.1371/journal.pone.0017184 for use under the terms of the Creative Commons CC BY 3.0 license (http://creativecommons.org/licenses/by/3.0/legalcode).

Question 9

Ulcerative colitis can cause people to experience urgency to defecate. In these cases, the disease process has most likely damaged the:

- O **A.** stomach.
- O **B.** ileum.
- O **C.** colon.
- O **D.** rectum.

Question 10

Ulcerative colitis damage stops before reaching the ileum. When observing the digestive tract beginning from the mouth, the first possible location of mucosal injury would be seen in the:

- O **A.** sigmoid colon.
- O **B.** transverse colon.
- O **C.** ascending colon.
- O **D.** descending colon.

Question 11

In a previous study, investigators compared the colons of patients with UC to those of healthy controls. They most likely found that in patients with UC, there was:

- O **A.** excess riboflavin production due to increased bacterial diversity.
- O **B.** excess vitamin B12 production due to increased bacterial diversity.
- O **C.** no change in riboflavin production due to selective bacterial overgrowth.
- O **D.** decreased vitamin B12 production due to selective bacterial overgrowth.

Question 12

If a patient with *H. pylori* develops gastric cancer and undergoes an operation to remove the stomach, which of the following functions will be completely lost without proper supplementation?

- O **A.** Production of gastrin
- O **B.** Break down of protein
- O **C.** Production of bicarbonate
- O **D.** Physical digestion

Question 13

The various layers of smooth muscle within the stomach allow it to effectively churn its contents. The control of this digestive process is most similar to that of:

- O **A.** chewing food.
- O **B.** esophageal peristalsis.
- O **C.** protein breakdown by pepsin.
- O **D.** absorption of carbohydrates.

Questions 14 - 17 do not refer to a passage and are independent of each other.

Question 14

Investigators studying digestive processes performed a series of experiments involving saliva. They likely concluded which of the following?

○ **A.** It does not share any similarities with pancreatic enzyme secretions.

○ **B.** Saliva lubricates the esophagus to aid in esophageal digestion.

○ **C.** Without saliva there is a lack of carbohydrate digestion.

○ **D.** Saliva aids in the first part of chemical digestion that occurs after eating.

Question 15

Which of the following best protects the stomach from the low pH of gastric fluids?

○ **A.** Chief cells

○ **B.** Goblet cells

○ **C.** Parietal cells

○ **D.** Enteroendocrine cells

Question 16

Liver cirrhosis, a type of severe liver damage, occurs with chronic alcoholism. Patients with chronic alcoholism are likely to experience:

   I. Increased absorption of fatty acids and cholesterol

   II. Decreased clotting

   III. Increased blood glucose levels between meals

○ **A.** I only

○ **B.** II only

○ **C.** I and III only

○ **D.** II and III only

Question 17

Which of the following is likely to be a result of damage to the liver?

   I. Increased vulnerability to toxins

   II. Reduced immune function

   III. Increased utilization of lipids for energy

○ **A.** I only

○ **B.** III only

○ **C.** I and II only

○ **D.** I, II, and III

Passage 4 (Questions 18-21)

Gallstone disease (GS) is the major manifestation of gallbladder diseases and is one of the most common digestive disorders worldwide. GS is one of the major risk factors for gallbladder cancer (GBC), which is the most common type of biliary tract cancer and the sixth most common form of digestive tract malignancy. GS can be classified into either cholesterol stones or pigment stones according to cholesterol content, and cholesterol gallstones are more common than pigment stones.

The liver is the major organ involved in the regulation of cholesterol metabolism. It can acquire cholesterol from plasma lipoproteins via endocytosis or selective cholesterol uptake mediated by the interactions of apolipoproteins with various cell surface molecules including low-density lipoprotein (LDL) receptor. After hepatic uptake, the cholesterol is transported efficiently through the liver, and is ultimately secreted both as bile salts and unesterified cholesterol into the bile.

Apolipoprotein B-100 (ApoB-100) is a key protein involved in lipid metabolism. It is the sole component of LDL particles and plays an important role in the homeostasis of LDL cholesterol in plasma. ApoB-100 is mainly synthesized in the liver and has an obligatory structural role in the formation of triglyceride-rich very low-density lipoprotein (VLDL). A recent study found that absence of ApoB-100 expression in intestine reduced GS formation.

The human ApoB-100 gene is 43 kb in length with an 81 bp signal sequence. Numerous polymorphisms have been identified in ApoB-100, including a single base alteration in exon 26 that has been demonstrated to be associated with inter-individual variability of lipid levels. In a genome-wide association study (GWAS), scientists scanned 500,000 SNPs in 280 individuals with GS and 360 controls and identified a single nucleotide polymorphism (SNP) in *ABCG8*, a cell membrane ATP-dependent transporter, as a susceptibility factor for human GS when inherited in an autosomal recessive manner. Scientists predicted this SNP could be used to provide prognostic information for patient treatment outcomes.

This passage is adapted from "Roles of ApoB-100 Gene Polymorphisms and the Risks of Gallstones and Gallbladder Cancer: A Meta-Analysis." Gong Y, Zhang L, Bie P, and Wang H. *PLoS ONE*. 2013. 8(4) doi:10.1371/journal.pone.0061456 for use under the terms of the Creative Commons CC BY 3.0 license (http://creativecommons.org/licenses/by/3.0/legalcode).

Question 18

Which of the following best characterizes the particle in which ApoB-100 plays a major structural role?

○ **A.** It contains the lowest concentration of cholesterol and is produced by enterocytes of the small intestine.

○ **B.** It contains the highest concentration of fatty acids of a particle produced by the liver.

○ **C.** It contains the highest protein to fatty acid ratio of circulating lipoproteins.

○ **D.** It contains triglycerides and cholesterol primarily absorbed from the systemic circulation.

Question 19

New onset of gallbladder cancer would most likely:

○ **A.** decrease the absorption of glucose.

○ **B.** increase the absorption of arginine.

○ **C.** decrease the absorption of Vitamin A.

○ **D.** increase the absorption of Ca^{2+}.

Question 20

Bile most likely improves fatty acid absorption by emulsification that first occurs in the:

○ **A.** duodenum.

○ **B.** ileum.

○ **C.** jejunum.

○ **D.** cecum.

Question 21

Cholesterol gallstones that obstruct the common bile duct are most likely to:

○ **A.** increase production of esterified bile salts.

○ **B.** increase the concentration of fatty acids stored in hepatocytes.

○ **C.** decrease the production of urobilinogen, a water-soluble product of red blood cell breakdown produced by the liver.

○ **D.** increase the elimination of lipid-soluble drugs.

Passage 5 (Questions 22–27)

Barrett's esophagus (BE) is defined as columnar metaplasia and the presence of goblet cells (GC) in the distal esophagus near the junction with the stomach. There is abundant evidence to suggest that cancer in BE develops via a columnar metaplasia/dysplasia/carcinoma pathogenic sequence. Columnar metaplasia occurs as a result of chemical/toxic damage secondary to reflux of gastric acid and bile into the distal esophagus, combined with release of inflammatory mediators. It has been proposed that BE-associated metaplastic columnar epithelium represents a successful adaptation against the noxious effects of acid and bile. Barrett's epithelium also possesses claudin-18 tight junctions that provide improved protection against acid permeation, and a crypt architecture that is believed to be tumor suppressive. Metaplastic columnar cells have been shown to maintain intracellular pH following prolonged and repeated acid exposure, and a previous gene expression study concluded that Barrett's epithelium overexpresses genes involved in defense and repair of reflux-related injury.

Given the changes in Barrett's epithelium throughout the metaplasia/dysplasia/carcinoma pathogenic sequence, scientists predicted that the number and genomic architecture of GC may predict future risk of adenocarcinoma. Researchers isolated GC from Barrett's epithelium and used digital karyotyping to assay for chromosomal ploidy. The number of goblet cells per crypt and their ploidy findings are shown in Figure 1.

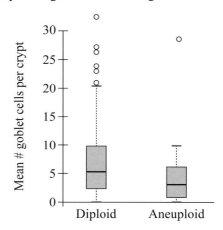

Figure 1 Relative number of diploid and aneuploid goblet cells in Barrett's epithelium

Mucous is produced from both non-goblet (mucinous) columnar cells and GC, but the relative contribution of each of these types of cells to the production of an adherent surface mucous layer in BE patients, and the protective effects of each type of mucin, have not been well characterized. Previous studies, however, have showed a strong association between DNA abnormalities, such as aneuploidy, and the disruption of intracellular organelles involved in mucous biosynthesis.

This passage is adapted from "High Goblet Cell Count Is Inversely Associated With Ploidy Abnormalities and Risk of Adenocarcinoma in Barrett's Esophagus." Srivastava A, Golden K, Sanchez C, Liu K, Fong P, et al.. *PLoS ONE.* 2015. 10(7) doi:10.1371/journal.pbio.0133403 for use under the terms of the Creative Commons CC BY 4.0 license (http://creativecommons.org/licenses/by/4.0/legalcode).

Question 22

Barrett's esophagus most likely results from a functional deficit in which of the following structures?

- ○ **A.** Pyloric sphincter
- ○ **B.** Cardiac sphincter
- ○ **C.** Fundus
- ○ **D.** Epiglottis

Question 23

An additional cause of Barrett's esophagus may be irritation of the esophageal lining by food particles. An association between which of the following digestive changes and BE would most strongly support this alternate hypothesis?

- ○ **A.** Decreased mastication of solid foods
- ○ **B.** Decreased secretion of acid from parietal cells
- ○ **C.** Increased amylase secretion from the parotid gland into the oral cavity
- ○ **D.** Increased chymotrypsin secretion from the pancreas

Question 24

Which of the following treatments would be effective in preventing Barrett's esophagus?

- I. Diphenhydramine, an anti-histamine
- II. Omeprazole, a proton pump inhibitor
- III. Netazepide, an gastrin receptor antagonist

- ○ **A.** I only
- ○ **B.** II only
- ○ **C.** I and II only
- ○ **D.** I, II, and III

Question 25

Which of the following statements best supports the data presented in Figure 1?

- ○ **A.** Barrett's esophagus has a higher rate of goblet cell non-balanced chromosomes than the normal esophagus.
- ○ **B.** Barrett's esophagus has a comparable rate of balanced chromosomes compared to the normal esophagus.
- ○ **C.** Increased chromosomal imbalance causes the dysplastic changes seen in Barrett's esophagus.
- ○ **D.** No conclusion about goblet cell chromosome balance can be drawn between Barrett's esophagus and normal esophagus.

Question 26

Which of the following findings would best support the conclusions drawn by the authors of the study presented in the passage?

- ○ **A.** BE-associated metaplastic epithelium secretes anions and bicarbonate.
- ○ **B.** BE-associated dysplastic epithelium secretes protons.
- ○ **C.** High potassium levels are found in the gastric juice of BE patients.
- ○ **D.** Low gastrin levels are associated with BE-associated dysplastic changes.

Question 27

Which portion of the stomach is most likely to have the highest concentration of free phenylalanine and tyrosine?

- ○ **A.** Fundus
- ○ **B.** Cardia
- ○ **C.** Pylorus
- ○ **D.** Body

Questions 28 - 31 do not refer to a passage and are independent of each other.

Question 28

Enteric nervous system stimulation is one of the major inputs to GI organs. Which of the following does NOT describe a consequence of stimulating these nerve fibers?

○ **A.** Enhanced peristaltic action of smooth muscle

○ **B.** Vasoconstriction of gastrointestinal blood vessels

○ **C.** Changes in hormone release

○ **D.** Increased GI tract fluid exchange

Question 29

Which of the following pairs correctly matches a part of the digestive system with its function?

○ **A.** Goblet cells – absorption of nutrients

○ **B.** Lacteal – transport of nutrients from the intestines

○ **C.** Brush border – secretion of mucus

○ **D.** Chief cell – secretion of HCl

Question 30

Which of the following is a difference between salivary and pancreatic amylase?

○ **A.** Only pancreatic amylase hydrolyzes polysaccharides to smaller sugars.

○ **B.** Pancreatic amylase plays a larger overall role in digestion.

○ **C.** Pancreatic amylase acts on polysaccharides before salivary amylase does.

○ **D.** Salivary amylase is capable of digesting polysaccharides down to monosaccharides while pancreatic amylase is not.

Question 31

Investigators studying the effects of the hormone gastrin ran a series of tests to determine its target and mechanism of action. They likely came to which of the following conclusions?

○ **A.** Gastrin's final target is the pancreas.

○ **B.** Gastrin release is stopped in response to distention of the stomach.

○ **C.** Gastrin stimulates the secretion of bases.

○ **D.** Gastrin production is stimulated by the parasympathetic nervous system.

Passage 6 (Questions 32-35)

Hirschsprung disease (HSCR) is a congenital disorder of the intestinal tract that is characterized by variable lengths of colorectal aganglionosis resulting from the failure of neural crest-derived cells to form the distal enteric nervous system. Although the most obvious consequence resulting from the absence of enteric ganglia is a defect in colonic motility, the most serious complication is the development of Hirschsprung-associated enterocolitis (HAEC). In patients with HSCR, enterocolitis occurs despite surgery to remove the aganglionic bowel, suggesting that the pathogenic mechanisms involved in HAEC extend beyond the region of aganglionosis.

The mucus layer coats the surface of the epithelium throughout the colon and consists of a mixture of water, complex glycosylated proteins (mucins), and antimicrobial proteins. Studies of the mucus layer in HSCR have shown changes in both mucins and secreted immunoglobulin in patients with HAEC. A study of mucin turnover in HSCR patients showed that development of enterocolitis was specifically related to an increase in the ratio of intracellular to secreted mucins.

Endothelin receptor B (Ednrb) knockout (KO) mice are a well-described model of colorectal aganglionosis that exhibit many of the features of human HSCR including megacolon and development of HAEC. Ednrb KO mice exhibit early alterations in the normal colonic and fecal microbiome prior to the onset of significant colitis. Additionally, Ednrb KO mice have more and larger goblet cells in the distal colon, while goblet cells in the proximal colon are smaller and fewer in number.

This passage was adapted from "Altered Goblet Cell Differentiation and Surface Mucus Properties in Hirschsprung Disease." Thiagarajah JR, Yildiz H, Carlson T, Thomas AR, Steiger C, et al. *PLoS ONE*. 2014. 9(6) doi:10.1371/journal.pone.0099944 for use under the terms of the Creative Commons CC BY 4.0 license (http://creativecommons.org/licenses/by/4.0/legalcode).

Question 32

During a resection, 30% of a patient's ascending colon is removed. Which of the following is most likely to be observed in the patient?

○ **A.** Reduced absorption of lipids

○ **B.** Increased resorption of water through the colon

○ **C.** Loss of fluids through feces

○ **D.** Inability to store feces

Question 33

If size of goblet cell is directly related to level of mucus secretion, which of the following would be observed in Ednrb KO mice?

○ **A.** Increased mucus secretion throughout the colon

○ **B.** Decreased mucus secretion throughout the colon

○ **C.** Increased mucus secretion in the proximal colon and decreased mucus secretion in the distal colon

○ **D.** Decreased mucus secretion in the proximal colon and increased mucus secretion in the distal colon

Question 34

Which of the following is most likely observed in enterocolitis?

○ **A.** Decreased mucin production

○ **B.** Increased mucin production

○ **C.** Increased mucin secretion

○ **D.** Reduced mucin secretion

Question 35

The bacterial changes in the colon of Ednrb KO mice are most likely related to which component of mucus?

   I. Mucins

   II. Antimicrobial proteins

   III. Immunoglobulins

○ **A.** I only

○ **B.** II only

○ **C.** I and II only

○ **D.** II and III only

Passage 7 (Questions 36-39)

The small G-protein Rab27A has been shown to regulate the intracellular trafficking of secretory granules in various cell types. In pancreatic beta-cells, Rab27A was shown to mediate the tight docking of insulin granules to the plasma membrane upon high glucose stimulation. Mutations of Rab27A are causal to type 2 Griscelli Syndrome, a rare, autosomal recessive disorder that results in pigmentary dilution of the skin and hair with the presence of large clumps of pigment in hair shafts and an accumulation of melanosomes in melanocytes.

Ashen mice, which lack the expression of Rab27A due to a spontaneous mutation, were used to investigate the function of Rab27A in pancreatic acinar cells. Isolated pancreatic acini were prepared from wild-type or ashen mouse pancreas, and amylase secretion was measured following CCK (cholecystokinin) treatment. Rab27A is present in mouse pancreatic acinar cells and partially co-localizes with Rab27B to the zymogen granule (ZG) membrane. Rab27A deficiency did not significantly affect the morphology of acini but showed decreased amylase release upon CCK treatment.

The other isoform of Rab27, Rab27B, has been found to mediate exocytosis in a large variety of secretory cells. Rab27B is abundantly expressed on the ZG membrane of mouse pancreatic acinar cells. Overexpression of Rab27B enhanced CCK induced amylase release from isolated rat pancreatic acini.

This passage was adapted from "Rab27A Is Present in Mouse Pancreatic Acinar Cells and Is Required for Digestive Enzyme Secretion." Hou Y, Ernst SA, Stuenkel EL, Lentz SI and Williams JA. *PLoS ONE*. 2015. 10(5) doi:10.1371/journal.pone.0125596 for use under the terms of the Creative Commons CC BY 4.0 license (http://creativecommons.org/licenses/by/4.0/legalcode).

Question 36

If pancreatic amylase release was inhibited, which of the following is most likely to occur?

○ **A.** Increased bile secretion from the liver

○ **B.** Reduced bile secretion from the liver

○ **C.** Increased glycogen levels in the liver

○ **D.** Reduced glycogen levels in the liver

Question 37

Based on the passage, which of the following would most likely be an effect of Rab27B genetic knockout in the pancreas?

○ **A.** Increased amylase release and less responsiveness to CCK

○ **B.** Increased amylase release and more responsiveness to CCK

○ **C.** Inhibition of amylase release and less responsiveness to CCK

○ **D.** Inhibition of amylase release and more responsiveness to CCK

Question 38

Enteropeptidase cleaves trypsinogen to trypsin. Which of the following would occur in an individual with a frameshift mutation in the enteropeptidase gene?

○ **A.** Reduced digestion of proteins

○ **B.** Reduced digestion of lipids

○ **C.** Reduced secretion of trypsinogen

○ **D.** Reduced secretion of trypsin

Question 39

Which of the following is most likely to be found in ashen mice?

    I. Increased sugar content in feces

    II. Increased blood sugar levels

    III. Fewer ketone bodies in the blood

○ **A.** I only

○ **B.** II only

○ **C.** I and II only

○ **D.** I, II, and III

Passage 8 (Questions 40-43)

The intestinal epithelium covering the gastrointestinal tract consists of a monolayer of enterocytes covered by a mucus gel layer. Together these two layers provide a dynamic and regulated barrier allowing selective passage of luminal contents into the intestinal wall. Loss of the epithelial/mucus layer integrity is a common feature in gastrointestinal diseases and intestinal ischemia encountered in various forms of shock.

The mucus gel layer, which ranges in thickness from 50–300 mm, is a hydrated polymeric gel composed of carbohydrates, lipids and protein. The major protein component of the mucus layer is mucin, which consists of several isoforms, both secreted and membrane associated. Mucin is believed to protect the epithelial surface of the small intestine from luminal digestive enzymes, abrasion by food particles, and pathogens by forming a barrier between the lumen and the intestinal epithelium. The epithelial cells also form a selective barrier to molecules found in the lumen; this barrier depends on the integrity of intercellular junctions and the extracellular plasma membrane proteins. Changes in the environment of epithelial cells make these molecules targets for proteolytic attack, cause disruption of cell structure components influencing intracellular signaling, and impair epithelial barrier function.

This passage was adapted from "Breakdown of Mucin as Barrier to Digestive Enzymes in the Ischemic Rat Small Intestine." Chang M, Alsaigh T, Kistler EB, Schmid-Schonbein GW. *PLoS ONE*. 2012. 7(6) doi:10.1371/journal.pone.0040087 for use under the terms of the Creative Commons CC BY 3.0 license (http://creativecommons.org/licenses/by/3.0/legalcode).

Question 40

Which enzyme would be most appropriate for researchers to use if they wanted to measure damage to junctions and membrane proteins following mucin breakdown?

○ **A.** Trypsin

○ **B.** Amylase

○ **C.** Lipase

○ **D.** Kinase

Question 41

Which of the following would be a systemic effect of damage to the intercellular junctions in the small intestine?

    I. Less efficient absorption of water

    II. Less efficient absorption of ions

    III. Less efficient absorption of macronutrients

○ **A.** I only

○ **B.** III only

○ **C.** I and II only

○ **D.** I, II, and III

Question 42

Which of the following would be an effective way to measure the integrity of a small intestine mucin membrane?

- O **A.** Measuring enterocyte apoptosis following exposure to toxic analogs of peptides
- O **B.** Measuring enterocyte apoptosis following exposure to toxic analogs of sugars
- O **C.** Measuring enterocyte growth following exposure to bacterial toxins
- O **D.** Measuring enterocyte apoptosis following exposure to bacterial toxins

Question 43

Due to an episode of ischemic bowel, a lacteal becomes obstructed and filled with pus. Absorption of which of the following nutrients will be most impaired in the villi with the obstructed lacteal?

- O **A.** Protein
- O **B.** Fat
- O **C.** Glucose
- O **D.** Water

Questions 44 - 47 do not refer to a passage and are independent of each other.

Question 44

Which of the following is NOT true regarding the regulation of the digestive system?

- O **A.** Hormones require access to the bloodstream in order to exert their effects.
- O **B.** The enteric nervous system regulates hormone release.
- O **C.** Hormones are released via a system of ducts.
- O **D.** The parasympathetic nervous system contributes to regulation.

Question 45

Celiac disease, an autoimmune disease that destroys the microvilli of the small intestine, is LEAST likely to cause:

- O **A.** decreased secretion of insulin from beta cells of the pancreas.
- O **B.** increased secretion of glucagon from alpha cells of the pancreas.
- O **C.** increased lipolysis in adipocytes.
- O **D.** increased storage of glucose-6-phosphate as glycogen in skeletal muscle cells.

Question 46

Researchers administered bethanecol, a muscarinic acetylcholine receptor agonist, to mice to better understand its effects on the digestive system. Which of the following observations is likely to be seen in treated versus control mice?

- O **A.** Decreased blood flow to the stomach
- O **B.** Increased small intestine peristalsis
- O **C.** Increased pH of the stomach
- O **D.** Decreased fluid exchange in the colon

Question 47

One main function of secretin is to:

- O **A.** prevent acid-catalyzed destruction of the duodenum wall.
- O **B.** decrease the secretion of trypsinogen.
- O **C.** decrease striated muscular contractions in the stomach.
- O **D.** increase the pH of the stomach.

Passage 9 (Questions 48-52)

Helicobacter pylori (*H. pylori*) is the major infectious cause of chronic stomach inflammation and plays a key role in the development of gastric cancer (GC). Inflammation of the gastric compartment associated with *H. pylori* infection reportedly afflicts numerous gastric cell types, including chief cells, G cells, mucus cells, and epithelial cells.

Evidence also suggests that *H. pylori* could directly regulate the levels of hunger-related peptide hormones leptin, which signals satiety, and ghrelin, which signals hunger. Epithelial cells of the gastric mucosa are amongst the first cellular barriers for *H. pylori* in the gastrointestinal tract. Engagement of the epithelial toll-like receptors (TLRs) that recognize bacterial lipopolysaccharides (LPS) may affect leptin, ghrelin, and inflammatory cytokine secretion. These cytokines include TNFα, interferon γ, and various interleukins (IL).

In order to confirm if leptin, ghrelin, insulin, and inflammatory cytokine levels are different at various disease states ranging from asymptomatic infection to gastric cancer, scientists collected 10 mL of blood and quantified peptide levels by western blot. The results are presented in Table 1.

Within each disease state, scientists also discovered that individuals with various allele frequencies for TLR single nucleotide polymorphism (SNP) rs4833095 had a different susceptibility to *H. pylori*-mediated disease progression. They found that 30% of individuals with a homozygous rs10004195 T allele were at increased risk of developing GC. They concluded that this SNP resulted in reduced activation of the innate immune system by *H. pylori* LPS, leading to increased inflammation and a higher risk of developing GC. Their proposed mechanism is presented in Figure 1.

	Asymptomatic	Non-ulcer dyspepsia (NUD)	Peptic ulcer disease	Gastric cancer (GC)	One-way ANOVA (p value)*
Leptin (ng/ml)	2.27 ± 0.71	5.1 ± 2.1	6.2 ± 2.8	8.5 ± 3.3	0.000
Ghrelin (pg/ml)	580.4 ± 50.7	477.2 ± 58.8	454.6 ± 35.4	435.1 ± 24.9	0.000
Insulin (mU/I)	38.7 ± 7.8	27.5 ± 8.7	24.7 ± 7.5	29.4 ± 9	0.000
TNF-α (ng/l)	133.5 ± 59.3	557.6 ± 62.2	687.7 ± 37.2	799 ± 23.3	0.000
IL-4 (pg/ml)	33.4 ± 16.6	129.6 ± 42.9	174.4 ± 54.3	286.2 ± 13.6	0.000
IL-8 (ng/l)	15.3 ± 5.7	52.3 ± 11.3	80.8 ± 32.3	238.5 ± 23.4	0.000

Table 1 Distribution (Mean and Standard Deviation) of Gut Hormones and Inflammatory Cytokines Based on Disease Status (Asymptomatic, NUD, PUD, GC)

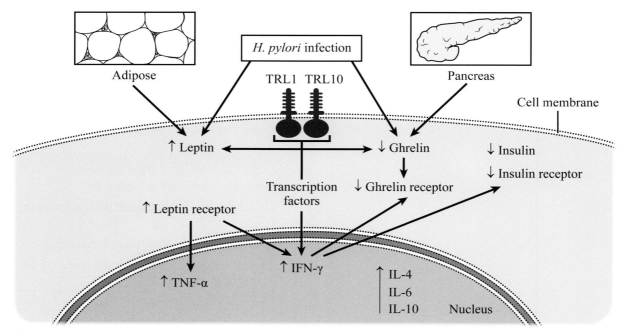

Figure 1 Proposed mechanism of the association of *H. pylori* infection with gastroduodenal diseases and gastric cancer (GC)

This passage was adapted from "Polymorphisms at Locus 4p14 of Toll-like Receptors *TLR-1* and *TLR-10* Confer Susceptibility of Gastric Carcinoma in *Helicobacter pylori* Infection." Ram M, Goh K, Leow A, Poh B, L M, et al. *PLoS ONE.* 2015. 10(11) doi:10.1371/journal.pone.0141865 for use under the terms of the Creative Commons CC BY 4.0 license (http://creativecommons.org/licenses/by/4.0/legalcode).

Next ▶

Question 48

Upon activation, ghrelin controls the level of IFN-γ by activating proteins that:

○ **A.** bind RNA.

○ **B.** bind DNA.

○ **C.** replicate RNA.

○ **D.** replicate DNA.

Question 49

Exocytosis of intracellular vesicles is likely to be greater in which cell type in asymptomatic persons versus persons with gastric cancer?

○ **A.** Beta cells

○ **B.** Alpha cells

○ **C.** Parietal cells

○ **D.** Chief cells

Question 50

H. pylori-mediated disruption of G cell functioning would lead to:

○ **A.** increased secretion of pepsinogen from chief cells.

○ **B.** decreased secretion of acid from parietal cells.

○ **C.** increased mucus secretion from mucus cells.

○ **D.** decreased leptin secretion from endothelial cells.

Question 51

In a separate experiment, researchers administered scopolamine, a muscarinic acetylcholine receptor antagonist. Which of the following observations is LEAST likely to be seen in treated versus control mice?

○ **A.** Decreased blood flow to the stomach

○ **B.** Increased small intestine peristalsis

○ **C.** Increased pH of the stomach

○ **D.** Decreased fluid exchange in the colon

Question 52

Recent studies have shown that *H. pylori* may also infect the duodenum and jejunum of the small intestine. Small intestine infection is likely to impact all of the following EXCEPT:

○ **A.** water reabsorption.

○ **B.** delivery of trypsinogen to the intestines.

○ **C.** solubilizing ingested fats.

○ **D.** absorption of glucose.

Passage 10 (Questions 53-56)

In celiac disease (CD), an autoimmune disease caused by an allergy to gluten, small intestinal epithelium damage occurs secondary to an immune insult and is characterized by blunting of the villi and crypt hyperplasia. Although ~70% of patients with acute CD recover a normal intestinal histology after they are on gluten free diet, some recover symptomatically but retain intestinal damage. These individuals are at higher risk of developing severe complications, including intestinal lymphoma, a cancer of the lymph nodes in lining of the gut.

In normal small intestinal epithelium, stem cells, defined as cells that have high expression of cell surface marker LGR5 (LGR5^{HIGH}), reside at the bottom of the human intestinal crypt. They produce immature progenitor cells (LGR5^{LOW}) that eventually differentiate into epithelial cells. Stem cells are intermingled with Paneth cells, up to position +4, with few outliers at the top of the microvillus (Figure 1).

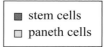

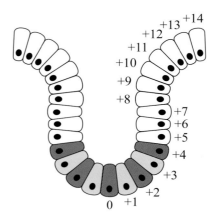

Figure 1 Schema of an intestinal crypt

Scientists investigated the localization of the stem cells and immature progenitor cells inside the crypts of normal human small intestine epithelium and the small intestine epithelium of CD patients. They plotted the number of LGR5^{LOW} and LGR5^{HIGH} cells as a function of position in the crypt and the results are presented in Figure 2.

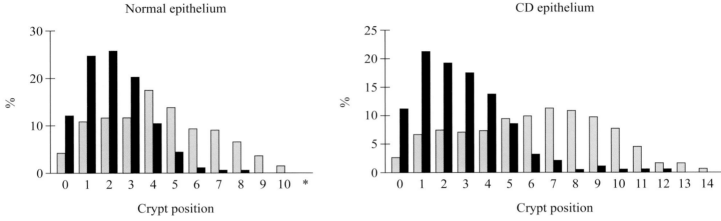

Figure 2 Distribution of LGR5^{LOW} and LGR5^{HIGH} cells in the intestinal crypts of normal and CD epithelia
(* = no LGR5 found at positions 11-14)

Scientists concluded that the celiac hyperplastic crypt is characterized by an expansion of the immature progenitor cells compartment as defined by the LGR5 stem cell marker, but no significant expansion of the intestinal stem cell population.

This passage is adapted from "Celiac Disease Histopathology Recapitulates Hedgehog Downregulation, Consistent With Wound Healing Process Activation." Senger S, Sapone A, Florentino M, Mazzarella G, Lauwers G, et al. *PLoS ONE*. 2015. 10(12) doi:10.1371/journal.pone.0144634 for use under the terms of the Creative Commons CC BY 4.0 license (http://creativecommons.org/licenses/by/4.0/legalcode).

Question 53

Celiac disease is LEAST likely to impact homeostasis of:

○ **A.** glucose absorption.

○ **B.** sodium absorption.

○ **C.** calcium absorption.

○ **D.** water absorption.

Question 54

Gluten, a mixture of complex proteins that provides elasticity to dough, is likely to be hydrolyzed by:

○ **A.** α-amylase.

○ **B.** trypsinogen.

○ **C.** pepsin.

○ **D.** lipase.

Question 55

Which of the following statements best described the features of cells found at position zero in Figure 1?

○ **A.** They are responsible for the majority of glucose absorption.

○ **B.** They have the ability to produce cells that differentiate into multiple cell types.

○ **C.** They form part of the innate immune system of the gut.

○ **D.** They are responsible for cholesterol absorption.

Question 56

Contraction of the gallbladder is most likely mediated by:

○ **A.** the arrival of chyme in the duodenum.

○ **B.** peristalsis of the esophagus.

○ **C.** release of protons from parietal cells.

○ **D.** delivery of lipase by the pancreatic duct.

Questions 57 - 59 do not refer to a passage and are independent of each other.

Question 57

People with familial adenomatous polyposis often have their colons removed as prophylaxis against colon cancer. Which of the following would be a concern following this procedure?

   I. Dehydration
  II. Electrolyte imbalance
 III. Vitamin deficiency

○ **A.** I only

○ **B.** II only

○ **C.** I and II only

○ **D.** I, II, and III

Question 58

A person with low blood sugar is treated with an oral glucose solution. Addition of what ion to this solution would most strongly facilitate restoration of blood sugar?

○ **A.** Potassium

○ **B.** Sodium

○ **C.** Calcium

○ **D.** Chloride

Question 59

The thoracic duct of the lymphatic system is severed following a surgical procedure. Which of the following saturated fatty acids will be best absorbed in this patient?

○ **A.** Behenic acid (C22)

○ **B.** Stearic acid (C18)

○ **C.** Lauric acid (C12)

○ **D.** Valeric acid (C5)

STOP. If you finish before time is called, check your work. You may go back to any question in this test.

ANSWERS & EXPLANATIONS for Test 5A can be found on p. 286.

LECTURE 5

The Digestive and Excretory Systems

MINI-TEST 5B

Time: 65 minutes
Questions 1–41

DIRECTIONS: Most of the questions in this test section are grouped with a passage. Read the passage, then select the best answer to each question. Some questions are independent of any passage and of one another. Select the best answer to each of these questions. If you are unsure of an answer, rule out incorrect choices and select from the remaining options. Indicate your selection beside the option you choose. A periodic table can be found on the last page of this book for you to use at any point during this test section.

Passage 1 (Questions 1-4)

Gallstones represent a highly prevalent condition. In the Western world, gallstones affect up to 20% of the population. 10–15% of the symptomatic patients have concomitant common-bile duct (CBD) stones, which can remain asymptomatic; however, they carry an increased risk of serious complications such as obstruction, acute cholangitis and pancreatitis. Given the potential serious complications of CBD stones, identification and careful follow-up of patients with recurring stones is necessary.

The biliary tree is a system of ducts that transmits secretions from the liver, gallbladder, and pancreas into the duodenum. The present study describes a new entity of the biliary tree, which was termed the oblique common bile duct (OCBD) and is characterized by a horizontal common bile duct course. 1,307 patients with common bile duct stones underwent imaging. The angle enclosed between the horizontal portion of the common bile duct (CBD) and the horizontal plane was measured (angle α). An oblique common bile duct (OCBD) was defined as a CBD with angle $\alpha < 45°$. The selected demographics and imaging findings are summarized in Table 1.

Table 1 Select Imaging Findings for Patients With OCBD vs. Controls

	OCBD	Controls
Common bile duct stones	100%	100%
Average age	72	67
Chronic pancreatitis	7.3%	< 1%
Biliary fistulae	5.1%	0%

This passage was adapted from "Oblique Bile Duct Predisposes to the Recurrence of Bile Duct Stones." Strnad P, von Figura G, Gruss R, Jareis K-M, Stiehl A, et al. 2013 *PLoS ONE* 8(1): e54601. doi:10.1371/journal.pone.0054601 for use under the terms of the Creative Commons CC BY 3.0 license (http://creativecommons.org/licenses/by/3.0/legalcode).

Question 1

In a follow up study, patients with recurrent CBD stones were treated with a cholecystectomy (removal of the gallbladder). As a result of this operation, these patients would be able to do all of the following EXCEPT:

○ **A.** synthesize bile.

○ **B.** store bile.

○ **C.** emulsify fat.

○ **D.** break down protein.

Question 2

As stones form within the common bile duct, they have the capacity to migrate. As a stone moves closer to the duodenum, which of the following functions might become compromised?

    I. Breakdown of fats

    II. Breakdown of proteins

    III. Breakdown of carbohydrates

○ **A.** I only

○ **B.** I and III only

○ **C.** II and III only

○ **D.** I, II and III

Question 3

Investigators found that one group of individuals had an average duodenal pH of less than 6. Which of the following results might explain this finding?

○ **A.** OCBD individuals have increased bicarbonate production due to decreased pancreatic activity.

○ **B.** Control individuals have increased bicarbonate production due high rates of chronic pancreatitis.

○ **C.** OCBD individuals have reduced bicarbonate production due to decreased pancreatic activity.

○ **D.** Control individuals have reduced bicarbonate production due to increased pancreatic activity.

Question 4

Bile forms specialized micelles that shuttle fat to the brush border. When in the blood, fatty acids are largely transported by which protein produced by the liver?

○ **A.** Albumin

○ **B.** Thrombin

○ **C.** Fibrinogen

○ **D.** Globulin

Passage 2 (Questions 5-8)

Type 2 diabetes mellitus (T2DM) is associated with a high incidence of non-alcoholic fatty liver disease (NAFLD). Non-alcoholic fatty liver disease (NAFLD) is understood as excessive lipid accumulation in the liver associated with obesity and insulin resistance, and is the most common chronic liver disease worldwide. No established pharmacological treatments are currently used for NAFLD, and medical interventions have focused on diet control and exercise.

Sodium-glucose cotransporter 2 (SGLT2) inhibitors are newly-developed oral antidiabetic drugs. SGLT2 is primarily expressed in renal proximal tubules, where it reabsorbs approximately 90% of glucose filtered at the renal glomeruli. In obesity, excess energy accumulates as triglycerides not only in adipose tissue but also ectopically in non-adipose tissues. Ectopic lipid accumulation in liver has strongly been associated with whole-body and tissue specific insulin resistance and inflammatory processes. However, it is completely unknown which lipids, in adipose tissue or liver, are more susceptible to the effect of urinary calorie loss induced by

SGLT2 inhibitors. It is also unclear how increased energy intake by hyperphagia is accumulated with SGLT2 inhibitor treatment, and how lipid accumulation affects systemic and tissue glucose metabolism. Researchers examined whether ipragliflozin, a competitive SGLT2 inhibitor, improved hepatic steatosis in an obese diabetic mouse model with insulin resistance (Figure 1). They further explored whether effects were dependent on body weight reduction.

Ipragliflozin consistently improved high-fat diet (HFD)-induced hyperglycemia and increased energy intake with hyperphagia. Compared with the control, epididymal fat weight was increased with ipragliflozin. There was a significant negative correlation between liver and epididymal fat weights in ipragliflozin treated mice.

This passage was adapted from "Ipragliflozin Improves Hepatic Steatosis in Obese Mice and Liver Dysfunction in Type 2 Diabetic Patients Irrespective of Body Weight Reduction." Komiya C, Tsuchiya K, Shiba K, Miyachi Y, Furuke S, et al. *PLoS ONE*. 2016. 11(3) doi:10.1371/journal.pone.0151511 for use under the terms of the Creative Commons CC BY 4.0 license (https://creativecommons.org/licenses/by/4.0/legalcode).

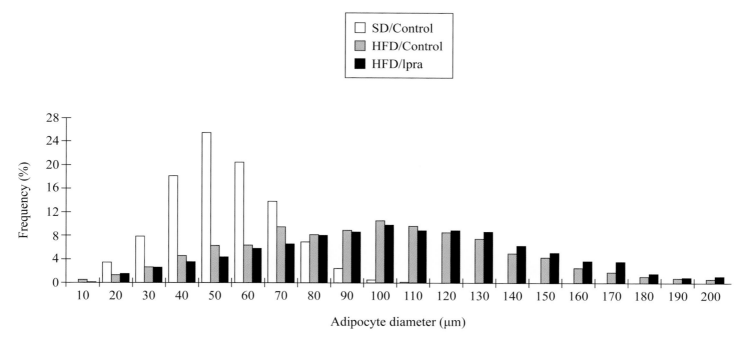

Figure 1 Histogram of adipocyte diameter (Note: SD = standard diet)

Question 5

Which of the following organs and enzymes would most likely have significantly increased activity in mice fed the HFD when compared to the standard diet?

- A. Stomach
- B. Gallbladder
- C. Colon
- D. Trypsin

Question 6

If secretin signaling were interrupted, which treatment administered to the duodenum would be most appropriate?

- A. Insulin
- B. Ipragliflozin
- C. Calcium carbonate
- D. Gastrin

Question 7

Which of the following molecules is most likely ipragliflozin?

○ **A.**

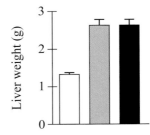

○ **B.**

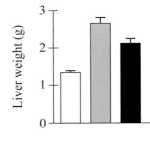

○ **C.**

○ **D.**

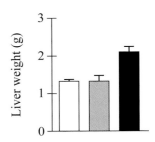

Question 8

Given the information in the passage, which of the following most likely depicts liver weight?

○ **A.**

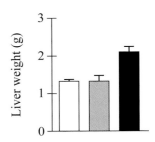

○ **B.**

○ **C.**

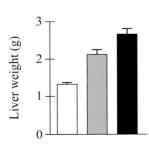

○ **D.**

Passage 3 (Questions 9-12)

Vitamin D and folate (folic acid, vitamin B9) are activated and degraded by ultraviolet (UV) radiation, respectively, and are necessary for human development and physiology. Genes controlling the levels of the vitamin D precursor 7-DHC and folate are likely to have been targets of selection as humans adapted to new diets and environments over time. Vitamin D regulates target gene expression in many tissues and has major roles in diverse physiological functions, being primarily responsible for calcium and phosphate homeostasis and bone remodeling. Vitamin D deficiency, which affects millions of people worldwide, has been associated with brittle and poorly formed bones in childhood, osteoporosis, a bone degradation disease of the elderly, and cardiovascular disease.

Production of the water soluble active form of vitamin D $(1-\alpha-25(OH)_2D_3)$ requires many chemical conversion steps in the skin, liver, and kidney. While it acts as a transcription factor in nearly all tissues, it plays crucial roles in the intestines to regulate the absorption of certain ions (Figure 1).

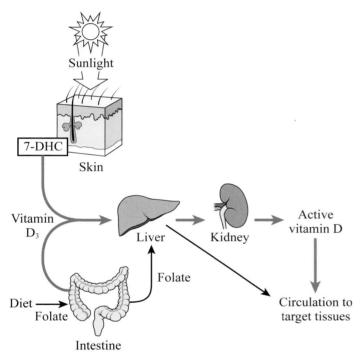

Figure 1 Organ systems involved in vitamin D and folate acquisition and metabolism

The biochemical pathway for the production of the active form of vitamin D is fairly well conserved through evolution. There is evidence that the active form of vitamin D and its receptor, VDR, evolved and specialized in the regulation of intestinal calcium absorption that is essential for proper mineralization of the skeleton particularly in environments that lacked sufficient intake of calcium. It is possible that these selective pressures lead to the evolution of target genes of vitamin D, such as *CXXC1*, *LRP5* and *RUNX2*, which help stimulate bone formation.

This passage is adapted from "Genes Regulated by Vitamin D in Bone Cells Are Positively Selected For in East Asians." Arciero E, Biagini S, Chen Y, Xue Y, Luiselli D, et al.. *PLoS ONE*. 2015. 10(12) doi:10.1371/journal.pbio.0146072 for use under the terms of the Creative Commons CC BY 4.0 license (http://creativecommons.org/licenses/by/4.0/legalcode).

Question 9

Damage to which of the following organs would hinder gut vitamin D absorption?

    I. Gallbladder

    II. Ileum

    III. Liver

○ **A.** I only

○ **B.** II only

○ **C.** I and III only

○ **D.** I, II, and III

Question 10

Decreased synthesis of vitamin D would be most likely to stimulate the exocytosis of:

○ **A.** PTH.

○ **B.** calcitonin.

○ **C.** GH.

○ **D.** prolactin.

Question 11

In an experiment to track the distribution of vitamin D metabolites, patients ingested 100 mg of $^{19}F-1-\alpha-25(OH)_2D_3$, a radiolabeled water soluble active form of vitamin D. The greatest concentration of excess $^{19}F-1-\alpha-25(OH)_2D_3$ would be found in:

○ **A.** the proximal convoluted tubule of the kidney.

○ **B.** the transverse colon of the large intestine.

○ **C.** the jejunum of the small intestine.

○ **D.** the common hepatic bile duct of the liver.

Question 12

Which of the following plots best depicts the relative concentrations of vitamin D and folate in the body?

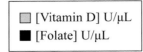

☐ [Vitamin D] U/μL
■ [Folate] U/μL

○ **A.**

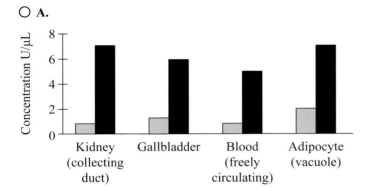

○ **B.**

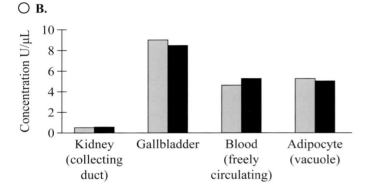

○ **C.**

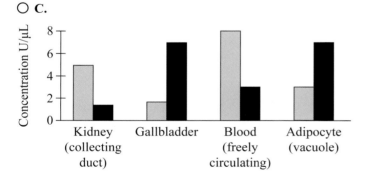

○ **D.**

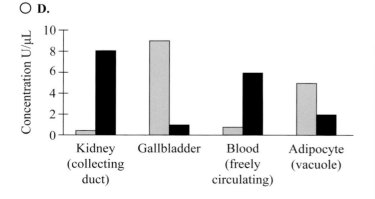

Questions 13 - 16 do not refer to a passage and are independent of each other.

Question 13

Which of the following correctly maps the path of filtrate through the kidney?

○ **A.** Loop of Henle, glomerulus, distal tubule, collecting duct

○ **B.** Proximal tubule, distal tubule, loop of Henle, collecting duct

○ **C.** Proximal tubule, loop of Henle, distal tubule, collecting duct

○ **D.** Glomerulus, loop of Henle, proximal tubule, collecting duct

Question 14

Which component of the excretory system does glucose pass through immediately before being reabsorbed by the bloodstream?

○ **A.** Bowman's capsule

○ **B.** Glomerulus

○ **C.** Loop of Henle

○ **D.** Afferent arteriole

Question 15

If a dehydrated person ingests a toxin that causes the salt concentration in the medulla of the kidney to more closely resemble that of the cortex, which of the following would be expected?

○ **A.** Aquaporins are inserted into the membrane of collecting duct cells to increase their permeability to water and produce concentrated urine.

○ **B.** Low osmolarity urine is produced and does not become concentrated when supplemental ADH is administered.

○ **C.** More salt passively diffuses into the less concentrated medulla as the filtrate flows through the descending limb of the loop of Henle.

○ **D.** The amount of sodium that is filtered by the glomerulus increases.

Question 16

A physician prescribes a drug that blocks the activity of a key ion transporter in the medulla of the nephron. Which of the following is most likely to occur after drug administration?

○ A. Less sodium will be reabsorbed in the loop of Henle which will eventually result in the production of more dilute urine.

○ B. Sodium excretion will be decreased due to the direct inhibition of the ion transporter by the drug.

○ C. Inhibition of the transporter will increase the concentration gradient found in the medulla and increase the kidney's ability to make concentrated urine.

○ D. A large osmolar gradient in the medulla will not be created due to the increased flow of water out of the ascending loop of Henle.

Passage 4 (Questions 17-20)

Netrin-1 is a laminin-related secreted protein that is widely expressed in many tissues, including kidney. Netrin-1 is also shown to increase kidney epithelial proliferation and migration and cancer development and progression. This protein binds to three distinct families of receptors, the DCC family (DCC and neogenin), the UNC5 family (UNC5A-D), and DSCAM, to mediate its biological effects in different tissues. Localization studies had determined that netrin-1 expression is restricted to vascular endothelial cells, and little or no expression was seen in the tubular epithelial cells.

It has been demonstrated that within hours after injury of the tubules, netrin-1 protein is induced and excreted into urine. To deduce the mechanism through which renal insult induced netrin-1 protein expression, mice were subjected to 30 minutes of ischemia followed by 3 and 6 hours of reperfusion (Figure 1).

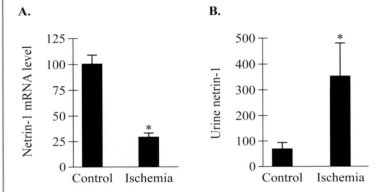

Figure 1 Netrin-1 mRNA (A) and protein (B) levels in kidneys of mice in the control group versus the ischemia reperfusion group

Pervanadate molecules were used to investigate the influence of cellular stress on netrin-1 production in mouse proximal tubular epithelial cells (TKPTS). The results are shown in Figure 2.

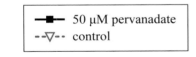

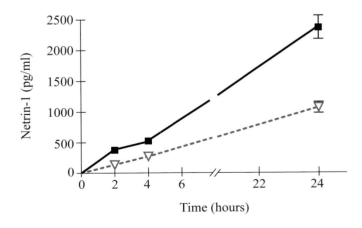

Figure 2 Pervanadate induces netrin-1 production in a time-dependent manner in TKPTS cells

Pervanadate is known to activate MAP kinases (MAPKs) in HeLa and smooth muscle cells, and the effect was measured in TKPTS cells by Western blot (Figure 3). TKPTS cells were treated with 50 mM pervanadate in the presence or absence of specific inhibitors of p38 MAP kinase (10 mM SB203580), ERK (10 mM U0126), or JNK (20 mM SP600125). Pervanadate was shown to have no effect on mRNA stability.

A.

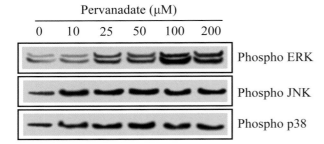

B.

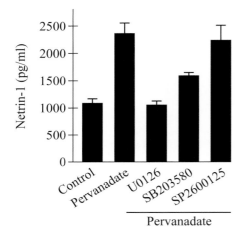

Figure 3 Western blot of MAPKs in the presence of pervanadate (A). Netrin-1 protein levels in the presence of pervanadate and specific inhibitors (B).

This passage was adapted from "Intracellular Kinases Mediate Increased Translation and Secretion of Netrin-1 from Renal Tubular Epithelial Cells." Jayakumar C, Mohamed R, Ranganathan PV, Ramesh G. *PLoS ONE*. 2011. 6(10): e26776 doi: 10.1371/journal.pone.0026776 for use under the terms of the Creative Commons CC BY 3.0 license (http://creativecommons.org/licenses/by/3.0/legalcode).

Question 17

Netrin-1 is induced and blood is filtered in the:

- ○ **A.** cortex and the renal corpuscle in the cortex, respectively.
- ○ **B.** medulla and the glomerulus in the cortex, respectively.
- ○ **C.** medulla and the Bowman's capsule in the cortex, respectively.
- ○ **D.** cortex and the glomerulus in the medulla, respectively.

Question 18

Netrin-1 induced from TKPTS cells first encounters:

- ○ **A.** the distal convoluted tubule.
- ○ **B.** the thick ascending limb.
- ○ **C.** the juxtaglomerular apparatus.
- ○ **D.** the collecting duct.

Question 19

Increased urine netrin-1 after kidney injury is likely caused by:

- ○ **A.** increased translation due to SB203580.
- ○ **B.** decreased transcription due to rapid mRNA turnover.
- ○ **C.** reabsorption of circulating netrin-1 produced from vascular endothelial cells.
- ○ **D.** increased translation due to post-transcriptional pathway enzyme phosphorylation.

Question 20

Which kinase has the greatest effect on netrin-1 production?

- ○ **A.** ERK
- ○ **B.** UNC5A-D
- ○ **C.** U0126
- ○ **D.** p38

Passage 5 (Questions 21-25)

Diabetic nephropathy is a leading cause of end-stage renal disease. It is often characterized by functional and structural changes in the glomerulus such as glomerular hyperfiltration and thickening of the glomerular basement membrane, ultimately progressing into glomerular sclerosis associated with an increased urinary excretion rate of albumin and renal dysfunction. However, it has been hypothesized that changes within the interstitium of the renal tubules are more important than dysfunction of the glomerulus in terms of renal dysfunction in diabetic nephropathy. Ninety percent of glucose filtered by the glomerulus is reabsorbed by a low-affinity/high capacity sodium-glucose cotransporter 2 (SGLT2), which is expressed mainly on S1 and S2 segment of renal proximal tubules (PCT).

First, researchers investigated the effect of the drug remogliflozin (RE) on SGLT2 activity and glucose excretion. All subjects received single oral doses of either RE or placebo separated by approximately 2 week intervals. In Part A, 10 healthy subjects participated in 5 dosing periods where they received RE or placebo. In Part B, 6 subjects with type 2 diabetes mellitus (T2DM) participated in 3 dose periods where they received RE or placebo. The results are summarized in Table 1.

Table 1   Urinary Glucose and Electrolyte Excretion After Single-dose Administration of Remoglifozin

Parameter	Placebo	Remogliflozin etabonate dose (mg)		
		20	50	500
Healthy subjects				
Urinary glucose excretion (mmol)	6.5 (18.6)[a]	67.1 (17.9)	96.7 (17.1)[b]	223 (49.5)
Filtered glucose excretion in urine (%)	0.9 (2.4)[a]	9.0 (2.2)	12.7 (3.7)[b]	34.2 (5.0)
Urinary sodium excretion (mmol)	162 (49.4)[a]	148 (64.0)	212 (67.6)[b]	143 (55.0)
Urinary chloride excretion (mmol)	141 (39.8)[a]	136 (56.6)	189 (51.4)[b]	126 (55)
T2DM subjects				
Urinary glucose excretion (mmol)	40.4 (62.4)[a]		384 (210)	642 (256)
Filtered glucose excretion in urine (%)	2.3 (3.6)[a]		15.9 (5.9)[c]	21.6 (9.1)
Urinary sodium excretion (mmol)	196 (39.2)[a]		173 (35.5)[c]	301 (128)

In addition, researchers examined whether insulin, high glucose, AGEs, or insulin inhibitor N-acetylcysteine (NAC) stimulated SGLT2 expression in cultured proximal tubular cells. Tubular cells were treated with the different concentrations of insulin. After 24 hours, proteins were extracted from tubular cells with lysis buffer, and then separated by SDS-PAGE and transferred to nitrocellulose membranes. The results are shown in Figure 1.

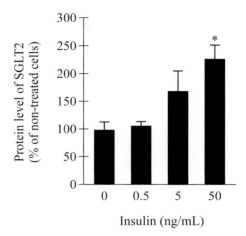

Figure 1   Effect of insulin on SGLT2 expression in tubular cells

Question 21

Which experimental approach would be MOST effective in measuring the effect of diabetic nephropathy on glomerular function?

- **A.** Quantification of the medullary osmotic gradient in a diabetic patient
- **B.** Attachment of a fluorescent tag to glucose molecules
- **C.** Quantification of urinary protein in diabetic patients
- **D.** Comparison of urine volume between healthy and diabetic patients

In order to determine the effect of antioxidant NAC on glucose excretion, tubular cells were treated with or without 50 ng/ml insulin in the presence or absence of 1 mM NAC for 24 h. Which graph most likely displays the results of this experiment?

○ **A.**

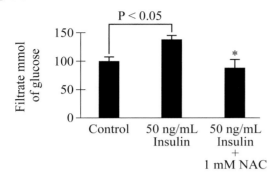

○ **B.**

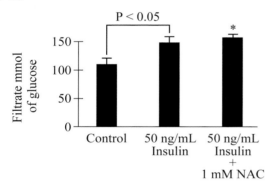

○ **C.**

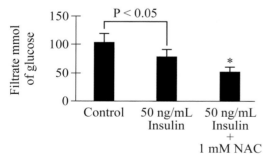

○ **D.**

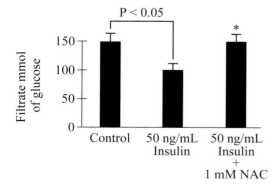

A student hypothesizes that patients being treated with RE will also experience an increase in frequency and volume of urination. Is this hypothesis reasonable?

○ **A.** Yes, increased osmolarity of the filtrate would cause decreased water excretion.

○ **B.** Yes, lack of glucose reabsorption inhibits water reabsorption in the loop of Henle.

○ **C.** No, electrolyte excretion and absorption is unaffected by RE treatment.

○ **D.** No, frequency of urination is unaffected by glucose in the filtrate.

The effects of administration of remoglifozin are most likely to increase:

○ **A.** with increasing filtrate depth into the medulla.

○ **B.** with increasing filtrate proximity to the cortex.

○ **C.** with increasing filtrate distance to the glomerulus.

○ **D.** with increasing filtrate proximity to the vasa recta.

Question 25

The effect of RE on electrolyte absorption and excretion was further explored in healthy patients by evaluating the activity of sodium/hydrogen exchange protein 1, SLC9A1, in the ascending and descending loop of Henle in varying concentration of RE. Which of the following displays the most likely results of the experiment?

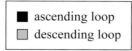

A.

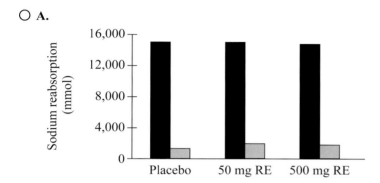

B.

C.

D.

Questions 26 - 28 do not refer to a passage and are independent of each other.

Question 26

Which of the following must occur in order to allow for the release of urine?

- ○ **A.** Relaxation of the bladder
- ○ **B.** Relaxation of the urinary sphincter
- ○ **C.** Contraction of the urinary sphincter
- ○ **D.** Relaxation of the ureter

Question 27

A patient with high-blood pressure consumes a meal that contains a large amount of sodium. Which of the following physiological responses is most likely?

- ○ **A.** More sodium will be excreted following stimulation of sodium channels in the distal tubule by aldosterone.
- ○ **B.** Water permeability in the collecting ducts will be enhanced.
- ○ **C.** The anterior pituitary gland will decrease ADH secretion to lower blood pressure by producing more dilute urine.
- ○ **D.** Renin will be released by the juxtaglomerular cells after sensing the high concentration of salt in the filtrate.

Question 28

Which of the following would most likely occur if the degree of fenestration of endothelial cells in the glomerulus were reduced?

- ○ **A.** Increased filtration due to increased permeability across the capillary wall
- ○ **B.** Increased filtration due to decreased permeability across the capillary wall
- ○ **C.** Decreased filtration due to increased permeability across the capillary wall
- ○ **D.** Decreased filtration due to decreased permeability across the capillary wall

Passage 6 (Questions 29-33)

The renin angiotensin system (RAS) is an important modulator of blood pressure (BP) and sodium homeostasis. Apart from other regions of the kidney, renin is synthesized in the connecting segment and collecting duct (CD) and secreted into the lumen of the collecting duct. Angiotensinogen and angiotensin converting enzyme are also expressed in the renal tubule, leading to luminal Angiotensin-II (Ang-II) synthesis, which can modulate electrolyte and water reabsorption and ultimately BP.

Previous studies have suggested that Ang-II is a potent stimulant of CD renin synthesis. In order to determine the role of CD renin in BP regulation, researchers developed gene-targeted mouse models with renin overexpression or ablation in the CD. Mice with CD-specific overexpression of renin demonstrated increased expression of membrane-bound epithelial Na channel (ENaC).

To further explore whether CD renin plays a role in Ang-II-independent hypertension, the researchers utilized the deoxycorticosterone acetate (DOCA) high salt model of experimental hypertension , and they measured the expression of renin in WT and collecting duct renin Knock-Out (KO) mice with and without DOCA treatment (Figure 1). After completing the study, researchers hypothesized that CD renin contributes to other forms of Ang-II independent hypertension, possibly due to abnormal nitric oxide (NO) synthesis and activity.

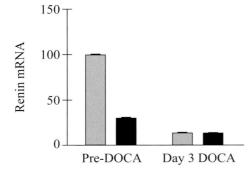

Figure 1 Medullary renin mRNA expression in WT and CD renin KO mice before and after DOCA-salt treatment

Question 29

Stimulation of the RAS is LEAST likely to:

- **A.** increase parasympathetic nervous system activity.
- **B.** decrease the concentration of circulating potassium.
- **C.** increase the secretion of aldosterone.
- **D.** increase arteriolar vasoconstriction.

Question 30

Damage to which of the following structures would most decrease circulating renin levels?

- **A.** Descending loop of Henle
- **B.** Thin ascending loop of Henle
- **C.** Thick ascending loop of Henle
- **D.** Juxtaglomerular apparatus

Question 31

Kidney RAS dysfunction may worsen pre-existing cardiac abnormalities. Decreased heart rate may be a potential side effect of:

   I. angiotensin-receptor agonists.
   II. angiotensin-converting-enzyme inhibitors.
   III. competitive antagonists of aldosterone.

- **A.** II only
- **B.** I and III only
- **C.** II and III only
- **D.** I, II, and III

Question 32

In a follow-up study, researchers found that CD renin decreased the flow of filtrate through the proximal convoluted tubule by 1 mL/minute. This additional experimental evidence:

- **A.** strengthens the finding that CD renin decreases sodium reabsorption.
- **B.** strengthens the finding that collecting segment renin decreases potassium secretion.
- **C.** weakens the finding that CD renin increases potassium secretion.
- **D.** neither strengthens nor weakens support for the role of CD renin in sodium homeostasis.

Question 33

Which of the following statements best summarizes the results of Figure 1?

- **A.** CD renin stimulates angiotensinogen activity to control blood pressure.
- **B.** Knockout of the renin gene in the CD leads to compensatory renin release before DOCA treatment.
- **C.** CD renin is unlikely to play a major role in hypertension caused by DOCA and high blood sodium levels.
- **D.** WT mice are unable to secrete CD renin in response to low sodium levels.

TEST 5B

Passage 7 (Questions 34-38)

The bladder has long been regarded as a transit and storage organ for urine in mammals. Normally, bladder urothelial cells are exposed to an inclement environment for a long time, under conditions such as high osmolality and high urea concentration. Urea is highly concentrated in urine up to more than 1000 mmol/L, representing about 45% of total urinary solutes.

Urea transporters (UT) belong to a family of membrane proteins that selectively transport urea. In mammals, at least seven urea transporters, UT-A1 to UT-A6 and UT-B, have been characterized. UT-B deletion causes urea accumulation in testis and early maturation of the male reproductive system.

Experiment 1

To determine the functional consequence of UT-B deficiency on urothelial cells, scientists examined urea concentrations in UT-B null and wild-type bladder urothelium, also known as the epithelium of the bladder. The results are presented in Figure 1.

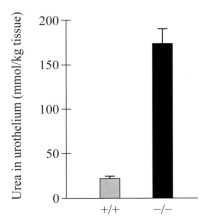

Figure 1 Urine concentration in wildtype (+/+) and UT-B null (−/−) bladder urothelium

Experiment 2

After determining that increased urea concentration induced DNA damage, scientists cultured urothelial cells in media containing urea at the following concentrations: 5, 37.5, 75, 150 or 300 mmol/L and used flow cytometry to detect the stage of the cell cycle each urothelial cell was in. The results are presented in Figure 2.

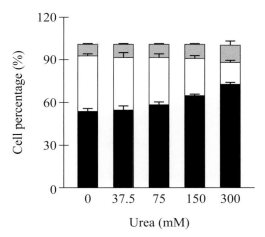

Figure 2 Percentage of cells at various cell stages after exposure to urea

UT-B has been shown to transport urea and urea analogues selectively without carrying ions and sugars, and urea has been shown to induce oxidative stress in several cell types, as evidenced by the appearance of 8-oxoguanine lesions and single-strand breaks in genomic DNA after urea exposure. The scientists concluded that UT-B deficiency could lead to an increase in bladder cancer in susceptible individuals.

This passage is adapted from "Urea Transporter UT-B Deletion Induces DNA Damage and Apoptosis in Mouse Bladder Urothelium." Dong Z, Ran J, Zhou H, Chen J, Lei T, et al. *PLoS ONE.* 2013. 8(10) doi:10.1371/journal.pone.0076952 for use under the terms of the Creative Commons CC BY 3.0 license (http://creativecommons.org/licenses/by/3.0/legalcode).

Question 34

Elimination of stored urine is most likely under the control of:

   I. the parasympathetic nervous system.

   II. the sympathetic nervous system.

   III. the somatic nervous system.

○ **A.** I only

○ **B.** I and III only

○ **C.** II and III only

○ **D.** I, II, and III

Question 35

In a follow-up experiment, scientists measured the concentration of NO in urothelial cells at two concentrations of arginine. The data presented below are most likely to:

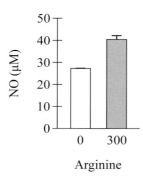

Arginine

- ○ **A.** support the authors' additional conclusion that increased urea increases the risk of bladder cancer.
- ○ **B.** challenge the authors' additional conclusion that UT-B knockout reduced urea concentration in the collecting duct.
- ○ **C.** support the authors' additional conclusion that increased arginine reflects a defect in the urea metabolism pathway.
- ○ **D.** challenge the authors' additional conclusion that decreased free radical content increases the risk of urothelial cancer.

Question 36

In addition to the bladder urothelium, UT-B is most likely to have the highest expression in:

- ○ **A.** the liver.
- ○ **B.** the pancreas.
- ○ **C.** the adrenal gland.
- ○ **D.** cardiac muscle.

Question 37

UT-B deficiency most likely leads to:

- ○ **A.** acidification of the urine stored in the bladder.
- ○ **B.** basification of the urine stored in the bladder.
- ○ **C.** no change in the pH of the urine stored in the bladder.
- ○ **D.** acidification of the urine passing through the ureter to the bladder.

Question 38

Renal reabsorption of urea is most likely to occur to the greatest extent in the:

- ○ **A.** ascending loop of Henle.
- ○ **B.** distal convoluted tubule.
- ○ **C.** proximal convoluted tubule.
- ○ **D.** descending loop of Henle.

Questions 39 - 41 do not refer to a passage and are independent of each other.

Question 39

Mice exposed to decreased levels of artificial sunlight, which lowers vitamin D levels, are likely to have impaired absorption of:

- ○ **A.** Na^+.
- ○ **B.** K^+.
- ○ **C.** PO_4^{3-}.
- ○ **D.** Mg^{2+}.

Question 40

The concentration of urine in the collecting duct:

- ○ **A.** creates the counter-current multiplier and increases urine osmolarity in the presence of ADH.
- ○ **B.** creates the counter-current multiplier and increases urine osmolarity in the absence of ADH.
- ○ **C.** is due to the corticopapillary osmotic gradient.
- ○ **D.** does not occur due to the impermeability of the collecting duct to solutes.

Question 41

Reabsorption of sodium independent of renin activity is most likely:

- ○ **A.** greater in the distal tubule compared to the proximal tubule.
- ○ **B.** greater in the thick ascending loop of Henle compared to the proximal tubule.
- ○ **C.** greater in the proximal tubule compared to the distal tubule.
- ○ **D.** greater in the collecting duct compared to the distal tubule.

STOP. If you finish before time is called, check your work. You may go back to any question in this test.

ANSWERS & EXPLANATIONS for Test 5B can be found on p. 286.

STOP

LECTURE 6

Muscle, Bone and Skin

TEST 6A

Time: 95 minutes
Questions 1–59

DIRECTIONS: Most of the questions in this test section are grouped with a passage. Read the passage, then select the best answer to each question. Some questions are independent of any passage and of one another. Select the best answer to each of these questions. If you are unsure of an answer, rule out incorrect choices and select from the remaining options. Indicate your selection beside the option you choose. A periodic table can be found on the last page of this book for you to use at any point during this test section.

Passage 1 (Questions 1-4)

Skeletal muscle has critical physiological functions including energy expenditure, metabolism, and physical strength. Skeletal muscles are divided into two isoforms based on their metabolism: type I fibers are red, with a slower contractile speed and greater fatigue resistance and have greater mitochondrial content, favoring oxidative respiration. On the other hand, type II fibers are white with a faster contractile speed and lower mitochondrial content and more easily become fatigued.

Denervation of peripheral motor nerves results in dysfunction of skeletal muscle contractility. These changes include a rapid loss of muscle mass and mitochondrial function during the first week after denervation. During long-term denervation, skeletal muscle undergoes atrophy resulting from the loss of neural input. Skeletal muscle atrophy is followed by an increase in fibrous and adipose connective tissue and subsequently the loss of muscle function.

The therapeutic treatment of skeletal muscle atrophy with naturally occurring compounds has recently received increasing attention. Pyrroloquinoline quinone (PQQ), a bacterially synthesized quinine, is a strong redox cofactor with multiple biological benefits that may modulate PGC-1α expression and mitochondrial electron transport chain (ETC) complex expression in skeletal muscle following denervation (Figure 1).

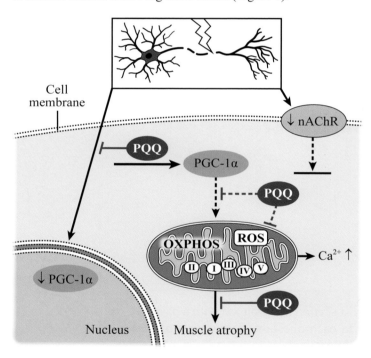

Figure 1 Summary of hindlimb denervation-stimulated signaling transduction leading to skeletal muscle twitch and atrophy and the possible actions of PQQ

Experiment 1

To confirm the role of PGC-1α, scientists transected the neuron to the hindlimb muscle and measured both the cross sectional area of the muscle and the expression of expression PGC-1α 10 days later. The results are shown in Figure 2.

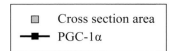
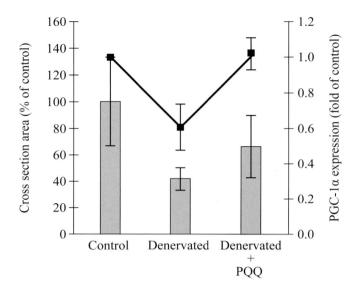

Figure 2 Cross sectional area of the hindlimb muscle and PGC-1α levels following denervation and PQQ treatment

The absence of motor recovery after nerve damage may result from a failure of synapse reformation after prolonged denervation rather than a failure of axonal growth. Many cellular structural alterations have been described after denervation, including changes in the number and size of mitochondria. Scientists speculated that activation of the mitochondrial oxidative phosphorylation (OXPHOS) pathway via PGC-1α may provide an additional avenue for novel treatments in the early stages of muscle denervation.

This passage is adapted from "Pyrroloquinoline Quinone Resists Denervation-Induced Skeletal Muscle Atrophy by Activating PGC-1A and Integrating Mitochondrial Electron Transport Chain Complexes." Kuo Y-T, Shih P-H, Kao S-H, Yeh G-C, and Lee H-M. *PLoS ONE.* 2015. 10(12) doi:10.1371/journal.pone.0143600 for use under the terms of the Creative Commons CC BY 4.0 license (http://creativecommons.org/licenses/by/4.0/legalcode).

Question 1

According to information contained in the passage, skeletal muscle atrophy is most likely caused by:

○ **A.** an increase in reactive oxygen species.

○ **B.** an increase in the acetylcholine released at the neuromuscular synapse.

○ **C.** a decrease in the intracellular sodium concentration that triggers muscle contractions.

○ **D.** demyelination of neurons by Schwann cells.

Question 2

Treatment with which of the following drugs would be LEAST likely to help reverse the early effects of muscle denervation?

    I. Varenicline, a nicotinic receptor agonist

    II. Neostigmine, an acetylcholinesterase inhibitor

    III. Pirenzepine, a muscarinic receptor antagonist

  ○ **A.** I only

  ○ **B.** III only

  ○ **C.** I and II only

  ○ **D.** II and III only

Question 3

Which of the following would be most likely to contain type I muscle fibers?

  ○ **A.** Diaphragm, an abdominal muscle that controls breathing

  ○ **B.** Triceps, an arm muscle than controls elbow extension

  ○ **C.** Biceps, an arm muscle that controls elbow contraction

  ○ **D.** Gluteus maximus, a hip muscle that controls leg extension

Question 4

According to Figure 2:

  ○ **A.** denervated muscle treated with PQQ has a greater fasciculus diameter than denervated muscle.

  ○ **B.** denervated muscle has a greater fiber width than denervated muscle treated with PQQ.

  ○ **C.** control muscle has a smaller myofibril width than denervated muscle.

  ○ **D.** control muscle has a smaller fasciculus diameter than denervated muscle treated with PQQ.

Passage 2 (Questions 5-9)

In skeletal muscle, intracellular Ca^{2+} is an important regulator of contraction as well as gene expression and metabolic processes. Because of the difficulties to obtain intact human muscle fibers, human myotubes have been extensively employed for studies of Ca^{2+}-dependent processes in human adult muscle. Despite this, it is unknown whether the Ca^{2+} handling properties of myotubes adequately represent those of adult muscle fibers.

In intact muscle fibers, electrically evoked action potentials activate the voltage sensitive Ca^{2+} channels (DHPR) in the t-tubules that in turn triggers the opening of the sarcoplasmic reticulum (SR) Ca^{2+} release channel (RyR1), resulting in an increase in Ca^{2+} concentration and force production.

To enable a comparison of the Ca^{2+}-handling properties of human muscle fibers and myotubes, a model was developed of dissected intact single muscle fibers obtained from human intercostal muscle biopsies. The intracellular Ca^{2+}-handling of human muscle fibers was compared with that of myotubes generated by the differentiation of primary human myoblasts obtained from vastus lateralis muscle biopsies. Two experiments were done.

Experiment 1

First, human myotubes and myoblasts were electrically stimulated to see if they would respond with an increase in $[Ca^{2+}]$, and the resultant Ca^{2+} concentrations were compared to those in human muscle fibers. Cells were stimulated electrically with a single 70 Hz, 350 millisecond train of current pulses (Figure 1).

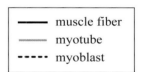

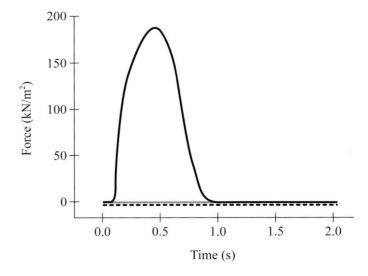

Figure 1 Force production following a single 70 Hz, 350 ms train of current pulses in a human intercostal muscle fiber (solid), myotube (grey) and myoblast (dashed black)

Experiment Two

Second, the mRNA abundance of the slow type skeletal muscle/β-cardiac myosin heavy chain (MHC I), type IIa MHC (MHC IIa), and type IIx MHC (MHC IIx) in human muscle fibers, myotubes, and myoblasts was investigated (Figure 2).

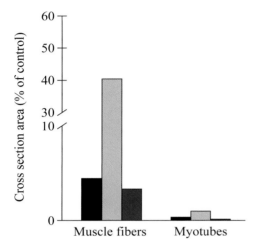

Figure 2 mRNA quantities of MHC I, MHC IIa, MHC IIx in muscle fibers and myotubes

Question 5

Which statement most likely correctly describes a characteristic of the muscle fibers dissected and used in this experiment?

○ **A.** Fibers were primarily white in color due to increased calcium storage

○ **B.** Fibers utilized primarily aerobic respiration and were slow to fatigue

○ **C.** Fibers contain large amounts of myoglobin to allow increased oxygen storage

○ **D.** Fibers contracted at high velocity but were quick to fatigue

Question 6

Which experimental data would NOT display dysfunction in activity of DHPR in the muscle cell?

○ **A.** Quantifying the change in ion concentration inside the sarcolemma

○ **B.** Measuring the rate of release of acetylcholine into the synapse

○ **C.** Quantifying the force generated by the contracting muscle fiber

○ **D.** Measuring the free energy change due to conformational change of cellular troponin

Question 7

What process does the electrical stimulation used in Experiment 1 imitate?

○ **A.** An impulse transmitted to the muscle fiber through release of ACh by the autonomic nervous system

○ **B.** An impulse transmitted to the muscle fiber through release of norepinephrine by the autonomic nervous system

○ **C.** An impulse transmitted to the muscle fiber through release of ACh by the somatic nervous system

○ **D.** An impulse transmitted to the muscle fiber through release of norepinephrine by the somatic nervous system

Question 8

Which of the following additional experiments would most strengthen the hypothesis that calcium handling processes differ between myotubes and muscle fibers?

○ **A.** Quantifying the relative abundance of mitochondria in the cells

○ **B.** Immunofluorescence staining used to display localization and arrangements of transmembrane proteins in the presynaptic neuron

○ **C.** Transmission electron micrographs displaying the presence or absence of ultrastructural arrangements like A and I bands

○ **D.** Measurement of the relative mRNA expression of the proteins associated with the thin filament of sarcomere

Question 9

The following additional graphs are given to display the localization of the proteins RyR and DHPR in muscle fibers (top) and myotubes (bottom). Which property of skeletal muscle do the following graphs suggest that myotubes lack?

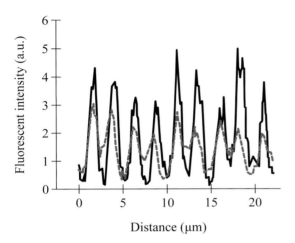

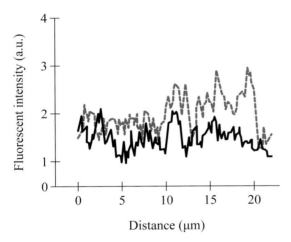

- **A.** Smooth contractile force created by evenly dispersed Ca^{2+} protein channels
- **B.** A regular and organized arrangement of proteins creating a striated pattern
- **C.** The repeating pattern of muscle cells separated by intercalated discs
- **D.** Voltage controlled release of calcium upon stimulation by the somatic nervous system

Passage 3 (Questions 10-13)

Loss off function mutations in the in the *dystrophin* gene are known to cause Duchenne's Muscular Dystrophy (DMD), an inherited disorder characterized by skeletal muscle and cardiac pathology. Boys typically present with symptoms of muscle weakness by age five, become wheelchair-bound by early to mid teens, and die from respiratory failure or heart disease in their late teens to early twenties. Women are rarely symptomatic from mutations in the *dystrophin* gene due to its location on the X chromosome.

Dystrophin is an important support protein that connects muscle fibers to a cell's extracellular matrix via protein complexes that span the sarcolemma. Deficiencies in dystrophin coupled with the inability of muscle regeneration to keep pace with destruction in DMD leads to fibrosis, a process that is mediated largely by transforming growth factor beta (TGF-β). Increased TGF-β signaling has been documented in both the mdx mouse and in the Golden Retriever models of DMD.

A recent study demonstrated the antagonism of TGF-β with losartan, an angiotensin II receptor blocker that has been shown to significantly reduce TGF-β activity in a number of disease models. Since losartan is a widely used antihypertensive drug that is considered safe for use in humans, researchers were interested in investigating its therapeutic potential on both the skeletal and cardiac muscle of dystrophic (mdx) mice.

To evaluate the effect of losartan on skeletal and cardiac muscle, researchers randomized male mdx mice to receive either standard drinking water or drinking water supplemented with losartan (0.6 g/L) for two years. At the end of the two year treatment phase, all surviving mice were sacrificed, and the extensor digitorum longus (EDL), soleus, and diaphragm muscles were extracted for mass, length, and maximum tetanic force analysis (Figure 1).

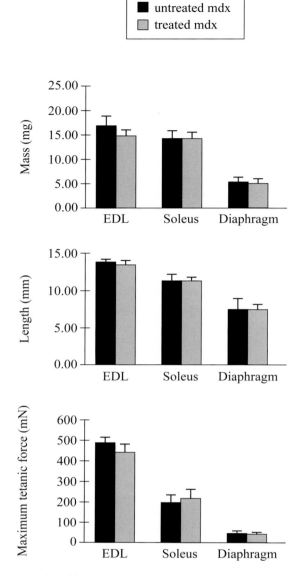

Figure 1 The effects of losartan treatment on the mass, length, and maximum tetanic force of mdx mouse skeletal muscles

Cardiac muscle was assessed via echocardiography (data not shown) and the expression of Nav1.5, a sodium channel, and gap junction protein connexin 40 (Cx40) was analyzed by Western blot (Figure 2). Protein levels of Nav1.5 and Cx40 were compared among untreated and treated mdx mice as well as untreated wild type (WT) mice.

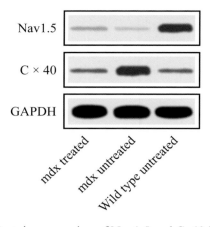

Figure 2 Protein expression of Nav1.5 and Cx40 in the cardiac muscle of treated mdx, untreated mdx, and untreated wild type mice

This passage was adapted from "Chronic Losartan Administration Reduces Mortality and Preserves Cardiac but not Skeletal Muscle Function in Dystrophic Mice." Bish, L T., Yarchoan, M, Sleeper, MM., Gazzara, JA., Morine, KJ., et al. *PLoS ONE*. 2015 6(6) doi:10.1371/journal.pone.0020856 for use under the Creative Commons CC BY 4.0 license (http://creativecommons.org/licenses/by/4.0/legalcode).

Question 10

Which of the following is/are most likely to be true about the EDL based on Figure 1 and the passage?

   I. The EDL produces the greatest force under muscle fatigue.

   II. The EDL has a fast contractile velocity.

   III. The EDL is mostly composed of Type I fibers.

- **A.** II only
- **B.** I and II only
- **C.** I and III only
- **D.** I, II, and III

Question 11

A woman with a mutant copy of the dystrophin gene and a man with DMD have 2 children, a boy and a girl. What is the probability that both children will have DMD?

- **A.** 0%
- **B.** 25%
- **C.** 50%
- **D.** 100%

Question 12

Based on the information in Figure 2, which of the following is most likely to be observed in patients with DMD?

- O **A.** Cardiomyopathy
- O **B.** Muscle weakness
- O **C.** Abnormal heart rhythm
- O **D.** Respiratory distress

Question 13

According to the passage, the dystrophin complex is found in the sarcolemma. Which of the following is another important feature of the sarcolemma?

- O **A.** It is a specialized form of the smooth endoplasmic reticulum.
- O **B.** It is a specialized form of the rough endoplasmic reticulum.
- O **C.** It is the smallest functional unit of the contractile apparatus in skeletal muscle.
- O **D.** It forms invaginations that allow the interior of the muscle cell to be depolarized.

Questions 14 - 17 do not refer to a passage and are independent of each other.

Question 14

Scientists discover a poison that blocks norepinephrine release from the presynaptic neuron. Which of the following processes would be negatively affected by this poison?

- O **A.** Increasing heart rate
- O **B.** Peristalsis of the esophagus
- O **C.** Contracting of the biceps
- O **D.** Relaxing diaphragm

Question 15

Which of the following exercises could be used to measure isometric strength of a muscle?

- O **A.** Leg press against a large amount of weight that cannot be overcome
- O **B.** Pushups to failure
- O **C.** Maximum weight biceps curl
- O **D.** Maximum weight bench press

Question 16

A separate snake venom, known as an α-neurotoxin, competitively inhibits the ACh receptor on muscle cells. Which of the following tracings most likely represents the voltage of the muscle cell after release of ACh from the motor neuron?

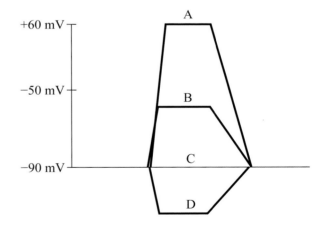

- O **A.** Curve A
- O **B.** Curve B
- O **C.** Curve C
- O **D.** Curve D

Question 17

Which of the following is LEAST likely to impact mobility?

○ **A.** Acetylcholinesterase is dysfunctional

○ **B.** A nonsense mutation occurs in the titin protein

○ **C.** An individual's cells have defective dense bodies

○ **D.** Efferent neurons suffer demyelination

Passage 4 (Questions 18-21)

Myogenic differentiation not only occurs during muscle development, but also during muscle regeneration. Upon acute muscle injury in athletic competitions or automobile accidents resident muscle stem cells, or satellite cells, become activated, proliferate, migrate to the site of damage and fuse with each other and existing myofibers to restore muscle structure. Injured muscle also releases numerous signaling molecules including growth and G-protein coupled receptor ligands. These signals promote regeneration in part by activating quiescent satellite cells and providing homing cues for migrating myoblasts and macrophages.

Many of these signals activate cAMP response element binding protein (CREB), and CREB activity is required for myogenic differentiation during embryogenesis. However, it is still unknown whether CREB activity is dynamically regulated in myoblasts after muscle injury and how CREB contributes to muscle regeneration. Better insight into differentiation may assist in repairing muscles after traumatic injury.

Experiment 1

Scientists hypothesized that CREB phosphorylation was activated in response to skeletal muscle injury and that activated CREB drives myoblast proliferation. To characterize the role of CREB in skeletal muscle regeneration, they injected the snake venom component cardiotoxin into the mouse gastrocnemius muscles. To monitor CREB transcriptional activity, they quantified mRNAs of two direct CREB target genes in muscle cells, *SIK1* and *NR4A2*. Both of these genes have been previously shown to contain consensus CREB binding sites that are occupied by CREB and phospho-CREB in multiple cell types, including C2C12 myoblasts. The results are shown in Figure 1.

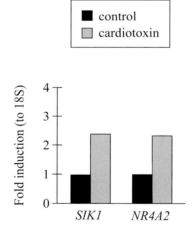

Figure 1 Expression of *SIK1* and *NR4A2* in mouse gastrocnemius after cardiotoxin injection

Experiment 2

In order to assess the *in vivo* effect of CREB activation, scientists used mice that contained a gain-of-function mutation in CREB (CREB-YF). They assessed myoblast proliferation and differentiation, two processes that occur as part of muscle regeneration, and the growth-curve assays of CREB-YF are shown in Figure 2.

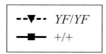

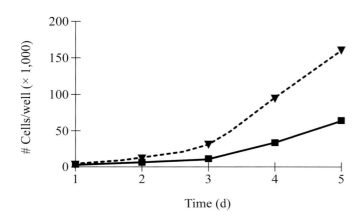

Figure 2 Effect of CREB activation on myoblast proliferation and differentiation

Question 18

Migrating satellite cells are likely to contribute most directly to repairing which organizational unit of skeletal muscle?

    I. Myofibril

    II. Muscle fiber

    III. Muscle fascicle

○ **A.** I only

○ **B.** II only

○ **C.** I and II only

○ **D.** II and III only

Question 19

Muscles with high expression of *SIK1* are likely to:

○ **A.** play a role in skin thermoregulation.

○ **B.** contribute to the return of extracellular fluid to the circulatory system.

○ **C.** assist in the delivery of blood to peripheral tissues.

○ **D.** experience fewer depolarizations at the neuromuscular junction.

Question 20

Injured muscle often distorts the architecture of the cross-sectional T-tubules. After injection with cardiotoxin, the muscle fascicle is:

○ **A.** unlikely to contract evenly across the fascicle width.

○ **B.** more likely to release more calcium from the sarcoplasmic reticulum.

○ **C.** more likely to become tetanic.

○ **D.** unlikely to return to a relaxed state.

Question 21

Sik1 phosphorylates histone acetylases to increase expression of muscle-specific genes, such as actin and myosin. In regenerating muscle, phosphorylated CREB would be expected to increase the density of which of the following structures the most?

○ **A.** M line

○ **B.** A band

○ **C.** Z line

○ **D.** I band

Passage 5 (Questions 22-26)

Conventional endurance (CE) exercise models (e.g., cycle ergometry and treadmill) are commonly used to assess the combined effects of endurance-type exercise and essential amino acid (EAA) supplementation on whole-body and skeletal muscle protein turnover. Protein supplements have been recommended to athletes to enhance nitrogen retention and retain muscle mass, as well as to prevent sports anemia and Delayed Onset Muscle Soreness (DOMS) by promoting an increased synthesis of hemoglobin, myoglobin, and mitochondria during aerobic training. Studies have shown that EAA supplementation spares whole-body protein and enhances skeletal muscle protein synthesis (MPS) in recovery from CE.

However, other studies have failed to observe this effect, and whether the effects of CE and EAA supplementation reflect whole body protein turnover and MPS responses to real-world sporting events, occupational tasks, or exercise training scenarios that include sustained and/or repeated bouts of weighted endurance-type exercise (i.e., load carriage, LC) have not been determined.

Experiment 1

Forty adults were randomly assigned to perform 90 minutes of absolute intensity-matched (2.2 ± 0.1 VO_2 $L \cdot m^{-1}$) LC (performed on a treadmill wearing a vest equal to 30% of individual body mass, mean $\pm$ SD load carried 24 ± 3 kg) or CE (cycle ergometry performed at the same absolute VO_2 as LC) exercise, during which EAA (10 g EAA, 3.6 g leucine) or control (CON) were consumed in four small doses over 90 minutes.

Whole-body protein flux, synthesis, breakdown, oxidation, and net balance were assessed to determine main effects of exercise mode, dietary treatment, and their interactions (Figure 1).

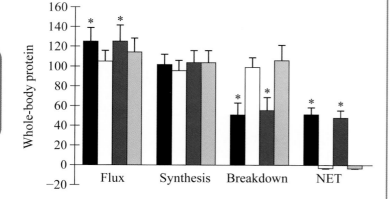

Figure 1 Whole-body protein turnover. Flux, synthesis, breakdown, oxidation, and net protein balance during recovery from 90 min

Experiment 2

Circulating plasma surrogates of muscle damage were assessed in participants at baseline and 195 min post-exercise, including creatine kinase (CK). CK catalyzes the reaction of creatine and ATP into phosphocreatine and ADP (Table 1).

Table 1 Effects of Load Carriage, Conventional Endurance Exercise, and Essential Amino Acid Supplementation on Surrogate Markers of Muscle Damage During Recovery (*Different from baseline within mode)

Creatine kinase	Baseline	195 minutes post exercise (PE)
LC-EAA	202.1 ± 15.7	272.0 ± 8.5*
LC-CON	209.7 ± 19.7	269.1 ± 16.2*
CE-EAA	175.0 ± 16.9	248.1 ± 16.9*
CE-CON	178.5 ± 12.2	275.2 ± 19.5*

Question 22

Researchers add periodic sprints to the CE exercise regimen. In comparison to weight lifting, muscle groups recruited during the sprinting period:

- **A.** appeared red in color and contracted at faster velocity.
- **B.** appeared white in color and contracted at a slower velocity.
- **C.** appeared red in color and contracted at an equal velocity.
- **D.** appeared white in color and contracted at a faster velocity.

Question 23

What control experiments could be included in Experiment 1 to confirm the conclusions of Figure 1?

I. Assessing LC-CON vs CE-CON's effects on serum cortisol over a 90 minute interval.

II. Assessing breakdown of the compound responsible for arresting muscle contraction in the absence of Ca^{2+} with a non-nutritive drink given at 4 incremental intervals during LC.

III. Assessing net flux in the compound responsible for initiating muscular contraction in the presence or absence of EAA during CE.

- **A.** I only
- **B.** II only
- **C.** II and III only
- **D.** I, II, and III

Question 24

Which other homeostatic processes would be LEAST likely to be affected by skeletal muscle protein breakdown during CE or LC?

○ **A.** increase in blood flow to peripheral tissue.

○ **B.** regulation of body temperature.

○ **C.** movement of chylomicrons to the thoracic duct.

○ **D.** maintenance of pressure in peripheral vasculature.

Question 25

Based on the passage, experimental muscle differs from cardiac muscle in that it:

○ **A.** lacks the ability to alter speed and strength of contraction.

○ **B.** retains the ability to alter the speed of muscular contraction.

○ **C.** will cease to contract with a removal of outside stimuli.

○ **D.** can increase in strength and size due to repeated contraction.

Question 26

Researchers measured the effect of exercise and diet on protein synthesis in mixed muscle groups. (*EAA different than CON, p < 0.05. † LC different than CE, p < 0.05.)

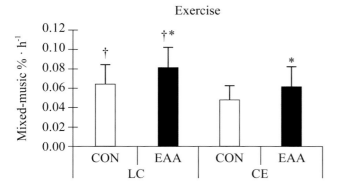

Based on their findings, LC exercise including EAA supplementation:

○ **A.** increases contractile strength of experimental muscle when compared to CON.

○ **B.** decreases contractile strength of experimental muscle when compared to CON.

○ **C.** decreases susceptibility of experimental muscle to fatigue when compared with CE.

○ **D.** increases susceptibility of experimental muscle to fatigue when compared with CE.

Questions 27 - 30 do not refer to a passage and are independent of each other.

Question 27

Myasthenia gravis is a disease in which the immune system attacks and destroys the neurotransmitter receptor proteins on the sarcolemma, resulting in muscle weakness. Which of the following methods of treatment would be LEAST effective in reducing the symptoms of the disease?

○ **A.** A drug suppressing the production of antibodies

○ **B.** A drug inhibiting the reuptake of ACh molecules into the presynaptic neuron

○ **C.** A drug upregulating the production of membrane proteins

○ **D.** A drug promoting the breakdown of synaptic ACh into fragment molecules

Question 28

The primary source of energy used to generate prolonged muscle contractions is generated by:

○ **A.** gluconeogenesis.

○ **B.** ketolysis.

○ **C.** glycolysis.

○ **D.** oxidative phosphorylation.

Question 29

Following exercise, which of the following physiological responses would be required for a return to homeostasis?

○ **A.** A drop in respiratory rate due to muscles no longer undergoing elevated oxidative phosphorylation

○ **B.** Free radicals build up in the blood and are removed through exhalation

○ **C.** An increase in respiratory rate due to buildup of carbon monoxide in the blood

○ **D.** The liver requires more oxygen to restore homeostasis

Question 30

Type I fibers may contract more slowly due to a decrease in velocity of the action potential in peripheral nerves. Which of the following best explains this finding?

○ **A.** Nerves to type I fibers have fewer associated oligodendrocytes.

○ **B.** Dendrites of the nerves to type I fibers have fewer sodium channels.

○ **C.** Nerves to type I fibers have fewer associated Schwann cells.

○ **D.** Axon terminals of the nerves to type I fibers have more ACh stored in intracellular vesicles.

Passage 6 (Questions 31-35)

Multiple sclerosis (MS) is characterized by complex and heterogeneous symptoms, often leading to reduced quality of life and impaired functional capacity. The latter is related to reduced muscle strength of predominantly the lower limbs. The mechanisms underlying the observed strength deficits are of muscular as well as neural origin.

Neurologically, central impairments of the central motor function are reported. At present, it remains unknown whether the reported observations are consequences of the disease per se, are caused by inactivity or are affected by a combination of both. At the cellular level the impact of MS on muscle fiber cross-sectional area (CSA) and muscle fiber proportion remains conflicting. To clarify the heterogeneous results of the existing literature in small groups of MS patients, the researchers aimed to investigate the effect of MS on muscle fiber CSA and proportion, muscle strength and body composition in a larger group of MS patients, compared with healthy controls (HC). It was hypothesized that MS would negatively affect skeletal muscle characteristics.

Researchers found that cross-sectional area of multiple types of muscle fibers was reduced. This was most pronounced in type I fibers. MS seems to negatively influence skeletal muscle fiber CSA, muscle strength and muscle mass of the lower limbs of mildly affected MS patients. These results emphasize the need for rehabilitation programs focusing on muscle preservation of the lower limb.

Table 1 Body and Muscle Characteristics

	Healthy controls	MS patients
Total fat mass (kg)	26.1	26.4
Total lean tissue (kg)	47.9	46.2
Bone density (Z-score)	0.2	–2.4
Isometric muscle strength (Nm)	140	108
Muscle fiber CSA (μm^2)	4621	3827

Question 31

Which of the following is the most likely cause of the change in bone density observed in MS patients?

- **A.** High calcitonin levels
- **B.** High blood calcium
- **C.** Vitamin D deficiency
- **D.** Increased amount of spongy bone

Question 32

Based on the results presented in Table 1, which of the following statements is most likely to be true?

- **A.** The fat and lean mass in the lower limbs of MS patients is similar to that of HCs.
- **B.** Decreased muscle mass leads to an increased in adipose tissue.
- **C.** All striated muscle cells are reduced in size.
- **D.** Exercises involving repetitive, forceful contractions could counteract some of the effects of MS.

Question 33

MS results in demyelination of the central nervous system. Which of the following is most likely to be an effect of this change?

- **A.** Reduced nerve conduction velocity due to increased saltatory conduction
- **B.** Reduced nerve conduction velocity due to decreased saltatory conduction
- **C.** Increased nerve conduction velocity due to increased saltatory conduction
- **D.** Increased nerve conduction velocity due to decreased saltatory conduction

Question 34

According to the study, performance of which of the following tasks would be most impaired in a person with MS?

- **A.** Swimming
- **B.** Weight lifting
- **C.** Sprinting
- **D.** Long distance bike racing

Question 35

Which of the following could explain the change in CSA in muscle fibers of MS patients?

  I. Reduced cell division
  II. Reduced actin synthesis
  III. Reduced H zone length

- **A.** I only
- **B.** II only
- **C.** I and II only
- **D.** II and III only

Passage 7 (Questions 36–39)

Human temperature is regulated within a very narrow range. When exposed to hyperthermic conditions, heat dissipation becomes vital for survival. During exercise, the primary mechanism of heat dissipation is evaporative heat loss secondary to sweat secretion from eccrine glands.

Studies have shown that physically trained athletes have enhanced capacity for sweat production as well as lowered skin surface temperature, which provide a certain physiological advantage when physical exercise is performed under extremely hot conditions.

The quantitative sudomotor axon reflex test (QSART) is a useful method for evaluating postganglionic sympathetic C fiber function. Iontophoresed acetylcholine (ACh) evokes a measurable and reliable sweat response that has been used to measure autonomic responses. Iontophoresis is a method of administering a drug through the skin without using an injection by an applied electric field. The QSART capsule allows for accurate quantification of directly activated (DIR, muscarinic receptor) and axon reflex-mediated (AXR, nicotinic receptor) sweat responses.

Thirty six subjects, including 20 sedentary controls and 16 long-distance runners were observed. Upon arrival at the climate chamber set to room temperature (25°C), each subject changed into light clothing and rested quietly for 1 hour. The drug solution 10% ACh was iontophoresed through the skin for 5 min at 2 mA constant current. Sweat output was calculated as the area under the curve 0–5 min AXR1, 6–11 min AXR2, 6–11 min (DIR) and expressed as mg/cm^2. The time lapse before onset of the AXR1 sweat response was measured as a response latency in minutes. VO$_2$ max, a measure of cardiovascular fitness, was determined while cycling (Figure 1).

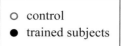

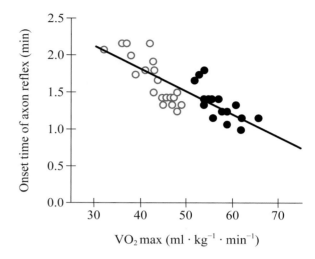

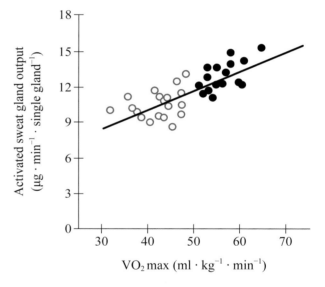

Figure 1 Correlation between VO$_2$ max and AXR1 sweat onset time and activated sweat gland output in the control subjects (white circles) and trained subjects (black circles)

This passage was adapted from "Long Distance Runners Present Upregulated Sweating Responses than Sedentary Counterparts." Lee J-B, Kim T-W, Min Y-K, Yang H-M. *PLoS ONE*. 2014. 9(4) doi:10.1371/journal.pone.0093976 for use under the terms of the Creative Commons CC BY 4.0 License (https://creativecommons.org/licenses/by/4.0/legalcode).

Question 36

Which of the following might also contribute to the lower skin temperature of endurance athletes?

    I. Dilated peripheral vasculature

    II. Stronger skeletal muscle

    III. Contracted hair erectile musculature

○ **A.** I only

○ **B.** I and II only

○ **C.** II and III only

○ **D.** III only

Question 37

Which of the following conclusions can be best interpreted from Figure 1?

○ **A.** Those with larger involuntary muscles produced more sweat than those with smaller involuntary muscles.

○ **B.** Those with larger involuntary muscle produced less sweat than those with smaller involuntary muscles.

○ **C.** Those with more voluntary muscle had a slower AXR1 than those with less voluntary muscle.

○ **D.** Those with more voluntary muscle had a faster AXR1 than those with less voluntary muscle.

Question 38

Why was ACh iontophoresed rather than applied topically to the surface of the skin?

○ **A.** Keratin in the dermis would have been unaffected by the neurotransmitter.

○ **B.** Nerve endings in the base of the epidermis would have interfered with the experiment.

○ **C.** Blood vessels responsible for maintaining cool skin temperature are in the dermis.

○ **D.** Eccrine glands are not found in the layers of the epidermis.

Question 39

Which layer of the skin does the QSART primarily stimulate?

○ **A.** Stratum corneum

○ **B.** Stratum spinosum

○ **C.** Dermis

○ **D.** Hypodermis

Passage 8 (Questions 40-43)

Myotonia refers to impaired muscle relaxation following a voluntary forceful contraction. It is found in several clinical disorders with different etiologies. Myotonic dystrophy type 1 (DM1) is the most common form of muscular dystrophy in adults, caused by an expansion of an unstable $(CTG)_n$ triplet repetition on chromosome 19 in the 3′ untranslated region (3′-UTR) of the gene encoding for myotonic dystrophy protein kinase (DMPK). It is an autosomal dominant inherited disorder with a peculiar and rare pattern of multisystemic clinical features, affecting skeletal muscles, heart, eyes, endocrine and central nervous systems.

Another myotonic disorder is Congenital Myotonia (CM), caused by a mutation in the skeletal muscle chloride channel ClCN1 that leads to reduced sarcolemmal chloride conductance from the interior to the exterior of the muscle cell.

DM1 patients often present with the abnormal presence of small conductance Ca-activated apamin-sensitive K^+ channels (SK3) in the muscle. These voltage independent channels are found to underlie the long lasting after-hyperpolarization (AHP) following the action potential in muscle cells. SK3 channels are abnormally expressed in DM1 muscle but not in CM muscle. Recently, a study in rats showed that chronic Neuromuscular Electrical Stimulation (NMES) of denervated soleus muscles down-regulates SK3 channels.

This passage was adapted from "Chronic Muscle Stimulation Improves Muscle Function and Reverts the Abnormal Surface EMG Pattern in Myotonic Dystrophy: A Pilot Study." Chisari C, Bertolucci F, Dalise S, and Rossi B. *Journal of NeuroEngineering and Rehabilitation*. 2013. 10(94) doi 10.1186/1743-0003-10-94 under the terms of the Creative Commons CC BY License 3.0 (http://creativecommons.org/licenses/by/3.0).

Question 40

Which experiment would best support the proposed mechanism by which NMES affects DM1 and CM patients?

○ **A.** Keep NEMS constant and measure the concentration of ClCN1 in increasing concentrations of calcium in the presence and absence of SK3.

○ **B.** Keep SK3 and ClCN1 constant and measure the length of time for sarcoplasmic reticulum (SR) reuptake of calcium at increasing frequencies of NEMS.

○ **C.** Measure the amount of NEMS used with increasing ClCN1, comparing between length of time for reuptake of calcium in the presence and absence of SK3.

○ **D.** Measure the length of time for reuptake of calcium to the SR with increasing use of NMES, comparing between patients with SK3 and ClCN1.

Question 41

Which of the following fails to occur in muscular myotonia?

○ **A.** SR release of calcium ions

○ **B.** SR reuptake of calcium ions

○ **C.** Mitochondrial production of ATP

○ **D.** Mitochondrial breakdown of ATP

Question 42

The use of NEMS mimics what physiological process?

○ **A.** An impulse begins in dendrites forming ganglia outside the spinal cord, passing to the axon terminals and releasing NE to the muscle.

○ **B.** An impulse begins in axon terminals forming ganglia outside the spinal cord, passing to the dendrites and releasing NE to the muscle.

○ **C.** An impulse begins in dendrites forming nuclei in the spinal cord, passing to the axon terminals and releasing ACh to the muscle.

○ **D.** An impulse begins in axon terminals forming nuclei in the spinal cord, to the dendrites and releasing ACh to the muscle.

Question 43

Researchers measured changes in function of cardiac tissue of DM1 patients. Which of the following is/are the most likely result(s) of this experiment?

  I. SK3 counteracts the effect of preexisting voltage-gated calcium channels

  II. SK3 exacerbates the effect of preexisting voltage-gated calcium channels

  III. The patient's heart is able to beat much faster than a healthy individual.

○ **A.** I only

○ **B.** I and III only

○ **C.** I, II, and III

○ **D.** II only

Questions 44 - 47 do not refer to a passage and are independent of each other.

Question 44

When comparing the muscles of a weightlifter and a long distance runner, which of the following differences would be expected?

○ **A.** The long distance runner will have more smooth muscle.

○ **B.** The long distance runner will have more type IIb fibers, while the weightlifter will have more type I fibers.

○ **C.** The weightlifter will have more type I and type IIb fibers.

○ **D.** The weightlifter will have more type IIb fibers, while the long distance runner will have more type I fibers.

Question 45

When observed under a microscope, centrally clustered myocyte nuclei indicate disease and peripherally scattered nuclei indicate good health. Could researchers use a measure of centrally located nuclei to characterize myocyte fibrosis in a study that tests only involuntary muscles?

○ **A.** Yes, because all involuntary muscle cells have single nuclei.

○ **B.** Yes, because all involuntary muscle cells have multiple nuclei.

○ **C.** No, because all involuntary muscle cells have single nuclei.

○ **D.** No, because all involuntary muscle cells have multiple nuclei.

Question 46

The joints in between phalanges are best described as:

○ **A.** Fibrous

○ **B.** Synovial

○ **C.** Cartilaginous

○ **D.** Ball and socket

Question 47

Osteoblasts are likely to differentiate from:

○ **A.** osteocytes.

○ **B.** erythrocytes.

○ **C.** leukocytes.

○ **D.** osteoprogenitor cells.

Passage 9 (Questions 48-52)

Adriamycin (doxorubicin) is an effective anti-cancer drug of which use is limited by the development of a dose-dependent cardiomyopathy and congestive heart failure. Cardiac tissue from animals and patients treated with doxorubicin are histologically characterized by swelling of the sarcoplasmic reticulum and mitochondria, cytoplasmic vacuolization, and widespread loss and disarray of sarcomeres.

Cardiac sarcomeres are highly organized structures and maintain a strict stoichiometry of myofilament proteins allowing efficient generation of contractile force. Myofilament stoichiometry, in turn, relies on the coordinated turnover of myofilament proteins that efficiently replaces worn out or damaged myofilament proteins. This equilibrium is presumably regulated by sarcomeric elements able to mechanically "sense" myofilament protein deficits and signals the cardiomyocyte to induce myofilament gene transcription.

Cardiac ankyrin repeat protein (CARP, ANKRD1) is a transcriptional regulatory protein that has been shown to be essential for sarcomere organization and is capable of sensing and relaying a muscle stretch signal to induce gene expression.

Adult rat ventricular myocytes (ARVMs) were isolated from male rats and were plated on laminin-coated culture dishes. To determine the susceptibility of CARP to doxorubicin, ARVMs were incubated at different concentrations of doxorubicin for 24 h and CARP levels analyzed by immunoblot (Figure 1).

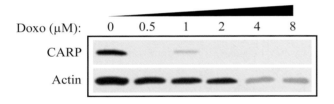

Figure 1 The effect of increasing concentrations of doxorubicin on actin and CARP in AVRMs

In addition, confocal images were taken from ARVMs and co-immunostained with CARP and either α-actinin (Z-line protein) or myomesin (M-line protein) to reveal CARP localization within the sarcomere (Figure 2).

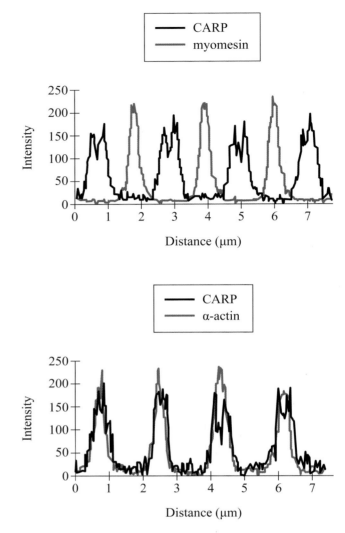

Figure 2 The Sarcomeric localization of CARP in AVRMs

Since GATA4 and CARP regulate sarcomere gene expression and GATA4 is upstream of CARP, researchers examined whether GATA4 overexpression could rescue the doxorobucin-induced sarcomere disarray phenotype. Experimental cells were infected with AdV-GATA4 for 24 h prior to doxorubicin, increasing levels of GATA4 levels (Figure 3).

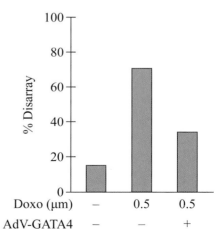

Figure 3 Percent sarcomere disarray in cells treated with doxorubicin and AdV-GATA4

Question 48

Which statement best describes how untreated experimental cardiac tissue synchronizes contractions between groups of cells?

- **A.** Intercalated discs between adjacent cells allow free flow of impulse ions
- **B.** Intercalated discs between adjacent cells allow free flow of signaling hormones
- **C.** Intercalated discs in the sarcoplasmic reticulum allow increased release of calcium
- **D.** Intercalated discs in the presynaptic neuron allow increased uptake of ACh

Question 49

Based on the information in the passage, cardiac ankyrin repeat protein is most likely to be found in which region of the sarcomere?

- **A.** I band
- **B.** H zone
- **C.** A band
- **D.** M line

Question 50

Patients with Duchenne Muscular Dystrophy (DMD) experience many of the same symptoms as those associated with doxorubicin treatment. Based on this statement, which of the following is LEAST likely to be associated with DMD?

- **A.** Decreased muscle strength, ultimately resulting in paralysis
- **B.** Increased susceptibility to muscular fatigue
- **C.** Loss of striation in cardiac muscle tissue
- **D.** Ineffective binding of myosin to actin filaments

Question 51

According to the passage, transcription of which of the following muscular components is LEAST likely to be correlated with cellular concentration of CARP?

- **A.** Thick filament
- **B.** Tropomyosin
- **C.** Thin filament
- **D.** Intermediate filament

Question 52

Which statement best describes how doxorubicin-induced mitochondrial dysfunction might first impact cardiac muscle tissue?

- **A.** Myosin heads are blocked from attachment to actin due to lack of cellular ATP.
- **B.** Myosin heads remain in cocked position due to lack of cellular ATP.
- **C.** Myosin heads remain attached to actin filaments due to lack of cellular ATP.
- **D.** Myosin heads cannot shift to the low energy bent state due lack of cellular ATP.

Passage 10 (Questions 53-56)

TNFα-converting enzyme (TACE) is a membrane-bound proteolytic enzyme with essential roles in the functional regulation of TNFα and epidermal growth factor receptor (EGFR) ligands. Previous studies have demonstrated critical roles for TACE *in vivo*, including epidermal development, immune response, and pathological neoangiogenesis. Complete TACE deficiency in mice was unexpectedly found to be embryonic lethal with defects resembling those found in epidermal growth factor receptor (EGFR)-deficient mice.

To understand the potential contribution of TACE in the skeletal development, scientists generated a mutant line in which TACE was specifically inactivated in chondrocytes by crossing *Tace^{flox/flox}* mice with a transgenic line in which the transcription of *cre* was driven by a chondrocyte-specific *COL2A1* promoter (*T/Col2* mice) (Figure 1).

A.

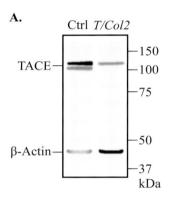

B.

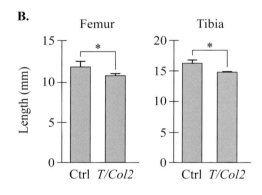

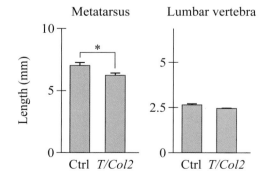

Figure 1 (A) Western blot analysis of TACE and β-Actin in primary chondrocytes in control (Ctrl) and *T/Col2* mutants. (B) Comparison of bone length at 8 weeks (adult)

Histological analyses revealed that *T/Col2* mice exhibited a longer hypertrophic zone in the growth plate during development. It was assessed whether the phenotype in the growth plate was derived from a decrease in chondrocyte proliferation in the *T/Col2* mice via 5-bromodeoxyuridine (BrdU) labeling (Figure 2).

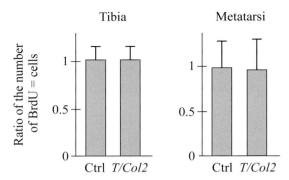

Figure 2 The ratio of the number of BrdU-positive chondrocytes in the proliferating zone of the tibia and metatarsus in Control and *T/Col2* mice

Scientists then stained the sections for tartrate-resistant acid phosphatase (TRAP), an osteoclast marker. Expression of genes involved in osteoclast activation and development in cartilage tissues lacking TACE were next examined, specifically *RANKL*, *OPG*, and *MMP13*. *RANKL* is an upregulator of osteoclastogenesis, *OPG* is a potent inhibitor of *RANKL*, and *MMP13* is a critical enzyme for cartilage matrix degradation during postnatal growth (Figure 3).

A.

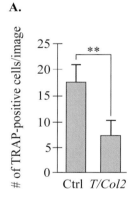

B.

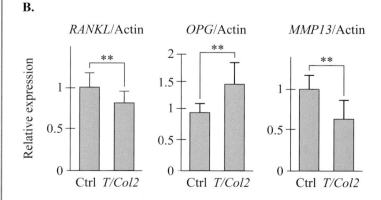

Figure 3 (A) The number of TRAP-positive cells at 3 weeks (B) Quantitative analysis of the levels of *RANKL*, *OPG*, and *MMP13* transcripts in the cartilage tissues

Further experimental data demonstrated that the TACE-EGFR pathway in chondrocytes regulates *RANKL*, *OPG*, and *MMP13* expression. The scientists concluded that abnormalities in this pathway are responsible for the skeletal defects observed.

This passage was adapted from "Conditional Inactivation of TNFα-Converting Enzyme in Chondrocytes Results in an Elongated Growth Plate and Shorter Long Bones." Saito K, Horiuchi K, Kimura T, Mzuno S, Yoda M, et al. *PLoS ONE*. 2013. 8(1) doi: 10.1371/journal.pone.0054853 for use under the terms of the Creative Commons CC BY 3.0 license (https://creativecommons.org/licenses/by/3.0/legalcode).

Question 53

Which of the following hormones would be the best to administer therapeutically to counteract the observed effect on the growth plate in *T/Col2* mice?

- **A.** PTH
- **B.** TSH
- **C.** Calcitonin
- **D.** Vitamin D

Question 54

What is the greatest absolute magnitude of change that would be expected to be seen at 10 weeks in *T/Col2* mice?

- **A.** Increase in metatarsis length
- **B.** Decrease in metatarsis length
- **C.** Decrease in humerus length
- **D.** Decrease in vertebral column length

Question 55

What is the most evident cause for elongation of the hypertrophic zone?

- **A.** Decreased number of osteoclasts
- **B.** Decreased activity of osteoclasts
- **C.** Increased activity of osteoblasts
- **D.** Decreased chondrocyte proliferation

Question 56

What additional information would most strengthen the scientists' final conclusion?

- **A.** TACE conditionally disrupted in monocytes produced mice with lengthened growth plates and reduced femur, tibia, and metatarsus length.
- **B.** EGFR knockout mice had lengthened growth plates and reduced femur, tibia, and metatarsus length.
- **C.** TACE knockout mice when compared to *T/Col2* mice produced mice with greater than 15% reduced femur, tibia, and metatarsus length.
- **D.** EGFR conditionally disrupted in macrophages produced mice with normal length growth plates and normal femur, tibia, and metatarsus length.

Questions 57 - 59 do not refer to a passage and are independent of each other.

Question 57

Elongation of bone that occurs during puberty is supported by which of the following glands?

- **A.** Hypothalamus
- **B.** Adrenal gland
- **C.** Thyroid gland
- **D.** Parathyroid gland

Question 58

Ewing's sarcoma is a type of bone cancer that often begins in the flat bones. With continued tumor growth and damage of its primary site, which of the following organs would be more likely to be affected?

- **A.** Pancreas
- **B.** Small intestines
- **C.** Heart
- **D.** Lungs

Question 59

Extended periods of starvation are most likely to:

- **A.** increase gluconeogenesis occurring in the yellow marrow of the bone.
- **B.** increase lipolysis occurring in the yellow marrow of the bone.
- **C.** decrease gluconeogenesis occurring in the yellow marrow of the bone.
- **D.** decrease glycogenolysis occurring in the yellow marrow of the bone.

STOP. If you finish before time is called, check your work. You may go back to any question in this test.

ANSWERS & EXPLANATIONS for Test 6A can be found on p. 310.

TEST 6A

LECTURE

6

Muscle, Bone and Skin

MINI-TEST 6B

Time: 65 minutes
Questions 1–41

DIRECTIONS: Most of the questions in this test section are grouped with a passage. Read the passage, then select the best answer to each question. Some questions are independent of any passage and of one another. Select the best answer to each of these questions. If you are unsure of an answer, rule out incorrect choices and select from the remaining options. Indicate your selection beside the option you choose. A periodic table can be found on the last page of this book for you to use at any point during this test section.

Passage 1 (Questions 1-5)

Fibroblast growth factor (FGF) and Wnt/β-catenin signaling play crucial roles during skeletal development. Mutations in human fibroblast growth factor receptor (FGFR) or mutations that render β-catenin constitutively active all cause skeletal defects consistent with a role in osteoblast differentiation and functioning. These defects are among the most common cause of inherited skeletal defects worldwide.

The bony skeleton initially develops either by ossification of a cartilage template (chondral ossification) or in the absence of a cartilage template (achondral ossification). During chondral bone development, osteoblasts differentiate in the perichondrium. Genetic analysis has identified a transcription factor Osx that acts in a transcriptional cascade during osteoblast differentiation (Figure 1). Osx levels are predicted to be regulated by FGF and Wnt/β-catenin pathways.

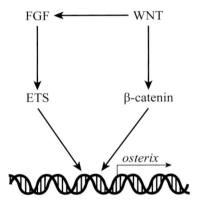

Figure 1 FGF and Wnt/β-Catenin signaling pathways interact to regulate osx transcription

Using zebrafish, an organism that closely recapitulates the bone formation in humans, scientists investigated whether FGF and Wnt/β-Catenin pathways act on osteoblast precursors to promote bone formation in the developing facial skeleton by regulating Osx. Three groups of zebrafish were used. The first group was treated with SU5402, an inhibitor of Wnt, while the second group expressed a dominant negative form of FGFR, meaning that the expressed protein antagonizes the activity of the wild type FGFR. The third group overexpressed wild type FGF. In each of the conditions, the expression of Osx was measured by PCR. The results are shown in Figure 2.

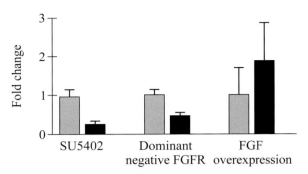

Figure 2 Effect of FGF and Wnt signaling on the expression of Osx

This passage is adapted from "Expression of *osterix* Is Regulated By FGF and Wnt/β-Catenin Signalling during Osteoblast Differentiation." Felber K, Elks P, Lecca M, and Roehl H. *PLoS ONE*. 2015. 10(12) doi:10.1371/journal.pone.0144982 for use under the terms of the Creative Commons CC BY 4.0 license (http://creativecommons.org/licenses/by/4.0/legalcode).

Question 1

Stimulation of which of the following glands is likely to oppose osteoblast activity?

○ **A.** Parathyroid gland

○ **B.** Thyroid gland

○ **C.** Adrenal gland

○ **D.** Pineal gland

Question 2

Overexpression of fibroblast growth factor in zebrafish is likely to increase the absorption of which of the following ions?

   I. Ca^{2+}

   II. PO_4^{3-}

   III. Mg^{2+}

○ **A.** I only

○ **B.** III only

○ **C.** I and II only

○ **D.** II and III only

Question 3

A frameshift mutation in Wnt in the second codon of exon one would most likely decrease the bone marrow concentration of which of the following cells?

○ **A.** Erythrocytes

○ **B.** Osteoclasts

○ **C.** Osteoprogenitor cells

○ **D.** Osteocytes

Question 4

Which of the following is LEAST likely to directly connect to chondral bone?

    I. Ligament

    II. Tendon

    III. Muscle

○ **A.** I only

○ **B.** III only

○ **C.** I and II only

○ **D.** II and III only

Question 5

In an additional experiment, scientists treated zebrafish with an agonist of FGFR. The experimental zebrafish were likely to show:

○ **A.** increased cranial bone density.

○ **B.** decreased skeletal bone density.

○ **C.** an increased number of bones.

○ **D.** a decreased number of bones.

Passage 2 (Questions 6-10)

Multiple myeloma (MM), a hematologic malignancy of terminally differentiated plasma cells, is closely associated with induction of osteolytic bone disease and skeletal complications. Osteolysis is localized to areas adjacent to tumor growth and is often characterized by increased activity of osteoclasts and suppression of osteoblastogenesis. Current standard management of MM bone disease is limited to the use of bisphosphonates.

While osteoclasts have been shown to promote myeloma cell survival and to protect the cells from spontaneous and drug-induced apoptosis, osteoblasts suppress myeloma cell growth and interfere with osteoclasts' stimulatory effects on myeloma cells. Treating MM with osteoblast-activating agents could simultaneously help control bone disease and myeloma cell growth.

Parathyroid hormone (PTH), when given intermittently, can prevent and reverse bone loss in osteoporotic animals and humans. It has been suggested that PTH promotes bone formation primarily by modulating Wnt signaling in bone cells. Researchers used severe combined immune deficiency (SCID) mouse models to study MM. These mice lack functional immune systems, and were implanted with a human femur into which primary human myeloma cells were injected. To investigate the effects of PTH on MM bone disease, researchers treated these SCID mice with daily PTH and measured resulting bone density (Figure 1).

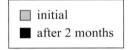

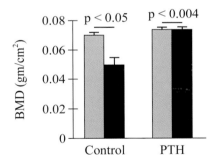

Figure 1 Bone mineral density (BMD) in a model of MM following PTH treatment

Question 6

Bisphosphonates are administered as one of the standard treatments of osteolysis. Which of the following is a possible effect of bisphosphonates?

    I. Decrease in bone density of jaw

    II. Stimulating osteoclast apoptosis

    III. Increased intestinal absorption of calcium

- ○ **A.** I only
- ○ **B.** II only
- ○ **C.** I and II only
- ○ **D.** II and III only

Question 7

Which of the following statements is supported by the results of Figure 1?

    I. PTH leads to maintenance of BMD over a 2 month period.

    II. Wnt signaling can activate osteoblasts.

    III. PTH causes BMD levels to increase over a 2 month period.

- ○ **A.** I only
- ○ **B.** II only
- ○ **C.** III only
- ○ **D.** I and II only

Question 8

MM often reduces the amount of functional red bone marrow due to an overgrowth of cancerous cells. Which of the following statements best describes the potential effects of this reduction in marrow?

    I. Anemia

    II. Reduced fat storage

    III. Breakdown of spongy bone

- ○ **A.** I only
- ○ **B.** II only
- ○ **C.** I and II only
- ○ **D.** II and III only

Question 9

Researchers tested various types of transplanted bones in order to grow the tumor. What type of bone did they eventually use in the experiment?

- ○ **A.** Flat
- ○ **B.** Short
- ○ **C.** Irregular
- ○ **D.** Long

Question 10

Bone cell activity is heavily dysregulated in MM. Which of the following is the best mechanism by which researchers could generate a population of cells to improve the condition of an MM patient?

- ○ **A.** Increase mitosis of osteoblasts
- ○ **B.** Increase mitosis of osteoclasts
- ○ **C.** Increase differentiation of osteoprogenitors
- ○ **D.** Decrease differentiation of osteoprogenitors

Questions 11 - 13 do not refer to a passage and are independent of each other.

Question 11

Based on the data in the following figure, increasing the dose of erythropoietin (Epo) is most likely to:

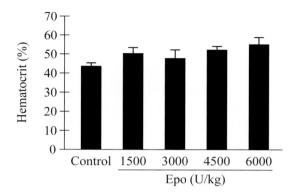

○ **A.** increase the volume of red blood cells per mL of blood.

○ **B.** decrease the volume of red blood cells per mL of blood.

○ **C.** increase the volume of platelets per mL of blood.

○ **D.** increase the volume of lymphocytes per mL of blood.

Question 12

Pachyonychia Congenita, a rare genetic disorder, features overexpression of the gene for the protein keratin. Which symptom is least likely associated with this disorder?

○ **A.** Thickening of the nail

○ **B.** Abnormally fast hair growth

○ **C.** Decreased thermal insulation

○ **D.** Decreased skin permeability to water

Question 13

Human bodies utilize endoskeletons instead of exoskeletons in order to:

○ **A.** better accommodate gradual physical growth.

○ **B.** completely protect internal soft tissue and organs.

○ **C.** regrow skeletal structure periodically to avoid damage.

○ **D.** provide structural support to the body.

Passage 3 (Questions 14-18)

The enhanced production of hematopoietic marrow has long been known to be associated with the conversion of fatty marrow to hematopoietic marrow at the expense of bone. This occurs particularly in the appendicular skeleton, and is associated with accelerated bone resorption observed in chronically bled animals. Similar findings may be responsible for progression of osteoporosis in postmenopausal women where chronic menstrual bleeding may persist for up to 35 years.

It has been demonstrated that blood loss, a condition that stimulates hematopoietic stem cells (HSCs), may also activate osteoprogenitor cells in the bone marrow to form bone. However, the mechanisms induced by direct marrow injury and bleeding to stimulate bone formation remain unclear. Blood loss can be quantified by hematocrit which is the volume percentage of red blood cells in the blood. Dilute blood would have a low hematocrit whereas concentrated blood has an elevated hematocrit.

Although erythropoietin (Epo) is best known for its role as a hematopoietic hormone, recent findings suggest that Epo receptors (EpoR) are expressed in non-hematopoietic tissues like endothelial cells and neurons. Scientists suspected that Epo was responsible for the increased bone formation seen after an acute bleed.

Experiment 1

To determine if the serum levels of Epo are able to increase during the same time frame that HSC activation occurs, animals were bled and 3 days later serum was collected. Additionally, saline solution and parathyroid hormone (PTH) were injected into two other animal groups, and 3 days later serum was collected. The Epo levels are shown in Figure 1.

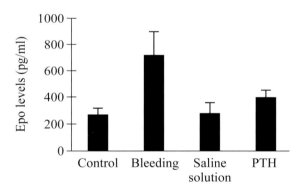

Figure 1 Epo levels in experimental animal cohorts

Experiment 2

To determine if Epo is able to signal through EpoR in HSCs, cells were cultured for 12 hours *in vitro* in the presence or absence of Epo. A western blot was done for EpoR expression, as well as two downstream targets of EpoR, phospho-Jak2 and phospho-Stat3. The results are shown in Figure 2.

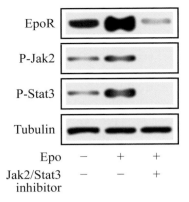

Figure 2 Western blot for EpoR, P-Jak2, and P-Stat3 in cultured HSCs

This passage is adapted from "Erythropoietin Couples Hematopoiesis with Bone Formation." Shiozawa Y, Jung Y, Ziegler A, Pedersen E, Wang J, et al. *PLoS ONE.* 2010. 5(5) doi:10.1371/journal.pone.0010853 for use under the terms of the Creative Commons CC BY 3.0 license (http://creativecommons.org/licenses/by/4.0/legalcode).

Question 14

Compared to mice treated with saline solution in Experiment 1, mice treated with PTH would be expected to have:

○ **A.** decreased bone density and increased hematocrit.

○ **B.** increased bone density and increased hematocrit.

○ **C.** increased bone density and decreased hematocrit.

○ **D.** decreased bone density and decreased hematocrit.

Question 15

According to information contained in the passage, animals that experience chronic blood loss are likely to have:

○ **A.** reduced red marrow and increased yellow marrow compared to control animals.

○ **B.** reduced red marrow and reduced yellow marrow compared to control animals.

○ **C.** increased red marrow and reduced yellow marrow compared to control animals.

○ **D.** increased red marrow and increased yellow marrow compared to control animals.

Question 16

In an additional experiment, scientists quantified the number of osteoblasts when mice were exposed to Epo or RANKL, a molecule known to stimulate osteoclast proliferation.

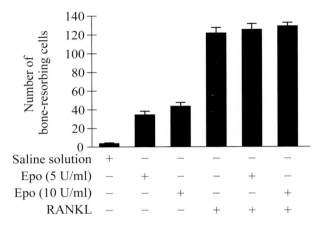

Compared to RANKL, Epo:

○ **A.** does not induce proliferation of osteoclasts.

○ **B.** induces less proliferation of osteoclasts, in a dose-dependent manner.

○ **C.** induces less proliferation of osteoclasts, in a dose-independent manner.

○ **D.** induces more proliferation of osteoblasts, in a dose-dependent manner.

Question 17

Blood loss is most likely to increase the differentiation of:

○ **A.** osteoprogenitor cells into osteoblasts.

○ **B.** osteoprogenitor cells into osteoclasts.

○ **C.** osteocytes into osteoblasts.

○ **D.** osteoblasts into osteoclasts.

Question 18

In order to measure the expression changes of *EPO*, the erythropoietin gene, scientists would most likely:

○ **A.** isolate the mRNA of fibroblasts in the kidney.

○ **B.** isolate the protein of red marrow in the bone.

○ **C.** isolate the mRNA of epithelial cells in the ureter.

○ **D.** isolate the DNA of yellow marrow in the bone.

Passage 4 (Questions 19-23)

Melanoma, a serious type of skin cancer, responds poorly to conventional therapy, such as irradiation and chemotherapy, but may be susceptible to therapy involving the immune system. Studies using the toll-like receptor (TLR) ligand cytosine-guanine oligodeoxynucleotides (CpG) as a TLR9 agonist or imiquimod as a TLR7 agonist in the melanoma setting, have shown encouraging results. Treatment-related skin bleaching may occur as an autoimmune side-effect of immunotherapy, which is considered an encouraging prognostic sign. Skin contact with phenols or catechols, such as monobenzone, induces depigmentation in susceptible individuals by interacting with tyrosinase, the key enzyme in melanocyte pigment synthesis.

Scientists postulated that monobenzone, by its selective interaction with melanocytes, induces melanocyte-specific autoimmunity that could result in killing melanoma cancer cells.

Experiment 1

Researchers combined the topical skin-bleaching agent monobenzone with immune-stimulating TLR7-agonist imiquimod and the TLR9-agonist CpG, designated as MIC-treatment. They inoculated C57BL/6 wildtype mice with 2.5×10^6 B16.F10 melanoma cells injected into the fat layer of the skin, and from day 2, treated these mice with monobenzone alone, the immunostimulatory adjuvants CpG and imiquimod combined (CI) or monobenzone with imiquimod and CpG (MIC). Melanoma tumor samples were stained for TNFα positive cells, which were taken to be killer T cells. Results are shown in Figure 1.

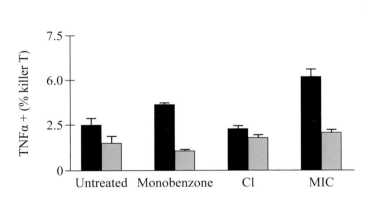

Figure 1 MIC treatment of subcutaneous B16.F10 melanoma induced melanoma-reactive CD8+ T cells and −NK cells

Experiment 2

In order to determine the long-term effects of MIC treatment, scientists again injected 2.5×10^6 B16.F10 melanoma cells subcutaneously in 7 mice. The tumors were allowed to grow under no treatment and MIC treatment conditions that began at various time points after tumor inoculation. The tumor size was measured at 100 days after melanoma cell injection and the results are shown in Figure 2.

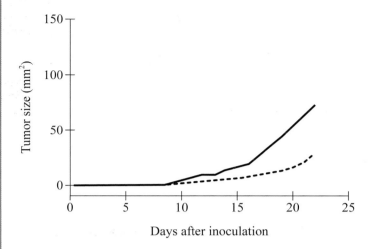

Figure 2 Growth of subcutaneous melanoma

This passage was adapted from "Effective Melanoma Immunotherapy in Mice by the Skin-Depigmenting Agent Monobenzone and the Adjuvants Imiquimod and CpG." van der Boorn J, Konijnenberg D, Tjin E, Picavet D, Meeuwenoord N, et al. *PLoS ONE*. 2010. 5(5) doi:10.1371/journal.pone.0010626 for use under the terms of the Creative Commons CC BY 3.0 license (http://creativecommons.org/licenses/by/3.0/legalcode).

Question 19

Melanoma tumors tend to be highly vascularized to provide amino acids and carbon backbones needed for rapid proliferation. Topical treatment with which of the following compounds could serve as an additional therapy for reducing tumor growth?

   I. Norepinephrine, a sympathetic agonist

   II. Bethanechol, a parasympathetic agonist

   III. Scopolamine, an acetylcholine antagonist

- **A.** I only
- **B.** I and III only
- **C.** II and III only
- **D.** I, II, and III

Question 20

Sun exposure in patients treated with monobenzone is most likely to result in:

- **A.** an increase in the number of DNA base substitutions in skin keratinocytes.
- **B.** an increase in the growth of hair and nails.
- **C.** a decrease in the impermeability of skin to water.
- **D.** a decrease in skin capillary vessel size.

Question 21

Scientists most likely injected B16.F10 melanoma cells:

- ○ **A.** within the avascular epithelial tissue.
- ○ **B.** between the avascular epithelial tissue and dermis.
- ○ **C.** between the skin stem cells and the dermis.
- ○ **D.** within the superficial fascia.

Question 22

Which of the following cell types is most important for activating the stained cells in Figure 1?

- ○ **A.** Melanocytes
- ○ **B.** Keratinocytes
- ○ **C.** Langerhans cells
- ○ **D.** Merkel cells

Question 23

Which of the following statements best explain the results of Experiment 2?

- ○ **A.** MIC-treated mice are likely to show less skin-bleaching compared to control mice.
- ○ **B.** MIC-treated mice likely have more Langerhans cells compared to control mice.
- ○ **C.** MIC-treated mice likely have lower intracellular tyrosine levels compared to control mice.
- ○ **D.** MIC-treated mice likely have reduced vitamin D synthesis compared to control mice.

Questions 24 - 27 do not refer to a passage and are independent of each other.

Question 24

Strabismus surgery attempts to correct alignment of the eyes by surgically altering the extraocular muscles which control the movement of the eye. Which of the following is least likely to be damaged during this procedure?

- ○ **A.** Ligaments
- ○ **B.** Insertion
- ○ **C.** Collagen
- ○ **D.** Tendon

Question 25

A student hypothesizes that vascular control plays a greater role than sweat in thermoregulation when ambient temperature is higher than 37°C. Is this reasonable?

- ○ **A.** Yes, because in higher temperatures sweat is less likely to evaporate from the skin.
- ○ **B.** Yes, because serum adrenaline is elevated at high ambient temperature.
- ○ **C.** No, because the difference between body and ambient temperature is reduced.
- ○ **D.** No, because exothermic heat loss from sweat is greater at high temperature.

Antidiuretic hormone raises systemic blood pressure through changes in blood vessel diameter. An increase in this hormone would most likely:

○ **A.** raise internal body temperature through vasoconstriction in superficial capillaries.

○ **B.** lower internal body temperature through vasodilation in superficial capillaries.

○ **C.** maintain internal body temperature through vasodilation in superficial capillaries.

○ **D.** lower internal body temperature through vasoconstriction in superficial capillaries.

The arrector pili are a collection of muscle around the hair shaft in the dermis whose structure resembles that in the vasculature. Which of the following would likely in cold conditions?

○ **A.** A decrease in stimulus by the somatic nervous system to the arrector pili

○ **B.** An increase in stimulus by the autonomic nervous system to the arrector pili

○ **C.** A decrease in stimulus by the autonomic nervous system to the arrector pili

○ **D.** An increase in stimulus by the somatic nervous system to the arrector pili

Passage 5 (Questions 28-32)

Chronological aging is a time-dependent biological process that leads to gradual changes in the structure and functions of all tissues that compose an organism. Skin is a valuable model to study aging in humans since it is widely affected by this process and is easily accessible.

Aged skin is characterized by a flattening of the dermal-epidermal junction and a marked atrophy and a loss of elasticity of the dermal connective tissue. In addition, it is associated with a reduction and disorganization of its major extracellular matrix components such as collagen and other elastic fibers. A histological characteristic of chronological aging in the epidermis is a decrease of tissue thickness. The observed age-related changes in fibroblasts include cell morphology, change in production of growth factors like monocyte chemoattractant protein (MCP-1), and expression of proteases involved in the degradation of the extracellular matrix such as MMPs.

Experiment 1

Fibroblasts were obtained from the superficial layer of the dermis, named "papillary dermis", and from the deeper dermal layer, named "reticular dermis'. Age of donors ranged from 19 to 74 years. Fibrobasts from the papillary dermis (Fp) and reticular dermis (Fr) were respectively isolated from superficial dermis (between the surface to 0.3 mm depth) and deep dermis (more than 0.7 mm depth). Age-related secretion of cytokines, matrix metalloproteinase (MMPs), and tissue inhibitor of metalloproteinase (TIMPs) by Fp and Fr was analyzed in a cohort of skin samples from 16 independent donors, ranging from 19 to 74 years old, by linear regression.

Experiment 2

The effect of Fp and Fr from young and old donors on skin reconstruction was evaluated in a reconstructed skin model comprising a dermal and epidermal equivalent. Keratinocytes from the same batch were seeded onto dermal equivalents containing either Fp or Fr from young or old donors. Histological sections revealed that young Fp were more potent to promote epidermal morphogenesis than Fr of similar age (Figure 1).

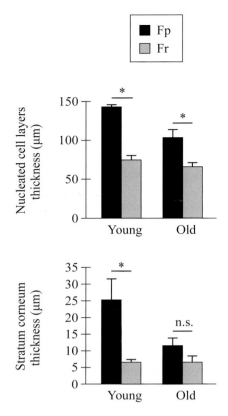

Figure 1 Age related impact of Fp and Fr on layers of reconstructed epidermal tissue thickness

Question 28

Which of the following functions of the epidermis would be likely to be impacted directly by aging?

   I. Regulation of water composition

   II. Decreased perfusion of surface capillaries

   III. Protection against foreign pathogens

○ **A.** I only

○ **B.** I and III only

○ **C.** I, II, and III

○ **D.** II and III only

Question 29

Based on the results of Experiment 2, rank the following in order of least to greatest ability to regulate internal water composition in a reconstructed skin model.

○ **A.** Young Fp, old Fr, young Fr, old Fp

○ **B.** Young Fp, young Fr, old Fr, old Fp

○ **C.** Old Fr, old Fp, young Fr, young Fp

○ **D.** Old Fr, young Fr, old Fp, young Fp

Question 30

Based on the information in the passage, which of the following has the most similar cellular composition and elasticity to the dermis?

○ **A.** Cartilage

○ **B.** Synovial joint fluid

○ **C.** Spongy bone

○ **D.** Tendon

Question 31

Aging is found to correlate with a breakdown of the matrix structure around sweat glands and hair follicles. Which of the following is likely to be the results of Experiment 1?

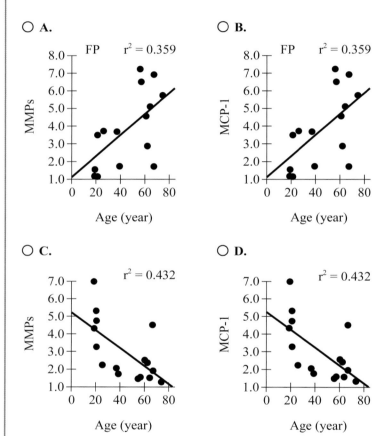

Question 32

In a separate experiment, aging was also found to correlate with thinning of the hypodermis. Which of the following would likely increase in elderly patients as a result of this phenomenon?

○ **A.** Excretion of sebaceous oil glands

○ **B.** Thickening of the epidermis

○ **C.** Vasodilation of surface capillaries

○ **D.** Contraction of smooth muscle in hair fiber follicles

Passage 6 (Questions 33-38)

Mammalian skin consists of epidermal and dermal layers separated by the basement membrane. Keratinocyte differentiation and interactions with the basement membrane and with neighboring cells within the epidermis play crucial roles in the structural integrity and development of skin. Non-enzymatic and enzymatic antioxidant substances protect the skin from the harmful effects of radical oxygen species (ROS), which are involved in several skin disorders like xeroderma pigmentosum (XP). XP is an autosomal recessive disorder characterized by multiple basal and epidermal skin malignancies. Selenium is a dietary micronutrient that often helps fight ROS to prevent cancer.

Experiment 1

Many of the protective effects of selenium are thought to be mediated by selenoproteins that contain selenium in the form of the amino acid, selenocysteine. Though human skin cells express about 10–15 different selenoproteins, their role in skin is poorly understood. In order to elucidate their involvement in skin development and function, epidermal knockout of *TRSP* was targeted in basal cells of several stratified epithelia (Figure 1).

Control   Knockout

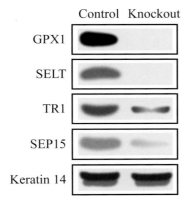

Figure 1 Effect of K14-mediated *TRSP* deletion on selenoprotein expression

Experiment 2

Defective keratinocyte adhesion and malformed hair follicles can trigger a wound healing response in skin, leading to infiltration of inflammatory cells. To test this possibility, scientists analyzed skin sections for the presence of granulocytes and macrophages. Macrophage infiltrates were significantly increased in knockout skin samples around some deformed hair follicles and at areas of dermal-epidermal separation. Additionally, hair follicles were composed of multiple concentric layers of keratinocytes around the developing hair shaft.

This passage is adapted from "Selenoproteins Are Essential for Proper Keratinocyte Function and Development." Sengupta A, Lichti U, Carlson B, Rysavage A, Gladyshev V, et al. *PLoS ONE*. 2010. 5(8) doi:10.1371/journal.pone.0012249 for use under the terms of the Creative Commons CC BY 3.0 license (http://creativecommons.org/licenses/by/4.0/legalcode).

Question 33

Which of the following proteins is most important for adherence of the epidermal layer?

- **A.** Hemidesmosomes
- **B.** Desmosomes
- **C.** Claudin
- **D.** Myosin

Question 34

Which of the following statements LEAST describes the role of keratinocytes in the skin?

- **A.** Production of a protein that decreases osmosis across the epidermis
- **B.** Production of a protein that decreases oxidative damage to DNA
- **C.** Prevents infection by bacteria and viruses
- **D.** Provides physical protection against abrasions

Question 35

TRSP knockout mice most likely have higher concentrations of dendritic cells:

- **A.** in the basal dermis.
- **B.** in the subcutaneous fat layer.
- **C.** in the stratum spinosum.
- **D.** in the stratum corneum.

Question 36

In mice with defective glutathione peroxidase 1 (GPX1) function, UV radiation to which of the following cell types would most likely lead to malignant transformation?

- **A.** Langerhans cell
- **B.** Merkel cell
- **C.** Epidermal stem cell
- **D.** Granular cell

Question 37

Selenocysteine-containing proteins most likely protect against ROS by:

- ○ **A.** oxidation of two selenocysteine amino acids to a diselenide bond.
- ○ **B.** reduction of a disulfide bond to two cysteine amino acids.
- ○ **C.** sequestering the ROS against the phospholipid bilayer.
- ○ **D.** increasing the expression of DNA repair enzymes.

Question 38

Which of the following additional experiments would most likely contradict the authors' findings in the passage?

- ○ **A.** After exposure to UV radiation, an antibody against oxidized GPX1 shows an increased signal compared to the no UV radiation condition.
- ○ **B.** After exposure to UV radiation, an antibody against reduced SEP15 shows a decreased signal compared to the no UV radiation condition.
- ○ **C.** After exposure to UV radiation, mRNA levels of *SELT* increase 5-fold compared to the no UV radiation condition.
- ○ **D.** After exposure to UV radiation, binding of TRSP to the *TR1* promoter decreases 3-fold compared to the no UV radiation condition.

Questions 39 - 41 do not refer to a passage and are independent of each other.

Question 39

The skin regulates body temperature by all of the following methods EXCEPT:

- ○ **A.** contraction of erectile muscles in the dermis.
- ○ **B.** vascular control of blood flow.
- ○ **C.** endothermic evaporation of sweat released by glands in the epidermis.
- ○ **D.** endothermic evaporation of sweat released by glands in the dermis.

Question 40

Skeletal muscle helps regulate body temperature via the shivering reflex. Which of the following processes is LEAST likely to accompany the shivering reflex under hypothermic conditions?

- ○ **A.** Stimulation of the thalamus by receptors in the skin and spinal cord
- ○ **B.** Production of glucose-1-P by glycogen phosphorylase
- ○ **C.** ACh mediated innervation of neuromuscular junctions
- ○ **D.** Increased metabolic rate due to rapid muscular contractions

Question 41

In which scenario would the skin's role in water retention be most compromised?

- ○ **A.** A reduction in production of keratin in the epidermis
- ○ **B.** An increase in production of sweat by eccrine glands in the dermis
- ○ **C.** A reduction in ACh causing widespread vasoconstriction
- ○ **D.** An increase in production of melanin in the epidermis

STOP. If you finish before time is called, check your work. You may go back to any question in this test.

ANSWERS & EXPLANATIONS for Mini-Test 6B can be found on p. 310.

WARM-UP

ANSWERS & EXPLANATIONS
Questions 1–5

ANSWER KEY
1. D
2. A
3. C
4. C
5. B

EXPLANATIONS FOR WARM-UP

Passage 1 (Questions 1-5)

1. **D is the best answer.** This question is somewhat complicated in light of the detail provided. The question is asking why the researchers would carry out a test that looks at the enzyme activity of an enzyme attached to an antibody that is added to the medium surrounding the apical surfaces. The idea of the test is that they are adding something to the apical surfaces and testing for its presence in the medium surrounding the basolateral surfaces. This type of test would help to clarify the permeability of intercellular junctions that normally function to inhibit the passage of fluid or large particles such as antibodies between these areas. Choice A is misleading, since anti-Nectin-1 antibodies are discussed in the passage. However, this type of test does not give any information about the efficacy of the anti-Nectin-1 antibodies, since this test is using anti-donkey antibodies. Choice B is tricky, since the passage indicates that the polarity of the cells was confirmed by immunodetection, a process that involves attaching antibodies to cell surfaces for visualization. However, this particular test measures permeability, since the particular antibodies used would not be expected to bind cell surface proteins on the apical side. Choice C is tempting, since it addresses permeability, but it would not be the best answer because the goal here is not to establish a baseline. As the passage discusses, the polarity of the cells used in the experimental model was confirmed by a measurement of paracellular permeability. This means that the researchers wished to show that the cells were similar to regular oral epithelia that restrict the passage of fluid through intercellular junctions, so choice D is the best answer.

2. **A is the best answer.** The passage explains that HIV proteins result in the disruption of tight junctions through the internalization of the tight junction proteins. This means that these proteins attached to the plasma membrane are endocytosed and carried inside the cell. Within the cell, these vesicles are frequently sent to lysosomes for degradation to recycle the components for future use. Since it addresses this scenario, choice A is a strong answer. The internalization and subsequent breakdown of these proteins would account for the thinning of the tight junction barrier. Choice B is misleading since the passage indicates that these HIV proteins cause the downregulation, or decreased production, of tight junction proteins. However, the HIV proteins are not downregulated as indicated by choice B. Choice C is tricky, since this effect explains the increase in viral entry discussed in the passage, but it does not explain the initial disruption of the tight junction barrier. Choice D is also tempting because it is true that there is greater permeability through the tight junctions, but this is the effect and not the cause of tight junction disruption.

3. **C is the best answer.** This question can be confusing due to the detail about hepatitis C, but this information is not necessary for answering the question. The question is asking for the stage of the HIV life cycle that may be mediated by gp120. The question stem indicates that this glycoprotein binds membrane receptors. The ability to bind specific receptors is critical to viral entry into the host cell. Since HIV is an enveloped virus, and gp120 is an envelope protein, choice A can be misleading. However, the viral envelope is derived from the lipid bilayer of the host cell and is not self-assembled in the same way a protein capsid of a virus is assembled. Choice B is also unlikely given the position of the protein on the outside of the virus and its ability to bind membrane receptors. It is true that HIV integrates its genome into the host genome, but there is no indication that this is mediated by gp120. Since viral invasion of the host cell is only possible through the specific attachment of the virus to the outside of the host cell, choice C is a strong answer. Choice D is a stage of the HIV life cycle that follows a period of dormancy and reactivation, though reactivation of a provirus is typically driven by factors such as stress that affect the environment of the host cell. Choice C is a better answer than choice D.

4. **C is the best answer.** This question refers to Figure 1 in the passage. It shows that there is minimal infection with HSV in the control population. The passage does not give detail about the control group, but it is possible to figure out what is done with the group through the use of logic. Choice A is misleading, since using inactive forms of the proteins leads to decreased levels of HSV infection as shown in the figure. However, this is already done for the tat/gp120 inactive group, so this cannot be the case for the control group. Choice B is a weaker answer, since the y-axis is a measure of HSV infection, and though it is reduced for the control group, the positive value for HSV infection indicates the cells were infected with HSV. Choice C is the best answer, since the control group is expected to mirror the normal epithelium with preserved tight junctions. This helps to provide a valid comparison for the other groups that show increased HSV infection as a result of tight junction permeability. Choice D is tempting, since the cause of increased HSV infection is mediated through the increase in Nectin-1 exposure. However, since the researchers are investigating the effect of increased exposure of Nectin-1 rather than increased production, the control group is expected to have the same expression of Nectin-1 with the difference being that the Nectin-1 is shielded from the virus particles by the tight and adherens junction proteins.

5. **B is the best answer.** HIV is a retrovirus that uses reverse transcriptase to form DNA from RNA. Without the knowledge that HIV carries single-stranded RNA, one can still correctly answer the question. Reverse transcriptase works by carrying out the exact reverse of transcription. This means that a single strand of RNA is copied as a template to make DNA. Choice A is a weaker answer since the single strand of RNA is copied to form a DNA-RNA hybrid and not double-stranded RNA. Choice B is a strong answer since it identifies the proper sequence that is expected for reverse transcription. Choice C is tricky given that one may not know the nature of the initial HIV genome. However, it is not possible for double-stranded RNA to be converted to DNA. In such a case, the double-stranded RNA would have to be converted to a single strand first to create a hybrid. Choice D is also a weaker answer for this reason. If HIV were to start off with double-stranded RNA, it would need to form single-stranded RNA before making the hybrid.

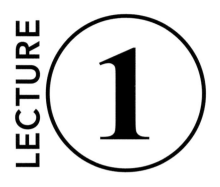

LECTURE

1

The Cell

TEST 1A

LECTURE 1 ANSWER KEY

TEST 1A		MINI-TEST 1B	
1. A	31. A	1. C	22. A
2. B	32. A	2. D	23. B
3. A	33. A	3. B	24. A
4. C	34. D	4. D	25. B
5. A	35. C	5. A	26. D
6. A	36. B	6. B	27. D
7. D	37. B	7. D	28. C
8. A	38. C	8. C	29. C
9. B	39. D	9. D	30. A
10. A	40. D	10. C	31. D
11. D	41. C	11. A	32. D
12. A	42. A	12. B	33. C
13. B	43. C	13. C	34. A
14. C	44. D	14. C	35. C
15. D	45. B	15. A	36. A
16. C	46. D	16. D	37. D
17. D	47. B	17. D	38. C
18. A	48. A	18. C	39. B
19. C	49. B	19. A	40. C
20. A	50. D	20. D	41. C
21. B	51. A	21. A	
22. B	52. D		
23. A	53. D		
24. D	54. A		
25. C	55. A		
26. C	56. D		
27. C	57. D		
28. B	58. D		
29. B	59. D		
30. D			

EXPLANATIONS FOR LECTURE 1

Passage 1 (Questions 1-4)

1. **A is the best answer.** According to the passage and the question, insertion of the EBV genome into the human genome disrupts proper transcription of tumor suppressor genes, which are genes that are responsible for maintaining DNA integrity and controlling proliferation. Disruption of transcription is unlikely to occur by insertion of the EBV genome at the 3′ untranslated region, which helps control translation initiation and other post-transcriptional processing of mRNA, so choice B is a weaker answer. Disruption of an enhancer could decrease transcription, so choice C is a possible answer. Insertion into a splice site for an exon would change the mRNA sequence and the amino acid sequence of the final protein that is translated but would not prevent transcription from occurring. Since this question is specifically asking for which choice would decrease the amount of transcription for these genes, choice D can be eliminated. If the genome was inserted into the promoter region, the sequences necessary for transcription factors to bind would become disrupted, decreasing the likelihood of transcription. Insertion into the promoter would be more likely to prevent transcription than insertion into an enhancer, as an enhancer serves to increase the basal levels of transcription. This makes choice A a better answer than choice C.

2. **B is the best answer.** The lysogenic phase of the viral life cycle is characterized by low protein expression, according to paragraph one. The latent phase is synonymous with the lysogenic phase and is the time where viral DNA integrates into the host chromosome, and a limited number of proteins are expressed, presumably to prevent detection of an infected cell by the host immune system. The best answer will be the epigenetic change that is LEAST likely to prevent protein expression. Methylation of C bases "mutes" transcription, which would prevent expression of many viral proteins. Because this is a possible mechanism during latency, option I can be eliminated, along with choices A and D. Methylation of histones may also "mute" transcription, but, at times, can activate transcription. The function of the methylation depends on which amino acid of the histone is methylated. Option III can likely be eliminated because the answer choice is not specific enough. Acetylation of histones opens up chromatin to increase transcription. This would increase, not decrease, viral protein production, making option II LEAST likely to be employed by viruses in the lysogenic phase. Option II must be part of the best answer, making choice B the best answer. Choice C can be eliminated because option II is not included as part of the answer.

3. **A is the best answer.** According to the first and second paragraphs of the passage, EBV is a DNA virus that has the potential to integrate into the host genome to become lysogenic, or latent. Once the viral DNA is integrated in the host genome, it lays dormant until the cell experiences stress or conditions that are favorable for viral replication. At this point, the virus becomes lytic and produces viral proteins. Because EBV is already a DNA virus, it does not need reverse transcriptase to convert its RNA into DNA, eliminating choice B. Viruses hijack the cellular machinery of host cells, meaning the viruses do not have their own ribosomes. This eliminates choice C. Inhibiting the host RNA polymerase would decrease transcription of the integrated viral DNA, acting similarly to a virus that is in a lysogenic, not lytic, phase. This eliminates choice D. Inhibiting an enzyme that transfers a methyl group to DNA would prevent the viral DNA from being methylated at C bases. Methylation at C bases "mutes" transcription, so preventing this addition could lead to transcriptionally active DNA that could create virus proteins. These proteins could be expressed on the cell surface, leading to destruction of the infected cell by the host immune system. Also notice that the compound is relatively hydrophobic and contains many aromatic rings that could participate in hydrophobic interactions with other nonpolar amino acids. Phenylalanine is a nonpolar amino acid that could pair with this relatively nonpolar compound. Choice A is the best answer.

4. **C is the best answer.** Figure 2 shows the percent of cells surviving with increasing doses of compound 11. Notice that the passage states that these cells were also co-incubated with adaptive immune system cells. At each concentration, more non-infected cells survive than EBV-infected cells. This eliminates choice A. Since the survival of host cells infected with EBV declines with increasing concentrations of compound 11, Figure 2 can also be interpreted as showing that survival of EBV-infected cells increases with decreasing concentrations of compound 11, so choice B can be eliminated. Increased concentrations of compound 11 result in a larger percentage of EBV-infected cells being killed, which makes choice C a strong option. While it is true that non-specific cell death of cells not infected with EBV is also seen at much higher concentrations, a substantial increase in EBV infected cell death is also observed, so the portion of the answer choice that states that non-infected cells are dying preferentially makes choice D a weaker answer.

Passage 2 (Questions 5-8)

5. **A is the best answer.** Figure 1 shows cell viability and viral count following infection with PR8 and VSV viruses. There is a clear relationship where cell viability increases in response to KIOM-C treatment. This makes choices C and D unlikely, as they state that KIOM-C does not affect cell viability. The lytic and lysogenic cycles are two types of life cycles for viruses. During the lytic cycle, the cellular machinery is hijacked by the virus to produce more viruses until the cell can no longer function and proceeds to lyse. The lysogenic cycle involves incorporation of viral DNA into the host genome, which allows the virus to remain dormant as the host cell divides and generates daughter cells whose nuclei contain viral genes. The lytic cycle is the type of life cycle that more prominently features cell death and impacts viability. Additionally, the lytic cycle produces new virus particles that are released into the extracellular environment. Since Figure 1 shows an increase in cell viability and a decrease in viral titer, which is a measure of the amount of virus particles in the extracellular fluid, choice A is a better answer than choice B.

6. **A is the best answer.** Based on the passage, this virus is a ssRNA virus, so any answer not beginning with RNA is unlikely. These are choice C and D. The passage states that Newcastle disease virus is a negative-sense, single stranded RNA virus. This means that the viral genome that is packaged into viral particles is unable to be directly translated into proteins. To generate viral proteins, the RNA-dependent RNA polymerase must generate a complementary strand (positive sense) of RNA. This positive strand can be translated by host ribosomes into proteins as well as serve as a template for the creation of more negative sense RNA strands, which act as the genomic RNA. This makes choice A a strong option. The life cycle of a positive-sense RNA virus is similar to a negative-sense virus, except that its genomic RNA that is found in the viral capsid can be directly translated by host ribosomes. Choice B is describing the life cycle of a positive-sense RNA virus and can be eliminated.

7. **D is the best answer.** Figure 1 shows cell viability and viral titer in samples following KIOM treatment. Viral titer is reduced by about 60% for PR8. This suggests that the presence of KIOM would inhibit the ability of the PR8 vector to infect cells and transfer the desired gene. This eliminates choices A and B. Similarly, viral titer is reduced 20% for VSV in the presence of KIOM. KIOM effectively reduces the ability of both viruses to infect cells. This rules out choice C and makes choice D the best answer.

8. **A is the best answer.** Viruses infect host cells, and these cells can undergo apoptosis, killing viral progeny before they are released. An effective viral treatment would not damage or affect healthy cells, making choices B and D less likely. Next, increasing apoptosis in infected cells would reduce the amount of virus. Decreasing apoptosis in infected cells would allow newly created viruses to escape and infect other cells, so choice B is unlikely, and choice A is the best answer. By increasing apoptotic signaling in infected cells, the damage of viral infection can be contained within that cell as newly formed viruses are unable to escape and infect other cells.

Passage 3 (Questions 9-13)

9. **B is the best answer.** The first step in choosing the best answer for this question is to determine where the virus is most likely to bind. Between the outer and inner phospholipid leaflets, the virus is most likely to bind to molecules on the outer leaflet, as this is the side of the cellular membrane that faces the extracellular environment. Thus, choices C and D can be eliminated. Of the two remaining options, a lipid and a glycoprotein, the virus is more likely to bind to a glycoprotein. This is because viruses have numerous receptors on their surfaces designed to bind glycoproteins, proteoglycans, carbohydrates, or proteins. Glycoproteins are primarily proteins that have sugar modifications added to them, while proteoglycans are primarily carbohydrates that have been modified by the addition of proteins. Viruses have receptors on their outer membrane or capsid that can interact with portions of the cell membrane and trigger endocytosis. Since lipids are not a normal target of these viral receptors, choice B is the best answer.

10. **A is the best answer.** According to paragraph two, DENV infects cells by binding to a receptor on the extracellular surface, as do many other viruses, causing endocytosis. This process is known as receptor-mediated endocytosis. Cholesterol is a component of the plasma membrane that helps maintain fluidity in cold temperatures and integrity of the membrane during warm temperatures. It is contained within the membrane and may be found in the endocytotic vesicle, but it is not a necessary molecule for endocytosis, making choice B a weaker answer. Tubulin is the protein that makes up microtubules which are important for numerous cell functions including mitosis and forming flagella, but tubulin does not play a role in receptor-mediated endocytosis, eliminating choice C. Myosin is a motor protein that assists in cytoskeletal rearrangement and intracellular transport. While it can help with cellular locomotion and vesicle transport, it does not have a critical role in receptor-mediated endocytosis, eliminating choice D. Receptor-mediated endocytosis is directed by a protein called clathrin that coats a plasma membrane pit once the receptor is engaged by a ligand. In this case, DENV binds a glycoprotein on the outside of the cell, triggering clathrin coating and endocytosis of the virus, making choice A the best answer choice.

11. **D is the best answer.** According to the question stem, type I interferon is able to induce the transcription of many different genes that defend against viral infection. The amplification of a particular signal occurs through a signal cascade that depends on intracellular second messengers that can activate or deactivate many enzymes. The molecule LEAST likely to contribute to a signaling cascade is the best answer for this question. cAMP and Ca^{2+} are both common intracellular second messengers. cAMP is formed from the nucleotide AMP after adenylate cyclase is stimulated by an activated G protein, and calcium is often released from the endoplasmic reticulum, eliminating choices A and C. The receptor serves as the initial starting point for a signaling cascade as it activates proteins inside the cell that can make or cause the release of second messengers. Thus, choice B can be eliminated. Choice D represents a version of cholesterol that is likely contained in the plasma membrane and not free to diffuse into the hydrophilic environment of the cytosol. It is least likely to serve as a second messenger, meaning it would not increase transcription, making choice D the best answer.

12. **A is the best answer.** Paragraph three provides additional information that helps link the new function of the mitochondria to viral infection. Under IFI6 expression, the mitochondrial membrane potential is stabilized and the activity of caspase-3 is reduced. No information is provided as to how the mitochondria could be acting to prevent viral infection. Additionally, the passage suggests that one of the major preventative measures of viral infection would be to block viral binding, not to manipulate mitochondria, eliminating choice B. Upregulation of IFI6 occurs by the binding of type I interferon to a receptor on the cell surface, which initiates a cascade that leads to increased transcription. No information in the passage links IFI6 expression with mitochondrial function, eliminating choice C. Mitochondria are capable of generating heat through a process called uncoupling, where the proton gradient is collapsed specifically to create heat. Choice D describes a function of mitochondria, but the passage notes that the mitochondrial membrane potential is retained in IFI6$^+$ cells, meaning that the electron transport chain is pumping protons that can be used to make ATP. Thus, choice D can be eliminated. IFI6 expression reduces the activity of caspase-3, a protein described to be involved in apoptosis. Apoptosis is the programmed cell death that occurs during embryogenesis and when cells are no longer viable. Thus, choice A is the best answer choice.

13. **B is the best answer.** The question stem details an experiment in which a non-competitive inhibitor is used to decrease the activity of IFI6. Decreased activity resembles the phenotype observed for the IFI6$^{-/-}$ cells on the graph in Figure 1. By looking at Figure 1, it can be seen that when IFI6 activity is absent, the expression of pro-apoptotic gene XAF1 is increased, likely leading to an increase in apoptosis, also known as programmed cell death. The mitotic spindle complex is associated with DNA replication and mitosis, which is not likely occurring in a cell that is under stress from an infection and undergoing apoptosis, eliminating choice A. A cell undergoing apoptosis is degrading the existing proteins in the cell, not creating new ones. As ribosomes are responsible for synthesizing new proteins, an increase in the number of ribosomes is unlikely, eliminating choice C. The passage does not provide information about mitochondrial DNA. One of the steps of apoptosis involved the packaging of DNA into small vesicles that can be taken up by neighboring cells. It is reasonable to predict that changes in mitochondrial DNA might be similar to those of the nuclear DNA and would undergo additional coiling, not uncoiling. While this makes choice D unlikely, it is still important to look at choice B to confirm it is the best answer. During apoptosis, the cellular membrane starts to project out and form blebs of cellular membrane that are cleaved off to form apoptotic bodies. Since apoptosis is expected to be seen in this experiment, it is likely that the scientist will observe the cells forming these blebs, which makes choice B the best answer.

Stand-alones (Questions 14-17)

14. **C is the best answer.** Prions are proteins that cause infection through replication of the misfolded proteins without the use of DNA or RNA. The question is asking for an appropriate method of testing the mechanism for this type of infection. Choice A is misleading, since while there may be a genetic component to prion infections, the model of infection in prion disease does not involve DNA or RNA. Instead, the misfolded proteins cause other proteins to be misfolded in a similar way. Affected cells may be genetically normal but can accumulate the misfolded proteins. Choice B is likewise misleading. There is unlikely to be any change in transcription in affected cells, since the method of infection does not involve increased transcription. Choice C is the best answer, because while such an experiment may only give limited information, the conformation of the protein could be helpful in determining its ability to interact with other proteins in a cell. Choice D could be reasonable if it was testing different combinations of amino acid sequences, but there is no reason to test the interaction of prions with nucleic acids. It is best to carefully read answer choices to avoid the mistake of misreading choice D as discussing amino acids.

15. **D is the best answer.** This test must be able to have positive results in one of the two types of pathogens and negative results in the other. Viruses have RNA or DNA, which is short of deoxyribose nucleic acid, at the center of their structure. Meanwhile, bacteria have circular chromosomes within a central nucleoid. Since it is possible for some viruses to have DNA, testing for it would not provide the physician with a definitive answer about the nature of the pathogen, making choice A unlikely. Proteins are found in bacteria and viruses. Viruses often have protein capsids, and proteins are found all over bacteria, which eliminates choice B. Nuclei are found in neither viruses nor bacteria, so a negative result would occur for both. Choice C is unlikely. Finally, choice D is the best answer because bacteria have ribosomes while viruses do not. When a virus infects a cell, it utilizes that cell's ribosomes to produce new viral proteins.

16. **C is the best answer.** Mutations can occur frequently within the genome, but rare mutations that inactivate vital genes are unlikely to have an effect on the phenotype of an individual because there is a second copy of the gene. This is especially true for mating that occurs between individuals from different populations as the likelihood of both mating partners carrying to rare mutation is much smaller in a large, diverse population. However, in a small inbred population, these mutated alleles can be in both mating partners and can be passed down to the offspring. Polymorphisms reflect the diversity in alleles for a given gene, and this type of mating is one in which there is a lack of diversity, so choice A can be eliminated. Choice B is tricky, as a population that is experiencing inbreeding has a decrease in gene flow, but gene flow, which results from outbreeding, is the transfer of alleles between the inbred population and an outside population, not within the inbred population. This makes choice B a weaker answer. The underlying cause of an increase in rare disorders in an inbred population is the increased homozygosity within that population. Choice D is also true of inbred populations, but choice C is a more direct explanation for the elevated rate of rare disorders as the observance of more homozygous individuals would increase the amount of individuals with two mutated alleles, so choice C is the best answer.

17. **D is the best answer.** This question may seem confusing given all the terminology. Also, all of the answer choices are true statements about evolution, but only one of them fully answers the question. The hint in the question stem is that the best answer should directly connect evolution with allopatric speciation which is mediated by geographic isolation and the unique environments each population experiences. Choice A is tempting because it discusses speciation and the role of selection, but it is a weaker choice because it does not address how speciation occurs by selection in different environments. Choice B is true but also neglects to address how this definition fits with allopatric speciation. Choice C is tempting given the focus on adaptations and speciation. However, this type of speciation is not due to geographic isolation. Choice D is the best answer, since this definition of evolution is linked to allopatric speciation through the mention of distinct pressures. The distinct pressures of the environment result in differences in selection in those environments, which contributes to evolution occurring through geographic isolation.

Passage 4 (Questions 18-21)

18. **A is the best answer.** Apoptosis is the organized cell death of damaged, infected, and/or old cells. Apoptosis of infected cells is initiated if certain immune cells detect viral peptides within a host. The presence of viral peptides implies the presence of CA HIV-1 RNA since RNA is required to generate proteins. Choice A is a potential answer because if more apoptosis is occurring, then more viral peptides and RNA must be present. Additionally, the passage indicates that an elevated level of CA HIV-1 RNA is indicative of reactivation of a previously latent infection. This would lead to more viruses entering the lytic cycle and causing more cell death. A low amount of CA HIV-1 RNA would be expected to trigger very little apoptosis, contradicting choice B. Given the role of apoptosis in combating viral infection, it should have some relation to the detection of virus, so choice C is unlikely. While it is possible that measuring the number of infected cells will not yield a precise estimate of the number of infected cells since some of the viruses will be in the latent phase and undetectable, the number of infected cells should still be related to detectable HIV-1 RNA, so choice D is also unlikely.

19. **C is the best answer.** The lytic phase is when the virus rampantly reproduces, preparing to burst from the cell. The lysogenic phase is when a virus lies dormant as host cells divide and indirectly reproduce the virus by replicating the host cells DNA that has the viral DNA incorporated into it. Viruses proliferate rapidly within a host during the lytic phase and then release themselves from the host cell, often causing the cell to lyse, which is why it is called the lytic phase. During the lytic phase, the host machinery, including DNA polymerase, RNA polymerase, and ribosomes, is used to generate new viruses. These characteristics rule out choices A and D. CA HIV-1 RNA would most likely be increased during the lytic phase, when transcription of viral genes is occurring rapidly, so choice C is the best answer. Choice B is a worse answer as the CA HIV-1 RNA would likely be undetectable when the virus is in the lysogenic phase.

20. **A is the best answer.** The reproductive process of HIV-1 consists of genetic incorporation into the DNA of the nucleus, and subsequent transcription by RNA polymerase and translation by ribosomes. Choices C and D do not include the nucleus, and are thus unlikely choices. Though all three organelles listed are heavily involved in protein packaging and creation, the nucleus is an equally important organelle. The key decision between choices A and B is determining whether free ribosomes or bound ribosomes are more important to viral translation. These proteins remain in the cell to form viruses which either bud out of the cell and are covered by a portion of the plasma membrane or cause the cell to lyse and release the naked viruses into the surrounding area. Bound ribosomes in the rough ER produce all secreted and membrane-bound proteins. Since these proteins are not packaged and secreted, choice A is the best answer.

21. **B is the best answer.** Based on the passage and background knowledge about how viruses operate, HIV-1 uses a specific receptor that is found on certain immune cells to enter the cell. This directly contradicts choices A and D, as viruses cannot infect all cells. Choices A and D can further be ruled out because they basically say the same thing. If the virus uses a receptor to enter a host cell that is constitutively expressed, then it is able to infect all cells. Whenever two answers reach the exact same conclusion, they are usually both incorrect. The receptor is used to cross the membrane, so it makes sense that an identical membrane-bound receptor is used by the majority of HIV viruses. Choice B is the best answer. Reverse transcriptase is an enzyme that is translated from the HIV genome, but is used to copy the HIV-1 RNA genome into a DNA compliment which can be incorporated into the host genome. This allows the virus to enter the lysogenic cycle, so Choice C can be eliminated. For example, both muscle and nerve cells can have acetylcholine receptors, but these are derived from very different populations of stem cells. This could be the case for the cells that HIV infects.

Passage 5 (Questions 22-25)

22. **B is the best answer.** Conjugation is the transfer of genetic material from one bacterium to another via a sex pilus. Transformation is the acquisition of DNA fragments from the environment. Transduction is the transfer of genes by viruses that incorporate whatever genes they are carrying into the host. The question describes direct pickup of nucleic acids by a cell without the involvement of another cell or a virus. Choice A is unlikely as conjugation is the transfer of genes from one bacterium to another via a sex pilus. Choice B is the best answer since transformation is the pickup of DNA from the environment by bacteria. Choice C is a term that describes gene transfer via viruses that accidentally transfer host genes in addition to or instead of the viral DNA when they infect another bacteria. Choice D is a distractor, as it describes a process by which bacteria divide, but binary fission does not acquire new DNA from the environment. Instead, a bacterium replicates its own DNA prior to dividing into two sister bacteria.

23. **A is the best answer.** *tetM* increases the fitness of bacteria that possess the plasmid when tetracycline is present because it confers resistance to tetracycline. In an environment devoid of tetracycline, this advantage goes away. When the advantage is gone, the levels of the plasmid are more likely to decrease, since there is no longer a positive selective pressure, and often bacteria without the plasmid can outcompete *tetM* containing bacteria in non-tetracycline conditions, so choice A is a strong answer. Choice B is unlikely because the removal of a massive selective pressure should cause some shift in the population. While it is true that *N. gonorrhoeae* would no longer have a selective advantage in the absence of tetracycline, this would result in the level of *tetM*-containing plasmids decreasing, not increasing as the answer choice states, so choice C can be eliminated. Choice D is unlikely because the change in the ratio of each type of bacteria occurs because of changes in the relative fitness of each group of bacteria. Once a single group of bacteria has lower fitness, its proportion within the population will decrease over generations. This change in the population is not due to a programmed mutation away from the once-favorable trait.

24. **D is the best answer.** Evolution is the change in a population's traits as a result of environmental factors. One key thing to remember is that evolution occurs by chance, and the best traits are determined and selected for by the environment. The bacteria do not "want" anything, ruling out choice A. Choice B is also unlikely since it is implied in the passage that the 25.2 plasmid prevalence was a result of antibiotic treatment and development of resistance in the population rather than manipulation by scientists. The passage states that the bacteria have 25.2 plasmids, making Choice C unlikely. Next, choice D is correct description of the process of evolution, as a higher proportion of bacteria with 25.2 plasmids survive and are able to pass on their genome to the next generation, so choice D is the best answer.

25. **C is the best answer.** Flagella and cilia are structures that cells use to move. Flagella resemble a long tail, while cilia are short, hair-like projections. Both of these organelles are involved in movement, and flagellar propulsion is often involved in chemotaxis. This makes choice A better answer than choice B, since ciliary beating is not as important for directed locomotion of bacteria. An even better answer is choice C, because chemotaxis is exactly what is described in the question. While flagella are heavily involved in movement up and down gradients, the process of responding to a concentration gradient and moving either towards or away from a certain product is defined as chemotaxis. Since this is the more precise answer, choice C is a stronger answer and choice B can be eliminated. Lastly, choice D describes a form of bacterial motion, but tumbling is a more random movement that is not responsive to chemical gradients, so choice D can be eliminated.

Stand-alones (Questions 26-29)

26. **C is the best answer.** It is important to recognize that bacteria grow in an exponential manner. The graph can be used to determine the time it takes for these bacteria to double just as a radioactive decay graph can be used to determine the half life of a radioactive sample. Specifically, it takes 0.5 hours for the bacteria to grow from approximately 13,000 colonies to 26,000 colonies on the graph. To increase from 6,400 colonies to 102,400 colonies, the bacteria must have doubled approximately four times. At 0.5 hours the number of colonies should be approximately 13,000 after undergoing one round of division, so choice A can be eliminated. After 1 hour there would be about 26,000 colonies, which eliminates choice B. After 2 hours, the bacteria have undergone approximately 4 rounds of binary fission and should total about 104,000 colonies. This estimate can be made if the initial colony count is rounded from 6,400 to 6,500. This is reasonably close to 102,400, making choice C the likely answer. If the bacteria grew for 2.5 hours, the colony population would have doubled 5 times to approximately 208,000. This is a much greater count than the one the student found, so choice D can be eliminated.

27. **C is the best answer.** The question states that sodium thioglycolate converts atmospheric oxygen to water, implying that it helps remove oxygen gas from the surroundings. Lack of oxygen produces an anoxic environment. Bacteria that do NOT require anoxic conditions to survive must be aerobic or at least aerotolerant. In other words, they either require O_2 for survival or can otherwise survive in its presence. Aerobic and aerotolerant bacteria are more likely to be found at the surface of the thioglycolate medium than bacteria that require anoxic conditions because the surface is more exposed to O_2. Option I should be included in the best answer because it depicts aerobic bacteria that require O_2 for survival and cannot proliferate in anoxic conditions. Option II should not be included in the best answer because it depicts anaerobic bacteria that are restricted to the bottom of the tube because of its lack of O_2. These bacteria require anoxic conditions and are not aerotolerant. This eliminates choices B and D. Option III should also be included in the best answer because it depicts aerotolerant bacteria, which appear scattered because they do not require O_2 for survival but can tolerate its presence. These aerotolerant bacteria are equally likely to survive in anoxic or oxygen rich environments. Choice A can be eliminated because it only includes option I. Choice C is the best answer because it includes both options I and III.

28. **B is the best answer.** The question requires some knowledge of endosymbiotic theory, but also recognition that there is uncertainty about many aspects. Endosymbiotic theory proposes that early eubacteria were phagocytosed by other cells, but not digested, and resulting in primitive versions of the membrane bound organelles seen in eukaryotes today that eventually evolved, like mitochondria and chloroplasts. This primarily applies to organelles with a double membrane and not organelles like the ER, lysosomes, or the Golgi complex, which more likely arose from parts of the cell membrane that localized characteristic proteins and drifted into the cytoplasm. Some archaea have histone bound DNA, but endosymbiotic theory postulates that mitochondria originated from early eubacteria, not archaea, so choice A can eliminated. In addition to being phagocytosed by early eukaryotic cells, the endosymbiotic theory suggests that pre-mitochondria began reducing their genome and relying on the host cell to provide many of the proteins required for survival. This is where the "symbiotic" portion of the name originates. Mitochondria are unlikely to be able to survive and reproduce outside of the cell since they no longer have the full genome that the original phagocytosed bacteria possessed. Choice B is the most compelling evidence against endosymbiotic theory. Since lysosomes are not proposed to have originated from early eubacteria, the presence of compounds inside lysosomes that are toxic to prokaryotes would neither hinder nor support the endosymbiotic theory, making choice C a weaker answer. Choice D also follows that same logic. The ER was likely part of the cell membrane that broke off and specialized since it doesn't have DNA of its own. This doesn't contradict endosymbiotic theory since some organelles could have arisen in other ways.

29. **B is the best answer.** Since these bacteria are the cause of gastric ulcers, it is safe to assume that the bacteria are found in the stomach of the infected patient. The stomach is maintained at a very low pH to assist in food digestion as well as protection against foreign microbes. Bacteria capable of surviving in the stomach have to be capable of surviving in a low pH environment, so choice A can be eliminated. The next three answer choices all address the shape of the bacteria, about which the question stem provides clues. A high surface to volume ratio provides support for the possibility of the bacteria being spiral-shaped, which is also called spirelli, or helical bacteria. This makes choice B a strong answer. Helical bacteria do not aggregate very commonly, and *H. pylori*, the typical ulcer-causing bacteria are spirelli. Choice C indicates that the bacteria might be sphere shaped, like *Streptococcus aureus*, which you can infer from the stem "coccus", meaning spherical. Some spherical bacteria aggregate. In choice D the main distinguishing factor between these bacteria would be the shape. *Lactobacillus* is a bacillus or rod shaped bacterium, which does not have a very high surface area to volume ratio, so choice D is a weaker answer.

30. D is the best answer. According to the first paragraph, GC is a gram-negative bacterium. Gram-negative bacteria have thin peptidoglycan cell walls that allow most of the gram stain to be washed off during the staining procedure. Gram-positive bacteria, by contrast, have thick peptidoglycan cell walls that would give a purple color. Because the wall is thin and GC would appear pink, not purple, choices A and B can be eliminated. Choice C can be eliminated because a pink-appearing cell would be gram-negative bacteria and have a thin cell wall. Choice D is the best answer because it appropriately pairs the result of a gram-stain for a thin-walled gram-negative bacterium.

31. A is the best answer. Development of antibiotic resistance is due to a selective pressure that causes certain bacteria that are more capable of reproducing in that specific environment to pass on their genome to the next generation. The selective pressure in the situation outlined by the question is the presence of a drug that inhibits formation of the bacterial cell wall, which causes the cell wall to be leaky. A mutation that would change the active site of the enzyme responsible for forming the cell wall could prevent a drug from inhibiting the enzyme. This makes choice A a strong answer. Increased methylation of a gene would decrease transcription of an enzyme, lowering the overall amount of transpeptidase in the bacterium. This would be the opposite of developing resistance, eliminating choice B. A mutation that deleted the TATA box in a promoter would also prevent or reduce expression of the gene. This would also be the opposite of developing resistance, eliminating choice C. A repressor is a region of DNA that interacts with proteins on a promoter to decrease the likelihood of expressing a given gene. Formation of a new repressor would decrease transpeptidase expression, which is also the opposite of resistance. This eliminates choice D.

32. A is the best answer. Paragraph three provides some functions of the Obg proteins, noting that they are important in ribosome function, DNA replication, and chromosomal separation. Prokaryotes do not have membrane-bound organelles, so an Obg inhibitor in bacteria could not prevent docking of ribosomes at the rough endoplasmic reticulum. This makes choice A a strong answer. In binary fission, the process by which a bacterium divides to form two identical cells, the singular bacterial chromosome is duplicated and one copy is segregated into each new bacterium. The exact method of segregation is still be elucidated, but the formation of the septal ring, which divides the two cells is a critical step in ensuring that each cell receives one chromosome. Choice B can be eliminated. Topoisomerase enzymes help unwind supercoiled DNA during DNA replication. Because Obg contributes to DNA replication, choice C can be eliminated. Ribosomal assembly and translation initiation involves association of the large and small ribosomal subunits. Since Obg proteins contribute to ribosomal function, choice D can be eliminated.

33. A is the best answer. According to paragraph two, Obg proteins are G proteins that have a high affinity for nucleotides. Inhibitors that resemble nucleotides are most likely to bind tightly in Obg proteins, preventing them from carrying out their enzymatic functions. The passage states that Obg proteins are GTPases, which as the name indicates, are capable of hydrolyzing GTP. ATP and GTP are very similar in structure, so an inhibitor that resembles either of these molecules is possibly going to be able to bind the Obg proteins. This makes choice A a strong answer. Calcium is often an intracellular second messenger that is able to activate or repress the action of other enzymes. The passage does not suggest that calcium is necessary for Obg action, making choice B less likely to be the best answer. Ubiquitin is a protein that tags proteins for destruction. It is not a nucleotide, eliminating choice C. Glucose-6-phosphate is the second molecule in the glycolysis pathway but does not resemble a nucleotide as much as ATP resembles a nucleotide. Choice A is a better answer choice than choice D.

Passage 7 (Questions 34-39)

34. D is the best answer. The question is worded in a detailed way so as to be confusing, but it is otherwise straightforward. The passage explains that antibiotic resistance is the result of the acquisition of different mutations. The question is asking for the evolutionary concept that best describes this process. Polymorphisms refer to different alleles for a given gene, so this concept does not relate to the acquisition of mutations but rather to the outcome of different mutations occurring within genes. Choice A is a weaker answer for this reason. Choice B is misleading since the process of acquiring mutations contributes to speciation over time. However, the acquisition of mutations for antibiotic resistance does not necessarily create new species of bacteria but rather different strains of the same species, so choice B can be eliminated. Genetic drift refers to the loss of alleles in a small population, so this is not relevant to the question and makes choice C a weaker answer. Choice D is the best answer since an evolutionary adaptation refers to the development of a feature that enhances the survival of an organism as is the case here.

35. C is the best answer. The passage explains that the carbapenem drugs work by inhibiting the enzymes that form the bacterial cell wall, similar to the mechanism of action of penicillin. However, unlike penicillin, which generally functions best against gram-positive bacteria with thick cell walls, these drugs are also used for *P. aeruginosa*, which is gram-negative. Choice A is a weaker answer since the drugs are effective against some gram-negative bacteria that have thin peptidoglycan layers. Choice B is misleading, since though the passage discusses the acquisition of resistance to the drug, the passage also states that carbapenem drugs are used for these types of infections, so they are likely to be effective in most but not all cases. Though choice C is phrased as a double negative, which makes it tricky, it is a strong answer. Since meropenem works in a similar way to penicillin, which functions best against gram-positive bacteria with thick cell walls, meropenem would be expected to also work well against these bacteria. Choice D also involves a double negative, but the statement is inaccurate. The passage indicates that strains that produce carbapenemase are resistant to the drug, so the drug would be expected to be ineffective against such strains.

36. B is the best answer. The question is asking for a possible finding that would relate to the classification of the bacteria as aerobic. Bacteria that are aerobic use oxygen for cellular respiration to generate energy, and the term aerobic often refers to bacteria that require oxygen to survive. However, some aerobic bacteria are facultative anaerobes and can survive without oxygen when oxygen is not readily available. Choice A is misleading because mitochondria carry out the final steps of cellular respiration in eukaryotic cells where oxygen is the terminal electron acceptor. The lack of mitochondria might indicate that these bacteria do not use oxygen for cellular respiration; however, all prokaryotic cells lack mitochondria, so the lack of mitochondria gives no indication about whether or not the bacteria are aerobic. The ability to survive in thick mucus indicates that the bacteria can survive with little or no oxygen, since oxygen will not penetrate the thick mucus well. This would lead to the conclusion that the bacteria are not obligate aerobes, since they can derive energy from their environments without using oxygen, so choice B is a strong answer. Choice C is misleading, since the ATP synthase for producing ATP is generally located in the mitochondria. However, since prokaryotes lack mitochondria, they generate ATP using a gradient across the cellular membrane. Choice D is true of these bacteria but is not relevant, since the shape of the bacteria would not help to determine whether or not the bacteria require oxygen for generating energy.

37. B is the best answer. This question is somewhat complex because it asks for the finding that in combination with the data in the passage would indicate that the resistance is caused by the insertion of a large segment of DNA. This type of change is possible in DNA transposition. The insertion sequence discussed by the passage is a type of transposon, which is a mobile segment of DNA that can insert in various regions of one or multiple chromosomes. Choice A is true, though this finding is already indicated in Figure 3. Also, this finding does not clarify why there is a downregulation of the porin. Choice B points to the presence of a transposon. Figure 1 shows that the *oprD* genes of the mutants are significantly longer than that of the parent strain. The finding that the additional sequence of DNA in a mutant carries a transposase gene that allows for the transposition of the piece of DNA helps to confirm that the resistance to meropenem is caused by transposition. This makes choice B a strong answer. Choice C is tricky, since the passage explains that upregulation of the efflux pump is associated with resistance, but this finding is not related to any of the data in the passage and does note describe an insertion sequence, making it a weaker answer. Choice D is misleading, since while it is true that there is no PCR product for this mutant, such a finding could be the result of an error in the experimental setup. While this finding could contradict the hypothesis that the resistance is caused by an insertion sequence because the experiment is designed to detect an insertion sequence, and it seems to be absent in that mutant, it does not lend evidence to the conclusion that antibiotic resistance is developed through insertion of a large segment of DNA. Choice D can be eliminated which makes choice B the best answer.

38. C is the best answer. The passage explains that porins are proteins that form large transmembrane channels for the passage of molecules such as the carbapenems. Since these molecules require special channels to traverse the membrane, they must be polar and thereby incapable of crossing the hydrophobic core of the plasma membrane. The inner portion of the channel would therefore be lined with amino acids that carry polar side groups and allow the passage of polar molecules to cross within the channel. Aromatic groups are hydrophobic, since they contain hydrocarbon rings, so choice A can be eliminated. The amino acids with R groups composed of all hydrocarbons can be classified as aliphatic. These R groups would be hydrophobic and unlikely to be found in the interior of a channel, so choice B can be eliminated. The polar amino acids are much more likely to compose the interior of a transmembrane channel and associate with other hydrophilic molecules as they pass through the channel, so choice C is a strong answer. The side chain groups facing the inner channel should be able to interact with the fluid and polar molecules traveling through the channel, so choice D can be eliminated since hydrophobic molecules will not strongly interact with polar molecules.

39. **D is the best answer.** This question is somewhat complex, since it requires an understanding of the experiments and the information in the passage. The sample PAO1 shows a PCR product equivalent to the parent strain PA42 in Figure 1, indicating that the sample contains a similar *oprD* gene to the PA42 strain. Choice A describes the sample well labeled "no template control" or NTC, but it would not describe PAO1, which is shown to contain DNA. Choice B is tricky, since logically, it would serve as a control sample. However, it would not make sense to use DNA from a different species, since this type of control would differ significantly from the mutant strains and an effective comparison could not be made. Choice C is tempting, since such a sample would be expected to be mostly similar to the mutants. However, if the isolate had been treated with a high dose of the drug, the bacteria would either be killed or be resistant to the antibiotic. There is no reason to compare the mutant strains to other strains resistant to the drug. The point of the experiment is to show how the bacteria develop resistance. To accomplish this, it is best to compare mutant isolates to bacteria that are susceptible to the drug. This helps to highlight the differences in the mutant isolates. Choice D is the best answer for this reason.

Passage 8 (Questions 40-43)

40. **D is the best answer.** The three types of eukaryotic host lipids mentioned in the first paragraph are phosphatidylcholine, sphingophospholipid and cholesterol. The first two are examples of phospholipids, which contain polar phosphate groups, so choice A can be eliminated. Since phospholipids have both a polar and a nonpolar region, they would not be considered hydrophobic because this implies they are entirely nonpolar, so choice B is not the best answer. Choice C is misleading, since phospholipids do form micelles when placed in water. However, micelles consist of a single layer of the lipids where the polar head groups are oriented towards the outside where the water is present, and the hydrophobic tails are on the inside. Amphipathic is the term used to describe molecules with both polar and nonpolar regions, so this is an accurate description of the phospholipids, so choice D is the best answer. Cholesterol is a major component of the plasma membrane, but its structure and function are different from that of phospholipids.

41. **C is the best answer.** This question is difficult because it requires an understanding of both the information and the data in the passage. Figure 2 shows that the lack of peroxisomes has little, if any, effect on the formation of inclusions within host cells. The caption indicates that this is a measure of bacterial infection and development. However, one cannot conclude from this that there is no change to the bacteria. The experimental results shown in Figure 2 are only one measure of bacterial infection, whereas other experiments may show a difference in the bacteria using alternative measures. Since the conclusion in choice A is too extreme given the lack of evidence, it can be eliminated. There is no evidence from the data that the replication of the bacteria is impaired, since there seems to be no change in the graph of Figure 2, so choice B is a weaker answer. Choice C is a strong answer, because it incorporates information from the passage with the results of the experiments. Figure 1 shows that the bacteria are closely associated with peroxisomes, which provides evidence that the bacteria interact with them. The passage explains that peroxisomes make ether lipids, and these are important precursors for bacteria-specific lipids. The loss of peroxisomes would be expected to affect the bacteria, which act as parasites by taking the ether lipids of the host. Choice D uses words from the passage regarding the loss of genes related to lipid synthesis in the bacteria, but this is not relevant to the *PEX19* mutation, which is part of the experimental design and is created by researchers to study the effect of peroxisome deficiency on *C. trachomatis* infection.

42. **A is the best answer.** The passage explains that the loss of genes related to lipid synthesis in the bacteria due to extensive genome reduction. This type of genetic change is the result of evolution whereby random mutations result in differences in the ability of the bacteria to replicate. Mutations that improve a bacterium's ability to replicate will result in more future generations having that same mutation. In the case of *C. trachomatis*, the reduction in unnecessary genes must have provided a reproductive advantage. This is the process that is most directly referred to in the passage, so choice A is a strong answer. Transduction is a major factor in the exchange of bacterial DNA and is carried out by bacteriophages, but it is not discussed in the passage, and usually results in the increase in genome size, not the reduction, so choice B can be eliminated. Choice C is tempting since it references a loss of genetic material. However, there is no evidence in the passage that these genes are on a plasmid. While it is true that the bacteria are highly adapted to the human cells, it is also true that the bacteria infect these cells and exploit them as parasites. A symbiotic relationship requires that both parties of the relationship benefit from it. Also, this type of relationship does not explain the underlying process of the genetic change. Choice D is a weaker answer and can be eliminated.

43. **C is the best answer.** This question can be tricky if not read carefully since it implies that the best answer is one that is based on information in the passage. The passage explains that plasmalogens are bacteria-specific ether lipids, and it also states that peroxisomes make ether lipids. While choice A is true of peroxisomes, the answer choice does not indicate the critical role for the formation of plasmalogens of synthesizing certain types of lipids in addition to storing them, so choice A is a weaker answer. Choice B describes a well-established function of peroxisomes, but it is not relevant to the question because the question is discussing the role of peroxisomes in lipid synthesis, so choice B can be eliminated. Choice C addresses information in the passage about lipid synthesis and provides a possible function for the peroxisomes in this process, so it is a strong answer. While the smooth endoplasmic reticulum is generally associated with lipid formation, the passage explains that peroxisomes also have a role in this pathway. Choice D is true regarding peroxisomes, and it may even be tempting because of the details in the passage about the association of peroxisomes and lipid droplets in the cytosol. However, this answer choice only discusses the transport or storage of lipids but not the synthesis of lipids. This makes choice D a weaker answer and leaves choice C as the best answer.

Stand-alones (Questions 44-47)

44. **D is the best answer.** Choice A is not likely to reveal viral infection because viruses are too small to be seen with a light microscope. They are many magnitudes smaller than eukaryotic and prokaryotic cells. Signal sequences are found on proteins that are translated by the rough ER. Since bacteria and viruses do not have organelles, a molecule that causes toxicity based on the presence of proteins with signal molecules is unlikely to cause an effect on either the bacteriophage or the bacteria. Choice B is a weaker answer. Increasing the temperature of incubation would potentially increase the effectiveness of certain reactions, which could have an effect on the ability for the bacteria to multiply, but it would not help distinguish between a normal bacterium and one infected by a bacteriophage. This makes choice C a weaker answer. Bacteria have plasmids and circular DNA, neither of which has exposed 3′ or 5′ ends. Viruses often have linear DNA or RNA, so they possess exposed 3′ ends in DNA. When the fluorescent tag is used on bacteria infected by bacteriophage, portions of the bacteria will fluoresce and be visible via fluorescent microscopy. If there is not infection, the bacteria will not fluoresce. Choice D is the best answer.

45. **B is the best answer.** This question is asking about the potential effects of a drug that significantly reduces the amount of cholesterol in the body. Cholesterol has a number of important functions including its role in maintaining the integrity of the plasma membrane. It is also converted to steroid hormones, which are important for signaling. Since cholesterol is a steroid hormone precursor, signaling between cells via lipophilic hormones is likely to be affected by a decrease in the amount of cholesterol available, so choice A can be eliminated. The synthesis of steroid hormones occurs in the smooth endoplasmic reticulum, not the rough endoplasmic reticulum, so the experimental drug would not affect synthesis in the rough endoplasmic reticulum. This makes choice B a strong answer. Choice C is misleading, since it implies that cholesterol is might only be in one of the leaflet layers, but cholesterol is integrated into both leaflets, which makes choice C a weaker answer. Steroid hormones derived from cholesterol easily cross the membrane to bind receptors within the cell to affect many functions including transcription, so choice D would also be affected by this experimental drug.

46. **D is the best answer.** There are two types of surface proteins: integral and peripheral. Integral proteins are permanently embedded within the lipid bilayer while peripheral proteins are temporarily associated with the lipid bilayer or integral proteins. In both cases, surface proteins are subject to diffusion across the surface of the plasma membrane as is described by the fluid mosaic model. Choices A and C can be eliminated because segregated color labels imply a lack of fluid, lateral movement. Choice B can also be eliminated because stable intermolecular interactions would hamper the tagged proteins' ability to diffuse randomly throughout the membrane and intermix. Choice D is the best answer because transient or temporary intermolecular interactions among membrane components allow membrane proteins to diffuse throughout the membrane. Initially, the labeled proteins on the fused cell's surface are segregated with red labeled proteins to one hemisphere and blue labeled proteins are located on the other. Over time the proteins diffuse across the surface in a random fashion and the labels intermix. The overlap of blue and red fluorescent light can be seen in the microscope as green fluorescent light. This makes choice D the best answer.

47. **B is the best answer.** This question focuses on the different functions of the mitochondria and can seem difficult because all three options are roles of the mitochondria. Each option should be evaluated to see if the description of its role is specifically true, and if this description matches the situation described. For option I, oxidative phosphorylation relies on the reactions of different proteins in the inner mitochondrial membrane to establish the hydrogen ion electrochemical gradient that ATP synthase can use to generate ATP. Additional surface area would theoretically allow for more sites of oxidative phosphorylation, and exporting cells require significant energy to fuel their metabolic processes, so option I is a true statement. For option II, cholesterol is a precursor for steroid hormones, and it is produced along the inner mitochondrial membrane, so this is also a true statement. Option III contains an inaccuracy. Ketone bodies are formed in the mitochondrial matrix, not the inner mitochondrial membranes. This means that it fails the first test, and is not a true statement. The fact that options I and II are true makes choice B the best answer. It is worth noting that even if the reader did not remember the specific site of cholesterol synthesis, this is enough information to eliminate half of the distractors.

Passage 9 (Questions 48-52)

48. **A is the best answer.** Figure 1 shows that domains 4 and 5 of NCX1.1 are transmembrane domains, meaning that they cross the plasma membrane. The plasma membrane is hydrophobic internally due to the lipid chains on the phospholipids. Amino acids that are strongly hydrophilic will likely not be found in the plasma membrane. Valine, V, is a hydrophobic amino acid and would be reasonably found in the transmembrane domain, eliminating choice B. Isoleucine, I, similar to valine, is hydrophobic and could also be found in the transmembrane domain, eliminating choice C. The final two choices are both amino acids that would not be ideally found in the plasma membrane. Serine, S, is a polar amino acid that is hydrophilic, while arginine, R, is both polar and positively charged. Because R has the additional positive charge over serine, it would be less likely to be found in the transmembrane domain, eliminating choice D and making choice A the best answer choice.

49. **B is the best answer.** According to paragraph three, wild-type CaMS allows NCX1.1 to localize to the exoplasmic side of the plasma membrane, which can also be referred to as the leaflet of the plasma membrane that faces the extracellular matrix. Deletion of CaMS allows NCX1.1 to traffic to the exoplasmic side of the plasma membrane in choice A. Because mutation of CaMS does not alter the localization of the protein, as compared to the wild-type CaMS, this would not support the role of CaMS in membrane localization, eliminating choice A. The cellular localization of proteins is usually determined by a sequence found at the N-terminus. If the N-terminus were mutated on NCX1.1, it could fail to localize to a particular portion of the membrane, but this does not comment on the role of CaMS in mediating that transport. Thus, while choice C may be true, it does not answer the question, eliminating choice C. In the presence of wild-type or mutant CaMS, NCX1.1 still localizes to the plasma membrane, but the side of the plasma membrane is different between wild-type and mutant. Thus, the difference between the two proteins is based on chemistry at the plasma membrane, not prior. Thus, choice D does not help answer the question about the role of CaMS in determining whether the transporter is on the cytosolic or exoplasmic side, eliminating choice D. Paragraph three describes that when CaMS is deleted, NCX1.1 is found on the cytosolic side instead of the extracellular side. If CaMS worked with a protein responsible for flipping charged proteins across the lipid bilayer, mutation of CaMS could prevent this protein from working, explaining the difference in distribution of NCX1.1 under the wild-type versus mutant conditions. Thus, choice B is the best answer choice.

50. **D is the best answer.** According to paragraph two, NCX1.1 is a transporter that exchanges one calcium ion for three sodium ions. Simple diffusion occurs without the use of proteins or transport molecules and is used by hydrophobic molecules like hormones to cross the plasma membrane. Because calcium is charged and uses a transporter, choice A can be eliminated. Passive diffusion utilizes a protein and allows an ion to flow down its concentration gradient without the assistance of a second gradient. Because NCX1.1 uses the sodium gradient to move calcium, choice B can be eliminated. Primary active transport uses the energy of ATP hydrolysis to drive the translocation of a molecule across the plasma membrane, usually against its concentration gradient. The passage does not describe the use of ATP by NCX1.1 to export calcium, eliminating choice C. Secondary active transport is the method of transport that couples the concentration gradient of one ion to drive the movement of a second ion. In the case of NCX1.1, the sodium gradient drives the translocation of calcium across the plasma membrane, in the absence of direct hydrolysis of ATP, making choice D the best answer choice.

51. **A is the best answer.** According to the question stem, the mutant V5A CaMS was expressed instead of the wild-type protein only in cardiac myocytes. According to Figure 2, which shows the current generated due to calcium movement across the plasma membrane, mutation the V5A CaMS mutant protein shows reduced calcium movement compared to wild-type CaMS. Muscles require calcium in order to allow actin and myosin to bind to initiate muscle fiber movement. Reduced calcium would slow muscle contract, leading to a decrease in heart rate, not an increase in heart rate, eliminating choice B. Because the question stem says that the mutant protein was only expressed in cardiac myocytes, choices C and D can be eliminated. A slower breathing rate would also be seen if the protein was expressed in other cell types, but the question stem eliminates choice D further. Because reduced calcium would lead to a decrease in the cardiac muscle contraction, choice A is the best answer.

52. **D is the best answer.** Actin is one of the proteins of the cytoskeleton and serves numerous roles in cellular trafficking and stability. Motor proteins like myosin interact with actin to transport vesicles like neurotransmitters along the length of cells, making option I true. Myosin and actin interaction also mediates muscle contraction, making option II true. Actin, along with other intermediate filaments, provide structural support to the cell at rest and during cellular migration. Thus, option III is true. The best answer will be the one that contains all of the options, making choice D the best answer.

Passage 10 (Questions 53-56)

53. **D is the best answer.** According to the last paragraph of the passage, the number of AV particles detected was reduced following knockdown of ATG proteins. Choice A is unlikely because the two half-statements contradict each other. If ATG proteins are unimportant to AVs, then AV detection should not change following knockdown. Next, the conclusion that can be drawn from this result is that ATG proteins play a key role in AV formation/function due to the effect of knocking them out. This statement makes choice B unlikely and choice D the best answer. Choice C is an unlikely answer because just like choice A, the two half-statements contradict each other. If ATG proteins are important, then they should have some noticeable impact.

54. **A is the best answer.** The best approach for this question is to analyze the results of Figure 1 and use these results to rule out incorrect answers. Figure 1 shows the effect of inhibition of autophagy through lysosomal enzymes. None of the treatments increase autophagy, ruling out choice B. While choice C may seem appealing, remember that the net increase in AVs is most likely compensation for the inhibition of autophagy. Though there are more AVs in the treatment group, autophagic activity is most likely not actually increased. Next, AVs are found in higher levels in the treated sample, not the control, contradicting choice D. Choice A is the best answer because it corresponds to the results of Figure 1, where the inhibited sample has increased levels of AV particles.

55. **A is the best answer.** LC3B is used by researchers to detect AVs. Thus, it makes sense that it would only be able to bind to something specific to AVs. This makes choice A the best answer. Choices B, C, and D are all more general than choice A. Binding to all DNA or all mRNA would not help with AV detection. Next, choice D is a tempting answer, but it would bind to all vacuoles rather than just AVs.

56. **D is the best answer.** Autophagy is the self-destruction of organelles for a variety of reasons. This can be to destroy damaged/infected organelles as in option I, recycle resources from old organelles that are no longer functioning well as in option II, and to facilitate apoptosis, the organized destruction of the cell. This makes the best answer choice D, all three options.

Stand-alones (Questions 57-59)

57. **D is the best answer.** Smooth ER is involved in toxin breakdown and fat storage. Alcohol can be broken down by the smooth ER, not produced by it, so choice A is a weaker answer. Lactate is a product of fermentation, which occurs in the cytoplasm, not the smooth ER, so choice B can be eliminated. Glucose is not produced by the smooth ER, which eliminates choice C. Triglycerides are the storage form of lipids, and are made by smooth ER. Choice D is the best answer.

58. **D is the best answer.** Since the antibody being used by the researcher is specific for tubulin, cells that are abundant in tubulin are expected to have a greater amount of fluorescence, and if viewed under a microscope, it is possible to see localization of the green fluorescence to areas where there is a higher concentration of tubulin. Cilia and flagella in eukaryotic cells are composed of tubulin. Prokaryotic cells also have flagella, but it is formed by a specific protein called flagellin. If a human cell sample was contaminated by a bacterial infection, it is highly possible that there is a larger amount of flagella in the sample, but since prokaryotic flagella are not composed of tubulin, the amount of green fluorescence observed should not increase. Choice A can be eliminated. Tubulin is the key structural component of eukaryotic cilia, so ciliated respiratory cells would be expected to display a high amount of fluorescence if subjected to this protocol, so choice B can be eliminated. While prokaryotes have a homolog of tubulin, it is unlikely that the antibody being used in this experiment will recognize these homologs if it is already specific for tubulin. This makes choice C a weaker answer. Since tubulin is the primary structural component of cilia and flagella whose main role is usually in motile processes, cells that utilized these functions are more likely to display a high level of green fluorescence. Choice D is the best answer.

59. **D is the best answer.** They key characteristic of a micelle is that it has a single layer of amphipathic molecules making up its surface. Choices A, B, and C are all lipid bilayers, meaning choice D is the best answer. Most organelle membranes tend to be lipid bilayers rather than single-layered micelles. While it might not be obvious that digested fats form micelles, the process of elimination can be used to find the best answer, since all of the other choices have bilayers.

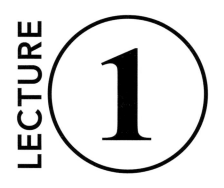

LECTURE

1

The Cell

MINI-TEST 1B

ANSWERS & EXPLANATIONS
Questions 1–41

Passage 1 (Questions 1-5)

1. **C is the best answer.** Some proteins outside the mitochondria are generated from mtDNA, while other mitochondrial proteins are generated from nuclear DNA. Generally, answers that make sweeping statements are weaker answers, and this rule holds true with choices A and B. Choice C accurately describes the source of mitochondrial proteins, as demonstrated by p66Shc in the passage. Next, all organelles, including the mitochondria, contain proteins, so choice D is unlikely.

2. **D is the best answer.** Some of the answers can be ruled out by analyzing Figure 1. In an environment that causes oxidative stress, the knockout has higher viability than the control, ruling out choices A and C. If removing expression of p66Shc leads to increased resistance to oxidative stress, then it makes sense that the normal function of p66Shc leads to vulnerability to ROS and oxidative stress. Choice B is unlikely since the cells become more vulnerable, which makes choice D the best answer.

3. **B is the best answer.** mtDNA is entirely inherited by the mother, ruling out option III, as sperm come from the father. In fact, all of the organelles of the zygote are already in the egg. The sperm's contribution to the zygote is only the paternal DNA. Option II is likely to be in the answer, as eggs are the female gamete. Next, somatic mutations are never inherited, so the mtDNA would not be expected to be inherited via this mechanism either. This makes option I less unlikely. Choice B, option II only, is the best answer.

4. **D is the best answer.** According to the passage, hydrogen peroxide damages the cell by inhibiting DNA repair and inducing mutations. It makes sense that this compound would do the most damage to the cell within the nucleus, where the DNA of the cell is stored. Choice D is the best answer. The nucleolus creates ribosomes, the rough ER creates secreted and membrane proteins, and lysosomes break down old cell parts. These organelles do not contain the DNA of the cell, making choices A, B, and C, less likely than choice D.

5. **A is the best answer.** A high level of ROS leads to damaged DNA, which, if severe enough, can result in the cell undergoing apoptosis. Lysosomes are heavily involved in apoptosis and serve as contained environments with low pH and enzymes for digestion of proteins. None of the other organelles listed are particularly involved with either DNA repair or apoptosis, so choice A is the best answer.

Passage 2 (Questions 6-9)

6. **B is the best answer.** Activating ERK1/2 signaling is stated to be favorable to the virus in the question stem. Thus, it is unlikely to destroy viral progeny, eliminating choices A and C. Next, apoptosis is the process of organized cell death, and can be triggered by the presence of virus in a cell. The virus is destroyed during apoptosis, so something favorable to viruses would likely prevent apoptosis. This makes choice B a better answer than choice D.

7. **D is the best answer.** The caption of Figure 1 states that U0126 is an inhibitor of ERK1/2 activation, meaning it decreases ERK1/2 signaling. This eliminates choices A and C. Next, the number of cells infected decreases following treatment with U0126. One possible mechanism to explain this is an increased rate of apoptosis for infected cells. Decreased apoptosis would not make sense given the results of Figure 1, so choice B is unlikely, and choice D is the best answer.

8. **C is the best answer.** Mitochondria have both an inner and outer membrane, so option I is true. Next, mtDNA is inherited from the mother since the egg is the primary source of mitochondria for the future cells of the offspring and the sperm primarily contributes the paternal DNA, ruling out option II. Finally, the folds in the mitochondria are called cristae, and they increase the surface area for increased production of ATP. Choice C is the best answer.

9. **D is the best answer.** This question is essentially asking which of the listed organelles is most important to lipid management. The Golgi apparatus is involved in packaging and secretion of proteins, not lipids, so choice A is unlikely. The nucleolus produces ribosomes, and ribosomes translate mRNA into protein, ruling out choices B and C. Finally, the smooth ER is the organelle that handles lipid processing and is the only organelle listed that is heavily involved with lipids. Choice D is the best answer.

Stand-alones (Questions 10-13)

10. **C is the best answer.** Choice A is unlikely as glucose is not generally transported into the mitochondria. Glycolysis occurs in the cytoplasm, so glucose would generally stay there. This also makes choice B unlikely as the process does not occur in the mitochondria. Generation of ATP would be decreased if the cristae are flattened. The cristae are folds in the mitochondria that increase surface area, increasing the area that can participate in the exchange of protons and generation of ATP by the electron transport chain. Choice C is a strong answer. Finally, fatty acid import into the cell depends on hormones, enzymes, and the properties of the cell membrane. Choice D is unlikely since mitochondria folds will not impact this.

11. **A is the best answer.** This question is a two-part question, and it is best to consider each part separately before picking an answer choice. Dehydration refers to a lack of water in the body, and this will result in a more concentrated extracellular fluid since there is not as much water to dilute the ions in the extracellular fluid. The extracellular fluid will be hypertonic to the cells and exert an osmotic pressure on the water inside the cells to pull water from the cells. If the cells in the brain attempt to compensate and maintain their size, they must hold on to the water in the cells. Choice A is the best answer, since it reflects the relationship between hypertonic and a higher osmotic pressure to pull fluid into the cells so as to counteract the pressure from the extracellular fluid. Choice B is a weaker answer, since the pressure would be increased and not decreased in an effort to compensate. Likewise, if the cells attempt to compensate, they must be hypertonic and not hypotonic to the extracellular fluid, so choices C and D can be eliminated. The size of the cells can be maintained because the extra ions inside the cells allow for more water to remain within the cells than would be expected if the cell did not make these adjustments and was exposed to a hypertonic extracellular fluid.

12. **B is the best answer.** When questions present information about the effects of an agent or syndrome and for a prediction, determining the net change to the cell is frequently the best strategy. In this question, the sodium-potassium pump is inhibited, which will result in an increase in intracellular Na^+. If intracellular Na^+ is usually low, then it could be used to facilitate the transfer of another ion against its gradient if Na^+ ions are allowed to move down their concentration gradient and into the cell. This is how the Na^+/Ca^{2+} exchanger operates. Many different channels use the Na^+ electrochemical gradient to provide power for their actions. If this pump is reversed by high levels of intracellular Na^+ due to the non-functional NKA, then it would now be exporting Na^+ in exchange for Ca^{2+}. Ca^{2+} is an important signaling molecule, so it is usually kept at a very low concentration in the cytosol by the actions of pumps which rapidly clear it, even against its concentration gradient. Therefore, the best answer will be one which is directly linked to higher intracellular Ca^{2+}. Choice A may be a tempting answer if the second part of the question stem is not considered, as inactivating NKA will alter the membrane potential. However, increased Ca^{2+} would result in more neurotransmitter release at synapses, making this a weaker answer choice. Increased intracellular calcium would increase the ability and strength with which a muscle can contract. Increased intracellular calcium is correctly associated with the prediction of increased muscle activity, making it a strong choice. An inhibited NKA pump would lead to a failure to reestablish normal Na^+/K^+ concentrations after an action potential, which would lead to weaker action potentials, not stronger ones. This makes choice C a weak answer. Choice D, localized pain relief, is not supported by any information in the question stem, and while it is possible that pain signals could not be communicated due to the inability of neurons to function properly, there are more severe consequences that would likely arise before this effect was achieves, so Choice D is a weaker answer choice. Choice B is the best answer.

13. **C is the best answer.** The rough endoplasmic reticulum is the primary site of protein synthesis for proteins that are exported out of the cell or to another intracellular organelle. The best answer will be the protein that would not be found either outside the cell or in the cytosol. Albumin is a secreted protein and makes up the majority of blood protein levels, eliminating choice A. Both the lysosome and Golgi apparatus are other membrane-bound organelles in the cell and would have proteins synthesized in the rough ER. Thus, choices B and D can be eliminated. Ribosomes that function to synthesize nuclear proteins are found in the cytosol. Once the nuclear proteins are synthesized, they are transported into the nucleus through nuclear pores. This is achieved independent of the rough endoplasmic reticulum, and the rate is unlikely to be affected by rough ER disruption, making choice C the best answer choice.

Passage 3 (Questions 14-17)

14. **C is the best answer.** The ribosomes studied in this experiment are cytoplasmic, unbound ribosomes, as opposed to the membrane-bound ribosomes of the rough ER. All ribosomes consist of two subunits composed of rRNA and proteins. In fact, rRNA stands for ribosomal RNA. This makes options I and II likely to be in the best answer. Next, the ribosomes on rough ER, not cytoplasmic ribosomes, are involved in production of secreted proteins, so option III is untrue. Choice C is the best answer.

15. **A is the best answer.** Ribosomal distribution requires intracellular transport mechanisms. Flagella and cilia are on outside of the membrane and involved in movement of the whole cell, so choices B and C are unlikely. Microtubules, on the other hand, are a platform for intracellular transport, making choice A likely. Next, the nucleolus is involved in production of ribosomes, and is a tempting choice. However, this is not the best answer because the nucleolus is not involved in transport of ribosomes, just the synthesis rRNA and the assembly of ribosomes.

16. **D is the best answer.** The ratio described in the question is close to one, meaning that ribosomes are found in equal numbers in both cells. While degrading the ribosomes and resynthesizing them would be one possible explanation for this equal distribution, lacking ribosomes in a newly formed cell would result in cell death since the cells would not be able to synthesize new proteins. This is supported by the observation in the passage that equal distribution of ribosomes in daughter cells is critical for cell survival. Choice A can be eliminated. Choices B and C are unlikely because they describe the behavior of chromosomes, not ribosomes. While it is possible that ribosomes undergo a similar mechanism as chromosomes to ensure proper segregation to each daughter cell, this is not discussed by the passage and has not been clearly elucidated, so choice B and C are weaker answers. Since the passage states that the ratio of ribosomes in both cells is approximately one, it is likely that the distribution of ribosomes is roughly equal, so choice D is the best answer.

17. **D is the best answer.** Figure 1 shows that during G_1, the distribution of cytoplasmic ribosomes near the cytoplasmic membrane and nuclear membrane is roughly equal. In G_2, there is a larger proportion of ribosomes near the nuclear membrane. This eliminates choices A and B. There is no surplus of ribosomes near the cytoplasmic membrane in G_2, so choice C is unlikely. It is likely that at some point between G_1 and G_2, ribosomes migrate towards the nuclear membrane, making choice D the best answer.

Passage 4 (Questions 18-22)

18. **C is the best answer.** Figure 2 is a western blot that shows the levels of tubulin in the trypanosome cell in the presence and absence of the various tubulin inhibitors. Notice that for compound 79, compound 11, and compound 12, the bars are at the same position and density, indicating that the protein content is the same between the conditions. A decrease in density would correspond to a reduction in protein content. Because the protein contain is relatively the same, choices A and B can be eliminated. Additionally, from the western blot, it would not be possible to determine whether a reduction in protein levels occurred due to a decrease in transcription or translation, further helping to eliminate these as possible answer choices. If compound 12 destabilized the tubulin polymers in order to prevent proliferation, the trypanosome would not be able to divide but would also contain the same concentration of tubulin, just in its monomer form, not polymer form. Because the levels of tubulin would remain the same, choice C is likely the best answer. Ubiquitination targets a protein for degradation by the proteasome, which would reduce cellular levels of tubulin. Figure 2 shows the levels are relatively constant, eliminating choice D. Choice C is the best answer.

19. **A is the best answer.** According to the question stem, some trypanosomes have become resistant to tubulin inhibitors, even when the inhibitor exists at a high concentration in the body. The structures of the tubulin inhibitors, as shown in Figure 1, are polar and relatively large, rending it unable to passively diffuse through the plasma membrane. Because the drug concentration is high outside the cell, energy will be required to pump a hydrophilic molecule across the plasma membrane, making choice A most likely to be the best answer. Because the tubulin inhibitor is going against its concentration gradient, not down its concentration gradient, choice B can be eliminated. Channels serve to mimic the hydration shell of molecules that are allowed to pass through them. These molecules move down their concentration gradients, which would be into the trypanosome in this scenario. Because the question stem indicates that the drug is being exported out of the trypanosome, choice C can be eliminated. Channels only allow molecules to move down their electrochemical gradients, eliminating choice D.

20. **D is the best answer.** The presence of tubulin inhibitors creates an evolutionary selective pressure that favors organisms that can survive in a selective environment. Trypanosomes that have a beneficial mutation in a gene that could confer resistance to the tubulin inhibitors would be more likely to survive. An example of a beneficial mutation would be an amino acid change in the site of the tubulin proteins to which the tubulin inhibitors formerly bound. A silent mutation does not change the amino acid sequence of a protein and would be less likely than a missense mutation to confer resistance to a small molecule. This eliminates choices A and B. A missense mutation changes the amino acid and could confer resistance if the amino acid change prevented the tubulin inhibitor molecule from binding tubulin. A gene is a set of DNA sequence that codes for a protein that is able to carry out a function in the cell. An allele is one version of a gene, defined by the exact nucleotide sequence of a given gene. A missense mutation would create a new allele within the tubulin gene, making choice D a better answer choice than choice C.

21. **A is the best answer.** According to paragraph one, trypanosomes are also eukaryotic cells, meaning they contain all features of other eukaryotic cells, such as neurons. Eukaryotes have membrane bound nuclei, so trypanosomes would be unlikely to contain non-membrane bound nuclei, making choice A a strong answer. DNA coiled around histones is a eukaryotic feature, eliminating choice B. While mRNA does not undergo post-transcriptional modification to a large extent in bacteria, it does in eukaryotes, eliminating choice C. Membrane bound organelles like the Golgi apparatus and mitochondria would also likely be found in both cells, eliminating choice D.

22. **A is the best answer.** The additional experiment performed by the researchers aims to determine whether compounds 12 or 79 can affect the number of trypanosome cells in the blood. According to the passage, these compounds are tubulin inhibitors. Tubulin is important in the separation of sister chromatids during anaphase of mitosis. Notice that it takes 4 to 5 days for the number of trypanosomes to increase in the blood during administration of compound 12. It takes 3 to 4 days for both the control and compound 79. This means compound 12 is more effective than compound 79 and the control at inhibiting tubulin. This makes choice A a strong answer. Tubulin is also an important component of flagella in eukaryotes. However, compound 12 is a more effective anti-tubulin inhibitor, eliminating choice B. Compared to control, administration of either compound 79 or 12 results in fewer trypanosomes per mL of blood, which means they are effective at controlling proliferation. This eliminates choice C. Because the number of trypanosomes begins to increase around days 3 to 4, even in the presence of the anti-tubulin compounds, this suggests that some of the trypanosomes have acquired ways to export the drug from the cell or now contain mutations that provide a survival advantage. This eliminates choice D and makes choice A the best answer.

Passage 5 (Questions 23-26)

23. **B is the best answer.** This question is asking about the voltage-gated potassium channels that are active during an action potential. It is not necessary to remember the direction of ion movements for an action potential to answer this question correctly. The hint in the passage is that these channels are activated by a change in voltage and not through ATP hydrolysis. This means that they are not accomplishing active transport. Glucose transport is a key example of facilitated diffusion where the glucose is transported by a carrier protein using an electrochemical gradient. The voltage-gated potassium channels are facilitating the diffusion of potassium ions down a gradient, so choice A is true of these channels. Since these channels are responsive to changes in voltage, they are unlikely to be stimulated to open by an external molecule. Ligand-gated channels are more likely to operate in this fashion. A classic example of this mechanism of stimulation is the binding of acetylcholine in the neuromuscular junction to ligand-gated sodium channels. Since the passage is describing a gated-channel that is responsive to changes in voltage, choice B is not a likely description for these channels, which makes it a strong answer. Choice C is true of these channels. Since ATP hydrolysis is not needed, the ions must be moving down an electrochemical gradient. Choice D is also true of these channels since ion channels must span the length of the bilayer in order to allow polar ions to traverse the plasma membrane, and such membrane proteins are referred to as intrinsic or integral proteins.

24. **A is the best answer.** The CFTR protein complex is a channel involved in the export of ions, as discussed in the passage. It must be a transmembrane channel for this reason, or else it would not be able to facilitate the passage of polar compounds across the hydrophobic core of the membrane. It is synthesized by ribosomes along the rough endoplasmic reticulum, and it is embedded in the membrane at this point. From there, it follows the normal path of vesicle transport. Option I is tricky because lysosomes are associated with the breakdown of cellular components. However, the lysosomes serve an important function in recycling compounds for future use, and the CFTR channel can be sent in a vesicle to the lysosomes for such a process. Glycosylation typically occurs in either the endoplasmic reticulum or the Golgi apparatus and not in secretory vesicles, so option II can be eliminated. Since the channel is a transmembrane channel, it will not be attached to the inner leaflet of the membrane but will be integrated into the membrane, so option III is inaccurate. Option IV is accurate, since the modifications involving the sugar groups attached to proteins occurs in the Golgi apparatus. Choice A is the best answer, since it contains both options I and IV, which are both possible for the CFTR channel. Choices B and C both contain option III and can be eliminated. Choice D includes option II, so it can be eliminated.

25. **B is the best answer.** This question is tricky because the answer choices are all somewhat valid independently, but not all of the choices are appropriate in light of the experimental design. The question is asking why amiloride is used in the experiment. As Table 1 shows, amiloride is a sodium channel blocker. Choice A is partially true in that the amiloride can serve as a comparison for the potassium channel blockers in order to assess how the latter can significantly inhibit hyaluronan export. However, the calcium channel blocker was also used, and it served as another point of comparison. This answer choice overreaches in saying that the use of amiloride serves to validate the experiment, since the calcium channel blocker could provide the same comparison. Choice B is a better answer because it more accurately reflects the point of looking at various channel blockers where the researchers can then make a conclusion about the potassium channel blockers by comparison. Still, at the outset, they would be interested in whether or not there is an effect on hyaluronan export through other channels, so the amiloride test would not necessarily be only a control group. Choice C is misleading. While inhibiting the sodium channel can provide information on its effect on the cell's ability to transport hyaluronan, the amiloride test does not give any information about the specific mechanism of ion transport in these cells. Choice D is tempting in light of the detail on the use of the drug in the question stem. However, the researchers are clearly focused on specific channel blockers in relation to hyaluronan export and not on how various therapeutics may affect the resting membrane potential. The last sentence of the passage states that the inhibitors were used to test the effects of the channels on membrane potential and hyaluronan export.

26. **D is the best answer.** Table 1 shows that glibenclamide selectively targets and blocks the ATP-dependent potassium channel. This means that the drug likely works by a mechanism related to this channel specifically. The ability of solutes to cross the membrane changes the resting membrane potential. Blocking a channel can thereby affect the membrane potential. Choice A is a weaker answer since the G protein-associated channel is not involved in this situation. The table shows that glibenclamide only targets the ATP-dependent channel. Choice B is tricky because the channel is regulated by the presence of ATP, and a drug blocking the formation of ATP could have an effect on the channel. However, cells rely on ATP for many processes, and such a drug could be lethal to a cell. It would be more likely that the drug would act selectively on the channel or a component related to the channel, so choice B is a weaker answer. Choice C is misleading because it mentions insulin, and the flow of calcium ions is related to insulin release. However, there is no evidence in the table or in the passage that glibenclamide inhibits the flow of calcium. In beta cells that release insulin, the inhibition of the potassium channel actually allows the calcium channels to open and raise the level of intracellular calcium. This information is not necessary to answer this question correctly but may be helpful to understand what is going on in this case. Choice D is the best answer since it proposes a mechanism in line with the information in the passage and in the table. The blockage of the channel has an effect on the membrane potential, and this is what leads to insulin release in patients treated with this drug.

Stand-alones (Questions 27-29)

27. **D is the best answer.** Marfan syndrome is a connective tissue disorder, and its effects are seen throughout the body. It is associated with defects in the aorta and heart valves, since the disorder can have lethal consequences when these areas are affected. Choice A would not be the best answer choice since blood vessels are lined by smooth and not skeletal muscle. There may be abnormalities in the smooth muscle as a result of the misfolded protein that can affect the growth and function of the surrounding smooth muscle cells. Choice B is tricky, since one may make the mistake of assuming the aorta contains cardiac muscle. Only the heart contains cardiac muscle, which is specialized to allow for rhythmic beating. The wall of the aorta is has a layer of smooth muscle. While epithelial cells make the basal lamina and proteins making up the extracellular matrix, they are not associated with making connective tissue, which weakens choice C. Choice D is the best answer, since fibroblasts make large amounts of elastin and collagen to make up the connective tissue. A study of this syndrome would benefit from focusing on these cells specifically.

28. **C is the best answer.** Gap junctions are intercellular junctions that form small channels for the passage of ions between cells. They are found in the heart where they are essential for the coordination of the cardiac muscle cells. They are also found in other cells throughout the body. In those cells, the purpose of the gap junctions is still the same. They allow for the passage of ions between cells, thereby allowing cells to communicate with one another. Epithelial cells contain gap junctions, but cell attachments are not directly associated with connexins. Desmosomes and tight junctions are more closely associated with this function, so choice A is not the best answer. Choice B is misleading since it is true that the skin is composed of epithelial cells, and it is true that these cells rest above an important sheet of extracellular matrix called the basal lamina that helps to keep the cells tethered. However, the gap junctions are unrelated to the basal lamina since gap junctions do not function in attaching these cells. Choice C is a better answer than choice A because the lack of gap junctions results in impaired cell-to-cell communication and signaling. The main function of gap junctions is to accommodate this type of signaling and not to just attach the cells to one another. Choice D is describing tight junctions, which serve to inhibit the flow of fluid between cells, so it can be eliminated.

29. **C is the best answer.** A single bacterial colony on a plate originates from one mother bacterium, so it is unlikely that Colony 1 and 2 are entirely different species, since they came from a single colony. Outbreeding means two unrelated individuals mating, so it makes this choice even less likely. Choice A is not the best answer. Conjugation is one way for bacteria to exchange genetic material with other, non-identical bacteria. If Colony 2 and Colony 1 conjugated with each other, it is possible for the random mutation in Colony 2 to be transferred to Colony 1. This would increase the fitness of Colony 1 plated on an antibiotic treated agar, so choice B can be eliminated. Random mutations occur frequently, and if Colony 2 developed a random mutation that Colony 1 did not, then all of the subsequent bacteria produced by Colony 2 via binary fission would have that beneficial mutation. Since the two colonies are isolated from one another, it is unlikely that this beneficial mutation could be transferred to Colony 1 via conjugation. This makes choice C a strong answer. Choice D is true of both colonies and is not a good explanation for why one colony survived while the other did not. This makes it a weaker answer.

Passage 6 (Questions 30-34)

30. **A is the best answer.** YC contains many hydroxyl groups that can serve as hydrogen bond donors and many oxygen atoms that can serve as hydrogen bonding acceptors. Leucine is a nonpolar amino acid that cannot participate in hydrogen bonding. It contains only hydrocarbons on its side chain, eliminating choice B. Valine is also a nonpolar amino acid that cannot participate in hydrogen bonding as it also only contains hydrocarbons on its side chain, eliminating choice C. Proline is a cyclic amino acid that sterically hinders the formation of alpha helices. It is also nonpolar due to the presence of hydrocarbons on its side chain and would be unable to participate in hydrogen bonding. Choice D can be eliminated. Hydrogen bonding occurs between H and N, F, or O. Serine, S, contains a hydroxyl group on the end of its side chain, making it a polar amino acid. The oxygen of the hydroxyl can serve as a hydrogen bond acceptor, while the hydrogen can serve as a hydrogen bond donor, making choice A the best answer.

31. **D is the best answer.** According to the passage, trypan blue-stained cells are apoptotic cells. Apoptosis is the process of organized cell death that occurs when cells are unable to repair mutated DNA or respond appropriately to pathogens like intracellular viruses and bacteria. Apoptosis also occurs during development and is necessary to remove cells that are no longer needed, such as those that form skin between the fingers. During apoptosis, chromatin condenses and endonucleases fragment DNA into specific lengths, making options I and II components of the best answer. The fragments of chromatin and DNA then aggregate into pieces of the plasma membrane that break off in a process called membrane blebbing, making option III a component of the best answer. Choice A can be eliminated because DNA fragmentation and membrane blebbing also occur during apoptosis. Choice B can be eliminated because membrane blebbing occurs as well. Choice C can be eliminated because chromatin condensation also occurs during apoptosis. Choice D is the best answer because it describes three of the processes that occur during apoptosis.

32. **D is the best answer.** The cytoskeleton is the network of proteins that maintains the structure of the cell and allows for the transport of intracellular vesicles and organelles. The cytoskeleton is composed of three components, including microtubules, intermediate filaments, and actin. Microtubules play a role in cell division by helping to separate chromosomes during anaphase and in the transport of intracellular vesicles by motor proteins like myosin, eliminating choice A. Intermediate filaments mainly support the structure of the cell, eliminating choice B, and actin polymerizes to allow movement of the cell, eliminating choice C. Glycoproteins are largely components of the extracellular matrix and allow for other cells to adhere and may serve as receptors in some instances. Glycoproteins do not serve as a main component of the intracellular cytoskeleton, making choice D the best answer.

33. **C is the best answer.** The basement membrane is where the basal part of the cell attaches to the extracellular matrix of the tissue. Gap junctions are apical connections between cells that allow the passage of ions and small molecules and are important for cell-to-cell communication. Because they do not mediate the basement membrane attachment, choice A can be eliminated. Desmosomes hold two cells together on the sides of cells and are part of the apical membrane of the cell. They are not responsible for basement membrane adhesion, eliminating choice B. Tight junctions are nearest the luminal side of a cell and form between two cells to prevent the diffusion of molecules between two cells. They do not mediate cellular attachment to the basement membrane, eliminating choice D. Hemidesmosomes are similar to desmosomes but are important in the attachment of a cell to the extracellular matrix of the basement membrane. Cancer cells would need to break down these structures in order to metastasize, making choice C the best answer.

34. **A is the best answer.** The data in Figure 3 show that increasing the concentration of YC results in decreased cellular locomotion. According to the passage, YC acts on AMPK, which acts on mTORC2 to regulate the actin cytoskeleton of the cell. Actin is primarily important for cellular locomotion and plays a major role in the metastasis of cancer cells, as supported by the passage. Because the passage implies that actin rearrangement is the most important mechanism used for cellular motion, an answer choice involving microtubules, which help separate the chromosomes in anaphase of mitosis, is less likely to be the best answer. Ubiquitination of proteins targets proteins for degradation by the proteasome, decreasing their concentration in the cell. Because the passage does not discuss the role of ubiquitin or protein degradation, choices C and D are less likely to be the best answer. Figure 3 supports the role of YC in cellular migration, not progression through the cell cycle, also helping to eliminate choice C as the best answer. Figure 3 also shows that increasing the concentration of YC results in decreased cellular motion. Because YC acts on mTORC2, which regulates actin, inhibition of mTORC2 would likely decrease the formation of actin polymers that allow the cell to move forward. This makes choice A the best answer choice.

Passage 7 (Questions 35-38)

35. **C is the best answer.** According to the passage, VE-cadherin is a critical adhesion molecule. Based on this, it seems that the protein would be enriched in cells that must be stationary and adherent to other cells and the ECM. Choice A is unlikely since rough ER creates membrane bound proteins like VE-cadherin. Thus, an inverse relationship would not be expected. There is no direct relationship between smooth ER and function/generation of VE-cadherin, so choice B is unlikely. Choice C is the best answer since flagella are involved in movement and motility of cells. A cell that needs to move around a lot would be unlikely to have high levels of VE-cadherin, so choice C is likely. Choice D is unlikely since almost all cells have only one nucleus.

36. **A is the best answer.** Figure 2 shows that knockout of VN reduces vessel permeability. Furthermore, Figure 1 shows that knockout of VN drastically reduces the number of macrophages that can exit the bloodstream. Vessel permeability seems to be directly related to the number of macrophages that can exit the bloodstream and go into the tissues. Since VN knockout reduces permeability choices B and D are unlikely. Next, choice A is a strong answer because a reduced ability of immune cells to leave the bloodstream would lower the proper response to a pathogen. Choice C is unlikely because immune response would not be expected to be enhanced if macrophages could not leave the bloodstream.

37. **D is the best answer.** Tight junctions are intercellular connections that prevent movement of most molecules. Tight junctions specifically prevent the movement from the apical side to the basilar side, or vice versa, that normally would occur at the border of two cells. This form of transport is called transcellular transport, so option I is true. Tight junctions are typically found in epithelial tissues because epithelial tissues are often meant to form a barrier, which makes option III true. Cardiac muscles transmit action potentials via movement of ions, and this is facilitated by gap junctions, which allow for this movement. Option II is also true and choice D is the best answer.

38. **C is the best answer.** Proteins and other large, polar signaling molecules have membrane-bound receptors because they are unable to pass through the lipid bilayer membrane. Thus, any intracellular answers, as in choices B and D, are unlikely. Even signaling molecules that do bind to intracellular receptors, like those in the nucleus and cytoplasm, do not typically exit the target cell by exocytosis. They typically are used to signal in the target cell and then can be degraded within the target cell. Choices A and C are both possible since they correctly identify the membrane as the site of the vitronectin receptor. When molecules bind to their receptors, the receptor-ligand complex is often taken into the cell by receptor-mediated endocytosis, so choice C is a better answer than choice A. Choice A is not the best answer because pinocytosis describes taking up of extracellular fluid in a random, nonselective manner. This is not what happens following receptor binding.

Stand-alones (Questions 39-41)

39. **B is the best answer.** The plasma membrane is made up of a phospholipid bilayer. Phospholipids have a polar, hydrophilic phosphate head and two non-polar, hydrophobic fatty acid chains that make up the "tails". Small, non-polar, and/or non-charged molecules are able to passively diffuse through the hydrophobic center of the bilayer. Choice A depicts benzene, a non-polar, and non-charged molecule that is likely capable of passing through the lipid membrane due to its hydrophobic properties. Choice B depicts glucose, which at first glance may seem as large as benzene, but is much larger given its hydroxyl functional groups. The polar properties of these groups coupled with glucose's relatively large size make it less likely to passively diffuse through the bilayer. Choice C depicts carbon dioxide, a relatively small, non-polar, and non-charged gas that is not hindered by the hydrophobic phospholipid tails and will most likely passively diffuse. Choice D depicts ethanol, which is a polar molecule like water but is relatively small and non-charged. Of the four choices, Choice A, C, and D can be eliminated because they are more likely to diffuse through the cell membrane due to their electrochemical properties than choice B. Choice B is the best answer because glucose is least likely to passively diffuse through the plasma membrane due to its size and the polarity of its many functional groups. Glucose requires facilitated diffusion to pass through most cell membranes.

40. **C is the best answer.** The question is asking why a vaccine using coat proteins might be ineffective against HIV. This question does not require memorization, and a hint is in the question stem. The question stem suggests that this particular vaccine would not be effective, indicating that there is something about the structure of HIV that would make the HPV vaccine ineffective. Choice A is true but is unrelated to the question since it does not explain why this particular type of vaccine would be ineffective. The increased ability to adapt means it may be difficult to target through all types of vaccines. Choice B is true but is also not relevant since the vaccine is meant to protect against infection before one is infected, so the effect on the immune system is more relevant for people who already have the virus. The coat proteins of an enveloped virus are shielded from the immune system by the envelope. This means that the use of a virus-like particle that only displays the coat proteins to the immune system would not allow for the immune system to develop an effective defense to future infection. This makes choice C a strong answer. Choice D is true of HIV, but it is not relevant to a vaccine. This explanation may clarify why HIV is difficult to treat for those who have it, but it does not explain why this vaccine would not work to prevent infection in the first place.

41. **C is the best answer.** The question is asking for the cell type that is typically responsible for the production of extracellular matrix components. Hyaluronan is an example of a specific glycosaminoglycan that can be made by epithelial cells, though there are many other types of large molecules that constitute the extracellular matrix. Epithelial cells are supported by the ECM but are not typically associated with forming the extracellular matrix, so choice A can be eliminated. Lymphocytes, as their name implies, are associated with the lymphatic system and travel within blood and lymph, so these would not be expected to form extracellular matrix. Choice B can be eliminated. Fibroblasts typically make elastin, collagen and other components to form the extracellular array of proteins and other components that attach cells together. Choice C is a strong answer since it accurately identifies the cell type associated with the production of these components. Choice D, neurons, are typically associated with other cells such as Schwann cells that form extracellular components such as the thick myelin sheath around neurons. Choice D can be eliminated, making choice C the best answer.

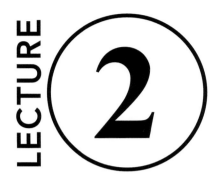

LECTURE

2

The Nervous System

TEST 2A

ANSWERS & EXPLANATIONS
Questions 1–59

LECTURE 2 ANSWER KEY

TEST 2A		MINI-TEST 2B	
1. B	31. C	1. C	22. A
2. B	32. C	2. B	23. A
3. D	33. B	3. B	24. D
4. B	34. C	4. C	25. B
5. D	35. C	5. B	26. D
6. D	36. B	6. C	27. A
7. B	37. D	7. A	28. B
8. A	38. D	8. D	29. B
9. B	39. D	9. D	30. A
10. C	40. C	10. B	31. C
11. D	41. D	11. B	32. A
12. A	42. D	12. D	33. B
13. C	43. A	13. A	34. C
14. C	44. B	14. C	35. B
15. C	45. D	15. C	36. C
16. C	46. B	16. D	37. D
17. D	47. B	17. D	38. B
18. A	48. B	18. D	39. B
19. C	49. A	19. A	40. A
20. A	50. D	20. D	41. A
21. C	51. D	21. D	
22. D	52. B		
23. D	53. C		
24. A	54. A		
25. C	55. D		
26. C	56. B		
27. D	57. D		
28. B	58. A		
29. C	59. B		
30. B			

EXPLANATIONS FOR LECTURE 2

Passage 1 (Questions 1-4)

1. **B is the best answer.** The resting membrane potential is a balance of the relative sodium and potassium concentrations inside and outside of the neuron. In general, potassium is high inside the neuron and sodium is high outside the neuron. A mutation that increased the permeability of the channel to K^+ at rest would allow more K^+ to leak out of the cell. The outward movement of K^+ hyperpolarizes the cell, as positive charge is leaving. Thus, the value of the resting potential will be more negative. This eliminates choices C and D. -120 mV is too much of a deviation from the normal resting potential to be the best answer. The equilibrium potential of potassium is around -84 mV, meaning that if potassium was the only ion giving rise to the membrane potential, -84 mV would be the value. Because some sodium still contributes to the neuron membrane potential, -120 mV would never be reached, eliminating choice A. The sodium/potassium pump would still be functioning, which would help prevent the membrane potential from deviating too much from the resting potential, also helping to eliminate choice A. Choice B is the best answer because it shows are more negative potential than the resting potential but still between the equilibrium potentials of potassium and sodium.

2. **B is the best answer.** According to paragraph one, Kv1.2 channels are found in the axon initial segment and the axon terminal. The axon hillock is the axon initial segment that determines whether an action potential will fire. Option I should be in the best answer. The synaptic button is the end of the axon where vesicles containing neurotransmitters fuse with the plasma membrane to deliver chemicals to the synaptic cleft. An action potential must also reach the axon terminal in order to allow the vesicles to fuse, meaning that option II should be contained in the best answer. The cell body does not contain Kv1.2 channels, according to the passage and is mostly responsible for maintaining the nutritional state of the cell. Option III will not be contained in the best answer. Choice A can be eliminated because it does not contain option II. Choices C and D can be eliminated because they contain option III. Choice B is the best answer because it contains both options I and II, but not option III.

3. **D is the best answer.** Potassium is a positively charged ion that needs a channel to flow through in order to cross the hydrophobic plasma membrane. Arginine, R, is also a positively charged amino acid and would likely repel, not attract K^+ into the channel, eliminating choice A. Lysine, K, is also a positively charged amino acid that would likely repel, not attract, K^+ into the channel, eliminating choice B. Alanine, A, is a hydrophobic amino acid and would avoid interacting with polar or positively charged ions. Alanine is unlikely to be found in the channel itself, eliminating choice C. Glutamate, E, is a negatively charged amino acid that could help attract the positive charge of K^+, allowing it to enter and flow through the channel. Thus, choice D is the best answer.

4. **B is the best answer.** Figure 2 provides the best information to help answer this question. The red curve represents the mutated Kv1.2. Notice that its current is much higher than the wild type channel, indicating that more ions move per unit time through the mutant channel, as compared to the wild type channel. Potassium channels are involved in repolarization of the neuron by allowing potassium to flow out of the neuron. Because they are involved in repolarization, not depolarization, choices C and D can be eliminated. Sodium channels are the primary drivers of depolarization in the neuron. A higher current would allow more ions to move in a shorter amount of time, allowing the membrane to return to a negative potential more rapidly. This would decrease the time of repolarization, eliminating choice A and making choice B the best answer.

Passage 2 (Questions 5-9)

5. **D is the best answer.** Neurons are the primary cells of the nervous system and may be damaged by GBS. However, the passage focuses only on myelin, so choice A is not the best answer. Astrocytes are found in the central nervous system (CNS) and perform many functions including providing nutrients to the neurons. The passage does not mention the CNS, so choice B is not the best answer. Oligodendrocytes are the cells that myelinate the CNS. They are not found in the peripheral nervous system, so choice C is not the best answer. The passage states the GBS is a demyelinating disease that affects the peripheral nervous system. The cells that myelinate the peripheral nervous system are Schwann cells, so choice D is the best answer.

6. **D is the best answer.** The passage states that GBS results in paralysis through demyelination of the peripheral nervous system. The autonomic nervous system has two branches: the sympathetic and parasympathetic. Both are involved in breathing through control bronchiole dilation and constriction, respectively. However, the primary muscle that controls breathing is the diaphragm which is a skeletal muscle, so it is part of the somatic nervous system. Choices A, B, and C are not wrong answers because the autonomic nervous system and its branches do have effects on breathing. However, choices A, B and C are not the best answers. This is a key feature of many MCAT® questions. Always read each answer choice to determine which answer is best.

7. **B is the best answer.** The passage states that GBS causes demyelination in the peripheral nervous system. Although the spinal cord is considered part of the central nervous system, this question can be answered by identifying which part of the spinal cord may have myelin. Myelin is the fat that surrounds the axons of neurons and gives nervous tissue a white color. In the spinal cord, the white matter is the outer layer, so choice B is a strong answer. This white matter represents the axons of neurons returning to the brain whereas the centralized gray matter is the cell bodies and glial cells that eventually send signals to the muscles. Choice A inaccurately identifies the location of white matter. Choices C and D refer to gray matter, which generally is not myelinated. So, choice B is the best answer.

8. **A is the best answer.** The question is asking which neurotransmitters would not be released in a person who has GBS. The passage states that GBS causes paralysis. Muscle movement is controlled by the somatic nervous system, which uses acetylcholine as its primary neurotransmitter. In GBS, neurons are demyelinated, which causes a slower and potentially ineffective propagation of the action potential. This means the excitatory signal cannot reach the axon terminal. This would cause less acetylcholine to be released, and option I is true. Epinephrine and norepinephrine are used by the sympathetic nervous system. There is no information in the passage that suggests that these would be affected so options II and III are not good answers. Dopamine is used primarily in the CNS and is involved in movement. The passage only mentions effects in the peripheral nervous system so option IV is not true and choice A is the best answer.

9. **B is the best answer.** In GBS, the myelin is destroyed so no signal is sent from the neuron to the muscle. Excitatory signals result in an increased chance that a signal will be sent to the next cell so choice A would have the opposite effect as GBS. Calcium influx at the axon terminal triggers neurotransmitter release. Without this, the signal will not be sent from the neuron to the muscle so choice B is a good answer. Acetylcholine (ACh) is the primary neurotransmitter used to signal skeletal muscle contraction. Anything that increases the amount of ACh will increase excitation of the muscles. A decrease in metabolism would increase the concentration of ACh so choice C is an opposite. The relative refractory period is the time in which it takes a greater electrical stimulation to trigger an action potential. Unlike the absolute refractory period, the relative refractory period can be overcome with a greater electrical excitation in the form of a huge depolarization. Since signals could still be sent during this time, choice D is not the best answer.

Passage 3 (Questions 10-13)

10. **C is the best answer.** Reflexes may operate in a negative feedback loop, as described in choice A. For instance, the stretch reflex contracts a stretched muscle to regain its resting length. Somatic muscle reflexes often involve contraction of one muscle group and extension of its antagonistic group, which makes choice B also true and unlikely to be the best answer. Reflexes cannot operate without either the brain or spinal cord, which makes choice C false and the best answer. Although not required, the spinal cord via interneurons or the brain via voluntary control can regulate reflexes, so choice D is also unlikely to be the best answer.

11. **D is the best answer.** Table 1 shows that diabetics had significantly less sensitive corneas than control, making choices A and B unlikely to be the best answer. If the eyes of diabetics took longer to become desensitized to corneal stimuli, as choice C describes, it is likely that they had a higher corneal sensitivity to begin with, which is not the case as shown in the figure. If diabetics have less sensitive corneas, then they are more likely to have weaker corneal reflexes since this reflex is stimulated by nerve endings on the corneal surface sensitive to touch. This makes choice D the best answer.

12. **A is the best answer.** Table 2 indicates that tear film stability, represented as NIBUT, is significantly correlated with lower neuropathy scores. The first sentence of the passage says that the neuropathy seen in diabetes leads to decreased sensation, so decreasing tear film stability in diabetics would lead to higher neuropathy scores and thus changes in the somatosensory system. Photoreceptors are in retina and do not belong to the somatosensory system, making choice A the best answer. Mechanoreceptors for touch, nociceptors for pain, and thermoreceptors for temperature are all part of the somatosensory system and can thus be correlated with neuropathy in diabetics, making choices B, C, and D less likely to be the best answer.

13. **C is the best answer.** This is a concept question that will be easier to answer upon thinking of an example for each option. Different neurotransmitters are released at different synapses, such as epinephrine for the sympathetic system and acetylcholine for both the parasympathetic and sympathetic nervous systems. The nervous system can change levels of neurotransmitters released by altering the activity of certain neurons, making option I true which eliminates choice B. Regulation of other organ systems is another key function of the nervous system, such as how the parasympathetic nervous system stimulates the urinary and gastrointestinal systems, which makes option II true and eliminates choice A and choice D. Option III is unlikely to be the best answer because sensory processing generally remains unchanged. The brain's perception of these processed stimuli may change. For instance, in this passage, the corneal reflex will follow the same route from the corneal nerve endings to the brain regardless of the external environment, but patients with diabetes may perceive less of this sensation.

Stand-alones (Questions 14-17)

14. C is the best answer. This question is asking for the big picture function of the nervous system, which can sometimes be lost when one focuses on the molecular mechanisms underpinning nervous system function. Choices A, B, C and D are all functions of the nervous system. The best choice will be the one that is the broadest and most encompassing. Choice A, B and D describe specific tasks that the nervous system accomplishes. Choice C describes the ultimate goal of all these individual tasks: to interact with the external world (by sensing, processing and reacting to stimuli) and to act as a method of communication within the body. This makes choice C the best answer.

15. C is the best answer. This question tests the concept of regulation. Specifically, this question tests regulation of other organ systems by the nervous system. Choice A essentially states that the hypothalamus plays an important role in temperature control which is a type of internal regulation, making Choice A unlikely to be the best answer. Choice B states that a branch of the nervous system stimulates other organ systems, making it unlikely to be the best answer. Choice C only mentions an isolated function of part of the central nervous system without stating whether it regulates other organ systems, so this is not an example of regulation and the best answer. Choice D shows how the brain can suppress, or regulate, the act of breathing, making it also unlikely to be the best answer.

16. C is the best answer. Section A of the figure shows the resting membrane potential of around -70 mV. Sections C and D represent the phases of the action potential where the membrane is repolarizing. This is due to the action of voltage-gated potassium channels, eliminating choice A. Section B is the depolarization step that is mediated by ligand-gated sodium channels, eliminating choice B. As this is the neuron action potential, not the cardiac action potential, there is no portion of the action potential that corresponds to calcium, eliminating choice D. The sodium/potassium pump is responsible for maintaining the resting membrane potential, making choice C the best answer.

17. D is the best answer. This question asks about the differences between chemical and electrical synapses. Chemical synapses consist of a neuron that releases neurotransmitters into the synapse, which then bind to receptors on the postsynaptic neuron. Electrical synapses are where electrical impulses jump from one neuron to another to communicate. Both types of synapses occur all over the nervous system, making choices A and B unlikely. At chemical synapses, there are distinct presynaptic terminals that release neurotransmitters into the synapse, and postsynaptic terminals that have receptors that neurotransmitters bind to. The communication only occurs in one direction, meaning they are unidirectional. Electrical synapses can communicate in both directions, making them bidirectional. If cell A and cell B are connected by an electrical synapse, then communication can go A→B and B→A. Thus, choice C is a weaker answer and choice D is the best answer.

Passage 4 (Questions 18-21)

18. A is the best answer. The best answer to this question will need to explain how myelin damage in the bipolar type I neurons can result in hearing damage. The passage states that MBPs are essential components of the myelin sheath. The loss of the MBPs will result in damage to the myelin. Myelin is essential because it serves to insulate axons to allow action potentials to propagate. The leakage of the ions will result in weaker action potentials that will not be able to release as much neurotransmitter into the synaptic cleft. Less neurotransmitter in the synaptic cleft will cause the post-synaptic cell to become less depolarized because there are less activating signals being passed on. If an action potential is not sent, the auditory stimulus will be lost because there is no information being passed on. Choice A is plausible because it provides a valid explanation for how myelin damage can lead to hearing loss. The determination of whether a neuron sends an action potential or not occurs at the axon hillock. Action potential firing has to do with the depolarization of the axon hillock which is unrelated to the presence of myelin. Choice A is better than choice B because it better explains how loss of MBPs can cause hearing deficits. Choice B can therefore be eliminated. Ion channels are located within the plasma membrane of the neuron. Ion channels need to be located in the plasma membrane in order to bring ions from the extracellular space into the intracellular space. The passage states that MBPs are components of the myelin which does not contain any ion channels. Choice C can be eliminated because it incorrectly associates MBPs with the ion channels. The resting membrane potential is established by the electrochemical gradient. This is governed by the ion channels located within the plasma membrane. The myelin on the axon has no influence on the resting membrane potential. Choice D can be eliminated because the resting membrane potential of neurons is not affected by reduction of MBPs. Choice A is the best answer because it explains how reduction of MBPs can cause hearing deficits.

19. **C is the best answer.** Myelin sheath damage of the auditory nerve will result in a reduction in the signals being transmitted from the ear to the brain. Myelin is required for successful action potential propagation, so the best answer will describe a situation where hearing loss can be attributed to factors other than damage to the auditory nerve. It would be expected that damage to the myelin sheath of the auditory nerve would result in decreased auditory cortex activation. The auditory cortex is where auditory information is processed. In order for a stimulus to be processed, it first needs to pass through the auditory nerve. Damage to the myelin sheath of the auditory nerve will result in less activation of the auditory cortex so choice A can be eliminated. The semicircular canals are a major component of the vestibular system. The vestibular system is important for detecting body movements. Damage to the semicircular canals would have no impact on hearing so choice B can be eliminated. Hair cells are the specialized mechanoreceptors that are responsible for detecting auditory stimulus. The hair cells function by taking the auditory stimulus and converting it into a neural signal that is then carried by the auditory nerve. A reduction in the number of hair cells would result in less information being carried by the auditory nerve. This is a plausible explanation for presbyacusis that does not involve myelin sheath damage. The amount of action potentials fired is related to how well a signal is detected. Increased action potential firing would mean that auditory stimuli are better detected which is the opposite of hearing loss. Choice D can therefore be eliminated. Choice C is the best answer because it provides a mechanism for presbyacusis that does not involve the myelin sheath of the auditory nerve.

20. **A is the best answer.** Dendrites will become depolarized when neurotransmitter is released into the synaptic cleft. This occurs when presynaptic neurons send an action potential which is then transferred to the dendrites of the postsynaptic neuron. When dealing with sensory systems, there is maximum depolarization when the sensory stimulus is best detected. Figure 1A contains the ABR threshold which is measured in decibels on the Y axis and it also has frequency measured in kilohertz on the X axis. The ABR threshold is the decibel level required to cause an auditory brainstem response which is an indicator of auditory nerve activation. The auditory system is most sensitive when the ABR threshold is low. This means that under low decibel conditions, there is still activation of the auditory nerve. The best answer to this question will be the frequency range that requires the lowest ABR threshold. Between 10 kHz and 30 kHz, the ABR threshold is at 20 dB which is the minimum of the graph. Choice A is plausible because it describes a frequency range that contains a low ABR threshold. Between the range of 5 kHz and 10 kHz, the ABR threshold ranges from 50 dB to 20 dB. Choice B can be eliminated because this frequency range requires a higher ABR threshold than choice A. The frequency range of 5 kHz to 10 kHz and 30 kHz to 40 kHz both contain ABR thresholds that are higher than between the frequency range of 10 kHz to 30 kHz so choice C can be eliminated. The depolarization of the dendrites will vary depending on the sensitivity of the auditory system. Figure 1A shows that different sound intensities are required to elicit an ABR. Choice A is better than choice D because the sensitivity of the auditory system will determine the dendrite depolarization at various frequencies. Choice A is the best answer because the frequency range of 10 kHz to 30 kHz requires the lowest ABR threshold.

21. **C is the best answer.** The passage states that the hair cells in addition to the bipolar type I neurons form the sensory receptors. ANS neurons form synapses on many tissues either as the sympathetic nervous system or the parasympathetic nervous system. Both of these systems regulate the function of the tissues that they innervate. The ANS takes signals from the central nervous system and passes them along to peripheral tissues. An afferent neuron is also called a sensory neuron. Its function is to bring information toward the central nervous system. An efferent neuron is also called a motor neuron or effector neuron. It brings information from the central nervous system to the peripheral tissues. The ANS is composed of efferent neurons whereas the bipolar type I neurons are afferent neurons. Choice A can be eliminated because it reverses the classifications. Choice B is essentially the same as choice A. A sensory neuron is an afferent neuron and an effector is an efferent neuron. Choice B can be eliminated because it does not correctly classify ANS neurons and the bipolar type I neurons. Choice C is a plausible answer because it correctly matches efferent with ANS neurons and afferent with bipolar type I neurons. A neuroglia cell is a support cell in the nervous system. It is not a type of neuron so choice D can be eliminated. Choice C is the best answer because it correctly classifies ANS neurons and bipolar type I neurons.

22. **D is the best answer.** Neurons are often described in terms of concentration cells because ions flow across the membrane due to electrochemical gradients. Ions will diffuse down their concentration gradients until they are eventually resisted by the electrical gradient that forms. The question stem indicates that there is a high intensity auditory stimulus so it can be assumed that an action potential will take place in the bipolar type I neuron. The flow of negative charge is equivalent to the flow of electrons. During an action potential, Na^+ ions first flow into the neuron and then K^+ ions flow out. In electrochemical cells, current is described in terms of the flow of positive charge and electrons always flow opposite this. During an action potential, there are only positively charged ions being exchanged between the neuron and the extracellular space; however, electrons always move in the opposite direction of positive charge. Saying that positive charge is moving into the neuron is exactly the same as saying that negative charge is leaving the neuron. Choice A can be eliminated because electrons always flow opposite positive charge. The current is defined by the movement of positive charge. Choice B can be eliminated because the current does not describe the flow of electrons. The resting membrane potential is partly established because negatively charged proteins cannot pass through the plasma membrane. This helps the membrane reach a negative resting potential. However, during an action potential these negatively charged proteins are different than the flow of electrons that is opposite the flow of positively charged ions. Choice C can be eliminated because it does not explain how electrons flow during an action potential. The first step of an action potential is for Na^+ ions to flow from the extracellular space into the cytosol of the neuron. This means that electrons will be flowing out of the neuron. Even though choice D only explains the first part of an action potential, it is the only answer the correctly describes the flow of electrons so choice D is the best answer.

Passage 5 (Questions 23-26)

23. **D is the best answer.** This question may seem more complex at first, but it is essentially testing where acetylcholine is used throughout the nervous system. Motor neurons primarily use acetylcholine so option I is likely to be in the right answer. Next, the sympathetic nervous system's preganglionic neurons use acetylcholine, while both preganglionic and postganglionic neurons use acetylcholine in the parasympathetic nervous system. Thus, all three of these components could be impacted by this deficiency, and choice D is the best answer.

24. **A is the best answer.** Figure 2 shows that apoptosis is drastically increased in SOD1 deficient mice. Apoptosis is organized cell death, and proper control of this process depends on cleanup after. This is the role of macrophages, and microglia are the macrophages of the nervous system. When they are not working correctly it is likely that apoptosed cells will not be properly disposed of and will release toxic contents into the extracellular space, damaging neighboring cells. Choice A is a strong answer. A deficiency in Schwann cells could increase the effect of reduced nerve conduction velocity. However, this is not examined in Figure 2, so choice B is less relevant to the question. B lymphocytes are involved in the adaptive immune response and produce antibodies against specific phagocytes. This is not particularly related to Figure 2, and additionally, antibodies do not generally get into the central nervous system or cerebrospinal fluid. Neutrophils are another prominent white blood cell and they phagocytose and degranulate in order to combat pathogens. They are not particularly involved in the steps of apoptosis, so choice D can be ruled out. Choice A is the best answer.

25. **C is the best answer.** Simple two neuron reflexes involve one synapse between a sensory neuron that receives a stimulus, and the motor neuron that carries out the response to the stimulus. Examples include the patellar and Achilles reflex. There is no interneuron involved in this type of reflex, making option II unlikely. This eliminates choices B and D. Neurons involving three or more neurons are classified as polysynaptic, as they involve more than one junction between neurons. These reflexes utilize interneurons, and reflexes that fall into this category include the flexor withdrawal reflex, which causes the body to withdraw from a harmful stimulus like pain. This particular three neuron reflex arc contains a sensory neuron, an interneuron, and a motor neuron. Both sensory neurons and motor neurons transmit signals via axons during this reflex. The sensory neuron receives a stimulus from the environment and then sends this information to a motor neuron via an axon. Next, the motor neuron axon terminates on muscle cells and brings about the motor response. Choice C is the best answer, as recording from the locations in both options I and III would result in useful information.

26. **C is the best answer.** SOD1 is a protein involved in preventing oxidative damage to cells, particularly DNA. A SOD1 deficient cell would be damaged and likely not functioning at full capacity. If anything, neurotransmitter concentration would be lower as protein synthesis would not be occurring as rapidly as normal. Choice A is unlikely. Neuron death would be increased as SOD1 is not present to prevent DNA damage, which is the opposite of choice B. Next, the resting potential is negative and dependent on moving more positive ions out than in. Lipid damage and lack of membrane integrity would cause all of the ions to equalize across the membrane, causing it to go from a regular resting potential of -70 mV towards 0 mV. This leads to an inability to maintain resting potential due to an increase in this value. Choice C is the best answer. Choice D is unlikely because the membrane potential would increase, or become less negative, not decrease.

Stand-alones (Questions 27-30)

27. **D is the best answer.** Ependymal cells are cells that use their many cilia to circulate cerebrospinal fluid throughout the nervous system. Microglia are the primary immune cells in the nervous system, making choice A unlikely. Myelination, which involves oligodendrocytes and Schwann cells, is the key factor is conduction velocity, making choice B not a strong answer. The blood brain barrier is maintained by astrocytes, not ependymal cells, so choice C is unlikely. Choice D is the best answer because when ependymal cells experience loss of function, the primary effect is on production of cerebrospinal fluid. Ependymal cells produce this fluid, and also circulate it with their many cilia.

28. **B is the best answer.** Nerve conduction velocity depends on myelination in many nerves. Myelin serves to insulate the processes of neurons and allow for salutatory conduction between nodes of Ranvier, which are unmyelinated areas between myelin sheaths. This increases nerve conduction velocity, so the cell most involved in myelination is most likely to be the best answer. Oligodendrocytes and Schwann cells are both involved in myelinating neurons, but Schwann cells are in the peripheral nervous system while oligodendrocytes are in the central nervous system. This distinction makes choice B a better answer than choice A. Microglia are immune cells and phagocytes within the nervous system. They do not as directly contribute to nerve conduction velocity, so choice C is less likely. Ependymal cells are involved in cerebrospinal fluid flow and production, using their cilia to beat the CSF and allowing it to flow throughout the nervous system. This is also not as related to conduction velocity, eliminating choice D.

29. **C is the best answer.** There are several major types of glia that are important to know. Microglia are the major immune cells of the nervous system and also perform phagocytic cleanup. Oligodendrocytes and Schwann cells form myelin sheaths throughout the nervous system. Choices A and B are unlikely as they identify other cell types. Choice C is the best answer because astrocytes are indeed heavily involved in the blood brain barrier. Ependymal cells have many cilia and beat them to circulate cerebrospinal fluid. Choice D is unlikely.

30. **B is the best answer.** Myelin wraps around axons and only leaves small sections of the plasma membrane exposed. The plasma membrane contains the ion channels which are essential for producing action potentials. The result of the myelin is that the action potential needs to jump from opening to opening because these are the only locations on the axon where the ion channels have access to the extracellular space. The areas with exposed plasma membrane are called nodes of Ranvier. The nodes of Ranvier facilitate the fast travel of action potentials because they contain ion channels. Choice A seems plausible because it describes a feature of neurons that increases action potential velocity. Saltatory conduction is the actual process of the jumping of the action potentials between nodes of Ranvier. Choice B is better than choice A because the nodes of Ranvier are only features of the neuron whereas saltatory conduction is the actual process that increases action potential velocity. Choice A can therefore be eliminated. Glial cells are what compose the myelin. Although important, the question is asking for a specific aspect of the myelin that is responsible for increasing action potential velocity so choice C can be eliminated. Electrical synapses are a specific type of synapse that does not use a neurotransmitter. They are very fast but they are not related to the presence of a myelin sheath. An electrical synapse forms because of specialized proteins contained within the plasma membrane so choice D can be eliminated. Choice B is the best answer because it identifies the process that is responsible for increasing the propagation velocity of an action potential.

Passage 6 (Questions 31-35)

31. **C is the best answer.** Figure 1 shows a clear increase in dopamine levels in the triple mutant. This immediately rules out choices A and B. While choice A could potentially be logical, as dopamine levels would drop if too much dopaminergic signaling occurred, it does not reflect the results in Figure 1. Next, there is no evidence provided regarding reuptake levels, making choice B unlikely. Although more dopamine would be in the synapse and actively signaling if it did not undergo reuptake, there is no evidence for this answer. Choice C is a good answer because it not only correctly interprets Figure 1, but also explains it in a plausible way. When a type of signaling is lost, cells will compensate by over-releasing the relevant neurotransmitter. Choice D is not the best answer as none of the experiments measure the ability to combat pathogens or present a relationship between those two variables.

32. **C is the best answer.** When receptors within the nervous system are over activated, like they would be with abnormally high DA, they can become desensitized and taken up into the cell. This reduces receptor count, ruling out choices A and B. Since receptor count would decrease, choices C and D are most likely. The genes knocked out in these mice are involved in neuronal survival, destruction of damaged mitochondria, and handling oxidative stress. Thus, knockout of these genes would lead to decreased resistance to oxidative stress. Choice C is a better answer than choice D.

33. **B is the best answer.** Based on Figure 1, the triple KO releases more DA than normal into the synapse, so potential reasons for this could be the neuron firing and releasing dopamine more often than normal. Potassium channels move potassium out of the cell, which decreases membrane potential since potassium ions are positive. This hyperpolarizes the neuron, making it harder to reach threshold and fire. Choice A is unlikely. Voltage-gated sodium channels open at a certain threshold and cause a massive influx of sodium cations. This causes the neuron to fire. If these channels were oversensitive, then it would be easier to reach threshold for the neuron and it would fire more frequently. Choice B is the best answer. Calcium channels cause influx of calcium that leads to release of dopamine vesicles. If they were blocked, dopamine would not be released, so choice C is unlikely. Lastly, vesicles must move towards the synapse and fuse with the membrane in order to release DA. Choice D is unlikely.

34. **C is the best answer.** Microglia are the phagocytes of the nervous system. DJ-1 and Parkin, according to the passage, are both neuroprotective. Parkin also destroys damaged mitochondria. None of these functions are linked to activation of the immune system, so choices A and B are unlikely. LPS is a bacterial endotoxin. This pathogenic molecule will activate microglia, so choice C is the best answer. Choice D is unlikely because SOD1 protects against oxidative stress. Microglia could potentially be activated in response to oxidative stress and apoptosis, but this is not as clear cut as microglial activation due to actual injection of a foreign toxin from bacteria.

35. **C is the best answer.** The major source of oxidative stress in neurons and most cells is the electron transport chain. This occurs along the inner mitochondrial membrane, so the most likely answer involves the mitochondria. Membrane lipids are a major component of plasma membranes. Most reactive oxygen species and other sources of oxidative stress are within the cell, so choice A is unlikely. For this reason, choice D is also unlikely. Nuclear proteins are a potential answer since DNA within the nucleus requires protection from oxidative stressors. It could make sense for SOD1 to be within the nucleus to deactivate oxidative stressors within the nucleus. Choice B is unlikely because the passage says that SOD1 needs to enter the source of oxidative stress, which is the mitochondria. Choice C is the best answer.

Passage 7 (Questions 36-39)

36. **B is the best answer.** Based on Figure 1, Ahi1 KO reduces serotonin release throughout the brain. This is indicated by lowered bars in each section of the brain. Serotonin, like all neurotransmitters, is released from the presynaptic neuron following an influx of calcium ions. Thus, choice B is a better answer than choice A. Considering choice C, it does seem that Ahi1 plays a key role in serotonin release based on the effect of knocking out Ahi1 in Figure 1. However, choice C does not explain this relationship at all, so it does not answer the question and is not the best answer. Finally, serotonin reuptake does indeed occur in the presynaptic neuron, but there is no evidence that Ahi1 has a relationship with the level of reuptake.

37. **D is the best answer.** The antidepressant, which should counteract the underlying causes of depression, acts to increase serotonin. The KO mice used in this study are modeling depression. Based on Figure 1, serotonin levels are significantly reduced in the Ahi1 KO. A potential conclusion that can be drawn from Figure 1 is that reduced serotonin levels lead to depression. If an antidepressant works to combat depression through increasing levels of serotonin, then the conclusion of the study is supported. Choice A is unlikely because the results do not indicate that depression could be caused by increased serotonin, they indicate the opposite. Choices B and C can be eliminated because both the mechanism of the antidepressant and the result of the experiment indicate that low serotonin is associated with depression. Choice D is the best answer because the results indicate that serotonin is reduced in a model of depression.

38. **D is the best answer.** The brainstem is involved in primarily autonomic regulation. This includes regulation of the cardiac and respiratory systems. Choice A is unlikely because memory is primarily a function of the hippocampus and cerebrum. Combating hypothermia would require regulation of temperature, and this is a function of the hypothalamus. Water balance is also a function of this brain region, so choices B and C are unlikely. In fact, the hypothalamus can be thought of as one of the main structures that maintains homeostasis of many factors throughout the body. Finally, choice D is the best answer because the brainstem does indeed control the cardiac system.

39. **D is the best answer.** Figure 1 shows the serotonin levels in each brain region. These include the hypothalamus, the hippocampus, and the thalamus. The thalamus is involved in sensory connections, and the thalamus only shows a modest increase in Figure 1, making choice A unlikely. The hippocampus is primarily involved in memory, and the hypothalamus maintains homeostasis. The region least affected by Ahi1 KO based on a comparison of control and treatment bars is the hippocampus. This makes choice B seem like a strong answer. Choice C is asking about the hypothalamus, and this shows a less significant decrease than choice B, making it unlikely. However, this question is a trick! The question actually asks about dopamine. There is no data provided on dopamine distribution throughout the brain, so the best answer is choice D.

Passage 8 (Questions 40-44)

40. **C is the best answer.** Figure 1 shows that the astrocyte specific targeting works by preferentially transducing astrocytes with ZsGreen. This is shown by the higher bar for astrocytes. The experiment only measures the level of ZsGreen. It is important to not confuse this with actual levels of astrocytes. Choices A and B are unlikely as the experiment does not say much about the population. Choice C is a solid answer because astrocyte specific targeting does indeed work based on the higher astrocyte bar compared to microglia. Choice D is the opposite of this most likely correct statement, so it is not a strong answer.

41. **D is the best answer.** A major characteristic of neurons is that they are typically in the G_0 phase and do not undergo division. However, glia are capable of division and undergo mitosis regularly. The passage states that lentiviruses are ideal for transduction because they can transduce both dividing and nondividing cells. This makes choices A and B unlikely, as it seems that both neurons and glia are able to be transduced. This very reasoning also makes choice D the best answer, and choice C unlikely.

42. **D is the best answer.** Various cells of the immune system are involved in combatting viruses. Choice A is unlikely because neurons are not primarily involved in the immune response. Next, microglia are not found outside the nervous system, so choice B is unlikely. Choice C is a distractor as beta cells secrete insulin, and are not directly involved in the immune system. NK cells specialize in targeting virally infected cells, so choice D is the best answer.

43. **A is the best answer.** VSV-G-ZsGreen is shown in Figure 1 as approximately equally transducing astrocytes and microglia. Because VSV-G-ZsGreen does not have a targeting component like the astrocyte specific antibody, it should transduce all cells equally. Choice A is the best answer. Choices B and C are unlikely because there is no preference of the specific molecule towards any membrane markers or glia or neurons. Choice D is unlikely because it is a more extreme version of choice B. In choice D, no neurons would be transduced and only astrocytes would be transduced. This would only be possible if lentiviruses did not transduce nondividing cells, which contradicts the passage.

44. **B is the best answer.** The first step in an action potential firing is the opening of voltage gated sodium channels. Sodium is in excess on the outside of the membrane, so increasing this gradient will accelerate the speed at which the membrane jumps up. The question asks what would slow down the action potential, so choice A is unlikely. Choice B, a reduction in the gradient would actually slow down the action potential, and choice B is a solid answer. Remember the role of each ion in a neuron's action potential! While sodium is involved in the firing and upswing, potassium movement decreases the membrane potential, repolarizes the cell, and eventually returns it to resting potential. Choices C and D are unlikely because they concern potassium.

Stand-alones (Questions 45-48)

45. **D is the best answer.** A reflex arc generally involves a sensory or afferent neuron first to detect a stimulus, making choice A less likely to be the best answer. Interneurons may be involved in the transfer of signals from sensory to motor neuron and typically reside in the spinal cord. This makes choice B also unlikely to be the best answer. In the final step of a reflex arc, motor or efferent neurons, either directly from sensory neurons or via interneurons, send a response to the muscle to either contract or relax. Thus, choice C is also unlikely to be the best answer. This makes choice D the best answer.

46. **B is the best answer.** Humans have different types of reflexes that serve to prevent injury. If the body feels that it is being stretched too far, a sensory neuron will send a signal to an interneuron in the spinal cord which will then communicate with a motor neuron that corrects the problem. The best answer to this question will describe how reflexes can be modified to allow for different body positions. Interneurons play an essential role in the reflex arc, but they do more to cause the reflex to happen than to stop it. Without the interneuron, the reflex would not take place and the gymnast would have no trouble achieving the position so choice A can be eliminated. The supraspinal neurons are located in the central nervous system and project to different reflex arcs. These neurons have the ability to change how sensitive the reflex is which is helpful for gymnasts. Choice B is plausible because it provides a valid mechanism for altering the reflex. Often times, the central nervous system is involved with modulating standard responses. All humans contain reflexes that prevent injury. Reflexes are essential for simple behaviors such as walking. Choice C can be eliminated because reflex arcs are essential for all types of movements. Additionally, the word "lacking" is very strong, which also makes choice C a poor answer. The sympathetic nervous system is involved with the flight or fight response. The sympathetic nervous system generally enhances our reflexes and prepares us to avoid harm. Choice D can be eliminated because it is unlikely that the sympathetic nervous system would enhance mobility. Choice B is the best answer because the supraspinal neurons will best alter the reflex to assist the gymnast.

47. **B is the best answer.** The sympathetic (SNS) and parasympathetic nervous systems (PNS) are two competing branches of the autonomic nervous system. Sympathetic innervation is associated with flight or flight situations with high stress and a high need to physical activity and survival instincts. This results in a shunting of blood away from the digestive system and towards muscles, lungs, the heart, which are crucial to maintaining activity. The parasympathetic is the opposite, and is active during less active rest and digest situations. Choice A is unlikely because it describes a situation where the PNS would be more active after a meal. Choice B is a potential answer since running a marathon is a high stress activity that would require maximal resource devotion to muscles, and the cardiovascular system. Choices C and D, like choice A, are more sedentary and less likely to feature sympathetic innervation. This makes choice B the best answer.

48. **B is the best answer.** The thalamus is a sensory relay center, so it will be active in processing taste, or gustatory, sensation. Choice A can be eliminated for this reason. Choice B is the best answer, since the cerebellum has many pathways involved in motor control and coordination, but it does not relate to taste. It is important not to confuse the cerebellum with the cerebrum, which is involved in many higher-level functions and plays a role in sensation as well. Choice C can be tricky if one forgets that smell is involved with eating, but since smell is such an important part of the sensation involved with eating, this choice can be eliminated. The temporal lobe contains the olfactory cortex, so this too is active in eating, and choice D is not the best answer.

Passage 9 (Questions 49-52)

49. **A is the best answer.** According to Figure 1, increased expression of fibronectin corresponds to patients with GO. Paragraph one states that patients with GO have corneal clouding, which means it would be denser than the normal cornea. The cornea is nonvascular and made from collagen. Normally, the cornea is clear and has a refractive index greater than air at about 1.4. The greater the index of refraction, the more the light bends when it enters a new medium. Increase clouding would increase the density of the cornea, further increasing the index of refraction. Because light bends when it enters the cornea, the light is considered to refract, not reflect, eliminating choices C and D. The increase in density results in the greater bending of light due to the increase in index of refraction, eliminating option B and making option A the best answer.

50. **D is the best answer.** An image is produced when light hits the retina and is transmitted to the occipital lobe of the brain to be interpreted. Rods and cones are the two cell types in the retina that absorb the light to initiate the transmission process. These cells contain pigments, which undergo a chemical change when light hits them. Vitamin A is the precursor to all pigments and can absorb visible light. Vitamin A is also a fat soluble vitamin, along with vitamins D, E, and K. Autoimmune disease of the heart is likely to have significant consequences but does not explicitly pertain to the eye or affect light absorption, making option I less likely to be part of the best answer. The liver produces bile salts, which are responsible for solubilizing fat. If bile salt production was hindered, vitamin A would be less likely to be absorbed, which would impair pigment production and impact vision. Option II is a component of the best answer for that reason. Similarly, absorption of fat and fat-soluble vitamins occurs in the ileum of the small intestine, making option III part of the best answer. Choice A can be eliminated because the small intestine is involved in vitamin A absorption. Choice B can be eliminated because the liver is involved in bile salt production, which allows for vitamin A absorption. Choice C can be eliminated because autoimmune disease of the heart would not specifically create a visual deficit. Choice D is the best answer because both the liver and small intestine are involved in processes that allow for vitamin A absorption.

51. **D is the best answer.** When photons of light hit the retina, they are absorbed by visual pigments. The pigment in rod cells is called rhodopsin and has a cofactor called retinal, which comes from vitamin A. Once light is absorbed, retinal isomerizes and causes the membrane of rod cells to become less permeable to sodium ions, which normally keep the cell depolarized. Because the cell is now less permeable, it hyperpolarizes, which would make its membrane potential more negative. Curves A and B would be produced by increased permeability to sodium, not decreased permeability, eliminating choices A and B as the best answer. Choice C shows no change in membrane voltage, which would only occur if the rod cell had not yet been excited by a photon of light. Because the question stem says that the rod cell was excited, choice C can be eliminated. Choice D is the only answer choice that shows a hyperpolarization upon absorbing a photon, making choice D the best answer.

52. **B is the best answer.** Hydrogen peroxide treatment of cells, according to Figure 2, increases the release of CTGF, one of the factors that increases clouding in the cornea, lens, and vitreous humor. Increased clouding would result in less light hitting the back of the retina, meaning that fewer photoreceptors would be activated. Upon activation, photoreceptors hyperpolarize, decreasing the amount of glutamate, a neurotransmitter that they release. Because glutamate, not acetylcholine, is the neurotransmitter used between the photoreceptors and bipolar cells, choices A and C can be eliminated. On bipolar cells are hyperpolarized, or inhibited, by the activity of glutamate. Because less light hits the retina, more glutamate will be released from photoreceptor cells, serving to inhibit on bipolar cells. Because the cells are inhibited, choice D can be eliminated and choice B is the best answer.

Passage 10 (Questions 53-56)

53. **C is the best answer.** According to the passage, CSPGs form on the retina, resulting in attraction of glia and formation of a barrier. The model of mouse used in the study should be those that best mimic how vision is lost due to glial scars. Rods and cones are photoreceptors in the retina. Rods are used for peripheral vision and cones detect color. Choices A and B are potential answers as they model some form of retinal degeneration. Choice C is an even more likely answer because the retina is affected, and the passage explicitly states that glial scars envelop the entire retina. These masses of cells would block, or at least heavily distort light hitting the retina. This would lead to blindness, making choice C a great answer. Choice D is another possibility just like choices A and B. However, there is no evidence provided that this is how glial scars cause blindness.

54. **A is the best answer.** Based on the passage, gliosis leads to an increase of intermediate filaments. This question is really asking what intermediate filaments do, and what occurs when they are overexpressed. Choice A is likely because intermediate filaments are vital to stability and rigidity of the cytoskeleton. Motility typically involves organelles like cilia and flagella. These organelles consist primarily of microtubules, not intermediate filaments, so choices B and C can be eliminated. Microtubules consist of tubulin and are involved in intracellular transport, while intermediate filaments are often composed of keratin. Another common cytoskeletal element is the microfilament, a narrow actin fiber that functions in changing cell shape. Choice D is not a likely answer since the cell membrane primarily is composed of lipids, with some other molecules spread throughout.

55. **D is the best answer.** This question primarily concerns Figure 1, as it shows photoreceptor counts at early, middle, and late age in WT and mutant mice. Choice A is not reflected in the results of Figure 1, as there is a mild change in photoreceptor count from early to middle to late age. This is indicated by the lower bars as time progresses. Choice B is unlikely because the decrease in bar height over time is more dramatic in the retinitis pigmentosa model compared to the Leber congenital amaurosis model. Choice C can be most easily ruled out based on the significantly lower photoreceptor counts in mutant models. Lastly, choice D is the best answer since the change from early age to later stages is largest in the retinitis pigmentosa model.

56. **B is the best answer.** Ciliary muscles are muscles in the eye that contract and extend to change the shape of the lens. They adjust their activity in response to how far away a person is looking. The change in shape changes the focusing power of the eye, allowing light to properly hit the retina. Option II is extremely likely. Option I is not likely because adjusting to changing levels of light requires smooth muscles in the iris to change the size of the pupil. This does not involve ciliary muscles. Next, color vision depends on cone cells, not any particular muscle group. Option III is not likely, and choice B is the best answer.

Stand-alones (Questions 57-59)

57. **D is the best answer.** The brainstem structure that is closest to the diencephalon, which includes the thalamus and hypothalamus, is the midbrain, which sits atop the pons and medulla. The midbrain serves as a relay station for visual and auditory inputs, so damage to the midbrain would likely affect hearing and vision. This makes options I and III true so choice A, choice B, and choice C are less likely to be the best answer. Olfaction, option III, is not transmitted to one of the lobes of the brain, but rather to the olfactory bulb, a structure that lies just above the nasal cavity. Only option I and option III are true, which makes choice D the best answer.

58. **A is the best answer.** The right hemisphere is more involved in negative emotion while the left hemisphere is more involved in positive emotion, making choice A the best answer and choice B and choice C less likely to be the best answer. When there are two answer choices that are completely opposite, it is often the case that one of them is the best answer. The language centers in the brain are in the left hemisphere, making choice D less likely to be the best answer.

59. **B is the best answer.** As more accumulation occurs in the medulla, it makes sense that the functions that are associated with this region of the brain would become impaired. Temperature control is primarily a function of the hypothalamus, as this region regulates many basic physiological needs. Choice A is unlikely. Control of blood pressure is a major function of the medulla, which is heavily involved in cardiovascular and respiratory control. Key functions regulated by this part of the brain include breathing, heart rate, and blood pressure. This is done by altering parasympathetic and sympathetic innervation to the heart and the vasculature. Choice B is the best answer. The cerebellum is involved in coordination and movement, so choice C is unlikely. Lastly, water balance is another basic physiological need controlled by the hypothalamus, so choice D is unlikely.

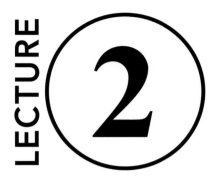

The Nervous System

MINI-TEST 2B

ANSWERS & EXPLANATIONS
Questions 1–41

Passage 1 (Questions 1-4)

1. **C is the best answer.** Compare each answer choice to the purpose of the retina. Light enters the eye at the pupil, and some of the first layers that it crosses includes the cornea and lens. Problems with the lens, like cataracts, can impair the entry of light into the eye. Choice A is unlikely. Next, the refraction of light onto the back of the eye cannot depend on the retina because the retina is the back of the eye. It is primarily the cornea and lens that refract light, so choice B is unlikely. Choice C is a great answer because it exactly describes what function the retina performs. Choice D, the adjustment of the eye between various distances, is accommodated by ciliary muscles that change the shape of the lens. This is not describing the retina, so choice D can be eliminated.

2. **B is the best answer.** According to the passage text, one of the primary mechanisms of cell death in response to NMDAR activation is through a massive influx of calcium ions from the outside of the cell. Excitatory signals are those that could potentially cause a neuron to release neurotransmitters. Release of neurotransmitters requires an influx of calcium. Thus, excitatory signaling should increase the harmful calcium influx, while inhibitory signaling should decrease it. Choice A is unlikely and choice B is a potential answer since it addresses part of the calcium issue. Choices C and D are unlikely as sodium is not suggested to play a role in induced cell death. This makes choice B the best answer, as it is the only one that positively impacts the abnormally high levels of intracellular calcium.

3. **B is the best answer.** At most chemical synapses, neurotransmitter reuptake occurs in order to recycle the components that make up neurotransmitters. Option I concerns this phenomenon, but is factually inaccurate. Reuptake does occur, but it is done by the presynaptic cell. This makes sense as the re-prefix implies that this is brought back to the neuron that secreted it. The neurotransmitter are first secreted by the presynaptic cell, and then undergo reuptake to be recycled. The postsynaptic cell would not reuptake since it did not release the neurotransmitter in the first place. Furthermore, the actual cell that initially released the neurotransmitters would be the cell that can utilize these materials in the future. Option I is false, ruling out choice C. Options II and III concern positive ion flow in the postsynaptic neuron. They cannot both be true because potassium and sodium are more concentrated on opposite sides of the membrane due to the sodium/potassium pump. This rules out choice D. The sodium potassium pump moves three sodium ions out and two potassium ions into the cell. This means that the cell most likely has more potassium and less sodium within the cell. When NMDARs activate and allow positive ions to flow down their gradients, sodium will flow in and potassium will flow out. Thus, choice A is a weaker answer and choice B is the best answer.

4. **C is the best answer.** Cone cells are retinal cells that detect color. Choice A is unlikely as the colored part of the eye is the iris, and the color is not due to the retina. Choice B is not the best answer because rod cells, not cones, are the photoreceptors involved in peripheral vision. Choices C and D both correctly identify the role of cones as color detection. However, choice C is the best answer because cones are indeed concentrated in the fovea, not the optic nerve.

Passage 2 (Questions 5-9)

5. **B is the best answer.** In the one face experiment, the face moves between conditions A, B, C, and D, from the top of the screen to the bottom of the screen. The ventral pathway, also known as the "what" pathway, projects to the temporal lobe and is involved in object recognition, and should show a relatively constant signal, as the face is the object recognized in each condition. In contrast, the dorsal pathway, also known as the "where" pathway, projects to the parietal cortex and is more involved in perceiving the location of objects. As the location of the face on the screen changes between conditions A and B, it is likely that the activity in the dorsal pathway would increase, making choice B likely to be the best answer. The optic nerve relays visual information from the retina to the brain. The intensity of the stimulus does not change in the experiment, just the location of the face, meaning the optic nerve is likely to be equally active as the amount of light does not change. This eliminates choice C. The lateral geniculate nucleus receives the optic nerve, preserves the visual map created by the ganglion cells, and projects the information to the primary visual cortex. It is not involved in interpretation of the images from the eye, though it serves as a relay point between the optic nerve and the occipital lobe. This makes choice D less likely than choice B to be the best answer.

6. **C is the best answer.** The question suggests that PET imaging may be useful in confirming that two pathways are involved in coordinating eye movement in response to noise and that these two pathways may integrate information to make detecting an object's location more efficient. The primary visual cortex has two main pathways, the ventral "what" pathway that projects to the temporal lobe, and the dorsal "where" pathway that projects to the parietal lobe. Because vision projects to the temporal lobe as well, choice A can be eliminated. The cerebellum is involved in the coordination of movement, but not necessarily the processing of visual or auditory information, making choice B less likely to be the best answer. The auditory cortex is located in the temporal love and receives information from the medial geniculate nucleus of the thalamus. Because processing of sound involves the temporal lobe and the processing of vision involves both the parietal and temporal lobes, scientists would most likely measure the FDG signal in these areas, making choice C most likely to be the best answer. The frontal lobe is involved in cognition and planning, but it is not the main lobe for visual or auditory processing, eliminating choice D.

7. **A is the best answer.** Signal detection theory focuses on how an organism differentiates important or meaningful stimuli from those that are not of interest in an environment. Visual stimuli of faces would be a meaningful stimulus, especially compared to background noise. Notice that the brain is activated in response to a face or multiple faces in the experiment, compared to background. This suggests that the brain is actively differentiating the face from the noise, supporting the signal detection theory. This makes choice A most likely to be the best answer and eliminates choice B, which suggests the opposite. Weber's Law states that a stimulus must have a certain change in intensity in order to be recognized. An experiment designed to test Weber's Law would have light of different intensity in the various conditions, instead of movement of the face at the same stimulus intensity. This makes choices C and D less likely to be the best answer.

8. **D is the best answer.** In the two face experimental condition, two of the panels contain faces and two of the panels are blurred background. Between conditions A, B, and C of the two face experimental condition, the two faces move from the top of the screen to the bottom of the screen together. The brain must be able to distinguish that two of the four panels are faces and that the faces change position on the screen. This is the principle of parallel processing, where the brain uses multiple pathways to convey information about the same stimulus. Bipolar cells receive information from their associated photoreceptors and may be inhibited or excited by changes in the amount of glutamate released by the photoreceptors. The bipolar cells are crucial to visual recognition, as they are the first step in processing what visual fields are active. This eliminates choice A. Horizontal cells also affect bipolar cells by providing information from photoreceptors at the edge of a bipolar cells' receptive field, which is the distinct area of visual information to which a cell responds. The integration of the vertical information from the bipolar cell's associated photoreceptor and the horizontal information from the horizontal cell gives the eye the ability to focus on changes and edges in the visual field, making horizontal cells also a part of distinguishing unique shapes. This eliminates choice B. Ganglion cells receive input from the bipolar cells and are the sensory neurons that produce action potentials, making them critical to transmitting the visual stimulus to the brain. The different types of ganglion cells split the visual information into two distinct pathways: one that detects and processes information about motion and one that is concerned with the form of the stimulus. These are the dorsal and ventral pathways, respectively. The importance of all three cell types makes choice D the best answer.

9. **D is the best answer.** Awareness of the body's location and movement is described as the kinesthetic sense, which works with all sensory organs to give an overall sensation of the body in relationship to the environment. Action potentials from the retina help to transmit visual information, which can be used by a participant to predict the distance between him- or herself and the screen, making option I a component of the best answer. The vestibular system detects changes in body position, as well as the body's relative orientation to gravity, and would be important in determining whether the screen and faces were upside down or rightside up compared to the participant, making option II part of the best answer. An awareness of posture and body position also comes from the major muscle groups, which relay information about stretch and position in space. Option III is part of the best answer. The kinesthetic sense involves visual, auditory, vestibular, and many other senses to allow the body to have an accurate representation of its position, making choice D the best answer.

Stand-alones (Questions 10-12)

10. **B is the best answer.** Blood flow is increased to certain parts of the brain that are more metabolically active. In patients who have a lesion in one of the language centers, blood flow would be expected to be lower than control during attempts to use language. This makes neither choice A nor choice C likely to be the best answer. Choice B is the best answer because speaking requires use of language, and this patient would have decreased metabolic activity and thus blood flow in the language center while speaking when compared to control. The awake state of the brain has little to do with blood flow in the language center and is not otherwise mentioned in the question stem, making choice D a distractor and unlikely to be the best answer.

11. **B is the best answer.** The forebrain is one of the structures in the brain that is distinguished from the midbrain and hindbrain during human development. It includes all the brain structures except the midbrain, pons, medulla, and cerebellum. Thus, any answer choice that states a function exclusive to one of these structures is likely to be the best answer. The motor cortex is part of the cerebrum of the brain, which is part of the forebrain, making choice A less likely to be the best answer. Regulation of the cardiovascular and respiratory systems via chemoreceptors is performed by the medulla, making choice B likely to be the best answer. The occipital lobe is also part of the cerebrum, making choice C less likely to be the best answer. Cognition is performed mainly by the frontal cortex, which is part of the cerebrum, making choice D unlikely to be the best answer.

12. **D is the best answer.** Photoreceptors are a type of neuron. Like most neurons, they do not divide, so choices A and B are unlikely. Additionally, using levels of cell division to detect light would be far too slow and ineffective. Signals that result in vision are fairly instant and have very low latency. This means that there is limited lag time from light entering the eye to the signal being processed in the brain. These electromagnetic receptors detect light and send electrical impulses through the optic nerve to the brain. This information is then processed as vision. When the light stimulus is decreased, it is most likely that the amount of photoreceptor firing will be directly related. This makes choice C unlikely and choice D the best answer.

Passage 3 (Questions 13-16)

13. A is the best answer. The fluid, also known as the endolymph, that exists in the inner ear surrounds the hair cells and is rich in potassium. When the hair cells move, they open ion channels that are physically connected to the hair cell movement. These channels are selective to allow potassium to flow from its high concentration in the endolymph into the cell. This is the signal that indicates that a sound is being heard at a particular frequency. Calcium current is important in generating the cardiac action potential but not in transducing sound signaling, eliminating choices C and D. Prestin-deficient hair cells are less likely to move to allow the hair cell channel to open, meaning a decreased potassium current would be seen, not an increased potassium current. This eliminates choice B and makes choice A the best answer choice.

14. C is the best answer. The end of the first paragraph notes that the maternal grandfather and this baby boy are both affected by the genetic disease but not the two parents. An autosomal dominant disease would be expected to be found in each generation, including the parents. Because the parents are unaffected, option I can be eliminated. Eliminating option I eliminates choices B and D. An autosomal recessive disease would be expected to skip a generation and should affect males and females equally. Because the pedigree is small, it is possible that another child born to the unaffected parents could be female and could inherit the disease. Option II is possible, making it a component of the best answer. X-linked recessive diseases tend to skip generations, like autosomal recessive diseases do, and predominantly affect males. The "grandfather-to-grandson" transmission is an inheritance pattern that suggests an X-linked recessive disease, making option III part of the best answer. Choice C is the best answer because it contains both options II and III that could display this pattern of inheritance.

15. C is the best answer. The question stem suggests that an additional test is given to patients to test for hearing loss. According to paragraph two, prestin shortens apical hair cells, which would prevent them from moving in the tectorial membrane. The apical end of the cochlea is responsible for vibrating with low frequency sounds, meaning that patients with normal prestin should be able to discriminate between these frequencies but patients with mutated prestin would not. High frequency sounds are detected at the basal end, not the apical end, eliminating choice A. The normal prestin protein should allow for the detection of high and low sounds but this does not support the role of prestin in hearing loss, making choice C less likely to be the best answer. Choice D describes the vestibular system, which senses the position of the body and allows the body to react to changes. The passage does not suggest that prestin mutations hamper the vestibular system, making choice D less likely to be the best answer. Because prestin mutations predominantly affect the apical end, not the basal end of the cochlea, they will affect the detection of lower frequencies more than higher frequencies, which should be more normal. This makes choice C the best answer choice.

16. D is the best answer. According to the question stem, the transcranial stimulation device produces vibrations of the bones of the middle ear by vibrating the bone of the skull. This vibration of the middle ear bones would allow for the tympanic membrane to vibrate, creating waves in the fluid of the inner ear that could move hair cells to detect sound. In prestin-dependent hearing loss, the problem is with the hair cells directly, not the conduction of sound from the outer ear to the inner ear. Regardless of how the membrane was moved to create sound waves, the hair cells would be unable to detect them. This treatment would not restore the ability to hear high frequency sounds, eliminating choice A. Additionally, it would not restore the ability to hear low frequency sounds, eliminating choices B and C. Because the problem is with detection of vibrations by the hair cells directly, this treatment which corrects conductive hearing loss would be ineffective, making choice D the best answer choice.

Passage 4 (Questions 17-21)

17. D is the best answer. According to the passage, NF2 is an autosomal dominant disease with complete penetrance. This means even if only one copy of the NF2 disease gene is present, the child will have the disease. The father is heterozygous, meaning he has one healthy allele and one disease allele, while the mother is homozygous, meaning she has two diseased alleles. No matter what, the child will inherit one of the mother's diseased alleles. Thus, choice A, 100% chance of being healthy, is impossible. If the disease was autosomal recessive, then the probability would be 50%, as there is a 50% chance of getting either allele from the father. However, since the disease is actually autosomal dominant, choice B is unlikely. Choice C is impossible because the child will have the disease no matter what due to the mother's homozygosity, meaning choice D is the best answer.

18. D is the best answer. The most ideal experimental setup in this case is to keep all things constant except for the hearing status, and then compare what factors led to this difference. Choices A, B, and C all depict familial relationships between deaf and hearing individuals. The closest in terms of genetics is choice C, making it a better answer than choices A and B. Choice D is an interesting case where a deaf and a hearing ear are observed within the same individual. This is an even better case, because within that individual, so many factors are held constant outside of the status of the ears. Choice D is the best answer.

19. **A is the best answer.** Hair cells are key cells that detect vibrations. These cells are located in the organ of Corti, which is a part of the cochlea. Choice A is a very likely answer. The semicircular canals are in the inner ear and play a larger role in the vestibular system, maintaining balance and orientation. They are not directly involved in hearing, making choice B unlikely. The malleus is a bone in the middle ear. Hair cells are located in the inner ear, so choice C can be ruled out. Finally, the pinna is the skin and cartilage that forms the external ear, and this is also not the location of hair cells. The pinna may have actual hairs on it, but it does not have hair cells, making choice D unlikely.

20. **D is the best answer.** According to the passage, CVSs associated with NF cause damage to the vestibular system. The vestibular system is responsible for balance and orientation, so choice A would be impaired and is not a strong answer. Next, hearing impairment is often associated with speech impairment, so choice B can be ruled out. According to the passage, NF2 patients have damaged hair cells. Hair cells detect sound waves and fire, sending signals into the auditory nerve and to the brain. Damage to hair cells would inhibit one of the steps of this process. Choice C is unlikely. Finally, there is no reason to believe taste would be impaired, so choice D is the best answer.

21. **D is the best answer.** Choices A and B present the same model in different, but very related species. The question suggests some key difference between rats and mice in modeling NF2. However, this is a trick, as there is no suggestion that the species of model, especially between rat and mouse, would play a large role. This in fact makes choices A and B unlikely since they are essentially very similar. The passage states that hair cell degeneration and deafness in NF2 is likely due to an excess of intralabrynthine protein in the inner ear. Choices C and D are quite similar, except for the fact that choice C involves overexpression all over the body, while overexpression in choice D is localized to the inner ear, the primary disease site in NF2. This makes choice D a better answer, and the best answer overall.

Passage 5 (Questions 22-25)

22. **A is the best answer.** According to paragraph one, ionizing radiation may damage the inner ear, in addition to other sites in the brain to cause problems with balance. The occipital lobe is located at the back of the head and helps with vision, eliminating choice B. The frontal lobe is located at the front and top of the head and helps with higher order thinking, such as decision making, eliminating choice C. The parietal lobe is located on the side of the head, towards to the top and helps with touch, eliminating choice D. The cerebellum is located at the back and base of the head and helps coordinate motor information coming from the cortex to fine tune movements. Balance is required when two or more muscles oppose each other in their actions to create a stable movement, especially when walking. Choice A is the best answer choice.

23. **A is the best answer.** Figure 1 helps provide information to help answer this question that is about sound intensity. Otoliths are organs in the semicircular canals in the inner ear. They are involved in the vestibular system, which is responsible for detecting changes in position and signaling the body to make necessary adjustments to maintain balance. Because the question asks about hearing thresholds, not balance, choices C and D are less likely to be the best answer. Figure 1 shows that mice also treated with PrC-210 IP could hear sounds at a lower decibel (dB) level than radiation treated mice. Decibels are the unit of sound intensity. Because they guinea pigs treated with PrC-210 IP hear a lower dB level, the organ of Corti would vibrate at a lower sound intensity. The organ of Corti vibrates based on sound waves to generate action potentials in the auditory nerve, making choice A the best answer choice and eliminating choice B.

24. **D is the best answer.** When auditory information travels through the nervous system, it undergoes processing and integration at each stage to build a more complex signal. Auditory signals begin at the auditory nerve then proceed to the cochlear nuclei in the medulla. At this point, sound information is only coming from one ear and cannot be used to recognize patterns, eliminating choice A. After the cochlear nuclei, axons move to the inferior colliculus, where some auditory information from each ear is sent to the opposite hemisphere. The information at this point is a small mix of both ears but has not undergone any processing, eliminating choice B. The medial geniculate nucleus of the thalamus further integrates both ears but still does not process the information, eliminating choice C. The auditory nucleus in the temporal lobe is responsible from receiving information from the thalamus and detecting patterns in sounds that allow a person to link a sound to a particular experience or scenario. Choice D is the best answer.

25. **B is the best answer.** The person described in the question probably has trouble with the vestibular system, which helps with maintaining balance. The vestibular system works with the kinesthetic sense, which gives a person an overall sensation of the body. The dizziness is likely a result of problems in this system. The organ of Corti is responsible for changing pressure waves from a sound wave into movement of stereocilia, or hair cells, that allow for an action potential to form to transmit sound information. Because the person does not have problems hearing high or low pitched sounds, choice A can be eliminated. The semicircular canals are part of the vestibular system but are more involved in twisting of the head than tilting and linear acceleration, which cause the dizziness. Choice C is less likely than choice B to be the best answer. The stapes bone is one of the bones of the middle ear that helps transmit sound. Because the person does not have trouble with hearing, the stapes is unlikely to be involved, eliminating choice D. The otolith organs detect tilting and linear acceleration. Defects in the otolith organs would probably impair the kinesthetic sense, preventing the body from having an awareness of location and movement, making choice B the best answer choice.

Stand-alones (Questions 26-29)

26. **D is the best answer.** The lens is responsible for focusing the image on the retina. When the ciliary muscle contracts, the lens becomes more spherical and decreases the focal length, which is a way of saying how far the image is formed from the lens. When the ciliary muscle relaxes, the lens becomes less spherical, or flattens, increasing the focal length. According to the question stem, patients display lens flattening and would have a lens with an increased focal length, meaning the image formed would be further from the lens, eliminating choices A and C. The image produced by an object comes from real light that has reflected off of an object. When it enters the eye, the image inverts and produces a real image at the back of the eye, eliminating choice A and making choice D the best answer choice.

27. **A is the best answer.** The auditory cells of the ear rely on the movement of hair cells, called stereocilia, to open and close attached potassium channels. When the hair cells become displaced by sound waves that move the organ of Corti, they are able to transmit action potentials to the auditory nerve and up to the brain. Phosphate is primarily involved in regulating the production of bone, eliminating choice B. Similar to phosphate, calcium is important in building bone. High calcium levels may cause increased bone formation but would not necessarily decrease hearing, eliminating choice C. Magnesium is a co-factor for many enzymes and may also help regulate the stability of some plasma membranes. Unlike potassium, which allow for the action potential to form for hair cells, magnesium is not involved, eliminating choice D. When the hair cells open the potassium channels, potassium ions flow down their concentration gradient, resulting in the formation of an action potential in the auditory nerve. Lower than normal potassium levels may prevent this from happening as strongly, decreasing the ability to hear and making choice A the best answer choice.

28. **B is the best answer.** After ganglion cells are excited in the retina, their axons gather to form the optic nerve, which leaves the eye to convey visual information to the brain. The optic nerve synapses at the lateral geniculate nucleus (LGN) of the thalamus, which preserves the visual map created by the ganglion cells. The LGN does not integrate or process information but serves as an intermediate relay point to the primary visual cortex. The primary visual cortex is located in the occipital lobe and receives input from the LGN. It is specialized for the detection of specific aspects of the visual stimulus, including lines and edges of different orientations. This is called feature detection. Damage to the primary visual cortex would prevent the detection of some of these orientation features, making choice B the best answer. The medial geniculate nucleus of the thalamus receives auditory stimuli, not visual stimuli, eliminating choice C. The semicircular canal is part of the vestibular system that is responsible for detecting changes in position and relaying these signals to the body to maintain balance. It does not play a role in transmitting visual stimuli, eliminating choice D.

29. **B is the best answer.** Pheromones are involved in subconscious behaviors, especially aggression and sexual behavior. This makes choice A unlikely to be the best answer. They also may be involved in social interaction and timing of menstrual cycles, making choice B the best answer. They are processed by the amygdala and hypothalamus, not thalamus; so choice C is unlikely to be the best answer. They are detected by chemoreceptors that are related but separate from olfactory chemoreceptors, which makes choice D unlikely to be the best answer.

Passage 6 (Questions 30-34)

30. **A is the best answer.** This question is asking for an interpretation of Figure 1, which shows the levels of the tested miRNA in neurons and glia. According to paragraph 3, a higher level of miRNA indicates a lower level of the troublesome and tumorigenic NF-1 protein. The level of miRNA is least in Schwann cells, then astrocytes and relatively higher in neurons. It is likely that Schwann cells have a higher level of NF-1 protein and are therefore most susceptible to tumors. Schwann cells are glial cells in the peripheral nervous system, making choice A a strong answer. Since neuronal cells have a relatively higher level of miRNA and therefor a lower level of NF-1, they are less likely to develop tumors, eliminating choice B. Astrocytes are glial cells that provide structural support to CNS neurons and help balance metabolites. Based on the data in Figure 1, Schwann cells are more likely to develop tumors than astrocytes, eliminating choice C. Choice D can be eliminated for the same reason as choice B, making choice A the best answer.

31. **C is the best answer.** The vestibular system is involved in coordination and position sense. It relies on the inner ear, the eyes, and certain parts of the brain. The nerve that innervates the inner ear is the vestibulocochlear nerve, also known as cranial nerve VIII. It eventually splits into the vestibular nerve which is responsible for the vestibular sense and the cochlear nerve which is responsible for hearing. It is unlikely the MCAT® will require memorization the cranial nerves but recognition of the nerves involved in the special senses is important. If a person lost their vestibular sense, or sense of position in the environment, it stands to reason that he or she may be unstable while walking. Option III is consistent with vestibular nerve dysfunction, so Choice A and D can be eliminated. That leaves choice B and C, meaning that either option I or option II must be true. A person's sense of smell is mediated by the olfactory bulb and cranial nerve I, which is far from the location of the vestibular system. Option I is unlikely and can be eliminated. Since the vestibular nerve and the cochlear nerve originate from the same nerve and are in close proximity to one another, a mass originating from a vestibular nerve would likely impact cochlear nerve function as well. Compression of the cochlear nerve could lead to hearing loss, making option II a consistent symptom. Since both option II and III are true, choice C is the best answer.

32. **A is the best answer.** Nociceptors are sensory receptors that convey painful stimuli to the body. The passage explains that in addition to regulating NF-1 production, each of the proteins discussed have additional functions. MiR-103 is involved in the pain pathway, which means that it likely interacts with nociceptors in come capacity. Choice A is a strong answer. MiR-137 exists in synapses and regulates the development of neurons and dendrites. It is less likely to interact with nociceptors, eliminating choice B. MiR-128 is involved in the fear pathways and is less likely than miR-103 to interact with nociceptors. Choice C can be eliminated. *U6* RNA was used as the control variable for the gel electrophoresis. It is not an endogenous RNA and does not interact with nociceptors. Choice A is the best answer.

33. **B is the best answer.** According to the passage, miR-137 regulates neuronal maturation and dendritic morphogenesis, and regulates the production of NF-1. The absence of miR-137 might lead to increased NF-1 production, which is tumorigenic. However, it is possible that miR-103 and miR-128 could compensate for it's absence. Choice A is a possible answer. Dendrites are responsible for receiving signals to the neuron. The many dendrites of a neuron can receive signals from multiple inputs. These inputs are integrated in a process called summation, which only allows the receiving neuron to fire if all the stimuli together call for a response. This prevents the neuron from firing in response to every stimulus, meaningful or otherwise. Since miR-137 is responsible for dendritic morphogenesis, its absence might result in dendritic dysfunction and malfunctioning of input integration process. Choice B is a strong answer. Based on Figure 1, miR-137 is not found in Schwann cells, which provide neurons of the peripheral nervous system with myelin sheaths. Since miR-137 is not responsible for myelin sheath production in the peripheral nervous system, there is no mechanism to slow down action potential propagation in the peripheral nervous system. Choice C can be eliminated. MiR-137 does regulate neuronal maturation and the passage does not specify what neuronal networks in particular would be affected. It is possible that in the absence of miR-137 neurons in the speech center would not mature properly leading to speech disabilities. However, this is a less direct connection between miR-137 and its function than choice B. This makes choice B the best answer.

34. **C is the best answer.** To answer this question, identify the answer choice that describes a phenomenon that occurs during a reflex. A reflex is a quick response to a stimulus which can occur without the direction of the central nervous system. A commonly studied reflex is the stretch reflex: when a muscle is stretched, a sensory neuron activates a motor neuron in the spinal cord to contract the muscle, returning it to its resting position. This is an example of a negative feedback loop. Choice A describes a phenomenon that does not occur in a reflex. If the feedback loop was positive, the motor neuron would cause the muscle to stretch even more in response to the initial stretching. Choice A can be eliminated. The supraspinal circuits, as their name suggests is above the spinal cord. The classic reflex loop goes only to the spinal cord. While inhibitory input from supraspinal circuits can be used to control the sensitivity and speed of the reflex, it is not part of the core reflex circuit. Choice B can be eliminated. Choice C describes the primary purpose of a reflex: a response that works independently of the central nervous system to quickly react to the environment in an effort to prevent tissue damage. Choice C is a strong answer. Reflexes do not activate the parasympathetic nervous system. Choice D can be eliminated. Choice C is the best answer.

Passage 7 (Questions 35-38)

35. **B is the best answer.** It is not necessary to know any details about quinine to answer the question. Figure 1 shows that there is a strong nerve response to the quinine in KO and wild-type mice, indicating that the two populations are similar. Accordingly, the test serves as a control in that it provides a comparison for the sucrose tests where there is a clearly diminished response to the sucrose in KO mice. Choice A overreaches by stating that the responses are identical, though this is not accurate. The point of the quinine test is to show that the responses are similar with regards to other gustatory pathways, indicating that the specific A2B deficit affects sweet sensation. Choice B is the best answer, since it clarifies this point, and it also highlights the importance of the control in providing evidence that the design is valid. The fact that there is intact signaling from quinine helps to demonstrate that action potential formation is preserved in KO mice. Action potentials represent waves of depolarizations along neurons following receptor activity that causes an influx of sodium cations. The defect in signaling is limited to the response to sweet stimulation due to the absence of the adenosine receptor, but other cellular components related to action potentials are unaffected. Choice C is somewhat true in that the NaCl test may demonstrate intact signaling for the salty pathway, though the quinine test provides additional information by showing how signaling is maintained in the bitter pathway. Choice D is true but is not the best answer, since it falls short of explaining the use of quinine as a control in the way that choice B does.

36. **C is the best answer.** The question states that the proposed mechanism of signaling for salty taste involves the entry of sodium ions into the cell. Using information from neuron action potentials, it is possible to reason out how the signal would be generated. Action potentials start with a rapid influx of sodium into the cell causing a depolarization. Potassium, which is usually concentrated inside the cells, then rushes out to return the cell towards the resting voltage. Action potentials propagate along neurons until reaching the end of the axon. At this point, calcium rushes into the cell and triggers the release of synaptic vesicles. Choice A is inaccurate, since sodium ions are positively charged, and entry of sodium into the cell causes a depolarization from the negative resting state and not a hyperpolarization. Choice B is accurate with regards to the depolarization, though it is inaccurate when describing the direction of flow of potassium ions. Choice C is the best answer, since it accurately describes both the effect on the voltage and also the secondary effect of the release of neurotransmitters from their vesicles. Choice D can be misleading, since disinhibition of tonically firing neurons is equivalent to activating neurons that are not usually active. This choice can be eliminated, however, since sodium entry causes depolarization and not hyperpolarization. It is also worth noting that photoreceptors are hyperpolarized in response to light, though that is not the case with gustatory receptors.

37. **D is the best answer.** The last paragraph explains that the ATP released by taste receptor cells is converted to adenosine that then acts on receptors on the initial taste receptor cells. This presumably leads to increased release of ATP or other signals acting on the gustatory neurons adjacent to the taste cells. When the sweet receptors are blocked, there will be no chemoreceptor activity, and no ATP will be released by the taste cells. Choice A is partially true for the KO group, though the blocker would also eliminated the response in the wild-type group, so there will be no difference between the groups. Choice B is partially true with regards to the equal effect. However, it is not the best answer, since a potent blocker would be expected to eliminate and not merely diminish the responses. Choice C is not accurate, since there is no reason why the blocker would affect the wild-type group primarily. Choice D is the best answer. In the absence of sweet receptor activity, ATP will not be released by the taste receptor cells. The loss of the adenosine receptor is irrelevant when no adenosine is present, so there will be no difference between the groups.

38. **B is the best answer.** The figure shows that the response to 30 mM of sucralose is similar to that of 300 mM of sucrose. The fact that the response is diminished in the KO mice in either case lends support to the fact that they both signal through the sweet pathway, since the adenosine receptors discussed in the passage are unique to the cells containing the sweet receptors. Choice A is not the best answer, since the concentration of sucralose required for a strong response is significantly lower than what is required with sucrose. Choice B is the best answer. Based on Figure 1, it would seem that sucralose is at least ten times as effective as sucrose. Choice C is not supported by the graph, since the diminished response in the KO group is evidence that the adenosine receptor is involved in sucralose signaling. In the absence of the A2B receptor, the response in notably diminished. Choice D is misleading, since the response to quinine is clearly the strongest. However, the lack of a difference in the KO group gives evidence to the fact that quinine triggers a taste response separate from the sweet response. If it were to signal by the sweet receptors, quinine would show a diminished response in the KO group.

Stand-alones (Questions 39-41)

39. **B is the best answer.** Choice A has the term "all," which highlights it as a weaker answer since it is virtually impossible to competitively inhibit all receptors. It is also unlikely that olfaction is diminished greatly by blockade of one receptor, since perception of smell integrates a multitude of types of olfactory chemoreceptors in the nasal cavity. This makes choice B the best answer. There is no evidence that blockade of one chemical enhances olfactory perception of other chemicals, making choice C unlikely to be the best answer. Since choice B is a strong answer, choice D is unlikely to be the best answer.

40. **A is the best answer.** The correct pathway for transmission of olfactory stimuli to the brain is from the olfactory chemoreceptors to the olfactory nerve to the olfactory bulb directly to the piriform or olfactory cortex in the temporal lobe, making choice A the best answer. It bypasses the thalamus, making choice B unlikely to be the best answer. Choice C has the olfactory bulb and nerve in reverse order and omits the chemoreceptors, making it less likely to be the best answer.

41. **A is the best answer.** Psychophysics is the study of human perception of external stimuli, which is prone to subjectivity due to individual experiences and prior knowledge of the phenomenon being tested. This makes A the best answer. Signals do need a minimal threshold to be detected, making choice B less likely to be the best answer. Signals can escape detection, making choice C less likely to be the best answer. Adjacent stimuli can cause signals to register inaccurately, as in the case of optical illusions, making choice D less likely to be the best answer.

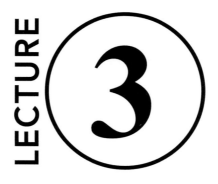

LECTURE ③

The Endocrine System

TEST 3A

ANSWERS & EXPLANATIONS
Questions 1–59

LECTURE 3 ANSWER KEY

TEST 3A		MINI-TEST 3B	
1. A	31. A	1. A	22. B
2. D	32. A	2. B	23. C
3. C	33. B	3. B	24. B
4. A	34. C	4. C	25. A
5. B	35. A	5. B	26. C
6. C	36. D	6. A	27. D
7. C	37. D	7. D	28. A
8. C	38. A	8. B	29. A
9. D	39. C	9. C	30. A
10. B	40. B	10. A	31. B
11. B	41. B	11. A	32. A
12. A	42. B	12. D	33. B
13. C	43. A	13. D	34. D
14. D	44. A	14. A	35. A
15. B	45. A	15. A	36. C
16. A	46. C	16. B	37. B
17. A	47. A	17. C	38. D
18. B	48. D	18. B	39. D
19. A	49. C	19. D	40. B
20. B	50. B	20. C	41. D
21. B	51. C	21. C	
22. D	52. D		
23. A	53. D		
24. D	54. C		
25. C	55. B		
26. C	56. A		
27. A	57. A		
28. A	58. D		
29. C	59. B		
30. B			

EXPLANATIONS FOR LECTURE 3

Passage 1 (Questions 1-4)

1. **A is the best answer.** Based on Figure 2, participants with active Cushing's disease in the absence of DLP have telomere lengths of greater than 8000 bp. According to the passage, the primary symptom of Cushing's disease is elevated blood cortisol, the stress hormone secreted by the adrenal cortex. Cortisol is a nonpolar stress hormone with long term effects. The elevation in heart rate from a nonpolar hormone would not be fleeting, as opposed to polar hormones like epinephrine and norepinephrine, eliminating option I. Cortisol increases gluconeogenesis, the production of glucose, in order to increase energy for the body to respond to the stressor, making option II a strong answer. Cortisol has anti-inflammatory properties, and would act to depress the immune system, not enhance it, eliminating Option III. Cortisol would not affect blood volume, eliminating option IV. Choice A, II only, is the best answer.

2. **D is the best answer.** Cushing's syndrome is caused by an overproduction of the hormone cortisol. Cortisol production is controlled by the hypothalamus, which releases corticotropin-releasing hormone (CRH) to the anterior pituitary. In response to this stimulus, the anterior pituitary releases adrenocorticotropic hormone (ACTH), which then travels through the blood to the adrenal cortex and stimulates the production of cortisol. Choice A is very vague but may refer to the adrenal medulla which is derived from nervous tissue. Impaired neural tissue migration may affect the function of the adrenal medulla which is responsible for secreting norepinephrine and epinephrine. Cortisol is made by the adrenal cortex so this would not cause dysfunctional production of cortisol, eliminating choice A. A tumor on the posterior pituitary would affect oxytocin and antidiuretic hormone, not cortisol, eliminating choice B. Abnormally high gonadotropin releasing hormone GnRH secretion would affect follicle stimulating hormone, luteinizing hormone, estrogen, progesterone, and testosterone, but not cortisol, eliminating choice C. A tumor on the anterior pituitary gland could cause increased ACTH production, which would lead to overproduction of cortisol and the symptoms of Cushing's disease, making choice D the best answer.

3. **C is the best answer.** Cortisol production is controlled by the hypothalamus, which releases corticotropin releasing hormone (CRH) to the anterior pituitary. In response to this stimulus, the anterior pituitary releases adrenocorticotropic hormone (ACTH), which then travels through the blood to the adrenal cortex and stimulates the production of cortisol. Antidiuretic hormone (ADH) is released from nervous tissue in the posterior pituitary, and unlike cortisol does not utilize an endocrine-based negative feedback system, eliminating choice A. Prolactin, like ADH, is released by nervous tissue at the posterior pituitary, eliminating choice B for the same reason as choice A. Estrogen stimulation begins at the hypothalamus with gonadotropin releasing hormone (GnRH). GnRH stimulates production of luteinizing hormone and follicle stimulating hormone (FSH), which in turn stimulate estrogen. This hormonal axis is very similar to that of cortisol, and choice C is a strong answer. FSH is a hormone released from the anterior pituitary gland that stimulates the production of estrogen; it is only controlled by one hormone, GnRH, and is not as strong of an answer as choice C. Choice D can be eliminated.

4. **A is the best answer.** The conclusions of this experiment are that high levels of cortisol can cause oxidative damage to telomeres. Cardiovascular risk factors like hypertension and dyslipidemia are correlated with shortened telomeres. Injuries are primarily healed through cellular division, whether in the skin, muscle, or bone. If telomeres are shortened, cellular division is also likely inhibited due to more cells in senescence. If hypertension is correlated with shortened telomeres, then healing time should be increased, not reduced. Choice A is a strong answer. If telomeres are shortened in patients with dyslipidemia, a cardiovascular risk factor, then cellular division should be reduced due to more cells in senescence, eliminating choice B. Elderly patients would likely have shortened telomeres due to the aging process, and a correlation between heart disease and shortened telomeres would strengthen the conclusions of this passage. Increased cellular senescence is related to an increase in the shortening of the telomeres. The passage concludes that high cortisol is correlated with short telomeres. In stressful environmental situations, cortisol production is increased, and thus a correlation between these situations and increased senescence would strengthen the conclusions of the study.

5. **B is the best answer.** The results of Experiment 2 are found in Figure 1. The table shows that individuals with CAH had elevated blood pressure compared to the control subjects. Aldosterone is a mineralocorticoid that is secreted by the adrenal cortex, and it works to increase blood pressure by altering sodium permeability in the kidney. When sodium is absorbed, water follows, and this raises plasma volume. In an individual with low blood pressure, aldosterone would increase in an effort to raise blood pressure. The passage states that people with CAH have impaired ability to synthesize aldosterone and must ingest mineralocorticoids. The first thing to notice is that the data in Figure 1 are not statistically significant. Although p values were not given, the mean measurements +/− the standard deviation leads to ranges that significantly overlap. Based on the data, there is no way to comment on aldosterone levels and choice A can be eliminated. Choice B is consistent with the data and is a strong answer choice. Choice C is an overgeneralization that cannot be assessed based on the data in Figure 1 so this choice can be eliminated. Likewise, choice D is an overgeneralization that cannot be concluded from the data.

6. **C is the best answer.** There are two broad categories of feedback that govern many biological pathways—positive and negative feedback. In positive feedback, an end product feeds back to stimulate more activity of a given pathway. In negative feedback, the end product feeds back to down regulate the pathway's activity. Much of the endocrine system operates via a negative feedback mechanism in order to regulate the amount of hormones released at any given time. In the case of the hypothalamic-pituitary-adrenal axis, in response to CRH release from the hypothalamus, the pituitary releases ACTH which promotes the release of cortisol from the adrenal gland. CRH is released when the body senses a need for cortisol. When levels are sufficiently high, cortisol can feedback at the level of the pituitary and hypothalamus to shut down further release of the stimulatory hormones. The relationship described here is that of a negative feedback loop. If cortisol were abnormally low due to CAH, ACTH would be very high in an attempt to raise the body's cortisol. Choices A and B can be eliminated because ACTH would be expected to be increased. Choice C is the best answer because it correctly characterizes the increase in ACTH as well as recognizes that this would be due to a lack of negative feedback from cortisol. ACTH and cortisol do not interact by positive feedback, so choice D can be eliminated.

7. **C is the best answer.** Aldosterone is the main mineralocorticoid that is secreted from the adrenal cortex. It functions to change the permeability of the nephron to sodium, causing sodium and water to be retained. This raises plasma volume and helps raise the blood pressure. The kidney can sense low plasma volumes and induces a cascade that leads to aldosterone secretion in order to raise blood pressure. Looking to Figure 1, it can be seen that individual A described in the question stem has a lower blood pressure than individual B. Therefore, it would be expected that individual A would require more aldosterone due to the fact that they have a lower blood pressure. Choice A can be eliminated because individual B would not be expected to have higher aldosterone levels because he has a higher blood pressure. Choice B can be eliminated because although individual A might be expected to have more aldosterone, he does not have a higher blood pressure. Choice C is a strong answer because individual A has a lower blood pressure and would thus be expected to have a higher aldosterone level. Choice D can be eliminated because aldosterone is regulated by blood pressure, so two individuals with significantly different blood pressures would be expected to have differing levels of aldosterone.

8. **C is the best answer.** Paragraph 1 states that patients with CAH have higher levels of circulating androgens, so masculine findings not normally found in women could aid in making the diagnosis of CAH. A lack of measurable cortisol in the blood would be observed in male and female patients with CAH, so choice A is not the best answer. Testosterone can help promote closure of the epiphyseal plate, but this would occur in both men and women exposed to testosterone, so choice B would not help specifically diagnose a woman with CAH. Women typically do not have visible facial hair growth on the chin and lip. This pattern of hair growth is associated with male secondary sexual characteristics that are the product of elevated testosterone. Therefore, this abnormal finding is a result of elevated androgens and could be very helpful in making the diagnosis. Changes in blood pressure as they relate to lower aldosterone and cortisol levels would not be specific to one gender over another, eliminating choice D and leaving choice C as the best answer.

Passage 3 (Questions 9-12)

9. **D is the best answer.** CRH is released from the hypothalamus, travels in the portal system connecting the hypothalamus and anterior pituitary, and causes the release of ACTH from the anterior pituitary. The graph of ACTH levels in Figure 1 provides the best information about CRH release, as CRH levels directly determine the ACTH that would be released into the systemic circulation of the blood. While Figure 1 does not provide clear error bars to judge significance, all the answer choices require a determination of relative levels between the three groups. In Figure 1, ACTH levels throughout the day appear to be relatively similar between the three trial groups, meaning that CRH levels are likely similar between the three groups. Because healthy controls are not higher than premanifest patients, choice A can be eliminated. Similarly, because stage II/III patients are not higher than premanifest patients, choice B can be eliminated. While healthy controls and premanifest patients appear to have similar levels, the ACTH levels, and thus, CRH levels, are not higher than stage II/III patients, eliminating choice C. Figure 1 shows a relatively similar levels of the hormones between the three groups, making choice D the best answer choice.

10. **B is the best answer.** The endocrine system has an intricate system for regulating the levels of hormones in the blood in an attempt to maintain homeostasis. In general, the endocrine system is characterized by negative feedback that acts to decrease the secretion of hormones once the concentration of the end product reaches high levels. Figure 1 provides the best information to help assess the strength of the negative feedback mechanism during different times of the day. CRH release from the hypothalamus drives ACTH release from the anterior pituitary, causing cortisol release from the adrenal glands. Thus, cortisol is the end product that would regulate the negative feedback. The highest level of cortisol most likely corresponds to the strongest negative feedback. Cortisol levels are the lowest at midnight, meaning the negative feedback is likely low as well, eliminating choice A. Cortisol levels peak around 8:00 AM and progressively fall throughout the day. Because the levels of cortisol are not the highest at 2:00 PM or 9:00 PM, the negative feedback is likely at an intermediate level, eliminating choices C and D, respectively. The peak of cortisol in the blood occurs around 8:00 AM according to Figure 1. Because cortisol is the end product of the HPA axis, negative inhibition is likely the strongest here, preventing the release of more CRH and ACTH from the hypothalamus and adrenal gland, respectively. Thus, choice B is the best answer choice.

11. **B is the best answer.** Excess ACTH released from the anterior pituitary due to a tumor would cause high levels of cortisol to be released from the adrenal glands. One of the effects of cortisol is to increase the circulating levels of glucose, eliminating choice A. Increased glucose in the blood would lead to decreased levels of circulating glucagon, instead of increased levels of glucagon, eliminating choice C. Thus, both choices A and C represent the same physiologic effect, decreasing both their likelihoods of being the best answer. Remember that glucagon is released when the circulating glucose levels are low. High cortisol levels would negatively feedback onto the hypothalamus, preventing the release of CRH instead of increasing its release. Thus, choice D can be eliminated. High levels of circulating glucose lead to high levels of insulin, which acts to try and restore the blood glucose levels to normal. Insulin acts on all cells of the body to increase the expression of the glucose transporter on the cell surface. The increased concentration of glucose transporters pulls more glucose out of the blood, restoring the circulating levels back to normal. Thus, choice B is the best answer.

12. **A is the best answer.** Cortisol is a hydrophobic steroid hormone that is not able to travel in the blood without the assistance of a carrier protein that allows it to become soluble in the blood. According to the passage, hypothalamus dysfunction can lead to high cortisol that has been seen in some Huntington's disease patients. In order to get high cortisol, high CRH would be required, eliminating choice B. Both FSH and TSH, while hormones, are not discussed in the HPA axis of this passage and may or may not be seen in conjunction with high cortisol levels in Huntington's disease. Because the passage does not specifically discuss these, choices C and D are less likely to be the best answer. Increased transcription and translation of steroid carrier proteins would occur in the liver in order to solvate the higher levels of cortisol produced from the adrenal glands, making choice A the best answer.

Stand-alones (Questions 13-16)

13. **C is the best answer.** Many hormones, products of endocrine glands, are slow to degrade and have long lasting responses, such as estrogen or cortisol. Choice A can be eliminated. Not all glands use positive feedback loops with hormones released by other glands. Negative feedback loops are more common in the endocrine system. Choice B can be eliminated. All glands control DNA transcription and translation, whether they have intracellular or surface protein receptors, making choice C a strong answer. Not all glands are groups of cells controlled by nervous tissue. The posterior pituitary gland, for example, is nervous tissue originating in the CNS releasing hormones into the blood stream.

14. **D is the best answer.** Endocrine glands secrete hormone products via the blood stream. Exocrine glands release enzymatic products via a ductal system. The adrenal cortex is responsible for secreting two major classes of hormones—mineralocorticoids and glucocorticoids. Choice A can be eliminated because the adrenal cortex is not an exocrine gland. Choice B can be eliminated because although the cortex is an endocrine gland, it does not release its product through ducts. Choice C can also be eliminated because the adrenal cortex is not an exocrine gland. Choice D is the best answer because the adrenal cortex releases hormones, and because these hormones are distributed throughout the body, these glands much have a rich blood supply for dissemination.

15. **B is the best answer.** In the brain, epinephrine can act as a neurotransmitter, acting across synapses. Option I will be in the best answer. The adrenal medulla synthesizes epinephrine and releases it in the blood, meaning that epinephrine acts as a hormone. Option II will be in the best answer. Epinephrine binds a cell surface receptor, which utilizes a second messenger system. Epinephrine itself is not the second messenger, so option III will not be in the best answer. Epinephrine is a tyrosine derivative, also called a catecholamine. Since it does not have multiple amino acids bound through peptide bonds, it is not a peptide. Option IV will not be in the best answer. Choice B, I and II only, is the best answer.

16. **A is the best answer.** ACTH is a polypeptide tropic hormone that binds to an extracellular receptor, leading to GDP for GTP exchange of a coupled G protein and setting off downstream cascade events that eventually result in increased gene transcription. While this question appears to test specifics of ACTH, the identity of ACTH as a peptide helps establish the best answer. Because ACTH is a peptide that would be large and charged, it would be unable to cross the plasma membrane by diffusion like steroid hormones. Thus, ACTH could not bind a cytosolic receptor, eliminating choice B. Nuclear receptors are bound by tyrosine-based steroid hormones that need to cross both the plasma membrane and the nuclear membrane. Because ACTH is a charged peptide, it would be unable to cross both these membranes, eliminating choice C. Binding of an endoplasmic reticulum receptor would require crossing the plasma membrane, which ACTH is unable to do, eliminating choice A. The charged nature of ACTH requires that it bind an extracellular receptor to trigger internal signaling, making choice A the best answer choice.

Passage 4 (Questions 17-21)

17. **A is the best answer.** Iodine carries a -1 charge as a simple ion and is the main co-factor in both the thyroid hormones, T_3, also known as triiodothyronine, and T_4, also known as thyroxine. T_3 contains three iodine atoms, while T_4 contains four iodine atoms. Thyroid cells are the only cells in the body that can absorb iodine and it is used as a co-factor to catalyze reactions related to metabolism and basal metabolic rate. This makes choice A the best answer. Cobalt (Co^{2+}) is an essential co-factor in vitamins like B12, which are important for the normal functioning of the brain and nervous system. Cobalt is not the unique co-factor of the thyroid, eliminating choice B. Magnesium (Mg^{2+}) is crucial to stabilizing the charge of ATP in phosphorylation and dephosphoryaltion reactions, as well as playing a major role in stabilizing enzyme active sites and some DNA conformations. Magnesium is also not unique to the thyroid, eliminating choice C. Chloride (Cl^-) often moves across membranes with positively charged ions, such as with sodium in the ascending loop of Henle in the kidney, but does not commonly serve as a co-factor, making choice D unlikely to be the best answer. For the MCAT®, the unique role of iodine in the functioning of the thyroid hormones is important to remember.

18. **B is the best answer.** This question focuses on regulation and negative feedback pathways in the hypothalamaus-pituitary-thyroid axis. The hypothalamus is responsible for releasing thyroid releasing hormone (TRH), which travels through the portal circulation in the brain to the anterior pituitary to stimulate the release of thyroid stimulating hormone (TSH), which then travels to the thyroid to induce formation and release of thyroid hormones T_3 and T_4. Principles of regulation show that low levels of effector hormones T_3 and T_4 lead to increased levels of TRH and TSH, to attempt to increase the production and secretion of T_3 and T_4 back to physiologic levels. This would imply that TSH levels should be higher, not lower, than normal, eliminating choice A. TRH levels would likely be elevated due to decreased negative feedback from low levels of T_3 and T_4. Choice B is the best answer. Corticotropin-releasing hormone (CRH) is released from the hypothalamus and serves to stimulate the anterior pituitary to release adrenocorticotropic hormone (ACTH), which acts on the adrenal gland. The circulating levels of T_3 and T_4 do not impact CRH release, eliminating choice C. Prolactin is the hormone that stimulates breast milk production and is not involved in the regulation of thyroid hormones, eliminating choice D.

19. **A is the best answer.** The western blot shown in Figure 1 provides information that helps answer this question. Notice that TRβ expression is high in thyroid cells only and liver cancer cells, while TRα expression is high only in liver cancer cells. If T_4 bound preferentially to TRα receptors, increased TSH release, which would increase the transcription of genes leading to the production of T_4, would most likely affects cells that expressed TRα. In Figure 1, these cells are liver cancer cells. According to the passage, activation of the TRs may lead to increased apoptosis, or cell death. As TRα is only expressed in liver cancer cells, increased death would only be seen in these cells, not thyroid cells, eliminating choice A. Thyroid cancer cells do not express TRα, so they are unlikely to show increased cell death, eliminating choices B and C. Liver cancer cells express TRα, which according to the passage, could be bound by thyroid hormones. This means these cells should undergo increased apoptosis, or increased, not decreased, eliminating choice D.

20. **B is the best answer.** Hyperthyroidism suggests that they thyroid gland is overactive. The thyroid gland is a gland in the neck that secretes two hormones, T_3 and T_4. The main purpose of these hormones is to set the basal metabolic rate of the body, or the base rate that they body burns calories to maintain physiologic processes. Increased levels of the thyroid hormones would increase activation of the cells, leading to a rise in the basal metabolic rate. A rapid heartbeat would be a symptom of over-activation of the cardiac muscle, making choice A less likely to be the best answer. If cells have a higher metabolic rate, they are likely to need additional glucose to push through glycolysis, the citric acid cycle, and oxidative phosphorylation to generate additional ATP. This would lead to decreased blood glucose levels, making choice B most likely to be the best answer. Increased activation of cells would lead to breakdown of stored fats and, eventually, proteins. Decreased body weight would be the rest of the breakdown of these energy stores, needed to fuel the higher energy requirements of a greater basal metabolic rate. This eliminates choice C. A higher basal metabolic rate would generate additional ATP as described above. Because the creation of ATP is not 100% energy efficient, some of the energy put into generating ATP creates heat. This would lead to a higher than normal body temperature, eliminating choice D.

21. **B is the best answer.** The western blot in Figure 2 helps to answer this question. Notice that both T_3 and FTI increase the presence of GTP-bound RhoB. The presence of GTP-bound RhoB is at moderate levels with the addition of T_3 to the culture dish and at low levels with the addition of FTI to the culture dish. Upon addition of both to the culture dish, the presence of GTP-bound RhoB increase dramatically, as shown by the hyperintense band on the western blot. The description of Experiment 2 notes that GTP-bound RhoB is activated by binding of the thyroid hormones to TRs, leading to the increased death of cancer cells. If FTI inhibited the action of T_3, the band in lane 4 of the western blot would not be hyperintense, eliminating choice A. Because the simultaneous addition of T_3 and FTI drastically increases the presence of GTP-bound RhoB above that of T_3 or FTI alone, this is likely synergistic agonism, making choice B the best answer. The passage does not discuss the negative or positive regulatory effects of thyroid hormone binding on a cancer cell on the overall endocrine system, weakening choices C and D. Additionally, Experiment 2 does not provide expression levels of TSH or TRH, which would come from the anterior pituitary and hypothalamus, respectively.

Passage 5 (Questions 22-26)

22. **D is the best answer.** According to the passage, adults mainly have a set number of adipocytes. They do not grow or reduce in number, but rather change size. The S phase involves synthesis of organelles and DNA is preparation for cell division. The M phase stands for mitosis and includes all of the phases of cell division. Choices A and B are unlikely since adipocytes are not preparing for or completing cell division. G_1 is also a preparation phase for mitosis, involving growth in size and synthesis of mRNA and proteins, so choice C can be eliminated. The G_0 phase is a relatively dormant phase in the cell cycle. Choice D is the best answer since adipocytes do not divide.

23. **A is the best answer.** Figure 1 shows that FABP4 mRNA is increased following administration of epinephrine in embryonic stem cells. The dose of epinephrine is meant to simulate stress. This result suggests that stress, which releases epinephrine, can cause an increase of adipocyte formation in the womb. Choice A is a great answer. Choice B is not the best answer based on the increase of an adipocyte marker following simulated stress. There is an important fact in the passage regarding adult adipocyte growth. In adults, new adipocytes do not form. They only change in size in response to signals from the body. Thus, formation would not decrease or increase in adults, meaning choices C and D are unlikely.

24. **D is the best answer.** FABP4 mRNA levels are used to detect adipocyte formation. While FABP4 mRNA is used to measure differentiation into adipocytes, it does not necessarily say anything about growth rate or formation of new cells. The increased number of adipocytes formed could just be more embryonic stem cells shifting towards an adipocyte path. Choices A and B are unlikely since they are conclusions about cell division. Choice C regards differentiation of cells. As cells become more specified and more committed to a certain fate, like becoming an adipocyte, their ability to differentiate decreases. FABP4 mRNA is an indicator of having been committed to becoming an adipocyte. Thus, the levels of this mRNA should be inversely correlated with ability to differentiate into a large variety of cells. Choice C is unlikely and choice D is the best answer.

25. **C is the best answer.** Receptors for hormones are located in different positions based on the composition of that hormone. Peptide hormones are polar and hydrophilic. This prevents them from being able to cross the membrane freely, so their receptors are typically on the membrane. Next, steroid hormones are lipid-based, and are hydrophobic. They can easily cross the membrane, so their receptors can be anywhere inside the cell. Choices A, B, and D describe locations within the cell, so they could be targets for steroid hormones. However, insulin is a peptide hormone. This makes choice C the best answer.

26. **C is the best answer.** Epinephrine is associated with stressful scenarios and induces the "fight or flight" response. These situations call for increased resource devotion to muscles, lungs, and heart, with decreased resource devotion to organs in the digestive system. Thus, both options I and II are likely. One of the ways that the body controls resource dedication is through controlling blood flow. Since options I and II are likely, choices A and B are most likely incorrect. Next, increasing water retention is a function of ADH, not epinephrine, so choice D is unlikely and choice C is the best answer. ADH regulates water balance by increasing water reabsorption in the collecting ducts, leading to more concentrated urine and reduced excretion of water.

Stand-alones (Questions 27-30)

27. **A is the best answer.** Steroid hormones require a carrier protein to make them soluble in the blood in order to be transported to target organs. End-stage liver disease prevents the production of these proteins, preventing adequate levels of circulating steroid hormones. The pancreas, not the liver, is the main producer of insulin and glucagon, eliminating choice B. Water-soluble compounds are eliminated in the kidney into the urine, while fat-soluble metabolites are excreted into the bile in the liver, eliminating choice C. The gland that secretes hormones is the site of negative feedback. For example, high cortisol levels from the adrenal glands feed back to the hypothalamus and anterior pituitary to prevent formation of CRH and ACTH, respectively, which would continue to produce cortisol in the adrenal glands. Thus, choice D can be eliminated. The liver is the main site of carrier molecule synthesis for hydrophobic hormones. If the liver function was decreased due to disease, fewer steroid hormones would circulate, making choice A the best answer choice.

28. **A is the best answer.** Cortisol is a steroid hormone that is responsible for regulating glucose mobilization. It is produced in the adrenal cortex along with the mineralocorticoid aldosterone. Therefore, choice A is a strong answer because it states that cortisol is made in the medulla, not the cortex. Cortisol is known to regulate glucose mobilization, so choice B can be eliminated. Cortisol is a steroid hormone, which means it is derived from cholesterol and is largely hydrophobic. Its hydrophobicity allows it to traverse cell membranes and bind to intracellular receptors that ultimately act within cell nuclei, allowing choice C to be eliminated as it is a true statement. The adrenal cortex releases cortisol in response to stressors, and cortisol is also able to have continued action as a long term response in the presence of chronic stressors. Therefore, choice D can be eliminated, leaving choice A as the best answer.

29. **C is the best answer.** P and E_2 are steroid hormones, while FSH and LH are peptide hormones. These are two major classes of hormones that make up the majority of these signaling molecules in the body. Steroid hormones are nonpolar, and are hard to dissolve in the blood. They require binding proteins to transport them, while peptide hormones do not. Steroid hormones also can diffuse across cell membranes and bind to cytosolic receptors, while most peptide hormones bind to membrane-bound receptors. Thus, choices A, B, and D all represent distinctions between these two classes of hormones. All endocrine hormones, by definition, travel to target cells through the blood. Choice C is the best answer.

30. **B is the best answer.** If the receptor protein was located in the cytoplasm, the hormone or stimulator must have been nonpolar. FSH is a protein hormone, and would not have been able to cross the lipid bilayer to stimulate this response, eliminating choice A. Prostaglandins effect their response locally, and are nonpolar molecules able to cross the lipid bilayer and stimulate a cell by a receptor protein, making choice B a strong answer. Cortisol is a nonpolar hormone, but would not cause a purely local response, as it would circulate throughout the body to all tissues with the proper receptor proteins, eliminating choice C. Calcitonin is a protein based hormone, and is also polar, and would not have crossed the lipid bilayer, eliminating choice D.

Passage 6 (Questions 31-34)

31. **A is the best answer.** The data presented in Figure 1 come from an experiment designed to test the effect of the plasmid alone and the plasmid expressing three genes known to help transform cells into insulin-producing cells. After a gene is transcribed into mRNA, the mRNA must be translated into protein in order to act on the cell. mRNA levels can be increased or decreased by the miRNAs mentioned in the last paragraph of the passage, meaning it would be important to determine whether the mRNA was translated into protein. A western blot uses an antibody directed against a protein target and could detect Glut2 and Gck levels and correlate them with mRNA levels. This makes choice A an strong answer choice. Staining for additional mRNA levels of glucagon would not show the effect of the plasmid on actually changing the protein levels of enzymes responsible for processing glucose in the cell, eliminating choice B. Replication of the experiment in a different cell line would be important but not as important as correlating changes in mRNA levels with changes in actual protein levels that would carry out the functions in the cell. This eliminates choice C. The increased expression of *Glut2* and *Gck* could result from increasing the number of copies of a gene. However, the passage does not suggest that B13 cells would undergo this type of mutation that would cause duplication of certain portions of the chromosome, eliminating choice D.

32. **A is the best answer.** According to the first sentence of the passage, T1D is an autoimmune disease. Autoimmune diseases result from the body attacking its own cells after aberrantly recognizing an antigen that it should not. Killer T cells recognize peptides in the content of MHC Class I. If a T cell recognized a peptide antigen that was from a normal cell, it would erroneously try and kill the cell. If this cell type was a β cell of the pancreas that produced insulin, T1D would result, making choice A the best answer. Autoimmune diseases can also be caused when antibodies recognize self- antigens. α cells, however, secrete glucagon, not insulin, and elimination of these cells would not cause the loss of β cells seen in T1D. This eliminates choice B. The passage does not imply that the innate immune system is part of the pathogenesis of T1D, making choice C less likely to be the best answer. Additionally, the passage states that T1D is caused by an autoimmune disease, which would be mediated by the adaptive immune system. Macrophages are part of the innate immune system, making choice D a weaker answer. Additionally, T1D does not result from loss of α cells, as choice D suggests, helping to further eliminate it as the best answer. Notice that this question can simply be answered by knowing that insulin is produced by β cells. Only choice A describes the destruction of β cells.

33. **B is the best answer.** Figure 2 shows the relative levels of two microRNAs in the enzyme-producing, or exocrine, pancreas, the islets of Langerhans that contains the endocrine pancreas, as well as the B13 cells from Figure 1. miR-2137 levels are higher in the exocrine pancreas, while miR-204-5p levels are higher in the endocrine pancreas. Because microRNAs are described to affect the stability of mRNA, they would likely modulate the levels of the proteins produced by the endocrine and exocrine pancreas. Chymotrypsin helps to break down proteins and is secreted from the exocrine pancreas. miR-2137 expression is higher in the exocrine pancreas, option I is part of the best answer. Similarly, miR-204-5p levels are higher in the endocrine pancreas, suggesting that production or secretion of hormones could be affected. Option II is part of the best answer. Somatostatin is a hormone released by δ cells of the pancreas and serves to prevent insulin and glucagon release. miR-2137 levels are low in the endocrine pancreas compared to miR-204-5p levels, meaning it is less likely to affect endocrine function, eliminating option III, and with it choices C and D. Choice B is a better answer choice than choice A because it contains both options I and II.

34. **C is the best answer.** Increased secretion of insulin occurs when the bloodstream contains a higher than normal concentration of glucose, typically after a meal. This indicates the "rest and digest" side of the nervous system, as opposed to the "fight or flight" side. The parasympathetic nervous system, not the sympathetic nervous system, drives digestion and the movement of food throughout the gastrointestinal system. Increased sympathetic stimulation and increased digestion do not occur together, eliminating choices A and D. Decreased parasympathetic stimulation of smooth muscle that surrounds the tissue of the intestines would be the opposite of the actions expected during "rest and digest," eliminating choice B. The ciliary muscles are found in the eye and control the shape of the lens. Parasympathetic stimulation causes the ciliary muscle to contract which thickens the shape of the lens which makes the eye more prepared for near vision. It is helpful to think about the evolutionary reason that this may occur. When the sympathetic nervous system, the "fight or flight" system is activated, distance vision would be important so that a person could identify and escape from a threat. When the parasympathetic, the "rest and digest" system is activated, near vision may be important to ensure a person is not eating anything that is poisonous.

Passage 7 (Questions 35-38)

35. **A is the best answer.** According to paragraph one, acromegaly is caused by over-secretion of GH, or growth hormone. GH is released from the anterior pituitary and causes the elongation of bones at the epiphyseal plate. Release of GH is under the direct control of growth hormone releasing hormone, GHRH, from the hypothalamus, making choice A likely to be the best answer. GnRH, or gonadotropin-releasing hormone, controls the release of luteinizing hormone (LH) and follicle-stimulating hormone (FSH) from the anterior pituitary, but does not modulate GH levels, eliminating choice B. Calcitonin is released from the parathyroid glands and causes a decrease in blood calcium levels and an increase in bone density. It does not impact bone growth, but rather bone density, eliminating choice C. Prolactin results in the production of milk from the mammary glands and does not impact bone growth or bone density, eliminating choice D.

36. **D is the best answer.** Figure 1 provides the best information to help answer this question. Notice that the telomere shortening rate does not change appreciably with an increase in GH levels, while the telomere shortening rate drastically increases when IGF-1 levels increase. As GH levels do not impact telomere shortening, choice A can be eliminated. Increased IGF-1, not decreased IGF-1, results in altered telomere length, eliminating choice B. As with choice A, because GH levels do not impact telomere length, choice C can be eliminated. Increasing the level of IGF-1 from 100 ng/mL to 500 ng/mL causes an increase in telomere shortening, making choice D the best answer. Notice that binding location of the factor was not necessary to answer this question, but it can be used to confirm the best answer. IGF-1 is most likely to be similar to insulin, which is a peptide hormone, meaning that it would bind a cell-surface receptor. It would be unlikely to bind a cytoplasmic receptor, as it would be large and polar, meaning it would be unable to diffuse through the plasma membrane.

37. **D is the best answer.** The western blot in Figure 2, along with the mRNA levels quantified in the question figure, help provide information to answer this question. Remember that in a western blot, the density of the band corresponds to the amount of protein, which relatively correlates to the amount of mRNA. If protein levels do not change, it is likely that mRNA levels also do not change when conditions are varied. In Figure 2, the band intensity of p53 does not change with an increase in GH, though it does increase with an increase in IGF-1. This should correspond to relatively stable levels of p53 and p21 mRNA in the question figure under increasing GH levels and increased p53 and p21 mRNA levels under increasing IGF-1 levels. The scientists conclude that increased IGF-1 levels, not increased GH levels, leads to acromegaly, eliminating choices A and B. While choice C does state the findings of the scientists, notice that Figure 2, and thus the corollary data in Figure 3, pertain to Laron syndrome, not acromegaly. This means that the additional data provided by the question stem would not help support or deny the authors' findings regarding acromegaly, making choice D a better answer choice than choice C.

38. **A is the best answer.** The posterior pituitary is responsible for releasing vasopressin, also known as anti-diuretic hormone (ADH). ADH increases the transport of water across the collecting duct, resulting in an increase in blood pressure. Compression of the posterior pituitary would most likely lead to decreased ADH release, preventing ADH from acting on the collecting duct of the kidney, resulting in decreased blood pressure. This makes choice A the best answer. As a result of decreased blood pressure due to decreased ADH release, blood vessels would constrict to maintain perfusion of tissues, eliminating choice B. The ascending loop of Henle would also increase transport of sodium in an attempt to promote the passive reabsorption of water to raise blood volume, eliminating choice C. Decreased filtration at the level of the glomerulus would also likely occur, in an effort to preserve blood volume, making choice D less likely to be the best answer.

Passage 8 (Questions 39-42)

39. **C is the best answer.** Another hormone that begins with a p, parathyroid hormone (PTH), is responsible for stimulating bone breakdown, eliminating choice A. The basal metabolic rate is regulated by thyroid hormone, released from the thyroid glands in the neck. As basal metabolic rate is not determined by prolactin levels, choice B can be eliminated. Prolactin is one of the hormones released from the anterior pituitary and is responsible for increasing the production of milk from breast mammary glands in response to suckling. Choice C is most likely the best answer. Oxytocin, a hormone released from the posterior pituitary gland, is responsible for increasing the release of milk from the mammary glands, as well as uterine contractions, eliminating choice D.

40. **B is the best answer.** If Experiment 1 were repeated with thyroid cancer cells and an antibody directed against thyroid hormone, T_3, the western blot would show the expression and cytoplasmic or nuclear localization of thyroid hormone. An antibody directed against thyroid hormone would not bind parathyroid hormone, preventing any information about parathyroid hormone from appearing on the western blot. This eliminates choice A. Thyroid hormone is a non-polar hormone that diffuses to the nucleus of target cells to bind its receptor in the nucleus. Thyroid hormone staining would be the strongest in the nucleus, likely making choice B the best answer. As with staining for parathyroid hormone, the repeat of Experiment 1 would not provide information about prolactin levels, eliminating choice C. Because thyroid hormone diffuses to the nucleus, the thyroid hormone receptor is most likely to be found in the nucleus as well, meaning staining would be the strongest there and not at the cellular membrane. This eliminates choice D.

41. **B is the best answer.** PHPT patients show high levels of circulating parathyroid hormone, which helps to increase the circulating levels of calcium whey they are abnormally low. In addition to breaking down bone, PTH helps to stimulate additional reabsorption of calcium from the gut and kidney, while causing a decrease in phosphate reabsorption in the kidney. PTH serves to release calcium from the bone by stimulating osteoclasts, cells that break down bone. This eliminates choice A. As PTH prevents reabsorption of phosphate in the kidney, the concentrations of phosphate in the kidney are likely to be elevated above normal, making choice B the most probable answer. PTH increases calcium reabsorption, eliminating choice D. Decreased bone density would result from decreased bony matrix as a result of bone breakdown. Osteoclasts break down bone to cause this decreased density, eliminating choice D.

42. **B is the best answer.** A western blot is an experimental technique where an antibody binds a specific sequence of amino acids, called an epitope, to label the presence of a protein and provide a relative estimate of its abundance. The column corresponding to tumor six shows two bands, one at 80 kDa and one at 65 kDa. Because an antibody binds a specific amino acid sequence, it would not bind two epitopes, eliminating choice A. Also notice that the western blot is against the receptor for prolactin, a hormone released from the anterior pituitary. If the prolactin receptor had two isoforms of the gene, two protein products would be possible, one that is longer than another and a shorter protein that would result from alternative splicing of the RNA transcript. The antibody would bind the same epitope on both isoforms, leading to the two band pattern. This makes choice B most likely to be the best answer. Similar to choice A, the antibody is unlikely to bind three unique epitopes, eliminating choice C. Choice D notes that the antibody would bind only one isoform, but also says that the receptor is released from the anterior pituitary. Prolactin itself is released from the anterior pituitary, not its receptor, which is located in the target cells. This eliminates choice D and makes choice B the best answer.

Stand-alones (Questions 43-46)

43. **A is the best answer.** According to the information contained in the question stem, the *DOI2* gene participates in the conversion of thyroid hormone T_4 to a second thyroid hormone T_3. This question focuses on regulation both on the endocrine system on the whole and within the cell. Principles of regulation suggest that when the protein products of a gene are at a lower than average concentration, both gene transcription and mRNA translation would increase to restore the gene to normal physiologic levels. Increasing TSH release would increase the concentration of the TSH hormone, which would bind a nuclear thyroid hormone nuclear receptor. As a nuclear receptor, it is most likely that this thyroid hormone receptor would bind DNA and increase the transcription of target genes like *DOI2*. In addition, decrease methylation would decrease the heterochromatin proportion of the promoter, leading to increased transcription, further helping to support choice A as the best answer. Decreased TRH release would lead to decreased TSH release from the anterior pituitary, leading to decreased transcription, eliminating choice B. Decreased ubiquitination of T_3 would keep levels of T_3 raised, as ubiquitination leads to degradation of the protein by the proteasome. Increased protein concentrations would lead to negative feedback, leading to overall decreased transcription of the *DOI2* gene, eliminating choice C. Similarly, increasing mRNA translation of T_3 mRNA would lead to higher levels of the T_3 protein, leading to similar effects as seen in choice C. This eliminates choice D.

44. **A is the best answer.** Growth hormone is released from the anterior pituitary and drives the longitudinal growth of long bones at the epiphyseal plate, which lies at the junction of the metaphysis and the diaphysis of long bones. This makes option I a component of the best answer, eliminating choices B and D. Acid secretion in the stomach is under the control of gastrin, not GH. As gastrin does not lead to increased growth of long bones, option II can be eliminated from the best answer, along with choice B. While process of elimination does not require that option III be considered as part of the best answer, similarly to option II, lipogenesis is not increased by the levels of growth hormone, but rather by the circulating levels of fatty acids. Additionally, GH has been shown to increase fatty acid breakdown, not fatty acid synthesis, further eliminating option III.

45. **A is the best answer.** Parathyroid hormone (PTH) is typically released from the parathyroid glands when circulating calcium levels are low. In PHTP patients PTH is elevated without regard to calcium levels. PTH serves to increase bone breakdown to release calcium and phosphate, making choice A most likely to be the best answer. Phosphate is a component of the bony matrix and increased breakdown of the bone would also release additional phosphate, eliminating choice B. PTH increases osteoclast activity in order to release calcium. The circulating calcium levels would be abnormally high, not low, in PHPT patients, eliminating choices C and D. Negative feedback mechanisms are crucial to the endocrine system. In the case of PTH, high circulating calcium levels typically would lead to decreased release of PTH. In contrast, low circulating levels of calcium would lead to increased PTH release. In the former case, high calcium levels are exerting negative feedback on the synthesis and release of PTH from the parathyroid gland. PHPT is a disease state in which the negative feedback loops are impaired causing excess PTH release regardless of calcium concentration.

46. **C is the best answer.** By introducing extra testosterone into the blood, the endocrine system is tricked into thinking that it is producing enough and initiates the negative feedback loop to lower production of additional testosterone by the testes. While the use of supplemental testosterone would result in elevated testosterone levels, this change would most likely be due to direct effect of adding more testosterone to the blood, thus increasing the concentration. Since this is confused in choice A, it is a weaker answer. Similarly, answer choice B explains a situation that would result from positive feedback. Since luteinizing hormone (LH) stimulates the testes to produce testosterone, its secretion by the anterior pituitary will be decreased when testosterone is so choice B can be eliminated. Choice C is a vague but true answer. When levels of testosterone are low, the hypothalamus is stimulated to secrete gonadotropin releasing hormone, or GnRH, which acts on the anterior pituitary and stimulates it to secrete LH. Therefore, if testosterone is low, secretion of GnRH is decreased which is stated by choice C. The hypothalamus is stimulated by neuronal inputs which result in the release of certain hormones. The hormones secreted by the hypothalamus travel along specialized neurons which terminate in the anterior pituitary gland. This specialized delivery system prevents them from being released into the systemic circulation. Additionally, the anterior pituitary, not the hypothalamus, is responsible for the release of LH, allowing choice D to be eliminated.

Passage 9 (Questions 47-50)

47. **A is the best answer.** Apoptosis is the mechanism by which a cell commits suicide, and is caused both by preprogrammed information in the DNA as well as by external signals. According to the passage, the trigger for cellular apoptosis in the anterior pituitary is external, induced by the rise of estrogen. As both Choices C and D describe an internal response system, they can be eliminated. The lactotropes and somatotropes that undergo apoptosis are healthy cells that undergo apoptosis or proliferation in response to hormonal signaling, making choice A a strong answer. The cells in question are not damaged, eliminating choice B.

48. **D is the best answer.** Prolactin is a polar peptide hormone, and can dissolve freely in blood stream. In addition, due to its polarity, it cannot freely dissolve through the membrane and must be received by a membrane-bound receptor. Choice A describes hormones released by the hypothalamus travelling to the anterior pituitary, and thus can be eliminated. Choice B describes how hydrophobic hormones travel and misidentifies the mechanism by which a hydrophobic hormone would likely affect its target tissue. Choice C also describes how lipid hormones travel but unlike choice B, correctly pairs them with intracellular action. Since prolactin is not a hydrophobic hormone, choices B and C can be eliminated. Prolactin travels free floating through the blood stream and is received by membrane-bound receptors, making choice D the strongest answer choice.

49. **C is the best answer.** mERα is a membrane-associated estrogen receptor that induces cellular apoptosis. Recognize that steroid hormones do not typically act on membrane bound receptors. This is an unusual exception that was studied in the passage. E2-BSA is a type of estrogen that is unable to enter the cellular membrane, and thus would only affect membrane-bound receptors. If mERα induces apoptosis, then with increased E2-BSA concentration, there should be increased cellular apoptosis. If mERα does not induce apoptosis, then increased E2-BSA concentration will have no effect. Choice A describes an experiment that would determine whether or not mERα was involved in apoptosis, but it would not be able to distinguish whether membrane or intracellular receptors caused this programmed cell death. Choice B again would not distinguish between intracellular and membrane-bound induced apoptosis, as it is the concentration of normal estrogen that is increasing. Choice C has E2-BSA as the independent variable and holds E2 constant, making it a strong answer choice. Choice D would not elicit the role of membrane bound estrogen receptors, and can be eliminated.

50. **B is the best answer.** Prolactin, the hormone secreted by lactotropes, is important in lactation following birth, also known as parturition. Typically this hormone is inhibited by a hormone released by the hypothalamus called Prolactin Inhibiting Factor, or PIF. Following birth, secretion of this hormone is inhibited, allowing prolactin to be secreted and lactation induced. This question can be answered with that information or by process of elimination. Choice A describes how lactotrope secretion would be elevated due to estrogen, which deviates from the conclusions of the passage and can be eliminated. Choice B describes the process by which prolactin production is stimulated, or an inhibition of PIF at the hypothalamus, making this choice a strong answer. Choices C and D both describe lactotrope apoptosis which would decrease the amount of prolactin. Prolactin PROmotes LACTation and is very important after giving birth. Since choices C and D would reduce prolactin levels, those answers can be eliminated.

Passage 10 (Questions 51-56)

51. **C is the best answer.** The question is asking for an understanding of what the symptoms of PCOS are, which are described by the passage as anovulatory infertility, meaning that the oocyte is not ovulated and the individual becomes infertile. The correct answer choice likely will describe how FSH injection causes ovulation to occur. Choice A can be eliminated, as though a thickening of the endometrium would cause increased fertility, only LH could be responsible for stimulating the corpus luteum, not FSH. Choice B is incorrect, as a dramatic decrease in LH and inhibition of the luteal surge would cause a lack of ovulation, not addressing the main cause of infertility in PCOS-affected individuals. Choice C displays how FSH increases the amount of estrogen, which enters into a positive feedback loop with LH, eventually leading to the luteal surge that causes ovulation. Choice C is likely the correct answer. Finally, though choice D is a correct statement, it would not cause the oocyte to be more likely to ovulate, which is what is required to override the symptoms of PCOS. Choice C is a better answer than choice D.

52. **D is the best answer.** The question is asking for the connection between either the elevated progesterone or testosterone in DHEA-treated mice and the activity of the reproductive organs. Referring to Figure 1, the both serum levels of progesterone and testosterone are elevated in DHEA mice. One strategy for solving this question would be to make note of all the structures in the female reproductive system that would be affected by heightening or lowering of this hormone before reading the answer choices. The follicle, choice A, is stimulated by the production of FSH, something that is decreased in DHEA-treated mice and thus can be eliminated. The endomysium, a structure in the musculoskeletal system and choice B, is also introduced as a distractor and can be eliminated. The fimbriae, the structures retrieving the oocyte from the ovary or choice C, are not affected by hormonal control and can be eliminated. Finally, choice D, the endometrium, is directly affected by an increase in serum progesterone, and is the best answer.

53. **D is the best answer.** The question is asking for which hormone would be used to lower blood serum glucose levels in the DHEA-treated mice; the first three hormones would all increase blood glucose, which would exacerbate the symptoms of PCOS in DHEA-treated mice. The only answer choice that would decrease serum glucose is insulin, making choice D the best answer.

54. **C is the best answer.** The question is asking which data in the experiment displays that a reduction of PCOS symptomology occurs when rFSH is administered. The lack of change between rFSH + DHEA mice and just DHEA-treated mice in terms of LH, choice B, displays that the rFSH had little effect on mice hormone levels. This strengthens the conclusion that it was unsuccessful, not weakens it, eliminating this answer choice. Answer A and C are a pair and should be addressed in tandem. Figure 2 shows that the cysts are decreased in the presence of rFSH, eliminating choice A. The decrease in cysts displays the success of the administration of rFSH, making Choice C the best answer. The increased serum progesterone does not answer whether or not the experiment was successful, eliminating choice D.

55. **B is the best answer.** The question is asking for what type of molecule is decreased with the addition of DHEA + rFSH. The question must be answered in reference to Figure 1, which displays that LH production is decreased and that progesterone production is increased. Since the question is asking which hormone is decreased, it is looking for the composition of luteinizing hormone, a peptide. A peptide cannot passively diffuse through a cell membrane, as it is a polar compound composed of amino acids. Answer choices A and D can be eliminated as they describe how lipid hormones communicate with their target cells. Answer choice C is eliminated as not applying to either class of hormones. Answer choice B is the best answer, describing correctly all peptide hormones.

56. **A is the best answer.** The question is asking for the differences between male and female reproductive structures as well as for an understanding of the hormonal control of reproduction in males. According to figure one, DHEA will increase the amount of progesterone and decrease the amount of LH. In males, LH is responsible for stimulating Leydig cells, then producing testosterone. If LH is decreased, testosterone is decreased; the answer to the question will likely be caused by a decrease in testosterone. Choice A describes a consequence of decreased testosterone, making it the likely correct answer. Choice B describes a consequence of decreased FSH, outside the scope of information given in the passage. Choice C would be caused by an increase in LH and increase in testosterone, the opposite of the scenario described. Choice D describes a phenomenon only found in females, the luteal phase, and is eliminated.

Stand-alones (Questions 57-59)

57. **A is the best answer.** The anterior pituitary gland secretes FSH and LH, both of which are stimulated by the hypothalamus by the hormone GnRH. If the hormones secreted by the pituitary gland decrease, then GnRH would likely increase to compensate. Choice A is the best answer. Choice B can be eliminated, as it would be lower in a case in which the pituitary gland releases less hormones. Choice C can be eliminated as well; oxytocin is a hormone secreted from the posterior pituitary and would likely be lower in such a case. Estrogen is a hormone secreted by the ovary in response to elevated FSH, and if this hormone was decreased, then it would likely also decrease. Choice D can be eliminated.

58. **D is the best answer.** The seminal fluid is added to sperm by the seminal vesicles in to the urethra. While the sperm travels from the epididymis to the vas deferens to the urethra, the seminal fluid is not added until the urethra. Choice A can be eliminated, as the epididymis and the vas deferens are located before the production of seminal fluid in the male reproductive tract. Choice B can be eliminated as well, as it reverse the location of the vas deferens and the epididymis. Choice C also misorders the components of the male reproductive system, and the semen does not travel through both the bulbourethral gland as well as the seminal vesicles. Finally, choice D is the best answer, as it represents the correct pathway of the seminal fluid through the male reproductive tract.

59. **B is the best answer.** While it is true that the corpus luteum produces large quantities of progesterone and estrogen to prevent the shedding of the lining, this occurs after ovulation, so choice A can be eliminated. Estrogen normally inhibits the production of luteinizing hormone (LH). However, immediately before ovulation, a large increase in estrogen stimulates a massive increase in the production of LH. This is what is known as the luteal surge and leads to release of an egg from the mature follicle. Since this event is the start of ovulation, choice B is a strong option. Meiosis II occurs after a sperm cell has successfully penetrated the zona pellucida, therefore choice C can be eliminated. Choice D is a tempting answer because the description of the hormones involved in luteal surge is accurate. However, the luteal surge is not responsible for the proliferation of the endometrium, but rather triggers ovulation. The proliferation of the endometrium is induced by rising levels of circulating estrogens. While the proliferation of the uterine endometrium occurs prior to ovulation, choice D incorrectly states that this is a result of the luteal surge so it can be eliminated.

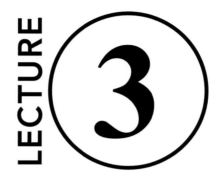

LECTURE

3

The Endocrine System

MINI-TEST 3B

ANSWERS & EXPLANATIONS
Questions 1–41

Passage 1 (Questions 1-4)

1. **A is the best answer.** The passage's key results are shown in Figure 1. These are that P and E_2 are decreased and FSH and LH stay constant in pregnant rats expose to TCS. LH surges do not occur during pregnancy, so no conclusions can be made about this. Next, uterine wall thickness is largely determined by estrogen. Maintenance is determined by progesterone. Given that both of these hormones are reduced, choice D seems very unlikely. Degeneration of the corpus luteum is a strong answer as this structure is maintained during normal pregnancy and is a major source of both hormones that were lowered following TCS exposure, P and E_2. Choice B seems unlikely as no changes are observed in FSH and LH, major reproductive hormones produced by the anterior pituitary.

2. **B is the best answer.** One way to narrow down answer choices in this question is to compare how E_2 and ER change, with how P and PR change, respectively. Both hormones decrease after TCS treatment in Figure 1. Furthermore, both receptors have increased mRNA expression according to the end of the passage. Since they all change in the same way, choices A and D are unlikely. Next, the endocrine system is full of examples of negative feedback, while positive feedback is relatively rare, making choice B more likely than choice C. Next, lowered hormone levels lead to increased expression of the receptors. This does not reflect positive feedback, as less positive feedback would lead to lower receptor expression. Choice B is the best answer, because as hormone levels decrease, reduced negative feedback could likely lead to increased receptor expression.

3. **B is the best answer.** According to the passage, HSD11B1 is involved in synthesizing cortisol. The right answer will likely have an answer that is opposite to the effects of cortisol. Cortisol stimulates gluconeogenesis in the liver to increase blood glucose levels. Thus, choice B is the best answer. Without cortisol, there will be reduced gluconeogenesis in the liver, and blood glucose levels will be lowered. Cortisol also induces synthesis of plasma proteins, so a reduction in cortisol would actually decrease plasma protein levels. Choice A is unlikely. Cortisol also has anti-inflammatory effects, which would be missing in a person with this mutation. This makes choice C unlikely. Similarly to how it mobilizes glucose, cortisol also increases energy availability throughout the body by mobilizing lipids and increasing blood levels. Choice D is unlikely since lipids would likely be lowered in the blood in a cortisol deficient person.

4. **C is the best answer.** This is really a question of what functions endoderm-derived organs have in the body. Endoderm forms the digestive tract, liver, pancreas, thymus, and thyroid. The thymus plays a key role in development of T cells, which are required for immunologic memory. Without the thymus, recurring infections are a very likely possibility. Option I should be in the correct answer. The pancreas secretes insulin and glucagon to control blood glucose levels. Additionally, the liver is the major reservoir of glucose, storing it as glycogen. Thus, glucose levels would be poorly controlled. Option II is likely to be in the right answer. Sensory organs are mainly ectoderm-derived, so deafness is less likely. Choice C is the best answer.

Passage 2 (Questions 5-8)

5. **B is the best answer.** According to Figure 1, cetrorelix causes a drop in the production of LH in experimental participants. Spermatocyte and spermatid production is increased by FSH stimulation of Sertoli cells in the seminiferous tubules. A drop in LH would not affect their production, eliminating choice A. Testosterone production is largely controlled by secretion of LH, and would decrease if LH decreased, making choice B a strong choice. Semen and seminal fluid production takes place at the prostate gland and bulbourethral gland, and is not controlled by hormones. Choice C would not be affected by a LH decrease and can be eliminated. The secondary male sex characteristics such as pubic hair and growth of larynx are controlled by testosterone production. A drop in LH would lower testosterone and would inhibit these developments, eliminating choice D.

6. **A is the best answer.** According to the passage, symptoms of RA are worsened when GnRH is stimulated. The primary feedback mechanism controlling GnRH secretion and therefore LH and FSH is estrogen secreted from the ovaries. When serum levels of estrogen are particularly high, such as immediately before ovulation, they create a positive feedback loop stimulating secretion of GnRH. This is one of the few positive feedback loops in the endocrine system. Elevated estrogen would worsen RA symptoms, making choice A a strong answer. Low estrogen levels in the blood act to inhibit GnRH secretion, such as during the follicular phase of the female reproductive cycle. This makes a worsening of RA symptoms unlikely, eliminating choice B. FSH does not inhibit or stimulate the secretion of GnRH, but rather is stimulated by GnRH. Low serum levels of GnRH would be associated with improvement of RA symptoms according to the passage so choice C can be eliminated. Low FSH would be due to low GnRH which is correlated with alleviation of RA symptoms, but again would not cause this, eliminating choice D.

7. **D is the best answer.** The primary purpose of measuring the effect of cetrorelix on LH was to determine if the drug successfully inhibited the production of GnRH. A suppression of LH would not necessarily indicate that RA symptoms were either alleviated or exacerbated. Instead, the effect on cetrorelix on markers of RA like CRP would suggest this, eliminating choice A. The purpose of measuring LH was to determine if GnRH was suppressed, not estrogen. Estrogen would be suppressed by successful use of cetrorelix, however, and though this is true, choice B is not the best answer when compared with choice D. During ovulation, a surge in LH stimulated by highly elevated serum estrogen causes the release of the secondary follicle from the ovary. Mimicking of ovulation would cause a stimulation of the GnRH hormonal axis, not inhibition, eliminating choice C. During the follicular phase, low levels of estrogen are secreted by the developing secondary follicle in the ovary. The low levels of estrogen act as a negative feedback mechanism that inhibits the production of GnRH at the hypothalamus, displaying the same effect as the cetrorelix. Choice D is the best answer.

8. **B is the best answer.** The dependent variables in Experiment 2 are IL-1β and TNF, both markers of inflammation. Cortisol is a hormone involved in the stress response which also has anti-inflammatory properties caused by its ability to depress the immune system. If protein receptors for cortisol were reduced, immune function would increase, increasing IL-1β and TNF, eliminating choice A. If cortisol receptors were increased, immune function would decrease, making choice B a strong answer. Antidiuretic hormone increases blood volume by increasing the permeability of the distal convoluted tubule of the kidney, but does not have an effect on immune function, eliminating both choices C and D.

Stand-alones (Questions 9-11)

9. **C is the best answer.** A sperm is composed of three parts: the head, midpiece, and tail. The head contains the genetic information as well as enzymes in the acrosome that digest the exterior of the oocyte, allowing the sperm to penetrate. If the sperm lacked these enzymes, it would be unable to fertilize the egg as a result of being unable to penetrate the exterior. Motility of the sperm is primarily driven by the presence of mitochondria in the midpiece to provide ATP for movement of the tail, eliminating choice A. Lack of enzymes would not affect sperm production, eliminating choice B. Sperm would be unable to penetrate the zona pellucida, making choice C a strong answer. While genetic information would be unable to fuse due to lack of these enzymes, choice C represents the direct consequence, and is a stronger answer than choice D.

10. **A is the best answer.** The cortical reaction occurs after the egg is fertilized by a single sperm cell. At this point, the egg produces several compounds that function to prevent additional sperm cells from fertilizing the egg. This process is call the cortical reaction. If it is being blocked, the possibility of multiple sperm cells fertilizing the egg increases which can result in the zygote having too many chromosomes, making choice A a strong option. Implantation of the blastocyst occurs well after the cortical reaction occurs which would make choice B a weaker option. Choice C also occurs well after the cortical reaction takes place and would not make for the best choice. Choice D is tricky because it also has to do with the fertilization step of reproduction. The difference is that choice D is referring to the acrosome reaction which allows the sperm cell to bury through the zona pellucida. Since the compound in the question inhibits the cortical reaction, choice A is a better option than choice D.

11. **A is the best answer.** Prenatal development, which is the first part of human physiological development, occurs in three distinct groups of time, often called trimesters. During the first trimester, major organs, including the special sensory organs that allow for vision, hearing, and taste, are forming. By the end of the ninth week of pregnancy, the major organs are developing in their final locations, marking the end of the first trimester. Rapid growth is characterized by the second trimester, where organs continue to grow. Growth is slowed during the third trimester, compared to the first and second trimesters, but the brain is still undergoing expansion prior to birth. The proliferation of cells that form the special sensory systems would most likely be the greatest during the times of rapid growth, characterized by the first and second trimesters, making choice A most likely to be the best answer. Growth is relatively slowed during the third trimester, making choice A a better answer choice than choice B. The first trimester is also characterized by rapid growth, making choice A more likely to be the best answer than choices C and D.

Passage 3 (Questions 12-16)

12. **D is the best answer.** The differentiation of a developing embryo is primarily affected by gene regulation, either through epigenetic mechanisms or induction by adjacent cells. The passage states that low dose NaF affects gene expression patterns, but does not affect viability or proliferation. Every cell contains the same genetic information, though depending on the cell's function different regions of the genome are either silenced or activated. Choice A, methylation of CpG islands, represents a mechanism of epigenetic control, and could thus feasibly represent a way that NaF could interact with the differentiation of the cells, eliminating choice A. Acetylation of histone tails is another mechanism of epigenetic control, and thus would also represent another technique that NaF could affect differentiation. Cell to cell communication, induction, is a primary way that cells commit to different lineages like the mesoderm, ectoderm, or endoderm, and thus could be a way that NaF affects differentiation. Finally, replication mutations like deletions of the genome are not a typical way that differentiation occurs, and would likely cause apoptosis of the cell. The passage states that exposure to NaF at low dose does not affect cell viability, making it unlikely that there are extensive mutations, eliminating choice D.

13. **D is the best answer.** The human embryonic stem cells used in this experiment were isolated from a blastocyst, which is a stage of embryogenesis where the embryo has become hollowed out and consists of two distinct regions of cells, that which will become the placenta, and that which will become the embryo. Option I, totipotent stem cells, are stem cells that could express any of their genes. The last structure in embryogenesis that contains totipotent stem cells is the morula, however, and the cells composing the blastocyst have been determined to either become the placenta or the embryo. Option I can be eliminated. Option II, or the inner cell mass, is one of the two distinct regions of the blastocyst, and is a strong answer. After the blastocyst is implanted into the uterine wall, it begins to secrete HCG from the region that will become the placenta. HCG, or human chorionic gonadotropin, stimulates the corpus luteum to continue secreting estrogen and progesterone. HCG would be likely to be found in the blastocyst, and is a strong answer. Choice A and B can be eliminated, as the blastocyst does not contain totipotent stem cells. Choice C can be eliminated, as both HCG and the inner cell mass are likely to be found near the blastocyst. Choice D is the best answer.

14. **A is the best answer.** Cell specialization describes how cells with the same genetic information express different sections of their genome, causing differences in shape, form, and function. This process occurs through determination and differentiation, in which regions of the genome are silenced or activated through epigenetic mechanisms or induction by other cells. A larger and flatter shape of the cells exposed to NaF would represent an alteration in cellular specialization, as shape is one of the most important characteristics of a specialized cell, like the difference in shape between a muscle cell and a neuron. Choice A is a strong answer. Decreased proliferation, while mentioned as a consequence of fluoride exposure, does not affect the differentiation of a cell, and choice B can be eliminated. Induction into the JNK pathway causes cellular apoptosis, and would cause a reduction in the number of cells, but would not necessarily affect differentiation. Alterations in the protein transcription pattern would change tissue specialization, but it is not mentioned in the passage, and thus is a weaker answer than choice A, eliminating choice D.

15. **A is the best answer.** The development of human embryonic stem cells (hESCs) into embryoid bodies (EBs) mimics the process of gastrulation. During gastrulation, the first cell movements occur as the cells move around the embryo to form three layers: the ectoderm, mesoderm, and endoderm. Choice A is a strong answer. The formation of the inner cell mass, what will later become the embryo, occurs during blastulation, not gastrulation, and choice B can be eliminated. Overproduction of NeuroD1 occurs only in cells treated by NaF, not healthy cells, and choice C can be eliminated. Organogenesis, or formation of the organs of the developing fetus, occurs after gastrulation, and choice D can be eliminated.

16. **B is the best answer.** In order to support the claim that fluoride directly affects IQ, a study would have to display that fluoride inhibits or negatively affects the process of neurulation, or the process during embryogenesis where the spinal cord and brain develop. Altered pH might cause a change in embryogenesis, but this study would not display a direct relationship between fluoride and neurulation, making choice A weaker answer. The neural plate develops from the ectoderm during neurulation due to induction, or cell to cell communication causing determination and differentiation. If fluoride affected this process, it would inhibit the development of the neural tube, which eventually becomes the central nervous system. Choice B is a strong answer. According to the passage, the transcription factor Brachyury is related to the mesoderm, so changes in its level would not directly support a claim that fluoride affects IQ, eliminating choice C. Neural crest cell migration is the process by which nervous tissues break away from the central nervous system and travel to tissues that contain nervous tissue throughout the body, like the adrenal medulla. A study displaying problems with this process would not necessarily display a deficit in IQ, eliminating answer choice D.

Passage 4 (Questions 17-20)

17. **C is the best answer.** A good positive control will provide a result that is both expected and is similar to the predicted response of the experimental groups. This gives the researcher confidence that the designed experiment is capable of acquiring the proper data needed to test the hypothesis. Choice A represents an additional test condition. Increasing the concentration of BPA, while likely to reduce the production of testosterone, has not been previously proven to work, so it would not make for the best positive control. Since the experiment is measuring the production of testosterone, the addition of a known concentration of testosterone could be used to check the accuracy of the measurement device, but not necessarily the effect that it has on the Leydig cell function, making choice B a weaker answer. The researchers hypothesize that the estrogen-like effect of BPA causes a reduction in the production of testosterone. By introducing a compound that has known estrogenic activity, the researchers can have more confidence that the experimental design is suitable for testing the hypothesis proposed. This makes choice C a strong option. Dibutyl Pthalate represents a new independent variable. The effect of this compound is not known as evidenced by its description as a potential ED. Since a positive control should have a known result, choice D is not the best answer.

18. **B is the best answer.** Prior to activation of the *SRY* gene, the gonads are capable of differentiating into testes or ovaries. The *SRY* gene induces the formation of the testes which will eventually produce testosterone. The direct action of the *SRY* gene is not likely to be the production of testosterone as this would occur later, after the testes have completely differentiated, making choice A a weaker option. To induce the formation of testes, a specific family of genes is expressed that will also give rise to the normal male characteristics. This can be accomplished if *SRY* codes for a unique transcription factor as described in choice B. Due to the lipophilic nature of estrogen, it is more likely to bind to a cytoplasmic receptor. Also, since *SRY* results in the formation of the testes, it is unlikely to produce a receptor for estrogen, the primary female sex hormone, making choice C less likely. Each cell contains the same DNA, but differing patterns of expression determine the phenotype of the cell. Choice D can be eliminated because it indicates that portions of the DNA no longer being used are degraded.

19. **D is the best answer.** The first step to answering this question is deciding what effect BPA has on Leydig cell function. The passage shows that BPA exposure causes a decrease in the production of testosterone by Leydig cells. With this in mind, the question can be simplified as asking about the potential effects of low testosterone production. While choice A indicates a phenotype (late onset of puberty) that might be associated with poorly functioning Leydig cells, it states that this would result in higher levels of testosterone being produced which contradicts the expected effect of BPA exposure. Choice A can be eliminated for this reason. Leydig cell malfunction could lead to indeterminate sex if testosterone production was severely impaired. BPA exposure was not described as a mutagen, but rather as an estrogen-like compound, and would not be expected to cause a mutation on the *SRY* gene making choice B less likely. Testosterone is not a peptide hormone so its synthesis is not mediated by ribosomes, which would eliminate choice C. The testes are responsible for producing sperm. Spermatogenesis requires a high concentration of testosterone, and if the effects of BPA were permanent, it is possible that the Leydig cells would be unable to produce enough testosterone for adequate sperm production. For this reason, choice D is the best answer.

20. **C is the best answer.** The best answer to this question should work with the data discussed in the passage to support the conclusion that TDS is potentially caused by fetal BPA exposure. For a chemical to have a direct effect on fetal development, it must cross the umbilical cord to gain access to the developing fetus. If BPA is unable to do so, then it would be difficult to conclude that BPA is disruptor of fetal development, making choice A a weak option. The results of the study depicted by choice B can be summarized as showing that the level of testosterone produced is largely dependent on genetic factors. This is because the monozygotic twins always experienced the same phenotype (level of testosterone produced) despite the presence of BPA. While this does not rule out the possibility of BPA as a factor in the development of TDS, it does indicate that genetics are largely at play since monozygotic twins have identical genetic material. In comparison, the study of dizygotic twins shows that the development of TDS is largely dictated by exposure to BPA since dizygotic twins share on average 50% of their genetic material, yet share a common prenatal environment. The high rate of TDS development in both dizygotic twins would show that the presence of BPA in the common prenatal environment is a factor in the development of TDS. This makes choice C a stronger answer than choice B which can now be eliminated. If the presence of BPA in the amniotic fluid of present-day women is the same as that found in the amniotic fluid from twenty years ago, then the elevated incidence of TDS is most likely independent of BPA exposure. Noting an increase in the amount BPA found in present-day woman would lend evidence to support the conclusion described in the question, but since there is no change, choice D is a weaker option.

Passage 5 (Questions 21-25)

21. **C is the best answer.** BMP4 is a transforming growth factor used in this experiment to induce differentiation into the mesoderm, a particular germ cell layer. Morulation, choice A, is the stage of embryogenesis in which the zygote undergoes cleavage, rapid cell division from one cell to 16. All cells of the morula remain totipotent at this stage of development, eliminating this answer choice. Blastulation, choice B, is the stage of embryogenesis in which the morula becomes a hollow fluid filled ball called the blastocyst; this stage of embryogenesis is still before that of the formation of germ cell layers, eliminating this answer choice. Gastrulation, choice C, is the stage of embryogenesis in which cells move about the embryo, forming the primitive streak and then the three germ cell layers, making this choice a strong answer. Neurulation, choice D, follows gastrulation, eliminating this answer.

22. **B is the best answer.** The strongest answer will display a tissue in the body that is derived from a layer other than the mesoderm that is negatively affected by DMD. Operating from a predetermined framework or hypothesis such as this one can help to avoid confusion when reading alternative answer choices. Experimental support for any hypothesis would be strongest when the data displays a clear connection between cause and effect, or DMD and dysfunction in a tissue derived from a germ cell layer other than the mesoderm. Tissues derived from the mesoderm include the muscles, skeletal system, blood vessels, and the kidneys. Tissues derived from the endoderm include the lining of the digestive tract, the pancreas, thymus, and the liver. Tissues derived from the ectoderm include the epidermis of the skin, the nervous system, and sense organs. Choice A describes an effect on cardiac tissue, which is derived from the mesoderm, and can be eliminated. Choice B describes an effect on neural tissue making this choice a strong answer, as this tissue is derived from the ectoderm. Choice C is also an effect on a tissue type derived from the mesoderm, skeletal muscle, and can be eliminated. Finally, choice D describes an effect on the kidneys, which is also the mesoderm, and can be eliminated.

23. **C is the best answer.** Cell specialization is the process by which a cell differentiates into a cell of a particular type, whether that is of the pancreas, muscle or bone. This does not explain how one cell that is differentiating could make the entire sample differentiate, eliminating choice A. Migration of cells is important in the movement of differentiated cells throughout the body; for example, this phenomenon is important in the movement of neural tissue from the neural crest to the adrenal cortex. Choice B can also be eliminated. Cell to cell communication is the process by which cells induce surrounding cells to differentiate into cells of the same type, making choice C a strong answer choice. Choice D, the downregulation of pluripotency markers, would occur as a cell becomes more specialized and ultimately differentiates, and can be eliminated.

24. **B is the best answer.** The question is asking for the use of stem cells in experiment one; hiPSCs, or human inducible pluripotent stem cells, are by definition pluripotent. Pluripotent cells have the ability to differentiate into any cell type except for that of the placenta. In order for cells to differentiate into that of the placenta, they must be totipotent. The only cells considered totipotent would be those of the embryo before blastulation, eliminating choice A. Choice B describes pluripotency, making this option a strong answer choice. Cells differentiated into the mesoderm would be considered multipotent, eliminating choice C. Finally, muscle cells would be considered the final differentiated muscle tissue, eliminating choice D.

25. **A is the best answer.** The question asks for an understanding of cellular determination, the process through which a cell becomes dedicated to a specific developmental path. Determination and later differentiation is caused by silencing of regions of the genome through epigenetic factors, making choice A a strong answer choice. During the initial stages of development, every cell in the morula is totipotent, meaning that each cell could differentiate into any type of specialized cell. The fate of a cell must be determined and is not inherent from the beginning of development, eliminating choice B. Although apoptosis is an important aspect of human development, particularly in the development of the neural system, it is not the primary mode of determination, eliminating choice C. Finally, determination of the fate of a particular cell is caused by epigenetic influence, not deletion of regions of the chromosome, eliminating choice D.

Stand-alones (Questions 26-29)

26. **C is the best answer.** During cleavage, the developing zygote divides rapidly without growing much in size. This makes option I a strong choice. After fertilization, the egg is swept into the fallopian tube where it begins to divide. These divisions do not enlarge the developing zygote significantly as described in option I, also making option II a strong option. During the second trimester, cleavage with little overall embryo growth is no longer occurring. It is in this stage that the embryo is getting larger in size, which makes option III a weaker option. Choice C is the best answer because it groups options I and II.

27. **D is the best answer.** The cell of the zygote undergoes cleavage, rapid stages of mitosis, repeatedly dividing from one cell until it is a mass of 16, called the morula. All of the cells in the morula remain totipotent, or are able to express all of their DNA, and thus the potency of the zygote does not change during the initial stages of cleavage. Choice A can be eliminated. In addition, throughout the initial stages of cleavage, the zygote does not change in shape, eliminating choice B. During fertilization and the initial stages of cleavage the zygote is located in the fallopian tube, and implants in the endometrium around the time of blastulation, eliminating choice C. The surface area of cells does greatly increase as the number of cells increases, making choice D the best answer.

28. **A is the best answer.** This question tests the existence of stem cell-driven regenerative capacities in various species, including humans. Humans can only undergo incomplete regeneration, which is the replacement of lost or injured tissues with new, different tissue. Complete regeneration is replacement with identical tissue, making choice A false and most likely to be the best answer. Salamanders can regrow limbs and tails, an ability that is especially useful when seeking escape after capture by a predator. This makes choice B true and unlikely to be the best answer. Parts of a flatworm are able to regenerate into new flatworms, making choice C also true and unlikely to be the best answer. In humans, blood loss or conditions that stimulate the immune system, such as illness, will stimulate white blood cells, or leukocytes, in the bone marrow to re-differentiate into the necessary subtypes for either routine replacement or to fight disease. This makes choice D also true and unlikely to be the best answer.

29. **A is the best answer.** Gastrulation is the formation of the three primary germ layers, the mesoderm, ectoderm, and endoderm. Differentiation is the process by which cells become fully specialized, and does not occur until the end of development, making choice A a strong answer. Determination, or commitment of a cell to a particular lineage, does occur at gastrulation, as cells commit to one of the three layers, eliminating choice B. Cell migration occurs, as cells move around the embryo to form the three layers of tissue, eliminating choice C. Cell-cell communication plays an important role in gastrulation, as adjacent cells induce surrounding cells to commit to the same germ cell layer, eliminating choice D.

Passage 6 (Questions 30-33)

30. **A is the best answer.** The passage states that N-cadherin is first expressed following implantation of the embryo. It would be expected that any structures formed prior to this step would be unaffected by the loss of N-cadherin function. Neural tube formation occurs during the third week in the gastrula. Since gastrulation occurs after implantation, a lack of N-cadherin activity could possibly affect neural tube formation, making choice A a strong option. Trophoblasts are another name for the cells that make up the trophectoderm. These cells develop prior to implantation and are more likely to require the proper function of E-cadherin, making choice B a weaker answer. The zona pellucida is a glycoprotein layer that surrounds the oocyte and is present until the blastocyst hatches from it to implant into the uterine wall. Because it is developed prior to implantation, choice C is a weaker choice. The inner cell mass which gives rise to the developing embryo is formed in the blastocyst prior to implantation. Since it occurs prior to implantation, it is less likely to be affected by an N-cadherin defect making choice D a weaker choice than choice A.

31. **B is the best answer.** Given the decrease in blastocyst formation in the EoNi embryos compared to the wild-type, it is likely that there is an increase in caspase-3 production. Since Igf1 signaling is responsible for a pro-survival response, an increase in apoptosis would correspond to a decrease in Igf1 signaling. Since Choice A states there is an increase in Igf1 signaling, it is a weaker choice. Cells that have been severely damaged will often undergo apoptosis. Since caspase-3 is a protein produced in apoptosis, and the inability to form blastocysts corresponds to an increase in the level of apoptosis, choice B is a strong answer. While the passage does not directly refer to activity of E-cadherin in morula development, it does indicate that E-cad plays a major role in the formation of the blastocyst which occurs after the morula is fully formed. Choice C is more vague and a weaker option than choice B. The rescue of the NoEi phenotype by administration of extra Igf1 would decrease the level of apoptosis in the developing gastrula. This would correspond to a decrease in the level of caspase-3 which makes choice D a weaker choice.

32. **A is the best answer.** Cell adhesion molecules are a class of proteins that are found on the surface of cells. They are able to bind certain molecules on other cells and in the extracellular matrix and transmit information about the surrounding environment back to the cell. Depending on the signal, alterations in the cells shape, movement, gene expression, or proliferation can occur. A role of cadherins in transmitting information to a cell about the extracellular environment and neighboring cells is critical for successful development, making choice A a strong option. Given that cadherins are found on the plasma membrane, transmission of a lipophilic hormone signal would not be expected, making choice B a weaker option. Choice C is describing the role of the placenta which forms from the cells of the trophectoderm. While the formation of the trophectoderm is dependent on cadherins, choice C is weaker than choice A because it describes a more indirect function of cadherins. While cadherins can have a role in altering gene expression, they are bound to the plasma membrane and are unable to act as transcription factors directly, making choice D a weaker choice.

33. **B is the best answer.** Blocking the activity of Igf1 would result in an inability to form the blastocysts due to an increased level of apoptosis. Choice A represents the normally functioning E-cadherins and would be capable of forming a blastocyst, making it a weaker choice. E-cad$^{-/-}$ on the other hand would not be able to form a blastocyst as shown by data in Table 1. It is also unresponsive to Igf1 which would be expected if the receptor is being blocked as described in the question, making choice B a strong answer. The EoNi$^{ki/ki}$ have a reduce rate of blastocyst formation compared to the wild-type, but is still successful 80 percent of the time. Since blocking the Igf1 receptor would prevent blastocyst formation, choice C is a weaker choice. The NoEi$^{ki/ki}$ genotype displays a complete loss of blastocyst formation under normal conditions as would be expected if the Igf1 receptor was blocked. The difference between choice B and choice D is that in the NoEi$^{ki/ki}$ embryos, administration of Igf1 was able to stimulate the successful formation of blastocysts. If the receptor is blocked, addition of Igf1 would not be expected to change the phenotype. For this reason, choice D is a weaker answer than choice B.

Passage 7 (Questions 34-38)

34. **D is the best answer.** According to Figure 2 and the information contained in the passage, mFrz8CRD is a specific inhibitor of Wnt. Comparing between the untreated and mFrz8CRD treated CB cells in Figure 2, notice that mFrz8CRD prevents the formation of cells that express Snail2 and HNK-1, which are both markers of neural crest cells. Neural crest cells are the cells of the ectoderm that are close to the neural tube and migrate away from the tube to form the accessory cells to the peripheral nervous system, cells of the adrenal medulla, and the C cells of the thyroid. As neural crest cells are responsible for forming the cells of the adrenal medulla and the C cells of the thyroid, choices A and B can be eliminated. Schwann cells are accessory cells of the peripheral nervous system that myelinate peripheral nervous system axons. They also are derived from neural crest cells, eliminating choice C. The lining of the ileum is formed from endoderm and is a specialized type of epithelial cell. In Figure 2, cells that express Ker, a marker of an epidermal cell, are found in both conditions, meaning mFrz8CRD treatment would not prevent the formation of epidermal cells that could like the small intestine, making choice D the best answer.

35. **A is the best answer.** Information contained in the passage discusses a chick embryo at stage 4 and notes that is at a late gastrula stage, where neural crest cells have already begun to form. The three tissue types, ectoderm, mesoderm, and endoderm form during a process called gastrulation, which, in humans, occurs three weeks after fertilization. In the gastrula stage, all three tissue types have formed. Stage 5 would indicate a later time point during embryologic development and the best answer would be the one that would occur after formation of the gastrula was completed. The gastrula develops into a neurula though induction, where the notochord causes the overlying ectoderm to thicken and fold into the neural plate, which will eventually become the neural tube that forms the spinal cord, brain, and most of the nervous system. Choice A is most likely the best answer, as it describes neurulation. The formation of the primitive streak occurs before the gastrula is completely formed, meaning it would have to occur before stage 4 in the embryo, eliminating choice B. Migration of endodermal cells from the primitive streak occur during first cell movements, as cells begin to slowly move around the embryo. As only the endoderm and ectoderm are present in an embryo at this point, it would likely be before stage 4, eliminating choice C. The last stage of gastrulation is the formation of the mesoderm, which completes the process of gastrulation and makes an embryo stage 4, according to the passage. Stage 5 would likely have additional neurological development, making choice A a better answer choice than choice D.

36. **C is the best answer.** Snail2$^+$ cells are neural crest cells, according to information contained in the passage. Neural crest cells for the peripheral nervous system, including the neurons and supporting cells like Schwann cells that myelinate the peripheral nervous system neurons to improve the speed of action potential conduction. Motor development begins in a cephalocaudal and proximodistal pattern. This means that the direction of development is from the head to the toe, or cephalocaudal, and from the trunk to the fingers and toes, or proximodistal. The pectoralis major is the main muscle of the chest and would be important for helping maintain posture and arm movement. Compared to the muscles of the head and neck, a child would develop control over these contractions later, making choice A a weaker answer choice. Control over the biceps muscle would come after control of the pectoralis major muscle, eliminating choice B. Control over the sternocleidomastoid muscle of the neck would likely be the first developed of the choices listed, making choice C most likely to be the best answer. The gastrocnemius muscle of the lower leg is the most distal of the choices listed and control over its contraction and movement would likely be the last to be fully developed, eliminating choice D.

37. **B is the best answer.** Reproduction occurs in four stages: fertilization of the egg by sperm, implantation of the blastocyst into the uterine wall, development of the fetus in the uterus, and birth of the fetus. Figure 3 shows that exposure of the RB to Wnt3A turns cells of the RB from epidermal cells that express Ker to neural crest cells that express Snail2 and HNK-1. This means more neural crest cells are forming and less epidermal cells are forming in the RB. The stage 4 embryo discussed in the passage is a late stage gastrula, meaning it has already formed three germ layers and would be implanted in the uterine wall. After fertilization but before implantation, the developing cell is a blastocyst, which is a hollow ball that is filled with fluid and has a mass of cells on one side that have not differentiated into the germ layers. Choice A can be eliminated. After implantation the cell mass starts to differentiate the cell mass into the three germ layers. Exposure of the RB to Wnt3A would decrease the number of epidermal cells formed and increase the number of neural crest cells formed, likely making choice B the best answer. According to information contained in paragraph one, most of the neural crest cell fate decisions are made at and around stage 4 in the embryo, which means it is less likely that additional cell fate decisions are made after the neural tube is formed or after birth, making choices C and D less likely to be the best answer.

38. **D is the best answer.** HNK-1 positive cells are neural crest cells and neural crest cells help control many of the organs and developmental changes seen in adolescence. Adolescence is marked by rapid and dramatic physical development during puberty, which eventually leads to sexual maturity. Some dopamine is produced from the adrenal medulla, an endocrine gland formed from neural crest cells, has been shown to cause behavioral changes during puberty, such as increased risk-taking behavior and novelty seeking, eliminating choice A. The sympathetic and parasympathetic nervous systems contain peripheral nervous system neurons formed from neural crest cells that migrated to the sex organs of the body. Increased responsiveness and control of sexual functioning is part of puberty, eliminating choice B. Calcitonin is released from the C cells of the thyroid, which is an endocrine organ formed from neural crest cells. Calcitonin serves to decrease the circulating levels of calcium, helping to return calcium to the bone, which is undergoing periods of rapid growth during puberty. This eliminates choice C. Serotonin expression in the hippocampus would most likely be modulated by the ectoderm cells that formed the brain, not the neural crest cells that migrated away from the neural tube during development. This makes choice D most likely to be the best answer.

Stand-alones (Questions 39-41)

39. **D is the best answer.** Cell migration is the process by which different types of specialized tissue developed during embryogenesis move to their respective regions of the developed body. Thus, the correct answer is likely a tissue in the body that was developed in one region and had to migrate to a different one. Choice D is the best answer, as the nervous tissue in the adrenal medulla developed during neurulation and migrated to the kidneys. Neural crest cells are formed at the neural tube and migrate and differentiate into melanocytes, craniofacial bones, smooth muscle, and the adrenal medulla. Neural crest cells themselves do not rely on migration, their final cell products do. So, choice C is not as strong as choice D. While choice A and B are types of nervous tissue developed during neurulation, neither of them need to move to a different region of the body, and can thus be eliminated.

40. **B is the best answer.** There are three germ layers that differentiate into different parts of the body. Adipocytes are fat cells and are typically of mesoderm origin. Ectoderm forms the epidermis, nervous system, and sense organs. Thus, choice A is unlikely. Choice B is a great answer because mesoderm forms the skeleton, muscles and fat. Choice C is endoderm, which forms the lining of tracts, liver, pancreas, thymus, and thyroid. Choice C is not a good answer. Choice D is unlikely since the tissues that are described are primarily come from mesoderm, not two different layers.

41. **D is the best answer.** In utero, or prenatal, development is roughly divided into the three trimesters spanning three months each. Growth, especially of the brain, is a major component of the third trimester, which makes choice A unlikely to be the best answer. The first trimester is characterized by organ development, which involves cell migration to their target location in the developing embryo. Thus, choice B and choice C are unlikely to be the best answer. The brain continues to develop postnatally, and its incomplete development at parturition, or birth, minimizes skull size and facilitates passage through the birth canal. Choice D is true and most likely to be the best answer.

LECTURE

4

The Circulatory, Respiratory, and Immune Systems

TEST 4A

ANSWERS & EXPLANATIONS
Questions 1–59

LECTURE 4 ANSWER KEY

TEST 4A		MINI-TEST 4B	
1. C	31. A	1. A	22. A
2. C	32. D	2. C	23. A
3. A	33. A	3. A	24. B
4. C	34. C	4. C	25. C
5. A	35. B	5. A	26. C
6. B	36. D	6. C	27. A
7. D	37. D	7. D	28. B
8. C	38. A	8. B	29. A
9. B	39. C	9. B	30. A
10. A	40. D	10. C	31. C
11. D	41. A	11. B	32. D
12. B	42. D	12. A	33. C
13. D	43. C	13. B	34. A
14. C	44. C	14. C	35. C
15. A	45. D	15. B	36. A
16. B	46. C	16. B	37. D
17. C	47. B	17. C	38. A
18. A	48. A	18. A	39. D
19. D	49. C	19. D	40. A
20. A	50. A	20. D	41. D
21. D	51. C	21. D	
22. D	52. B		
23. A	53. B		
24. B	54. A		
25. A	55. D		
26. A	56. C		
27. A	57. C		
28. C	58. C		
29. B	59. D		
30. A			

EXPLANATIONS FOR LECTURE 4

Passage 1 (Questions 1-4)

1. **C is the best answer.** Figure 1 shows that p66Shc KO mice have increased desmosine levels compared to WT mice, even when both groups are exposed to CS. According to paragraph two, desmosine is an important component of elastin, which allows for the elastic recoil of the lungs. Elastic recoil exists during both inspiration and expiration. During inspiration, the elastic recoil works against the expansion of the lungs, while during expiration, the elastic recoil aids in expelling air from the lungs. The increased desmosine levels suggest that p66Shc KO mice have more elastin and would have higher elastic recoil. p66Shc KO mice would have increased elastic recoil of the lungs during expiration, but they would also have increased elastic recoil of the lungs during inspiration, making choice A less likely to be the best answer. The lungs would not experience decreased elastic recoil during inspiration, eliminating choice B. p66Shc KO mice with more elastin compared to WT would have increased recoil during expiration and inspiration, making choice C most likely to be the best answer. The lungs would experience increased elastic recoil during expiration, not decreased recoil, eliminating choice D.

2. **C is the best answer.** According to paragraph two, WT mice that have been exposed to CS for 7 months have a condition that resembles emphysema in humans, which is characterized by breakdown of the alveolar walls, which reduces the surface area over which oxygen and carbon dioxide diffusion can occur. The decrease in surface area means less oxygen would diffuse into the blood, resulting in decreased, not increased, blood oxygen levels. This eliminates choice A. In order to compensate for the decrease in circulating oxygen levels, the body would most likely synthesize the hormone erythropoietin, which increases the levels of circulating red blood cells, and thus increases the hematocrit. This eliminates choice B. The increase in hematocrit and decrease in blood oxygen levels matches the description in choice C, likely making it the best answer. Mice would not experience a decrease in hematocrit and increase in blood oxygen levels, but the opposite, eliminating choice D.

3. **A is the best answer.** According to paragraph two, WT mice have increased breakdown of the alveolar wall, meaning they have less surface area for gas diffusion. In addition to oxygen not being able to diffuse as effectively, carbon dioxide cannot escape the blood as effectively. Increased levels of carbon dioxide in the blood result in higher levels of carbonic acid, which lowers the pH of the blood. p66Shc KO mice do not display degradation of the alveolar wall, meaning they should relatively maintain the same surface area for diffusion to occur and be able to get rid of carbon dioxide. WT mice would show acidosis of the blood, while p66Shc KO mice would have normal blood pH, making choice A most likely to be the best answer choice. As the pH of the blood would decrease in WT mice, they should not have alkalosis, or an elevated pH in the blood, eliminating choice B. p66Shc KO mice do not show major changes in the alveolar walls, meaning their blood pH should be normal, eliminating choice C. Because WT mice should show blood acidosis, not blood alkalosis, choice D can be eliminated.

4. **C is the best answer.** The respiratory system begins with the nose that warms and humidifies the incoming air before it passes into the trachea. After the trachea, also known as the windpipe, the air flows into the left and right bronchi before splitting into bronchioles that end in alveoli. Mucus is produced by cells called Goblet cells, while epithelial cells are responsible for lining the various portions of the respiratory system. Apoptosis is a process of programmed cell death, and apoptosis of tracheal Goblet cells would suggest that less mucus, not more mucus, was being produced, eliminating choice A. Neither the question stem nor the passage suggest that epithelial cells undergo a change in number with smoking, making choice B less likely to be the best answer. Goblet cell proliferation would result in increased mucus production, making choice C most likely to be the best answer. As with choice B, the passage and question stem do not imply that the epithelial cells undergo a change in number, making choice D less likely to be the best answer.

Passage 2 (Questions 5-9)

5. **A is the best answer.** The purpose of surfactant in alveoli is to reduce the surface tension in the layer of water in the lungs. This surface tension is an attractive force between water molecules that pulls the lungs inward, favoring contraction. By replacing surfactant with water, the surface tension will increase, eliminating choices B and D. The increased surface tension makes it more difficult to inhale, due to an increase in collapsing pressure, which is given by the law of Laplace. Choice C can be eliminated, making choice A the best answer.

6. **B is the best answer.** Figure 3 shows that HAPE reduces diffusion capacity. Factors that affect diffusion according to Fick's Law are surface area, partial pressure differential, and thickness across the membrane where diffusion occurs. Diffusion = (Surface area) · (ΔP)/thickness. Increased surface area allows for more gas exchange to take place while an increase in partial pressure differential allows more oxygen to flow down its gradient. An increased thickness opposes rapid diffusion. Option I would increase the partial pressure differential of oxygen because the person would be receiving a higher level of oxygen than normal air. Option I would increase, not decrease diffusion capacity. Choice A and C can be eliminated. Option II would lead to decreased diffusion capacity as explained above. Option III, similar to option I, would increase the partial pressure differential of oxygen, which would increase diffusion capacity. Option IV may be seen in HAPE, but the question asks for a cause of reduced diffusion capacity, and blood in the pulmonary vein has already passed the lungs and does not affect diffusion. Eliminate choice D. Only option II would decrease diffusion capacity, making choice B the best answer.

7. **D is the best answer.** Henry's Law describes how much gas can be dissolved in a solution, and is given by C = P × solubility, where C is the concentration, P is the partial pressure of the gas, and solubility is constant for a given temperature. Note that this only describes dissolved gas, and NOT oxygen bound to hemoglobin. To solve this problem, first find the solubility constant. Concentration is given in the question, and partial pressure of O_2 at 490 m is given in Table 1.

Plug in the values to get:

$$3 \text{ mL } O_2/L = 100 \text{ mmHg} \cdot \text{solubility}$$

$$\text{solubility} = 3 \cdot 10^{-2} \text{ mL } O_2/L/\text{mmHg}$$

Since this solubility is constant at both 490 m and 4559 m, use the partial pressure of O_2 at 4559 m for the HAPE group in Table 2 to find the concentration at 4559 m.

$$3 \cdot 10^{-2} \text{ mL } O_2/L/\text{mmHg} \times 30 \text{ mmHg} = 0.90 \text{ mL } O_2/L$$

Choice A is half of the concentration at 490 m. Choice B incorrectly uses the partial pressure of O_2 of the control group. Choice C incorrectly uses the PCO_2 baseline values. Choice D is the best answer.

8. **C is the best answer.** Breathing rate is controlled by the medulla, which receives signals from chemoreceptors. Chemoreceptors sense changes in blood pH and blood gas content. Baroreceptors sense changes in pressure. Baroreceptors control cardiac function rather than respiratory function, so choices A and B can be eliminated. The central chemoreceptors located in the medulla are very sensitive to changes in pH which is caused by a change in CO_2. If CO_2 increases, H^+ increases, which reduces pH. Remember the complex equilibrium: $CO_2 + H_2O \leftrightarrow H_2CO_3 \leftrightarrow H^+ + HCO_3^-$. The hippocampus is primarily responsible for processes related to memory and does not specifically have receptors to detect PO_2 levels. Choice D can be eliminated and choice C is the best answer.

9. **B is the best answer.** Figure 1 shows that FVC, or the maximum volume of air that can be exhaled, is reduced in individuals with HAPE. Figure 2 shows that the residual volume, or the volume remaining in the lungs after exhalation, is increased in HAPE. Taken together, the most likely answer choice will be the one that involves a reduction in exhalation. Exhalation involves relaxation of the diaphragm, contraction of the internal intercostal muscles, and an increase in intrapleural pressure. The only option of these is choice B, making it the best answer. Diaphragm contraction, external intercostal contraction, and development of negative intrapleural pressure are all associated with inhalation, so choices A, C and D can be eliminated.

Passage 3 (Questions 10-13)

10. **A is the best answer.** Surfactant is a material composed of amphipathic lipids that coats the alveolar surface and breaks up the intermolecular forces between water molecules, resulting in lower surface tension. Surface tension on the alveolar surface tends to collapse the alveolus and oppose the expansion of the lung. Because the question stem notes that the potassium channels are thought to regulate surfactant levels, an inhibitor of the channel would most likely prevent surfactant formation or export onto the surface of the alveolus. This would decrease the amount of surfactant available to break apart water molecules, making it more difficult to expand the lungs. Because an increase in breathing difficulty, not a decrease, would be observed, choices C and D can be eliminated. The lungs expand during inspiration, not expiration, eliminating choice B and making choice A the best answer.

11.   **D is the best answer.** Under normal conditions, the elastic tension of the lungs allows the lungs to passively contract, expelling air from the lungs. During forced exhalation, muscle contraction decreases the diameter of the chest faster than passive relaxation alone. The muscles between the ribs, called the intercostal muscles, are an example of muscles that contract to forcibly exhale air. Dopamine receptors are located in the brain and help mediate connections between neurons. More information about dopamine is beyond the scope of the MCAT®, making choice A less likely to be the best answer. Both epinephrine and norepinephrine are receptors of the autonomic nervous system, meaning that they act on the smooth muscle that surrounds blood vessels and the intestines. Forced exhalation would occur with skeletal muscle, not smooth muscle, meaning that the somatic, not autonomic nervous system, would mediate forced chest contraction. This makes choices B and C less likely to be the best answer. Acetylcholine receptors are at the neuromuscular junction between the somatic nervous system and skeletal muscle. Blocking these receptors would prevent the action of acetylcholine, which would prevent the contraction of muscles that could mediate forced exhalation of the air in the lung. Choice D is the best answer choice.

12.   **B is the best answer.** According to Figure 2, patients with severe asthma are more likely to have an increased number of mucus-producing cells, which would result in thicker mucus. Mucus functions to trap particles, which are then cleared along with the mucus by the action of cilia. Thicker mucus would be more difficult to clear than thinner mucus. Thicker, not thinner mucus, would be seen in severe asthmatics, eliminating choice A. Because severe asthmatics have the highest number of mucus-producing cells according to Figure 2, choice B is a strong answer. The passage does not discuss how the number of cilia changes in asthmatics. Cilia function to move the mucus to the back of the pharynx to be swallowed or spit. Because the passage does not imply that the number of cilia change, rather that the number of mucus-producing goblet cells changes, choices C and D are less likely to be the best answers. This leaves choice B as the best answer choice.

13.   **D is the best answer.** The question stem asks about the effect of increasing the thickness of the alveolar wall on the diffusion of oxygen and carbon dioxide into and out of the blood, respectively. Changing these values will also affect the pH of the blood by determining the amount of oxygen received by the tissues. Because CO_2 is exhaled from the lungs, increasing the thickness of the alveolar wall will make it more difficult for carbon dioxide to be exhaled, making option I correct. Similarly, because oxygen crosses the alveolar wall to dissolve in the blood, an increased wall thickness would prevent the same amount of oxygen from crossing over in the same amount of time, decreasing the amount of oxygen dissolved in the blood. Option II is correct. The primary function of the circulatory system is to deliver oxygen and remove carbon dioxide from the tissues of the body. Impaired diffusion of oxygen and carbon dioxide at the level of the alveoli would impact the efficacy of the circulatory system, making option III correct. Since all three options are correct, choice D is the best answer.

Stand-alones (Questions 14-16)

14.   **C is the best answer.** The structure of the lung is intimately related to its function. The branching of the lung is a mechanism for exponentially increasing the lung's surface area. This gives the lung a greater capacity for gas exchange. Choice A is something needed to replicate a lung. In order to bring air into the lung, the diaphragm contracts, decreasing intrathoracic pressure and expanding the lungs. This generates a negative pressure in the lung and air flows in to fill it. Choice B is also a needed element for a synthetic lung. Breathing is an involuntary action mediated by the medulla oblongata. Although a person can hold their breath, ultimately the body initiates breathing automatically. An engineer trying to replicate the human lung would need a way for breathing to be automated. Imagine having to press a button every time a breath needed to be taken. Chances are this would severely limit a person's daily activities. Choice C is a strong answer. The purpose of breathing is to transfer oxygen from the air to the blood to reach the tissues in the body. Without ample vascularization, air would enter the lungs without achieving the ultimate goal of breathing. Choice D would be a very important part of the design. For this reason choice C is the best answer.

15.   **A is the best answer.** This question asks about the dynamics of how the diaphragm and rib cage create a pressure differential between the air outside the body and the air inside the lungs. The diaphragm is a muscle that separates the thorax from the abdomen. Its contraction increases the volume of the thorax, lowering the intrathoracic pressure, causing the lungs to expand downward to increase their volume. Increased lung volume decreases the pressure inside the lungs, allowing air at higher pressure outside the body to flow into the lungs. The most ATP would be burned during the most muscle contraction. Contraction of the diaphragm, coupled with the contraction of the external intercostal muscles, would be required to overcome the elastic resistance of the lungs and chest wall. The external intercostal muscles are found between the ribs. Choice A is a strong answer, as the most muscle contraction would be required to initiate inhalation and overcome the elastic recoil forces of the chest wall. The end of inhalation is when little additional expansion of the lungs would occur. The greatest change in volume occurs at the beginning of inhalation, meaning the muscles are contracting more in the beginning instead of the end. This makes choice A a better answer choice than choice B. Exhalation is generally a passive process due to the inward recoil of the chest wall and lungs. Forced exhalation can use some muscles, such as the internal intercostal muscles, but in general the process of exhalation does not require muscle contraction, eliminating choices C and D. Choice A is the best answer.

16. **B is the best answer.** A narrow trachea, or wind pipe, would prevent the easy movement of air from outside the body to the lungs. The respiratory system serves a number of functions, including control of blood pH, filtering of foreign particles from inhaled air, and warming and humidifying inhaled air. Decreased movement of oxygen into the lungs would also co-occur with decreased movement of carbon dioxide out of the lungs. The decreased oxygen would contribute to lower blood oxygen levels, raising lactic acid fermentation in cells, as they would need to convert pyruvate to lactate to regenerate NAD^+ for glycolysis. This increased lactate would lower the pH of the blood, not raise it. In addition, more carbonic acid would remain the blood, also contributing to a decreased pH. This eliminates choice A. A narrow trachea would require that the incoming air to be filtered over a greater surface area. Mucus and ciliary hairs help trap incoming particles and allow for their clearance, making choice B a strong answer. Reduced movement of air into the lungs would increase the breathing rate, in an effort to restore normal oxygen levels. This eliminates choice C. The circulatory system takes cues from the respiratory system and also measures the oxygen content of the blood. Reduced oxygen entering the lungs would reduce blood oxygen levels, causing the heart to compensate by beating faster to deliver the blood to target tissues. This eliminates choice D.

Passage 4 (Questions 17-20)

17. **C is the best answer.** Examine Figure 1 to see what it suggests about ACh and the immune system. VAChT facilitates ACh storage in secretory vesicles, so when VAChT is knocked out, the amount of ACh that a cell can release is reduced. Thus, Figure 1 is essentially saying that when there is less ACh, markers of inflammation increase. When ACh is present, and can have its normal function, the opposite should occur: reduction in immune activation and inflammation. Reduction of immune response could potentially include inhibition of macrophage activation, so option I is likely. Next, capillary permeability is key for inflammation because it allows immune cells to exit the bloodstream at the site of inflammation. This does not match with ACh turning down the immune response, so option II is unlikely. Lastly, neutrophil recruitment is another key step of inflammation, so it makes sense that ACh would reduce it. Choice C, which includes options I and III, is the best answer.

18. **A is the best answer.** According to the passage, ACh release from parasympathetic fibers results in bronchoconstriction. This reduces the cross-sectional area and increases the resistance of the airways. As a result, air flow is impeded and it becomes harder to breathe. This could certainly result in reduced ventilation, or total volume moved by the lungs, so choice A is likely. Blood pH depends primarily on clearance of carbon dioxide from the bloodstream. Carbon dioxide is moved through the blood primarily as carbonic acid , so it decreases the pH of the blood. In addition, carbon dioxide can be transported directly bound to hemoglobin, and dissolved directly in the blood. Reduced breathing could lead to less removal of carbon dioxide and greater levels of carbonic acid in the blood. This would decrease, not increase blood pH, so choice B is unlikely. Next, total lung capacity is the volume of the lungs when they are fully expanded. There is no way that obstructing the lungs would increase this value, so choice C is unlikely. Residual volume is the volume remaining in the lungs after completion of forced expiration. This would not decrease in response to bronchoconstriction, so choice D is unlikely, and choice A is the best answer.

19. **D is the best answer.** Choice A is a trick answer because macrophages are not adaptive immune cells. They play a role in antigen presentation to adaptive immune cells, but generally are involved in cleanup and phagocytosis. B cells are adaptive, and they respond to specific pathogens and secrete antibodies that help with the immune response. Choice B is unlikely because B cells pump out a large quantity of these proteins, but do not necessarily control inflammation and direct other cells to continue this response. $CD8^+$ T cells scan cells for damage to DNA and viral infection, and then cause those damaged cells to undergo apoptosis. These play a very specific role and do not cause inflammation, so choice C is unlikely. $CD4^+$ T cells are helper T cells that control the response to pathogens on a large scale. They maintain activity by reactivating other cells, increasing their immune function, and maintaining inflammation. Choice D is the best answer.

20. **A is the best answer.** If the right lung is blocked off, there will certainly be a reduced ability to oxygenate, which is reflected in all four answer choices. Perfusion is blood flow and ventilation is air flow. If the right bronchus, a major airway, is blocked, then air flow will be reduced and there will be more perfusion than ventilation. Choice A is a strong answer. Choice B is unlikely since it suggests the opposite relationship. It would be appropriate in a situation with decreased blood flow, like a clot in the lung. Choice C is unlikely because an airway block should not negatively impact red blood cell count. Additionally, cardiac output, or the volume of blood pumped by the heart, would also not be negatively impacted by blockage of the airway. Choice A is the best answer.

Passage 5 (Questions 21-25)

21. D is the best answer. Cytokines are molecules released by immune system cells that stimulate the immune system to fight infections. They may also work to control an overactive immune system to prevent unintentional damage to host cells. Vasodilation is an increase in the diameter of peripheral blood vessels and would decrease, not increase blood pressure, eliminating choice A. Movement, or chemotaxis, of B cells to the lungs would not explain the change in blood pressure upon sustained exposure to high cytokine levels. This fact makes choice B less likely to be the best answer. Interleukins are a type of cytokine, some of which serve to cause adaptive immune system cells like T cells to proliferate. Blood pressure changes are also unexplained by this finding, eliminating choice C. Mast cells are a type of innate immune system cell that can cause vasoconstriction or vasodilation. Prostaglandins are molecules released by mast cells that can cause blood vessels to dilate, reducing blood pressure. Choice D is the best answer.

22. D is the best answer. The patient presented in the passage has traveled to a region of lower oxygen concentration in the atmosphere, due to the higher altitude. One of the responses to high altitude is the increased production of an allosteric compound, 2, 3-bisphosphoglycerate, which helps to decrease the binding affinity of hemoglobin for oxygen. This decreased binding affinity allows hemoglobin to drop off more oxygen in the tissues, maintaining oxygenation even when the atmospheric concentrations of oxygen are lower. Because hemoglobin has four subunits, it exhibits cooperativity and has a sigmoidal dissociation curve. Myoglobin only has one subunit and exhibits no cooperativity. Curves A and B represent shifts in myoglobin and show no cooperativity, they can be eliminated. Choice C represents a right shift, which would allow for less oxygen to reach the tissues, eliminating it as the best answer. The left shift in the curve would allow the hemoglobin molecule to drop off more oxygen in the tissues, making choice D the best answer.

23. A is the best answer. The main job of the circulatory system is to deliver oxygen to the tissues and carry away carbon dioxide and other metabolic waste. In response to decreased oxygen, the physiologic response would be to increase oxygenation of the blood by increasing the breathing rate and increase heart rate to circulate more oxygenated blood per unit time. This combination makes choice A a strong answer. Choice B is less desirable because heart rate would increase not decrease. Choice C and D can be eliminated because breathing rate would be increased not decreased.

24. B is the best answer. As with most other metabolites and small molecules, these particles are filtered into the proximal convoluted tubule near the glomerulus of the kidney. Bicarbonate, or HCO_3^- is one of the products of the carbon dioxide and water addition reaction performed by carbonic anhydrase. Carbonic anhydrase is the main enzyme responsible for regulating blood pH. Inhibiting carbonic anhydrase would prevent bicarbonate from being broken down in the proximal convoluted, leading to its elimination from the body. This would allow the body to get rid of more carbon dioxide, without needing the lungs to work as hard to expel the increased carbon dioxide that would result from more anaerobic respiration in regions with decreased oxygen concentrations in the air. Because acetazolamide would decrease the work of breathing, choice A can be eliminated and choice B is a strong answer. According to paragraph two, the increased breathing rate seen at high altitudes is partly do to increased carbon dioxide in the blood. Changing this concentration of carbon dioxide should affect breathing rate, eliminating choices C and D. Additionally, it is difficult to choose between choices C and D, as they are essentially the same answer. This helps to further eliminate them as possible answer choices. Choice B is the best answer.

25. A is the best answer. Erythropoietin is a hormone released by the kidney that serves to increase the production of red blood cells from the bone marrow. For individuals that may travel to a high altitude climate and experience altitude sickness, an increased number of red blood cells that could carry oxygen may help to limit the effects of low oxygen concentration in the atmosphere. This makes choice A a likely answer. Epinephrine is a hormone that stimulates the sympathetic nervous system and would increase both breathing rate and heart rate. This might an adequate temporary response to hypoxemia, however it is less likely than erythropoietin to *prevent* altitude sickness, eliminating choice B. Glucagon stimulates the release of glucose into the bloodstream but does not affect blood pH, breathing rate, or heart rate, eliminating choice C as the best answer. Acetylcholine is neurotransmitter, not a hormone, eliminating choice D. Choice A is the best answer.

Stand-alones (Questions 26-29)

26. A is the best answer. The oxygen dissociation curve changes for hemoglobin with heat and concentrations of CO_2, H^+, and 2,3-BPG. As any of these increase, the curve shifts to the right which means that there is less affinity for O_2. K_a is a measure of affinity and will decrease. $K_D = 1/K_a$. Alternatively, K_D is the dissociation constant. It is the measure of the PO_2 at which 50% of the available binding sites on hemoglobin are bound. When the curve shifts to the right, a higher PO_2 is required to bind 50% of the binding sites, and the K_D increases. It is important to know that K_a and K_D are inversely related. That means that if one increases, the other must decrease. In a question like this, you can then immediately eliminate equivalent answer choices. If K_a increases, then K_D must decrease and vice versa. Choices B and C can be eliminated. Also, choice D can be ruled out since heat is generated from active skeletal muscle, and heat changes the equilibrium constant. This leaves choice A as the best answer without yet considering the effects of CO_2 and H^+ on hemoglobin. Choice A is the best answer.

27. A is the best answer. This question requires knowledge of the basic anatomy of the heart and circulation. Beginning from the inferior and superior vena cava, blood flows into the right atrium, through the tricuspid valve, into the right ventricle, through the pulmonary valve into the pulmonary artery followed by the pulmonary vein. It flows back into the heart into the left atrium, passes through the mitral (bicuspid) valve into the left ventricle and is pushed past the aortic valve into the aorta and on to the rest of the body. Since the left ventricle and aorta are not answer choices, the best answer will be the first choice that blood interacts with upon returning to the heart. Choice A, the tricuspid valve, comes before choices B, C and D in the heart circuit, making choice A the best answer.

28. C is the best answer. Capillary beds are the main route for nutrients, oxygen, water and other molecules to be transported to tissues in the body. Recall that capillaries are composed of a single layer of endothelial cells. Capillaries are equipped to communicate with surrounding tissue via four main routes: pinocytosis, fenestrations in the endothelial cell, movement between individual cells and diffusion across the endothelial cell membrane. To answer this question, first note whether or not the answer choice is one of the transmission routes used by capillaries, then consider if a water soluble molecule could use this method. Choices A, B, C and D are all transmission routes used by capillaries. Now look for the answer choice that is least likely to work for a hydrophilic molecule. Both choice A and choice B are compatible with hydrophilic molecules and can be eliminated. Remember that cell membranes are made of a lipid bilayer and are hydrophobic. It is unlikely that a water soluble drug could cross the membrane, making choice C a strong answer. Choice D is also a possibility for a hydrophilic drug, eliminating choice D. Choice C is the best answer.

29. B is the best answer. The respiratory and integumentary systems play an important role in thermoregulation. Increased respiratory rate, also known as panting, increases the rate of evaporation and can be a mechanism to dissipate heat. On a cool day, this would be the opposite of what a person would want to do to maintain their body temperature. Choice A can be eliminated. Optimal gas exchange occurs when the air that reaches the alveoli is warm and moist. Nasal and tracheal capillary beds vasodilate and dissipate heat onto incoming air to warm it up. On a cold day, this would be especially important, and the capillary beds would be vasodilated. This makes choice B a strong answer. Choice C is the opposite of what is expected and can be eliminated. Arterioles vasodilate and direct blood to the skin capillary beds to dissipate heat. Conversely, they vasoconstrict and shunt blood away from the skin capillary beds to conserve heat. On a cold day, the arterioles would most likely be vasoconstricted to conserve body heat, eliminating choice D. Choice B is the best answer.

Passage 6 (Questions 30-33)

30. A is the best answer. In contrast to the passage, where ethanol increases membrane fluidity of RBCs, the question stem states that chronic alcoholics actually have stiffer, rather than more fluid, RBC membranes. The best answer will help explain this contradiction in ethanol exposure and increased stiffness. Cholesterol is an important molecule that is synthesized in the liver and helps maintain the fluidity of the plasma membrane. Extensive liver damage is likely to affect the synthesis of cholesterol by decreasing the number of cells that can produce it. Chronic alcoholics could have lower cholesterol levels, which may stiffen the membranes of cells, making choice A a strong answer. Early on in the disease course, the RBCs of people that will develop chronic alcoholism are likely to behave similar to the cells used in the experiments in the passage. There is no evidence that the RBCs of chronic alcoholics were initially different from those of controls, making choice B less likely to be the best answer. According to paragraph three, increased fluidity is associated with a more spherical RBC and is inversely proportional to the surface area of the RBC. Because the RBCs of chronic alcoholics are stiffer, they are less likely to be spherical, eliminating choice C. Stiffer membranes that cannot deform should also have increased surface area, eliminating choice D. This leaves choice A as the best answer.

31. **A is the best answer.** Blood can be divided into two parts, the volume made up of red blood cells and the volume made up of plasma. Hematocrit is the percent volume of the blood that is made up of red blood cells, while plasma contains clotting factors, white blood cells, and other circulating molecules. Erythropoietin is a hormone that is secreted from the kidneys and acts in the bone marrow to increase the production of red blood cells. Because erythropoietin increases production of red blood cells, the hematocrit, or the volume of the blood made up of red blood cells, should also increase, making choice A a answer. Choice B is the opposite of what would occur with increased secretion of erythropoietin and can be eliminated. If the hematocrit increased, the volume of the plasma would likely decrease to preserve overall blood volume, eliminating choice C. Depending on the amount of red blood cells released into circulation by the increase in erythropoietin, the blood volume will either remain the same or slightly increase. Blood volume is tightly regulated by the kidney but a significant increase in hematocrit may increase the oncotic pressure of the blood, which is determined by the number of particles in the blood. An increase in oncotic pressure would draw some water back into the blood, slightly raising blood volume. Choice D describes the least likely effect of increased hematocrit on blood volume and can be eliminated. Choice A is the best answer.

32. **D is the best answer.** Hemoglobin is a protein in the cytoplasm of red blood cells that carries oxygen from the lungs to target tissues. Hemoglobin contains a heme cofactor that has an iron atom, Fe^{2+}, at its center. It is this iron atom that is responsible for associating with oxygen in the hemoglobin molecule. Molecular oxygen, O_2, does not have any hydrogen atoms that could contribute to hydrogen bonding, eliminating choice A. Metallic bonding occurs between many metal atoms and allows the electrons to be shared across all metal atoms. Because oxygen is a nonmetal, choice B can be eliminated. Covalent bonding occurs between two nonmetals. Because iron is a metallic element, choice C can be eliminated. The 2+ positive charge on iron would likely attract the electrons of the oxygen molecule, inducing a slightly negative charge at one end of the oxygen molecule. This dipole, induced by the Fe^{2+} in the heme cofactor, is what allows oxygen to associate with hemoglobin, making choice D the best answer.

33. **A is the best answer.** Information contained in paragraph three, in combination with Figures 2 and 3, provide the information necessary to answer this question. High blood alcohol levels around 0.5% are shown in Figure 1 to increase membrane fluidity and in Figure 2 to decrease hemoglobin content and concentration, which would decrease oxygen transport. These data support choice A, making it a strong answer According to Figure 1, even low blood alcohol levels at 0.1% have a statistically significant effect on membrane fluidity. Additionally, Figure 2 shows that hemoglobin content and concentration are decreased at this low level, which would decrease the amount of oxygen delivered to tissues. Choice B can be eliminated. Intermediate blood alcohol levels around 0.3% do show decreased membrane fluidity but also show decreased hemoglobin content and concentration. This would decrease the ability of the red blood cell to transport oxygen, eliminating choice C. Because the passage does not directly discuss carbon dioxide transport, choice D is less likely to be the best answer, as no data is presented. Additionally, some carbon dioxide is carried by the hemoglobin molecule from the tissues to the lungs for elimination. A decrease in hemoglobin should impair some of this transport, further eliminating choice D. Choice A is the best answer.

Passage 7 (Questions 34-37)

34. **C is the best answer.** Platelets and fibrinogen have important functions in coagulation. During clotting, platelets become sticky and begin to release chemicals and swell. Activated platelets stick to the endothelium of the blood vessel and to each other, forming a platelet plug. Polymerization of fibrinogen at the site of platelet accumulation leads to formation of a tight plug. Based on Figure 2, fibrinogen binding is inversely related to Dp-3-g concentration, indicating that Dp-3-g can inhibit fibrinogen from being recruited to the clot site. This rules out choices A and B. Next, since fibrinogen must be at the site of the clot in order to polymerize and form a tight plug, Dp-3-g decreases the tightness of the plug. Choice C is a better answer than choice D.

35. **B is the best answer.** A partial block in a blood vessel is similar to a decrease in radius of the vessel, as there is a smaller area for blood to flow through. Resistance is inversely proportional to radius to the fourth power. Any decrease in radius will dramatically increase resistance. Option I is likely to be in the correct answer. Next, this blockage by definition reduces cross-sectional area. The initial cross-sectional area is reduced by however large the blockage is. Option II is in the correct answer, and the only remaining choices are choices B and D. The blockage is effectively similar to vasoconstriction, which increases systemic vascular resistance and increases blood pressure, eliminating option III. Choice B is the best answer.

36. **D is the best answer.** The best answer will be one that will impact clotting dramatically and that is also tied to flow of blood. Resistance in vessels or tubes that carry fluid is primarily based on the dimensions of the tube. Even though there is no flow in a stationary sample, the vessels containing the blood would still have resistance, so choice A is unlikely. Next, megakaryocytes are the cells that form platelets. They certainly play a key role in clotting through production of platelets, but these cells are not found in the bloodstream. They are localized to the bone marrow, ruling out choice B. Fibrinogen is an example of a plasma protein that plays a key role in clotting. However, these would not be removed by lack of flow, so choice C can be ruled out. Shear stress is the pressure on the wall of a blood vessel as a result of blood flow. This will impact the wall of the artery where clotting takes place, and is dependent on flow, so choice D is the best answer.

37. **D is the best answer.** Platelets are the key clotting cells in the blood. Megakaryocytes break off pieces of their membrane and cytoplasm into the bloodstream, generating platelets. Based on the information in Figure 1 and 2, Dp-3-g treatment both reduces the size of a thrombus and binding of fibrinogen to the site of clotting. Choice A, B and C can be eliminated since all three of them include Dp-3-g treatment, which would likely worsen the platelet deficiency condition. Since megakaryocytes are platelet progenitors, megakaryocyte transplant would likely be a beneficial treatment, making choice D the best answer.

Passage 8 (Questions 38-42)

38. **A is the best answer.** Figure 1 shows the amount of sulfate anion (SO_4^{2-}) transferred into red blood cells over time. Red blood cells do not have a nucleus so choice A is a true statement and a strong answer. Sulfuric acid, H_2SO_4 is a strong acid but the sulfate anion itself is a base and nucleophile meaning choice B is inaccurate. According to the passage, the sulfate anion is utilizing an ion channel that is usually for Cl^-/HCO_3^- so the channel is not specific to sulfate and choice C is inaccurate. Albumin is a protein in the blood that transports many ions and organic molecules. The passage states that the transport occurs through the Cl^-/HCO_3^- ion channel. Ion channels are far too small for a protein such as albumin to be able to cross. Sulfate may bind to albumin, but in Figure 1, free sulfate anion must be crossing the cell membrane and choice D is not possible. This makes choice A the best answer.

39. **C is the best answer.** GSH, also known as glutathione, is a popular antioxidant that is produced by the body but can also be taken as a supplement. GSH has a free thiol group that can be oxidized with another GSH molecule to GS-SG. The correct answer choice must identify a reduction that is coupled to this oxidation. Choices A and B refer to deoxygenation and oxygenation respectively. These are transfers of oxygen but not of electrons, so neither is an oxidation. Methemoglobin is hemoglobin in which the iron is in the Fe^{3+} state as opposed to the Fe^{2+} state found in normal hemoglobin. Converting methemoglobin to oxyhemoglobin means converting Fe^{3+} to Fe^{2+} which is a reduction so choice C is a strong answer. This is likely not knowledge required by the MCAT®, and the passage can be used to deduce this information. The passage states that methemoglobin production is an oxidation so the opposite must be a reduction. Converting oxyhemoglobin to methemoglobin means converting Fe^{2+} to Fe^{3+} which is an oxidation and the opposite of what the question stem is asking for. Choice D can be eliminated in favor of choice C, which is the best answer

40. **D is the best answer.** The oxygen saturation curve of hemoglobin is experimentally determined and controlled by many factors. When a molecule changes the configuration of hemoglobin such that it holds on to oxygen less tightly, we observe that the curve shifts to right. Factors that shift the curve to the right can be predicted based on the needs of the tissue. Having hemoglobin release oxygen would be beneficial in tissues that need oxygen, such as the brain or metabolically active muscle. When metabolically active, CO_2 organic acids like lactate are produced. So, acid and CO_2 should signal oxygen offloading. Sulfuric acid is a strong acid so it would release H^+. Acid causes a right shift in the hemoglobin saturation curve so choices A and B are not the best answer. A right shift on the curve means that for the same pressure of oxygen, hemoglobin will be less saturated. This corresponds to oxygen offloading. This means choice C can be eliminated, and choice D is the best answer.

41. **A is the best answer.** White blood cells that are responsible for cleaning up debris often have peroxisomes full of molecules like H_2O_2, also known as peroxide, to help degrade the debris. Debris could include bacteria, dead cells, proteins, and other macromolecules. The white blood cells that clean up debris are known as phagocytes. The question is essentially asking which of the cells listed is a phagocyte. Neutrophils have many peroxisomes since they are involved in cleaning up debris. So, choice A is a good answer. Mast cells are known for releasing histamine. They do not typically clean up debris so they do not have many peroxisomes. Choice B is not the best answer. B cells produce antibodies. They are a type of white blood cell but not one that cleans up debris. Choice C is not the best answer. Platelets are small cells involved in clot formation. If they released H_2O_2, the clot would be destabilized. Choice D is not the best answer.

42. **D is the best answer.** This is a very challenging question that is has to be worked through completely. The ion channel in the passage is a Cl^-/HCO_3^- channel. In red blood cells, this channel pumps Cl^- out of cells when HCO_3^- is being taken up by the cell. This results in a chloride shift and is also known as the Hamburger effect. It occurs in situations where it is necessary to utilize carbonic anhydrase to make CO_2. In the tissue, there is already plenty of CO_2 present because cellular respiration is occurring, and carbonic anhydrase is running in the reverse direction to produce HCO_3^-, which is released by the red blood cell while Cl^- is taken up. This is the opposite of the question so choice A is not the best answer. If the blood was becoming more basic, HCO_3^- concentration must be rising so Cl^- must be absorbed by the red blood cell. This is the opposite of the question so choice B is not the best answer. Blood osmolarity is tightly regulated by the kidneys. Even though Cl^- is being released, HCO_3^- is leaving the blood so there is no direct change in osmolarity. This means choice C is not the best answer. If carbonic anhydrase is producing water, it is also producing CO_2. This occurs in the lungs and is associated with red blood cell uptake of HCO_3^- and release of Cl^-. This is consistent with the question, so choice D is the best answer.

Stand-alones (Questions 43-46)

43. **C is the best answer.** Blood vessels in the skin help to maintain body temperature by dilating to increase blood flow and allowing more heat to radiate out, or by constricting to limit blood flow and conserving heat. The autonomic nervous system primarily uses epinephrine and norepinephrine as its neurotransmitters, while the somatic nervous system uses acetylcholine at skeletal muscle. Because choices A and B contain acetylcholine as the signaling molecule, they can be eliminated as the best answers. Sympathetic stimulation of smooth muscle that surrounds blood vessels in the skin allows them to dilate to give off more heat. Increased radiation of heat would decrease the body temperature, making choice C the best answer and eliminating choice D because constriction conserves heat and increases body temperature.

44. **C is the best answer.** Albumin is the main osmotic protein in the blood, meaning it controls the flow of water in and out of the bloodstream based on its concentration in the blood. The increased albumin will increase the osmotic pressure of the blood. This means water will tend to flow into the bloodstream, increasing the blood volume of the body. Option I is most likely in the correct answer. Next, blood volume is directly correlated to blood pressure, so if blood volume increases, blood pressure should also increase. Option II is unlikely. Lastly, hematocrit is the ratio of the volume of red blood cells to the total volume of blood. An increase in blood volume, without any corresponding increase in erythrocytes would lead to a decreased ratio of red blood cell volume to total volume. Option III is true and choice C is the best answer.

45. **D is the best answer.** This researcher has synthesized a blood vessel akin to the capillary, which is lined by only one layer of endothelial cells. This question is essentially testing the function of endothelial cells and what can or cannot pass through them. Nutrient and gas exchange is one of the main functions of capillaries, making choice A incorrect. Thermoregulation, or heat exchange, is also a function of capillaries, eliminating choice B. Fluid exchange may occur across the endothelial cell wall and into the interstitial fluid, making choice C unlikely to be the best answer. Albumin is a large plasma protein that is unlikely to diffuse through the endothelial cell wall under physiological conditions, which makes choice D the best answer.

46. **C is the best answer.** Resistance increases at the borders of a blood vessel. In the middle, there is lamellar flow and low resistance. Therefore, the best answer would be the vessel with the smallest diameter. Arterioles and venules, choices A and B, are categories of small vessels on either side of the capillary beds. While it is possible to predict which of these would have higher resistance, that is beyond the MCAT® level, making it unlikely for either to be the right answer. Capillaries are the smallest blood vessels, and erythrocytes must often elastically deform to move into and through them. This would make the resistance here the greatest. Choice C is a strong answer. Choice D, lymphatics, can be eliminated because red blood cells do not enter them. Fluid and white blood cells operate in these compartments. Choice C is the best answer.

Passage 9 (Questions 47-50)

47. **B is the best answer.** According to the passage, Dox results in decreased delivery of blood to the heart muscle itself, causing a drop in oxygen and subsequent heart damage. The pulmonary artery is the only artery in the body that contains deoxygenated blood. It emerges from the right ventricle and proceeds to the lung in order to pick up oxygen. Because this vessel runs from the heart to the lungs, it does not supply blood to the heart itself, eliminating choice A. The coronary artery is responsible for bringing oxygenated blood to the heart muscle itself. If Dox decreased the diameter of the vessel, it could decrease the oxygenated blood supply to the heart, causing a drop in oxygen that could kill cardiac muscle cells. Choice B is a strong answer. The pulmonary vein is the only vein in the body that contains oxygenated blood. It is returning from the lungs to the left atrium but does not supply blood directly to the heart muscle, eliminating choice C. The vena cava is the vein with the largest diameter in the body. It brings deoxygenated blood from the body to the right atrium. Because it does not contain oxygenated blood, choice D can be eliminated. The main vessels to know are the vena cava, pulmonary artery, pulmonary vein, and aorta. If the functions of these vessels are known, they can be eliminated as the best answers, helping to elucidate choice B as the best answer.

48. **A is the best answer.** The resting heart rate is determined by the cyclical depolarization of a specialized group of cells, called the sinoatrial node, that are located in the right atrium. These cells have leaky channels that allow positive charge to build up in the nodal cells over time, leading to predictable contractions. The rate of this ion flow determines the resting heart rate, making choice A a strong answer. The atrioventricular node lies between the atrium and the ventricles and receives the action potential from the atrium before transmitting it to the ventricles. It is not responsible for setting the initial heart rate, eliminating choice B. The Purkinje fibers run through the left and right ventricles to coordinate contraction of the ventricles to deliver blood to the lungs and systemic circulation. They receive the signal from the Bundle of His but do not set the heart rate, eliminating choice C. The Bundle of His is a collection of fibers that run directly from the atrioventricular node and split into the Purkinje fibers that innervate the left and right ventricles. The Bundle of His runs in the muscle wall between the left and right ventricles but is not necessary for setting the resting heart rate, eliminating choice D. Choice A is the best answer.

49. **C is the best answer.** The action potential shown in the figure is that of the contractile cells of the heart. The segment marked choice A represents the resting state of the cardiac myocyte where the membrane is relatively impermeable to moving ions. Because calcium is not moving across the membrane, verapamil would have little effect, making choice A unlikely to be the best answer. The contractile cells are cardiac myocytes that initially depolarize due to the influx of sodium, shown in the segment marked B. Because verapamil blocks calcium channels, not sodium channels, choice B can be eliminated. Choice C marks the plateau phase of the action potential where calcium is entering the cell to help with muscle contraction. Verapamil would have the greatest effect on calcium flow during this segment, making choice C a likely answer. Potassium channels allow the efflux of potassium, helping to restore the membrane potential to a negative voltage. Potassium flow is shown in the segment marked D, eliminating choice D. Choice C is the best answer.

50. **A is the best answer.** The number of oxygen molecules bound to hemoglobin, the protein that is responsible for carrying oxygen through the blood, is dependent upon the partial pressure of oxygen. The vessel right before the lungs, the pulmonary artery, would have the lowest concentration of oxygen, making choice A a strong answer. In the lungs, the partial pressure of oxygen is the highest, meaning that nearly all hemoglobin molecules in red blood cells contain oxygen. The pulmonary vein is the vessel running from the lungs back to the heart. Because the red blood cells in the pulmonary vein were most recently in the lungs, they contain the highest number of hemoglobin molecules that contain oxygen. This eliminates choice B. The vena cava receives deoxygenated blood from the systemic circulation. Blood from the vena cava enters the right atrium and travels to the right ventricle. During this interval, it is able to distribute oxygen to some of the tissues of the heart that it flows through. By the time the blood reaches the pulmonary artery, it has even less oxygen than it did in the vena cava, eliminating choice C. The aorta contains highly oxygenated blood that has just exited the left ventricle. The left side of the heart receives oxygenated blood from the lungs, helping to eliminate choice D. Choice A is the best answer.

Passage 10 (Questions 51-55)

51. **C is the best answer.** Blood pressure and body fluid volume are directly related in the scope of the MCAT®. For instance, when blood volume increases, there is physically more matter (blood) in the circulatory system. Assuming the vessels do not change size, that increase in matter must correspond to an increase in pressure. Likewise, as body fluid volume decreases, blood pressure will decrease. In a patient with hemorrhage, there will be significant fluid loss which will result in a drop in blood pressure. Choices A and B can be eliminated. Systolic pressure occurs when the ventricles of the heart are contracting, and diastolic pressure occurs during the relaxation of the ventricles. This means that systolic pressure is higher than diastolic pressure. Choice D can be eliminated, and choice C is the best answer.

52. **B is the best answer.** Hematocrit is the *percentage* of red blood cells (RBCs) by volume in the blood. If the patient is suffering blood loss, whole blood will be leaving the body which reduces the *number* of red blood cells. The question notes that fluids are being administered into the blood circulation, which increases the volume of blood but not the number of red blood cells. This means that as a percentage of the total volume, RBCs will be lowered, meaning a decreased hematocrit. The information regarding the osmolality of the solution is extraneous. Choice B is the best answer.

53. **B is the best answer.** In a patient who is hemorrhaging, the body will attempt to conserve blood volume as much as possible in order to maintain the patient's blood pressure. As a result urine output will be minimal. The kidneys are involved in regulation of blood pressure through the actions of antidiuretic hormone (ADH) and the renin-angiotensin-aldosterone system (RAAS). The overall effect of ADH is to reduce the amount of urine volume. The pathway of the RAAS is as follows: renin is an enzyme released from the kidneys into the blood which converts angiotensinogen into angiotensin I. Angiotensin I is converted to angiotensin II by angiotensin-converting enzyme (ACE). Angiotensin II acts on the adrenal gland to increase aldosterone release. Aldosterone acts on the kidney to increase Na^+ resorption and K^+ secretion, which leads to increased K^+ excretion and decreased Na^+ in the urine. The Na^+ resorption ultimately leads to more fluid retention. During hemorrhage both ADH and the RAAS are activated by baroreceptors, which sense the decreased blood volume of the body. Although the RAAS will retain as much Na^+ as possible, the volume of urine output during hemorrhage will be so dramatically decreased that the concentration of Na^+ ($[Na^+]$) will be increased, despite having lower total amount of Na^+. Choice A can be eliminated. Since the RAAS is active in a hemorrhaging patient, one would expect increased K^+, making choice B a strong answer. As discussed, urine volume would be very minimal in a hemorrhaging patient, so choice C can be eliminated. Blood ADH will be elevated, but since ADH is a peptide, it should not be excreted in the urine. Peptides are too large to enter Bowman's capsule and should only be found in the urine if the nephron is damaged. Choice D can be eliminated. Choice B is the best answer.

54. **A is the best answer.** Gas exchange of O_2 and CO_2 occurs in the alveoli of the lungs. O_2 diffuses down its concentration gradient from the high oxygen content in the lungs to the deoxygenated blood of the neighboring capillaries. The deoxygenated blood carries the CO_2 waste from the tissues to the lungs, where the PCO_2 is lower. CO_2 follows its concentration gradient into the lungs, and is expelled from the body during expiration. Increasing respiration rate increases the amount of gas exchange that occurs. This increases arterial PO_2 and decreases arterial PCO_2, which explains the results of the graphs. Choices B and C can be eliminated. The effect of decreased PCO_2 is to lower the amount of H^+ in the blood. Remember the equilibrium equation:

$$CO_2 + H_2O \leftrightarrow H_2CO_3 \leftrightarrow H^+ + HCO_3^-$$

By lowering CO_2, the equation above is pulled to the left, reducing the amount of H^+ (strong acid) in the blood. This makes the blood more basic and raises the pH. Choice A is the best answer.

55. **D is the best answer.** With two part questions, if you do not remember both parts, begin by narrowing down answer choices as much as possible based on one part. The anterior pituitary releases the hormones FLATPG: FSH, LH, ACTH, TSH, prolactin, and GH. Choice A can be eliminated. While the hypothalamus is responsible for the synthesis of ADH, the posterior pituitary stores and releases ADH (as well as oxytocin) into the blood stream. Choice B can be eliminated. The juxtaglomerular apparatus in the kidneys releases the enzyme renin which regulates blood pressure and affects aldosterone, but the kidneys do not release ADH. Choice C can be eliminated. Based only on the first piece of information in the answer choice, choice D is the best answer. To support this, the effect of ADH is to make the collecting duct permeable to water so that more water can be retained. This action is done by adding aquaporins to the collecting duct, which is normally impermeable to water. This further eliminates choices B and C.

Stand-alones (Questions 56-59)

56. **C is the best answer.** Arteries and veins contain much of the same basic structure. Both have a smooth muscle component, as in choice A, though it is much thicker in arteries and arterioles than their venous equivalents. Choice B, a selectively permeable endothelial layer, is also present in both arteries and veins, eliminating it from consideration. Choice C, valves are unique features of veins and prevent backflow. Choice D, lymphatic vesicles are found in conjunction with arteries and veins in many tissues, following in the same paths. These blind ended ducts drain tissues, and empty into venous circulation. The specifics of whether they follow arteries, veins, or both varies by tissue, and is beyond the scope of the MCAT®. This makes choice C the best answer as it is the only unique feature of one of the two types of blood vessels listed.

57. **C is the best answer.** With thicker endothelial cell membranes, the rate of diffusion across these membranes would be decreased. Thus, the best answer would be a substance that is transported via diffusion across capillary walls. Albumin, choice A, is not the best answer since its size only allows for pinocytosis or passage through fenestrations. Sodium chloride, choice B, also is not the best answer because it exists in the body as ions, which are hydrophilic and cannot diffuse through the lipophilic cell membrane. Carbon dioxide, choice C, is a small, lipid-soluble, hydrophobic molecule that can pass through the membranes via diffusion and is most likely to be affected by a thicker endothelial membrane. Thus, it is a strong answer. Choice D, potassium, is also an ion and can be eliminated for the same reason as choice B. Choice C is the best answer.

58. **C is the best answer.** The right lymphatic duct drains lymphatic fluid from only the right arm and head. Obstruction would lead to a buildup of fluid proximally, which would ultimately flow into the interstitium, leading to a swollen appearance. A shriveled appearance may occur in cases of fluid depletion, not overload, eliminating choice A and choice B and making choice C the best answer. Choice D would be correct if the obstruction occurred at the thoracic duct, which drains lymphatic fluid from the rest of the body.

59. **D is the best answer.** Opposing forces act at the wall of an arteriole, capillary, and venule. The hydrostatic pressure, or the pressure exerted by the fluid inside the vessel, forces fluid out of the circulatory system and into the surrounding tissue. Osmotic pressure, by contrast, pulls fluid back into the vessels, as ions, proteins like albumin, and other cells make the blood hypertonic compared to the extracellular space. All the fluid that flows into the extracellular space must make its way back to the circulatory system and does so through the lymphatic system, eventually draining through the thoracic duct into the subclavian vein, a vein in the neck. Albumin resides in the blood vessels, not in the extracellular space, eliminating choice A. Constriction of the arteriole would increase the hydrostatic pressure, forcing more fluid out of the veins instead of compensating for the fluid already present. Constriction of the venule would raise the pressure in a similar manner. This eliminates choices B and C. Fluid returning to the circulation through the thoracic duct would offset the fluid flowing from the vessels into the interstitial space, making choice D the best answer.

LECTURE

4

The Circulatory, Respiratory, and Immune Systems

MINI-TEST 4B

ANSWERS & EXPLANATIONS
Questions 1–41

Passage 1 (Questions 1-4)

1. **A is the best answer.** According to the question stem, platelets may also contain RNA that could be used to measure the relative expression of certain genes. In order to isolate the platelets, the scientists would need to extract them from the plasma portion of blood. Blood is split into three main fractions, the plasma, the buffy coat, which contains the white blood cells and platelets, and the erythrocyte-containing fraction. In order to measure relative expression of a gene by a microarray, the RNA copies must be turned back into DNA. The enzyme that is responsible for this reaction is reverse transcriptase. Isolating platelets from the buffy coat, followed by copying the RNA to cDNA makes choice A a strong answer. RNA polymerase transcribes DNA into RNA but does not create new copies of the same RNA template, eliminating choice B. Additionally, the platelets are found in the buffy coat, not the plasma. The erythrocyte layer does not contain platelets but instead red blood cells. This eliminates choices C and D, leaving choice A as the best answer.

2. **C is the best answer.** According to paragraph three, CTCs can travel either as individual cells or clusters of 4-10 cells. In order to establish a metastatic tumor, it is reasonable to predict that these groups of CTCs become stuck when the lumen of a vessel gets too small for the cluster to pass. The aorta is the largest diameter artery in the body and would be unlikely to constrict the passage of a cell cluster compared to the smaller arteries, making choice A unlikely to be the best answer. The renal artery is smaller than the aorta but still larger than the smallest vessels, the capillaries, making choice B less likely to be the best answer. The lung capillaries would have the narrowest diameter, giving a cluster of CTCs the best chance at getting stuck and forming a distant metastasis. This makes choice C a strong answer. Similar to the aorta, the vena cava is a large diameter vein that brings blood back to the heart. The large diameter would prevent a small cluster of cells from becoming stuck, eliminating choice D. Choice C is the best answer.

3. **A is the best answer.** Clonal expansion is the process where a particular immune cell receives signals to proliferate. These signals occur when the immune cell recognizes a particular foreign antigen, such as an abnormal protein expressed on the surface of a cancer cell. Killer T cells directly lyse cells that display abnormal proteins on their cell surface. Isolating specific populations of killer T cells from the patient and expanding those T cells that recognize melanoma antigens is a feasible way of using the leukocyte layer to help the patient, making choice A a strong answer. Macrophages are innate immune system cells that do not directly respond to antigen stimulation to proliferate, making choice B less likely to be the best answer. Helper T cells will respond to antigen stimulation, but they do not directly lyse cells that express abnormal antigens, making choice C less likely than choice A to be the best answer. Natural killer cells are also innate immune cells that are not specific for certain antigens, eliminating choice D.

4. **C is the best answer.** The lymphatic system serves to transport extracellular fluid back to the blood by way of the lymph nodes. Additionally, the lymphatic system carries chylomicrons, which contain the greatest concentration of fatty acids and cholesterol from the small intestines to the blood stream. The lower pressure of the lymphatic system causes a slower velocity which would increase the likelihood that some CTCs would transit to distant organs without breaking apart. According to paragraph two, this increases the probability of forming a new tumor and eliminates choices A and B. The lymphatic system is rich in B cells, T cells, macrophages, and other cells of the immune system that would be able to survey circulating tumor cells and eliminate them during transit. This would decrease the likelihood of forming a metastasis, making choice C a likely answer. High levels of cellular fuels like triglycerides could help support the metabolism of CTCs that are no longer in a tissue environment. This eliminates choice D, leaving choice C as the best answer.

Passage 2 (Questions 5-8)

5. **A is the best answer.** The question stem describes a scenario where a person is introduced to a pathogen for the first time. Think first about the types of immunity: adaptive and innate. The adaptive or acquired immune response is specific and takes time to develop. Following an initial exposure, the "primary response" of the adaptive immune system prepares for a second exposure by synthesizing antigen specific T cells and B cells. The innate immune response, on the other hand, is non-specific and immediate. Part of the innate immune response is inflammation, which includes dilation of blood vessels and increased permeability of capillaries. If the endotoxin were suddenly introduced to a person's bloodstream this could cause a systemic inflammation response and dilate blood vessels all over the body, dropping the person's blood pressure. This life-threatening phenomenon is part of sepsis, which is briefly mentioned in the passage. Choice A is a promising answer. Based on the passage, natural antibodies are part of the innate immune response. They are already present in the body and ready to recognize pathogens using non-specific antigens. Choice B can be eliminated. Antibodies specific to the endotoxin would be part of the adaptive immune response and would not be in the body if this is the person's first exposure. Choice C can be eliminated. Choice D describes a phenomenon that does not occur in the human body. Choice D can also be eliminated and choice A is the best answer.

6. **C is the best answer.** When antibodies are generated in the body they must be tested to ensure that they can react to foreign antigens but not to self-antigens, or antigens from endogenous proteins. This ensures a robust immune system without developing autoimmunity. If antigen presentation as a whole were to fail, the entire immune system would fail because the immune system would not be alerted to the presence of pathogens in the body. Autoimmunity is over-activity of the immune system. Choice A would not precipitate an autoimmune condition and can be eliminated. Positive selection refers to the elimination of antibodies that do not react to foreign antigens in favor of those that do. Failure of positive selection would lead to antibodies that could not rally the immune system to react to antigens. Similar to choice A, this indolence of the immune system is the opposite of what might create an autoimmune condition. Choice B can be eliminated. Negative selection refers to the elimination of antibodies that react to self-antigens in favor of those that do not. This ensures that the immune system does not attack the body of the host. Failure of this process could lead to antibodies that create an autoimmune condition. Choice C is a strong answer. Choice D refers to the process which encompasses both negative and positive selection. Although it is a true answer choice, choice C is more specific and is the best answer choice.

7. **D is the best answer.** Figure 1 and especially Figure 2 seem to suggest that all women, with or without IBD, have a robust immune response to endotoxin for reasons that are not explained in the passage or by the data. Choice A and choice B specify the two diseases discussed in the passage. It is tempting to choose choice B since the passage describes CD to have deep patches, while UC has superficial patches, and Figure 2B shows a slightly higher average TEN % among CD patients. Between choice A and choice B, hold on to choice B for now. Macrophages form an important part of the innate immune system and are phagocytic cells which engulf pathogens. A connection between macrophage function and TEN % is not indicated in the passage though it is possible that impaired macrophage function could lead to a less robust immune system and a higher TEN %. Choice C is a weak answer. Choice D suits the general message of the data: TEN % is not a specific indicator for any of the diseases mentioned in the passage and can even be high in healthy control patients. Choice D is the best answer.

8. **B is the best answer.** First examine Figure 1 and Figure 2 and determine what conclusions can be made about the data. Based on the passage, TEN % acts as a way to measure the robustness of a person's immune response to the bacterial endotoxin. Recall that developing IBD leads to leakiness of the intestinal wall and thus chronic exposure to bacterial endotoxin. Figure 1 shows that TEN % increases in males with IBD while females with IBD seem to have already had a high TEN %. This suggests women have a more robust innate immune response to endotoxin, although it is not clear if this is due to exposure to endotoxin for a reason other than IBD or if their innate immune response is more robust than men's at baseline. Figure 2 shows that men with IBD (UC or CD) have higher TEN % than men without IBD (control), while women with IBD (UC or CD) seem to have the same TEN % as women without IBD (control). This data strengthens the finding in Figure 1 because it confirms a trend seen amongst IBD patients and compares them to a control group. Choice A states the opposite of what the data indicates since the controls in Figure 2A do not have a high TEN %. Choice A can be eliminated. Because women with and without IBD have high TEN %, choice B is a good candidate. Choice C might be tempting since circulating levels of endotoxin correlate with disease severity and women with IBD have a high TEN % from start, which might indicate a high initial exposure to endotoxin. However, this is undermined by the fact that healthy controls also have high a TEN %. Choice C is a weak answer. Choice D is the opposite of what the data indicates and can be eliminated, leaving choice B as the best answer.

Stand-alones (Questions 9-12)

9. **B is the best answer.** The lymphatic system is important for producing immune cells, like B cells, that help defend the body against pathogens. B cells are formed and mature in the lymph nodes of the lymphatic system and are activated by antigen presenting cells and helper T cells passing through the lymph nodes. Langerhans cells are specialized cells of the skin that uptake bacteria and other foreign particles and process them to be presented on MHC Class II molecules. In order to induce an immune response, cells of the immune system need to see the foreign antigen on these antigen presenting cells. Helper T cells engage antigen presenting cells and become activated. Once these helper T cells are activated, they then help activate B cells that recognize the same antigen to become differentiated and proliferate. As helper T cells, not Langerhans cells directly, are responsible for inducing B cell differentiation, choice A is unlikely to be the best answer. An antigen presenting cell like the Langerhans cell interacts with helper cells to stimulate an immune response, including antibody response by B cells. This makes choice B most likely to be the best answer. Plasma cells are memory B cells that secrete antibodies. However, they must have seen an antigen previously. Choice C can be eliminated because plasma cells will not secrete an antibody against an antigen that has not been seen. Antigen presenting cells primarily focus on uptaking foreign matter and processing it to present the antigens on MHC Class II molecules to T helper cells. Unlike killer T cells and macrophages, they do not focus on directly killing foreign pathogens, making choice D less likely to be the best answer compared to choice B.

10. **C is the best answer.** The lymphatic system is important for transporting fluid from the extracellular space back to the circulatory system, transporting absorbed fat and cholesterol from the gut in particles called chylomicrons, and helping to survey the body for infections. Cholesterol and fat are absorbed in the gut and packaged into particles called chylomicrons. Chylomicrons are too large to be transported directly from the gut epithelium to the blood stream and travel in the lymphatic system back to the circulation. Damage to the thoracic duct is likely to lower cholesterol and triglyceride levels in the blood, as fewer chylomicrons would reach circulation. This eliminates choices A and B. Glucose, however, is directly absorbed by the gut epithelium and transported in the blood. Damage to the lymphatics is least likely to impact the blood glucose value, as the lymphatics are not the main transport for glucose. This makes choice C most likely to be the best answer. Lymphocytes reside in the lymphatic system to help survey the body for infections. Damage to the thoracic duct would prevent some lymphocytes from returning to the blood circulation, eliminating choice D, and leaving choice C as the best answer.

11. **B is the best answer.** Lymphatic fluid flow is directly related to interstitial fluid pressure: as it rises, lymphatic fluid flow increases as well. Look for the answer choice that would cause interstitial fluid pressure to rise. A decrease in capillary permeability would cause more fluid to be retained in the circulatory flow and less fluid to leak into the interstitium. This would cause either no change in the interstitial fluid pressure or a drop, but certainly not an increase in pressure. Choice A can be eliminated. An increase in blood pressure would increase the pressure pushing fluid out of the capillaries and into the interstitium, increasing interstitial fluid pressure. Choice B is a promising answer. Choice C is directly the opposite of what would increase lymphatic fluid flow and can be eliminated. When the osmotic pressure in a capillary increases, the fluid in the interstitium would be drawn into the capillaries. This would cause a drop in the interstitial fluid pressure and thus a drop in the lymphatic fluid flow. Choice D can be eliminated and choice B is the best answer.

12. **A is the best answer.** The lymphatic system removes particles from the blood that are too large to be removed by capillaries, especially large proteins and glycerides. Choice A is a monoglyceride, as evidenced by the glycerol backbone and one fatty acid attached, so it a promising answer. Choice B and choice C are both small molecules that can be easily removed or exchanged by capillaries, so they can be eliminated. Choice D is an amino acid (glycine) and, although it is the building block for proteins, the glyceride in choice A is a larger molecule so is more likely to be removed by the lymphatic system than by a capillary. Choice D can be eliminated in favor of choice A.

Passage 3 (Questions 13-17)

13. **B is the best answer.** According to paragraph 3, TIM-3 becomes phosphorylated on the intracellular tyrosine residues and this phosphorylation serves to attract LCK and PLC, preventing them from activating T cell signaling pathways. While it is not as important that Cdk 4 is a cell cycle kinase, a kinase in general would likely augment the activity of TIM-3, assuming the kinase could serve to phosphorylate Y residues, making choice A less likely to be the best answer. On the other hand, if the phosphorylation on the Y residues of the TIM-3 molecule were removed by a phosphatase, TIM-3 would not be able to sequester proteins, preventing it from acting as effectively. This makes choice B a likely answer. PLC is an enzyme that helps cleave some lipids that are integrated into the plasma membrane in order to active two downstream signaling pathways. However, increases in PLC would not directly affect the ability of TIM-3 to attract and sequester proteins, as PLC does not act on the TIM-3 protein directly. Thus, choice C can be eliminated. As with choice A, a kinase would likely serve to help activate, not hinder, TIM-3 activity, eliminating choice D. Thus, choice B is the best answer choice.

14. **C is the best answer.** Immune system cells become activated when they are exposed to a peptide presented in a major histocompatibility complex (MHC) molecule. CD4$^+$ T helper cells are specifically activated when the peptide is presented in the context of MHC Class II. Eosinophils play a major role in allergy and parasite infections and do not serve as one of the major antigen presenting cells that could activate T cells, making choice A less likely to be the best answer. Similar to eosinophils, basophils play a role in allergy and also do not present antigens in the context of MHC Class II, eliminating choice B. Macrophages are one type of antigen presenting cell that takes up foreign particles in the microenvironment and processes them to present on MHC Class II. These peptides in the context of MHC Class II then contact the TCR of CD4$^+$ T helper cells to activate them, making choice C a likely answer choice. Mast cells contain membrane bound antibodies that cross-link upon exposure to an antigen to release high amounts of pro-inflammatory molecules that mediate allergic reactions. They are not responsible to antigen presenting, eliminating choice D. Choice C is the best answer.

15. **B is the best answer.** According to paragraph 3, the NFAT pathway is dependent upon calcium and serves to activate T cells. The best evidence for the role of the NFAT pathway in T cell responses would be one that inhibits activation of the pathway and observing a decrease in T cell response. The passage provides experimental evidence that TIM-3 serves to prevent activation of T cells. However, the passage does not directly discuss pathways other than the NFAT pathway. Evidence that the TIM-3 protein prevented NF-κB activity may prevent T cell activation but does not provide any information about the NFAT pathway, making choice A less likely to be the best answer. Paragraph three notes that calcium is involved in NFAT signaling. If a cytosolic compound could bind calcium, the NFAT pathway would be inhibited, even if the T cell received proper activation signals, leading to a decrease in activity. Choice B is a probably answer. Exogenous application of a cytokine, such as IL-2, has the potential to induce growth and proliferation of T cells. However, this finding may not be specific to the NFAT pathway, eliminating choice C. The question stem asks specifically about the activation of T cells, not B cells. Additionally, the CTLA-4 molecule is described in the passage to be associated with T cells and does not mention its presence or activity in B cells, eliminating choice D. Thus, choice B is the best answer choice.

16. **B is the best answer.** According to the passage, TIM-3 is an inhibitory molecule on T cells that serves to prevent their activation. Paragraph one provides some background information about the interaction between cancer cells and the tumor microenvironment and T cell activity. TIM-3 is one of many inhibitory molecules, including CTLA-4, LAG-3, and PD-1. Overexpression of TIM-3 may hinder some T cell activity but is unlikely to completely decrease T cell responses, as some of the other inhibitory ligands may not be yet expressed. Rapid proliferation of cancer cells would imply a complete lack of an immune response to cancer, likely caused by upregulation of all inhibitory molecules that would decrease T cell activation and activity. Because the question stem only notes that TIM-3 was overexpressed, it is less likely that rapid proliferation would occur, making choice A less likely to be the best answer choice. Choice B is an attractive answer because it accounts for the increase in tumor volume that would occur secondary to TIM-3, but is not as extreme as choice A. Keep choice B for now. Regression of tumor volume would imply that the immune reaction had grown stronger. Because TIM-3 is an inhibitory ligand, this represents the opposite of the proposed scenario, eliminating choice C. Stable disease would imply neither activation nor repression of the immune reaction. As TIM-3 is inhibitory, immune system suppression should be observed, eliminating choice D. This leaves choice B as the best answer.

17. **C is the best answer.** According to Figure 1, TIM-3 overexpression leads to drastically reduced levels of cytokine secretion by T cells. This decrease in secretion is likely to hamper recruitment of other immune system cells, lead to decreases in activation of adaptive immune system cells already present in the tumor microenvironment, and lead to decreases in antigen presentation and processing by antigen presenting cells. Plasma cells reside in the bone marrow and are a specialized B cell subset that synthesizes and secretes antibodies. As they reside in the bone marrow, they are unlikely to transit to the microenvironment under chemokine signaling, making choice A less likely to be the best answer. Basophils help mediate allergic reactions but still require growth cytokines to continue proliferating. Thus, it is plausible that decreases in cytokine secretion could cause increased cell death in innate immune system cells that are nearby, as they would not receive as many extracellular signals to stay alive. Thus, choice B can be eliminated. MHC Class II is used to present antigens that have been taken up from the microenvironment. Decreases in cytokines would serve to prevent robust activation of antigen presenting cells, decreasing the need to maintain high concentrations of MHC Class II. Thus, transcription of MHC II could decrease under conditions of reduced cytokines, making choice C a good answer choice. Decreases in cytokine and chemokine secretion would prevent B cell chemotaxis, not increase it. Thus, choice D can be eliminated in favor of choice C.

Passage 4 (Questions 18-21)

18. **A is the best answer.** This patient lacks B and T cells. B and T cells are two major cell types in the adaptive immune function. The specific role of B cells is to produce antibodies that combat infection. Meanwhile, T cells primarily control and coordinate other immune cells, and also scan for DNA damage and viral infection through MHC molecules on all human cells. When T and B cells are exposed to a pathogen that they can combat, they become active and proliferate. This process makes future instances of fighting off this pathogen much more efficient and effective, giving the person immunity. A vaccine would not work in this person because T and B cells in the adaptive immune system are required to have memory of pathogens and develop immunity. Option I is true. Option II is false since it states the opposite of option I. A person would not develop immunity following the initial exposure if they lacked these key cells that have memory. Next, option III is a distractor as the housekeeping function of macrophages is the role they play in removing wastes throughout various tissues. This is not significantly affected by T and B cells. Because only option I is true, choice A is the best answer.

19. **D is the best answer.** This transgenic mouse has a B cell deficiency, meaning this function must be replaced in some way. Choice A is a potential answer, because B cells primarily make antibodies. However, like all proteins, circulating antibodies turnover within the body so they must be remade regularly. Pro-inflammatory cytokines are not the major product of B cells, so choice B does not adequately replace this lost function. Choice B can be eliminated. Plasma cells are B cells that produce large amounts of antibodies. Injection of these cells will replace function as long as these cells can divide and survive, so choice C is a potential answer. Memory cells are B cells that reside typically in lymph nodes. They have great proliferative power and can undergo clonal selection, where appropriate B cells are activated and divide. Choice D is the best answer, since injection of memory cells could potentially provide lifetime B cell function.

20. **D is the best answer.** CVID is marked by loss of B cells. Based on the information in the passage, those CVID patients with inflammation have reduced B and T cell counts as well as increased innate immune activation and activity. MHC I is expressed on all cells and is used by certain cells to examine the integrity of the genome and check for potential viral infection. Because they are expressed on all cells, option I is unlikely. Next, B cell counts would be reduced, so it makes sense that B cell receptors, a protein only found on B cells, would be lowered. Option II is likely and choices B and D are the only ones that include option II. Next, granules are found in a variety of innate immune cells, including neutrophils, eosinophils, and basophils. These would be upregulated in CVID with inflammation, so option III is likely. Choice D is the best answer.

21. **D is the best answer.** Aplastic anemia results in damage to bone marrow stem cells, and this potentially limits their ability to divide and form the key blood cells of the body. Bone marrow stem cells differentiate into erythrocytes, megakaryocytes which form platelets, and all immune cells. Thus, damage to this population of key cells would reduce levels of all blood cells. This is the key conclusion to answering this question. With a reduced red blood cell count, hematocrit would be reduced. This is because hematocrit is a measure of the quantity of red blood cells. If red blood cells are reduced, oxygen carrying capacity is also reduced, so option I is unlikely. This eliminates choices A and C. Next, thrombocytopenia would be seen since the number of megakaryocytes would be reduced. This reduction limits production of platelets, and option II is likely to be in the correct answer. Option III is increased risk of infection. With an impaired ability to generate immune cells from the bone marrow, infection is certainly more likely, and any exposure to pathogens becomes more harmful. The best answer is choice D because it combines the two most likely options.

Passage 5 (Questions 22-26)

22. **A is the best answer.** The interactions between a B cell and a T cell help prime the T cell to secrete cytokines and other molecules that activate the antibody-producing capability of B cells. T helper cells are responsible for recognizing antigens presented on B cells with their T cell receptors. Short peptides, not long peptides, between 6 and 18 amino acids are processed and presented on MHC Class II molecules when a DC or macrophage engulfs a dying cancer cell. The MHC molecule is a protein structure designed to hold these peptides and does not catalyze any chemical reactions. The key distinguishing part between answer choices A and B is that the TCR is an example of a non-enzymatic peptide. Because short, not long, peptides are presented on a non-enzymatic, not enzymatic, protein, choice B can be eliminated. Polysaccharides are not presented on traditional MHC molecules like MHC class I and II, eliminating choice C. Fatty acids, regardless of whether they are long or short chained, are not presented on MHC class I or II, eliminating choice D. Because short, 6-18 amino acid peptides, are held in a non-enzymatic protein structure called MHC Class II, choice A is the best answer choice.

23. **A is the best answer.** According to the question stem, the initial IgM antibody has high avidity, meaning it can bind many antigens simultaneously, and low affinity, meaning it is not able to bind the antigen tightly. Knowing that avidity means the ability to bind multiple antigens is not necessary to answer this question but can help in distinguishing between the answer choices. In contrast, the IgG molecule depicted in Figure 1 has lower avidity but much higher affinity. The number of binding sites would be representative of the avidity, as each binding site could bind one antigen. The K_m would represent the affinity. A low K_m means that the antibody bound the antigen tightly, while a larger K_m implies that the antibody would bind the antigen less tightly. To match the information contained in the question stem, IgM should have a higher number of binding sites and a larger K_m compared to IgG. Because the number of binding sites, meaning the relative avidity, is the same in choice B, it can be eliminated. The K_m of both IgM and IgG is similar in choice C, making it less likely to be the best answer choice. Choice D describes the opposite of the information presented in the question stem, where IgM has a lower K_m and IgG has a higher avidity. This allows choice D to be eliminated. Choice A is the best answer choice because it matches IgM with the higher avidity and IgG with the lower K_m.

24. **B is the best answer.** Steroid-based molecules, typically hormones, are able to diffuse through the plasma membrane and would be unlikely to bind cell surface receptors. Additionally, movement of cytosolic proteins into the nucleus suggests that binding of TNFα modulates transcription in the nucleus, not translation, which takes place in the cytosol. This eliminates choice A. Peptides are large, charged molecules that would be unable to easily cross the plasma membrane, requiring them to bind extracellular receptors. Additionally, because they cause translocation of proteins to the nucleus, they are likely increasing the transcription of target genes, making choice B a strong answer. Lipid-derived molecules would also be able to diffuse through the lipophilic plasma membrane and are unlikely to bind cell surface receptors, eliminating choice C. Polysaccharides are polymers of sugars that are polar and hydrophobic. This means they are likely to bind an extracellular receptor. As with choice A, if the binding of TNFα causes proteins to translocate to the nucleus, then transcription is more likely to be involved than translation. Choice D can be eliminated in favor of choice B.

25. **C is the best answer.** According to the last paragraph, there is a 3 to 4 day lag after antigen exposure in which T cells are not robustly proliferating and activating B cells. T and B cells are part of the adaptive immune system, meaning they recognize specific antigens with high specificity. Because the immune system is engineered to adapt to all antigens, the populations that recognize a particular cancer antigen will likely vary in specificity. Clones that have different specificities will compete for access to the antigen and those that can bind the tightest will have the best chance at proliferating and surviving. Macrophages and dendritic cells are both antigen presenting cells. Dendritic cells are able to process and present peptide antigens more efficiently than macrophages, eliminating choice A as the best answer. The last paragraph notes that only antigen-experienced B cells migrate to germinal centers, eliminating choice B. T cell clones with the lowest dissociation constant, which can be thought of as similar to a K_m, would have the highest specificity for cancer antigens. During the time preceding robust T cell proliferation, the most fit T cell is likely being selected, making choice C a strong answer. T helper cells are responsible for helping to activate and mature B cells. DCs indirectly activate B cells by activating T cells, which in turn activate B cells. This eliminates choice D, leaving choice C as the best answer.

26. **C is the best answer.** Blocking inhibitory interactions would prevent T cells from being rendered inactive to cancer antigens. This means that more T cell populations would be active against cancer cells in patients treated with immunotherapy versus patients who were untreated. Because a single T cell population recognizes a unique peptide, more T cell populations would recognize more peptides. Failure to dampen the immune response prevents elimination of clones of T cells that react against the body's own antigens, causing autoimmune disease. This makes option I a component of the best answer. Increased rates of infection would imply that a patient's immune system was less active than normal. The question stem does not provide evidence to suggest that patients not receiving immunotherapy have less active immune systems than normal. Option II can be eliminated. A DNA sequence of the T cell receptor gene would create a unique combination of amino acids that would build a unique TCR peptide. The ability to recognize more antigens by preventing inactivation of T cells would imply a greater diversity of T cell receptor sequences, making option III a part of the best answer. Choice C is the best answer because it contains both options I and III.

Stand-alones (Questions 27-29)

27. **A is the best answer.** When a person is given a blood transfusion, their ABO type and their Rh- factor type must be compatible with the donor's ABO and Rh-factor type. Otherwise the recipient's body will recognize the antigens on the donor's red blood cells as foreign bodies and attack them. In this question, the recipient has type B, Rh (−) blood. This means that he/she does not have any Rh factor antigens, has the B antigen on the surface of his/her red blood cell and circulating antibodies against the A antigen. This means that the person cannot receive blood from a person who has A antigens or Rh antigens on their red blood cells. While Rh transfusion reactions are usually mild, it would still not be "safe" to give a person Rh (+) blood if he/she were Rh (−). Option I is O, Rh (−) which means that there are no antigens of concern on the donor's red blood cells. Keep choice A, C and D for now and eliminate choice B. Option II is AB, Rh (−), which means that there are A and B antigens on the red blood cell surface. Eliminate choice D. Option III does not have A antigens but it does have Rh antigens, which makes it not the best option. Choice C can be eliminated in favor of choice A.

28. **B is the best answer.** All lymphocytes are defined by their receptor, but the way they interact with other cells and the antigen that binds the receptor varies significantly. T cells have permanent membrane bound receptors that interact with MHC complexes. Choice A can be eliminated. B cells initially have membrane bound receptors, however after their proliferation and development, they are able to produce antibodies, which can be thought of as soluble B-cell receptors. Choice B is a promising answer. Neutrophils are phagocytic cells of the innate immune system. They have non-specific receptors, which are permanently associated with membrane. Choice C can be eliminated. NK cells are a special sub class of lymphocytes that function in the innate immune response. Like their analogs in the adaptive immune system, Killer T-Cells, their receptors are membrane bound. Choice D can be eliminated. This makes choice B the best answer choice.

29. **A is the best answer.** Molecular mimicry results when the peptide structure of a pathogen closely resembles that of a normal cellular protein. When a person becomes infected with a virus or bacteria, the immune system generates strongly binding T cells, and B cells that produce antigen-specific antibodies. However, these T cells and antibodies also recognize the closely related peptide that is normal. Thus, the body cannot distinguish between the pathogen and the normal protein and attacks both, causing autoimmune disease. It is unlikely that all host peptides would be eliminated from the body, though the immune system is now attacking normal tissue. Choice A seems like a strong answer. As mentioned, the immune system's attack on the normal protein would result in autoimmune disease, eliminating choice B. Plasma cells are antigen-specific B cells that would expand to produce antibodies specific to the pathogen peptide and also the normal human protein being mimicked, eliminating choice C. Host T cells would also now recognize this once normal peptide as now abnormal and mount an immune response. T cell proliferation would occur, as the T cell would become activated upon binding peptides that it recognizes, eliminating choice D. Choice A is the best answer choice.

Passage 6 (Questions 30-33)

30. **A is the best answer.** According to the passage, Treg cells are important for keeping the immune system in check in response to infection. Both the innate and adaptive immune systems are important for defending the body against pathogens like viruses and bacteria. Activation of the immune system helps to clear the infection, but overactivation of the immune system can lead to autoimmune disease. Treg cells limit activation of the immune system. MEK inhibitors would decrease the number of Treg cells, leading to less deactivation of T cells and increased immune system activation. Fewer cells that limit the activation of the immune system could result in autoimmune disease, making option I a component of the best answer. Activation of the immune system would decrease susceptibility to viral and bacterial illnesses. Since MEK inhibitors ultimately increase activation of the immune system, options II and III can be eliminated. Choice A is the best answer because only option I is true.

31. **C is the best answer.** There are several different types of T cells, but the two major subsets are $CD4^+$ T helper cells and $CD8^+$ T killer cells. $CD4^+$ T helper cells are responsible for stimulating other immune cells, like macrophages. Once activated, macrophages phagocytose pathogens and release cytokines that promote inflammation. This eliminates choice A. T helper cells also activate B cells, causing them to divide and differentiate into specialized B cells, called plasma cells and memory B cells. Plasma cells release antibodies that are specific to a given antigen. Choice B can be eliminated. $CD4^+$ T helper cells do not directly attack pathogens like bacteria, but rather activate other immune cells to complete this task. Choice C is a strong answer. Antigen presenting cells are responsible for activating $CD8^+$ T killer cells by presenting an antigen on MHC Class I molecules. When a $CD8^+$ T killer cell recognizes its cognate antigen, it becomes activated and can directly kill other cells that display that antigen. T helper cells do not directly bind $CD8^+$ T killer cells. Instead, $CD4^+$ T helper cells activate $CD8^+$ T killer cells indirectly by activating antigen presenting cells, which then activate $CD8^+$ T killer cells, eliminating choice D. Choice C is the best answer.

32. **D is the best answer.** Phagocytosis is the process of engulfing particles found outside the cell and internalizing them. Antigen presenting cells take these phagocytized molecules, process them, and load them onto MHC Class II molecules that sit on the cell surface and can activate B cells and T cells. Macrophages are phagocytic cells that are part of the innate immune system. They take up pathogens and process the proteins, which are then loaded onto MHC Class II molecules. This eliminates choice A. Dendritic cells are even better than macrophages at presenting extracellular proteins, eliminating choice B. Although B cells are primarily responsible for secreting antibodies, they are also able to take up foreign particles and present them on their cell surface via MHC Class II molecules, eliminating choice C. T cells are unable to phagocytize extracellular molecules but instead either help activate other immune cells, as in the case of T helper cells, or directly lyse infected cells, as in the case of T killer cells. Choice D is the best answer choice.

33. **C is the best answer.** In the early stages of infection, the T cell population is considered naïve, as it has not seen the antigen. Once the antigen is presented by an antigen presenting cell to $CD4^+$ T helper cells that recognize that antigen, those specific $CD4^+$ T cells begins to proliferate rapidly. $CD4^+$ T cells that bind the antigen the tightest are stimulated to proliferate more than the cells that bind the antigen less tightly. While the T cell receptor itself does not change, the affinity of the population as a whole would increase over time, as the T cells that bind the tightest are those that proliferate the most. This also means that the number of antigen-specific T cells would increase over time, not decrease or remain the same, eliminating choices A and D. Because the population-wide affinity would increase over time, choice B can be eliminated, making choice C the best answer. This process is generally called clonal selection. For T cells, clonal selection can occur in the thymus to negatively select against T cells that bind self-antigens too tightly. Outside the thymus, clonal selection can also occur upon the population of T cells that recognize a particular antigen with differing affinities.

Passage 7 (Questions 34-38)

34.   A is the best answer. Peptides that are produced from mutations in the genome of cancer cells are endogenous proteins that would be presented on major histocompatibility molecules for recognition by circulating lymphocytes. Endogenous proteins, derived either from processing and presentation of the cell's own proteins or from intracellular bacteria or viruses, are presented on MHC Class I molecules and are recognized by CD8$^+$ T-effector cells, making choice A a strong answer. Exogenous proteins, such as those from phagocytized bacteria, are processed and presented on MHC Class II. Because cancer proteins are endogenous, they would be less likely to be presented on MHC Class II, eliminating choice B. According to paragraph one, cervical cancer cells are epithelial cells. A T cell receptor (TCR) is found on circulating T cells and recognizes peptides presented in the content of MHC Class I or II molecules. Cervical cancer cells would not contain a TCR, eliminating choice C. Similarly, B cell receptors (BCRs) are found on circulating B cells, not on epithelial cells, eliminating choice D. Choice A remains as the best answer.

35.   C is the best answer. The question stem indicates that the curve should correspond to the proliferation of antigen-specific adaptive immune system T cells. Once an HPV antigen is processed and presented on MHC Class I molecules on an antigen presenting cell, circulating CD8$^+$ cells can detect the peptide in the MHC binding pocket and undergo significant proliferation if it recognizes the peptide. This process of immune surveillance and maturation of the T cell response takes upwards of 10-15 days to become strong enough to get logarithmic increases in T cell number. Curve A likely corresponds to a non-specific B cell that is secreting IgM but is now changing to an antigen-specific IgG secreting plasma cell, eliminating choice A. Choice B may also represent a similar B cell to choice A, though one that may be more specific for one of the viral antigens, making choice B less likely to be the best answer. It likely takes a few days before the antigen-specific T cell encounters its antigen held in MHC Class I. Once the T cell finds its cognate peptide, it would undergo rapid proliferation to increase cell number in a short period of time, as shown by the sharp slope around day 10 in curve C. Choice C is a likely answer. Choice D shows a linear rise in cell count, which would not correspond to an adaptive immune system cell that is highly stimulated by a viral antigen. Once stimulated, adaptive immune system cells undergo rapid proliferation, not a constant rate of proliferation, as exemplified by the constant slope. Thus, choice D can be eliminated, in favor of choice C.

36.   A is the best answer. According to Figure 1, the number of tumor free mice falls to around 80% on day 10 but rebounds to around 100% on day 20. Based on information contained in the passage, this most likely implies that the tumor formed but was subsequently cleared by the immune system in previously vaccinated mice. Once the antigen-specific response was established, the immune system could work to clear to tumor, helping mice that formerly had established tumors eliminate them. If the response were strongest around day 15, the immune system could possibly clear the tumor before the next measurement were made on day 20, making choice A a likely answer. Natural killer cells are innate immune system cells that do not recognize specific peptides in MHC molecules. If the NK population decreased around day 30, a slight decrease in the number of tumor free mice could be seen. Because the percentage stays constant at around 100% tumor free, choice B is unlikely to be the best answer. If macrophages were most efficient at antigen presentation shortly after cell injection, the curve would likely show no dip at all, because antigen-specific responses could be initiated earlier to eliminate the tumor, making choice C unlikely to be best answer. If TC-1 cells were incapable of establishing a tumor at all, no dip would be seen in either the vaccinated or unvaccinated mice. Because Figure 1 shows a dip in the vaccinated mice and a constant downward trend in the unvaccinated mice, choice D can be eliminated.

37.   D is the best answer. The third paragraph and Figure 2 provide the best information to help answer the question. T cells become activated when their TCRs bind their cognate peptides presented in the content of MHC molecules. According to the third paragraph, the [IFNγ] is proportional to T cell activation, meaning that the highest [IFNγ] corresponds to the T cell population experiencing the highest activation, or the tightest binding between its TCR and cognate peptide. The tightest binding is represented by the lowest K_m. According to Figure 2 in the E6E7 vaccinated cohort of mice, challenging mice T cells with E6 antigen causes an increase in interferon over baseline, but this increase is less than that of either E7 or E6E7, eliminating choice A. The T cells exposed to E7 alone or E6E7 both show an increase in interferon production over E6. However, the confidence interval bars on the E7 and E6E7 bars overlap, meaning that the result is indistinguishable between the two conditions. Thus, there is no way to tell if either E7 or E6E7 produces the strongest response, meaning choice D is the best answer.

38.   A is the best answer. The provided figure is an antibody that is produced by plasma cells and may attach to specific antigens on the surface of a cancer cell. The specificity of the antibody is determined by the ends of the light and heavy chains, around the location marked A, making choice A the best answer choice. Choice B assists in recognizing the MHC molecule but does not provide the highest specificity for the exact antigen. Thus, choice B can be eliminated. Choice C is the site of glycosylation of the heavy chain and does not bind the antigen, eliminating choice C. Choice D is the site of receptor engagement of an antibody by a phagocytic cell. It does not recognize the antigen, eliminating it as the best answer.

Stand-alones (Questions 39-41)

39. **D is the best answer.** While antibodies traditionally bind protein antigens, the arrangement of charges in the protein secondary structure of the antibody would not prevent it from binding sugars and fats, assuming these sugars and fats had an arrangement of functional groups that could bind the functional groups of the antibody. Because all three molecules could theoretically be bound by an antibody, depending on the arrangement of functional groups on the amino acids of the antibody, choice D is the best answer.

40. **A is the best answer.** The best answer to this question will be the answer choice that describes a secondary antibody against the part of an antibody that is the same for many antibodies. In other words, an antibody against the least differentiated part of antibodies. The heavy and light chains refer to the peptides that make up the antibody. The FC region has components of two heavy chains, while the Fab domains each contain a light chain and a part of a heavy chain. The Fc domain of an antibody is conserved between antibodies against any target, making it an excellent target for a secondary antibody. Choice A is a strong choice. The Fab domain is the portion of the antibody beyond the hinge regions which actually contains the receptors that bind to antigen, this makes it more likely to be differentiated, and therefore an inferior target, eliminating choice B. Because the light chain is a component of the Fab domain, it will also have differentiated regions and choice C can be eliminated. Similarly, at least part of the heavy chain is a part of the Fab domain, meaning it is partially differentiated. Choice A more specifically refers to the part of the heavy chain that is the same in all antibodies, and choice D can be eliminated. As choice A is the least variable, and also the most sterically accessible part of a bound antibody, it would make the best target.

41. **D is the best answer.** Antibodies are able to bind proteins on the bacterial cell wall, helping to target them for destruction. Macrophages can bind one end of the antibody molecule to help endocytose bacteria and degrade them, making option I a component of the best answer. Complement molecules can also assemble along the carbohydrates that are attached to the protein structure of the antibody, leading to direct lysis of the bacterial cell wall. This makes option II a component of the best answer, eliminating choice A. A separate type of antibody, called an IgA antibody, works at mucosal surfaces to prevent bacteria and viruses from attaching to endothelial cells to enter the blood stream. This makes option III a component of the best answer, eliminating choices B and C. Choice D is the best answer because it contains all three options, which are all mechanisms by which antibodies decrease the circulating levels of bacteria.

The Digestive and Excretory Systems

TEST 5A

ANSWERS & EXPLANATIONS
Questions 1–59

LECTURE 5 ANSWER KEY

TEST 5A		MINI-TEST 5B	
1. C	31. D	1. B	22. D
2. C	32. C	2. D	23. B
3. C	33. D	3. C	24. B
4. D	34. D	4. A	25. A
5. A	35. B	5. B	26. B
6. B	36. D	6. C	27. B
7. A	37. C	7. D	28. D
8. D	38. A	8. C	29. A
9. D	39. A	9. D	30. D
10. C	40. A	10. A	31. C
11. D	41. B	11. A	32. B
12. A	42. D	12. D	33. C
13. B	43. B	13. C	34. D
14. D	44. C	14. A	35. C
15. B	45. D	15. B	36. A
16. B	46. B	16. A	37. B
17. C	47. A	17. A	38. C
18. B	48. B	18. B	39. C
19. C	49. A	19. D	40. C
20. A	50. B	20. A	41. C
21. B	51. B	21. C	
22. B	52. A		
23. A	53. D		
24. D	54. C		
25. D	55. B		
26. A	56. A		
27. C	57. D		
28. B	58. B		
29. B	59. D		
30. B			

EXPLANATIONS FOR LECTURE 5

Passage 1 (Questions 1-4)

1. **C is the best answer.** The removal of the ileum and cecum may have consequences for patients as each part of the GI tract serves a specific set of functions. The ileum typically contains a variety of bacterial species that lives in a symbiotic relationship with the human body. While these bacteria live off partially digested food, they simultaneously produce molecules like vitamins K and B12. Therefore, investigators in the above study would likely find that patients without an ileum, and the bacteria that normally inhabit it, would be vitamin K deficient. This would make choice A less likely. In the study, these patients were also found to have decreased diversity of microbiota. This would suggest that certain species are eliminated during the removal of the ileum. Therefore, choice B is not the best answer because removal of the ileum would result in an increase in the relative percentage of the other species in the GI tract that survived the surgery and antibiotics. Patients without an ileum would not be found to have a surplus of vitamin B12 because without a terminal ileum, B12 cannot be absorbed into the body, making choice C a strong answer. Because the ileum also serves to take up bile acids and recycle them, over time it would be expected that these patients would have decreased availability of bile acids. Therefore, choice D can be eliminated, and choice C is left as the best answer.

2. **C is the best answer.** This question requires understanding of the anatomic subdivisions of the small and large intestines. The small intestine is comprised of three parts, most proximally the duodenum, then the jejunum, and finally the ileum. The colon is comprised of many sections, with the bolus beginning at the cecum and traversing the ascending, transverse, descending, and sigmoid colon all before reaching the rectum. Therefore, the removal of the ileocecal junction would involve the removal of the terminal small intestine and proximal large intestine. Both choices A and B can be eliminated because they do not correctly describe this anatomical area. Choice C correctly lists terminal small intestine as the area for removal. Finally, choice D can be eliminated because the proximal small intestine is left intact in this procedure, leaving choice C as the best answer.

3. **C is the best answer.** The rectum is primarily responsible for the storage of feces. The absorption of water is known to occur primarily within the large intestine, so it might be tempting to select choice A as the correct answer because the rectum is part of the large intestine. However, on the MCAT®, this function is typically associated with the more proximal large intestine, rather than the rectum, making choice A less likely. Choice B can be eliminated because acidification of the GI tract occurs in the stomach and is counteracted by secretions in the duodenum and small intestine. Problems with the rectum should not impact this aspect of GI functioning, eliminating choice B. Choice C, the inability to store feces, is the best answer because this is precisely the primary function of the rectum and could be lost with rectal problems. While the function listed in choice D is associated with the large intestine, much like choice A, electrolyte absorption is considered a function of the more proximal colon.

4. **D is the best answer.** Movement of a bolus through the large intestine is involuntary and controlled by a special subset of the nervous system known as the enteric nervous system. The enteric nervous system consists of a large network of neurons that surround GI organs. Therefore, choice A is true and can be eliminated. Choice B is true and can be eliminated because peristalsis, the action of the moving food through the GI tract, is caused by the rhythmic contraction of smooth muscle. Choice C can also be eliminated because the action of the enteric nervous system on the GI smooth muscle is not under voluntary control. Choice D should be selected as the best answer because movement of food within the large intestine is not controlled by the somatic nervous system as peristaltic action is involuntary.

Passage 2 (Questions 5-8)

5. **A is the best answer.** This question refers to the anatomy of the gastrointestinal system. Because cholera is transmitted via a fecal-oral route, the bacteria are first ingested in the mouth before traveling through the esophagus to the stomach. Once in the small intestine, they transit through the duodenum, jejunum, and then ileum before arriving at the cecum, which begins the large intestine. The large intestine is broken down into the ascending colon, transverse colon, descending colon, and rectum. Choice B can be eliminated because the jejunum comes after the duodenum in the digestive tract. Choice C can be eliminated because the descending colon comes after the transverse colon in the digestive tract. Choice D can be eliminated because the ileum comes after the jejunum. Choice A describes the anatomical path of ingested particles through the gastrointestinal tract, making it the best answer choice.

6. **B is the best answer.** According to information contained in the passage, cholera is primarily a disease of diarrhea, which consists of profuse water loss through malabsorption of water in the intestinal tract. Water reabsorption is largely the role of the large intestine, which includes the ascending colon, transverse colon, descending colon, and rectum. The jejunum is the site of mixing of digestive enzymes and chyme in the small intestine, eliminating choice A. The fundus of the stomach receives food from the esophagus but does not contribute to water regulation, eliminating choice C. The ileum is the site of absorption in the small intestine, eliminating choice D. The descending colon is one of the major sites of primary water regulation in the large intestine, making choice B the best answer choice.

7. **A is the best answer.** The large intestine regulates water reabsorption and electrolyte balance. Certain ions are absorbed in specific areas of the intestinal tract. Calcium is almost entirely absorbed in the duodenum by active transport and in the jejunum and ileum by passive transport. Additionally, vitamin D facilitates calcium absorption. By contrast, potassium and sodium absorption occurs heavily in the large intestine, as these ions have a strong tendency to follow the movement of water across cellular membranes. High levels of CT are predicted to cause profuse diarrhea, leading to water loss primarily from the large intestine, as predicted by Figure 1. Because the water would not be reabsorbed, the electrolyte levels of potassium and sodium would be greatly affected, eliminating options II and III from the best answer. As water reabsorption does not occur to the greatest extent in the small intestine and calcium is reabsorbed in the small intestine, the concentrations of calcium would be least affected of the three ions. Thus, option I should be a component of the best answer. Choice B can be eliminated because it contains option II, while choice C can be eliminated because it contains option III. Choice D can be eliminated because it contains both options II and III. Choice A is the best answer choice, as it only contains option I.

8. **D is the best answer.** The additional experimental evidence shows that binding of CT and TCP to the cAMP receptor leads to degradation of aquaporin channels. Phosphorylation and ubiquitination are the steps that precede degradation by the proteasome, meaning that aquaporin channels are hydrolyzed in these cells. As in the kidney collecting duct, aquaporin channels in the large intestines are responsible for transporting water from the intestinal lumen to the intestinal cells. However, this additional information only supports the role of CT and TCP in water regulation but does not provide any additional information as to the mechanism of action of anethole. Thus, choices A and B can be eliminated. The authors suggest that anethole decreases ToxT binding in Figure 2 by showing that TCP production decreases with increasing anethole concentrations, eliminating choice C. Because no additional information about anethole is provided by the further experiments, choice D is the best answer choice.

Passage 3 (Questions 9-13)

9. **D is the best answer.** The contents of the GI system move through the digestive tract and are stored in the rectum prior to elimination. Urgency to defecate can be caused by an inability to properly store this waste. The question stem also states that urgency to defecate can be a symptom of ulcerative colitis. Based on the passage, both choices A and B can be eliminated because ulcerative colitis does not extend beyond the ileum. Involvement of the GI tract proximal to the colon would not be the best answer. Damage to the colon could cause voluminous and watery diarrhea, as this segment of the digestive tract would no longer be able to serve its function of water and electrolyte absorption. Damage to the rectum would affect its ability to store feces, which would lead to a sense of urgency as GI contents move into the rectum from the colon. While colonic damage could lead to some perceived urgency, rectal involvement and the loss of ability to store feces would be the most likely source of this symptom. Choice D is a better answer than choice C.

10. **C is the best answer.** The ileum is the terminal segment of the small intestine, which means the first location of possible damage would be the first segment of the colon. The colon joins the small intestine via the cecum, ascends, moves across the abdomen transversely, descends, and joins the rectum via the sigmoid colon. Remember that the colon makes roughly an upside down 'U' shape, meaning the order is ascending, transverse, and then descending. Choice A can be eliminated because the sigmoid colon is the segment furthest from the ileum relative to the other choices. Choice B can be eliminated because the transverse colon represents a more medial segment of colon. In this case, when a question asks for an extreme, the answer is most likely one of the extremes. Choice C is a strong answer as it is one sections of colon closest to the small intestine. Choice D is not the best choice and should be eliminated as it is a more terminal segment of colon than the ascending colon, making choice C the best answer.

11. **D is the best answer.** As stated in the passage, damage in UC typically occurs in the rectum and colon. Furthermore, according to paragraph 2, reduced bacterial diversity has been observed in patients with inflammatory bowel disease. Choices A and B can be eliminated because the colons of individuals with IBD would be expected to contain reduced bacterial diversity. The passage also indicates that bacterial overgrowth can ensue in these patients. Colonic bacteria provide an essential source of vitamin K, vitamin B12, and riboflavin by converting colonic contents into these substances. A change in gut flora would be expected to alter the production of these substances in some way. Choice C is inconsistent with this logic and is not the best answer. Choice D is the best answer because bacterial overgrowth of species that do not produce vitamin B12 could prevent those that do from thriving, thereby driving down the colonic production of B12. This is the most likely answer to occur in a person with UC.

12. **A is the best answer.** The stomach serves a variety of functions that aid in both physical and chemical digestion. The G cells of the stomach secrete gastrin, which in turn stimulates parietal cells to secrete HCl. Choice A is a strong answer because gastrin is only produced by the G cells in the stomach. Choice B, breakdown of protein, can be eliminated because although the stomach secretes pepsin which is responsible for protein breakdown, the pancreas also secretes proteases like trypsin that serve a similar function. Based on this fact, removal of the stomach would not halt all protein breakdown. The stomach serves a secretory role by releasing intrinsic factor enzymes, and acid. Bicarbonate is not a major product of stomach secretions. Bicarbonate is primarily secreted by the pancreas and enters the GI tract in the small intestine, eliminating choice C. Choice D can be eliminated because although the churning of the stomach does provide a source of physical digestion, so does chewing of the food in the mouth. This function would not be completely lost. Because the stomach is not the sole location of this mechanical digestion, choice D can be eliminated, leaving choice A as the best answer.

13. **B is the best answer.** The process described in the question stem is the use of smooth muscles in the digestive process. Chewing food involves skeletal muscles and is controlled consciously. Although these processes both contribute to mechanical digestion of food, their control mechanisms are quite different. Choice A is unlikely to be correct. Choice B, esophageal peristalsis, describes a process of moving food from the mouth to the stomach. This is a strong answer as it also describes a process where smooth muscles are used to facilitate movement and digestion of food. The enzymatic breakdown of protein by pepsin describes a chemical digestion, which would not be analogous to the mechanical movement and digestion of smooth muscle. Choice D describes an absorptive process that is also more on the molecular level, ruling out choice D.

Stand-alones (Questions 14-17)

14. **D is the best answer.** Saliva is an important substance that is secreted by salivary glands in the mouth and contributes to the initial steps of food mixing and movement. Saliva contains salivary amylase that begins the breakdown of long, straight-chain carbohydrates within the mouth. The action of salivary amylase mimics the action the amylase that is later secreted by the pancreas and utilized for digestion of carbohydrates within the small intestine. Choice A is not true and can be eliminated. Saliva in the mouth also serves to coat the food bolus and helps it move down the esophagus by providing lubrication. Choice B may be a tempting answer but the last part of the statement is false, as no digestion occurs in the esophagus. If any part of the statement is false, it must be eliminated unless all other answer choices are worse options. As discussed above, salivary amylase is similar to pancreatic amylase. Even without the presence of salivary amylase, there would still be some carbohydrate breakdown in the duodenum, eliminating choice C. In fact, pancreatic amylase plays a more important role in this process. Salivary amylase provides the first source of chemical digestion within the body, so choice D should be selected as the best answer.

15. **B is the best answer.** The low pH of the stomach is crucial to process of breaking down food into smaller units that can be absorbed in the small intestine. Low pH acts to activate pepsinogen to pepsin and protect against harmful bacteria and other pathogens that enter through the oral route. The chief cells secrete pepsinogen and gastric lipase to begin the process of breaking down proteins and fats, respectively. They do not help protect the lining of the stomach, eliminating choice A. Parietal cells secrete the acid that makes the pH of the stomach low, eliminating choice C. Enteroendocrine cells release hormones like gastrin, histamine, and others that modulate the activity of various cells. They are not directly responsible for protecting the lining of the stomach, eliminating choice D. Goblet cells secrete mucus, which forms a protective barrier over the lining of the stomach wall. This makes them the most important in protecting stomach structures from low pH. Choice B is the best answer.

16. **B is the best answer.** Liver cirrhosis occurs after many years of sustained alcohol consumption and is often a condition of chronic alcoholics. In liver cirrhosis, normal hepatocytes die and are replaced by scar tissue in a process called fibrosis. The liver is responsible for making bile salts, which emulsify fat and cholesterol in the gut to allow it to be absorbed by the small intestine. Liver damage would impair bile salt production, decreasing, not increasing, fatty acid and cholesterol absorption. Option I can be eliminated. The liver also produces proteins that are necessary for blood clotting, such as fibrinogen, which is converted to fibrin in the clotting reaction. Liver damage would decrease the ability of the blood to clot, making option II a component of the best answer. Additionally, the liver also helps regulate blood glucose levels between meals by releasing glucose stored as glycogen and synthesizing new glucose molecules by gluconeogenesis. A decrease in the number of hepatocytes that can do these two processes would impair the regulation of blood glucose, eliminating option III. Choice A can be eliminated because a decrease in bile salts decreases fatty acid absorption. Choice C can be eliminated for the same reason and the fact that impaired glycogenolysis and gluconeogenesis would decrease blood glucose levels between meals. Choice D can also be eliminated due to impaired glycogenolysis and gluconeogenesis that is expected to be observed in patients with liver damage. Choice B is the best answer because a decrease in the production of clotting factors would hinder blood clotting.

17. **C is the best answer.** The liver plays many key roles in digestion and metabolism. Cells in the liver, particularly those with a large amount of smooth ER, are involved in detoxification. It would make sense that a damaged liver would be less able to process toxins, increasing vulnerability. Option I is likely, so choice B can be eliminated. Next, the liver plays a subtle role in immune function through the filtration of blood by the phagocytic function of Kupffer cells. Bacteria picked up from the gut can travel to the liver and can be phagocytosed, preventing contamination and infection of the rest of the body. The liver also produces complement proteins that play a role in fighting off pathogens. Option II is likely because the immune function of the liver would be diminished if there was damage, so eliminate choice A. Next, the liver is the major storage center of lipids and can mobilize fats for energy by making ketone bodies. This would be reduced, not increased, in the context of liver damage, so option III is not a strong conclusion. Choice C is a better answer than choice D.

Passage 4 (Questions 18-21)

18. **B is the best answer.** According to paragraph 3, Apo-B100 is synthesized in the liver and contributes to the structure and function of VLDL. VLDL is the lowest density lipoprotein produced by the liver and serves to carry triglycerides and cholesterol to the systemic circulation. Chylomicrons, not VLDLs, are produced by the enterocytes of the small intestine. Chylomicrons transport fat and cholesterol from the gut, through the lymphatic system, to the bloodstream. Once the chylomicrons enter circulation, they are taken up by the liver, and the cholesterol and fatty acid components are packaged into VLDL particles that return to systemic circulation. The enterocytes produce chylomicrons, not VLDL, eliminating choice A. The liver produces and recycles VLDL, intermediate density lipoproteins (IDLs), low density lipoproteins (LDLs), and high density lipoproteins (HDLs). The highest concentration of fatty acids is found in the VLDLs, making choice B most likely to be the best answer. HDLs, not VLDLs, contain the highest protein to fatty acid ratio of the circulating lipoproteins, eliminating choice C. HDLs, not VLDLs, are also responsible for picking up excess fatty acids and cholesterol that has been deposited in the arteries and veins of the systemic circulation. This eliminates choice D, and makes choice B the best answer.

19. **C is the best answer.** The gallbladder is the site of storage of bile that is produced by the liver. Bile aids in the absorption of fat and cholesterol, as well as vitamins that are fat soluble. Glucose is absorbed by the enterocytes of the small intestine. Glucose absorption is not dependent upon bile, eliminating choice A. Amino acids are charged molecules as they have a positively charged amino group and a negatively charged carboxyl group, as well as occasional charge and polarity of their side chains. They do not require bile salts to be absorbed, making choice B less likely to be the best answer. Vitamins A, D, E, and K are fat soluble vitamins that rely on the emulsification of fat by bile salts in order for the vitamins to be absorbed. Gallbladder cancer would most likely decrease the amount of bile reaching the small intestine, resulting in a decrease in the amount of vitamin A absorption. Calcium, as a charged ion, does not require bile to be solvated, meaning gallbladder cancer would be less likely to impact its absorption, eliminating choice D.

20. **A is the best answer.** Bile is produced by the liver, stored in the gallbladder, and secreted via the bile duct into the small intestine. Bile specifically enters the small intestine at the duodenum and is mixed with chyme that exits from the stomach. Since bile is secreted into the duodenum, choice A is most likely the best answer. The ileum is the primary site of macromolecule absorption and is not the first site of bile entry into the small intestine, eliminating choice B. The jejunum is immediately after the duodenum and serves to mix chyme with digestive enzymes released from the pancreas. Bile, however, first enters the small intestine in the duodenum, making choice A a better answer than choice C. The cecum is the most proximal part of the large intestine, and bile enters before this point, eliminating choice D.

21. **B is the best answer.** Obstruction of the common bile duct would lead to the back-up of bile in the gallbladder, eventually preventing the liver from appropriately excreting bile. This would most likely decrease the amount of esterified bile salts being produced, as the concentration of bile salt products would be higher than normal in the liver hepatocytes. This makes choice A less likely to be the best answer. Fatty acids and cholesterol are components of bile salts. If bile salts cannot be produced at the normal rate, the reactants of the reactions that result in bile production will increase in concentration and remain in the hepatocyte. Think of this like an equilibrium problem using Le Chatelier's principle. A backup of bile excretion would lead to fatty acid storage in the hepatocyte, making choice B most likely to be the best answer. Because the liver is responsible for eliminating fat-soluble metabolites in the bile, gallstones are unlikely to impact the elimination of water-soluble products, making choice C less likely to be the best answer. Reduced production and secretion of bile that would result from an obstructed bile duct would prevent elimination of fat-soluble drugs and metabolic products, eliminating choice D.

Passage 5 (Questions 22-27)

22. **B is the best answer.** Barrett's esophagus is the result of a deficit in the functioning and integrity of the distal esophagus. The pyloric sphincter separates the stomach from the duodenum of the small intestine, which is not the anatomical region of concern in Barrett's esophagus, eliminating choice A. The cardiac sphincter is a band of smooth muscle that helps separate the lower esophagus from the stomach. Decreased integrity of the cardiac sphincter would allow stomach acid to interact with the lower esophagus, possibly causing Barrett's esophagus and making choice B most likely to be the best answer. The fundus of the stomach receives food from the lower esophagus, but it is not responsible for creating a barrier between the lower esophagus and the stomach, eliminating choice C. The epiglottis is a flap of tissue that covers the trachea to prevent food from entering the airway. As Barrett's esophagus impacts the lower esophagus, not the trachea, choice D can be eliminated.

23. **A is the best answer.** The additional hypothesis suggests that irritation due to poorly chewed solid foods may increase the risk of Barrett's esophagus. Mastication is the process of chewing solid foods into smaller pieces in order to aid digestion. Failure to chew food into small enough pieces could result in irritation, supporting the additional hypothesis, and making choice A most likely to be the best answer. The passage suggests that Barrett's esophagus results from acid entering the lower esophagus. Decreased secretion of acid from parietal cells would increase the pH of the stomach, likely leading to less damage in the lower esophagus and eliminating choice B. Amylase is an enzyme that breaks down starch. Increased secretion of amylase would encourage the breakdown of starches, making some food particles smaller, and eliminating choice C. The pancreas releases digestive enzymes into the small intestine and does not interact with the esophagus, eliminating choice D.

24. **D is the best answer.** Barrett's esophagus is caused by reflux of stomach acid and bile into the lower esophagus, according to information contained in the passage. Decreasing the production of acid in the stomach would decrease the compensatory changes in the distal esophagus, likely helping to prevent Barrett's esophagus. Gastric acid secretion is promoted by histamine. An anti-histamine compound would prevent additional release of stomach acid, increasing the pH of the stomach contents and helping to prevent Barrett's esophagus. This makes option I a component of the best answer. A proton pump inhibitor would prevent protons from entering the stomach lumen to acidify the contents, making option II a component of the best answer. Gastrin also promotes release of stomach acid into the stomach lumen. An antagonist prevents gastrin from activating the gastrin receptor and reduces acidification of the lumen, making option III a component of the best answer. As choice D contains all three options, it is the best answer.

25. **D is the best answer.** Figure 1 presents the number of goblet cells that have a diploid number of chromosomes and the number of goblet cells that have an aneuploidy number of chromosomes. Aneuploidy is the state of having an imbalance between the number of chromosomes and can occur when part of a chromosome is lost or gained. Cancer often has chromosomal imbalances that confer a selective growth advantage by increasing the number of copies of genes that increase proliferation and survival. Notice that Figure 1, however, does not include any number of diploid or aneuploid goblet cell counts from the normal esophagus. It is reasonable to conclude from information contained in the passage that the normal esophagus would contain few, if any, goblet cells, but Figure 1 does not provide any comparison between the normal esophagus and Barrett's esophagus. Barrett's esophagus has cells that do not contain balanced chromosome sets and are aneuploidy. However, because data from the normal esophagus is not included in Figure 1, choices A and B can be eliminated. Figure 1 only presents the number of goblet cells with certain chromosomal states but does not provide causative information about the genetic changes and the formation of Barrett's esophagus, making choice C less likely to be the best answer. As Figure 1 does not directly provide information that compares the normal esophagus to Barrett's esophagus, choice D is the best answer.

26. **A is the best answer.** According to information contained in the passage, Barrett's esophagus is a compensatory change to increased stomach acid and bile that enters the lower esophagus. Goblet cells become numerous in the distal esophagus in order to secrete mucus to protect the esophageal lining from the acid. Acid is formed from HCl, which dissociates into protons and chloride ions in solution. Anions, bicarbonate in particular, would be able to neutralize excess protons, helping to lower the acidity of the lower esophagus. This additional finding would support the authors' conclusions, likely making choice A the best answer. Secretion of additional protons in BE would worsen the symptoms and cause additional dysplastic changes. A finding of proton secretion by BE-associated epithelium would not support the authors' conclusions, and choice B can be eliminated. The stomach is acidified by a proton pump that pumps protons into the lumen in exchange for potassium. High potassium levels in the gastric juice would suggest the pump is not actively moving protons into the lumen, which would lead to a higher pH in the gastric juice and less damage to the lower esophagus. This is counter to the conclusions drawn by the authors, eliminating choice C. Low gastrin levels would prevent the acidification of the stomach lumen, leading to reduced damage to the lower esophagus. This eliminates choice D and makes choice A the best answer.

27. **C is the best answer.** One of the main functions of the stomach is to begin the breakdown of ingested food and help churn the food into chyme, which will enter the small intestine for further digestion and absorption. The fundus and cardia of the stomach receive food from the esophagus that has not had a chance to encounter stomach acid or pepsin, which is activated by the low pH of the stomach from its inactive form, pepsinogen, which is released from chief cells in the stomach wall. Proteins are unlikely to have been broken down at this point into their individual amino acids, such as phenylalanine and tyrosine, eliminating choices A and B. The pylorus is the distal-most portion of the stomach, where the ingested food has had the longest amount of time to be exposed to pepsin. The rhythmic contractions of the pylorus help mix and churn the food to increase the surface area over which pepsin can act, likely allowing more proteins to be broken down into individual amino acids and making choice C most likely to be the best answer. The body of the stomach is also a site of mixing and digestion, but the food in the body has had less exposure to pepsin than the food in the pylorus, making choice D less likely to be the best answer compared to choice C.

Stand-alones (Questions 28-31)

28. **B is the best answer.** The enteric nervous system is a large network of neurons that serves to stimulate digestive processes. Through peristaltic action of smooth muscle, a bolus can move more readily through the digestive tract. This would contribute positively to digestion, eliminating choice A. When any organ is more active, its oxygen demand is higher and thus requires more blood flow. Vasoconstriction of the GI vessels would deprive the digestive organs of oxygen and reduce absorption of nutrients, hindering digestion. Choice B is a strong answer because vasoconstriction would not promote digestion and for that reason would not be a likely result of enteric nerve stimulation. Vasoconstriction would reduce blood supply to the digestive system. Stimulation of the enteric system would likely increase hormone release to promote adequate digestion and absorption. Therefore, choice C is true and can be eliminated. Fluid exchange is also a vital process that occurs within the digestive tract, and enteric nerve stimulation would promote this function, eliminating choice D. This leaves choice B as the best answer.

29. **B is the best answer.** There are many specific cell types and structures in the digestive system that play specific roles. Goblet cells secrete mucus, making choice A unlikely. In addition to the digestive tract, these cells are also found in the respiratory tract. Lacteals are lymph vessels that transport digested fat molecules from the intestines. Choice B is likely to be correct since it correctly matches the name and function. The brush border is a layer of microvilli on the surface of the small intestine. These maximize surface area for exchange and absorption of nutrients. They do not secrete mucus, so choice C is unlikely. Next, chief cells secrete digestive enzymes like pepsinogen, but it is actually parietal cells that control secretion of acid. Choice D is unlikely, and choice A is the best answer.

30. **B is the best answer.** Salivary and pancreatic amylases both digest sugars. This digestion tends to turn polysaccharides into disaccharides and trisaccharides, or 2 and 3 part sugars. Choice A is a weak answer. Next, pancreatic amylase tends to play a larger role in digestion. This enzyme degrades a much larger quantity of carbohydrates and is more powerful, so choice B is a likely answer. Choice C is unlikely based on the structure of the digestive system. Salivary amylase starts acting as soon as food enters the mouth, while pancreatic amylase acts further into the GI tract, starting at the small intestine. Choice D is not the best answer since brush border enzymes, not either of these amylases, degrade polymers into monosaccharides before absorption. This eliminates choice D.

31. **D is the best answer.** Gastrin is released in response to vagal input from the parasympathetic nervous system. It is released from G cells, which are located in the stomach and acts on parietal cells to increase acid production. Choice A can be eliminated because parietal cells are located in the stomach, so the final target of gastrin is within the stomach, not the pancreas. Gastrin can also be released in response to stretch of the stomach, signaling that food is present and acid is needed to break it down. Choice B can be eliminated since mechanical stretch of the stomach would increase, rather than stop gastrin secretion. Gastrin is also known to stimulate the release of HCl, an acid, not a base, so choice C can be eliminated. Gastrin production is stimulated by parasympathetic inputs, and choice D is the best answer.

Passage 6 (Questions 32-35)

32. **C is the best answer.** Lipid absorption occurs in the small intestine and depends on bile that is produced by the liver and stored in the gallbladder. These are unrelated to the ascending colon, so choice A is not the best answer. Water resorption does indeed occur in the colon, but a removal of 30% of the ascending colon should reduce this activity, as the length and surface area along which this process can occur is reduced. Choice B is unlikely. Choice C is the best answer because reduced water reabsorption should lead to excretion of more water in feces. The rectum is the part of the large intestine that stores feces, so storage of feces should be unaffected by resection of the ascending colon. Choice D is a weak answer.

33. **D is the best answer.** According to the passage, Ednrb KO mice have more and larger goblet cells in the distal colon while goblet cells in the proximal colon are smaller and fewer in number. The distal and proximal colon goblet cells change in opposite ways, so it is extremely unlikely that mucus secretion changes are constant throughout the whole colon. Thus, choices A and B are unlikely. Next, choice C is unlikely because goblet cells are reduced in number and size in the proximal colon. Additionally, goblet cells in the distal colon are increased in size and number. Choice D is the best answer because changes to goblet cells in the proximal and distal colon indicate the mucus will be reduced proximally and increased distally.

34. **D is the best answer.** According to the passage, enterocolitis is related to an increase in the ratio of intracellular to secreted mucins. Secreted proteins like mucins would be made in the ribosomes of the rough ER, and packaged, processed, and modified in the Golgi network. They can then be stored in exocytotic vesicles and be secreted in response to certain signals. There is no comment made on the quantity of mucin made, so no assumptions can be drawn regarding mucin production. This is reinforced by the fact that one part of the mucin produced has increased, while the other part has decreased. Choices A and B are unlikely. Next, mucin secretion has been impacted here as the ratio of intracellular to secreted mucin has changed. Higher intracellular and lower secreted mucin means that less mucin is being secreted, making choice C unlikely. Choice D is likely, as this would lead to the ratio observed in enterocolitis.

35. **B is the best answer.** The bacteria in the colon are most likely to change due to immunological molecules. Mucins are glycosylated proteins and no immune function is implied by the passage, so option I is unlikely. Antimicrobial proteins have their function in the name. They kill microbes, and this would certainly change the environment of the gut. Option II is likely to be the best answer. Next, immunoglobulins are antibodies, which are immune molecules that are secreted into the gut as well as other parts of the body like the bloodstream. These are immune proteins that are likely to impact bacterial growth. However, they are not one of the three components of mucus, so option III can be ruled out, and choice B is the best answer.

Passage 7 (Questions 36-39)

36. **D is the best answer.** Pancreatic amylase is key to digesting polysaccharides into smaller subunits that can be absorbed in the small intestine and utilized in the body. If release was inhibited, there would be less breakdown and fewer carbohydrates ready for absorption. Bile is produced by the liver and stored in the gallbladder. This substance is used to emulsify fats into micelles that can be digested. Bile is primarily made of water and bile salts. Since polysaccharides are not fats, bile is not expected to play a major role in their digestion or absorption. Choices A and B can be eliminated. Choice C is unlikely because a reduced amount of saccharide absorption will reduce glycogen levels in the liver as the body compensates for the decreased absorption. Less intake leads to less storage. This is why choice D is the best answer. The reduced breakdown of polysaccharides by amylase leads to reduced absorption, which means less storage is possible.

37. **C is the best answer.** Rab27B overexpression enhances CCK induced amylase secretion according to the end of the passage. This means that Rab27B plays some sort of intermediate role between detecting CCK and release of amylase from pancreatic acini. If Rab27B was knocked out, meaning it is no longer expressed, then a step between CCK detection and amylase release would not be carried out. Thus, the responsiveness to CCK would decrease. Choices B and D can be eliminated. It also means that CCK would not be able to cause amylase release. This matches best with choice C. Choice A is unlikely since amylase release is a response to CCK, so they should be directly correlated.

38. **A is the best answer.** Frameshift mutations generally lead to severe losses of function. Enteropeptidase cleaves trypsin from its zymogen form to its active form. Digestive enzymes are stored and secreted as inactive zymogens so that they do not damage the cells that secrete them. They are only activated once they are in the gastrointestinal tract and in position to digest their target macromolecules. Since trypsin digests proteins, and it would be less activated with dysfunctional enteropeptidase, choice A is a strong answer. Trypsin is not involved in digestion of lipids, so choice B is unlikely. The main enzyme that digests lipids is lipase. Trypsinogen is secreted, but this is not controlled by enteropeptidase, ruling out choice C. Choice D can be eliminated because trypsin is not secreted. Trypsinogen, the zymogen form of trypsin, is secreted. Choice A is the best answer.

39. **A is the best answer.** Ashen mice are missing Rab27A, reducing their level of pancreatic amylase and reducing breakdown of sugars. This means that fewer sugars will be absorbed in the small intestine and more will pass through the gut and be found in the feces. Option I is likely to be in the best answer. Option II can be eliminated because reduced absorption of sugars should reduce blood sugar levels. Ketone bodies are the result of reduced sugar levels and are a molecule through which energy can be transferred throughout the body. If sugar levels are reduced, then ketone bodies should be found in higher levels. This contradicts option III, so option III is unlikely, and choice A is the best answer.

Passage 8 (Questions 40-43)

40. A is the best answer. This question is asking about how to set up an experiment in order to measure damage to the outside of enterocytes. According to the passage, these membrane junctions are damaged by proteolytic attack. Proteolytic attack is basically cleavage of proteins by enzymes, so it makes sense to use an enzyme that digests proteins in this experimental setup. An example of such an enzyme is trypsin, and choice A is a strong answer. Amylase, choice B, is a major digestive enzyme that processes sugars. Lipase is involved in fat breakdown. Finally, kinases are a category of enzymes that phosphorylate proteins, often in signaling pathways. These choices would not damage membranes and would not be useful in such an experiment.

41. B is the best answer. To answer this question, consider where the major absorption of each of these molecules occurs. The colon is responsible for the majority of water and ion absorption, as these are the major functions of the large intestine. Thus, damage to the small intestine would not necessarily cause options I or II. Considering option III, absorption of macronutrients occurs mostly in the small intestine. Damage to the junctions in this part of the gastrointestinal tract would cause problems in absorption. As nutrients are transported into the enterocytes from the intestinal lumen, damaged intercellular junctions could potentially let these macronutrients leak back out and impair absorption. Since only option III is true, choice B is the best answer.

42. D is the best answer. The small intestine normally absorbs peptides and sugars to transmit them to the bloodstream. Toxins that look like peptides and sugars will be absorbed readily by the small intestine, and even a healthy small intestine would become damaged as these types of molecules are absorbed. This lack of ability to differentiate in terms of integrity makes choices A and B unlikely. Next, bacterial toxins would be more likely to damage cells if the integrity of the mucin membrane was damaged. The deciding factor between choices C and D is whether to measure growth or apoptosis. Apoptosis is a better indicator of damage than growth, as apoptosis is programmed cell death in response to damage. Choice D is the best answer.

43. B is the best answer. Lacteals are lymphatic vessels in villi that are involved in the absorption of nutrients. Proteins move into intestinal membrane cells and then directly into the bloodstream, so choice A is unlikely. Next, fats actually go into lacteals and travel through the lymphatic system after they are taken up by intestinal cells. Choice B is a strong answer. Glucose follows a similar path as protein, so choice C can be ruled out. Finally, water does not enter the lacteals, so choice D can be eliminated.

Stand-alones (Questions 44-47)

44. C is the best answer. The digestive system is controlled by nervous system impulses that lead to the production of many regulatory hormones. The hormones that are involved in digestion are part of the endocrine system, meaning that they need to travel through the bloodstream to exert their effects, eliminating choice A. The enteric nervous system is a special branch of the nervous system that helps regulate functions like peristalsis, blood flow to digestive organs, and hormone release. Choice B is true and can be eliminated. Choice C states that the hormones that regulate digestion require a system of ducts for their release. This is not accurate and better describes hormones that are released as part of the exocrine system, which are unrelated to digestion. Release into a duct versus release into the bloodstream is the defining difference between exocrine and endocrine signaling. In addition to the enteric nervous system, the parasympathetic nervous system provides inputs from the vagus nerve that help the stomach prepare for digestion. Choice D can be eliminated, and choice C is left as the best answer.

45. D is the best answer. The microvilli of the small intestine greatly increase the surface area of absorption for molecules like glucose. Disruption of microvilli leads to decreased absorption of glucose, which lowers blood glucose levels. Insulin is secreted in response to high levels of glucose, so insulin levels are likely to be lower. Thus, decreased insulin should be observed, eliminating choice A. Glucagon is released when blood glucose is low. In celiac disease, impaired absorption of glucose would likely lower blood glucose levels, inducing glucagon release, eliminating choice B. Due to lowered glucose levels, cells would likely begin to break down fats to generate acetyl-CoA for the citric acid cycle and ATP generation. Thus, choice C can be eliminated. Storage of excess glucose as glycogen occurs in the presence of high glucose concentrations. As absorption would be impaired, there would be no excess glucose to store, making choice D the best answer choice.

46. B is the best answer. The parasympathetic nervous system, mostly the vagus nerve, is responsible for mediating the effects of the nervous system on digestion. Parasympathetic nervous system activation stimulates digestion and is mediated by acetylcholine release from the vagus nerve. If an acetylcholine receptor agonist were used, it would stimulate digestive system action. This increase in stimulation would result in increased blood flow to the stomach, eliminating choice A. Since acetylcholine also stimulates G cells to release gastrin that stimulates acid production in the stomach, increased stimulation of G cells would lead to more acid secretion and a lower pH, eliminating choice C. Fluid exchange, including water, would also likely increase in the large intestine, eliminating choice D. Increased peristalsis occurs upon stimulation by the parasympathetic nervous system. Increasing this stimulation by a receptor agonist would lead to increased, not decreased, peristalsis, making choice B the best answer.

47. **A is the best answer.** Secretin is produced by the duodenum, and its release is stimulated by the arrival of acid in the small intestine. Secretin acts on the pancreas to increase, not decrease, the release of digestive enzymes, such as the zymogen trypsinogen, eliminating choice B. Secretin does not target the stomach, so it does not impact the muscular contractions of the stomach, eliminating choice C. Additionally, the stomach muscle is not under voluntary control, meaning that it is characterized by smooth muscle, not striated muscle, further eliminating choice C. Secretin does not impact stomach pH, eliminating choice D. In addition to stimulating the release of digestive enzymes from the pancreas, secretin also drives the secretion of sodium bicarbonate, which helps to neutralize the acid of the stomach that is present in the chyme. Thus, secretin acts to neutralize acid that may destroy the duodenal wall, making choice A the best answer.

Passage 9 (Questions 48-52)

48. **B is the best answer.** Figure 1 provides information that helps answer this question. According to Figure 1, *H. pylori* infection decreases the activation of ghrelin and increases the activation of leptin. Paragraph one also notes that leptin and ghrelin are protein hormones. Because they are protein hormones, they are likely to be charged and hydrophilic. This means they are unable to cross the plasma membrane and must bind extracellular receptors. Using Figure 1 as a guide, ghrelin and leptin then activate intracellular transcription factors that translocate to the nucleus to increase IFN-γ levels. Transcription factors are primarily responsible for binding sites on DNA, increasing the transcription of particular genes, leading to higher levels of the target protein. Transcription factors are unlikely to bind RNA over DNA, eliminating choice A. Replication of RNA occurs by an RNA-dependent RNA polymerase, which some viruses contain. However, eukaryotic cells do not undergo RNA replication directly, eliminating choice C. DNA polymerases, not transcription factors, are responsible for replicating DNA, eliminating choice D. Transcription factors bind specific sequences of DNA, helping to recruit the machinery responsible for RNA transcription. Increased transcription generally leads to increased protein production, making choice B the best answer choice.

49. **A is the best answer.** Table 1 provides the information needed to help answer this question. According to Table 1, levels of insulin are significantly higher in asymptomatic persons than in persons with gastric cancer. Alpha cells secrete glucagon, which acts opposite to insulin to raise blood glucose levels. When insulin levels are high, as they are in asymptomatic persons, glucagon levels are likely to be low, meaning that less glucagon would be exocytosed from alpha cells in the pancreas. These two signaling molecules can be thought of as antagonistic. Thus, choice B can be eliminated. Parietal cells secrete HCl. Insulin is produced in the pancreas by special exocrine cells called beta cells secrete HCl into the lumen of the stomach. The passage states that many gastric cell types may be affected by *H. pylori* invasion, so it is feasible that parietal cells may also be affected. However, ions, such as H⁺, are secreted via membrane-bound transporters, not vesicular transport, eliminating choice C. Additionally, the passage only states that the cell types may be affected but does not provide any information about how the acidity of the stomach changes in GC, further making choice C less likely to be the best answer. As with choice C, it is possible that chief cells are affected as well. However, the passage does not provide any information about how the concentration of pepsinogen would change in the stomach, making choice D less likely to be the best answer. Beta cells of the pancreas secrete insulin. Insulin levels are highest in asymptomatic persons as compared to those with ulcers or GC. Insulin is synthesized then transported out of the cell via vesicles. Thus, persons with higher insulin levels in the blood likely have greater production of insulin and thus greater exocytosis of intracellular vesicles filled with insulin, making choice A the best answer choice.

50. **B is the best answer.** G cells are cells of the stomach that receive stimulation from the parasympathetic nervous system and induce the release of HCl from parietal cells. G cells affect the acidification of the stomach through parietal cells, but not through the release of the zymogen pepsinogen from chief cells, eliminating choice A. Mucus secretion would reasonably be higher in more acidic stomach conditions, as the increased mucus would serve as a thicker barrier for the stomach lining. If G cell functioning was compromised, the parietal cells would secrete less acid and the stomach would be less acidic. Thus, if mucus secretion changes at all, it is most likely to decrease, rather than increase, eliminating choice C. Table 1 helps with determining whether choice D is the best answer choice. According to the leptin row in Table 1, patients with GC have the highest levels of leptin. GC likely represents the most dysfunctional spectrum of *H. pylori* infection, resulting in increased, not decreased leptin production, helping to eliminate choice D. Additionally, no link is made between G cell functioning, acid content of the stomach, and leptin secretion, further eliminating choice D. G cells stimulate the release of acid from parietal cells of the stomach. If G cells became dysfunctional, a decrease in the secretion of acid is likely to be seen, making choice B the best answer choice.

51. **B is the best answer.** The parasympathetic nervous system, specifically the vagus nerve, is responsible for mediating the effects of nervous system on digestion. Parasympathetic nervous system activation stimulates digestion and is mediated by acetylcholine release from the vagus nerve. If acetylcholine receptor antagonists were used, it would appear to the digestive system that no parasympathetic stimulation was occurring. This decrease in stimulation would result in decreased blood flow to the stomach, eliminating choice A. As acetylcholine also stimulates G cells to release gastrin that stimulates acid production in the stomach, decreased stimulation of G cells would lead to less acid secretion and a higher pH, eliminating choice C. Fluid exchange, including water, would also likely decrease in the large intestine, which includes the colon, eliminating choice D. Increased peristalsis occurs upon stimulation by the parasympathetic nervous system. Removal of this parasympathetic stimulation would lead to decreased, not increased peristalsis, making choice B the best answer.

52. **A is the best answer.** The duodenum receives the chyme from the stomach, allows it to mix with bile salts delivered by the bile duct and pancreatic enzymes delivered by the pancreatic duct. Trypsinogen is a zymogen enzyme that is produced by the pancreas and released into the small intestine. Compromised integrity of the cells of the duodenum and jejunum may prevent delivery of trypsinogen to the intestines by blocking the duct by which it enters the small intestine, eliminating choice B. The solubility of ingested fats is increased by bile salts delivered into the beginning of the small intestine by the bile duct. Before entering the small intestine, bile is stored in the gallbladder. Disruption of the duodenum could prevent delivery of bile salts, leading to decreased solubility of fats, eliminating choice C. The jejunum is responsible for some absorption of molecules like glucose, in addition to mixing the contents in the small intestine. Thus, choice D can be eliminated. Water reabsorption occurs in the large intestine, not the small intestine. Infection of *H. pylori* in the small intestine is thus less likely to impact water reabsorption in the large intestine, making choice A the best answer choice.

Passage 10 (Questions 53-56)

53. **D is the best answer.** According to paragraph one, celiac disease is a disease of the small intestine, which is responsible for receiving chyme from the stomach, adding digestive enzymes, and absorbing monomers of various macronutrients. Glucose is a carbohydrate monomer, which would be absorbed by the microvilli of the small intestine, which are blunted in celiac disease. Choice A can be eliminated. Sodium and calcium are both ions that are absorbed in the ileum of the small intestine. Microvilli blunting would decrease the surface area available for absorption, eliminating choices B and C as the best answer. Water is primarily reabsorbed in the large intestine. Because celiac disease is a small intestine disease, not a large intestine disease, water homeostasis would be least affected, making choice D the best answer.

54. **C is the best answer.** According to the question stem, gluten is a mix of complex proteins. Proteins are strings of amino acids linked by peptide bonds and need to be broken down by enzymes in the gut before they are absorbed as amino acid monomers in the small intestine. α-amylase is found in the mouth and helps to break down carbohydrates into smaller polysaccharides and monosaccharides. It does not break down proteins, eliminating choice A. Trypsinogen is a zymogen, meaning it is an inactive form of an enzyme. Many of the pancreatic enzymes are released in zymogen form to prevent damaging the pancreatic cells that produce and secrete them. In its inactive form, trypsinogen would not able to cleave proteins, eliminating choice B. Lipase is the enzyme responsible for breaking down fats, not proteins, eliminating choice D. Pepsin is a protease operating in the stomach that breaks down larger proteins into amino acids that can be further broken down and absorbed in the small intestine, making choice C the best answer. Pepsinogen is its zymogen and is produced in the stomach and activated by the low pH of gastric juice. It is responsible for activating the other zymogens released from the pancreas.

55. **B is the best answer.** According to Figure 1, the cells at position zero are stem cells, which are also found in dark grey towards the bottom of the intestinal crypts. Stems cells are undifferentiated cells that have a nearly unlimited ability to proliferate and produce cells that can migrate and differentiate into epithelial cells, Paneth cells, and other cell types. Epithelial cells are differentiated cells that are responsible for absorbing most molecules in the gut but are not stem cells, eliminating choice A. Paneth cells are cells that produce molecules that help defend the gut epithelium against pathogens like bacteria and viruses. Paneth cells are also differentiated and do not have the ability to further proliferate to a great extent, eliminating choice C. Epithelial cells are also responsible for absorbing cholesterol and fats, eliminating choice D. One of the features of stem cells is that they have the ability to divide to create daughter cells that can differentiate into many other cell types, making choice B the best answer.

56. **A is the best answer.** The gallbladder is responsible for storing bile salts, which are produced by the liver. Once chyme, the mixture of partially digested food and gastric juices, exits the pyloric sphincter at the end of the stomach, it enters the first part of the small intestine, the duodenum. Bile salts and bicarbonate from the pancreas help to neutralize the acid and being to solvate fats, which can be absorbed later in the small intestine. Peristalsis, also known as coordinated contraction, of the esophagus helps move food from the mouth to the stomach but is not directly responsible for stimulating gallbladder contraction, eliminating choice B. The arrival of food, as well as hormones like gastrin and histamine, encourage the release of acid from the parietal cells of the stomach. The acid helps to begin breaking down food macromolecules but does not lead to gallbladder contraction, eliminating choice C. Lipase is the enzyme responsible for breaking down larger fats into smaller molecules. Delivered by the pancreatic duct, lipase breaks down the fats in the micelles formed by the bile salts but does not directly cause gallbladder contraction, eliminating choice D. The arrival of chyme in the duodenum stimulates the release of the hormone cholecystokinin, which causes the gallbladder to contract and release bile salts into the small intestine, making choice A the best answer. This answer also makes the most sense as the arrival of chyme in the duodenum is exactly when bile salts would be needed.

Stand-alones (Questions 57-59)

57. **D is the best answer.** Consider the major functions of the large intestine. These should all be impaired if a significant portion of this organ is removed. The major functions of the large intestine are water absorption and electrolyte absorption. These would both be impaired following a colectomy (removal of the colon). Options I and II are likely to be the best answer. Next, certain vitamins, like K and B12, are produced by bacteria in the large intestine and absorbed there as well. Option III is also true, so choice D is the best answer.

58. **B is the best answer.** Consider what role ions play in restoring the glucose levels of this person. The patient would like to maximize glucose absorption in the intestines. The key to answering this question is recognizing which ion is cotransported across the intestinal membrane with glucose. This ion is sodium, so choice B is the best answer. Glucose transporters move both sodium ions and glucose across the membrane for absorption, so adding sodium to the solution facilitates glucose transport and absorption. None of the other listed ions are directly involved in transport or absorption of glucose, so choices A, C, and D are unlikely.

59. **D is the best answer.** The thoracic duct is the major route by which lymph rejoins blood circulation. This is important to fat absorption because fatty acids are absorbed by lacteals in villi. These lacteals are lymph vessels, and to reach the liver to be processed, the fats must pass through the thoracic duct. Longer fatty acids, like those in choices A, B, and C, use this lacteal pathway. This is because their long hydrophobic chains are unable to dissolve in blood. The absorption of these would be impaired, making these choices unlikely to be part of the best answer. Choice D is a short chain fatty acid based on the number of carbons that valeric acid has. These fatty acids are polar enough due to short tail length and can directly diffuse into blood from the inside of the intestinal lining cell. Therefore, choice D is the best answer.

LECTURE

The Digestive and Excretory Systems

MINI-TEST 5B

ANSWERS & EXPLANATIONS
Questions 1–41

Passage 1 (Questions 1-4)

1. **B is the best answer.** Bile is produced in the liver and stored in the gallbladder. In response to chyme entering the duodenum, the gallbladder contracts to release bile through a series of ducts into the duodenum to emulsify the fat present and allow for breakdown and absorption of this nutrient. Without a gallbladder, the liver will continue to produce bile, eliminating choice A. Following a cholecystectomy, there would no longer be an organ in which to store the bile, making choice B a strong answer. Because bile can still be synthesized by the liver, the body still has the capacity to emulsify fats in the duodenum, eliminating choice C. The breakdown of proteins relies on the release of various proteases from the stomach and pancreas. Removal of the gallbladder should not impact the pancreatic secretion of proteases, so choice D is not a strong answer and can be eliminated. Based on the above analysis, choice B is the best answer.

2. **D is the best answer.** Bile is stored in the gallbladder and released through a series of ducts in response to food in the duodenum. Bile first moves through the cystic duct, then into the common bile duct, and finally through the hepatopancreatic ampulla before being released into the duodenum. Pancreatic enzymes are released into the pancreatic duct, which also empties into the duodenum via the hepatopancreatic ampulla. Therefore, if a bile stone were to become lodged in the hepatopancreatic ampulla, both bile and pancreatic enzymes would fail to enter the duodenum and exert their effects. It would be expected that there would be defects in fat breakdown due to a lack of pancreatic lipase, so option I is true, and choice C should be eliminated. Option II is true because this blockage would also lead to a defect in protein degradation due to a lack of pancreatic proteases, such as trypsin. Because choices A and B do not included option II, they can be eliminated. Finally, option III is true as carbohydrate degradation would be impaired due to a lack of pancreatic amylase. All three options are true, leaving choice D as the best answer.

3. **C is the best answer.** This question requires knowledge of one of the major pancreatic secretions, bicarbonate. The pancreas is responsible for producing bicarbonate in order to neutralize the acidic pH of the food bolus as it moves from to stomach to the small intestine. Therefore, changes in pancreatic function can disrupt the normal production of bicarbonate. Without bicarbonate, the pH in the duodenum will decrease. Choice A can be eliminated because a decrease in pancreatic activity would lead to less bicarbonate production and a lower duodenal pH. Choice B can be eliminated because, according to Table 1, the control population has a <1% rate of chronic pancreatitis. Choice C is a strong answer because decreased pancreatic activity could lead to limited bicarbonate production in these individuals. This finding would explain a low duodenal pH. Choice D can be eliminated because although reduced bicarbonate production would lead to a decreased pH, this would most likely not result from increased pancreatic activity.

4. **A is the best answer.** The liver is responsible for production of a variety of proteins included albumin, thrombin, fibrinogen, and globulins. Choice A is a strong answer because albumin is a protein that is responsible for carrying free fatty acids within the blood. Both thrombin and fibrinogen are synthesized by the liver and serve important roles in the blood clotting cascade. Despite the fact that they are found in the blood, they are not responsible for the transport of fatty acids in the blood, so choices B and C can be eliminated. Globulins are a group of proteins that are produced by the liver and have various functions. However, they are generally not responsible for transport of fatty acids, so choice D can be eliminated, leaving choice A as the best answer.

Passage 2 (Questions 5-8)

5. **B is the best answer.** The HFD has more fat than the standard diet, so the best answer to this question is the organ involved primarily in fat metabolism. The stomach is involved in acid secretion and mixing of food, but it would not have increased activity to a higher fat content of food. Choice A can be eliminated. The colon is primarily involved in water and electrolyte balance rather than fat absorption, so choice C can be eliminated. Trypsin is an enzyme that degrades protein rather than fat, so choice D can be eliminated. The gallbladder stores bile acids, which are necessary for fat digestion, and would be more active in the HFD compared to the standard diet. The gallbladder would be more actively introducing bile acids into the small intestine in response to the HFD. Choice B is the best answer.

6. **C is the best answer.** Secretin signaling stimulates the pancreas to increase secretion of bicarbonate and causes decreased gastric H^+ secretion. If this signaling were interrupted, a new source of base, or an inhibition of acid secretion would be necessary to prevent damage due to lowering of the pH in the intestines. Insulin is involved in glucose metabolism, and would not have a major effect on the acid/base balance of the GI tract, so choice A can be eliminated. Ipragliflozin primarily affects glucose transport at the kidneys well after it has been absorbed and would be expected to have little effect on the GI tract, so choice B can be eliminated. Gastrin promotes H^+ secretion of the stomach, which would exacerbate the problem of lacking bicarbonate, so choice D can be eliminated. The carbonate ion is a weak base that is a great buffer, so administration of calcium carbonate would help to offset the lack of bicarbonate secretion due to interrupted secretin signaling. Choice C is the best answer.

7. **D is the best answer.** Ipragliflozin is a sodium-glucose transporter inhibitor, meaning that it most likely resembles glucose with additional functional groups. Choice A is an inhibitor that has a fructose substrate, which can be inferred from the furan in the middle of the molecule. Glucose in its ring form is a pyranose, so choice A can be eliminated. Choice B is thyrotropin-releasing hormone (TRH), which is a modified tripeptide rather than a modified glucose. This makes choice B unlikely. Choice C is sucrose, a naturally occurring disaccharide. While it does contain glucose, it is unlikely that a naturally occurring disaccharide would inhibit a critical transporter in biological systems. In fact, sucrose is broken down and absorbed in the GI tract. Choice D is the best answer, as it contains a modified glucose molecule that would likely function as an inhibitor of a glucose transporter.

8. **C is the best answer.** Paragraph two mentions that in obesity, triglycerides accumulate in both adipose tissue and the liver. It can be inferred that both high fat diets would have higher liver weight than the standard diet. Choice B can be eliminated, since the HFD/control should be higher in weight than the SD/control. The final paragraph and Figure 1 provide information to determine whether the control or ipragliflozin would have a higher weight. Figure 1 shows that the ipragliflozin has a higher frequency of larger adipocytes, while the final sentence states that there is an inverse relationship between liver and epididymal fat. Since epididymal weight was increased with ipragliflozin, liver weight should be reduced. This means that the ipragliflozin-treated mice would have a lower liver weight than that of the HFD/control mice, making choice C the best answer.

Passage 3 (Questions 9-12)

9. **D is the best answer.** Vitamin D, along with vitamins A, E, and K, are fat-soluble vitamins that can only be absorbed after being made soluble in the gut. The bile salts that are released into the small intestine are responsible for solubilizing the fat-soluble vitamins. The gallbladder is the storage site for bile salts. Damage to the gallbladder that would prevent bile salts from exiting into the small intestine would decrease vitamin D absorption , making option I a component of the best answer. The ileum is the location of the small intestine that is responsible for absorbing bile salts, meaning that damage to the ileum would hinder absorption, regardless of the presence or absence of bile salts. This makes option II a component of the best answer. The liver is the site of production of bile salts. Damage to the liver that would decrease bile salt production would decrease vitamin D absorption, making option III a component of the best answer. Choice A can be eliminated because damage to both the ileum and liver would hamper vitamin D absorption. Choice B can be eliminated because bile salt production and storage involve the liver and gallbladder, respectively. Choice C can be eliminated because the ileum is the site of absorption of solvated vitamin D. Choice D is the best answer because it contains the options that correspond to production, storage, and absorption of bile salts that solvate the fat-soluble vitamins A, D, E, and K.

10. **A is the best answer.** According to the last paragraph, vitamin D is essential for proper absorption of calcium in the gut. Calcium is one component of bones that gives bone compressive strength and is also key to the proper functioning of neurons and muscle cells. Decreased synthesis of vitamin D would impair absorption of calcium, leading to lower than normal levels of circulating Ca^{2+}. PTH, parathyroid hormone, is released in response to decreased levels of calcium. Deficient synthesis of vitamin D would impair absorption of calcium, likely raising PTH levels in the blood to maintain calcium homeostasis. This means that exocytosis of PTH from the parathyroid cells would increase, making choice A a strong answer. Calcitonin acts to decrease blood calcium levels when circulating calcium is too high. Because circulating calcium would be too low in vitamin D deficient patients, choice B is the opposite and can be eliminated. GH, growth hormone, stimulates the lengthening of bone and other metabolic processes related to growth. The link between GH and vitamin D is not discussed in the passage, making it less likely to be the best answer. Additionally, if circulating levels of calcium were too low, it would likely prevent, not stimulate, the release of GH, as the necessary building blocks for bone would not be present. Prolactin is a hormone that induces the formation of milk in breast tissue and is not related to vitamin D, eliminating choice D, and leaving choice A as the best answer.

11. **A is the best answer.** While this experimental question seems detailed and specific, the key to answering this question lies in knowing how water-soluble and fat-soluble metabolites are eliminated from the body. Nearly all small molecules that are water soluble are filtered into the proximal convoluted tubule of the kidney. Excess ^{19}F-1-α-25(OH)$_2$D$_3$ is likely to be filtered here, making choice A a strong answer choice. The transverse colon of the large intestine is not responsible for eliminating any particular molecules but is primarily responsible for water reabsorption, eliminating choice B. The jejunum of the ileum is the primary site of mixing of bile salts, chyme, and digestive enzymes released from the pancreas. It does not play a role in excretion, but it instead serves to prepare molecules for absorption in the ileum. This eliminates choice C. The common hepatic bile duct runs from the liver to the gallbladder, the main site of storage of bile. The liver helps to remove metabolites that are fat-soluble, meaning those that cannot travel through the blood and be eliminated in the kidney. Choice D can be eliminated, leaving choice A as the best answer.

12. **D is the best answer.** The key difference between vitamin D and folate is that one is fat-soluble and one is water-soluble. Fat-soluble molecules are able to concentrate in hydrophobic environments, while water-soluble molecules are able to concentrate in hydrophilic environments. The absolute concentration is not important but rather the relative ratio of fat-soluble vitamin D to water-soluble folate in each tissue. The gallbladder is the storage of bile, which solvates fats and other hydrophobic molecules. Vitamin D should be in higher concentration here, eliminating choice A. The collecting duct of the kidney is where water soluble metabolites would be concentrated, meaning that the concentration of folate would be higher than vitamin D. This eliminates choice C as the best answer. The blood is an aqueous environment that should have higher levels of hydrophilic molecules like folate compared to hydrophobic molecules like vitamin D. Both plots B and D show higher levels of folate, meaning that the concentration in the adipocyte, or fat cell, will help determine the best answer. Vitamin D should accumulate in the high-fat environment of vacuoles within fat cells that store lipids. This makes choice D more likely than choice B to be the best answer because choice D shows a much higher concentration of vitamin D in the adipocyte.

Stand-alones (Questions 13-16)

13. **C is the best answer.** The filtrate passes through a series of subdivisions of the nephron. First, blood is delivered to the glomerulus. Then it passes through the proximal tubule, through the loop of Henle, and then through the distal tubule. The filtrate then makes its way to the collecting duct. The answer choice that provides the correct order is choice C. Choice A can be eliminated because the loop of Henle is not the first location where the filtrate passes nor does it precede the glomerulus. Choice B can be eliminated because the distal tubule does not precede the loop of Henle. Choice D can also be eliminated because the loop of Henle does not precede the proximal tubule.

14. **A is the best answer.** Glucose is reabsorbed in the proximal convoluted tubule (PCT) of the nephron of the kidney. Glucose would travel from the afferent arteriole to the glomerulus to Bowman's capsule to the PCT. The last component of the nephron the glucose would travel through would be Bowman's capsule, making choice A a strong answer. The glomerulus is before the Bowman's capsule, eliminating choice B. Glucose never travels through the loop of Henle, as it is absorbed at the proximal convoluted tubule, eliminating choice C. The afferent arteriole is before the glomerulus, eliminating choice D.

15. **B is the best answer.** Because this patient is dehydrated, he or she would be expected to produce concentrated urine by reabsorbing water in the collecting ducts following ADH signaling. Choice A would be the normal response to dehydration by the kidney, but since the medulla is at a lower salt concentration than normal, water will not be drawn out of the tubule resulting in more dilute urine than would be expected given the hydration status, making it a weaker choice. Choice B addresses the fact that the urine will remain dilute (low osmolarity). Because supplemental ADH does not improve the kidney's ability to concentrate the urine, the kidney is either unable to respond to ADH, or the action of aquaporins is insufficient. In this case, the increase in membrane aquaporins yields no change in urine concentration because the medullary gradient is no longer present to draw the water out of the filtrate. This makes choice B a strong answer. The descending limb of the loop of Henle is highly permeable to water, but impermeable to ions. Choice C states that ions would passively diffuse out of this portion of the kidney, which makes this a weak choice. The amount of sodium that is filtered by the glomerulus is related to renal blood flow. As long as the pressure in the glomerulus remains the same, changes in the medulla will not affect the filtration rate, making choice D a weaker choice than choice B.

16. **A is the best answer.** The loop of Henle has two portions, the descending and ascending limbs, which are both in the medulla. The descending limb is permeable to water but impermeable to ions. The opposite is true for the ascending limb and its ion transporter will be targeted by the drug mentioned in the question stem. The normal role of this transporter is to pump sodium, potassium, and chloride ions out of the filtrate and into the medulla. By inhibiting this function, the osmolarity of the medulla will be lowered which will decrease the ability of the collecting duct to reabsorb water or produce a highly concentrated urine, making Choice A a strong answer. Because this transporter reabsorbs ions from the filtrate, if it is inhibited, more sodium will be delivered to the collecting ducts and excreted, which is the opposite of Choice B. Choice C confuses the role of the transporter and implies that it acts to secrete ions into the filtrate. Choice C is essentially the opposite of Choice A and is a weaker answer. Choice D correctly states that the normal osmolar gradient will not be formed, but it attributes this failure to an increase in the amount of water in the medulla rather than a decrease in the amount of ions that are pumped into the medulla, which makes it a weaker choice. Choice A is the best answer.

Passage 4 (Questions 17-20)

17. **A is the best answer.** This question requires knowledge of the nephron, and the cortex and medulla of the kidney. Remember that the medulla is always the inner region of an organ (for instance the adrenal medulla) and the cortex is the outer layer. The renal corpuscle, proximal tubule, and distal tubule are in the cortex, while the loop of Henle and the collecting duct are in the medulla. In the experiment, netrin-1 was induced in proximal tubular epithelial cells (TKPTS). The proximal tubule is located in the cortex, so choices B and C can be eliminated. Filtration of blood in the kidneys occurs in the renal corpuscle which contains the glomerulus. This structural information does not allow elimination of choice A or D, since they are both correct. The location of the renal corpuscle is in the cortex, not the medulla, so choice A is the best answer.

18. **B is the best answer.** This question requires following the filtrate through the nephron as it would normally flow, starting with the glomerulus. After the glomerulus comes the proximal convoluted tubule, where netrin-1 is induced. It would then flow through the descending limb of the loop of Henle, to the ascending limb, and to the distal convoluted tubule. Remember that the juxtaglomerular apparatus connects renal corpuscle and the beginning of the distal convoluted tubule. Finally, the filtrate flows to the collecting duct before being excreted in the urine. Of the choices listed, the first structure that would be encountered by netrin-1 from TKPTS cells would be the thick ascending limb, making choice B the best answer.

19. **D is the best answer.** This question requires synthesis of the passage information and experiment data. Figure 1 shows that urine netrin-1 increases while mRNA decreases. This does not allow elimination of any answer choices yet. Figure 2 shows that pervanadate increases netrin-1 production. Figure 3B shows that inhibitors of kinases can reduce the amount of netrin-1 produced in the presence of pervanadate. Kinases phosphorylate amino acids, so this means that when specific phosphorylation is inhibited, netrin-1 translation is reduced. Choice D summarizes this result and is the best answer. While SB203580 causes increased netrin-1, this is only the case in the experiment. The question asks for increased urine netrin-1 after kidney injury, where the inhibitors added by the researchers are likely not present, so choice A can be eliminated. Choice B is tempting since mRNA is reduced when netrin-1 production is increased, however there is no support for this causal relationship given in the passage. Choice C can be eliminated since reabsorption would reduce, not increase, the amount of urine netrin-1.

20. **A is the best answer.** First eliminate answer choices that are not kinases. UNC5A-D is described in the first paragraph as a receptor for netrin-1. This is not explicitly a kinase and there is no indication that it affects netrin-1 production, so choice B can be eliminated. U0126 is described as a kinase inhibitor, rather than a kinase, so choice C can be eliminated. Figure 3B shows the relative effects of inhibiting a kinase in the pathway of netrin-1 production. Since the inhibition of ERK lowers netrin-1 production more than the inhibition of p38, ERK will have a greater effect. Choice D can be eliminated leaving choice A as the best answer.

Passage 5 (Questions 21-25)

21. **C is the best answer.** The osmotic gradient in the medulla is created by the counter current in the loop of Henle, and dysfunction in this would be more indicative of a problem here than a problem in the glomerulus. Choice A can be eliminated. Dysfunction in the absorption and excretion of glucose molecules would be more likely to be an issue in the proximal convoluted tubule, not the glomerulus, eliminating choice B. The glomerulus filters blood via small pores known as fenestrations, allowing smaller molecules to travel into the filtrate but blocking larger molecules like proteins and blood cells. In a healthy glomerulus, protein should be blocked from entering the filtrate by the small size of the fenestrations, so protein content in the urine would indicate glomerular dysfunction by increasing size of the pores, making choice C a strong answer. Urine volume is more likely to be affected by the loop of Henle, not the glomerulus, eliminating choice D.

22. **D is the best answer.** According to Figure 2, with increased concentration of insulin, there is increased transcription of the protein SGLT2. With increased SGLT2, a transport protein in the proximal convoluted tubule, there would be increased reabsorption of glucose and decreased urine concentration of glucose. The best answer should correlate an increase in insulin with a decrease in urine glucose excretion. As both Choice A and Choice B display the opposite phenomenon, they can be eliminated. According to the passage, NAC is an inhibitor of insulin, and would therefore likely reverse the effect of insulin on filtrate glucose concentration. Choice C displays the presence of NAC compounding the effect of insulin, with even less glucose in the filtrate, and can be eliminated. Choice D displays both insulin reducing the presence of glucose in the filtrate as well as NAC reversing the effect of insulin, and is the best answer.

23. **B is the best answer.** Frequency of urination increases in patients treated with RE due to an increase in the osmolarity of the filtrate due to an excess of glucose molecules. This increase in frequency of urination is called polyuria. Increased concentration of the filtrate causes decreased difference in the difference in osmolarity between the descending loop of Henle and the medulla of the kidney. Less water is reabsorbed into the bloodstream due to the decreased osmotic gradient, increasing frequency of urination. Increased osmolarity of the filtrate should cause increased water excretion, eliminating choice A. The increase in glucose in the filtrate causes less water reabsorption in the loop of Henle, making choice B a strong answer. While electrolyte excretion and absorption is not affected by RE, glucose can still affect water volume in urine, eliminating choice C. While frequency may or may not be affected by excess glucose in the urine, volume will definitely be affected, eliminating choice D.

24. **B is the best answer.** The primary effects of remoglifozin administration occur in the proximal convoluted tubule, a section of the nephron located in the cortex of the kidney. Remoglifozin does not affect electrolyte absorption, eliminating choice A. As all glucose absorption occurs in the proximal convoluted tubule (PCT) in the cortex of the kidney, choice B is a strong choice. As the filtrate moves away from the glomerulus, it moves away from the PCT, eliminating choice C. Finally, the vasa recta are primarily found in the medulla of the kidney, and as RE does not affect electrolyte absorption and thus the loop of Henle, the vasa recta would likely be less affected than the PCT. Choice D can be eliminated.

25. **A is the best answer.** The question sets up an experiment measuring the effect of RE on sodium absorption in the nephron. According to Table 1, RE has no significant effect on the excretion of any of the electrolytes in a healthy individual. The amount of sodium absorbed should be the same in the results for any of the doses of RE in a healthy patient. The loop of Henle creates an osmolarity gradient in the medulla by pumping salt out of the ascending loop and absorbing water out of the descending loop. Thus, in a normal individual the amount of sodium reabsorbed by the blood should be greatest in the ascending loop, and lowest in the descending loop. Because RE should have no effect on the absorption of sodium in the loop of Henle, both choices B and C can be eliminated. In choice A, the amount of sodium absorbed in the ascending loop is greater in all cases than in the descending loop, which based on the former conclusions about sodium absorption and the passage's conclusions on the effects of RE is a strong answer. Choice D represents the opposite of choice A, and because more sodium should be absorbed in the ascending loop than the descending loop, choice D can be eliminated.

Stand-alones (Questions 26-28)

26. **B is the best answer.** In order for urine to be released from the body, several steps must occur. In order to expel urine, the bladder needs to contract. This is the opposite of what is stated in choice A, eliminating this answer. Unless voiding, the bladder keeps the urethra closed by contracting the urinary sphincter muscle. During urination, the urinary sphincter muscle relaxes, and the bladder contracts to release the urine. Therefore, choice B would promote the release of urine, while choice C would prevent the release of urine. The ureter is the structure that carries the contents of the renal pelvis to the bladder. Contraction and relaxation of this structure does not contribute to control of urination, therefore, choice D can be eliminated, leaving choice B as the best answer.

27. **B is the best answer.** A meal with a large amount of sodium will ultimately cause an increase in the concentration of sodium in the blood. The kidney can respond to sodium levels by adjusting the amount of sodium that is reabsorbed in the distal portions of the tubule system. With an elevated blood sodium, less sodium will be reabsorbed which contradicts choice A, making it a weak answer. Higher plasma levels of sodium will be sensed by the brain which will release ADH. This signal will result in the insertion of aquaporins into the collecting duct and an increase in water reabsorption, which makes choice B a strong answer. Since the ADH secretion is expected to be enhanced, choice C is a weak answer. Monitoring of the sodium concentration in the filtrate is performed by the juxtaglomerular apparatus. When sodium is low, renin is released in an attempt to raise blood pressure and increase the GFR. Since the concentration of sodium is expected to be high in the proposed situation, renin would not be expected to be released, eliminating choice D. Choice B is the best answer.

28. **D is the best answer.** The glomerular capillaries are fenestrated, meaning there are small pores that allow for bulk flow across into the Bowman's capsule. This is called filtration, and the fluid that exits will be filtered and altered to finally become urine. Meanwhile, blood cells and plasma proteins are generally retained. Because filtration occurs by passing through these fenestrations, reduction of fenestrations would reduce filtration. Choices A and B can be eliminated for this reason. Decreased filtration is the result of decreased, not increased, permeability across the capillary wall. Fewer fenestrations means less filtrate can and will cross the membrane into the Bowman's capsule. Choice D is the best answer.

Passage 6 (Questions 29-33)

29. **A is the best answer.** Angiotensin II plays many roles in the regulation of blood pressure through its effects on various organs. Angiotensin II is able to stimulate sympathetic activity, leading to vasoconstriction and increased blood pressure. As choice A is the opposite of increasing sympathetic activity, it is most likely the best answer. An increase in tubular sodium reabsorption comes at the expense of potassium excretion, as sodium is absorbed through a sodium/potassium exchanger. Choice B can be eliminated. Angiotensin II also stimulates the release of aldosterone from the adrenal cortex, eliminating choice C. The arteriolar vasoconstriction seen with RAS activation helps to increase and maintain a higher blood pressure, eliminating choice D.

30. **D is the best answer.** In addition to collecting segment and collecting duct renin excretion as detailed in the passage, renin is also secreted from other segments of the kidney in response to decreases in renal perfusion. The descending loop of Henle is responsible for water reabsorption, not renin secretion, eliminating choice A. The thin and thick ascending loops of Henle are impermeable to water and ions, except sodium, potassium, and chloride. In the thin ascending loop of Henle, sodium and chloride cross by diffusion, while in the thick ascending loop of Henle, sodium, potassium, and chloride are actively reabsorbed. The ascending loop of Henle does not play a primary role in renin secretion, eliminating choices B and C. The juxtaglomerular apparatus contains specialized cells that sense perfusion of the kidney and synthesize and secrete renin in response to decreased perfusion. Damage to this area would most likely decrease circulating renin levels, making choice D the best answer.

31. **C is the best answer.** Medications that are used to control blood pressure and circulating sodium levels also have an impact on the levels of circulating potassium, which can lead to failed homeostatic control of blood circulation. Decreased heart rate implies that cardiac activity has decreased. High potassium levels hyperpolarize cardiac muscle, making an action potential less likely to occur, ultimately resulting in fewer contractions per minute. Angiotensin-receptor agonists would activate the absorption of sodium and the excretion of potassium in the collecting duct, which would result in lower, not higher, blood potassium levels. Option I can be eliminated. Angiotensin-converting-enzyme inhibitors would lower the levels of angiotensin II, leading to less reabsorption of sodium and increased retention of potassium, which could result in hyperpolarization of the cardiac muscle. Option II is part of the best answer. Aldosterone also stimulates the reabsorption of sodium and the excretion of potassium. A competitive inhibitor of aldosterone would decrease its efficacy, leading to decreased sodium reabsorption and decreased potassium excretion. Option III is a component of the best answer. Choice C is the best answer, as it includes options II and III, but not option I.

32. **B is the best answer.** The additional experiment shows that glomerular filtration is reduced by CD renin. According to the last sentence of the passage, the authors suggest that CD renin may work by impairing nitrous oxide synthesis and activity. NO plays a role in vasodilation and the effect of vasodilation in the kidney is more often pronounced at the efferent arteriole. A greater increase in diameter of the efferent arteriole would decrease the pressure in the blood vessels in the glomerulus, leading to decreased glomerular filtration and retention of more sodium in the blood. The authors suggest this occurs through an Angiotensin-II independent manner, indicating that active sodium reabsorption is not the main mediator of the increased blood sodium levels. Remember that, normally, angiotensin II leads to aldosterone secretion, which increases sodium re-uptake in the collecting duct. The authors do not conclude that CD renin decreases sodium absorption, especially because CD renin increases the expression of sodium channels, eliminating choice A. With more sodium in the blood due to decreased initial filtration, the collecting segment and duct would have less sodium it needed to actively reabsorb, leading to retention of potassium. Choice B is most likely the best answer. Choice C can be eliminated, as it is the opposite of the best answer, choice B. The authors imply that CD renin does alter the levels of sodium in the blood, though not to the extent of juxtaglomerular renin does. This eliminates choice D as the best answer.

33. **C is the best answer.** Figure 1 shows that renin expression is lower in KO mice compared to controls pre-DOCA treatment and equivalent to controls upon DOCA treatment. The effect of CD renin on angiotensinogen activity is not depicted in Figure 1, as neither the activity of the enzyme nor the concentration of angiotensin-II is measured. This makes choice A less likely to be the best answer. Knock out of the renin gene in the CD leads to decreased renin expression, not increased renin expression, eliminating choice B. Notice that the expression of renin is comparable between the control and KO mice under DOCA treatment. This indicates that renin expression from the CD likely does not contribute greatly to hypertension, as the renin levels are equivalent between control and KO mice upon DOCA treatment in Figure 1. Choice C is most likely to be the best answer. WT mice should be able to secrete renin in response to low sodium levels, as the passage does not imply that WT mice have a defect of any sort. This eliminates choice D.

Passage 7 (Questions 34-38)

34. **D is the best answer.** One purpose of the bladder is to store urine until elimination. Bladder contraction falls under the control of the parasympathetic, sympathetic, and somatic nervous system. The elimination of urine falls under the "rest-and-digest" half of the autonomic nervous system, making option I a component of the best answer. The sympathetic nervous system helps relax the bladder and allow it to fill, storing urine before elimination, and making option II a component of the best answer. The somatic nervous system serves as the final control for urine elimination. It is responsible for preventing the uncontrolled release of urine from the bladder, making option III a component of the best answer. As options I, II, and III, describe control over urine elimination and storage, choice D is most likely to be the best answer.

35. **C is the best answer.** In the additional experiment conducted by the scientists, an increase in urea concentration led to an increase in NO concentration. Because the passage does not assess the relative risk of cancer at various concentrations of NO or urea, choice A is less likely to be the best answer. Scientists have only measured the concentration of urea, NO, and UT-B in the bladder, not in the cells that line the collecting duct of the kidney or the ureter, making choice B less likely to be the best answer. According to the urea cycle, the nitrogen in the arginine amino acid may be used in one of two ways. The nitrogen may be used to create NO, which mediates vasodilation, or the nitrogen may be eliminated via urea. The nitrogen is preferably eliminated via urea. As the concentration of arginine increases, the NO concentration also increases, suggesting that there is a defect in the urea elimination pathway, as the excess nitrogen in arginine should be eliminated as urea, not NO. This makes choice C most likely to be the best answer. The scientists do not provide evidence that NO or any other free radicals increase the risk of urothelial cancer. While this may be true, the additional experimental evidence does not support this conclusion, eliminating choice D.

36. **A is the best answer.** UT-B, according to the passage, is responsible for the movement of urea across the cellular membrane. In addition to the bladder and kidney, the liver is also responsible for eliminating nitrogenous waste, making choice A most likely to be the best answer. The pancreas is responsible for secreting digestive enzymes, bicarbonate, and hormones that regulate blood glucose levels. It is not responsible for controlling the concentration of urea in the blood, eliminating choice B. The adrenal glands secrete cortisol and mineralocorticoids that control the circulating levels of stress hormones and sex steroids. The adrenal gland is not primarily responsible for controlling blood urea concentrations, eliminating choice C. Cardiac muscle is responsible for creating the rhythmic contractions of the heart but not the control of nitrogen elimination, making choice D less likely to be the best answer. Choice A is the best answer.

37. **B is the best answer.** UT-B is responsible for transporting urea out of the bladder back into the interstitial space, decreasing the concentration of urea in the bladder. Urea is a weak base and serves to raise the pH of the urine. Deficiency of UT-B would keep levels of urea artificially high in the bladder, leading to a higher pH, not a lower pH. Acidification is a lower pH, eliminating choice A and making choice B most likely to be the best answer. As the concentration of urea would increase in the bladder compared to individuals with normal levels of UT-B, a change in pH would most likely occur, eliminating choice C. As with choice A, increased urea concentrations in the bladder would lead to increases in pH, not decreases, eliminating choice D. Choice B is the best answer.

38. **C is the best answer.** The kidney is primarily responsible for the permanent removal of soluble nitrogenous waste. The ascending loop of Henle is responsible for the reabsorption of sodium and potassium, but not urea, eliminating choice A. The distal convoluted tubule does assist in reabsorbing ions that were not first absorbed in the proximal convoluted tubule. However, most reabsorption occurs in the proximal convoluted tubule, making choice C more likely than choice B to be the best answer. Urea is freely filtered in glomerulus and around 50% is reabsorbed in the proximal convoluted tubule of the kidney, along with many other freely filtered ions, glucose, and amino acids. This makes choice C most likely to be the best answer. The descending loop of Henle helps to reabsorb water, but it is not the main site of urea reabsorption, eliminating choice D. Choice C is the best answer.

Stand-alones (Questions 39-41)

39. C is the best answer. Sodium and potassium are two of the main electrolytes of the blood and their absorption is heavily regulated by the kidney and large intestine. Their absorption is primarily regulated by the movement of water in the kidney and large intestine, eliminating choices A and B, respectively. Magnesium is primarily reabsorbed in the loop of Henle in the kidney and occurs by paracellular diffusion that is not impacted by vitamin D levels. Thus, choice D can be eliminated. Vitamin D is made and altered in many locations throughout the body and undergoes an important reaction in the skin upon exposure to light. The modified vitamin D is then able to help increase the absorption of calcium and phosphate, which are the raw building materials of bone. Decreased levels of vitamin D are thus likely to impair the reabsorption of phosphate, making choice C the best answer choice.

40. C is the best answer. Urine is concentrated in the collecting duct when ADH is present. ADH increases the permeability of the collecting duct to water, so water can flow out as the filtrate goes down the collecting duct. The reason that this can occur is due to the corticopapillary osmotic gradient, meaning the osmolarity surrounding the nephron increases as the nephron descends into the medulla. This allows water to continue to diffuse out as the filtrate descends into the medulla and eventually is excreted. The osmotic gradient is created by the counter-current multiplier effect, which occurs in the loop of Henle, not the collecting duct. Choices A and B can be eliminated. Choice D can be eliminated since concentration of urine does occur in the collecting duct. Choice C correctly describes the cause of concentration of urine.

41. C is the best answer. Ions are filtered out of the blood and into Bowman's space and are first reabsorbed at the proximal convoluted tubule. The proximal convoluted tubule reabsorbs around 67% of the sodium that is filtered. The distal convoluted tubule reabsorbs little sodium, around 5%, eliminating choice A. The thick ascending loop of Henle is able to actively reabsorb about 25% of the filtered sodium, eliminating choice B. The main site of ion reabsorption is the proximal convoluted tubule, making choice C most likely to be the best answer. The collecting duct generally reabsorbs the least amount of sodium at around 3% or less, eliminating choice D. Knowledge of the exact percentages is not necessary for the MCAT®, but it is important to know where the majority of reabsorption takes place. As the filtrate flows through the excretory system, it first passes through the proximal tubule, which is where most reabsorption should take place, given the high ion concentration and active reabsorption. As it continues to flow through the excretory system, less sodium would be present to reabsorb, so it makes sense that more distal sites would reabsorb less sodium than more proximal sites.

LECTURE

6

Muscle, Bone and Skin

TEST 6A

ANSWERS & EXPLANATIONS
Questions 1–59

LECTURE 6 ANSWER KEY

TEST 6A		MINI-TEST 6B	
1. A	31. C	1. A	22. C
2. B	32. D	2. C	23. B
3. A	33. B	3. D	24. A
4. A	34. D	4. B	25. C
5. D	35. B	5. A	26. A
6. B	36. A	6. D	27. B
7. C	37. A	7. D	28. B
8. D	38. D	8. A	29. D
9. B	39. C	9. D	30. A
10. B	40. D	10. C	31. A
11. B	41. B	11. A	32. D
12. C	42. C	12. C	33. A
13. D	43. B	13. A	34. B
14. A	44. D	14. A	35. A
15. A	45. C	15. C	36. C
16. B	46. B	16. C	37. A
17. C	47. D	17. A	38. D
18. C	48. A	18. A	39. C
19. D	49. A	19. A	40. A
20. A	50. A	20. A	41. A
21. B	51. D	21. D	
22. D	52. C		
23. B	53. A		
24. D	54. C		
25. C	55. A		
26. A	56. D		
27. D	57. A		
28. D	58. D		
29. D	59. B		
30. C			

EXPLANATIONS FOR LECTURE 6

Passage 1 (Questions 1-4)

1. **A is the best answer.** Figure 1 and paragraph three help provide information necessary to answer this question. According to paragraph three, PQQ has been a promising agent to treat muscle loss due to denervation because it helps control the redox state of the cell. The redox state is the balance of oxidative molecules, like reactive oxygen species (ROS) and reducing molecules that help keep the cytosol at a particular oxidation state. Additionally, Figure 1 shows that PQQ blocks the cellular damage caused by ROS, helping to prologue the life of the muscle cell. A denervated muscle cell would show less acetylcholine in the neuromuscular synapse because it would have fewer neurons synapsing to it, eliminating choice B. Calcium, not sodium, is responsible for muscle contractions, eliminating choice C. Demyelination of peripheral nervous system neurons by damage to Schwann cells could be one mechanism of causing muscle atrophy. The passage, however, does not discuss demyelination at the main cause, instead focusing on the metabolic and intracellular redox state as the key to muscle cell survival. Choice D is less likely to be the best answer for this reason. An increase in reactive oxygen species would change the redox state of the cell, allowing for protein damage that could cause the cell to die. PQQ helps balance this increase in ROS to decrease their harmful effects. Choice A is the best answer.

2. **B is the best answer.** The neuromuscular junction is comprised of the axon terminal of a neuron and the muscle plasma membrane. Remember that an agonist acts like the natural substrate for a receptor and would activate the receptor, while an antagonist blocks the action of the receptor. Acetylcholine is the main neurotransmitter that allows for depolarization of the muscle cell and spreading of the action potential through the T tubules to allow calcium to enter the muscle. Nicotinic acetylcholine receptors are found in the central nervous system neurons. Nicotinic receptor agonists could increase the firing of these neurons, allowing the peripheral neuron synapsing with a muscle to release more ACh into the synaptic cleft, eliminating option I from the best answer. An acetylcholinesterase inhibitor would block the breakdown of acetylcholine, increasing the local concentration of ACh in the neuromuscular junction, eliminating option II from the best answer. A muscarinic receptor antagonist would block the effects of ACh at the neuromuscular junction, preventing the muscle cell from undergoing action potentials and making option III part of the best answer. Choice A can be eliminated because a nicotinic receptor agonist would improve muscle function. Choice C can be eliminated because both a nicotinic receptor agonist and an acetylcholinesterase inhibitor would stimulate muscle contraction. Choice D can be eliminated be an acetylcholinesterase inhibitor would stimulate muscle contraction. Choice B is the best answer because a receptor antagonist would resemble the effects of denervation, likely making symptoms worse for the patient.

3. **A is the best answer.** According to the first paragraph, type I muscle fibers are used for muscles that contract slowly and are not easily fatigued. Type II muscle fibers can contract quickly but often are unable to sustain quick contractions for an extended period of time. The triceps and biceps act as an opposite pair. When the triceps contracts, the biceps relaxes and vice versa. Both are able to use oxygen efficiently and contract quickly, as they are skeletal muscle, making choices B and C less likely to be the best answer. The gluteus maximus is also a skeletal muscle that helps control the movement of the legs, making choice D less likely to be the best answer. In general, skeletal muscle is more likely to be type II in order to generate quick muscle contractions. The diaphragm is a slow contracting muscle that determines the rate of breathing. It does not become easily fatigued, making choice A the best example of a type I fiber.

4. **A is the best answer.** This question asks about the organization of muscle. The smallest unit of organization is the myofibril, which bands together to form fibrils, which band together to form a fasciculus. According to Figure 2, denervated muscle has the smallest cross sectional area, followed by denervated muscle that has been treated with PQQ, followed by control muscle that is still innervated. The cross sectional area of all three levels of organization should be smaller in the denervated than the denervated treated with PQQ. Additionally, all three levels of organization should be smaller in the denervated treated with PQQ than the control. Choice B can be eliminated because the fiber width should be smaller in the denervated muscle. Choice C can be eliminated because the control muscle should have a greater myofibril width than denervated muscle. Choice D can be eliminated because the control muscle should have a greater fasciculus diameter than denervated muscle treated with PQQ. Choice A is the best answer because it reflects that treated denervated muscle should have a greater with than denervated muscle alone.

Passage 2 (Questions 5-9)

5.   D is the best answer. The question is asking for which fiber type is predominant in the skeletal muscle fibers used in this experiment. Based on the information in Figure 2, the most predominant type of muscle fiber in the skeletal muscle used in the experiment was Type IIa fibers. Type II fibers, also known as fast twitch, are quick to fatigue due to a relative lack of mitochondria. Type I fibers, or slow twitch fibers, are slow to fatigue, rich in mitochondria, and are red in color. Choice A describes a trait of type IIb fibers; however, the white appearance is caused by lack of myoglobin, not calcium. Choices B and C both describe characteristics of type I fibers, and can thus be eliminated. Thus, choice D must be the best answer. If two choices are saying the same thing, they are either both correct or both incorrect, and should be considered together. Two answer choices that say the same thing are more likely to both be incorrect than both be correct.

6.   B is the best answer. The question is asking first for the function of DHPR in the cell, which can be found in the information in the passage. DHPR is a protein on the t-tubules that allows the release of calcium. During a typical muscular contraction, first, the presynaptic neuron releases neurotransmitter into the synapse. The neurotransmitter then activates ion channels in the sarcolemma, causing depolarization of the membrane. The action potential on the sarcolemma is propagated into the muscle through the t-tubules, where the DHPR protein is located. Any stage of muscular contraction following the depolarization of the sarcolemma at the t-tubule would be inhibited by dysfunction of DHPR, and thus any choice referring to a process after this point could be used to display the activity of the protein. As DHPR is a protein on the sarcolemma associated with action potentials, it would change the ion concentration due to its activity, thus eliminating choice A. Choice B, release of the neurotransmitter into the synapse, would still occur even if DHPR was dysfunctional, making this choice the best answer. Muscular contraction is the last stage, and thus would be inhibited by faulty DHPR, eliminating this choice. Finally, the calcium ions causing the conformational change of troponin is stimulated by the activity of DHPR, and thus choice D can be eliminated.

7.   C is the best answer. The question is asking for the type of innervation common in skeletal muscle fibers as well as the way that an impulse is transmitted from a neuron to a muscle cell. Skeletal muscle is innervated by the somatic nervous system, and thus choices A and B can be eliminated. In contrast, cardiac and smooth muscle, both involuntary, are primarily innervated by the autonomic nervous system. Neurotransmitters such as ACh or norepinephrine are released into the synapse to pass an electrical impulse from the presynaptic neuron to the target muscle tissue. The question asks which type of neurotransmitter is used by the somatic nervous system. Acetylcholine, a neurotransmitter, is used by both the somatic nervous system and the parasympathetic nervous system. In addition, ACh is used by the preganglionic synapse of the sympathetic nervous system. Norepinephrine, on the other hand, is used by the sympathetic nervous system at the postganglionic synapse. Choice D can be eliminated, making choice C the best answer.

8.   D is the best answer. The question is asking for an understanding of the different process calcium is involved in muscle contraction. Choice A can be eliminated, as it describes a characteristic that would display a differential use of ATP. Choice B can be eliminated, as it would display differences in the handling of acetylcholine. Choice C can be eliminated, as it would add information about structural differences. Only choice D would give further information about the role of calcium in muscle contraction, as the proteins tropomyosin and troponin are regulated by calcium.

9.   B is the best answer. The question is asking both for a general interpretation of the graphs displayed as well as knowledge of the distinctions between smooth, skeletal, and cardiac muscle cells. The graph of a muscle fiber displays a distinct repetitive arrangement showing regions of increased proteins and regions of relative absence the graph of myotubes does not display. Thus, one can expect the answer choice might have to do with some kind of spatial arrangement unique to skeletal muscle. Choice A is less likely, as calcium proteins are not evenly dispersed throughout skeletal muscle. It could be misleading, however, as it represents one interpretation of the graph given of myotubes. Choice B is more likely, as it describes the unique striated pattern of skeletal muscle. Choice C is less likely, as intercalated discs are a unique characteristic of cardiac muscle. Choice D is also not the best answer, as it is information outside the scope of the graphs given.

Passage 3 (Questions 10-13)

10. **B is the best answer.** Of the many conditions depicted in Figure 1, maximum tetanic force is of greatest relevance to this question. A muscle achieves physiological tetanus when it receives impulses in rapid succession, preventing complete contraction-relaxation cycles. The force produced at maximal tetanus can be used to categorize different muscles based on fiber type. Option I should be included in the best answer because EDL produced the greatest force at muscle fatigue for both untreated and treated mdx mice. Given that the EDL produces the greatest force at muscle fatigue, one can infer that it is composed mostly of Type II fibers and can eliminate any choices that include option III. This eliminates choices C and D. Option II should also be included in the best answer because Type II fibers not only produce greater force than Type I fibers, they also have a faster contractile velocity and are less resistant to fatigue. Although choice A meets the fast contractile velocity criteria, it can be eliminated because it does not refer to the EDL's force production. Choice B is the best answer because it covers both the fast contractile velocity criteria and states that the EDL produces the greatest force.

11. **B is the best answer.** The passage states that DMD rarely affects women due to the *dystrophin* gene's location on the X chromosome, implying an X-linked recessive pattern of inheritance. A woman with a mutant copy of the dystrophin gene would have the sex genotype XX*, where X* denotes the chromosome with the dystrophin mutation. The man with DMD would have a sex genotype of X*Y. A mating between the two may yield the following genotypes: X*X, X*X*, XY, and X*Y. The possibility of a DMD genotype for progeny of either sex eliminates choice A. The probability of having a child of either sex is 50% each. Out of the two possible progeny genotypes for each sex, one yields a DMD genotype. Therefore, there is a 50% chance that the couple would have son with DMD and a 50% chance they would have a daughter with DMD. Since both matings are independent, the probability of having both a son and a daughter with DMD can be calculated using the "AND RULE." $0.50 \times 0.50 = 0.25$, making choice B the best possible answer. The question specifies the probability of the couple having both a son and daughter with DMD. Choice C can be eliminated because there is a 50% chance that any child would have Like choice A, choice D may be eliminated due to the possibility of having healthy children of either sex.

12. **C is the best answer.** Figure 2 is a Western blot analysis of Nav1.5, a sodium channel, and Cx40, a gap junction protein among untreated dystrophic mice, treated dystrophic mice, and untreated wild type mice. Western blots detect the relative expression levels of protein where a darker band indicates a higher concentration of protein than a lighter band. The expression of Nav1.5 is significantly higher in untreated wild type mice than in untreated mdx mice, whereas the opposite is true of Cx40 expression. According to the passage, choice A, cardiomyopathy, is often seen in patients with DMD. Choice A can be eliminated because it does not relate to the results of the experiment. Choice B can be eliminated because it is a symptom related to skeletal muscle and cannot be deduced from measurements of cardiac proteins. As a sodium channel and gap junction protein, Nav1.5 and Cx40, respectively, are important components of the heart's electrical conduction pathway. Therefore, a difference in protein levels among dystrophic mice is most likely to disrupt normal electrical conduction and lead to arrhythmia, making choice C the best possible answer. Although choice D, like choice A, is explicitly stated as a symptom of DMD in the article, it can be eliminated because it does not relate to the results of the experiment.

13. **D is the best answer.** The sarcolemma is the skeletal myocyte equivalent of a plasma membrane and should not be confused with the sarcoplasmic reticulum or sarcomeres. Choice A can be eliminated because it describes the sarcoplasmic reticulum, an smooth ER derived organelle that is responsible for increasing the intramuscular concentration of calcium upon innervation. Choice B can also be eliminated because it too describes the sarcoplasmic reticulum, albeit erroneously as a specialized form of the rough ER. Choice C describes a sarcomere, which is composed of alternating strands of thick and thin filaments that can be visualized as striations in skeletal and cardiac muscle. Choice D is the best answer because it describes T-tubules, which are infolded regions of the sarcolemma that allow action potentials to uniformly spread to all regions of the muscle cell.

Stand-alones (Questions 14-17)

14. **A is the best answer.** Norepinephrine is used by the sympathetic nervous system, so a poison blocking its release would inhibit any process requiring the activity of the sympathetic nervous system. Choice A represents the primary responsibility of the sympathetic nervous system, fight of flight, and is the best answer. The esophagus is composed of smooth muscle, which is innervated by both parasympathetic and sympathetic nerves. Peristalsis is a process representative of the primary functions of the parasympathetic nervous system, or "rest and digest", and thus uses acetylcholine. Choice B can be thus eliminated. Choices C and D are both processes occurring in skeletal muscle, which are both controlled by the somatic nervous system using ACh and would be unaffected. Thus, both of these choices can be eliminated.

15. **A is the best answer.** There are several different types of muscle contraction. During concentric contraction, the muscle shortens. Eccentric contraction involves the muscle lengthening. Isometric contraction on the other hand involves no change in muscle length. Choice A involves the muscle fibers in the legs increasing in force but maintaining a constant length as there is a weight that cannot be moved. Choice A is a good answer. Pushups are a dynamic motion, so it is unlikely that muscle length remains constant. This is the case for choices C and D as well. Remember that the issue here is not whether a maximal weight is used or a weight that can be repeated multiple times as in the case of the pushups. Choices B, C, and D are unlikely, and choice A is the best answer.

16. **B is the best answer.** According to the question stem, a nerve toxin blocks the post-synaptic acetylcholine receptor on the muscle. If the ACh receptor is engaged on a muscle cell, calcium is able to flood out of the sarcoplasmic reticulum to initiate a muscle contraction. However, if the receptor is blocked by a toxin, preventing the ACh from binding, an action potential would not be reached, eliminating choice A. It is unlikely that the toxin saturates every single post-synaptic receptor to prevent any change in membrane voltage. This makes choice B a better answer choice than choice C, as some depolarization would occur, but not enough to trigger an action potential. There is no indication that the toxin opens channels that would allow potassium to flow out of the cell, eliminating choice D, which represents hyperpolarization.

17. **C is the best answer.** Choice A is likely to cause motor defects because a dysfunctional acetylcholinesterase enzyme would prevent degradation of acetylcholine and would result in constant stimulation at the neuromuscular junction. This would lead to stiff muscles initially but as the ion concentrations in the muscle become altered, the muscles would become flaccid. Choice B is also not the best answer because a nonsense mutation, which would likely truncate titin, would be catastrophic to the structure of skeletal muscle fibers, which require the protein to anchor myosin. Choice C indicates a defect in a structure found in smooth muscle, which while important to the body, does not impact mobility. Choice D would cause a loss of mobility because efferent neurons are responsible for carrying nerve impulses to the muscle.

Passage 4 (Questions 18-21)

18. **C is the best answer.** This question requires an understanding of the organizational structure of a muscle. A myofibril is a collection of myosin and actin inside a multi-nucleated muscle cell called a muscle fiber. The satellite cell is a differentiated muscle stem cell, according to the passage, and would likely contribute both intracellular components like myosin and actin, as well as plasma membrane components that surround the fibers, nuclei, sarcoplasmic reticulum, and other intracellular organelles. Contribution of intracellular proteins makes option I a component of the best answer, while contribution to the plasma membrane makes option II part of the best answer. As the satellite cell contributes some plasma membrane components, it also likely contributes to the T-tubule system, a network of invaginated plasma membrane that helps disperse an action potential evenly across the muscle. A muscle fascicle is a collection of muscle fibers. While the satellite cell contributes directly to the muscle fiber, it does not directly add or repair a muscle fascicle, making option III less likely to be the best answer. Choices A and B can be eliminates, as both options I and II are components of the best answer. Choice C is the best answer, as it contains both options I and II, eliminating choice D, which contains option III.

19. **D is the best answer.** In Experiment 1, the researchers use cardiotoxin to induce muscle death. Upon administration of cardiotoxin, the expression of *SIK1* rises, indicating that the muscle is damaged, and is unlikely to contribute heavily to the normal functions attributed to skeletal muscle. Smooth muscle, not skeletal muscle, surrounds arteries and veins and contributes to vasodilation and vasoconstriction that help regulate body temperature. This eliminates choice A. Skeletal muscle does play a role in helping move lymph back to the circulatory system. However, muscle that has high expression of *SIK1* is likely damaged and unable to perform its normal function, eliminating choice B. Similar to helping return lymph to the circulatory system, the skeletal muscle also functions in moving blood through tissues, eliminating choice C, as muscle with high expression of *SIK1* is damaged. Muscle that is damaged is unlikely to respond to neuronal input and may have reduced connections to the nervous system until the damaged muscle is repaired. This makes choice D the best answer.

20. **A is the best answer.** T-tubules are invaginations of the plasma membrane that help to transmit an action potential at the neuromuscular junction evenly across the width of the muscle fascicle. If the T-tubule network is distorted, the action potential will not reach each point of the muscle in a coordinated manner, prevent smooth contraction, and making choice A most likely to be the best answer. As the muscle is less likely to contract after damage with cardiotoxin, less calcium, not more calcium, would be released from the sarcoplasmic reticulum, eliminating choice B. Tetanus is a state of constant contraction, stimulated by repeated action potentials that occur very close in time. Damaged muscle is unlikely to respond to neural stimulation and the distortion of the T-tubule network makes it even less likely that parts of the muscle will contract. Without undergoing repeated contraction, tetanus would not occur, eliminating choice C. A relaxed state of a muscle is when it is not contracting. Damaged muscle will be unable to contract, making it more likely that it remains in a relaxed state, eliminating choice D and making choice A the best answer choice.

21. **B is the best answer.** The answer choices are all components of the sarcomere, the contractile unit of the muscle. Increased expression of a gene would imply that more protein product was being formed to help heal the damaged muscle. The sarcomere with the greatest concentration of both actin and myosin would most likely gain the greatest density compared to the other sections. The M line represents the middle of the myosin thick fiber segment and would be expected to increase in density as more myosin protein is added to repair the muscle fascicle. The A band represents the overlap between myosin and actin, where the motor action will pull the two Z lines closer together. As more actin and myosin would be added to this same region, the density would increase more than that of the M line, making choice B a better answer choice than choice A. The Z line is the border of the sarcomere, where the actin fibers are bound. It would not be expected to change in density, as the Z line is primarily made up of the cell membrane, eliminating choice C. The I band is the region of actin on either side of the Z line, before interacting with myosin. An increase in density would be expected as the actin polymers were rebuilt, but the density increase would not be as dramatic as would be seen in the A band, making choice B a better answer choice than choice D.

Passage 5 (Questions 22-26)

22. **D is the best answer.** Each type of skeletal muscle fiber is specialized for different tasks. Type I muscle fibers are slow twitch and slow to fatigue, useful for endurance. Type I fibers are red in color due to an abundance of myoglobin. Type II fibers are quick to contract and to fatigue, useful in sprints. The muscle group most useful in sprinting would be type II fibers, which are white in color, eliminating choices A and C. The fibers most useful in sprinting would contract a quicker velocity, eliminating choice B. The fibers most used in sprinting would be white in color and quick to contract, making choice D the best answer.

23. **B is the best answer.** Experiment One is measuring the effect of two different types of exercise (LC and CE) and the administration of a nutritive essential amino acid (EAA) drink on total body protein flux. A control experiment is typically intended to minimize the effects of other variables besides the independent variable on the dependent variable. The type of exercise and presence of protein supplementation were independent variables in this experiment, and the amount of protein flux was the dependent variable. Assessing the effect of the control drink during LC and CE exercise on cortisol, a hormone involved in the physiological stress response, is unrelated to the experiment one. Option I can be eliminated. Introducing a control drink that contains no protein administered at the same increments of time as the EAA would be able to display that EAA is causing the changes in net protein breakdown and synthesis. The compound responsible for arresting muscular contraction in the absence of ATP is tropomyosin, which covers the active sites on the actin filament in the absence of calcium. Tropomyosin is a protein in the sarcomere, and would be representative of this experiments' dependent variable, protein flux, making option II a strong answer. Option III represents a control experiment that would display the difference between the types of exercise, regardless of the addition of the drink. However, the molecule responsible for initiating skeletal muscular contraction could be either acetylcholine or calcium, in either case, not a protein. Thus, this would not be representative of the experiment's dependent variable, eliminating option III.

24. **D is the best answer.** Skeletal muscle has many functions. First, skeletal muscle aids in circulation of blood throughout the body, as contracting skeletal muscle helps squeeze both blood and lymph through their respective vessels. Blood flow is assisted in flowing to peripheral tissue, eliminating choice A. In addition, skeletal muscle helps in regulating body temperature, as skeletal muscle can contract to generate heat in a process called the shivering reflex, eliminating choice B. Chylomicrons are transported from the intestines to veins via the lymphatic system, as triglyceride particles packaged this way are too large to be absorbed into the intestinal capillaries. Skeletal muscle aids in squeezing lymphatic vessels, which would aid in transport of chylomicrons throughout the body, eliminating choice C. Smooth muscle is the primary type of muscle that would affect the maintenance of pressure in vasculature. Though skeletal muscle does have some effect on the pressure of the vasculature through its assistance in blood flow, this is least relevant compared to the other choices. Choice D is the best answer.

25. **C is the best answer.** Experimental muscle was skeletal muscle, which differs from cardiac in that it is voluntary muscle, not involuntary. Voluntary muscle is consciously controlled, and is able change both the speed and strength of contraction, eliminating choice A. Involuntary muscle is not consciously controlled; however, the speed of the contraction can still be altered. Both the parasympathetic and sympathetic nervous system can increase or decrease heart rate, eliminating choice B. When stimulus from outside is removed, cardiac muscle can still contract due to the presence of the SA and AV nodes. Skeletal muscle will cease to contract without outside nervous stimulus, making choice C a strong answer. Both cardiac and skeletal muscle will grow stronger due to repeated contraction, a process known as hypertrophy, eliminating choice D.

26. **A is the best answer.** The graph displays that the addition of EAA increased protein synthesis in the muscle groups when compared to the control, and LC exercise increased protein synthesis over the control (CON). The functional unit of skeletal muscle, the sarcomere, is composed of several different protein fibers, including myosin, actin, troponin, and tropomyosin. An increase in muscle protein synthesis in skeletal muscle would increase the number of sarcomeres, increasing myofibril size. Increased myofibril size through increased protein synthesis would likely lead to increased contractile strength of the muscle fiber, making choice A a good answer. LC increases protein synthesis when compared to the control, increasing the strength of contractions of the muscle fiber, eliminating choice B. Muscle fatigue is caused by a lack of oxygen molecules in the muscle fibers; while performance of LC or CE might cause a decreased susceptibility to fatigue, the information that would confirm this hypothesis is not included in the graph given in this question. Increased muscle protein content would have no effect on the susceptibility to fatigue, eliminating choices C and D.

Stand-alones (Questions 27-30)

27. **D is the best answer.** The question is asking for which drug would exacerbate the effects of a loss of the receptor proteins on the postsynaptic muscle cell. Choice A would mitigate symptoms, as it would suppress the antibodies that are responsible for the disease. Choice B would also mitigate symptoms, as it would cause acetylcholine (ACh) to stay in the postsynaptic space for a longer period of time, increasing the odds that it would bind to the remaining receptors. Choice C would also counteract the effects of the disease, as it would cause more membrane proteins to be created, counteracting the destruction inflicted by the antibodies. Finally, choice D is the best answer, as it is the only choice that would make the symptoms of the disease worse by making it even less likely that ACh would bind to postsynaptic proteins.

28. **D is the best answer.** Muscle contraction requires two important molecules, ATP and calcium. ATP hydrolysis into ADP + P_i allows myosin to bind tightly to actin, triggering the muscle power stroke when the two contact. Calcium allows the myosin/actin binding site of be open after calcium binds troponin C. Gluconeogenesis is the building up of glucose, not the breakdown of glucose. Gluconeogenesis requires ATP, which would lower the intracellular ATP available for muscle contractions, eliminating choice A. Ketolysis is the breakdown of ketones. The brain and red blood cells are able to break down ketones but they do not provide a significant source of energy for skeletal muscle, eliminating choice B. Glycolysis produces 2 net ATP per glucose molecule broken down in comparison to ≈ 32-34 ATP per molecule of glucose in oxidative phosphorylation. Because oxidative phosphorylation is more efficient at ATP production, it provides the primary source of ATP, making choice D the best answer over choice C.

29. **D is the best answer.** Following exercise, there is an oxygen debt created when the intake of oxygen is not sufficient for the quantity of ATP being consumed by the muscles. Some anaerobic ATP production occurs and results in a buildup of lactic acid. After exercise lactic acid is transported to the liver through the bloodstream and requires oxygen to be metabolized back to glucose via the Cori cycle. Due to the oxygen demands for lactic acid metabolism, respiratory rate increases even after cessation of exercise. Choice A is not likely because nearly all strenuous exercise will create an oxygen debt. Choice B is not likely because free radicals are usually bound or neutralized by antioxidants and then excreted, not exhaled. The first portion of choice C is correct, respiratory rate does increase, but carbon monoxide is only found in the blood after prolonged inhalation of combustion products, such as during a fire. Carbon dioxide is the byproduct of oxidative phosphorylation found in the blood so choice C is a weaker answer. This leaves choice D, which is the best answer, because the liver will create primary elevated demand for oxygen in order to metabolize lactate left over from exercising.

30. **C is the best answer.** Myelin is the fatty sheath that wraps around neurons to insulate them and allow them to transmit action potentials via saltatory conduction. Saltatory conduction allows an action potential to skip between the nodes of Ranvier, where it is regenerated and propagated down the neuron. Oligodendrocytes myelinate central nervous system neurons, not peripheral nervous system neurons, eliminating choice A. Decreasing the number of sodium channels would decrease the likelihood that an action potential would fire at all but would not change the speed of the action potential moving along the axon of a neuron, eliminating choice B. Acetylcholine (ACh) release into the synaptic cleft causes depolarization in the dendrites of the postsynaptic neuron. Increased ACh release due to more vesicles would increase the chance that the postsynaptic neuron would fire but would not change the velocity of the action potential down the axon, eliminating choice D. Schwann cells myelinate peripheral nervous system axons. A decrease in the number of Schwann cells would lead to lower myelination and slow the action potential, making choice C the best answer choice.

Passage 6 (Questions 31-35)

31. C is the best answer. Calcium is regulated generally in order to keep blood levels normal. This is done through parathyroid hormone, which moves calcium from the bone to the blood, and calcitonin, which causes deposition of calcium into bone. High calcitonin would most likely increase bone density, and would definitely not cause a reduction in bone density, so choice A in unlikely. Next, high blood calcium levels are unlikely to occur in a person that is low on calcium, as indicated by low bone density. Choice B can be ruled out. Vitamin D is required for calcium absorption through the digestive system, so vitamin D deficiency could potentially be a cause of reduced bone density. Spongy bone is the type of bone surrounded by compact bone. Though it may sound right, as the name spongy bone suggests low density, these types of bone are distinct, and bone density loss does not necessarily increase the amount of spongy bone. Though choice C is far from a certainly, vitamin D deficiency is a common cause of bone density loss, and is the only choice that makes sense in this case.

32. D is the best answer. Choices A and B focus on the lean and fat mass of individuals. The table shows no difference in total lean body mass and total body fat mass. This might hint towards choice A. However, this is actually not a conclusion that can be drawn as these values are for the whole body. Additionally, the passage states that loss of muscle is most dramatic in the lower limbs. Perhaps, there is compensation due to greater use of upper limbs. There is also no evidence to support choice B, making it unlikely. Choice C is challenging. There is loss in CSA of all skeletal muscle fiber types. However, remember that cardiac muscle is also striated. There is no data presented regarding cardiac muscle, so choice C can be ruled out. Choice D is the best answer because repetitive, forceful contractions cause muscle fibers to hypertrophy, or increase in size and CSA. This would counteract the reduction in CSA shown in Table 1.

33. B is the best answer. Myelin sheaths are key components of many axons in the nervous system. They are maintained by oligodendrocytes and Schwann cells. These structures insulate the projections from the soma of a neuron. There are also gaps between sheaths called nodes of Ranvier. Action potentials can jump from node to node in a process called saltatory conduction. This speeds up the conduction of the action potential to the next cell. Demyelination removes the possibility of performing this kind of propagation, making choices A and C unlikely. Next, since myelin sheaths allow for faster conduction, choice B is a better answer than choice D. Demyelination, or destruction of myelin sheaths, reduces conduction velocity.

34. D is the best answer. This question is really asking about activities associated with individual types of skeletal muscle. The passage shows that CSA is most reduced in type I fibers. These are slow oxidative fibers. Type I fibers use aerobic metabolism, produce a low amount of force, but do not fatigue and can be used for a very long time. Since these fibers are most significantly lost, these kinds of activities are likely to be most impaired. Choice A is a possibility, as swimming can be a long, aerobic activity. Weight lifting is a high intensity, short duration activity. This is more likely to depend on type IIb fibers, which are fast glycolytic fibers that contract quickly, generate a lot of force, and fatigue quickly. Sprinting is similar in that type II fibers will be most important. Choices B and C are unlikely. A long distance bike race is even more of a long duration activity, especially since long distance is specified. Thus, choice D is a better answer than choice A.

35. B is the best answer. Each individual muscle fiber is one cell. This study measured cross-sectional area of fibers, not the whole muscle. Thus, they were measuring individual cells, and researchers observed that the CSA of individual fibers was reduced in MS. This indicates that individual cells are smaller. No conclusions can be drawn about cell division, and skeletal muscle cells do not generally divide, so option I can be ruled out. Option II is likely, as actin is one of the key components of muscle fibers. Reduced synthesis would reduce the thickness or CSA of fibers. Lastly, option III is unlikely because the H zone within a sarcomere has more to do with the length than CSA. This is the area with only thick filament, and reduces in size during muscle contraction. Choice B is the best answer.

Passage 7 (Questions 36-39)

36. A is the best answer. In order for a trait to contribute to lower skin temperature, it must act to rid the body of heat, not conserve it. Dilated peripheral vasculature, option I, would increase the amount of blood in surface capillaries and increase the amount of heat available to radiate from the body to the surrounding environment. Option I would cause decreased surface skin temperature, making it a strong answer. Shivering, or rapid contraction of skeletal muscle, breaks down ATP in an exothermic process primarily used by the body to generate heat. Stronger skeletal muscle would increase the body's ability to produce heat, but not to lose it, eliminating option II. Contraction of the hair erectile musculature would create a layer of heat trapped against the outside of the skin, elevating the surface temperature, not lowering it, eliminating option III. Choice A, I only, is the best answer.

37. **A is the best answer.** According to Figure 1, participants with a higher VO$_2$ max produced sweat more quickly than those with a lower VO$_2$ max. VO$_2$ max is a measure of cardiovascular fitness, or the strength of cardiac muscle in the heart and the vasculature. Both cardiac and smooth muscle are considered involuntary, as they are not under conscious control. Stronger involuntary muscle, or stronger cardiac muscle, would lead to muscular hypertrophy, not multiplication. In other words, stronger muscle cells increase in size, not number. Larger muscle, or higher VO$_2$ max, would correlate with more sweat production, making choice A a strong answer. Larger muscle, or higher VO$_2$ max, would not correlate with less sweat production, eliminating choice B. The figure shows that stronger muscle, or higher VO$_2$ max, is correlated with a quicker AXR1 time, or speed to begin sweating. More voluntary muscles does not necessarily equate to stronger muscles, eliminating choices C and D.

38. **D is the best answer.** According to the passage, iontophoresis is a method of drug administration where an electric field is used to cause a medication to move through the skin without use of an injection. In this experiment, QSART was used to apply ACh to the nerve endings around eccrine sweat glands in the dermis. Keratin, a waterproofing protein, is produced primarily in the epidermis, not the dermis, eliminating choice A. All nerve endings are found in the dermis, not the epidermis, eliminating choice B. While blood vessels responsible for cooling skin temperature are found in the dermis, these vessels would not have had an effect on this experiment, as the primary goal was to measure changes in sweat production. Choice C can be eliminated. Eccrine sweat glands, the glands primarily targeted in this experiment, are found in the dermis, not the epidermis. In order to determine the effect of ACh on sweat production, the drug would have had to penetrate the epidermis, making choice D the best answer.

39. **C is the best answer.** The quantitative sudomotor axon reflex test (QSART) is a device used in this experiment to measure the effect of iontophoresed ACh on the sweat glands of the dermis in trained and sedentary individuals. The stratum corneum is the outermost layer of the epidermis, composed entirely of dead cells. There are no blood vessels, sweat glands, or nerve endings here, and choice A can be eliminated. The stratum spinosum is the fourth layer of the epidermis, which again contains no blood vessels, sweat glands, or nerve endings, eliminating choice B. The dermis is composed of connective tissue and contains the sweat glands, blood vessels, sensory organs, and nerves, and is a strong answer. The hypodermis is a layer of fatty tissue important in thermoregulation and insulation, but contains no sweat glands, and choice D can be eliminated.

Passage 8 (Questions 40-43)

40. **D is the best answer.** According to the passage, NEMS reduces the number of SK3 channels. This would counteract the effect of DM1, allowing muscles to relax and therefore reducing the length of time needed for calcium to reenter the SR. NEMS would not affect the symptoms of CM patients, whose myotonia is primarily caused by C1CN1. Therefore, the best experiment must have NMES as the independent variable, the length of time needed for calcium to reenter as the dependent variable, and a comparison between patients with SK3 and C1CN1. Choice A would keep NEMS constant, and therefore would not be able to display whether an increase or decrease in electric stimulation affects the symptoms of myotonia. NEMS is not used here as the independent variable, eliminating choice A. The experiment should be measuring the effect of NEMS on SK3, ideally reducing this protein channel. If the experiment keeps the amount of this channel constant, this prevents the experiment from displaying whether or not NEMS successfully changes the channel concentration. Choice B can be eliminated. Choice C has NEMS as the dependent variable, when it should be independent, eliminating choice C. Choice D presents the measuring of the length of time of calcium reabsorption with increasing use of NEMS, the appropriate dependent and independent variables. In addition, neither SK3 nor C1CN1 are held constant, allowing a fluctuation which would display whether NEMS has an effect on CM or DM1 patients. Choice D is the best answer.

41. **B is the best answer.** Muscular myotonia is defined as the inability of a muscular fiber to relax after a strong contraction. During a muscular contraction, an action potential at the sarcomere causes the release of calcium ions from the sarcoplasmic reticulum. These calcium ions attach to troponin and allow myosin heads to bind to the actin filament, allowing muscular contraction to occur. When nervous stimulus ends, calcium ions are pumped back into the SR, causing tropomyosin to again cover the active site on the actin filament and preventing the attachment of myosin heads. The mitochondria in muscular tissue produce ATP, the compound fueling muscular contraction. ATP is important in powering the attachment and detachment of the myosin heads from the actin filament. Myotonia is not primarily related to fatigue of the muscular cell due to lack of ATP, but instead to an inability to relax. This is more likely related to a continued stimulation of the muscle cell, eliminating choices C and D. If the SR was unable to release calcium ions, myosin fibers would be unable to bind to actin and the muscle would be unable to contract. If the muscle cannot contract, it will never reach the stage where it would not be able to relax, eliminating choice A. If the SR cannot reuptake calcium, myosin fibers will never stop binding to actin, or will be unable to relax. As the primary problem in myotonia is the muscle inability to relax, choice B is the best answer.

42. **C is the best answer.** The muscles in this experiment are skeletal muscle, and thus are primarily controlled by motor neurons. A motor neuron originates in the spinal cord, where a collection of cell bodies is called a nucleus. The stimulus is passed from the dendrites around the cell body along the axon to the axon terminal, where acetylcholine (ACh) is released into the synaptic cleft to stimulate the muscle. Neurons that innervate the autonomic system form collections of cell bodies outside the spinal cord, called ganglia. Somatic nerves do not have ganglia. In addition, motor neurons do not use the neurotransmitter NE, eliminating choices A. The impulse begins in the dendrites, not the ganglia, eliminating choice B. The impulse begins in the dendrites in the spinal cord, passing along the axon to the axon terminal which then releases ACh, making choice C a strong answer. The impulse begins in the dendrites, not the axon terminal, eliminating choice D.

43. **B is the best answer.** Cardiac tissue is unique in that it has voltage-gated calcium channels that allow the influx of positively charged calcium ions into muscle cells. This causes the interior of the cell to maintain a positive charge for a longer period of time, making it slower to repolarize. This characteristic of cardiac tissue is important, as it prevents the heart from beating too quickly. SK3, an abnormal channel only present in individuals presenting with DM1, allows the calcium-stimulated flow of positively charged potassium ions out of the muscle cell. This flow of positive ions out of the heart tissue would counteract the effect of preexisting calcium channels, making option I a strong answer. This also eliminates option II, the opposite of option I. The calcium channels in cardiac tissue allow increased positive polarization of cardiac tissue, slowing repolarization and slowing the beating of the heart. By counteracting these channels, a patient's heart can beat much faster than normal, making option III a strong answer. Choice B, options I and III, is the best answer.

Stand-alones (Questions 44-47)

44. **D is the best answer.** The various fiber types all serve different roles. Type I fibers are fatigue resistant, and are slow oxidative fibers. Type IIb are fast, generate a lot of force, and are very prone to fatigue. Lifting weights is a relatively anaerobic activity requiring lots of force, so the dominant fiber in the weightlifter will be type IIb. Next, long distance runners must maintain their running speed for large amounts of time, so fatigue resistant fibers will be found in high levels. This is reflected in choice D. Choice B is the opposite of this. Choice C is unlikely because the weightlifter would not have more of both types of fibers. Lastly, smooth muscle is unrelated to the activities described in the question, so choice A is a distractor.

45. **C is the best answer.** Choice A can be eliminated because measuring the number of centrally located nuclei is only useful for muscle cells that have more than one nucleus. Skeletal muscles are voluntary muscles that are innervated by the somatic nervous system. Cardiac and smooth muscles are involuntary and are regulated by the autonomic nervous system. Choices B and D can be eliminated because neither cardiac nor smooth muscle cells contain multiple nuclei. Choice C is therefore the best possible answer because knowing the location of the lone nucleus in involuntary muscle cells is not useful in measuring muscular fibrosis.

46. **B is the best answer.** Fibrous joints connect bones that are held together with connective tissue, allowing for little movement. Examples are found in the skull and connecting teeth to the mandible. The phalanges (fingers) have significant movement and choice A can be eliminated. Synovial joints allow the greatest amount of movement, and are filled with synovial fluid. These are the most common joints and include phalanges, shoulder, elbow, and others. Choice B is a strong answer, but not necessarily the best answer, so continue eliminating the remaining answer choices. Cartilaginous joints connect bones together by cartilage, allowing for slight movement. Examples are found in the pelvis and the vertebrae. Choice C can be eliminated. Ball and socket joints are a subtype of synovial joint that describe the shoulder and the junction of the femur with the pelvis. Choice D can be eliminated, leaving choice B as the best answer.

47. **D is the best answer.** Osteoblasts, cells that are responsible for building bone, come from a progenitor cell that has the ability to differentiate into multiple cell types. Osteoblasts differentiate into osteocytes once they have secreted bony matrix. They are surrounded by a bony matrix called the periosteum and help maintain the bone but do not form new bone, eliminating choice A. Erythrocytes are differentiated cells that contain hemoglobin that carry oxygen in the blood stream, eliminating choice B as the best answer choice. Leukocytes, or white blood cells like T and B cells, are also differentiated cells that help fight infections, helping to eliminate choice C as the best answer choice. Osteoblasts come from progenitor cells called osteoprogenitor cells, which can become both osteoblasts and later osteocytes, as well as osteoclasts, cells which degrade bone. This makes choice D the best answer.

Passage 9 (Questions 48-52)

48. **A is the best answer.** The question is asking for an understanding of the function of intercalated discs, which are gap junctions between adjoining cardiac muscle cells that allow action potentials to be passed along the sarcolemma across multiple cells. A gap junction is a type of cellular junction that allows small molecules and ions to flow between adjoining cells. An action potential is propagated by depolarization of a membrane due to the flow of ions from the extracellular to the intracellular space. Choice A states that intercalated discs allow the flow of ions between adjacent cells, making this the best answer. Choice B states that the junctions allow hormones to flow between cells; however, an action potential is created by ions, not hormones, and thus this choice can be eliminated. Choice C and D can be eliminated, as both place intercalated discs in the wrong membrane, whether that is the sarcoplasmic reticulum or the presynaptic membrane.

49. **A is the best answer.** According to Figure 2, CARP is most likely to be in the same region as α-actinin, a protein in the Z-line. The Z-line is the region of the sarcomere at which the actin filaments attach. The I band consists of all the regions of the sarcomere containing actin, and contains the Z-line within it. As CARP localizes to the Z-line, choice A is the best answer. Choice B, the H zone, is the region of the sarcomere containing myosin, and can be eliminated. Choice C, the A band, is the region at which myosin attaches, and can be eliminated. Choice D, the M line, is where myomesin is located, and can be eliminated.

50. **A is the best answer.** According to the passage, doxorubicin treatment is associated with mitochondrial dysfunction, heart failure, and sarcomere disarray. If the symptoms of DMD and doxorubicin are shared, the correct answer must be symptom not listed as one associated with doxorubicin in the passage. Choice A, though a tempting distractor, is the best answer; the question is asking for symptoms that are associated with doxorubicin treatment as are listed in this passage, and there is no mention of any skeletal muscle dysfunction, only cardiac. Choice B can be eliminated, as the passage lists mitochondrial dysfunction as a symptom of doxorubicin treatment, which would cause quicker fatigue due to a deficit of oxygen. Choice C can also be eliminated, as sarcomere disarray in cardiac tissue is associated with doxorubicin treatment which would cause loss of striations. Finally, choice D can be eliminated, as lack of cellular ATP due to mitochondrial dysfunction would cause ineffective binding of myosin to actin filaments.

51. **D is the best answer.** According to the passage, CARP is a regulatory protein that stimulates transcription of the filaments of a sarcomere in a cardiac cell. A component would only be correlated with the concentration of CARP if it is part of the components of a cardiac cells sarcomere. The sarcomere is composed of the thin and thick filaments as well as tropomyosin. Intermediate filaments are only found in smooth muscle cells, and would thus not be correlated with the concentration of CARP.

52. **C is the best answer.** The question asks for an understanding of the purpose of mitochondria in a muscle cell as well as how ATP impacts the sliding filament model. Each choice represents a step in the activation, binding, and detachment of the myosin head. If mitochondria are dysfunctional, there would likely be a deficit of cellular ATP. The best answer would be the answer in which the depletion of ATP would first directly affect the proper function of the myosin head, or detachment. Myosin heads are blocked from attachment to actin due to a deficit of calcium and resulting lack of conformational change of troponin, and thus choice A can be eliminated. The myosin head is converted from cocked position to the relaxed state by expelling its ADP and phosphate group. While this step would be affected by a lack of cellular ATP, it would not be the first step affected by it, as this would be the step in which binding of freshly produced ATP directly affects the contractile apparatus. As the ATP is depleted in the cell with dysfunctional mitochondria, more and more myosin heads will remain attached to the actin filaments. Additional molecules of ATP are required for the detachment of the myosin heads from the actin filament, making answer choice C the best answer. Choice D is a reiteration of Choice B, which is caused by the detachment of the ADP and phosphate group, eliminating this choice.

Passage 10 (Questions 53-56)

53. **A is the best answer.** The question asks how to counteract the enlargement in growth plates in *T/Col2* mice during development. The cause of the enlarged growth plates is demonstrated to be a reduction in the number of osteoclasts. The correct answer will be a hormone that upregulates osteoclast number and/or activity. PTH (parathyroid hormone) is released from the parathyroid gland and acts on bone and kidney to increase serum Ca^{2+}. PTH acts on osteoclasts in bone by increasing their bone-resorbing activity and stimulates their proliferation, making choice A a strong option. TSH (thyroid-stimulating hormone) is released from the anterior pituitary and acts on the thyroid gland to increase T_3 and T_4 secretion, which in turn regulates metabolism, but not bone. Choice B can be eliminated. Calcitonin is also released from the thyroid gland, in response to increased serum Ca^{2+} levels. Calcitonin reduces osteoclast activity, so choice C can be eliminated. Vitamin D increases plasma Ca^{2+} levels primarily by increasing the amount of dietary Ca^{2+} absorbed in the intestine. Although vitamin D does work with PTH on osteoclasts to stimulate bone resorption, this activity is minor and the overall effect on bone is increased mineralization. Choice D can be eliminated, and choice A is the best answer.

54. **C is the best answer.** The question requires close inspection of Figure 1B. The figure shows a statistically significant decrease in length of femur, tibia, and metatarsus in mice at 8 weeks, while no significant change in vertebra length. Figure 1 shows that eight weeks indicates that the mice are adults, so the increase in growth plate length during development is not the focus of the question. With this information, the answer choice must include a decrease in bone length, eliminating choice A. Since vertebrae showed no significant changes, choice D can be eliminated. In determining the between choice B and C, bone type and relative length must be considered. Figure 1B shows that the significant changes in bone length all occurred in long bones, and the humerus is a long bone, so it can be reasonably assumed to follow the same pattern. The figure also shows that the change in length was a 10% decrease for all bones shown, and the question stem asks for magnitude of change. The longer bone of the remaining choices, the humerus, will decrease by the greatest magnitude in *T/Col2* mice according to the passage information. Choice C is the best answer.

55. **A is the best answer.** This question can be answered by interpretation of Figures 2 and 3. Figure 3A illustrates that *T/Col2* mice have a lower number of TRAP-positive cells. The preceding paragraph defines TRAP as an osteoclast marker. Figure 3B shows that *T/Col2* mice have decreased RANKL, which upregulates osteoclastogenesis, and increased OPG, which inhibits RANKL. Mmp-13 is lower in *T/Col2* mice, which means there is less cartilage degradation. With this information, choice C can be eliminated since osteoblast activity is not demonstrated to be affected by the passage information. Choice D can be eliminated, since chondrocyte proliferation was mentioned earlier in the passage, and Figure 2 shows no significant difference in *T/Col2* mice compared to controls. Osteoclast number is explicitly shown to decrease in Figure 3A, and the decrease in RANKL reduces the creation of new osteoclasts. While osteoclast activity may increase, there is no direct support for this conclusion, so choice B can be eliminated, and choice A is the best answer.

56. **D is the best answer.** The final conclusion of the scientists, stated another way, is that abnormalities in a specific pathway in a specific cell type are responsible for the observed skeletal phenotype. Disrupting a different pathway and finding the same phenotype would indicate that TACE-EGFR is not responsible. Disrupting the TACE-EGFR pathway in a different cell type while producing the same results would indicate that it is not specific to chondrocytes, also invalidating the conclusion. Choice A shows a disruption in the TACE-EGFR pathway in a different cell type, monocytes, produces a similar phenotype. This information would weaken the final conclusion, since the chondrocyte location of the pathway appears less important. Choice B states that removing EGFR completely would result in the *T/Col2* phenotype, while choice C shows that removing TACE completely would magnify the observed effects of *T/Col2* mice. While both of these choices appear to support the scientists' conclusion, the final sentence of the first paragraph states that complete TACE or EGFR deficiency results in dead mice. Since these options are not viable, choice B and C can be eliminated. Choice D presents the situation where disruption of the TACE-EGFR pathway in a different cell type produces normal mice. This would strengthen the conclusion that the pathway in chondrocytes is responsible for the observed defects, making choice D the best answer.

Stand-alones (Questions 57-59)

57. **A is the best answer.** Bone elongation occurs at the epiphyseal plate and is under the control of a hormone called growth hormone. The adrenal glands release hormones that help control sodium, cortisol, and sex hormone levels in the blood but are not directly responsible for releasing growth hormone, eliminating choice B. The thyroid gland secretes hormones that regulate the basal metabolic rate of the body. T_3 and T_4 do not cause the elongation of bones, eliminating choice C. The parathyroid gland is necessary for regulation of circulating calcium levels. Increased parathyroid hormone (PTH) release leads to bone breakdown, not bone elongation, eliminating choice D. The hypothalamus releases growth hormone releasing hormone (GHRH), which allows the release of growth hormone (GH) from the anterior pituitary. GH acts at the epiphyseal plate to support bone elongation, making choice A the best answer choice.

58. **D is the best answer.** Damage at the primary site, assuming that this tumor is growing in the flat bones as stated in the question stem, would injure the flat bone and likely lead to fracture. Flat bones include bones of the skull, sternum, ribs, and shoulder blades; their primary function is to protect their adjacent organ(s). The pancreas sits posterior to the stomach and is not protected directly by any bones, so choice A can be eliminated. The small intestines are also in the abdominal cavity and not protected directly by any bones, eliminating choice B as well. The heart does sit in the thoracic cavity and is surrounded by the ribs, which are flat bones and thus a possible site of growth of the sarcoma, but the lungs overlie the heart and are larger in mass. Thus, choice C can be eliminated, making choice D the best answer.

59. **B is the best answer.** The yellow marrow of the bone is filled with fat cells, called adipocytes, that can release fatty acids into the blood during times of starvation. Gluconeogenesis only occurs in the liver, and to some small extent, in the kidney cortex. Because yellow marrow cannot undergo gluconeogenesis, choices A and C can be eliminated. An increase in lipolysis of stored fatty acids would allow the bone marrow fat cells to help restore energy balance to other organs during periods of starvation. This makes choice B the most likely answer. During periods of low glucose intake, cells would likely be breaking down stored energy forms, like glycogen. Increased, not decreased, glycogenolysis would be characteristic of yellow bone marrow cells, eliminating choice D.

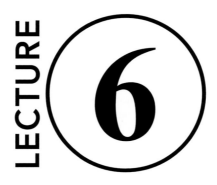

LECTURE

6

Muscle, Bone and Skin

MINI-TEST 6B

ANSWERS & EXPLANATIONS
Questions 1–41

Passage 1 (Questions 1-5)

1. **A is the best answer.** Osteoblasts are cells that promote the formation of bond by secreting collagen and other factors that ossify, or form bone, with minerals like calcium and phosphorus. The complex of these molecules is often called the bony matrix. Calcium is thus an important mineral to forming bone and glands that regulate the intracellular supply of calcium would affect the bone-forming outcome of osteoblast activity. The thyroid gland releases hormones T_3 and T_4, which serve to increase the basal metabolic rate of cells. They are not involved in regulating blood calcium or phosphorus, eliminating choice B. The adrenal gland secretes many hormones, including those that regulate cortisol, or stress hormone, levels, along with those that regulate sodium levels. Because the adrenal gland is not involved in calcium regulation, choice C can be eliminated. The pineal gland is located in the brain and releases melatonin, a hormone that regulates the sleep-wake cycle. Melatonin does not regulate calcium levels, eliminating choice D. The parathyroid gland releases parathyroid hormone (PTH), which results in the breakdown of bone to increase blood calcium levels. Because osteoblasts build bone, the stimulation of the parathyroid gland, which breaks down bone, would oppose the activity of osteoblasts, making choice A the best answer choice.

2. **C is the best answer.** In Figure 2, the overexpression of fibroblast growth factor (FGF) leads to the overexpression of *osx*. According to the passage, osx regulates osteoblast differentiation, leading to more cells that promote bone formation. An increase in the number of cells that build bone would likely increase the requirement for bone building materials, like calcium and phosphate, which make up the bony matrix in addition to products secreted directly from the osteoblast. Choice A can be eliminated because phosphate, option II, is also needed, along with calcium, to build bone. Choice B can be eliminated because magnesium, option III, is not a crucial component of the bone matrix. Choice D can be eliminated for the same reason. Choice C is the best answer choice because the bony matrix is partially made up of calcium and phosphate, options I and II, which are both absorbed in the gut and kidney. An increase in the number of cells that build bone would require an increase in the molecules that help form bone.

3. **D is the best answer.** According to the passage and Figure 1, both FGF and Wnt/β-catenin serve in the differentiation process of osteoblasts. Osteoblasts are cells that secrete protein factors that complex with calcium and phosphate to form solid bone. Once they have secreted bony matrix all around them, they cease being osteoblasts and differentiate into osteocytes, which help to maintain the bone environment but are not responsible for actively building new bone. A frameshift mutation creates a nonfunctional protein, especially when the frameshift mutation is early on in the protein, like the one described in the first exon of the question stem. Erythrocytes are red blood cells which do not differentiate from osteoprogenitor cells, eliminating choice A as the best answer choice. Osteoclasts differentiate from osteoprogenitor cells, not osteoblasts. Because Wnt plays a role in osteoblast differentiation, which eventually become osteocytes not osteoclasts, choice B can be eliminated. Osteoprogenitor cells are the stem cells of the bone that can differentiate into both osteoblasts and osteoclasts. Wnt and FGF impact the formation of osteoblast, not osteoprogenitor cells, making choice C less likely to be the best answer. Osteocytes are differentiated osteoblasts. A nonfunctional protein that prevented osteoblast differentiation would also prevent the increase in the number of osteocytes, making choice D the best answer choice.

4. **B is the best answer.** A ligament is a tough, fibrous connective tissue that forms between two bones to hold them in close proximity. The reference to chondral bone, versus achondral bone, is irrelevant to answer the question. Because a ligament connects two bones together, option I can be eliminated. A tendon connects muscle fibers to a bone via a tough fibrous connective tissue. Because a tendon also directly connects to bone, option II can be eliminated from the best answer. Muscles do not directly connect to bones but instead connect via connective tissue called tendons, making option III a component of the best answer. Choice A can be eliminated because ligaments connect bone to bone. Choice C can be eliminated for the same reason. Choice D can be eliminated because, while muscles do not directly connect to bone, tendons do. Choice B is the best answer because only muscle does not directly connect to bone, either chondral or achondral.

5. **A is the best answer.** According to the questions stem, zebrafish were treated with a molecule that activates the fibroblast growth factor receptor (FGFR). Molecules that activate receptors are called agonists and would mimic binding of the normal ligand FGF to the receptor. Increased activation of FGFR would mimic the overexpression of FGF. Using Figure 2, overexpression of FGF leads to increased expression of *osx*, which increases the building of bone by promoting the differentiation of osteoblasts. An increased number of osteoblasts would increase, not decrease, bone density, eliminating choice B. The number of bone building cells is not likely to impact the number of bones, but rather the density of the bones that do exist, helping to eliminate choices C and D as the best answer. An increased number of osteoblasts would create more bone matrix, leading to denser bone. Dense bone is important for structural support, making choice A the best answer choice.

6. **D is the best answer.** Osteolysis, breaking down the word, is a decrease in bone (osteo-) density as a result of increased osteoclast (-lysis) activity. Because bisphosphonates treat osteolysis, they should counteract the symptoms of osteolysis. It is unlikely that bisphosphonates, which treat a condition that lowers bone density, would further lower bone density. Option I is unlikely. Next, apoptosis is the organized death of cells. Osteoclast death would reduce the number of these cells that break down bone. This would help to restore bone density, making option II likely. Calcium absorption is key to bone density and extra calcium is moved from blood into bone. Option III is likely and choice D is the best answer.

7. **D is the best answer.** Option I states that PTH leads to maintenance of BMD over the two months. Based on the graph, PTH treatment leads to maintenance of BMD since there is two change in bar height over the two months in the experimental group. Option I is very likely, making choice A or D the most plausible answer. Wnt signaling promotes bone formation. Increasing bone formation can be done in two ways, by either increasing osteoblast or decreasing osteoclast activity. This makes option II very likely, and narrows down the answer to choice D. Considering option III, it contradicts the likely true option I, so choice C can be eliminated. Additionally, PTH does not increase BMD levels based on Figure 1.

8. **A is the best answer.** Red bone marrow is located in spongy bone and is the site of red blood cell development. Option I is likely because anemia is by definition a reduction in the levels of red blood cells. If the site where red blood cells develop and mature is dysfunctional, then red blood cell counts should decrease. Next, fat storage does occur in bone marrow, but this is in the yellow bone marrow, not red bone marrow. Option II is false for this reason. At this point, it is clear based on the options that choice A is the best answer. To confirm, examine option III. This is a trick answer. Spongy bone does indeed hold red bone marrow, which is affected by MM. However, there is no evidence to suggest a relationship between reduced functional marrow and a change or reduction in bone strength. This makes option III unlikely and choice A the best answer.

9. **D is the best answer.** According to the passage, the researchers used femur bones to grow tumors and model MM. Flat bones include the skull, shoulders, and sternum. These provide organ support, and choice A is unlikely. Short bones include the ankle and wrist bones, and are cuboidal in shape. These do not include the femur so choice B can be ruled out. Irregular bone is not regularly shaped and contains spongy and compact bone. Examples of this type include the bones of the middle ear, making choice C unlikely. Choice D is the best answer because the majority of bones in limbs are long bones. These include the femur in the upper leg.

10. **C is the best answer.** One important fact to remember about osteoblasts and is that they do not undergo regular mitosis. It may be helpful to remember that osteoblasts become osteocytes when they become trapped within the matrix that they secrete. Following this transformation no mitosis occurs, so choice A is unlikely. Next, osteoclasts would not help in this scenario based on the fact that they reduce bone density, which would make MM worse. Choice B is unlikely. Osteoblasts differentiate from osteoprogenitor cells, which are a variety of cells that work to repair or grow bone. This makes choices C and D possible at this point. MM patients that are supplemented with PTH, a hormone that increases osteoblast activity, seem to improve. This suggests that a higher number of osteoblasts would improve MM. This makes choice C a better answer than choice D.

Stand-alones (Questions 11-13)

11. **A is the best answer.** The hematocrit is the volume of the blood that is occupied by red blood cells. The remainder of the blood is composed of plasma, which includes nutrients, immune system cells, and platelets. Notice that the hematocrit increases as the dose of Epo rises from 1500 U/kg to 6000 U/kg, meaning the volume of blood occupied by red blood cells is increasing. This makes choice A the best answer. Increasing Epo does not reduce hematocrit, eliminating choice B. Platelets are fragments of cells that help to stop bleeding by serving in the blood clotting reaction. An increase in hematocrit would come with a decrease in plasma, decreasing the volume of platelets per mL and eliminating choice C. Lymphocytes, such as B and T cells, are also found in the plasma and would be reduced in situations of increased hematocrit, eliminating choice D.

12. **C is the best answer.** Keratin is a protein primarily found in the epidermis important in protection of the body and waterproofing of the skin. Nails are composed of keratinized cells, and would likely grow more quickly if keratin production increased, eliminating choice A. Hair is a column of keratinized cells, and if keratin production increased hair growth would likely increase as well, eliminating choice B. Thermal regulation primarily is controlled by insulation of the hypodermis and vasodilation and constriction in the dermis. It is largely unaffected by keratin content, making choice C a strong answer. Keratin functions as a waterproofing agent in the cells, and thus in a situation with increased keratin, skin would be more waterproof, eliminating choice D.

13. **A is the best answer.** Endoskeletons and exoskeletons describe the type of skeletal structure of an organism. Endoskeletons are internal skeletal structures, typically found in vertebrates. Exoskeletons, on the other hand, encase the entire organism, found in arthropods like insects. As an exoskeleton does not grow with the organism it encases, it does not allow for easy physical growth and must be shed. Endoskeletons facilitate gradual growth, making choice A a strong answer. Exoskeletons are a hard outer casing and completely protect their contents. Endoskeletons cannot accomplish this, eliminating choice B. Endoskeletons do not regrow periodically, like exoskeletons, eliminating choice C. Endoskeletons do provide structural support to the body, but exoskeletons accomplish the same purpose, so this statement does not represent a difference between the types of skeletal structure, eliminating choice D.

Passage 3 (Questions 14-18)

14. **A is the best answer.** Use the data presented in Figure 1 to help estimate the effect of PTH treatment on bone density and hematocrit. PTH, or parathyroid hormone, is released into the blood by the parathyroid glands when calcium levels are low. PTH increases the resorption, or breakdown, or bone, which would lead to a decrease in bone density. Figure 1 shows that PTH stimulates Epo levels over that of the saline solution treatment. Epo is responsible for stimulating red blood cell production and would increase the volume of the blood that corresponds to red blood cells, the hematocrit. Because bone density decreases and hematocrit increases, choice A is the best answer. Increased bone density would occur in the absence, not presence, of PTH, eliminating choice B. Epo stimulates red blood cell production to raise hematocrit, eliminating choices C and D.

15. **C is the best answer.** According to the first paragraph, chronically bled animals show conversion of fatty marrow to hematopoietic marrow. Fatty marrow, or yellow marrow, serves as a reservoir of fats and energy in the skeleton, while the hematopoietic marrow, or red marrow, serves to produce red blood cells and other cells like immune system cells. The increase in red marrow is likely due to the increased need of red blood cells that results from chronic bleeding. Because red marrow is likely to increase, not decrease, choices A and B can be eliminated. Because the amount of marrow in the bone is divided between red and yellow marrow, a growth of red marrow must come at the expense of yellow marrow, making choice C a better answer choice than choice D.

16. **C is the best answer.** This additional experiment that was performed by the scientists looks at the number of osteoclasts under conditions of Epo and RANKL. Notice that the number of osteoclasts increases under both Epo and RANKL exposure, compared to control. This finding eliminates choice A. RANKL increases the number of osteoclasts significantly more than Epo. The addition of 5 U/ml of Epo increases the number of osteoclasts by around 8-fold, while the addition of 10 U/ml of Epo increases the number of osteoclasts by around 10-fold. In contrast, the addition of RANKL increases the number of osteoclasts by 30-fold or more. Because the number of osteoclasts increases with increasing Epo dose and Epo induces less proliferation than RANKL, choice B is the best answer. As the number of osteoclasts increases when Epo changes from 5 U/ml to 10 U/ml, choice C can be eliminated. Notice that Epo induces an increase in the number of bone-resorbing cells, or cells that break down existing bone. Osteoblasts build bone, not break it down, eliminating choice D.

17. **A is the best answer.** The second paragraph implies that blood loss is known to stimulate hematopoietic stem cells to divide and differentiate into osteoprogenitor cells, which are the cells that give rise to osteoblasts. The function of osteoblasts is to build bone, making choice A the best answer. Osteoclasts do not differentiate from osteoprogenitor cells but rather from macrophages. This makes sense because macrophages also clean up tissues during infections. Because osteoprogenitor cells do not differentiate into osteoclasts, choice B can be eliminated. Osteocytes are mature osteoblasts that have become sealed in the bony matrix they have created. They do not become osteoblasts again, eliminating choice C. Osteoclasts would break down bone, not build bone. Because blood loss serves to stimulate bone growth, choice D can be eliminated.

18. **A is the best answer.** Epo is a hormone produced in the kidney in response to low oxygen levels in the blood. It travels through the blood to the bone marrow, where it acts on hematopoietic stem cells to increase their proliferation to generate new red blood cells. In order to measure how the expression of a gene changes, scientists would most likely isolate the mRNA of the *EPO* gene, making choice A the best answer. Red marrow does not produce Epo but instead responds to changes in the Epo levels, eliminating choice B. The ureter is the tube that connects the kidney to the bladder and serves to transport urine for elimination. Because the ureter is not sensing oxygen levels as blood passes through the kidney for filtering, cells located here are less likely that cells in the kidney itself to be responsible for releasing Epo. This makes choice C less likely to be the best answer compared to choice A. Yellow marrow does not make or respond to Epo, based on the information provided in the passage. Yellow marrow instead stores fat. This eliminates choice D.

Passage 4 (Questions 19-23)

19. A is the best answer. Sympathetic nervous system stimulation to the skin results in vasoconstriction that reduces the diameter of a blood vessel by contracting the smooth muscle surrounding it. This would decrease the flow of blood into the tumor and reduce the tumor's ability to obtain the amino acids and carbon molecules it needs for growth. This makes option I a component of the best answer. A parasympathetic agonist would act similar to a sympathetic antagonist and allow the diameter of the blood vessels to increase. As this is the opposite of reducing tumor growth, eliminating option II. An acetylcholine antagonist would prevent contraction of smooth muscle around the blood vessel, allowing the vessel to remain more dilated and increasing blood flow. This is the opposite of the desired effect, eliminating option III. Choice A is the best answer, as it contains only option I.

20. A is the best answer. One of the main function is skin is to serve as a protective barrier to abrasion, pathogens like viruses and bacteria, chemicals, and ultraviolet radiation. The skin protects against UV-induced damage by using melanocytes that produce a pigment melanin that is able to absorb the UV radiation before it creates free radicals that are able to damage DNA. Monobenzone causes skin bleaching as a side-effect of the treatment and would remove the protective pigment, causing an increased number of DNA mutations. This makes choice A the best answer. The passage does not discuss whether monobenzone affects the proliferation rate of cells, so choice B is less likely to be the best answer. Because the skin barrier itself is not damaged by monobenzone treatment, patients likely retain impermeability to water, eliminating choice C. Capillaries do not contain smooth muscle surrounding them, so the vessel size is unlikely to change, regardless of whether monobenzone treatment is used or not. This eliminates choice D.

21. D is the best answer. According to Experiment 1, the scientists injected the melanoma cells that would form the tumor subcutaneously, which is below the level of both the epidermis and dermis. Choosing the best answer requires the knowledge of the skin layer and structure. The avascular epithelial tissue layer is the epidermis and faces the external environment, eliminating choice A. The epidermis, or avascular epithelial layer, directly opposes the dermis, which contains blood vessels, sensory neurons, and a variety of cell types that help protect the body from damage. Because this is still within the dermis and epidermis, choice B can be eliminated. Stem cells form the bottom layer of the epidermis and proliferate to produce cells that form the avascular layer important for physical protection. This eliminates choice C. The superficial fascia, or subcutaneous layer, is characterized by a fat layer that helps to maintain body heat and separates the dermis and epidermis from the deeper tissues of the body. Because scientists injected cells into the subcutaneous layer, choice D is the best answer.

22. C is the best answer. Figure 1 shows the percentage of cells that are TNFα positive and are taken to be killer T cells. Melanocytes are responsible for transferring melanin, or skin pigment, to keratinocytes and do not play a role in modulating the immune system of the skin. This eliminates choice A. Keratinocytes are the outermost cell type of the skin and provide a physical barrier to the external environment. They also do not control the immune system of the skin, eliminating choice B. Langerhans cells are specialized macrophages of the skin that ingest dead and dying cells, in addition to foreign pathogens, and process antigens to activate T cells. These cells would be most important for activating the T cells in Figure 1, making choice C the best answer. Merkel cells attach to sensory neurons and function in the sensation of touch but not the immune system. This eliminates choice D.

23. B is the best answer. MIC treatment results in an autoimmune-like reaction according to paragraphs one and two that induces skin-bleaching. This eliminates choice A. Langerhans cells are the immune macrophages of the skin that would take up dead and dying melanocytes as a result of MIC treatment. Because the tumor volume is less in the MIC-treated mice compared to the control mice, the immune system of the skin is doing a better job at controlling the tumor growth than the immune system of control mice. One reason for this increased control could be an increased number of Langerhans cells, making choice B the best answer. Inhibiting tyrosinase, an enzyme important in melanin synthesis, would cause reactant levels of tyrosine to increase, not decrease, in MIC-treated mice. This eliminates choice C. Vitamin D synthesis occurs when UV radiation is able to activate a molecule in the skin that is a precursor to vitamin D. Decreased levels of melanin would allow more UV radiation to be absorbed by this precursor molecule, increasing vitamin D synthesis. This eliminates choice D.

Stand-alones (Questions 24-27)

24. A is the best answer. This question is asking "what is least connected to muscle?" Insertion is the distal muscle attachment point. Since the muscles controlling eye movement are being surgically altered, it is likely that the insertion of these muscles will be damaged, eliminating choice B. Tendons connect muscle to bone, and it is reasonable to assume that they can be damaged in some form due to this procedure, eliminating choice D. Collagen is a fibrous protein with a high percentage of glycine, alanine, proline, and 4-hydroxyproline wrapped in tight coils. It makes up a large portion of the connective tissue of both ligaments and tendons, so it can be eliminated along with choice D. Choice A is the best answer because ligaments, in general, connect bone to bone. The suspensory ligaments of the eye are inside the eye and unlikely to be damaged during an extraocular (outside the eye) procedure.

25. **C is the best answer.** Vasodilation and vasoconstriction are important physiological methods of thermoregulation. When blood capillaries dilate, more heat is lost through radiation from the 98°F or 37°C internal heat of the body to the environment. If the difference between body temperature and environmental temperature is reduced, less heat will be lost due to radiation. The ability to lose heat through evaporation is compromised mainly in high humidity, not necessarily heat, eliminating choice A. Vasodilation and constriction are compromised in high temperatures more than sweat in thermogenesis, so choice B can be eliminated. The reduction in heat difference between internal temperature and external temperature is the primary cause for compromised ability to lose heat via vasculature control, making choice C a strong answer. The heat loss due to sweat evaporation is endothermic, meaning heat is required for the phase change of water. This removes heat from the surface of the skin. Choice D states that sweat evaporation is exothermic, and can be eliminated.

26. **A is the best answer.** Vasoconstriction, or decreased diameter of blood vessels, is one the primary techniques of the body to raise blood pressure. If ADH increases, blood pressure increases through vasoconstriction. Vasoconstriction in surface capillaries causes conservation of internal body temperature, raising it. Choice A is a strong answer. Vasodilation would cause lower body temperature, but ADH primarily works by vasoconstriction, eliminating choice B. An increase in vessel dilation would change body temperature, as this is one of the primary techniques the body uses to lose internal heat, eliminating choice C. Vasoconstriction would cause the body to either maintain or raise internal heat, eliminating choice D.

27. **B is the best answer.** In cold conditions, the muscle surrounding the hair follicle should contract, making the hair perpendicular to the surface of the skin and trapping a layer of warm air on the surface of the skin. The vasculature contains smooth muscle, which is innervated by the autonomic nervous system. The stimulus to this smooth muscle would increase in these conditions, eliminating choices A and C. In addition, the smooth muscle of the arrector pili is innervated by the autonomic nervous system, not the somatic, eliminating choice D. B is the best answer.

Passage 5 (Questions 28-32)

28. **B is the best answer.** The epidermis is the uppermost layer of the skin, consisting many layers of keratinized cells responsible for protection against foreign pathogens and regulation of water composition of the body. The waterproofing of the epidermis is due to the presence of increasing levels of keratin, a protein that functions to seal in the body's water. Thinning of the layers of the epidermis would decrease the body's ability to seal in water due to a reduction in layers of keratin sealed epithelial cells, making option I a strong answer. The epidermis is avascular, and thus a thinning of the epidermis would have little direct effect on blood flow, eliminating option II. The epidermis is responsible for the protection of the body, preventing entry of foreign pathogens by creating a thick physical barrier of cells. A thinning of the epidermis would hinder the skin's ability to perform this particular function, making option III a strong answer. Choice B, or options I and III, is the best answer.

29. **D is the best answer.** According to the results of Experiment 2, each of the fibroblasts differ in their ability to promote the morphogenesis and thickening of the epidermis. The fibroblast that promotes the thickest epidermis would have the greatest ability to regulate the body's composition of water, this is the young Fp. This fibroblast is followed in ability to promote the thickening of the epidermis by the old Fp, then the young Fr, then the old Fr. Choice A places the young Fp as the least able to promote skin morphogenesis, and can be eliminated. Choice B can be eliminated for the same reason as choice B. The young reticular fibroblasts are less able to promote morphogenesis than the old papillary fibroblasts, eliminating choice C. Choice D places the fibroblasts in the most likely order, and is the best answer.

30. **A is the best answer.** According to the passage, the dermis is a flexible and elastic layer of the skin composed of collagen and connective tissue produced by fibroblasts. Cartilage is a flexible, strong connective tissue composed of collagen, like the dermis, making choice A a strong answer. Synovial joint fluid is a type of gelatinous fluid found in the synovial joint that cushions impact on the joint. The dermis is not a fluid substance, instead a matrix of flexible tissue, eliminating choice B. Spongy bone is composed of a hardened calcium/phosphate matrix, and is unlike the flexible collagen of the dermis, eliminating choice C. A tendon is a tough, inelastic band of connective tissue connecting a muscle to bone; while both are composed and connective tissue, a tendon is inelastic, and is less similar to the dermis than cartilage, eliminating choice D.

31. **A is the best answer.** According to the passage, MMPs are proteins that are correlated with the breakdown of the extracellular matrix and MCP-1 is related to cellular growth. If aging is related to the breakdown of the tissue surrounding hair follicles and sweat glands, it would be directly correlated with an increase in the protein that degrades the extracellular matrix of the dermis. Choice A displays that as age increases, MMPs increase, which would correspond to a breakdown in extracellular matrix, making choice A a strong answer. Choice B displays that as age increases MCP-1 increases, which would cause increased cellular growth, a result not correlated with breakdown around hair follicles. Choice B can be eliminated. Choice C is displays a decrease in MMPs as age increases, which would correlate to less breakdown in cellular matrix, ruling out choice C. Like choice B, the question does not show a correlation between aging and cell growth, making choice D a weak answer.

32. **D is the best answer.** The primary function of the hypodermis, a layer of fat found beneath the dermis, is heat insulation. If the hypodermis was too thin, elderly patients would be less capable of regulating body temperature and would experience a drop in core temperature. Thus, patients would likely display an increase in other physiological techniques used to increase temperature. Excretion of oil glands is unrelated to temperature, and if anything, would cause heat loss through evaporation, eliminating choice A. A thickening of the epidermis typically occurs in response to surface friction on the skin to create a callus, and is unlikely to occur to insulate body heat, making choice B a weak answer. Vasodilation of the surface capillaries would reduce the temperature of the body by increasing blood flow to the extremities and allowing more heat loss, ruling out choice C. A contraction of muscles in the hair follicle fibers would cause hair to stand on end, creating an insulated layer of heat on the surface of the skin, making choice D the best answer.

Passage 6 (Questions 33-38)

33. **A is the best answer.** The epidermis consists of multiple layers of stratified squamous epithelium composed primary of keratinocytes. The basal layer of cells of the epidermis interacts with the basement membrane in order to secure the epidermis to the underlying tissue. Hemidesmosomes are the most important molecule on the basal layer of cells that interacts with the basement membrane to secure the epidermis, making choice A the best answer choice. Desmosomes are important for intercellular connections within the epidermis, but they are not responsible for mediating adherence of the basal epidermis to the basement membrane, eliminating choice B. Claudins are important proteins that contribute to the tight junction between cells, preventing the passive movement of molecules. They do not connect the epidermis to the basement membrane, eliminating choice C. Myosin is a protein that is involved in muscle contraction. It does not mediate connections between cells, eliminating choice D.

34. **B is the best answer.** The epidermis is the outer layer of the skin, which is mainly composed of keratinocytes. Keratinocytes produce the protein keratin, which helps to waterproof the skin by prevent water from moving between cells. As osmosis is the movement of water from high concentrations to lower concentrations, choice A can be eliminated. Melanin is a protein produced by melanocytes that absorbs harmful UV radiation that can cause oxidative molecules to be generated inside cells. Melanocytes then pass the melanin they produce to keratinocytes to help decrease UV radiation absorption. These oxidative molecules can then go on to damage DNA. As melanocytes, not keratinocytes, produce melanin, choice B is the best answer. The physical barrier provided by the keratinocyte later prevents organisms such as bacteria and viruses from entering the body, as well as protecting deeper structures from damage. These functions eliminate choices C and D.

35. **A is the best answer.** According to Experiment 2, *TRSP* knockout mice have an increased number of macrophages around hair follicles. Specialized dendritic cells in the skin are called Langerhans cells, which act as macrophages to take up particles in the surrounding environment and present these antigens to immune system cells. In order to best answer this question, it is important to know that dendritic cells, like Langerhans cells, act as macrophages and that hair follicles are located in the basal skin layer. While the hair shaft is located in the epidermis, the hair follicle itself is located in the dermal layer, near the basal side, making choice A the best answer. The subcutaneous fat is below the dermis and does not contain hair follicles, eliminating choice B. The stratum spinosum is in the epidermis, not the dermis, and contains spinous cells that produce keratin. Hair follicles are not found in the epidermis, eliminating choice C. The stratus corneum contains keratinized cells that form the outermost layer of the skin and are responsible for physical protection. This layer also does not contain hair follicles, eliminating choice D.

36. **C is the best answer.** According to the first paragraph, proteins that contain selenocysteine help to prevent damage to DNA, proteins, and lipids by ROS. ROS can be generated when UV radiation is not absorbed by melanin and passes into other cells of the epidermal and dermal layers. As ROS can damage DNA, causing mutations, it can be the source of a new cancer. Langerhans cells are the dendritic cells of the epidermis and are responsible for endocytosing dead and dying cells, as well as pathogens such as viruses and bacteria. Damage to Langerhans cells could decrease the ability of the immune system to respond to local invaders or survey the epithelium for cells that may be cancerous. Langerhans cells, however, do not divide, so DNA damage would be unlikely to propagate to future cells, making choice A less likely to be the best answer. Merkel cells attach to sensory neurons and function in the sensation of touch. Damage to these cells would be less likely to produce cancer, eliminating choice B. Stem cells of the skin constantly divide to produce new keratinocytes that are able to migrate through the epidermis to protect the body from physical abrasion. DNA damage to stem cells that constantly divide could produce a cancer cell that also continues to divide, making choice C a better answer choice than choice A. Granular cells are in the stratum granulosum of the epidermis and are transiting to the stratum corneum to be fully keratinized and serve for physical protection. They are not dividing, so damage to these cells is unlikely to cause cancer, eliminating choice D.

37. **A is the best answer.** According to the passage, selenocysteine, containing the selenium atom, helps prevent cancer by decreasing the harmful effects of ROS. This question requires knowledge of both amino acids and chemistry. Cysteine amino acids contain a sulfur atom that is able to covalently bond to another sulfur atom in a second cysteine to create a disulfide bond. Two hydrogens are lost, one on each cysteine, making this reaction an oxidation. Notice on the periodic table that sulfur and selenium are in the same column, meaning they share chemical properties. It is likely that selenium could reach similarly to sulfur to absorb oxidative species in the cytosol. If the cytosol has a high concentration of oxidizing species, like ROS, these could react with the selenocysteine amino acids to form a bond similar to a disulfide bond, a diselenide bond. This would neutralize the ROS, making choice A likely to be the best answer. ROS would oxidize amino acids, not reduce them, eliminating choice B. The passage does not suggest that the enzyme sequesters ROS. In contrast, ROS sequestration against the plasma membrane would likely lead to further damage of the plasma membrane, increasing the negative effects of ROS. This eliminates choice C. The passage also does not show that selenocysteine-containing proteins are transcription factors, or factors that bind DNA to increase the expression of genes. This eliminates choice D.

38. **D is the best answer.** The authors of the passage suggest that selenocysteine-containing proteins help reduce the damaging effects of ROS by lowering their concentration in the cell. ROS would oxidize a selenocysteine-containing protein, such as GPX1, so a western blot should show an increased signal compared to the no UV radiation condition. This eliminates choice A, which would support the authors' findings. Similarly, SEP15 would become oxidized, decreasing the concentration of reduced SEP15 and increasing the concentration of oxidized SEP15. Choice B can be eliminated because it also supports the authors' findings. Transcription of *SELT*, a selenocysteine-containing protein in Experiment 1, would rise to help create more SELT protein to combat the ROS. Choice C can be eliminated because it supports the authors' conclusions. Transcription of proteins that mediate protection against ROS would be increased, not decreased, upon exposure to UV radiation. This would lead to increased binding of a transcription factor, such as TRSP, to the promotor of genes like *TR1*. As increased binding, not decreased binding, would be expected, choice D would contradict the authors' findings and is the best answer.

Stand-alones (Questions 39-41)

39. **C is the best answer.** Skin regulates body temperatures using a variety of methods. The best answer for this question will discuss a method that is NOT used by the skin to regulate body temperature. Choice A can be eliminated because contraction of the erectile musculature in the dermal layer causes hair to stand up and trap a blanket of warm air around the skin. Choice B can also be eliminated because vasodilation of capillaries increases blood flow to the skin, thereby promoting heat loss. Vasoconstriction decreases blood flow to the skin and has the opposite effect. Both choices C and D discuss sweat glands. Indeed, there are two types of sweat glands, eccrine and apocrine, respectively. Choice C is the best answer because eccrine sweat glands, found in the epidermis, are responsible for the release of sweat over the entire surface of the skin in response to sweat. Choice D can be eliminated because apocrine sweat glands are located in the dermis and produce foul smelling sweat in response to stress.

40. **A is the best answer.** Choice A is the best answer because the shivering reflex is a thermoregulatory mechanism during which receptors in the skin and spinal cord detect low external temperatures and stimulate the hypothalamus, not the thalamus. Choice B can be eliminated because under extremely cold conditions, excessive muscular contractions would necessitate the break down of glycogen into glucose. Glycogen phosphorylase is an enzyme involved in this process. Choice C can also be eliminated because the shivering reflex occurs via rapid innervation of skeletal muscles via the somatic nervous system. An increase in the rate of muscular increases the metabolic rate by necessitating the replenishment of rapidly depleting ATP.

41. **A is the best answer.** The primary method the skin uses to retain water is through the production of keratin in the epidermis, a protein that functions as a type of waterproofing. If keratin was reduced, this would dramatically affect the skins ability to retain water, making choice A a strong answer. While an increase in production of sweat might cause some water loss, it would not affect the primary method the skin uses to retain water. Choice B is a weaker answer than choice A. Widespread vasoconstriction would reduce the amount of heat loss occurring through radiation at the surface of the skin, but is not likely to affect water loss, eliminating choice C. An increase in melanin would affect the coloration of the skin, but is not likely affect water loss, eliminating choice D.

BIOLOGICAL SCIENCES

DIRECTIONS. Most questions in the Biological Sciences test are organized into groups, each preceded by a descriptive passage. After studying the passage, select the one best answer to each question in the group. Some questions are not based on a descriptive passage and are also independent of each other. You must also select the one best answer to these questions. If you are not certain of an answer, eliminate the alternatives that you know to be incorrect and then select an answer from the remaining alternatives. A periodic table is provided for your use. You may consult it whenever you wish.

PERIODIC TABLE OF THE ELEMENTS

1 H 1.0																	2 He 4.0
3 Li 6.9	4 Be 9.0											5 B 10.8	6 C 12.0	7 N 14.0	8 O 16.0	9 F 19.0	10 Ne 20.2
11 Na 23.0	12 Mg 24.3											13 Al 27.0	14 Si 28.1	15 P 31.0	16 S 32.1	17 Cl 35.5	18 Ar 39.9
19 K 39.1	20 Ca 40.1	21 Sc 45.0	22 Ti 47.9	23 V 50.9	24 Cr 52.0	25 Mn 54.9	26 Fe 55.8	27 Co 58.9	28 Ni 58.7	29 Cu 63.5	30 Zn 65.4	31 Ga 69.7	32 Ge 72.6	33 As 74.9	34 Se 79.0	35 Br 79.9	36 Kr 83.8
37 Rb 85.5	38 Sr 87.6	39 Y 88.9	40 Zr 91.2	41 Nb 92.9	42 Mo 95.9	43 Tc (98)	44 Ru 101.1	45 Rh 102.9	46 Pd 106.4	47 Ag 107.9	48 Cd 112.4	49 In 114.8	50 Sn 118.7	51 Sb 121.8	52 Te 127.6	53 I 126.9	54 Xe 131.3
55 Cs 132.9	56 Ba 137.3	57 La* 138.9	72 Hf 178.5	73 Ta 180.9	74 W 183.9	75 Re 186.2	76 Os 190.2	77 Ir 192.2	78 Pt 195.1	79 Au 197.0	80 Hg 200.6	81 Tl 204.4	82 Pb 207.2	83 Bi 209.0	84 Po (209)	85 At (210)	86 Rn (222)
87 Fr (223)	88 Ra 226.0	89 Ac= 227.0	104 Unq (261)	105 Unp (262)	106 Unh (263)	107 Uns (262)	108 Uno (265)	109 Une (267)									

	58 Ce 140.1	59 Pr 140.9	60 Nd 144.2	61 Pm (145)	62 Sm 150.4	63 Eu 152.0	64 Gd 157.3	65 Tb 158.9	66 Dy 162.5	67 Ho 164.9	68 Er 167.3	69 Tm 168.9	70 Yb 173.0	71 Lu 175.0
*														
=	90 Th 232.0	91 Pa (231)	92 U 238.0	93 Np (237)	94 Pu (244)	95 Am (243)	96 Cm (247)	97 Bk (247)	98 Cf (251)	99 Es (252)	100 Fm (257)	101 Md (258)	102 No (259)	103 Lr (260)